LITERARY GLOBALISM

Anglo-American Fiction Set in France

Carolyn A. Durham

Lewisburg
Bucknell University Presses

©2005 by Rosemont Publishing & Printing Corp.

All rights reserved. Authorization to photocopy items for internal or personal use, or the internal or personal use of specific clients, is granted by the copyright owner, provided that a base fee of $10.00, plus eight cents per page, per copy is paid directly to the Copyright Clearance Center, 222 Rosewood Drive, Danvers, Massachusetts 01923.[0-8387-5608-5/05 $10.00 + 8¢ pp, pc.]

Associated University Presses
2010 Eastpark Boulevard
Cranbury, NJ 08512

The paper used in this publication meets the requirements of the American National Standard for Permanence of Paper for Printed Library Materials Z39.48-1984.

Library of Congress Cataloging-in-Publication Data

Durham, Carolyn A.
   Literary globalism : Anglo-American fiction set in France / Carolyn A. Durham.
   p. cm.
   Includes bibliographical references (p.) and index.
   ISBN 0-8387-5608-5 (alk. paper)
1. English fiction—20th century—History and criticism. 2. France—In literature. 3. English fiction—21st century—History and criticism. 4. France—Foreign public opinion, American. 5. American fiction—History and criticism. 6. France—Foreign public opinion, British. 7. American fiction—French influences. 8. English fiction—French influences. I. Title.

PR129.F8D87 2005
813'.54093244—dc22

2004027217

PRINTED IN THE UNITED STATES OF AMERICA

For John—
and all Anglo-American Francophiles

Contents

Acknowledgments	9
Introduction	13
1. The New International Novel: Diane Johnson's *Le Divorce* and *Le Mariage*	25
2. Intertextual Travel and Translation: Rose Tremain's *The Way I Found Her*	41
3. Routes and Roots: Postmodern Paradox in Joanne Harris's *Chocolat*	61
4. Back to the Future: Nation and Nostalgia in Joanne Harris's *Blackberry Wine*	78
5. Mosaics of the Might-Have-Been: Metaphor, Migration, and Multiculturalism in Claire Messud's *The Last Life*	98
6. Modernism and Mystery: The Curious Case of the Lost Generation	118
7. Museum, Maze, Madhouse: Sarah Smith's "Theatre du Monde"	134
8. The Re-Zoning of Gay Paris: Edmund White's *The Married Man*	164
Conclusion: Diane Johnson's *L'Affaire*	193
Notes	211
Bibliography	245
Further Reading	255
Index	257

Acknowledgments

I AM GRATEFUL TO THE COLLEGE OF WOOSTER FOR SUPPORTING THE research leave in 2000–2001 that allowed me to begin work on this project, and for providing additional funding from the Henry Luce III Fund for Distinguished Scholarship, which granted me release time in the spring and fall of 2003 to complete the writing of this book. A grant from the Faculty Development Fund in the summer of 2003 enabled me to complete my research in Paris. I want to thank my students and my colleagues for the many ways in which they have challenged and encouraged my thinking and my scholarship. I am particularly grateful for the help, intelligence, and curiosity of my student assistants, Adrienne Brayman, Noël Hollinger, and Arete Moodey, who patiently helped me track down references and reviews over a period of several years.

    I thank Diane Johnson for permission to quote from *Le Divorce*, *Le Mariage*, and *L'Affaire*; Claire Messud for permission to quote from *The Last Life*; Sarah Smith for permission to quote from *The Knowledge of Water* and *Citizen of the Country*; and Edmund White for permission to quote from *The Married Man*. I thank the Random House Group Limited for permission to quote from *Blackberry Wine* and *Chocolat* by Joanne Harris published by Black Swann. The quotations from *Chocolat* by Joanne Harris, copyright © 1999 by Joanne Harris, are also used by permission of Viking Penguin, a division of Penguin Group (USA) Inc. I thank Rose Tremain, Chatto and Windus, and Farrar, Straus and Giroux for permission to quote from *The Way I Found Her* (copyright © 1997 by Rose Tremain). I am grateful to Joanne Harris, Claire Messud, and especially Diane Johnson for their willingness to speak with me; one of the great pleasures in writing this book lies in having met some of the novelists considered therein. Earlier versions of sections of chapters 1, 2, 5, and 6 appeared in *French Politics*; *Culture and Society*; *Contemporary Literature*;

JNT: Journal of Narrative Theory; and *Twentieth-Century Literature*. An earlier version of a portion of the conclusion to this book first appeared in *SITES: Contemporary French and Francophone Studies*, published by Taylor and Francis *(http://www.tandf.co.uk/journals)*. I thank the editors of these journals for their willingness to publish my work and for permission to reprint parts of it here. Conferences sponsored by Middlebury College, the University of Louisville, the University of Texas at San Antonio, the Midwest Modern Language Association, the South Central Modern Language Association, and the Modern Language Association provided a forum for presenting work in progress.

Like all books, this one could not have been written without the support of some very special people. I am particularly grateful to Edward Knox, whose work in a similar area encouraged my own, for his unfailing collegiality and professional generosity. The conference he hosted at Middlebury College on "Déjà Views: How Americans Look at France" in the fall of 2001 and the special issue of *French Politics, Culture and Society* he subsequently edited provided a stimulating intellectual context for my own work. I thank my French friends–especially Christine, Paul, Vincent, and Denis Guérin, Catherine Duras, and Michèle Valencia–for sharing their France and their views of the United States with me, almost always over excellent food and wine. Closer to home, Deb Shostak, Nancy Grace, Tom and Terry Prendergast, and Mark Wilson offered me not only the many pleasures of friendship on a daily basis but also the shared conviction that research and scholarship are of unquestionable value. Most of all, I thank John Gabriele for a life filled with love, language, literature, and laughter.

LITERARY
GLOBALISM

Introduction

*America is my country but France is my home
and Paris is my home town.*
—Gertrude Stein[1]

IN JUNE OF 2003, SHAKESPEARE AND COMPANY, THE ENGLISH-LANGUAGE bookstore in Paris, held its first literary festival: "Lost, Beat and New: Three Generations of Parisian Literary Tradition." As the festival program notes, the fact that neither the bookstore, "the meeting place of Anglophone literati," nor the city, a "mythical refuge for aspiring artists," had ever before hosted an event designed to celebrate both places as the home base and source of inspiration for three successive waves of American and British expatriate writers does indeed seem to be "an anomaly" in need of rectification.[2] At the same time, however, virtually everything about Shakespeare and Company is anomalous, and, with the exception of the festival itself, almost nothing about the bookstore could be described as original. As such, it serves as an ideal venue for the introduction of a book devoted to contemporary Anglo-American fiction set in France.

From the beginning the shop owned by Sylvia Beach was apparently "unlike any other."[3] The version often recalled today as the original—the store that stood at number 12, rue de l'Odéon, for twenty years (1921–41) —was in fact already a reproduction of the first Shakespeare and Company, which Beach had opened two years earlier on rue Dupuytren. This spatial mobility, evident long before George Whitman changed the name of his first bookshop on rue de la Bûcherie to Shakespeare and Company ten years after Beach closed her second store, has also always found further reflection in both the multiplicity and the ambivalence of the shop's sense of identity. The place described in the title of Beach's own memoir as "an American Bookshop in Paris," is, of course, named for England's most famous writer and owes its own fame to the controversial publication of the best-known novel of his Irish counterpart. The international reputations of William Shakespeare and James Joyce are fully consistent with the space of the shop itself, which stocked English-language books regardless of national origin and sold them equally indiscriminately to a clientele composed of as many, if not more, French and European readers as American and British ones. The diverse origins of the shop's customers were echoed in the different places figuratively contained within the very limited physical space of the store itself. At once bookstore, lending library, literary salon, and neighborhood clubhouse, Shakespeare and Company also became home to the first wave of Anglophone expatriate writers, the "Lost Generation" of Ernest Hemingway and Gertrude Stein, who, among many others, including Joyce and Beach herself, migrated to Paris in the 1920s and 1930s.

Stein, who stayed the longest, was still in France in the 1940s to welcome the forerunners of the second generation of Anglophone expatriates, itself this time an eclectic collection of primarily Beat poets (Lawrence Ferlinghetti, Allen Ginsberg, William S. Burroughs) and black Americans (Richard Wright, James Baldwin, Chester Himes) who would frequent a Shakespeare and Company under new ownership and in a new location.[4] By chance, Walt Whitman's photo and several of his early manuscripts were always prominently displayed on the walls of Beach's bookshops, and in 1926 she organized an exhibition in honor of one of her favorite poets. Whitman, the quintessential American writer, whose wanderlust and love of the open road largely belonged to a literary persona, nonetheless wrote passionately about France, a country he had never visited; identified himself as "a real Parisian";[5] and at the time of the Paris exposition enjoyed far greater acclaim and influence in his adopted country than in his native land. Thus, even though George Whitman is almost certainly not Walt Whitman's illegitimate grandson, great nephew, or any other relative, despite persistent Paris gossip to the contrary, there is still a certain inescapable logic, what one might even call a kind of poetic justice, in the fact that a wanderer named Whitman finally settled down in Paris to run an English-language bookstore known as Shakespeare and Company. If George Whitman's right to use that designation is as tenuous as his alleged descent from the poet whose name he shares, his decision to call his only descendant "Sylvia Beach Whitman" suggests that Shakespeare and Company will continue to stand at the metaphoric crossroads of the many paths that lead from past to present and connect America to France.[6]

Just as the current owner of Shakespeare and Company has in some sense realized Walt Whitman's desire to live in Paris, so too has the bookstore reached at least one of its possible literary destinations. Today the former locus of modernism exists in a decidedly postmodern space. The bookstore's original capacity to adapt a single setting to the satisfaction of multiple needs is now reflected in a geographical location whose indefinite and flexible boundaries extend well beyond the store itself. Spreading over three stories and spilling onto the surrounding area outside, where many of the events of the 2003 literary festival took place, Shakespeare and Company is not only the home of a bookstore, but also, and at once, the site of an antiquarian shop, a memorial library, a reading room, a writing workshop, a free hotel, and a private apartment—all interconnected, if not superimposed, and the whole curiously configured in an odd, irregular shape as difficult to map as its contents are to describe.[7] The early twentieth-century visitors to Beach's shop on the rue Dupuytren already entered a complex space, one both distinctively cultural, the "quintessence of the literary bookshop," and comfortably domestic, "of an authentic homeyness," and yet, at the same time, somehow always more fantastic than real, "picturesque beyond the imagination of any designer of stage or movie set."[8] At the dawn of the twenty-first century, the tourists, students, and literary scholars who carefully thread their way down the crowded corridors and up the cluttered staircases of Whitman's store to browse through the books, now both new and used and sometimes in French as well as English, which line the dusty shelves or sit in random piles on tables and beds, simultaneously find themselves in a museum, a historical monument, and a haunted house.[9]

Although Whitman's Shakespeare and Company devoted its first literary festival to "three generations of Parisian literary tradition" and consecrated somewhat more time to the "Lost Generation" and the "Beat Generation," the overall shape of the event, like that of the site that sponsored it, primarily reflected both the character and the importance of the "New Generation." Consistent with a postmodern world of copies and imitations, the festival organized an exposition in which the bookstore was reproduced yet again, this time in miniature. In a visible clash of styles and cultures, the entrance to this fourth replica of Shakespeare and Company lay beyond the elegant and imposing facade of the *Mairie du Veme*, the town hall that sits on the Place du Panthéon next door to France's grandiose monument to its former heroes. Within the exhibit itself, however, and despite the signs that attempted to distinguish among the three generations on display, the reduced dimensions of the gallery erased the continuity of a literary tradition to foreground the juxtaposition of past and present within the same palimpsestic and heterogeneous space. Ethan Gilsdorf, an American expatriate poet, has recently noted the essential integrity of "Lost, Beat and New" experienced by contemporary artists: "Writers who move to Paris today are haunted by the legacy of those who have previously made the pilgrimage."[10]

Similarly, the tribute to high culture inherent in a festival with modernist roots simultaneously celebrated popular culture and even postmodern kitsch. Next to such venerable relics as photos of Beach and Hemingway and postcards from Joyce and Ferlinghetti hung apologetic letters written by formerly ungrateful lost youths whom Whitman had once lodged in the bookstore for free. In a curious confusion of real life and performance art, I was unable to decide whether the two dirty and disheveled human beings who lay stretched out in the middle of the exhibit on the day I visited, blocking parts of it with an indifference worthy of their remarkably self-centered conversation, were current beneficiaries of the bookstore's hospitality, chance passersby, homeless vagrants, or actors hired for the occasion. Much of the festival itself took place in an outdoor tent where literary historians, scholars, and critics forsook the traditional academic lecture to read from their published works in yet another example of postmodern repetition. Several of the invited specialists also doubled as tour guides, leading culturally diverse groups of festival participants on "literary walks" featuring not only the former residences of expatriate artists but also stops for Berthillon ice cream and pitches for favorite restaurants passed along the way.

Shakespeare and Company's celebration of the "New Generation" specifically included only three of the twelve novelists discussed in these pages. Moreover, the participation of Diane Johnson and Edmund White, whose recent work stands, like bookends, at the boundaries of this study, was tangential at best—White's former apartment figured on the tour of île St. Louis, Johnson hosted a private reception for festival participants. Claire Messud alone took part in the festival's series of scheduled readings. Yet, despite the focus of the festival and the history of the bookstore that hosted it, there is nothing surprising in the noticeable absence from the program of Anglophone writers of fiction. The current generation of British and American expatriates, like the previous one, includes a significant number of poets, no fewer than seven of whom read from their work during the final days of "Lost, Beat and New."[11] Furthermore, the "Third Wave" participants included writers of Russian, Chinese, and Middle Eastern descent as well as those of Anglo-American origin.[12] The selection of Messud, who currently holds three passports and chose to read the only passage from *The Last Life* set entirely in Algeria, thus confirms a pattern increasingly characteristic of the cosmopolitan world of the early twenty-first century. In this context, one of the distinguishing features of *Literary Globalism* lies in its focus on contemporary Anglophone fiction set primarily in France.[13]

Shakespeare and Company sponsors one additional auxiliary activity that contributes to its metaphorical importance at the threshold of this book. Founded in 2002 to identify a website designed to publish the work of the writers and artists who pass through Whitman's bookstore, *Kilometer Zero* has since expanded to include a print magazine, an artists' residence, and a program of readings and exhibits held throughout Paris. Most importantly, however, the name reminds us that in its current location, directly across from the square in front of the cathedral of Notre Dame, the bookstore itself literally stands at *kilomètre zéro*, the unique geographical point that marks the origin of every road in France, the spot at which, figuratively speaking, world travelers either begin their journey or reach their destination—or both. A sampling of Paris's various descriptions—"the West's most seductive city," "the cosmopolitan Other, an alien site ... the great escape," "the crowning symbol, the concrete manifestation, of a foreign civilization" — reminds us that the capital of France has a textual presence as important as its physical being.[14] Paris has long enjoyed a literary existence as a mythical place of both promise and nostalgia, a paradoxical site of "departures, arrivals, transits," of inseparable "dwelling/traveling"[15] that makes it the perfect, indeed, the only possible setting both for a bookstore like Shakespeare and Company and for the novels of a new generation of Anglo-American writers. If today's expatriates still move to Paris for a variety of familiar financial, aesthetic, and ideological reasons, they single out the city's historical importance as a "crossroads of many cultures, a center for exiles" and its contemporary significance as a place "that mirrors all the changes going on throughout the world."[16] In Gilsdorf's synthesis, Paris is at once the hub of Europe and the multicultural center of a newly globalized universe, the same dual role it plays in the fiction discussed in this book: "The capital city of the only country that straddles both northern and southern Europe, Paris absorbs the influences of every culture that passes through it, including America's pop-culture imperialism."[17]

Just as Shakespeare and Company serves as a microcosm of Paris, so too it acts as an objective correlative for this book. The chapters that follow will further clarify the metaphoric importance I have attached to the bookstore at the beginning of this critical study. Perhaps the single most significant pattern that connects the texts discussed here involves the construction of the novel as an essentially spatial entity, whose capacity to contain diversity within unity recalls the eclectic form and functions of the bookstore's own successive locales. Like the shop and its owners, the central characters, often the narrators, of these texts are always travelers—wanderers, foreigners, expatriates, runaways, migrants, homeless men and women—who collectively inhabit "the new world order of mobility" that James Clifford identifies simply as "postmodernity."[18] Like the patrons of Shakespeare and Company, they are also often readers who inhabit an intertextual universe of citations and allusions, many of which reference the work and the lives of previous generations of Anglophone expatriates, notably Henry James's international novel and, especially, Gertrude Stein's famous salon. In imitation of an American bookstore named for an English writer and located in Paris, I have juxtaposed British and American novels set in France in the interest of respecting their authors' own international, cross-cultural, and cosmopolitan typographies and their shared ambivalence about boundaries and identities, including those of nations. As Shakespeare and Company's recent festival illustrates, Paris remains a city of literary readings and expositions, and I will use several more in the pages ahead to contextualize my critical readings of individual novels.

The subsequent chapters constitute a sequence of interrelated essays. Together, they create an emergent picture of a distinctive category of contemporary Anglo-American fiction, but I have also structured each essay to allow it to be read independently of the others. Although this inevitably means that I may on occasion repeat a specific reference to one of the critics and theorists—James Clifford, Homi Bhabha, John Tomlinson, Malcolm Bradbury, Linda Hutcheon, Brian McHale, among many others—whose ideas I have found most pertinent to my own discussion, the reader will find that the change of context leads to a progressively enriched understanding of the whole. Indeed, I have sought to enact in the design of this book the "complex connectivity," which defines "globalization" itself for Tomlinson.[19] As in the place that many still consider, "in the spirit of its predecessor, the best bookshop around,"[20] I have wanted different kinds of works to inhabit the same space so that general patterns gradually emerge from close textual analysis, and individual novels determine their own critical and theoretical frameworks.

However unoriginal, the resurgence of Anglophone fiction set in France can also seem curiously anomalous in a contemporary climate marked by the simultaneous revitalization of France's traditional role as the ally that America and Britain most love to hate. Nonetheless, over fifty of these novels have been published in the last ten to fifteen years, even if the specific geographical setting is in some cases largely irrelevant.[21] Among those texts in which France matters, albeit as an imaginary construct as often as a real place, I have selected works that serve as both representative and distinctive examples of a broader trend within the literature of globalization. I have primarily chosen mainstream novels, which enjoyed both critical and popular success and which also adapted a number of postmodern textual strategies, usually associated with highly experimental fiction, to the form of the traditional novel of character, plot, place, and, especially, manners.[22] Although these novels focus on France and above all Paris, they are also part of a wider American and European phenomenon. A recent call for papers for a multidisciplinary conference on "Voyages" signals an evolution in which Edward Said's "traveling theory" has expanded into Clifford's "traveling cultures";[23] Foster Rhea Dulles's pioneering work on tourism has similarly led to an increasingly popular critical and theoretical location, inhabited by John Urry and Dean MacCannell, among others. Stuart Hall identifies "traveling films" as a present and future cinematic genre, and Alison Russell has recently studied the growing importance of nonfictional travel writing in the late twentieth century. In this context, it would indeed be astonishing if a "new generation of travel novelists" were not ready for discovery as well.[24]

My opening discussion focuses on Diane Johnson's *Le Divorce* (1997) and *Le Mariage* (2000), which serve as a particularly fruitful context in which to illustrate a number of thematic interests and narrative strategies that will prove to be recurrent in contemporary English-language fiction set in France. The successive appearance of the two novels reflects in and of itself the emergence of a trend, just as the subsequent publication of *L'Affaire* (2003), a third novel whose portrait of France informs the conclusion to this book, demonstrates its continuing importance. The first two novels in Johnson's series of three are also interrelated in ways that reveal an evolution, visible elsewhere as well, from an explicit reliance on cross-cultural and comparative structures toward the development of a more broadly international and cosmopolitan framework, better reflective of an age of globalization. Long a well-known and highly regarded novelist and critic, since the publication of *Le Divorce* Johnson has enjoyed an increased prominence within the Anglophone community of Paris-based writers, which has accorded her a stature not unlike that once enjoyed by Gertrude Stein. Johnson's cultural commentary on France and Franco-American relations is now sought by publications as diverse as the *International Herald Tribune* and *Gourmet Magazine*, and she was the first writer contacted when Shakespeare and Company decided to hold a literary festival.[25]

At the same time, Johnson's work also allows for an initial consideration of the profound changes that the international novel inherited from Henry James, whose *Portrait of a Lady* is rewritten within *Le Divorce*, has undergone in a globalized world of altered Franco-American relations. More generally, Johnson establishes the practice of incorporating French texts into Anglophone fictions—Benjamin Constant's *Adolphe* in *Le Divorce* and Jean Renoir's *Rules of the Game* in *Le Mariage*—as a key strategy for constructing literary worlds that exceed conventional national and narrative boundaries. The subsequent analysis in the second essay of Rose Tremain's *The Way I Found Her* (1997), whose novels have won literary prizes in France as well as England, furthers this discussion of intertextuality and literary influence. Tremain not only rewrites *Le Grand Meaulnes*, Alain-Fournier's celebrated novel of adolescence, but she also employs extensive literary and cultural borrowing and the visible practice of translation to create both an international corpus of texts and a cosmopolitan community of readers, traits characteristic of the work of others as well.

Johnson's fiction also reveals the importance within the literature of globalization of the geography of France, in particular, and of spatial configuration, both literal and metaphoric, in general. In *Le Divorce* and *Le Mariage*, EuroDisney and the Paris flea market provide examples, like Shakespeare and Company, of a recurrent imagery of diversity in unity, equally reflective of a globalized world and of the formal structure of the postmodern novel. Two essays devoted to Joanne Harris's *Chocolat* (1999) and *Blackberry Wine* (2000), which, like Johnson's French novels, feature the same location and some of the same characters, explore Harris's metaphoric use of the space of provincial France to represent postmodernity as a world of mobility and rootlessness in which individuals are perpetually trapped between home and the loss of home. In keeping with the tension between the self-reflective and the referential, which is broadly characteristic of Anglophone novels set in France, Harris draws on the codes and conventions of an international amalgam of folk and fairy tales to comment on the reality of France, England, and Europe at the turn of the twenty-first century and to create a new model for a global culture, at once transnational, transcultural, and multilingual. At the same time, however, her work also both recalls and renews the *roman du terroir* or regional novel of Jean Giono and Marcel Pagnol. The parallelism that Harris's novels establish between literary and culinary discourses further links them to the many books about French food and wine, which constitute another significant category of Anglophone books about France and whose contemporary practitioners (Patricia Wells, Mort Rosenblum, Peter Mayle, and Harriet Welty Rochefort), like their fellow novelists, also reprise an earlier tradition.

Despite distinctive differences from Harris's fiction, Claire Messud's *The Last Life* (1999), the focus of my fifth essay, also qualifies as a traveling novel. Messud's text combines a classical coming-of-age story, also characteristic of Tremain's *The Way I Found Her* and yet another discernible subgroup within contemporary English-language fiction set in France, with national allegory. The private story of Messud's young narrator serves as an analogy for the history of France; in recovering her family's personal past, she simultaneously explores the nation's repression of its memories of colonial Algeria and the contemporary anxiety over immigration, multiculturalism, and racial violence that are its enduring consequences. In keeping with a pattern that is equally evident in Johnson's fiction and that we will see again in Edmund White's *The Married Man* (2000), another traveling novel, *The Last Life* foregrounds the constructed nature of national identity and the imaginary or metaphorical character of nations, an idea that has been widely explored in historical and cultural studies since Benedict Anderson's pioneering work on "imagined communities."[26] Like Johnson and others, Messud establishes a structural homology between "France" and "America" and imagines each as a metaphoric repository of myths and imagery whose diverse elements the other can freely borrow and recombine.

The sixth essay is devoted to a selection of the many recent mysteries and detective novels set in Paris. Lest the presence of popular fiction in a study of the mainstream novel seem out of place, the juxtaposition of the two categories in fact serves to foreground a common literary model. Within postmodern theory, the novel of mystery and detection has come to represent an international and hybrid art form that transcends both geographic and generic boundaries, and virtually all of the novels discussed here incorporate some of its conventions, notably, as in the case of Johnson and Tremain, the association of violence with cultural transgression. The specific group of Anglophone mysteries analyzed here confirms the same fascination with those American and British writers who played a significant role in France's cultural and literary past that is evident in Shakespeare and Company's own history and in its 2003 literary festival. Walter Satterthwait's *Masquerade* (1998), Howard Engel's *Murder in Montparnasse* (1999), and Tony Hays's *Murder in the Latin Quarter* (1993) are all set in the cosmopolitan Paris of the "Lost Generation." Fictional characters frequent Gertrude Stein's famous salon and interact with fictionalized versions of Stein, Joyce, Hemingway, and other legendary figures of the era, as the expatriate community of the turn of one century is recreated for the globally literate readers of another. This meeting of modernism and postmodernity sets the reader adrift in a whirlpool of free-floating intertextual allusions, recycled from multiple sources, rewritten, and parodied. The mysteries pay particular attention to the geography of Paris, the privileged location of the detective novel since Edgar Allan Poe invented the genre, and they portray crimes and characters that call into question the meaning of national identity in an international world.

Stein's Paris salon, frequented a decade earlier by Colette, Picasso, and Apollinaire, also figures at the center of Sarah's Smith's trilogy of historical novels: *The Vanished Child* (1992), *The Knowledge of Water* (1996), and *The Citizen of the Country* (2000). In keeping with the capacity of Shakespeare and Company for metamorphosis and renewal, Smith's fictional series moves beyond conventional boundaries of genre and geography to construct and deconstruct an internationally mobile community of 1905–11 as representative of the globally diverse universe of postmodernity. Smith recreates the novel as a form of André Malraux's *musée imaginaire* in which the museum, once the site of closure, coherence, and homogeneity, metaphorically opens up to reveal a wealth of heterogeneous texts in random juxtaposition. In the related space of what we might call the "imaginary library," the landscape of postmodernity is represented by a vast intertextual network of interconnected literary works, which reflects both the tunnels of the new subway under construction below Paris and the underground maze whose passageways mine the geography of provincial France. Once again a narrative of nation, Smith's fiction illustrates the fluidity of national identity as her protagonist, successively missing and then permanently displaced, evolves into the cosmopolitan "citizen of the world" of the final volume of the trilogy.

In the last essay, the similarities and differences between Johnson's version of James's international novel and that illustrated by White's *The Married Man* allow us to explore a final time the patterns of both continuity and change that characterize recent English-language fiction set in France. Like the famous figure of the Parisian *flâneur*, White leads us on a stroll through both Paris and the larger world of globalization to show us that the contemporary experience of postmodernity, characterized by ambivalence as much as alienation, can be lived positively as well as negatively. White, like Johnson and Messud, also juxtaposes the extended exploration of contemporary America to the parallel portrait of France in order to explore the meaning of expatriation in a postmodern world. *The Married Man*, whose narrator openly declares that "a love affair between foreigners is always as much about the mutual seduction of two cultures as a meeting between two people,"[27] provides perhaps the most extensive and innovative illustration of the revival and revision of the conventional Jamesian narrative of cross-cultural romance, common to virtually all of the works discussed in *Literary Globalism*. The substitution of a gay couple for the traditional heterosexual relationship and the analogies established between a homosexual lifestyle and postnational identity link White's novel not only to the earlier work of André Gide and Jean Genet but also to a series of novels that constitute another distinctive subcategory within Anglophone fiction set in France: Philippe Tapon's *A Parisian from Kansas* (1998), Patricia Duncker's *Hallucinating Foucault* (1996), Matthew Stadler's *Allan Stein* (1999), and Monique Truong's *The Book of Salt* (2003). Like the geographical zone beyond borders created within *The Married Man*, the book itself exists in a similarly postmodern space, in and in between a number of different texts.

Taken together, the essays in *Literary Globalism* suggest that in the late twentieth and early twenty-first centuries even mainstream English-language fiction can no longer be contained within conventional boundaries, whether narrative, national, or even, perhaps, linguistic. In an increasingly globalized world of constant border crossing and cultural borrowing, notions of national origin and native language no longer retain the same meaning. That the novels of Johnson, Tremain, Harris, Messud, and White, among others, have not only sold well in France but were translated with unusual rapidity no doubt confirms the interest shared by Francophone and Anglophone readers in exploring literary and cultural constructions set within the cosmopolitan space of postmodernity. Since England and the United States, unlike France, publish relatively few translations,[28] Anglo-Americans can be increasingly expected to experience the foreign primarily through their own language and literature. At the same time, however, English is fast becoming the international language of a culturally unified Europe, what the journalist Kristin Hohendel characterizes as "the passport to a community beyond geographical, cultural, and national identity."[29] Indeed, even as English-language bookstores like Shakespeare and Company proliferate in Paris, a variety of French bookstores have begun to compete with them.[30] By the summer of 2003, not only had the highly commercial FNAC significantly increased its already large selection of English-language books but the traditionally academic Gibert Joseph had opened an entire room devoted to British and American novels in the original. Messud believes that Anglo-American novels set in Paris reflect the fact that national identity applies to fewer and fewer people today: "Quite what the theoretical implications of that reality are, I have no idea. I'm not sure that publishers, the media, the critics, etc. have yet caught up—people still want very much for a book, or an author, to be pigeon-holed, and one of those pigeon-holes is 'national identity'" (personal communication). *Literary Globalism: Anglo-American Fiction Set in France* represents one such attempt to "catch up."

1
The New International Novel: Diane Johnson's *Le Divorce* and *Le Mariage*

IN THE OPENING PAGES OF DIANE JOHNSON'S *LE MARIAGE*, FRENCH BRIDE-to-be Anne-Sophie d'Argel surveys the room in an attempt to determine the *raison-d'être* for the first of the many gatherings of Americans in Paris that she and her fiancé Tim Nolinger will attend in the chapters to come: "Was this a reception for . . . someone who had written a book, another book, about France? *Zut*, they produced them endlessly, anglophones and their books. Even Tim threatened to write one."[1] As someone whose own behavior and beliefs are "patterned after books" (12–13), Anne-Sophie is no doubt particularly well positioned to provide not only a self-referential description of the book we are about to read but also to identify what has indeed become an ever broader and, of late, increasingly diverse cultural and literary trend. It is hardly surprising then that Tim, American journalist and "would-be novelist" (4), should experience both pressure to participate and uncertainty about the kind of contribution he might make: "Shouldn't he have a long project? Write a novel? About what? Or a book about European politics? All he really knew about was being in France—its history, wine, social conditions" (128).

Outside of fiction as well, the last fifteen years have been characterized by the publication of a steady stream of studies devoted to questions of nation, nationalism, and national identity; and the turn of the century appears to be marked by continued, even renewed, interest in such issues. In part, no doubt, because scholars have increasingly promoted the use of comparative methodologies and cross-cultural approaches to an understanding of national identity, works about France and the United States, each of which has traditionally defined its own cultural specificity in relation to that of the other country, have figured prominently in this corpus. The particular category defined by Anne-Sophie would alone include, for example, Theodore Zeldin's *The French* (1983), Richard Bernstein's *Fragile Glory: A Portrait of France and the French* (1990), Robert Daly's *Portraits of France* (1991), and Richard F. Kuisel's *Seducing the French: The Dilemma of Americanization* (1991), to cite only a few of the best known of the Anglophone books about France. Although the occasional autobiography (Alice Kaplan's *French Lessons: A Memoir* [1993]), travelogue (Nicholas Delbanco's *Running in Place: Scenes from the South of France* [1989]), and even novel (Linda Ashour's *Speaking in Tongues* [1988]) also found their way into print during this period, until recently the field was largely dominated by the work of cultural historians, anthropologists, sociologists, and professional journalists. Indeed, a turn toward a more personal approach to France and the French with a noticeable increase in the output of essayists (Adam Gopnik, David Sedaris), memoirists (Art Buchwald, Edmund White), and especially novelists constitutes the first of two significant shifts in direction that have marked this category of texts in the last few years.

The second change involves both a broadening and a refocusing within the general context of studies of nation to embrace a number of recent works that reconfigure questions of national identity and cultural specificity within the larger framework of globalization. The vast majority of these works concentrate almost exclusively on the economic or political dimensions of the phenomenon; moreover, the few books that do profess an interest in "cultural globalization," such as Thomas Friedman's best-selling *The Lexus and the Olive Tree* (1999) and even, despite its title, John Tomlinson's *Globalization and Culture* (1999), tend to two approaches, both of which arguably distance us, albeit in different ways, from the realm and the range of culture.[2] Either "cultural globalization" becomes something else than what it is—culture is equated with "environmentalism"—or it becomes something less than what it could be; that is, culture is reduced to "popular culture." In the latter case, the tendency to focus almost exclusively on visual media—television, advertising, movies—essentially ignores the domain of the written text. Not even international bestsellers à la Peter Mayle, to cite a particularly pertinent example, enter into the discussion.

Certainly the serious novel is conspicuous only by its absence, since the difference between "low" and "high" culture plays a key role in a general understanding of the contemporary globalized world as one in which the homogenizing tendencies of mass art have overwhelmed the presumed distinctiveness of national literatures. Yet, if advertising texts, to borrow a key example from Tomlinson, owe their cultural significance to the fact that "people make use of" them in the same way that "they use novels," it would seem self-evident that novels themselves must also "remain significant cultural texts."[3] Moreover, it is the serious—and not the popular—novel that logically holds special promise as the cultural form most likely to evolve in ways that will reflect the "complex connectivity" that Tomlinson considers to be the defining feature of globalization.[4] As Rob Kroes reminds us, prevalent representations of popular and elite culture are based on a "double standard"; in fact, they are grounded in an ironic reversal, an essential contradiction, that erases the original intentions of modern literature:

> What is often held against the emerging international mass, or pop, culture is precisely its international, if not cosmopolitan, character. Clearly this is a case of double standards. At the level of high culture, most clearly in its modernist phase, there has always been this dream of transcending the local, the provincial, and the national, or in social terms, to transgress the narrow bounds of the bourgeois world and to enter a realm that is nothing if not international: the transcendence lay in being truly "European" or "cosmopolitan."[5]

As we enter the newly globalized world of the twenty-first century, the contemporary Anglo-American novel once again reflects the ambition to enter an international realm, to be "European" or "cosmopolitan."[6] I wish to propose a reading of Diane Johnson's *Le Divorce* (1997) and *Le Mariage* (2000) that will serve as one example of what, as I noted above, constitutes a discernible pattern within recent and current publications of English-language fiction. Johnson offers a particularly apt illustration of this phenomenon for a number of reasons. In the first place, the successive appearance of *Le Divorce* and *Le Mariage* reproduces the pattern in and of itself and thus already bears witness to its importance.[7] Moreover, the two novels are interrelated in ways that also allow for an exploration of the passage I have described from the explicit use of direct cross-cultural comparison to more diffuse forms of literary globalism. In this context, Johnson's frequent characterization as a relatively traditional novelist, whose works, including *Le Divorce* and *Le Mariage*, can be classified within such established genres as the "comic novel" or "the novel of manners" and compared to the realist fiction of the nineteenth century, is also of importance. I will argue that her novels nonetheless highlight certain textual strategies shared by other contemporary writers of "Anglophone books about France," which, although they differ from novel to novel, can nonetheless all be grouped under the rubric of "postmodernism," viewed, as a result, as the literary counterpart of globalization.

In addition, Johnson is a well established writer, whose last two novels nonetheless achieved an unusual degree of critical and popular success. *Le Divorce* was not only a finalist for the 1997 National Book Award but also, and perhaps more importantly, brought Johnson, by her own admission, an unprecedented number of readers: "It was the first time in my life that I might be sitting next to someone at a dinner party or on an airplane, and if I admitted that I had written this book, they would have read it."[8] The particular kind of novel represented by *Le Divorce* and *Le Mariage* would therefore appear to have arrived at a moment in time when there is a considerable degree of coincidence between text and context, between what these novels have to offer and what an identifiable group of serious readers finds to be of interest. It is relevant to recall in this context that a number of recent scholars have proposed, with Ella Shohat and Robert Stam, that "beliefs about nations often crystallize in the form of stories" and, with Friedman, that the best way to reach an understanding of globalization is "through stories."[9]

In identifying storytelling as a "ubiquitous human activity" in an essay now some twenty-five years old, Louis Mink also argued that the kinds of stories that get told vary from culture to culture, just as those that get repeated within a particular culture significantly shape its national consciousness.[10] Given the frequently expressed concern that the process of globalization will produce a general homogenization of world culture, one might wonder if the stories that nations tell will also begin to resemble each other—somewhat more, that is, than they clearly already do. Neither the story of the American in Paris nor the narrative of cross-cultural romance, both of which not only reappear but begin to proliferate internally within *Le Divorce* and *Le Mariage*, is in any way original in and of itself, although the renewed popularity of both is certainly of interest. In *The Married Man*, another contemporary version of the same old story, Edmund White's narrator openly declares that "a love affair between foreigners is always as much about the mutual seduction of two cultures as a meeting between two people."[11] Given the nature of the historic relationship between France and the United States, which Tom Bishop qualifies as "more that of a love affair than that of a friendship," it is hardly surprising that the Franco-American couple has been featured with particular frequency in this romantic plot.[12] In contemporary Anglophone novels about France, this private relationship most frequently serves to metaphorize national and cultural differences.

In Johnson's fiction, cross-cultural romance achieves near mythic status by virtue of its elevation to the level of a depersonalized, general model, coupled with its simultaneous reproduction in a seemingly endless stream of variants. In *Le Divorce*, Isabel Walker spends six months in Paris with her stepsister Roxy, whose husband, Charles-Henri de Persand, has just left her for another woman, Magda Tellman, who is also married to an American. Isabel herself will have flings with several young Frenchmen and a love affair with Edgar de Persand, Charles-Henri's elderly uncle. In the background, Charles-Henri's sister Charlotte will run off to London with her English lover; several other Franco-American couples of Roxy's acquaintance will also split up; and by the end of the novel Roxy herself appears to be attracted to yet another potential French husband. If Isabel seeks to convince us that the characters in her narrative are "not generic Americans" (2), the hero of *Le Mariage*, in contrast, is explicitly introduced as "a generic young man," indistinguishable from "dozens of Americans like him in Paris" (6); and he is engaged to a woman who is described as "a compendium of received French ideas" (171). The lives of Tim and Anne-Sophie are interwoven with those of two other Americans in Paris, the filmmaker Serge Cray and Clara Holly, his wife, who has an affair with their neighbor, Antoine de Persand, yet another of Charles-Henri's siblings.

In keeping with characters like Antoine who move from one novel to the next, the titles of *Le Divorce* and *Le Mariage* are clearly interchangeable and function together to announce the troubled dynamics of cross-cultural romance in Johnson's fictional world. In a pattern more reminiscent, at least in the abstract, of a Racinian tragedy than of a comic novel of manners, every relationship, regardless of the form it takes at any particular moment, is in some way unsuitable; potentially, if not yet actually, unhappy; and always doomed to end, if not to fail. The most common complication, that of adultery, suggests that the merging of different cultures produces an impure, an "adulterated," mixture, which almost invariably explodes in violence and destruction. Marital infidelity consistently provokes acts deemed illegal or even openly criminal, as if the betrayal of one's lover or spouse amounted to something like high treason.

Thus Roxy, eight months pregnant, attempts to kill herself; and she remains the primary suspect in Charles-Henri's death, even after another American, Magda's husband, is arrested for his murder. Isabel is taken into police custody as Tellman's accomplice, while he holds the rest of the family hostage in the Château de la Belle au Bois Dormant in EuroDisney. Clara's husband publicly stages an attempt to murder his wife at Tim and Anne-Sophie's rehearsal dinner, and Clara is first verbally assaulted and physically threatened at the local post office and then condemned to prison for the desecration of a national monument—all by virtue of having bought a dilapidated chateau that once belonged to Madame du Barry, or of denying local hunters their right of access to her property, or maybe both. In short, anti-Americanism among the French, who perceive "the innate American desire for hegemony [to be] expressed by private citizens as much as in actions by the state" (*Le Mariage*, 196), is understandably rampant in Johnson's novels; and the American community, which spends much of its time and energy raising money to defend U.S. citizens against "irrational persecution by an entire nation" (*Le Mariage*, 222), is, equally understandably, strongly isolationist.

But *what* happens in *Le Divorce* and *Le Mariage*—and clearly rather a lot does—is far less important than *where* it occurs, and I mean this both literally and metaphorically and in a number of different ways. Although fiction is traditionally viewed as a primarily temporal medium, Johnson and her fellow novelists immediately call our attention to the construction of their novels as predominantly spatial entities with a complex geography of their own. In the opening "Prologue" to *Le Divorce* (1–3), a first-person narrator with the promising name of Isabel "Walker" takes us on a tour both of Paris and of the novel to come. Isabel, a film school dropout who conceives of her story "as a sort of film," offers us a credit sequence constructed as a visual montage of characters and scenes that constitute the raw material whose subsequent rearrangement will engender the novel. An initial high angle shot "establishes" only our presence in a generic "foreign city"; not until the camera moves in to reveal "the cliches of Frenchness"— baguettes, berets, poodles, and "perhaps the Eiffel Tower"—can the place be identified as Paris. Subsequent close-ups, however, immediately challenge the accuracy of stereotypes as geographical signposts: "we become aware that some of the people we are seeing are not French, that among all the Gallic bustle are many Americans," who, at a distance, can easily be "mistaken for European."[13] A second look at the picture as a whole reveals that the landscape is also haunted by literary expatriates of the past: "There are, also, certain ghosts of Hemingway and Gertrude Stein, Janet Flanner, Fitzgerald, Edith Wharton, James Baldwin, James Jones—all of them . . . conscious of a connection to Europe. Europe, repository of something they wish to know."[14]

The image of Europe as "repository" is one of the key controlling metaphors of Johnson's fiction, one that will be reconfigured in a number of different ways and take on a number of alternative shapes in *Le Divorce* and *Le Mariage*. In its most politically realistic configuration, the main characters of Johnson's first novel—Isabel, Roxy, Edgar—are all increasingly obsessed with the image of the Balkans, which reproduces the interpersonal tensions of divorce and marriage on an international scale. Made up of so many places as to be no place at all, an artificially unified site of irreconcilable differences, a space of perpetually shifting borders in constant internal flux, the Balkans are the repository of a failed vision of "Europe"—paralyzed, endlessly torn apart, by the inability to move beyond national, cultural, and ethnic identities to create a cosmopolitan whole. Its example drives Isabel to reject nationality, to redefine her "transplanted" American self as "a person without a country" (309).[15] In other Anglophone novels about France, such characteristic mobility and rootlessness of American characters in France figure what Aamir Mufti and Ella Shohat call the postmodern paradox of "home and loss of home," represented in contemporary criticism by the metaphoric figure of the migrant.[16]

Isabel's crisis of identity also has a more immediate cause in the painting of Saint Ursula, a free-floating object in constant motion throughout the novel, which functions as an objective correlative of Isabel's own situation. The painting, by an unknown artist, is variously attributed, claimed by several different potential owners, and finally sold at public auction to an unidentified buyer.[17] Hence Isabel's outrage when the Persand family attempts to keep Saint Ursula from leaving France, on the grounds that "it is a French picture, after all":

> This horrible idea gave me a glimpse into the stupid Serbs, crazed Irishmen, all those moronic brutes in the Balkans, all those fanatic Arabs in their identical costumes, all deranged by this really limiting idea, the dismal, lazy-minded habit of nationality, and I saw that I would never understand it. Maybe I had some crude new-World mentality that prevented me from seeing the charm of belonging to any nation at all. (195)

Books, like countries, are the repositories of knowledge; and the creation of an imaginary "Europe" is very much a literary ambition, as *Le Divorce*'s opening evocation of a pantheon of expatriate writers reminds us. Like other postmodern novelists of globalization, for whom "France" is often evoked as a cultural and historical *patrimoine*, Johnson uses intertextuality as one strategy for constructing a fictional world characterized by the "complex connectivity" that underlies the process of globalization.[18] With one important exception, to which I will return, intertextuality in Johnson's work is rarely explicit or sustained; rather, it functions evocatively and allusively to provoke a kind of Proustian displacement in the memory of the reader. Antoine Compagnon describes the epigraph as "the quintessence of quotation," whose function is to announce a relationship between the book we are reading and an earlier text in order to establish "une liaison qui accouple ou même confond deux systèmes" [a connection that couples or even confuses the two systems].[19] (I have cited Compagnon in the original since the suggestive sexuality of the process as described in French seems eminently suitable to refer to a novel that is structured around the intercultural "liaisons" of its characters.) In *Le Divorce* an extensive network of epigraphs substitutes for chapter titles. The quotations are of sufficient length and so closely allied with the content of the chapters they introduce that they resemble the captions that accompany photographs or the capsule summaries that sometimes precede newspaper articles.[20] This would be of little interest were it not for the fact that virtually all of the epigraphs are taken from French writers, so that a contemporary American novel becomes in some significant sense repositioned within a French literary tradition. Readers who follow the itinerary of the transhistorical and transcultural voyage that is proposed to them will be transported into an imaginary literary space beyond all conventional boundaries.

References and allusions to Henry James, who wrote "Anglophone books about France" at the turn of the twentieth century, logically abound in the new version of such texts that have appeared at the dawn of the twenty-first century.[21] Few readers of *Le Divorce* are likely to miss the novel's internal referencing of James's *The Portrait of a Lady* (1882); analogies of name and of situation make of Isabel Walker the contemporary counterpart or "remake" of Isabel Archer. Both come to Europe from America at the request of relatives but in search of knowledge; both value independence and freedom; both are characterized by their intelligence, curiosity, and resourcefulness. Both fall in love (or believe that they have). One marries unhappily and would willingly abandon her husband; the other has an affair she is unhappy to see end and believes she will be abandoned. It may seem excessive to compare the one's lover to the other's husband, but in fact "oncle Edgar" has something of Gilbert Osmond's "European" character—a certain rigidity and preoccupation with tradition and form—and Edgar, too, actively seeks to (re)shape his Isabel's mind.

Clearly such similarities operate only at a very general level and to very different consequences—a hundred years later, notably, Isabel Walker is the narrator of her own story. They serve primarily to remind us that reading is an activity that allows one to cross borders, that its shared practice creates an international conversation and a potentially cosmopolitan consciousness. In confirmation, readers of *Le Divorce* have the added pleasure of discovering that Johnson's novel is in fact simultaneously contextualized by another text, Benjamin Constant's *Adolphe*, whose influence within its own national canon rivals that of James; indeed, Constant's subjective, psychological tale of cruelty is frequently cited as the very paradigm of an "indelibly French" novel.[22] Thirteen of the thirty-five epigraphs in *Le Divorce* come from *Adolphe* (no other source appears more than once). Because Johnson's quotations reference passages from throughout Constant's novel, she metaphorically recreates his text within her own and revises both through their superimposition; as readers, we inhabit a cross-cultural echo chamber, an intertextual "virtual reality." Nor is Constant's influence either gratuitous or merely decorative. Once we perceive the shadow of *Adolphe* hovering above *Le Divorce*, we are less likely to find Roxy's suicide attempt and Charles-Henri's murder as incongruous as they otherwise tend to appear. Moreover, the presence of what Constant himself described as "the awful relationship [which is] that of a man who no longer loves and a woman who does not want to cease being loved"[23] reminds us that Isabel initially conceives of her narrative as "Roxy's story" rather than her own; moreover, her immediate revision of this assertion is expressed in terms that are equally revelatory in this context: "Perhaps it isn't Roxy's story so much as the story of *an intersection* of all our lives," including, I would suggest, those of characters in similarly patterned novels (100, my emphasis).

In Anne-Sophie, *Le Mariage* offers us a particularly appropriate diegetic reader; in ironic counterpoint to all those Anglophones who write books about France, Tim's fiancee is a French woman who reads works by Anglophone writers. Anne-Sophie is also a seriously unreliable reader whose culturally biased summaries of the novels she is reading can be amusingly perplexing. Clearly, the presence of multinational characters in fiction will not necessarily prevent chauvinistic (mis)readings nor produce cosmopolitan readers. Anne-Sophie always identifies with the character she most closely resembles by virtue of gender and nationality and then assumes, in total disregard for the internal coherence of the fictional world, that this is a compelling intradiegetic necessity rather than a highly subjective extradiegetic choice. Thus, *The Ambassadors* (41), *Jane Eyre* (99), and *The Sun Almost Rises* all become books about "French girls" to varying degrees of success. Anne-Sophie is particularly puzzled by the reputation of Hemingway's novel—"It said on the jacket this stupid book was required reading for every college freshman in America, imagine!"—given its glaring weaknesses of plot and plausibility: "a story that had begun promisingly enough with a poor French girl . . . disappointingly veered off to become the story of the main character, Jake, who was not at all like Tim" (173). As for Anne-Sophie's own symbolic standing among American women in Paris as "the perfect Française" (202), it is an entirely fictional construct based on the actions and the advice of the sophisticated, worldly heroines of her mother's best-selling historical novels.

In addition to Estelle D'Argel, who, despite an international reputation in a genre popular worldwide, would nonetheless appear to be a characteristically "Franco-Française" novelist (indeed, she is explicitly modeled on Colette), there are two other figures of the writer in *Le Mariage* who help us understand Johnson's conception of fiction in the globalized present. Whatever his literary ambitions, for the moment Tim Nolinger is still a journalist, albeit one of unusual range. In fact, to be exact, the man introduced as "the American journalist Thomas Ackroyd Nolinger" (4) is half European and only "ostensibly" a journalist (5). More accurately described as "a wanderer," his mixed heritage and cosmopolitan upbringing have left him "unsuited for fitting into either culture" (4): "Tim had never had a strong feeling of nationality. Though his passport declared him unequivocally American, he had never felt the need for deciding whether he was American or really European, and he thought that the whole subject of nationality was arbitrary and divisive" (254).[24] It is precisely Tim's in-between status, his ability to "wander," both literally and intellectually, in an intercultural space beyond national borders, that accounts for his success as a writer. Tim regularly contributes to two different news magazines, one ideologically conservative, the other politically liberal. Moreover, what Tim jokingly dismisses as "a kind of curse," that is, the fact that he "can usually see both sides" (157), does not result in the alternating or even the simultaneous submission of essays on different subjects. Rather, depending on point of view and structuring principle, the identical situation, the same set of raw data, reveal themselves to be the "repository" of multiple and diverse versions of one "virtual" story.[25]

Appropriately, since the notion of *auterism* or film authorship is similarly based on the identification of patterns of renewal and repetition within an individual director's body of work, one of Tim's primary narrative functions in *Le Mariage* is to gain access to the renowned but reclusive *auteur*, Serge Cray. As in *Le Divorce*, Johnson privileges the medium of film in seeking analogies for the expansive structure and the infinite capacity to contain that she imagines for a contemporary "cosmopolitan" or "European" international novel.[26] In language that recalls the importance of spatial metaphors in Johnson's work, Cray rhapsodizes about the advantages of film as a means of creative expression; the movement of the frames and the width of the screen are "so beautiful compared to the crampedness, crabbedness of books" (90).[27] Still, Cray also loves books—and not just for "their role as forerunners of films" (90). He collects ancient manuscripts and incunabula, and it is in his role as a collector that Tim first succeeds in approaching him: "Collecting as a logical extension of the role of *auteur*? Filmmaking as a form of collecting, in the sense that it was an accretion of images and ideas?" (6). Despite Tim's fear that such notions may be "too flimsy to stick" even in his own mind (6), a timely occurrence of the very "serendipity" (14) that leads Tim to Cray—and to a large extent determines the structure of *Le Mariage* as a whole—confirms Tim's theory of the contemporary artist as collector. In her two most recent films *Les Glaneurs et la Glaneuse* (2000) and *Deux Ans après* (2002), Agnès Varda explores the metaphor of "gleaning"—the selection and gathering of what remains of value among objects that have been discarded, rejected, or left behind—as a reflection both of the human condition in the modern world and of her own filmmaking practice.

Cray is merely the last and the most representative of Johnson's collectors, who are already present in the background and in secondary roles in *Le Divorce* before they multiply in number, increase in importance, and move center stage in *Le Mariage*. What unites all of them is their collective presence within the metaphoric space that serves as both *mise-en-abyme* for Johnson's fiction and microcosm of a globalized world. In what might well be most accurately described as "flea market novels," le Marché aux Puces de St. Ouen functions as a crossroads at which both characters and plots intersect. Cheval-Art, the stand where Anne-Sophie sells "horsey artifacts" (8) in *Le Mariage*, becomes, for example, the locus at which she and Tim cross paths with Delia and Gabriel, American collectors on a buying trip, transitional figures who serve as a conduit to the world of Clara and Cray. In both *Le Divorce* and *Le Mariage*, the flea market functions as a crime scene, at once a passageway for the movement of stolen goods and the site of theft and murder.[28] Geographical origin of the "complex connectivity"[29] that structures the thematic excess of Johnson's novels and allows the curious juxtaposition of domestic relationships and violent acts, the flea market also functions in *Le Mariage* as the auto-generative source of the raw material of the novel itself. In an internal duplication of this larger process, Cray comes to *le marché aux puces*, as if it were a vast prop room on a film studio lot, to pick up what he needs for the sets of his film. That many of the same objects subsequently migrate into the decor of his own home confirms that this is the ambiguous world of postmodernity where authenticity is always in question.

But the flea market is not only the metaphoric container and generator of fiction; it is also the repository of the image of Europe—of Europe itself as repository. During Delia's visit to the *marché aux puces*, she steps into "a cavernous warehouse space stacked with furniture and cartons" (27), whose internal reproduction, on a smaller scale, of the market as a whole concentrates its evocative power:

> In the dim early light, it was a magic cavern, a backstage, a magician's attic. Pictures in broken gilt frames and furniture were stacked along the walls to teetering heights, draped with padded cloths. Pieces of faded fresco suggested windows, vistas beyond, a palm tree made of tin grew from a box in the corner, a herd of heads of antlered animals were hung along the rafters. This mysterious world suggested all the places Delia had never been. (27)

On the example of a Europe still under construction at the dawn of the twenty-first century, the flea market offers a compelling image of national specificity and international diversity contained within a global space of unity. Made up of countless individual stalls, the *marché aux puces* is constructed on a model of markets within markets, whose external boundaries and internal configurations are determined by the particular kind of merchandise displayed by each. Although some signs of the bargains, cheap imported goods, and economic diversity, which characterized the flea market in an earlier era, still remain visible on its outskirts, the contemporary *marché aux puces* featured in Johnson's work specializes in luxury goods, in keeping with global economic prosperity—statuary, porcelain, curios, *bijoux*, chandeliers, marble busts, antique furniture, even "entire rooms of woodwork peeled off the walls of castles" (*Le Divorce*, 214)[30]—which attract an internationally mixed and cosmopolitan clientele of buyers, collectors, and tourists. Johnson's characters experience it as a vast commercial market, a museum, an open-air restaurant, or a pleasant place to take a stroll. With its acres of alleys and curious juxtaposition of heterogeneous "climates," *le marché aux puces* is quite literally comparable to a city, indeed, a country—maybe even a continent. It has its own addresses, directories, street signs, maps, and tourist guides—Gabriel will, in fact, take up temporary residence as Anne-Sophie's neighbor in the warehouse described above.

In *Le Divorce*, in contrast, where the division of property is still largely determined by national origins and Franco-American differences, the *marché aux puces* is unquestionably French territory. For Roxy and Isabel, the market represents a degree of "human materialism" they would have found "unimaginable" in the United States—perhaps, speculates Isabel, because "America just hasn't had a long enough history to accumulate all those objects" (217). Similarly, their visiting parents specifically love the market for its comforting foreignness: "they knew it couldn't happen in California" (217). Consistent with a world still structured by cross-cultural oppositions, in the first of her French novels Johnson positions a metaphoric EuroDisney as the American counterpart to the *marché aux puces*. Like the flea market—and, of course, like "America" itself—EuroDisney also constitutes a unified geographical space that contains diverse regions or "lands" within its borders, marked by intersecting streets and distinctive architectural styles. The park has an eclectic residential population and attracts an international clientele to its luxury hotels and restaurants. A preeminently commercial enterprise, EuroDisney is simultaneously a playground for children and adults alike; it markets not only its own brand of distinctive merchandise but also a variety of special attractions and theatrical performances. After six months in "the make-believe world of France," Isabel finds herself unexpectedly at home in this more familiar fantasy world: "we had a nice time, it was all so decorative and sweet, an idealized America, and I had to admit it was nice to be back in America, especially America refined to its ideal essence" (263).[31]

"America refined to its ideal essence," however, always appears to include the possibility of violence, a theory confirmed in *Le Mariage*, where dramatic tension once again reaches its climax and conclusion in a space in which the "make-believe" and the "real" are temporarily superimposed. In keeping with the "flair" anticipated from "a great *auteur* and *metteur en scène*" (291), Serge Cray entertains his guests at Tim and Anne-Sophie's rehearsal dinner with a clip from a remastered print of Jean Renoir's *La Règle du jeu*. Although the analogies between Renoir's "great classic" and Johnson's novel will have occurred to most readers long before they arrive at the chapter entitled "The Rules of the Game," we are still likely to concur with Tim that "it seemed a damned strange movie to show at a wedding party" (299), particularly since the scene that Cray chooses to project is taken from the hunt and not, as one might expect, from the costume ball.[32] Or rather, Cray succeeds in having it both ways, since the spectators of Renoir's film find themselves momentarily displaced into—and within—the world of the film: "For an eerie moment, they were the company in the film, this was the hall of the little marquis, these were the guests now dressed in dinner clothes, reviewing an entertainment of which they had been a part that afternoon. An eerie effect, one that surely Cray was aware of" (300). Indeed, Cray, like his rival Antoine de Persand, is clearly "remembering the rest of the Renoir film" (302). As he points a shotgun at his unfaithful wife—in Cray's remake, Clara, rather than her lover, is cast in the role of the rabbit—his guests, like those in *La Règle du jeu,* "continue to watch with interest, not sure this was not the beginning of a skit or entertainment" (304).

This single example in Johnson's two novels of the explicit, specific, and sustained use of an intertextual analogy is ultimately less exceptional than it initially appears. The reference to *La Règle du jeu* confirms once again the importance evident in her recent work of establishing patterns of "complex connectivity" in an age in which neither nations nor novels can be contained within conventionally fixed boundaries, whether spatial, cultural, or textual. The many parallels between *Le Mariage* and the film interpreted by Cray as "an allegory of marriage" (301) serve less to recall a similar subject matter than to highlight the extensive structural and metaphoric networks that link characters, themes, and plotlines in Johnson's novel. For François Truffaut, principal theoretician of the concept of film authorship, *La Règle du jeu* was "certainly the film that sparked the careers of the greatest number of directors," and Serge Cray is no exception.[33] Indeed, the sequence he projects from Renoir's film explicitly recalls his own work, both in terms of the violence it portrays and in the technique used to portray it: "The horrifying length of the sequence was worthy of Cray himself, whose reluctance to leave a scene was one of his most characteristic mannerisms, almost a film tic" (300). Cray's vision of film also depends upon the expression of abstract ideas, such that the "hypothetical movie" he has been researching for years, ostensibly about "America as a nation in right-wing revolt," would, in fact, result in "a film of enormous sweep" that would "by extension reflect all the protest lying in the hearts of all patriots in all the world, and the depravity of all oppression" (89).

One might wonder why anyone would think that a movie about America, even an abstract, allegorical America, could achieve such extraordinary range, although Johnson's ironic description is surely meant to evoke the exaggerated sense of its own universal importance and international influence that is all too often reflected in the discourse of the actual country—much to the exasperation of other nations, those of Europe, in particular, and France, most of all. If the first wave of contemporary "Anglophone books about France" readily fits into a long tradition of cross-cultural comparison and analysis, how are we to explain their continued importance within the much less clear-cut geographical and cultural context of globalization? If it is plausible to see the work of Johnson and others in terms of a revival and revision of a "cosmopolitan" and specifically "European" novel, what is "France," on the one hand, and "America," on the other, doing in this imaginary space, let alone dominating it? Part of Johnson's value as illustration of a broader literary trend is to begin to point the way to some possible answers. If Benjamin Franklin's conviction that France is everyone's second country still rings true, globalization— widely referred to as "Americanization"—has meant that American popular culture is rapidly becoming "everyone's second culture"[34] and English an international language. Johnson's use of spatial metaphors and intertextual allusions to portray "America" and "Europe" as comparable, indeed, superimposable, locations reflects the degree to which they must be seen, according to Kroes and other contemporary cultural historians, as "metaphorical constructs"; more importantly, it also allows Johnson to configure "America" as the "constituent element" of European culture it has become.[35]

In this context, the presence of "EuroDisney" in *Le Divorce*, some years after the park had been officially rebaptized as "Disneyland Paris," certainly results from a deliberate and meaningful choice. In Johnson's version, EuroDisney is precisely not the "embarrassing, envious, derivative collection of cardboard castles, an American dream of old-world splendor," which Isabel expects to find, but rather a surprisingly harmless, amiable, optimistic, and very pretty "America" (262–63). In other words, EuroDisney does not represent an American dream of Europe but rather a European dream of America. In contrast, by portraying anti-Americanism, in the form of envy of European culture, as an American trait, Johnson points to the ambiguities of contemporary globalism, itself perhaps best understood as something like a metaphor, a voyage only begun, constantly changing direction and in which nothing is ever quite what—or where—it seems.[36]

In *Le Mariage*, in keeping not only with the connotations of the title but also with the fact that a French word names an Anglophone novel, surface differences between "Europe" and "America" are ultimately bridged by an underlying structural similarity of a scope and a nature not unrelated to the process of globalization itself.[37] What allows Cray to believe that a film about "America" will be of international import is the progressive revelation in the course of the novel that "the developing pattern of anti-Americanism in Europe, paralleled, paradoxically, the rise of antigovernment ferment at home in America" (222). The latter turns out to thrive amidst the multiple stalls of the Sweet Home Antique Barn run by "the consorted cults of Oregon" (162), the repository of such a confusing mixture of goods, groups, and motives that Tim despairs of ever understanding "the connection among these things" (213). The American equivalent of the *marché aux puces*, this new configuration of space offers, like Johnson's cosmopolitan fiction, "a way of imposing order on the random materials of the chaotic world" (5). Selecting elements indiscriminately from American and European culture, *Le Divorce* and *Le Mariage* recombine and rearrange them in a fashion that Kroes qualifies as distinctively postmodern: "For America to fulfill its salvage mission, it has to treat Europe's culture . . . as one large *objet trouvé*, recasting, duplicating, multiplying, crossbreeding, and massmarketing it."[38]

2
Intertextual Travel and Translation: Rose Tremain's *The Way I Found Her*

"*IF YOU UNDERSTAND WHAT IS* PRIME, *ESPECIALLY WHEN WHAT IS PRIME APPEARS random or accidental, then you are getting somewhere in your understanding of the world*," writes Lewis Little, the thirteen-year-old narrator of Rose Tremain's *The Way I Found Her*, in the notebook he keeps to record his thoughts and observations during a summer vacation spent in Paris.[1] As both confirmation and illustration of Lewis's insight, I want to move into the world of Tremain's 1997 novel by relating an apparently random discovery of my own, made during a walk through Paris not unlike those that Lewis frequently undertakes. Indeed, anyone strolling in or by the Jardin du Luxembourg in the fall of the year 2000 would have come upon the same unusual exhibit.

"La Terre vue du ciel" ("Earth From Above"), consisting of over 150 aerial photographs taken by Yann Arthus-Bertrand in seventy-six different countries over a five-year period, was conceived to reflect the diversity of the world at the turn of the century and to bear witness to the state of the planet for future generations. Intentions so clearly defined, however, in the catalog and in the written commentary, which accompanied the exhibit, in fact resulted in a postmodern experience of visual disjunction. If conventional boundaries, both geographic and aesthetic, were first challenged by the transformation of the metal gratings of a public park into the site of an art gallery or a museum, the simultaneous display of artificial representations of the natural world within the space of nature itself was perhaps even more disorienting.[2] In a further disruption of perspective, one looked up at photos that had been taken looking down, and which, moreover, did not immediately reveal either their true content or even their mimetic origins. Rather, the passerby was initially seduced by pure form and composition—lines, shapes, textures, and colors, organized into seemingly abstract patterns and geometric designs, to which the beauty of the places actually represented seemed almost irrelevant.

Meanwhile, however, in keeping with postmodern rules of reproduction and repetition, the clearly multilingual and cosmopolitan public attracted to this corner of the Jardin du Luxembourg also had access to a variant model of the same exhibit. Visitors were able to walk about on a map of the world, mounted on a platform in front of the Senate, which allowed them to look down, this time from the perspective of the photographer, upon the geographic locales identified by miniature versions of the same images whose enlargements hung nearby. On the several occasions on which I was present, they used this scaffolding as inspiration; it served to orient their own memories and to support their own stories of international travel.

Consciously constructed as a puzzle of perspective to be solved by an actively engaged reader, Tremain's novel also fuses the abstract and the representational, explores the boundaries between imagination and vision, encourages storytelling, and offers another image of the diversity of the world contained within the unified space of art. But beyond the many specific parallels between my reading of "La Terre vue du ciel" and my understanding of *The Way I Found Her*, to which I will return, what is "prime" in this apparently random juxtaposition of a French photographer of reality and an English writer of fiction is the way in which both construct works that can be considered representative of a newly globalized world. An Anglophone novel set primarily in France, like Diane Johnson's *Le Divorce* and *Le Mariage*, *The Way I Found Her* similarly foregrounds certain characteristically postmodern textual strategies that confirm the simultaneous emergence of a particular novel of globalization in England and the United States.

In keeping with the potential for loss of direction implicit in the enigmatic title of *The Way I Found Her*, Tremain appropriately, if serendipitously, frames Lewis Little's first-person narrative between an initial dedication to a friend who "navigated along the route" and a final acknowledgment of an artist whose Paris watercolors "inspired many of the trails [she] followed on the ground." In a novel that is indeed importantly structured by travel and the geography of Paris, Lewis accompanies his beautiful mother Alice, the current English translator of Valentina Gavril's best-selling medieval romances, when she is summoned from their home in Devon to Paris to practice an unusual written version of "simultaneous translation" that will allow Valentina's still unfinished but eagerly awaited new novel to appear in French and English at the same time. Often left alone, Lewis takes long walks through Paris with Valentina's dog Sergei, discusses existentialism with the roofer Didier who is replacing the slates outside Lewis's attic bedroom, and discovers the existence of Benin and the problems of illegal immigration through his friendship with Valentina's African house cleaner Babba. Increasingly neglected by Alice, whose unexplained absences curiously coincide with Didier's failure to show up for work, Lewis's primary preoccupation is his growing obsession with Valentina, who functions at once as a substitute source of maternal affection, an object of romantic attachment, and a focus of sexual fantasy. When Valentina suddenly disappears, Lewis sets out on a dangerous quest to solve the mystery, which leads to his own kidnapping, endangers both of their lives, and concludes in a daring attempt to escape that costs Valentina her life.

If paintings seen by Tremain herself guide the search that she has her hero undertake in the fictional streets of Paris, it is literature read within the novel that in fact determines "the way he finds her." A variation of the *narrateur-témoin* of French fiction, initially more witness than actor, Lewis is an attentive and astute observer of the world around him;[3] and he repeatedly calls our attention to the significance of point of view and to the effects of perspective. What he likes best about his attic room at the top of Valentina's apartment is the round window, from which he can contemplate, all at the same time, the sky above, the street below, and the roofs opposite. "If a window is round," he writes his father, "you expect to see more interesting things out of it than out of a normal window" (41). The most interesting thing framed in Lewis's unusual window is the scaffolding cage that Didier has constructed just beyond. Before long, Lewis has begun to climb out of his window and to spend the night on the roof, which affords him a unique vantage point: "Hardly anybody knows what the world looks like from their own rooftop" (57). In Tremain's postmodern metafiction, the emphasis placed on vision, on how it is framed and what underlies it, functions metaphorically to draw the reader's attention to the framework and the scaffolding that support her own novel. From his rooftop position, Lewis plunges into the world of fiction; he spends his nights, whether in the attic or on the roof, reading a number of different texts.

The most important of these is Alain-Fournier's *Le Grand Meaulnes*,[4] which Lewis buys on his second day in Paris from a *bouquiniste* (secondhand bookseller) who "looked quite miserable to part with it" (23). The seller's attachment no doubt figures that of the book's previous owner(s), for Lewis appropriately purchases a used copy of a novel that has been read and reread by successive generations of adolescents throughout the world since its publication in 1913. Lewis's decision to buy the book is in fact directly motivated by speculation about the boy he imagines to have been his own age when he wrote his name ("Paul Berger, 1961") inside the front cover:

> [He] could be a writer himself by now, the kind of writer no one has heard of but who makes a puny living writing the books he once liked to read. The favourite authors of this kind of writer are all dead, but he still tries to become like them. He doesn't notice that the world he's writing about no longer exists. Paul Berger might be on his tenth attempt to rewrite *Le Grand Meaulnes*. (22)

Any hint of disillusion in Lewis's words should be attributed to a postmodern love of paradox, since this passage is in fact one of the most visibly self-referential in a novel whose discourse is riddled with allusions to other texts and to the practices of reading and writing. Tremain, like Lewis, unquestionably shares Paul Berger's hypothetical nostalgia for a certain kind of literature, here epitomized by Alain-Fournier's famous novel, which is grounded not in reality but in the power of the imagination, in the codes and conventions consistently produced and reproduced within this very body of literature. *The Way I Found Her* is nothing less than Tremain's own attempt to rewrite *Le Grand Meaulnes*.

To begin with, Lewis's progressive reading of *Le Grand Meaulnes*—"the story of Meaulnes gradually unfolding in [his] attic room" (25)—is incorporated into Tremain's novel as an activity on which he reports on a daily basis, both to us and to those around him. Alain-Fournier's novel functions to establish a network among a diverse group of fellow readers, ranging from a British schoolteacher to a French photographer to a Russian kidnapper, whose common memories of the same text not only connect them to Lewis, but implicitly to each other as well, in something like a model of a culturally united European community. As prototypical reader, Lewis consumes novels in a manner characteristic of his age and of youth in general; indeed, adult nostalgia may well be directed as much toward *how* he reads as toward *what* he reads. Lewis practices what Karlheinz Stierle calls a "quasi-pragmatic reception of fictional texts" in which the naive reader willingly surrenders to the illusory power of the fictional world.[5]

Lewis himself is astonished by "the power a book can exert over [his] psyche" (159). He worries about what will happen to characters whose fate directly concerns him—"I was getting quite fond of the narrator of the story, François" (45); "I was starting to identify with François" (55)—and who come increasingly to function as imaginary confidants and eventually as models for his own behavior. When he first ventures out on the roof, for example, he compares his own fear to that he believes François (but not Meaulnes) would have felt (56); frustrated by Alice's unexplained absences, he wonders what François would have done if his mother had begun to behave erratically (178); when he feels like crying, "only the resolution to act like François Seurel, who never blubbed, not even when things started to get sad" keeps him from giving in (139); and his determination to find Valentina, in the face of general indifference to her disappearance, is maintained by the conviction that "I am François Seurel: I never give up" (184). Understandably, then, Lewis finds himself seriously annoyed when he is confronted with the nuanced, distanced, and rather condescending readings of *Le Grand Meaulnes* offered by a certain adult world, here represented by his schoolteacher father: "*The book has been criticized, of course, for its melodramatic and sentimental flavour, but I have always found it rather moving,*" writes Hugh, in a letter that leaves Lewis so "totally pissed off" he is unable to read to the end (59).

Whether readers of *The Way I Found Her* respond with Lewis's passionate engagement or with Hugh's critical objectivity, Tremain clearly assumes a familiarity on our part as well with *Le Grand Meaulnes*. That she imagines the existence of an extradiegetic community of readers, comparable to the intradiegetic one that she creates within her own text, reinforces the possibility that the contemporary novel can evolve to reflect the "complex connectivity" that John Tomlinson singles out in *Globalization and Culture* (1999) as the defining feature of an emergent cultural globalism.[6] Although many readers of Tremain will remember *Le Grand Meaulnes* and others will be led either to read or to reread the novel, I do not mean to suggest that someone who has never heard of Alain-Fournier before picking up Tremain's book will be unable to understand or to appreciate *The Way I Found Her*. This is clearly not the case, since Tremain recreates *Le Grand Meaulnes* within her own novel in at least two different forms. If Lewis's detailed description of the events and the characters of François's narrative, coupled with his literal and extensive quotation of particular passages, constitute what we might (for the moment) consider the "original version" of Alain-Fournier's novel, then Tremain's own story is the simultaneous "remake." Intertextuality itself creates a shared literary experience, which functions not only to unite representative readers within *The Way I Found Her*, but to draw actual readers into this fictional world as well. The perception that the activities of reading and writing are interconnected, indeed, inseparable, which Lewis attributes to Paul Berger, is extended to Tremain's own readers, who are invited, if not required, to become active collaborators in the (re-)creation of both text and intertext.

Initially, *Le Grand Meaulnes* appears to function relatively conventionally as a *mise-en-abyme* for Tremain's narrative. *The Way I Found Her* is also recounted in the first person by an adolescent narrator, the only child of a provincial schoolteacher and a mother whom he calls by her first name. In keeping with its role as intertextual "scaffold," Alain-Fournier's novel explicitly informs the structure of Tremain's, which is also divided into three parts, followed by an epilogue. Moreover, Lewis, like François, tells his story in the past and the opening descriptions of both novels are marked by troubling imagery that evokes nostalgia and foreshadows coming tragedy. Tremain uses explicit examples of auto-referentiality early in the novel to teach us how to read her metafiction. Thus, to confirm a point I made above, whether or not we have ever read *Le Grand Meaulnes*, Valentina's reaction to its opening passage, which Lewis reads aloud to her, immediately alerts us to the parallelism of the text they are reading and the one we are reading. Valentina's reflection, "When you begin a book and you already know in the first line that everything is in the past, this makes you worry so for the character" (25), both echoes Lewis's initial pronouncement, "I don't want to talk about the present" (3), and suggests how we might interpret it. From this point on, readers of Tremain will inevitably seek new connections on their own each time Alain-Fournier's novel reappears.

Like François, whose life is forever changed by the arrival of Meaulnes, Lewis's "real life" begins when he meets Valentina (4). Just as Lewis abandons a beloved toy, which represents "the boy I was when I imagined Elroy was real," upon leaving England, François's separation from his habitual activities and attachments to become Meaulnes's companion similarly announces the end of childhood. Lewis's attic room, located next to a locked storeroom containing a clutter of curious objects of another era (185–86), recalls both the *grenier* (attic) François shares with Meaulnes and the abandoned furniture and costumes in the "chambre de Wellington" where Meaulnes falls asleep in the *domaine mystérieux* (mysterious domain). Certainly Meaulnes's and François's joint quest to find Yvonne de Galais prefigures Lewis's determination to track down Valentina after her disappearance; and "the way he finds her" requires that he literally reenact a scene from Alain-Fournier's novel to solve "the puzzle" he is sent by "the most literary kidnappers in the Western world" (258): "*Lewis, Meaulnes can tell you where to meet Valentine*" (253). Moreover, he is advised in this endeavor by an avuncular neighbor, Moinel, who shares the same name as François's "Aunt Moinelle," who also reveals important information about the whereabouts of the character Valentine in *Le Grand Meaulnes*. If

Valentina, who is blond, appears to be named for *Valentine Blonde*au, the passion she provokes and even, once again, her name, Valentina *Gavril*, appear equally well designed to evoke Yvonne de *Galais*.

In short, *The Way I Found Her* contains a vast network of clear, often explicit, and consistently recognizable references to *Le Grand Meaulnes*, about whose presence informed readers are quite likely to be in full agreement. Yet, not only do these allusions, despite their sheer number and, especially, their essential structuring importance, leave a great deal of what Tremain's novel is (also) about unaccounted for, but her decision to incorporate Alain-Fournier's text in a constantly fragmented and ultimately incomplete form must be seen as both deliberate and significant. My own decision not to provide a linear account nor even a fully cohesive description of *Le Grand Meaulnes* stems less from my interest in postmodern imitation and repetition than in the impossibility of the task and, more importantly, in the inevitable infidelity to the original text that would result from the endeavor.

On the one hand, what makes *Le Grand Meaulnes* such a memorable novel is, as I have already suggested, a certain general, even generic, power and appeal that unites readers beyond national, historical, cultural, and linguistic boundaries. Alain-Fournier draws on the "master tropes"[7] of an international, if not a universal, literary tradition to create a text that is at once an adventure, a romance, a tragedy, and a psychologically realistic account of adolescence. On the other hand, however, and largely as a result, *Le Grand Meaulnes* is also a profoundly mysterious text whose complexity and ambiguity leave it constantly open to interpretation and reinterpretation. John Fowles's afterword to the New American Library's translation of *Le Grand Meaulnes* is revealingly characteristic of a common critical response to the novel; he chooses to limit himself to an almost exclusively autobiographical reading, safely grounded in the author's own revelations. Subsequently, however, Fowles acknowledges that the reader may be wondering why he has "said so little about what the book 'really means' " and states his conviction that "books of this category . . . ought to mean what you, ordinary reader, think they mean."[8]

If such a belief points to what Fowles characterizes as "strongly heretical views on the value of literary analysis for the ordinary reader,"[9] Tremain shares in this heresy. Lewis again provides the model for a second level of collaborative and creative participation in which the reader of *The Way I Found Her* is summoned to a more broadly formal and thematic reflection. Like Lewis, we are expected to "like mysteries" and "solving things" and to be "good at it" (127): "I like mysteries. Unfinished knowledge. Most people have to be told everything straight away, get it all explained and wrapped up. But I like to work it out for myself, like in a chess game" (89). Because, as Fowles points out, interpretation of "books of this category" is a highly subjective endeavor and because I would not presume to spoil the pleasure that Tremain offers all "ordinary" readers, I will limit my remarks to one primary example of my own particular interest in the "unfinished knowledge" of Alain-Fournier's and Tremain's interconnected novels.

François's example proves to be least helpful to Lewis in coming to some understanding of what is perhaps most important to him, his mother's motives and behavior:

> I thought, what would François have done if Millie had taken the poney and trap and said she was going to Vierzon, say, and then he'd found out she'd been in the back room of the bakery in Sainte-Agathe? . . . He would have just lain in his attic, listening to the wind, trying to figure out why. And eventually, he would have discovered why.
>
> But Millie is a really different character from Alice. François always seems to know more or less what Millie is going to do and feel, but with Alice no one ever knows. (178)

Indeed, one of the things that is most curious about Alice, within the context of Tremain's novel and in dramatic contrast to other characters, is the fact that she really doesn't seem to have much of anything to do with the intertextual world of *Le Grand Meaulnes*. In fact, despite her own profession and the love of French she shares with her son, Alice never even acknowledges that he is reading Alain-Fournier's novel. Yet, precisely because this discontinuity seems inexplicable and therefore becomes a constant underlying concern, a "mystery" readers are meant to "work out" for themselves, we, like Lewis and François, keep "trying to figure out why" Tremain appears to disrupt the established patterns of her own novel.

The ambiguity generally characteristic of both *Le Grand Meaulnes* and *The Way I Found Her* becomes particularly remarkable at the end of the two texts. That Yvonne de Galais and Valentina Gavril should die tragic deaths and that the narrators of both novels should be transformed into solitary and unhappy figures, paralyzed by the memory of the past, would not in and of itself challenge our understanding, were it not for the fact that other characters, whom we have been encouraged to see as far less deserving, not only survive, but even seem destined to "live happily ever after." At the conclusion to *Le Grand Meaulnes*, for example, we are left to resolve the contradiction between the final image of Frantz and Valentine, reunited and settled in their own home, with our knowledge that every misfortune in the novel can reasonably be attributed to Frantz's extravagance, immaturity, and egotism. Whether or not it is fully satisfying in emotional terms, one plausible explanation available to us lies in our understanding that Frantz, despite—or rather—fully in keeping with the "flaws" I have just ascribed to him, is the single character who has remained constantly faithful to his adolescent dreams and commitments, who has never betrayed either his love for Valentine or his faith in Meaulnes.

If, on the one hand, the analogy with *The Way I Found Her* seems to elucidate the role of Alice, on the other hand, it simultaneously increases, rather than resolves, the ambivalence characteristic of Tremain's fictional world. Alice, selfish, capricious, and irresponsible in her own way, is nonetheless, like her counterpart in *Le Grand Meaulnes*, the only character at the end of Tremain's novel who retains at least the potential to find happiness. At the same time, however, in this case she is also guilty of the one fault that is unforgivable in the moral universe shared by François Seurel and Lewis Little. Unlike Frantz, Alice does not believe in the primacy of the imagination, and, as a result, she betrays the dreams and the ideals of those around her. When Valentina disappears and Lewis seeks an ally in his mother, she repeatedly dismisses his concerns as delusion: "You imagine things" (123); "[You're] whirling off into fantasy"; "You've always had a nervous imagination" (125).

It is appropriate to judge Alice by Alain-Fournier's standards, since Lewis implicitly invites us to do so by the parallel he draws. He goes back to reading *Le Grand Meaulnes* after Valentina's disappearance to find François (too) "on a quest to find someone." This time, however, François functions as counterpoint to Alice, rather than as model for Lewis, who quickly points out that "it wasn't really his quest, but Meaulnes'." Still, although François has never met the people involved and has no real evidence "that they exist," he unquestionably accepts his friend's dream as his own: "He never says, 'Listen, Augustin, perhaps you dreamt up this fantastic [adventure]; . . . perhaps you fell asleep in the cart when you got lost, and had the most brilliant dream of your life?' He just makes all that the centre of his existence" (158–59). In contrast, Alice's indifference and her refusal to help Lewis force him to act alone and to take ever greater risks. Lewis's reading of the chapter in *Le Grand Meaulnes* entitled "Je trahis" ("My Betrayal") is preceded and followed by successive scenes in which he must actively prevent Alice from confessing to marital infidelity (242–43, 255–56). Indeed, adulterous betrayal of her husband and son, who should be "the centre of [her] existence," is a deception whose insertion into the lives of François and his mother is literally unimaginable. The ellipsis in the quotation with which I began this discussion marks the omission of a reflection that Lewis cannot attribute to François: "He would never have said: 'Millie, you're betraying us'" (178).

In essence, just as we come to understand how Alice fits into Tremain's primary intertextual reference, her insertion turns out to reverse the very terms of existence of Alain-Fournier's world, offering us something like a mirror image. This is, of course, fully in keeping with the nature of intertextuality, which Julia Kristeva defined over twenty-five years ago as a process of "transposition" in which one signifying system is not only incorporated into another but, more importantly, significantly altered by virtue of this incorporation.[10] Again, to take only one example, closely related to the puzzle of Alice's presence, Tremain both realizes and rewrites a broader maternal thematics inherited from Alain-Fournier. Written prior to World War I, *Le Grand Meaulnes* displays, in the words of Karen D. Levy, "the wistful charm of an Impressionist painting" and appears "nonthreatening for readers of all ages," despite the undercurrent of violence and the obsession with death that already mark Alain-Fournier's text.[11] At the dawn of the twenty-first century, poetic suggestion has given way to verbal directness and romantic idolatry to sexual desire.

In the masculine world of *Le Grand Meaulnes*, female figures of all ages are simultaneously idealized and de-eroticized by their constant association with domestic and, especially, maternal imagery. *The Way I Found Her* also opens with a description highly reminiscent of the recurrent dream that haunts *Le Grand Meaulnes*, in which Meaulnes awakens in his childhood bedroom, transformed by the light streaming into it, to see a young woman sewing near the window. At the moment in which Lewis first notices his mother's "fantastic, gorgeous beauty," he observes her from his bed "sitting in my room, by my window, trying to mend my Action Man . . . . with the sun on her crazy hair" (3–4).[12] Subsequently, however, the hidden and repressed eroticism of the mother-son relationship in Alain-Fournier's novel, marked by the influence of Freudian psychoanalysis, comes to the foreground and to realization in *The Way I Found Her* through the substitution of Valentina for Alice.[13] Although Lewis, rather than Valentina, reads the bedtime story, her nightly visits to his attic room are clearly modeled on those of a parent to a child; on the occasions when she fails to appear, however, she inspires explicit and detailed masturbatory fantasies (see, for example, 44 and 207). When Lewis first sees Valentina in a bathing suit, her body generates a curiously sexualized metaphor of rebirth: "the most beautiful thing in the world would be to be born out of Valentina's vagina and be lifted up on to her stomach and given one of her huge breasts to suck and kept there on her breast with my lips round her milky nipple, sucking and sucking until I passed into oblivion" (51). A similar dynamics marks the actual scene of "incest": the kidnappers allow Lewis to spend the night with his "mummy"; he and Valentina make love as gently as "a parent who rocks a child" (341); and their escape attempt begins with another symbolic rebirth: "it was as if I was lifting her out and back into the world" (344).

Although the incorporation of *Le Grand Meaulnes* into *The Way I Found Her* is unquestionably "prime," I have potentially made Tremain's strategy of intertextuality appear at once more coherent and considerably less complex than it actually is. Kristeva's theory of the text as an internal network of sign systems also assumes that the literary text is situated in relation to the many other signifying systems that operate within a cultural context.[14] Tremain in fact practices textual borrowing on a scale consistent with postmodern excess and hybridity and with the border crossings and the "complex connectivity" reflective of both an emergent European community and a newly globalized world. At the beginning of part 2 of *The Way I Found Her*, Lewis returns to the same *bouquiniste* and buys a second book, which he reads at the same time and in somewhat the same way as *Le Grand Meaulnes*. The purchase by an English boy of a Russian novel in a French translation aptly figures the expansion of an international community beyond geographic and linguistic boundaries, and the "packaging" of Dostoevsky's *Crime et châtiment* serves as a particularly appropriate and engaging metaphor for the postmodern practice of intertextuality: "He handed me *Crime and Punishment* wrapped in a bag from Prisunic.... If you're a writer, I thought, you can't ever predict where your work is going to end up or what it will be wrapped in" (110).[15]

In part, no doubt, because of Valentina's recent disappearance, Lewis is particularly interested in the detective Porphiry Petrovich: "I'd decided he'd be my role model from now on: I'd follow every single trail and never give up until Valentina was found" (145). (In contrast, Lewis judges that Raskolnikov's lack of hope makes him—at least at this point in Tremain's novel—Lewis's "exact opposite" [142].) If *Le Grand Meaulnes* and *Crime and Punishment* might seem to represent incompatible discourses—even Lewis, for example, attributes the difficulty he has understanding existentialism to the fact that "nobody talked about political systems in *Le Grand Meaulnes*" (87)—the juxtaposition of the two novels in fact exposes the common literary model that informs them both. Within postmodern theory, the mystery novel and/or the detective story have come to serve as representative of an international and a hybrid art form, one that transcends both geographic and generic boundaries; requires the reader's active engagement in the realization of the text; and functions therefore, by definition, as a self-referential metaphor for the conception and the reception of the written text.[16] In an introduction to the work of Estelle Monbrun, whose own recent examples of the cross-cultural *polar* traverse national and aesthetic boundaries, Pierre Verdaguer stresses the thematic and stylistic flexibility of the form: "Il permet tous les amalgames et peut à l'occasion favoriser la juxtaposition de registres culturels dont on signale d'ordinaire l'incompatibilité" (It allows every kind of mixture and can sometimes support the juxtaposition of cultural registers usually deemed incompatible).[17]

Tremain's own textual "amalgam" of investigations into enigma, crime, and death not only positions versions of *Le Grand Meaulnes* and *Crime and Punishment* alongside Lewis's story of "The Way I Found Her" but also incorporates a number of other variants of the pattern. Valentina's "Medieval Romances" reproduce the generic conventions of the mystery within the realm of popular culture and in the process foreground the formulaic nature of both: "A little terror, a little chivalry, a lot of fucking, a happy ending" (18). Indeed, Moinel and others initially assume that Valentina has simply reproduced one more time the plot of novels that are "all the same" in engineering her own disappearance (13); and, in fact, although she has not authored this particular text, Valentina also assumes that the kidnapping has its origin in literature: "They think they're big-time villains. They've read some crime novels, I expect" (278).[18]

Once Lewis begins to investigate Valentina's latest romance as a potential source of clues to her disappearance, Tremain's novel crosses disciplinary as well as national boundaries to combine a series of nonfictional texts with its already diverse fictions. In an internal duplication of the task imposed on the reader by the comparison of *Le Grand Meaulnes* and *The Way I Found Her*, Lewis simultaneously reads *Pour l'amour d'Isabelle* ("For Isabelle's Sake") and *La Vie secrète de Catherine la Grande* ("The Secret Life of Catherine the Great"), the text from which Valentina, on the model of Tremain, borrows. Although the latter work is historical rather than fictional, Lewis finds that its author, Gregory Panin (Grisha), "looked like some crazed American writer of the kind my father read—Kurt Vonnegut or Joseph Heller.... In fact, he was a crazed Russian writer" (91). When Lewis breaks into Valentina's computer files, texts rapidly multiply. Notably, he discovers *A Propos d'Alice Little*, an essay devoted to the effects of his mother's beauty, which reads like another version of his own, frequently cited, notebook (117); and *Un Mas de Provence* ("A Provençal Farmhouse"), "a kind of diary" that is also a travelogue (146).

If, on the one hand, Tremain's use of intertextuality reflects the postmodern position that "reality" is always discursive in nature,[19] *The Way I Found Her* also destabilizes what Linda Hutcheon considers to be the most radical of distinctions, that between life and art.[20] This breakdown is initially figured within the novel by Didier, whose self-description as an existentialist might be said to necessitate, even to generate, the subsequent appearance of *Crime and Punishment* within the text. Reading the story of Raskolnikov leads Lewis to a better understanding of Didier's philosophy, which in its turn brings into Tremain's novel the notions of guilt and responsibility, which figure centrally not only in Lewis's interpretation of Alice's behavior but also in his understanding of his own role in Valentina's disappearance and death.

Unlike *Le Grand Meaulnes*, *Crime and Punishment* is less of interest in its own right than as a representative example of a particular kind of literature and as a source of raw material; Dostoevsky's novel dispenses elements of a realist literary tradition explicitly associated with and coded as "Russianness." Realism and idealism, a fiction that is "true to life" and a fiction that creates an alternative reality in the world of the imagination, function as competing discourses in *The Way I Found Her*. Although Valentina has lived in France for thirty-eight of her forty-one years, she still struggles to escape not only from what she calls the "prison" of her "old life," recreated within Paris by the miserable *café-charbon* (café-coal bunker) of her Russian emigrant parents (18), but also from the misfortunes of contemporary Russia, recalled by the bitterness and envy both of her lover Grisha and of her ex-husband Alexis. Indeed, she believes that the first would like to kill her (103–4), and she is literally reimprisoned by the second.

Still, Valentina fears the literary consequences of this harsh reality far more than the actual conditions. Having married Alexis to live in "the world of the poet" (292), she discovers that his poems are so depressing that they inspire her both to become a writer herself and, more importantly, to write beyond national, cultural, and (auto)biographical boundaries:

> So I thought, if he can write, so can I. But I will write something that a *lot* of people want to read. Alexis's poems were so *Russian*, so much about suffering and prison and grey skies. And I knew I didn't want to write about these things. You see how terrible our history is? . . . And I didn't want to write about my own life either. Because what was in my own life except work in the café and seeing my father struggling backwards and forwards from the coal cellar with his sacks of coal? Who would have read a novel about these things? No one. (309)

Ironically, Lewis—and the readers he represents—have, of course, already read this unwritten novel or, at least, the raw material that would inform it, within *The Way I Found Her*; and Lewis's response to the many stories Valentina tells him and us about her past is always to encourage her to set aside her medieval romances and write about her father's life. His final answer to her objections, quoted above, goes well beyond his own personal pleasure as a reader: "I started to say that Dostoevsky had written about suffering and poverty in *Crime and Punishment* and so many hundreds of thousands of readers had read it that it now had the status of a 'world classic' " (310).

Tremain's novel clearly challenges Valentina's belief in the possibility of containing literature within the boundaries of rigid oppositional categories—national *or* international, formulaic *or* unique, realistic *or* escapist, fictional *or* autobiographical. At the same time, her work reflects less a fusion or conflation of high and low culture, which informs much of postmodern theory, than the juxtaposition and coexistence of a wide range of diverse and heterogeneous texts and, especially, the right to enjoy them all. If the first position might be said to support the views of those who still fear that cultural globalization could lead to the loss of national identities, the second offers an appropriate literary analogy to the formation of a new European community.

The forces that seem designed to pull Valentina back down to earth, in keeping with the material reality of her Russian origins, ultimately triumph to deny her the "happy ending" she accords to her fictional heroines. She overcomes her fear of heights to follow Lewis out onto the roof beyond his attic cell, only to be distracted at the precise moment she is about to imitate his flight to freedom and to fall to her death instead. Although I think most readers of *The Way I Found Her* are likely to be surprised by this sudden descent into tragedy, it is, in fact, overdetermined within Tremain's novel by a curious and repetitive thematics, which foreshadows not simply Lewis's future unhappiness but the specific event that will cause it. From the moment Lewis first looks out his rooftop window in Paris, Tremain's text is haunted by recurrent references to the relationship between human beings and what lies either above or below. Despite the diversity of this network, whose allusions include, for example, kite flying (15), trapezes (35), the height of the Arch de la Défense (35), Michelangelo's painting the ceiling of the Sistine Chapel (46), Dorothy's house "blown into the sky" in *The Wizard of Oz* (83), Grisha's odd way of "watching sky" as he walks (100), Alice's and Didier's disappearance into their "private sky" (182; see also 154), and Lewis's past as an academic "high-flyer" (351), among others, the most important leitmotif repeats the dynamics of freedom and fatality that inform the conclusion of Tremain's novel.

Indeed, the words *fly* and *fall* appear in constant juxtaposition throughout the text. On the one hand, Didier, the roofer who believes in human freedom, has a tatoo representing himself as "Didier-l'oiseau" (Didier-the-Bird), because "there are times in life when you need to fly" (27) and "being alone, unattached, in the air, is the ultimate freedom" (87). On the other hand, he cannot escape the memory of his father falling to his death from the dome of the Salpêtrière hospital (see 70–71, 88–89, 263) in circumstances that both recall Lantier's fall in Zola's *L'Assommoir* (1877) and announce that of Valentina. Lewis too, despite his youth and his fascination with rooftops and the possibility of flight, is equally aware of the dangers, both literal and metaphoric: "I had a sudden scary vision of the void beyond the cage behind me and how falling through the air is one of the things that human beings seriously dread" (112).

In what may appear to be a risky flight of fantasy of my own, I want to propose that the massive web of words and images that weave flying and falling into the fabric of Tremain's novel serve another function beyond their evident contributions to the revelation of character and to the coherence of plot. On the model of the explicit analogies to *The Wizard of Oz* and to *L'Assommoir* (which, like *Le Grand Meaulnes* and *Crime and Punishment*, once again link the creation of an imaginary world to a tradition of literary realism), they point to an unidentified, a "secret" source of intertextuality that underlies *The Way I Found Her*. In imitation of the kidnapping message that Alexis sends Lewis, and which I paraphrase here, Tremain has set her readers "a puzzle," and she knows we'll solve it, because that's what we have become good at, "solving puzzles" (see 254).

Although I have not come across any such reference in reviews of *The Way I Found Her*, I think it probable that readers almost immediately connect characters named "Lewis" and "Alice Little" with Lewis Carroll and his young friend, Alice Liddell, for whom he wrote *Alice's Adventures in Wonderland* and *Through the Looking-Glass*, but I would also suggest that allusions that seem random, even accidental, only gradually reveal themselves to be "prime." Tremain's insistence on calling our attention to the possibility of falling into a void, flying into adventure, or both simultaneously, convince me that the narrative of the way Lewis grows up intentionally recalls Alice's metaphoric journey out of childhood, which begins by a long fall down a rabbit hole.[21] Like Charles Dodgson, Lewis loves mathematics and attempts to use mathematical principles to resolve psychological dilemmas, to "convert interior anxiety into maths" (56).[22] His thorough and lucid investigations into the secrets of the enigmatic world in which he has been abandoned by the adults around him recall Alice's attempts to make sense of the random occurrences and anarchic disorder of Wonderland. The behavior of Lewis's mother is as puzzling, capricious, and infuriating to her son as that of any of the characters or creatures encountered by Dodgson's Alice. Lewis's victory over Alexis in the game of chess in which his own and Valentina's lives are at stake repeats the analogy between chess and life that structures *Through the Looking Glass*. Both Lewis and Alice play white; he wins to become Valentina's lover, she to be crowned queen.[23] More generally, the fictions of Tremain and Carroll are equally dissonant in tone and content; random acts of violence and premonitions of death coexist with the naive confidence and fanciful interpretations of their young heroes. Often cited as a precursor of postmodernism, Carroll also practices intertextuality, parodying other contemporary writers, for example, or rewriting nursery rhymes.[24]

I am well aware that these examples of possible connections between *The Way I Found Her* and Lewis Carroll's stories of Alice in Wonderland represent a highly selective and inevitably subjective choice. Moreover, they are presented in a manner that must seem every bit as illogical and fanciful, as thoroughly mixed up, as the lawless world through which Alice travels. That, in fact, is the point. The intertextual incorporation of *Alice in Wonderland* into *The Way I Found Her* functions as a kind of summary of Tremain's understanding of the emergent literature of globalization. The palimpsestic texture of her novel, which results from a practice of borrowing already so excessive as to be potentially endless, suggests the "complex connectivity" of a cosmopolitan world and of an international community of readers.

The "wonder" Tremain allows the latter to experience in discovering an unidentified literary source on their own opens up a postmodern space in which reading and writing merge and the reader becomes an authentic collaborator in the construction of text and context. Like the meaning of the aerial photographs exposed in the jardin du Luxembourg, the patterns that emerge from our reading depend upon perspective and presuppositions; given the mobility of themes, stories, narrative codes, and generic conventions that cross fixed boundaries and elude former categories, there can be no one definitive order. One of Tremain's essential insights about the future of culture in a globalized Europe is that literature can become international in reach without losing the national specificity of its origins. Given the ambivalent position of England within the European community—notably, Lewis watches a television show in Paris about "Europe," which includes no references to his native country, "as if England wasn't really part of Europe" (227)—it seems both necessary that an internationally known classic of English literature appear alongside its French and Russian counterparts in Tremain's postmodern "bricolage" and yet equally appropriate that Alice's adventures should only gradually emerge from behind those of François and Raskolnikov. At the same time, of course, all three works represent national variations on that most broadly international and culturally fluid of forms, the novel of detection and mystery.

Finally, and not least importantly, Lewis Carroll's work exhibits a linguistic playfulness that makes language visible and foregrounds its autonomy long before Alice goes *Through the Looking Glass* to attempt to communicate with Humpty Dumpty:

> "When *I* use a word," Humpty Dumpty said, in rather a scornful tone, "it means just what I choose it to mean—neither more nor less."
> "The question is," said Alice, "whether you *can* make words mean so many different things."
> "The question is," said Humpty Dumpty, "which is to be master—that's all."[25]

In *The Way I Found Her*, Lewis Little reaches the remarkably similar conclusion that "secret language equals power" and determines to acquire as many "secret languages" as possible to serve as his "prime weapons in life" (48). Moreover, Lewis's realization, which results from his inability to understand a conversation in Russian between Valentina and her mother, explicitly equates power, the right "to be master," with knowledge of a foreign language or languages. Lewis, whose multiple roles as representative reader, as we have already seen, valorize the novel both as a source of illusion and identification and as an enigma to be interpreted is also always aware of the text as a conscious linguistic construction. Alice, Valentina, and Lewis are all described at various points as "good at languages"; and although only Alice is a professional translator, in different ways Lewis and Valentina also practice the art of translation.

Lewis reads *Crime and Punishment* in a French translation, but what one might therefore expect to be a comparable reading of *Le Grand Meaulnes* in the French original is rendered considerably more complex by the fact that he actually sets out to translate Alain-Fournier's novel into English.[26] In reading Tremain's text, as a result, we encounter at regular intervals italicized passages of "the Lewis Little Version" of *Le Grand Meaulnes* (23). If this strategy in and of itself directs our attention beyond what is signified through language to how language functions as a signifying system, Lewis also shows us the complexity and the ambiguity involved in the passage from one language to another:

> *J'avais quinze ans. C'était un froid dimanche de Novembre, le premier jour d'automne qui fit songer à l'hiver* . . . I moved round and round this sentence, trying translations. 'I was fifteen', or 'I was fifteen years old.' 'It was a cold Sunday in November,' or 'It was a cold November Sunday'; 'the first day of autumn,' no, 'the first autumn day,' no, 'the first day of *this* autumn . . . which made you [or 'he'? or 'one'? or 'everyone'?] dream of [or 'have thoughts about'? or 'remember'?] winter [or 'the winter']. (23)[27]

This text, in which possible solutions are rejected by the word *no* and brackets open up to introduce alternative versions, is curiously reminiscent of some of the practices of such experimental novelists as Raymond Roussel and Alain Robbe-Grillet, in whose works language functions to generate meaning. Appropriately, then, even Lewis's very first attempt at translation leads him to raise serious questions about authorship and originality: "Did Mum, as a translator, have to be a kind of writer herself, a kind of poet, in order to make a choice instinctively, as if the words came from her and not the original author"? (23).[28]

As he begins to translate *Le Grand Meaulnes*, Lewis explains the difficulty of what he also calls "reading" French by the fact that every word seems to have three dimensions (23), an insight that might be applied on a much broader scale to *The Way I Found Her*. The thematics of infidelity, betrayal, violence, and death, which I explored earlier in relation to form and content in Tremain's novel, also informs her telling of the specific story of language. If Valentina not only insists on having her English translator close at hand but also constantly interrupts her to challenge her translation, it is not only because "she thinks she owns [her]" (36), as Alice believes, but because Valentina has been betrayed in the past. She accuses Gail O'Hara, an American feminist who preceded Alice, of secretly attempting to change her women characters to make them appear more feminist (18, 290). As a result, Valentina openly acknowledges, much to Lewis's—and especially to Alice's—shock, that "she killed that translator" (18). Moreover, Valentina clearly feels no guilt about a "murder" (eventually explained as the unlimited provision of heroin to a drug addict) that she regards as an act of self-defense: "Why help someone to live, if they are killing you?" (290). In contrast, Valentina is guilty of a second crime, also related to translation, to which she never confesses, despite the many opportunities Lewis offers her. In the course of investigating her kidnapping, he has learned why her latest novel is so different from and so much better than her previous books that, in Alice's words, "it's as if it's been written by someone else" (34). Indeed, Lewis discovers that substantial portions of *Pour l'amour d'Isabelle* have been borrowed from the Russian version of *La Vie secrète de Catherine la Grande*: "Virtually everything, supposedly original, that Valentina had written so far . . . was based on . . . Grisha's book" (244).

In Tremain's novel, as in most postmodern art, questions of origin, originality, authenticity, and authorship are at once central and constantly open to challenge and revision. Characteristically, *The Way I Found Her* essentially raises a number of questions and identifies a series of paradoxes. For example, in keeping with the Italian proverb (*traduttore, tradittore*), translation, however faithful, is always to some degree an act of betrayal; at the same time therefore, and by definition, it is always an act of creativity as well. As Tremain has Lewis show us, translation consists of making responsible choices (a process that in the context of this novel might be qualified as existentialist). No two translations are ever identical, and yet a change in a single word can alter meaning, however subtly. In keeping with the ambiguity inherent in the word *original*, translation occurs in relation to a preexistent text, yet both the translation and the text translated are arguably authentic works of art. In a further paradox, mistranslation, which Valentina deplores as the murder of the author and for which she is willing to kill, differs relatively little from plagiarism. They are mirror images of each other, at once oppositional and identical. In plagiarism, one attributes to oneself the language and ideas of another; in mistranslation, one attributes to another one's own language and ideas. (In either instance, the question is "which is to be master.") In Valentina's case, plagiarism is motivated by the realization of what has always been her greatest fear, "that she would eventually run out of stories" (14, see also 319). Does this make the death of the author a foregone conclusion at the end of *The Way I Found Her* or is Valentina's "fall" her punishment for having metaphorically "killed" Grisha in her turn? Is Tremain's extensive use of intertextuality a sign that she too has "run out of stories"? Does her novel also read "as if it's been written by someone else"?

More importantly, in an increasingly globalized world of border crossings and constant cultural borrowing, can notions of national origin and native language still retain either meaning or significance? If it is already somewhat startling to see *Le Grand Meaulnes* identified as "a unique and uniquely French novel" in the same review that praises *The Way I Found Her* as Tremain's "translation" of Alain-Fournier's text,[29] Fowles goes even further, paradoxically characterizing the novel as "very nearly untranslatable" into English.[30] French playwrights Jean-Christophe Bailly and Michel Deutsch recently declared in an editorial in *Libération* that to speak of "foreign authors" is atavistic in an era that is "fundamentally already 'translated,'"[31] which suggests that translation has become the very condition of (re)writing in a postmodern world. Certainly, translation is what allows books to "travel" internationally and to create the "complex connectivity" among readers of different nations that is and will be characteristic of cultural globalization. In this context, Tremain's *The Way I Found Her* and the many other contemporary Anglophone novels about France (and Europe), which it resembles, once again play an exemplary role.[32] For, as a number of journalists and scholars have noted with increasing frequency and full consciousness of the irony, English is fast becoming the international *lingua franca* of a culturally unified Europe, what Kristin Hohendel characterizes as "the passport to a community beyond geographical, cultural, and national identity."[33]

In conclusion, I want briefly to return to the place from which I first set out on this journey through *The Way I Found Her* in order to reposition the image of the diversity of the world, which I encountered in the Jardin du Luxembourg, within the unified space of Tremain's novel, where it has always been. When Lewis first arrives in Paris, he makes an identical discovery to my own in another garden, the Jardin des Plantes, where he finds that different parts of the terrain have been sculpted and planted to resemble Africa, China, Corsica, the high Alps, or the Great Plains: "We sat down in the middle of China" (32). By the end of Lewis's summer in Paris, when he is imprisoned in a tiny attic cell, he has learned to conjure up the geography of the world within the space of his own imagination. If his early walks through Switzerland take him into a stereotypical landscape of "cows with bells around their necks, *edelweiss* flowers, groves of larch, people chopping wood for the winter, the high mountains covered with snow" (238), his last recorded walk through London rivals Arthus-Bertrand's aerial photographs of the "Earth from Above." Lewis's vision achieves the clarity and composition of art: "This imaginary London got such a grip on my mind, it was like I was a movie camera going along and getting everything into itself on film. . . . As well as *seeing* these things I was also *composing* them into frames and going in and out of close-up shots and wide shots" (308).

3
Routes and Roots: Postmodern Paradox in Joanne Harris's *Chocolat*

"*TRAVEL FAR ENOUGH, JOE USED TO SAY, AND ALL RULES ARE SUSPENDED*" (69), recalls Jay MacKintosh in Joanne Harris's second novel, whose publication less than two years after her first encourages us to view *Chocolat* (1999) and *Blackberry Wine* (2000) as the fictional equivalent of traveling companions.[1] The particular moment at which Jay believes that he has finally begun to understand what his old friend "Jackapple Joe" may have meant by words spoken twenty-five years earlier coincides with his own passage through the figurative spaces of what James Clifford has recently identified in *Routes: Travel and Translation in the Late Twentieth Century* (1997) as "postmodernity, the new world order of mobility, of rootless histories":[2]

> The things which bind us to the places and faces of home no longer applied. He could be anyone. Going anywhere—at airports, railway stations, bus stations—no one asks questions. People reach a state of near-invisibility. He was just another passenger here, one of thousands. No one would recognize him. No one had ever heard of him. (69)

For Vianne Rocher, the narrator of *Chocolat*, Jay's temporary location has been the defining condition of her entire life, marked by the "love of new places, the gypsy wanderlust" that has taken her "all over Europe and farther" (25).

Yet, in Harris's parallel novels, both Vianne and Jay abandon the routes of Europe and America to put down roots in *la France profonde*; they lead their fictional lives as residents of Lansquenet-sous-Tannes, an imaginary village of less than two hundred people situated deep in the southwestern heartland of rural France. This literary paradox has a critical counterpart in the corrective that John Tomlinson proposes in *Globalization and Culture* (1999) to Clifford's analysis of postmodernity, cited above. Rather than reversing the traditional priority between "roots and routes," as Tomlinson argues that Clifford does by conceptualizing postmodern culture as "rootless nomadic movement," Tomlinson believes that "we need to see 'roots and routes' as always coexistent in culture and both as subject to transformation in global modernity." Indeed, according to Tomlinson, "the transformation of localities themselves" figures most importantly in globalization's cultural impact.[3]

The multidisciplinary intersection at which cultural anthropology, political theory, and contemporary fiction converge in the work of Clifford, Tomlinson, and Harris corresponds to the emergence in recent years of a discernible pattern of texts devoted to questions of nation and national identity, increasingly configured within the larger framework of globalization. In the case of England alone, notes Jeffrey Richards in *Films and British National Identity* (1997), the "massive and continuing" interest in "Britishness," which first arose in the 1980s, was newly reflected in "an unending stream of 'state of the nation' books and articles" at the approach of the millennium.[4] The same phenomenon has been equally evident in relation to France; since Theodore Zeldin's *The French* appeared in 1983, "Frenchness" has been the subject of a significant body of work produced by cultural historians, anthropologists, sociologists, essayists, and journalists.[5] Moreover, such studies, like those of Richards and Zeldin, have not only tended to focus on England, France, and the United States, in particular, but also to explore French and Anglo-American identities, within the context of a globalized Europe, both through explicit cross-cultural comparison and, increasingly, within fictional as well as nonfictional works. The successive publication of Harris's two novels, set either exclusively (*Chocolat*) or primarily (*Blackberry Wine*) in France, followed by the release in December 2000 of Lasse Hallström's film version of *Chocolat*, demonstrates once again the contemporary importance of the pattern already discernible in the recent novels of Diane Johnson and Rose Tremain.[6]

Scenes of arrival figure as particularly significant in the literature of travel, whether ethnographic or fictional, and the version of the trope that brings Vianne Rocher to Lansquenet-sous-Tannes at the beginning of Harris's first novel introduces her as the very embodiment of Clifford's notion of postmodernity. She and her six-year-old daughter Anouk come "on the wind of the carnival" to stay "For a time. Till the wind changes" (1, 7). Within the space of a few sentences, "the woman" and "the child," suddenly exposed as outsiders by the narrator herself, are described as "strangers, transients . . . . *other*, foreign, indefinably strange . . . . a curiosity . . . a part of the carnival" (2–3). Carnivals travel too, of course, and everywhere they look much the same, implies Vianne, recalling those that she and Anouk have already seen in Paris, New York, and Vienna. Moreover, a festival that lies beyond national specificity and during which "all rules are suspended," as Jackapple Joe might put it, recurs within *Chocolat* to provide the model on which all the principal events of the novel are patterned.

Separated into carefully dated sections, which cover the six-week period from Shrove Tuesday (February 11) to Easter Monday (March 31),[7] the first-person narration of *Chocolat* is shared by—or rather, divided between—Vianne, who opens her "chocolaterie artisinale" on Valentine's Day, and Francis Reynaud, the priest whose church is directly across the square from "La Céleste Praline." The alternating accounts of the local *curé* and the newcomer he increasingly views as a threat to his own power within the community are distinguished by typeface. If this difference made visible serves primarily to reflect the growing rivalry that locks the two declared enemies in a struggle for influence over the citizens of Lansquenet-sous-Tannes, a battle whose outcome will determine to what extent this particular locality will be "subject to transformation in global modernity,"[8] it is nicely suggestive as well of a certain postmodern taste for the ornamental and the theatrical, equally evident in Reynaud's sermons and in Vianne's display windows. We come to know the residents of the village as they pass through the adjacent but hostile territories of the Catholic church and the chocolate shop. In this deeply divided community, almost anyone whom Vianne befriends turns out to be either Reynaud's enemy or closely related to one of his allies. Two occurrences, in particular, cause divergent interests to result in active conflict and ultimately to erupt in violence: Vianne's plans to hold her "own carnival," a "Grand Festival du Chocolat" (81), on Easter Sunday and the establishment of a "floating carnival" (104) of houseboats moored along the riverfront. Even as Vianne and the "carnival people" (23) settle in, *Chocolat*'s narrative structure nonetheless continues to allow for temporal and spatial displacement as contemporary events simultaneously lead Vianne to rethink the circumstances of her mother's life and force Reynaud to remember, indeed to relive, the mysterious tragedy that occurred during his thirteenth summer.

The tendency of reviewers and readers alike to classify Harris's fiction under the rubric of "fairy tales for adults" was retroactively reinforced in the case of *Chocolat* by the publication of *Blackberry Wine*, whose comparison to Harris's first novel left some of her fans disappointed, notably by what one reader perceived as the "dark undercurrents" of the second novel.[9] In reviewing *Chocolat* for *The New York Times*, for example, Nancy Willard refers, in rapid succession, to folktales, the fables of La Fontaine, traditional seventeenth-century French fairy tales, morality plays, and "magic realism" in order to convey the flavor of the novel.[10] But if Vianne herself does indeed retain the literal capacity to function as a standard fairy tale figure, in imitation of her own mother, a "witch" able to see the past and to predict the future, the daughter has rebelled to become what her mother would have dismissed with disdain as "a tame alchemist, . . . working domestic magic when [she] could have wielded marvels" (35). For Vianne "art" and "sorcery" exist in all cooking (40), but the transformation of "base chocolate" into "fool's-gold," which distinguishes her own chosen profession, results, in particular, in "a kind of alchemy," "a layman's magic," which she believes might have delighted even her mother (41). Nor, in fact, would such shared pleasure be at all surprising, since augury, her mother's speciality, essentially identifies her as an unusually sensitive interpreter of signs—as a metaphor, in other words, for the ideal reader—and it is in the realm of literary magic that Vianne both remains her mother's daughter and acts as Harris's own diegetic representative within the novel.

Chocolat unfolds in the space opened up between the carnival cart, decorated with "scenes from fairy tales" (1), which mesmerizes Anouk at the beginning of the novel, and the book of fairy tales, from which Vianne reads to her daughter, that appears at its end (239). Indeed, the passing *char* marks *Chocolat* immediately as a postmodern metafiction, for the "gingerbread house all icing and gilded cardboard, a witch in the doorway" (1), which embellishes the cart, reappears in dark chocolate as the "magnificent centerpiece" of Vianne's first window display (17), doubly engendered by the story of "Hansel and Gretel" and its carnival reproduction.[11] In a similar crossing of boundaries between reality and fiction, Vianne's second display introduces "a cluster of houseboats" into the legend of the Pied Piper, whose chocolate version also resembles one of the river people, docked along the Tannes, whom she has befriended (82–83).

Although the multiple confections on view in La Céleste Praline are undoubtedly delicious, both in look and in taste, the many descriptive passages in *Chocolat* serve less to convey the variety and the richness of the candy described than those same qualities of the language used to describe it. Harris foregrounds the generative power and the autonomous appeal of her own prose, both by her characteristic strategy of enumeration and by her narrator's self-referential insistence on the pleasure of words themselves. Listen, for example, to Francis Reynaud, whose years of sensory deprivation and days of near total abstinence come to an abrupt end when he breaks into Vianne's shop on Easter morning: "The names are entrancing: *Bitter orange cracknell. Apricot marzipan roll. Cerisette russe. White rum truffle. Manon blanc. Nipples of Venus.* . . . Again I linger over the names. *Crème de cassis. Three nut cluster.* I select a dark nugget from a tray marked *Eastern Journey.* . . . I take another, from a tray marked *Pêche au miel millefleurs*" (235).

The most important legacy passed down from mother to daughter (from narrator to listener, from writer to reader) in *Chocolat* is the indiscriminate love of stories, all of which coexist in the narrative space of the novel, as do the scenes they inspire in the display windows of La Céleste Praline. Vianne's "*Grand Festival du Chocolat,*" the dramatic focal point of the novel, originates, explicitly and complexly, in the fictions of Easter that she remembers hearing from her mother:

> All stories delighted her—Jesus and Eostre and Ali Baba working the homespun of folklore into the bright fabric of belief again and again. . . .
> And I, her daughter, listening wide-eyed to her charming apocrypha, with tales of Mithras and Baldur the Beautiful and Osiris and Quetzalcoatl all interwoven with stories of flying chocolates and flying carpets and the Triple Goddess and Aladdin's crystal cave of wonders and the cave from which Jesus rose after three days, amen, abracadabra, amen. (80)

For Ella Shohat and Robert Stam, as noted earlier, "beliefs about nations often crystallize in the form of stories," an understanding through narrative that Thomas Friedman also regards as the best way to comprehend globalization.[12] The stories that enchant Vianne and her mother suggest the generic power of fiction and folklore to fill up the space(s) between, as well as within, the local and the global. The dominant imagery of fabric ("homespun," "fabric," "interwoven") and of flight ("flying"), which binds together not only the passage cited above but also informs the metaphoric structure of *Chocolat* as a whole, identifies the strategy of intertextuality as an exemplary postmodern practice, whose simultaneous links to "roots" and to "routes" paradoxically make of world literature a way to leave home and to (re)create community at one and the same time, in keeping with Tomlinson's definition of contemporary globalization as a condition of "complex connectivity."[13]

In this and similar passages, Harris crosses the boundaries between the sacred and the secular, the serious and the fanciful, the literary and the cultural; and she metaphorically tours the world to create and to explore an intertextual and multicultural domain of storytelling, whose geographical origins encompass Scandinavia (Baldur), Iran (Mithras), Egypt (Osiris), pre-Columbian Mexico (Quetzalcoatl), Arabia (Aladdin), Persia (Ali Baba), ancient Greece (Eostre), and Jordan (Jesus). Her postmodern celebration of archetypes and variants—the absence here of any hierarchy makes such a distinction meaningless—clearly challenges the oftexpressed fear that globalization will lead to increased cultural homogeneity and uniformity; at the same time, however, Harris's textual *bricolage* also illustrates that an essential corpus of literary forms, figures, codes, and conventions can and will travel afar and adapt successfully to diverse localities.[14] Appropriately, Harris privileges figures of resurrection and renewal in her panoply of literary types (e.g., Baldur, Osiris, Quetzalcoatl). Just as Vianne perceives her chocolate shop as "a throwback to times when the world was a wider, wilder place" (42), Harris's revival of the oral tales at the origins of literature paradoxically serves to project a new ambition for the novel of the twenty-first century. In the "wider, wilder" world of contemporary globalization, Harris, like other practiners of what can be called an international, intercultural, or "European" novel, offers us a model of mainstream fiction that lays claim to an international transcendence of the local and the national, once characteristic of "high art" but now almost exclusively attributed to an increasingly standardized "popular culture."[15]

Whereas some cultural critics, the French in particular, continue to bemoan the disappearance of an original folk culture, revered as authentic and nationalist, in the wake of the spread of modern mass culture, dismissed as artificial and amorphous,[16] in *National Identity* (more specifically, in the aptly titled—and punctuated—chapter called "Beyond National Identity?") the British historian Anthony D. Smith convincingly outlines a cultural framework that *Chocolat* illustrates to perfection. As the only viable alternative to national identity, Smith describes the development of a "global culture" whose "pastiche of post-modern motifs, themes, and style . . . draw their contents from revivals of earlier folk or national motifs and styles, torn from their original context."[17] This "new cosmopolitanism"—"inherently eclectic," "fluid and shapeless," "universal and timeless," distinctive "not only in its worldwide diffusion but also in the degree of its self-consciousness and self-parody"—constitutes a "giant *bricolage*," highly reminiscent of the form and content of Harris's first novel.[18]

Lest the analysis of a single passage seem inconclusive as evidence, let me cite a second, parallel example. Asked by one of her regular customers what she "believes," Vianne responds with a transcultural and transnational amalgamation of beliefs; once again, she neither limits, orders, or discriminates among diverse possibilities:

> Magic carpet rides, rune magic, Ali Baba and visions of the Holy Mother, astral travel and the future in the dregs of a glass of red wine . . .
> Buddha. Frodo's journey into Mordor. The transubstantiation of the sacrament. Dorothy and Toto. The Easter Bunny. Space aliens. The Thing in the closet. The Resurrection and the Life at the turn of a card . . . I've believed them all at one time or another. Or pretended to. Or pretended not to. (135)

Smith's characterization of the reality behind the rhetoric of European cultural commonality, which, he argues, underlies and informs the more visible economic and political content of a "New Europe," strongly echoes Harris's version (her vision) of literary globalism: "This is not the planned 'unity in diversity' beloved of official Europeanism, but a rich, inchoate *mélange* of cultural assumptions, forms, and traditions, a cultural heritage that creates sentiments of affinity between [*sic*] the peoples of Europe."[19]

In this second example of the particular mixture of cultural suppositions inherited by the heroine of *Chocolat*, the dominant motif of "flight," noted earlier, is further reinforced through a multiplicity of allusions, both literal (magic carpet rides, astral travel) and metaphoric (transubstantiation, resurrection) to processes of movement, travel, change. In contrast, the role of what I called "fabric" might seem to be reflected only in the coexistence of diverse and contradictory traditions within the same textual space ("unity in diversity"), were it not, that is, for the specifically literary references to J. R. R. Tolkien's *The Hobbit* and L. Frank Baum's *The Wizard of Oz*, which serve, especially in the context of Harris's novel, to reconfirm the interdependence of "roots and routes." Dorothy's journey famously concludes in the conviction that "there's no place like home," a sentiment surely echoed by Fredo, a reluctant traveler to begin with. In the introduction to *Dangerous Liaisons*, a collection of essays on nation and postcolonialism, Aamir Mufti and Ella Shohat also reference Dorothy's closing mantra, reinterpreted as desire rather than reality. In contemporary criticism, they argue, "home and the loss of home," represented by the metaphoric figure of the migrant, "constitute a recurring motif of modernity." Mufti and Shohat's challenge to Dorothy—"Is there still a place called home?"—is echoed by Emily Apter throughout her discussion of the prospect of a "New Europe" in *Continental Drift*; and Homi K. Bhabha has recently explored what he calls "unhomeliness," a word whose very awkwardness reflects the sense of estrangement to which it refers, in modern fiction.[20]

Vianne's actual stay in Lansquenet—and the possibility that she might actually be able to stay in Lansquenet—raise questions and reveal tensions similar to those of interest to contemporary cultural critics and theorists. Vianne *Rocher*, despite the suggestion of stability embedded in her name (rock, in English), has known only "stopping places," at best "temporary homes," in the "long flight across the world" that has defined her entire life (140). Clifford conceptualizes postmodernity as "a frame for negative and positive visions of travel: travel, negatively viewed as transience, superficiality, tourism, exile, and rootlessness . . . ; travel positively conceived as exploration, research, escape, transforming encounter."[21] A similar understanding of the complexity of the experience is evident in *Chocolat*, conveyed throughout, as in the opening pages, by lexical variation. Those who, like Vianne, sometimes see themselves as "a race apart, we the travelers" (141) are variously referred to in the course of the novel as any or all of the following: strangers, transients, tourists, intruders, aliens, the unwanted, truants, outsiders, scavengers, undesirables, gypsies, carnival people, Spaniards, tinkers, *pieds-noirs*, newcomers, vagrants, fugitives, itinerants, adventurers, exiles, thieves, deportees, Arabs, interlopers.

Although Vianne's ambivalence about routes and roots, about home and loss of home, is real, the emphasis that the vocabulary of the novel as a whole places on Clifford's "bad travel" is also consistent with the evolution of her own thinking since her mother's death and, more importantly, since her daughter's subsequent birth.[22] People, unlike places, notes Vianne, foreshadowing Jay MacKintosh's sense of "near-invisibility," gradually "lose their identity," until their passage becomes "ghostlike," leaving "no trace" (142). In keeping with the constantly changing names in the registers of hotels—for Clifford, the "figure of the postmodern"[23]—Vianne and her mother change their names as they move, "drifting from one regional variant to another: Yvonne, Jeanne, Johanne, Giovanna, Anne, Anouchka . . . ." (25). Or, perhaps, even, almost certainly, S*ylviane Caillou* (stone, pebble, in English), whose name recurs most often in her mother's file of newspaper clippings about children who have disappeared: "So easy to lose a child, she told me" (214).

If this story is only "make-believe" (215), as Vianne can sometimes convince herself, the tales of "Hansel and Gretel" and "The Pied Piper," which inspire her window displays, offer other fictional versions of the same reality. Already caught between the less ambiguous poles figured by her mother and her daughter, Vianne also occupies both positions at once.

The paradoxical figure of postmodernism, par excellence, she will always be part uprooted child, part rootless adult. In *The Great Cat Massacre*, Robert Darnton reads French folktales as a realistic guide to the everyday life of the ancient peasantry in pre-Revolutionary France. Moreover, Darnton argues that what he identifies as an essential plot of "Frenchness" persists up to the present as "a master theme of French culture in general."[24] Much like the writers who first recorded the fairy tale tradition under Louis XIV—many of whom, despite the prominence today of Charles Perrault, were women—Harris's modern "fairy tale of France" reinscribes the dominant codes and conventions of the genre in order to comment on the actual circumstances of France and Europe at the turn of the century.[25]

Within days of her arrival in Lansquenet-sous-Tannes, Vianne begins to realize that the "enchanted village" (4) she entered hides a more complicated reality, one suitably configured by the geography of the town. Behind the picturesque perfection of a church on a central square and a main street lined with shops lies Les Marauds, a "tiny slum" unable to attract the tourists whose gaze might transform its marshlands; its stink of sewage; its decrepit, often derelict, houses; and its river platforms of rotting wood into "mere quaintness and rustic decay" (21–22).[26] In keeping with its name, Les Marauds is reportedly peopled with "bad" travelers—marauders, vagabonds, scavengers who live on what the river provides. Yet, this "complex place" (21) simultaneously constitutes "an oasis" for the children of Lansequenet, an enchanted world that provides the ideal setting for acting out make-believe adventures and gathering "purloined treasures" (49).

The traveler was as common a sight on the roads and in the folktales of pre-Revolutionary France as in the rootless, nomadic world of postmodernity and its literature. In the oral tradition examined by Darnton, the vagabond hero typically outwits a stronger, richer, and more powerful enemy to restore order and/or to bring about change. In Harris's contemporary version of the paradigmatic plot, the role of the ogre, a.k.a. the wealthy bourgeois, is played by Francis Reynaud, who is capable of the murderous violence of the former and displays the same arrogant abuse of authority as the latter; Reynaud is literally "out-witted," that is, driven mad, by Vianne and her chocolate shop.[27] The choice of the priest as enemy is at once consistent with the strongly anticlerical tradition of the French peasant tales, with the carnivalesque reversal of the conventional representatives of "good" and "evil," and with the reality of the sharply diminished influence of the Catholic church in modern France. On the other hand, even though France has often been referred to as "a nation of shopkeepers," their metaphoric rise to heroism in *Chocolat* may seem somewhat more puzzling. But if the conflict between the conservative right and the liberal left in France has historically positioned the village priest in opposition to the public schoolteacher, of late the bakery has replaced the church, at least in practice, as what is essential to the very definition of a village.[28]

"Francis" Reynaud incarnates a vision of France as a unified, hierarchical, ordered society, whose very roots are threatened, both by a growing number of immigrants and their native-born children unwilling to have their distinctiveness assimilated into a generic "Frenchness" and by the potential erasure of the famous French "difference" through the absorption of France into the larger European community. Under similar circumstances, of course, England has also felt its national autonomy and identity to be menaced and has at times responded in equally defensive and protective ways. Certainly, Reynaud is xenophobic, as evidenced by the "nationalist platitudes" (62) he begins to spout from the pulpit upon the arrival of the first houseboats:

> They are vagrants. They have no respect and no values. They are the river gypsies, spreaders of disease, thieves, liars, murderers when they can get away with it. Let them stay, and they will spoil everything . . . . All our education. Their children will run with ours until everything we have done for them is ruined. They will steal our children's minds away. Teach them hatred and disrespect for the church. Teach them laziness and avoidance of responsibility. Teach them crime and the pleasure of drugs. (63)

The vitriolic, irrational hatred expressed by Reynaud no doubt affords Harris an opportunity to condemn not only the attitudes encouraged in France by followers of Jean-Marie Le Pen's *Front National* but also the general revival throughout Western Europe of neo-Nazi sentiments in the last few years.[29] Although Reynaud does establish a hierarchy of horrible possibilities in the case of the river people, who may not come from urban France, as first assumed, but "worse, further afield, from Algeria and Morocco" (62), ultimately race, national origin, urban influence, and even foreignness itself provide only convenient codes for what Reynaud really despises. Thus, paradoxically, especially in a country where language ability and national identity often appear to be inseparable, Vianne's native French somehow makes it equally impossible for her to "fit in" in Lansquenet; Reynaud finds her accent "pure, almost too pure for a Frenchwoman," either a sign that she comes from Paris or "even across the border" (11), the two alternatives clearly interchangeable for the local priest. Ultimately, Reynaud does not distinguish between the dangerous outsider(s) he targets initially and those residents of the village who make them welcome; the latter are denounced by name in his weekly sermons under their evocative—and provocatively inappropriate—identification as Vianne's "collaborators" (101).

What Reynaud in fact represents is simply the fear of change, that is, the unwelcome arrival on traditional French soil of (post)modernity itself. Harris's understanding of the timeless ability of a mythic French heartland (*la France profonde*) to stand in for France as a whole will be more fully explored in *Blackberry Wine*, but her first novel already codes Reynaud's (unhealthy) attachment to the past in conventional terms of "Frenchness." Generally perceived as a country that has been geographically blessed, France typically configures its national identity in spatial terms; and the most frequently cited metaphor, both within France and in cross-cultural and comparative contexts, is certainly the French garden. In contrast to the circuitous paths and the profusion of unrelated foliage common to its unruly English counterpart, the linear alleyways and the perfectly symmetrical rows of balanced plantings, which are characteristic of *le jardin à la française*, connote the order, hierarchy, artifice, and mastery of *la civilisation* itself.[30] In repeated passages in *Chocolat*, gardening provides the dominant imagery for Reynaud's will to control and to preserve, until he is finally transformed into a literal gardener as well.

The garden in the churchyard functions as microcosm and *mise-en-abyme* for Lansquenet (i.e., France) as well as for the world of the novel as a whole. Reynaud, increasingly disturbed by the sensory "riot" of colors and smells that invasive herbs, weeds, and wildflowers have created in a "hitherto orderly garden," desperately cuts and prunes and purchases "docile plants" to fill in the empty spaces: "I would like orderly rows of shrubs and flowers, perhaps with a box hedge around the whole. This profusion seems somehow wrong, irreverent, a savage thrusting of life, one plant choking another in a vain attempt at dominance. We were given mastery over these things, the Bible tells us" (175–76). Like the postmodern traveler, weeds and wildflowers thrive even when, perhaps especially when, they are uprooted; and their metaphoric ability to take to the road, to move and to adapt to a changing environment, makes them difficult, if not impossible, to contain within the artificial borders of any single geographical entity, albeit a nation. Plants—or people—with a will of their own are hard to control through the arbitrary imposition of external authority. Such, arguably, is the dilemma facing a globalized world and a New Europe, whose tensions have increasingly found expression of late in the form of disputes over the regulation of goods, rather than people, and of food and plant products in particular, a development of particular importance in relation to *Blackberry Wine*. By chance, however, the very first action taken by the European Union redefined *chocolat*, over the objections and to the general dismay of the French, to include the "cheap grade," made up of "fifteen percent cocoa solids—twenty for the dark—with a sticky aftertaste of fat and sugar" that even Francis Reynaud rejects with horror (235).

Although Reynaud perceives Vianne as a stranger who "has nothing in common" with the citizens of Lansquenet (11), an outsider whose mere presence "break[s] down . . . community spirit" (118), in fact, "La Céleste Praline" becomes the geographical matrix of a newly imagined sense of community, redefined in function of contemporary reality. As a place that is at once "home" and "not home," where Vianne both lives and works, on the one hand; and as a place that is at once shop and café, whose customers, residents and "vagrants" alike, both come to buy and stay to taste, on the other hand; it recalls the complex interdependence of "roots and routes" in theories of the postmodern. In addition, this is a place that can and will "travel," which has already existed, like Vianne herself, in different places and under different names and whose multiple versions and transformative ability further illustrate postmodernism's characteristic challenge to presumptions of authenticity and uniqueness.

Like the French garden, which is carefully cultivated to look always the same, Reynaud's conception of an "original" Lansquenet requires his constant tending to keep it static, immobile, a village stopped in time. As in Tremain's *The Way I Found Her*, intertextual references to Lewis Carroll's *Alice in Wonderland* recur several times in *Chocolat* and serve to connect, in paradoxical postmodern fashion, the two characters—Reynaud, the permanent guardian of the past, and Vianne's mother, the perpetual seeker of the new—who would indeed seem to have nothing in common. Like Alice and the Red Queen of *Through the Looking Glass*, with whom Vianne dreams that Reynaud walks through Disneyland (112), they run faster and faster only to discover that they are, at best, still in the same place.[31] In contrast, Vianne's arrival in Lansquenet puts an end to her mother's futile movement in order to set Reynaud's village in motion: "Everything's on the move. . . . Speeding up, like an old clock, being wound up after years of telling the same time" (88, see also 24).

What Vianne herself must come to understand is that forward movement can be simultaneously centripetal, at least, even necessarily, in the paradoxical universe of postmodernity. As her own narrative reveals, "flight" and "fabric" are not only reconcilable; to a significant extent they are mutually interdependent. Vianne finally realizes that this is the very knowledge that her mother ceaselessly sought to escape, the fact, that is, that no matter how often you move, how fast you run, or how far you go, you cannot avoid contact, connections, caring, even commitment: "Was this what she fled? . . . the thousands of tiny intersections of her life with others, the broken connections, the links in spite of themselves, the *responsibilities*? (113, Harris's emphasis; see also 58, 151). In keeping with Clifford's redefinition of postmodern "location," the time and space of Vianne's life (of Harris's novel) is constructed as "an itinerary" rather than "a bounded site,"[32] a series of encounters *and* farewells, of arrivals *and* departures, of meeting and meeting *again*. Like the heroes of the stories she loves in all their variant versions, Vianne often senses "something familiar" about new acquaintances, as if she might have already known them elsewhere: "Lisbon, Paris, Florence, Rome. So many people. So many lives intersected, fleetingly crisscrossed, brushed by the mad weftwarp of our itinerary" (57–58). Similarly, as Vianne begins to learn the names and to recognize the faces of her customers, she experiences what can be most appropriately described as a process of "*dis*-estrangement": "the first secret skeins of histories twisting together to form the umbilical that will eventually bind us" (21).

Recipes and menus, part of the "domestic magic" that Vianne substitutes for her mother's charms and philters, have the power both to create a concentric world and to orient movement. Vianne keeps a collection of "cookery cards," "glossy clippings" of discovery and reunion that counterbalance her mother's file on loss and disappearance: "I carried recipes in my head like maps. . . . Cookery cards anchored us, placed landmarks on the bleak borders" (40, see also 223). Vianne's delight in "incanting the names of never-tasted dishes like mantras" reflects the same self-reflective pleasure in language evident in the enumeration of the chocolates in her shop and reveals the same linguistic and cultural diversity as the international corpus of stories she also carries with her (223).[33] Most importantly, just as storytelling leads to the "complex connectivity" characteristic of globalization,[34] so too a recipe (from the Latin *recipere*) implies an exchange, a giver and a receiver. What allows Vianne to achieve what Reynaud, to his increasing frustration, cannot, to make friends and to (re)create an inclusive community in Lansquenet, is the "truth" she learned as a necessary qualification for her "profession" (no doubt that of a multitalented "maker of magic"): "the process of giving is without limits" (21).

The man whom Vianne originally mistakes for a fellow traveler will in fact turn out to be the only stranger of the two, even though Reynaud was born in Lansquenet. Figured in Vianne's tarot cards as The Hermit, the village priest is driven mad by his own willful alienation from everyone around him. Whereas Vianne's first-person narrative is often spoken in the plural "we" to include either her mother or her daughter until finally, on the day of the chocolate festival, she is able to represent the collective voice of the community as a whole (238), Reynaud tells his story to someone with whom all communication is impossible, who can neither hear nor respond. The terrible isolation of his alter ego, Lansquenet's former priest who lies in a coma for which Reynaud himself is responsible, functions as a poignant metaphor for the latter's own estrangement from the community: "This is the truth of hell, stripped of its gaudy medievalisms. This loss of contact" (12). Night after night, Reynaud watches the parties in Les Marauds from the distant shadows, increasingly tormented by his desire to take part: "I find myself wondering what my own voice would sound like among those others, my own laughter meshed with [theirs], and the night is suddenly very lonely, very cold, very empty. If only I could, I thought. Walk out from my hiding place and join them" (128). Rather, Reynaud's mad invasion of the chocolate shop on Easter Sunday ironically transforms him alone, of all the characters in *Chocolat*, into the prototypical "bad traveler"—the marauder, the intruder, the thief.

In a characteristic twist of postmodern paradox, if the "complex connectivity" recreated in Lansquenet is, as Tomlinson suggests, the defining characteristic of contemporary globalization, it remains at the same time an essential component of traditional "Frenchness."[35] Using Harris's vocabulary of connection (of "fabric"), Raymonde Carroll makes a convincing argument in *Evidences invisibles* that the French, in contrast to Anglo-Americans, construct a world based on the cultural premise that "*je existe dans un réseau*" ("*I* exist in a network").[36] Carroll, however, tends to see "culture" as unalterable, more likely to disappear than to adapt to social change; in contrast, Harris's fictional village illustrates the "transformation of localities," which Tomlinson has singled out as among the most significant impacts of globalization. Moreover, once Vianne sets events in motion, the changes that occur in Lansquenet also confirm Tomlinson's belief that both "roots and routes" are "subject to transformation in global modernity."[37] As a result of yet another kind of "real magic"—"simply the focusing of the mind toward a desired objective"—the villagers begin to take control of their own lives (125). Thus, an increase in self-worth allows Roux, one of the river people, and Joséphine, a battered wife, to stay in Lansquenet, to stop running away, to dare to put down roots, even as Reynaud and Muscat, Josephine's abusive husband and the arsonist who destroyed Roux's boat, are metaphorically expelled from the community and flee into exile. Significantly, Vianne herself is also changed. We understand that she will probably not stay permanently in Lansquenet (*Chocolat* itself remains open-ended but she will indeed have moved on by the time the hero of *Blackberry Wine* arrives a few years later). Or rather, this time Vianne will finally be able both to stay *and* to leave. She and Anouk have "progressed": there will be no more hotels; "the way" has perhaps been "paved" for them to stay elsewhere, by the sea or the river, somewhere no doubt less "rooted"; and, if not, then, most importantly of all, concludes Vianne, "this time we can take so much of Lansquenet with us" (241).[38]

Chocolat concludes shortly after the chocolate festival, consecrated by Radio-Gascogne as "a charming local tradition" (241); and indeed, it has become an annual occurrence by the time Harris returns to Lansquenet-sous-Tannes in *Blackberry Wine* (204). Since readers of the two novels, however, don't actually get to attend "*Le Grand Festival du Chocolat*," nor finally even to hear about it in any detail, I want to end this essay with a brief description of an analogous event, which I am convinced resembles the celebration planned by Vianne, particularly as her festival can be expected to travel to other communities and to evolve over time. Both the paradoxes of postmodernism and the dislocations of contemporary globalization surely allow for just such a series of displacements: the substitution of reader for writer; the transformation of fiction into reality; the transgression of multiple boundaries, literal as well as metaphoric.

In the fall of 2000, Paris hosted the "6ᵉ Salon du Chocolat," which inhabited an appropriately designated exhibition "space" (the "espace Eiffel-Branly") near the Eiffel Tower from October 28 to November 1. Variously qualified, in English, as an "international event" and a "European Chocolate Show," the Salon du Chocolat did indeed provide entry to what seemed to be at once a microcosm of the globalized world and a metaphor for postmodernity itself. A map allowed the visitor to navigate the streets, avenues, boulevards, and squares of this real "enchanted village," whose charming names—"Hall aux Delices" (Hall of Delights), "Rue des Douceurs" (Street of Sweets), "Place Fondante," Boulevard des Croqueurs" (Boulevard of Crunchers)—might have come straight out of *Chocolat*. By a fortuitous coincidence, the "avenue Quetazcoatl," named for the heroine of one of Vianne's favorite tales, led to an exposition on the history of chocolate ("Des Précolombiens aux Internautes"), which projected a path from its pre-Columbian origins into a futuristic twenty-first century.

The *mise-en-abyme* effect, created by the juxtaposition within the perimeters of the Salon as a whole of exhibition spaces of various sizes, was reinforced by the postmodern *bricolage* of incompatible styles and contents that they represented. Like the "Céleste Praline" and Vianne's Easter festival, the Salon du Chocolat was, of course, a preeminently commercial enterprise, whose many stalls, sponsored by those whose job it is to make and to sell chocolate, were designed to entice the passerby with the same tempting siren call to "*Try me. Test me. Taste me*" that drives Reynaud into madness in Harris's novel (18, 234). Yet, just as in *Chocolat*, mundane and materialistic motives disappeared in face of the "art" and the "sorcery" of chocolate making. One "artisan" constructed fragile, ruffled skirts for Spanish flamenco dancers; another carved huge blocks of solid chocolate into statuary; a third created extravagant *pièces montées* as delicate as fine lace. Indeed, the (con)fusion of reality and imitation generally characterized this postmodern world of illusion, whose own "magnificent centerpiece" was a huge white chocolate reproduction of the cathedral of Notre Dame, complete with sculpture and gargoyles and virtually indistinguishable from the original.[39] A scale model of the Statue of Liberty represented America, and a typical Japanese garden spread out next to a stand that featured chocolate "sushi"; in the space of the Ivory Coast, it was impossible to tell from any distance which masks and carved figurines might actually be made of wood.

As in the world of the carnival, where "all rules are suspended," "high" and "low" culture coexisted, as did the serious and the frivolous. In the "Salle des conférences" professors, diplomats, doctors, and writers joined chefs and nutritionists to offer a series of lectures on such lofty subjects as "L'Imaginaire du chocolat aux 16e et 17e siècles" (The Imaginative Universe of Chocolate in the 16th and 17th Centuries) and "Les Origines sacrées du chocolat" (The Sacred Origins of Chocolate). The metaphoric repetition of the formula "Chocolate and . . . " led to such variously predictable or disconcerting hybrids as "Thé et chocolat" (Tea and Chocolate), "Rhum et chocolat" (Rum and Chocolate), "Chocolat et santé" (Chocolate and Health), and "Gibier et chocolat" (Game and Chocolate). The "Musée du cacao" displayed "hundreds of different molds," like those contained in Vianne's kitchen (83); and an admirable collection of finely crafted silver and china chocolate makers (*chocolatières*) collided with old cocoa boxes and a century of advertising posters. In the "Galérie d'art," Mickey Mouse, depicted as an orchestra conductor, stood next to chocolate busts of famous composers.[40]

The high point of postmodern parody may have been the "Expo Robes," featuring mannequins dressed by collaborative teams of "chocolatiers-artistes" and fashion designers of the stature of Courrèges, Balmain, Lagerfeld, and Ungaro, who produced what *La Revue du chocolat* described, in language astonishingly reminiscent of Harris's novel, as a *"transformation presque alchimique* du chocolat en vêtement irréel et *magique"* (an "almost alchemical transformation of chocolate into an unreal and magical garment").[41] Certainly, the pure theatricality of a spectacle, which was essentially indistinguishable from an actual *haute couture défilé de mode* (high fashion show) in the totally impractical celebration of artistic self-representation common to both, had an appealing sense of turn-of-the-century irony. Less divorced from reality was what one might call the *pièce de résistance* of this decidedly eclectic gourmet meal. In what might have been an "adults only" section of the Salon (had it not taken place in France), the counterpart of "Chocoland" where children were invited to mingle with "les personnages M&M's," enlarged photographs of nude models, their bodies strategically—or not—sprinkled or swirled with chocolate, afforded a preview of a 2001 pin-up calendar. The last thing I saw was one of the daily special events, a simulacrum of an African tribal ritual whose featured performance by a dancer who leapt about and swallowed cigarettes to musical accompaniment confirmed the many similarities between the Salon du Chocolat and Lansquenet's first chocolate festival, even given the little we are told about the latter. Notably, Harris's celebration is compared to a carnival and includes special events for children, a parade, craft stalls of various kinds, chocolate put to myriad uses, jugglers, music and dancing, and even "fire eaters" (238–39).

4
Back to the Future: Nation and Nostalgia in Joanne Harris's *Blackberry Wine*

WHEN HIS ARRIVAL IN FRANCE SIMULTANEOUSLY REVIVES HIS ABILITY TO write, the English novelist Jay MacKintosh discovers that his only supply of paper consists of an unfinished draft left over from fourteen years of false starts. Thus the hero of Joanne Harris's *Blackberry Wine* types the beginning of the long-awaited "sequel" to his first novel, *Jackapple Joe*, international bestseller and critical success, on the blank side of the pages of "the old, abandoned manuscript . . . , translating it, reversing it" with what he describes both as "his own layman's alchemy" and his own version of "maps and traveling."[1] One of many examples in Harris's second novel of the eponymous Joe's conviction that "nothing ever really disappears" (72), this magical transformation and metaphoric journey, common to Jay and to his recycled text, might also be said, in keeping with the self-referentiality and the irony characteristic of *Blackberry Wine* (2000), to figure that book's own relationship to *Chocolat* (1999). Although readers of Harris's first novel had to wait less than two years for her second, *Chocolat* also brought its author "affection from a public hungry for more" and even, as in the case of *Jackapple Joe*, a Hollywood film adaption (3).[2] Indeed, a scene toward the end of Harris's first novel almost seems to announce its transmutation into the second; tasting real chocolate for the first time in his life, the narrator is overcome with its evocative quality: "There are layers of flavor like the bouquet of a fine wine" (235).[3]

In contrast to most theorists of globalization, Anthony D. Smith argues in *National Identity* that in the case of a globalized Europe the promise of cooperation has always been premised on much broader cultural assumptions and traditions than its current expression in predominantly economic and political terms might suggest. Indeed, Smith describes "the conviction of a European pattern or patterns of culture" as the one constant in a region otherwise still characterized by frequent disagreements and divisions. Smith is fully aware, however, that the absence of a common language might seem to constitute a serious obstacle to the realization of cultural commonality.[4] In that case, it might also help to explain the total absence of any discussion of written literature in the very few works that do address cultural globalization. Characteristically, for example, in *Globalization and Culture*, John Tomlinson doubly restricts its range, first to the realm of "popular culture" and then to visual media alone.[5] Of particular interest, then, in light of the recent tendency to write about France in English, is Smith's hypothesis that the transcultural function of a *lingua franca* might well be served by the extension of certain "prestige languages," which he identifies, in the case of Europe, as French and English.[6]

Certainly, French words and phrases appear on occasion in Harris's novels and in the many other texts patterned on a similar transcultural model. At times, moreover, one has almost the same sensation of having lost touch with conventional standards of logic, though clearly not with reality itself, as when one encounters what has become an increasingly common characterization of the ever more prevalent phenomenon of films made in English by directors of French nationality. Throughout the fall and winter of 2000–01, for example, and without any apparent sense of irony, the weekly guide *Pariscope* referred to Arnaud Desplechin's *Esther Kahn* as a "comédie dramatique française (version originale en anglais)" (French dramatic comedy [original English version]). By such eminently postmodern standards of paradox, *Chocolat* and *Blackberry Wine* might well be described as "French" novels (indeed, the first is titled in French), which, like Jay's own manuscript, have been "translated," in every sense of the term, into English.[7] Smith believes that a "global" culture will be postmodern, by definition: highly self-conscious and self-parodic, "the new cosmopolitanism is inherently eclectic and in motion. Its shape is constantly changing."[8] In keeping with this prediction and in direct contrast to the threat of cultural homogenization, often associated with the globalization of popular culture, Harris's parallel novels offer a particularly compelling illustration, not only of the variety possible within mainstream fiction, even when it has much in common, but also of its ability to reflect the rapidly changing conditions of the contemporary world.[9]

In *Blackberry Wine*, Jay MacKintosh takes up residence in Lansquenet-sous-Tannes, an imaginary village of two hundred residents deep in the heartland of rural France, some five years after Vianne Rocher, his counterpart in *Chocolat*, has moved on, leaving her "Grand Festival du Chocolat" to become an annual Easter event. What Radio-Gascogne already pronounced "a charming local tradition" in its very first year,[10] this celebration, based on customs and stories dating back to pre-Colombian days, may in retrospect have been an early symptom in Harris's work of the reawakening of an entire nation's nostalgic attachment to the past, evident throughout France in recent years in the revival of regional celebrations.[11] In contrast to Vianne, who has spent her entire life as a traveler, an exemplary figure of what James Clifford has qualified as a "new world order of mobility,"[12] Jay not only comes to Lansquenet to stay, but he settles into the eighteenth-century chateau he has purchased sight unseen with a strong sense of *déjà vu*, as if he were returning both home and to the past.

In keeping with the word *nostalgia*, which haunts the pages of *Blackberry Wine*, Jay's need to go back in order to move forward determines the narrative structure of Harris's third-person novel. Jay's story is told in sixty-one chapters, which alternate between the three summers of his adolescence spent in Kirby Monckton in northern England (1975–77) and the first six months of his present life in the south of France (spring–summer 1999). Jay's existence in Kirby Monckton centers around Pog Hill Lane, where he is befriended by an eccentric old man, nicknamed "Jackapple Joe," who tells him wonderful stories of his world travels while he tries to teach him the "everyday magic" of gardening and the "layman's alchemy" of making wine. Joe's charms, rituals, and talismans seem to protect Jay both from the emotional neglect of his own parents and the physical violence threatened by a local gang of youths, until the day that Joe's own inexplicable disappearance leaves Jay feeling definitively abandoned and uncontrollably angry. Twenty-two years later, when Jay flees London and heads to Lansquenet in pursuit of Joe's dream of owning a French orchard and vineyard, an apparition of the old man reappears to counsel him, as Jay attempts to fit into a divided community and to penetrate the secrets of Marise d'Api, his mysterious neighbor.

Although the existence of a growing number of Anglophone novels about France is apparent, the explanation of the phenomenon is much more elusive. Engaging in their own form of nostalgia, reviewers tend to cite the example of a canon of earlier expatriate writers, from Henry James to Ernest Hemingway to Henry Miller, in identifying the re-emergence of an "international novel" at the turn of another century. Certainly the hypothesis of literary influence is a plausible one, especially in the case of serious fiction; and indeed some of the novels in question incorporate not only direct references but even extensive networks of intertextual allusion to the work of their predecessors.[13] In that case, however, one might expect to encounter more frequent speculation about a contemporary phenomenon that might be called the "Peter Mayle effect." At the very least, Mayle's best-selling books about Provence can be assumed to have helped create a potential audience for any similar works that followed. Moreover, if Mayle's reputation was established in the early nineties on the basis of two nonfictional works, *A Year in Provence* and *Toujours Provence*, he subsequently turned to fiction, as explicitly announced in the title of *Hotel Pastis: A Novel of Provence*.[14]

The problem, of course, is that there is arguably not a lot to be said about Mayle's popular, accessible, and generally diverting texts, beyond the fact of their remarkable success. In most cases, they bear only a superficial resemblance to the work of the writers I have identified here, but even though this is largely the case with Harris as well, there is one important difference: *Blackberry Wine* at once conceals and reveals a familiarity with both Mayle's work and his reputation. Take, for example, *A Year in Provence*, which tells the story of the author's transformation from Londoner to the newest resident (and wine grower) of a small village in the south of France—a tale, in short, not unlike Jay's own. Or, alternatively, take Jay's mysterious Lansquenet neighbor; Marise d'Api turns out to have a past plotted like a melodrama, whose paradoxical combination of total implausibility and absolute predictability is not without recalling Mayle's own highly formulaic fiction. Harris enters into a kind of playful dialogue, characteristic of postmodern fiction, with Mayle—less with specific texts he has written than with what the writer and his writing have come to represent. She makes this relationship explicit in a parodic aside toward the end of *Blackberry Wine*, when Kerry, Jay's ambitious former girlfriend, turns up unexpectedly in Lansquenet-sous-Tannes. To Joe's horror, she has come to film an episode of a new television show, *Pastures New*, which "is going to be all about British people living abroad" (319–20). "Forget what Peter Mayle did for Provence," she enthuses. "Before you know it, people will be flocking here" (330).

In *French Resistance: The French-American Culture Wars*, Jean-Philippe Mathy offers an interpretation of Mayle that makes his work the repository of Anglo-American nostalgia for "a precapitalist, bucolic, small-town France," whose survival is increasingly threatened—notably, by people like Kerry and especially, of course, by Mayle himself:

> The best-selling success of Peter Mayle's books on Provence show that what the educated readers of *The New York Times Book Review* expect

from France and the French is not any kind of philosophical *aggiornamento* or yet one more description of the postmodern apocalypse they are routinely reminded they live in, but precisely the opposite, a reprieve from modernity, the eternal unchanging values of a rural, aristocratic, premodern *civilisation*.[15]

Mathy provides a fruitful context for beginning to engage the distinctiveness and the complexity of *Blackberry Wine*, precisely because his words might seem at first glance to apply to Harris's novel as well. (To some extent, they are relevant to Jay, as we will see, who is a somewhat less ambitious and successful novelist than his creator.) In particular, Harris's work does not offer any "reprieve" from the (post)modernity in which she grounds her vision of rural France nor is Lansquenet-sous-Tannes in any sense the locus of "eternal, unchanging values."

If Mathy's language doesn't apply to Harris's novel, my own, upon further reflection, does. The reference above to a "fruitful context" turns out to be an unintentional but meaningful play on words, since the expression serves to describe *Blackberry Wine* as a whole, as well as to identify a figure frequently reproduced within. Whether more deliberate or not, the choice of a deep purple cover to contain the hardback edition of the text provides an especially satisfying and equally significant metaphor, whose suggestion of self-reflexivity is immediately confirmed by the first sentence of the novel: "Wine talks; ask anyone" (1). A statement, which sounds at once like a proverb and a methodological principle, introduces an opening paragraph that functions as both genesis and *mise-en-abyme*. The importance of the passage, confirmed by its periodic reprise in variant forms throughout the novel, justifies near-verbatim quotation:

> Wine talks; ask anyone. . . . It ventriloquizes. It has a million voices. It unleashes the tongue, teasing out secrets . . . It shouts, rants, whispers. It speaks of great plans, tragic loves and terrible betrayals. It screams with laughter. It chuckles softly to itself. It weeps in front of its own reflection. It revives summers long past and memories best forgotten. Every bottle a whiff of other times, other places, . . . Everyday magic, Joe had called it. The transformation of base matter into the stuff of dream. Layman's alchemy. (1; see also 88, 102)

Wine might be said to represent not only the narrator of this passage but of the entire novel, whose contents are gradually released from the six bottles of Joe's "Specials" that Jay has recovered from Pog Hill Lane and kept "for nostalgia's sake" (2). More importantly, the metamorphosis of referential narrative into metafiction is instantaneous as Harris's characteristic practice of enumeration merges with a self-descriptive verbal vocabulary to transform the fluency of wine into the autonomous celebration of language and literature.

A similar superimposition of two systems of meaning informs *The Flavors of Modernity*, a recent critical study of "Food and the Novel." Gian-Paolo Biasin's investigation into the parallelism of literary and culinary discourses originates in "the fundamental fact that the human mouth is the ambiguous locus of two oralities: one articulates the voice, language; the other satisfies a need, the ingestion of food for survival . . . but also for pleasure."[16] Biasin's discussion of what he calls "the literary genre of modernity" is premised on the belief that the "culinary signs" constituted by eating and drinking, by food and wine, typically produce a novel that is at once referential and self-referential; in representing reality and illuminating everyday life, "such a novel also talks, metaphorically, metonymically, and metanarratively, of itself, of its own being as literature, a system of verbal signs that construct possible worlds."[17] Although Biasin's book focuses on Italian fiction, it should already be evident that *Blackberry Wine* promises to provide a particularly apt illustration of his argument. Similarly, it is difficult to imagine a more suitable real world location to serve as matrix for the linguistic and gastronomical hybrid he describes than France, a country in which native language and national identity are historically inseparable and whose cultural prestige no doubt depends in equal measure on the international reputation of its food, its wine, and its writers. That some of the latter take the former as their subject matter is clear from the number of references to the critical and theoretical work of French authors that appear in *The Flavors of Modernity*.

Still, if France's destiny is unusually dependent upon how the nation feeds itself, to paraphrase Anthelme Brillat-Savarin's famous aphorism, books in English are well represented among the many devoted to France and its cuisine.[18] Indeed, a category of writing, whose tendency to escape conventional disciplinary and generic boundaries is once again characteristic of postmodern mobility, has also flourished of late among the works of a new literature of globalization. Moreover, recent examples, such as those of Patricia Wells or Mort Rosenblum, also reprise an earlier tradition, perhaps best illustrated by M. J. K. Fisher's essays; and the provinces and Provence, in particular, serve as a privileged setting both then and now. In the case of *Blackberry Wine*, Harris's ability not only to generate a self-contained world out of what Roland Barthes once described as the "boisson-totem" (totemic drink) of the French nation,[19] but also to represent the actual conditions of contemporary Europe, may ultimately have less to do with the cross-cultural analogy she establishes between two villages of different nationalities than with the fact that the same elements that once constituted traditional French identity have become—increasingly and within a remarkably short period of time—the focus of broader concerns about globalization. What Biasin describes as the "rapidly, at times vertiginously changing mentality," reflected in the literary itinerary he traces from the nineteenth century to the present,[20] might better characterize the evolution of reality that informs the passage from *Chocolat* to *Blackberry Wine*, a question to which I shall return.

If the initial passage of Harris's second novel is essentially self-reflective and self-contained, the first of the *Specials* opened by Jay releases the past and permits its artistic re-creation. The scent and the taste of "Jackapple '75" awaken sensations, emotions, and images of such force and vividness that not only can Jay suddenly recall every forgotten detail of Pog Hill Lane, but "for a second the illusion was so strong, that he was actually *there* in that vanished place" (12). The subsequent chapter, which takes us back for the first time to the summer of 1975 in Kirby Monckton, confirms this imaginary displacement in time and space. Moreover, although we are still in England and in the fictional world of both a British novelist and her diegetic representative, Harris already evokes France through its literary tradition. For an international community of readers, this reenactment of a scene of *la mémoire involontaire* (involuntary memory), like the sense of *déjà vu* that haunts Jay in other settings, is inseparable from the name and work of Marcel Proust. Similarly, sensory stimulation frequently leads to imaginary journeys and to the return of the past in a number of Charles Baudelaire's best-known poems. Notably, the first paragraph of Harris's novel depends upon an associative network, linking sensation to "secrets" and to "memories," that is strongly reminiscent of the structure of Baudelaire's "Spleen" ("J'ai plus de souvenirs que si j'avais mille ans").[21] Such intertextual allusions, common in postmodern literature, serve to unite readers beyond national, historical, cultural, and linguistic boundaries, in keeping with the "complex connectivity" that Tomlinson considers to be the defining feature of contemporary globalization.[22]

More immediately relevant is the generic resemblance that links *Chocolat* and *Blackberry Wine* to an early twentieth-century movement in French literature, which led to a series of "regional novels" or *romans du terroir*. This work was inherently nostalgic, as seen, for example, in Jean Giono's lyrical exaltation of the natural world and peasant life or in Marcel Pagnol's folkloric portrayal of provincial Marseille. Although Harris writes in English about British characters, her contemporary revision nonetheless returns the regional novel to its roots in *la France profonde*. Jay's absolute conviction that Joe's garden and his own creativity can only be restored in and by this particular place, the "real counterpart" to the idealized settings of his books (35), is on the order of self-evident truth, given the almost mythological attachment of the French to the agricultural heartland of the nation. Indeed, as more and more people abandon the farms and villages of France, in what the historian Richard F. Kuisel, among others, describes as "the most striking feature of the 'New France,'"[23] the *terroir* (both *soil* and *region* in English) has become more imaginary in reality than in fiction. The "logical corollary" to the disappearance of *la France profonde*, notes Kuisel, is an intensification of the same nostalgia that haunts Jay,[24] for whom it represents, in keeping with the full semantic range of the word, not simply the longing for the past but also an acute sense of "homesickness," reflective of a world, more thoroughly explored in Harris's first novel, in which "loss of home" has become, in the words of Aamir Mufti and Ella Shohat, "the recurring motif of modernity."[25]

Perhaps it is France's reputation as what Benjamin Franklin called "everyone's second country" that explains why, of late, it is so often Anglo-American writers who lament the alteration of the traditional French landscape. In the suggestively titled "Where are the Berets of Yesterday?," Alan Riding argues that France "enjoys a privileged place in the imagination of educated Britons and Americans" precisely because of its celebrated difference, *l'exception française*.[26] Thus Richard Bernstein delivers "An Elegy for the French Difference" as an afterword to *Fragile Glory*, Kuisel evokes "The France We Have Lost" in a recent essay collection, and Jonathan Fenby speaks of "a nation at risk" in a new book called *France on the Brink*.[27] Jay too is initially disappointed when his Lansquenet neighbors fail to fulfill comically exaggerated expectations worthy of Peter Mayle's most committedly naive fans. Invited to dinner by Georges and Caro Clairmont, Jay looks forward to a simple meal of homemade terrines, red wine, olives, pimentos, and soup in earthenware bowls, served by the local builder's wife, "who would be small and drab in an apron and head scarf, or sweet-faced and rosy . . . blushing with pleasure at his compliments" (145). To his astonishment, Jay is in fact greeted by "a plump, elegant lady, twin-setted and stillettoed in powder blue," who welcomes him into an interior of "relentless chintziness" where the food, as ornate as the house—*soufflé au champagne, vol-au-vents, gésiers farcis, boeuf en croûte*—leaves him "secretly longing for the homemade terrine and the olives of his fantasy" (145–47). Moreover, far from accepting Jay as the *"mec sympathique, pas du tout prétentieux"* ("nice guy, quite unpretentious") he hopes to be, the Clairmonts and their friends view the famous writer as the cultural salvation of the village (145).

Harris portrays Lansquenet-sous-Tannes as a divided community in both *Chocolat* and *Blackberry Wine*, but the source of tension differs in the two novels in ways that correspond to an equally rapid evolution over the last few years in the political and cultural climate beyond literature. Both Vianne and Jay are at once newcomers, outsiders, foreigners, and strangers; but their presence in Lansquenet fuels somewhat different anxieties. Vianne's arrival arouses the xenophobic hostility and chauvinism of those citizens, represented by the local priest, who fear that the increased presence in France of immigrants, deemed unassimilable, threatens the very identity of the nation. Whether intentionally or not, *Chocolat* indirectly evokes attitudes that led to the rise in France of Jean-Marie Le Pen's *le Front national* and to the reawakening of neo-Nazi sentiments across Europe. In contrast, in both the fictional France of *Blackberry Wine* and its referential counterpart, the opposition between native and foreign, national and alien, has been replaced by the conflict between rural and urban, local and global; and fear of transformation from within has displaced the threat of change introduced from without. Increasingly, the specters of a unified Europe and a globalized world seem to constitute a more immediate danger to national autonomy and integrity than immigration and the pressures of multiculturalism.[28] Let me stress that neither the situation I have just described nor the reaction(s) to it are in any sense uniquely French. In part, "France" functions as a powerful metaphor in the British fiction of a new literary globalism precisely because England has faced and continues to face many of the same dilemmas, a fact that the cross-cultural perspective of *Blackberry Wine* usefully emphasizes.[29]

Although Harris's novel does not in any sense promote a static, timeless world of traditional values and lifestyles, it does suggest that certain kinds of changes will prove far more destructive to France's heartland than the literal disappearance of family farms and provincial villages. The enemy, so recently an (African) immigrant, now takes the shape of Parisians, wealthy investors, tourists, and, ultimately, one's own neighbors, a category that includes the countries of the European Union. The Clairmonts' nightmarish alternative to Lansquenet's inevitable decline is epitomized by Le Pinet, "the local success story," a village of comparable size transformed into a haven for "wealthy English tourists." If "an enterprising couple from Paris" built the first holiday homes, the villagers' own eagerness to benefit from "the new tourist trade" accounts for subsequent expansion. A summary of Harris's comically detailed description of Le Pinet's current assets includes the following: gift shops, fast food outlets, Michelin ranked restaurants, luxury hotels, swimming pools, local buildings suddenly discovered to be "historically significant," shopping centers, riding clubs, health spas, the right to host the filming of a television series, and, as the French say, *j'en passe* (148–50). Jay understands all too well "the worst of it, the momentum [that] sweeps everyone along" (330). When he returns to Pog Hill Lane in 1999, he finds the former mining community under development by a riverside building project, whose plans include a visitors' center, "where tourists could descend an especially converted mine shaft or ride a barge on the newly cleaned canal" (306).

This is not, of course, a fictional fantasy, despite Harris's ironic account of the transformation of "real" villages into a postmodern hybrid of local folklore, theme park, vacation paradise, and souvenir shop. Rosenblum, for example, describes the crash landing of the medieval village of Conques in the late twentieth century as a result of the commercial success of the town's own plan "to sell itself to mass tourism."[30] Of particular significance is Kuisel's report on Laurence Wylie's return visit thirty-three years later to Roussillon, the 1950 star of *Village in the Vaucluse*, French scholarship's most celebrated equivalent of Lansquenet and Pog Hill Lane. Among scholars, too, the views prove interestingly divided; what for Kuisel illustrates the loss of a way of life reads, even in his own summary of Wylie's words, as a much more ambiguous development: "Writing in 1987, Wylie explains how the old village, once marked by polyculture farms, isolation, and fear of outsiders, a lack of amenities, and anxiety about the future, has become a wealthy resort community with cosmopolitan residents, boutiques, and a sense of connection with the region, and nation, and the world."[31]

There is nothing surprising in the fact that food and wine should be the dominant focus of the nostalgia aroused in Jay by his visit to the Clairmonts, despite the equal banality of their clothing and their conversation. His anticipated "potluck" (145), that is, a meal made up of whatever happens to be readily available, represents a *cuisine du terroir*, composed of authentic, local products, native to southwestern France. The dishes that Caro actually serves, although ostensibly, even originally, characteristic of France, exemplify an international *haute cuisine*, now featured on the menus of "continental" restaurants worldwide and still French in name only. It is precisely this contrast between local authenticity and European and/or global standardization that has turned "food" (broadly understood) into the latest focus of anxiety and protest in France.[32] To take yet another Anglophone book as example, *A Goose in Toulouse and Other Culinary Adventures*, Rosenblum's tour of the provinces at the turn of the new century, reveals a prevalent, persistent fear throughout the country that the regulations imposed by the new European Union will enforce a uniformity of standards, both of production and of product definition, that will make it financially impossible and perhaps even illegal to maintain the regional variety and the high quality of the ingredients on which the survival of a distinctive *cuisine du terroir* depends. If Rosenblum concentrates on a view already common to farmers, merchants, wine growers, chefs, and restaurateurs, there is strong evidence that their concerns are more generally shared and their cause widely supported by a vast majority of their customers and consumers, rural and urban, provincial and Parisian, alike.[33]

Surely no better example exists than the rapid ascension of José Bové, head of *La Confédération Paysanne* (Peasant Confederation), to the stature of national hero, a reincarnation of Astérix, the clever underdog of French popular culture who triumphs over a more powerful enemy by wit and wile—or, in the case of Bové, by organizing an attack on a local McDonalds in the summer of 1999.[34] Although most readers will no doubt inevitably be struck by certain intriguing parallels between Bové and Jackapple Joe, the near-mythological folk hero of *Blackberry Wine*, this may well be a case in which fiction is more likely to have generated reality—or, at least, preceded it—than vice versa; certainly Joe belongs to the world of fairy tales and folklore that Harris first evokes in *Chocolat*.[35] Most importantly, however, whereas Bové is, after all, something of a *terroriste*, albeit a relatively harmless and unusually popular one, Joe might better be described as a *"terroiriste,"* to borrow a term coined by Adam Gopnick.[36] On Pog Hill Lane, he engages in the time-consuming and labor-intensive work necessary to the cultivation of a garden designed to preserve the rich, natural variety of the plant world from extinction. Among the "millions of seeds" he has collected are "thousands and thousands of potatoes" and "over three hundred species of onion alone," as well as "a bewildering treasure store" of other vegetables, herbs, and fruit trees:

> Of all the millions of varieties of fruit and vegetables once grown, only a few dozen are still commonly used. Some of these seeds would grow plants which were already extinct in the wild, Joe said, their properties forgotten by everyone but a handful of experts.
>
> "It's your intensive farming does it," he would say, . . . "Too much specialization kills off variety. 'Sides, people don't want variety. They want everythin' to look the same. . . . There's things growin' here that you wouldn't find anywhere else in the whole of England, . . . and there's seeds in that chest of mine that you might not find anywhere else in the whole world." (54)

Despite Jay's enthusiasm at the thought that "arcane, forgotten things" might be growing in Pog Hill Lane (55) and the clearly accurate reference above to the results of modern methods of farming, I must confess that my reading of *Blackberry Wine* nonetheless positioned the man whom Kerry eulogizes as Britain's "favorite gardener" (311) squarely within the province of fiction, and even, of fantasy, in keeping with Joe's own references to his vocation as "everyday magic" and "layman's alchemy." Imagine my delight, then, to discover his real-life counterpart—a much closer copy than Bové—in a new English-language book about France. In *Paris to the Moon*, Gopnik describes his friend Antoine Jacobsohn as a "vegetable scholar," who holds a research fellowship at the "Museum of Vegetable Culture" in a suburb of Paris. He likes to present friends with an "idealized poster" of the twenty-four types of radishes native to the Ile-de-France; he writes nostalgically about "the lost monstrous spinach" of Viroflay and the flat onions of Verdus; and he is shocked at the lack of variety in the produce sold in the huge wholesale food market outside Paris. In short, in a curious incidence of postmodern boundary crossing, Antoine Jacobsohn sounds an awfully lot like Jackapple Joe: "So many radishes gone; the artichokes of Paris, almost gone; the turnips of Vaugirard, gone. There's a variety of beans that one reads about all the time in the nineteenth-century texts. But gone! We've kept some seedlings of the plants in the museum, and they could be revived."[37]

Still, there is, once again, an important difference. A truly devoted "terroiriste," like Antoine, finds diversity meaningful only within the context of a particular locality; value depends upon authenticity of origin. Harris's novel, in contrast, ultimately projects a vision more consistent with postmodern reality, a world of mobility, imitation, and reproduction in which what Linda Hutcheon calls the "interrogations of the impulse to sameness" no longer depend upon either originality or place of origin.[38] By the end of *Blackberry Wine*, Lansquenet-sous-Tannes has become a microcosmic model of a successfully unified Europe in which place-specific traditions have been uprooted, transformed, and recombined to produce an exemplary global culture whose cosmopolitan heterogeneity offers an alternative both to national cultures and to standardized world culture.[39] The exotic contents of Joe's seed chest, which unexpectedly turn up one day with Jay's mail, have been gathered from all over the world to be brought to fruition in the fertile soil of southwestern France. Appropriately, Jay is either evasive when asked about the "origins" of seeds that have literally both come from everywhere and appeared out of nowhere; or, alternatively, in an example of postmodern paradox, reminiscent of "French" films made in English, he describes them as "rediscovered originals" (354).

If Lansquenet's future is thus guaranteed by the cultivation of "old varieties" of vegetables (357), this is nonetheless neither a simple revival of the past nor a return to the *terroir*. Rather, it represents a case of postmodern hybridity, a version of the seemingly self-contradictory "world terroir," which chef Alain Ducasse posits as the ideal cuisine in a world of obsolete borders and limitless possibilities[40] or a variant on the practice of "retro-innovation," by which the celebrated baker Lionel Poilâne similarly proposed to retain the best of the old to add to the new.[41] In marked contrast, Jay's initial effort to "seal the perimeters" of Lansquenet proves as futile as did Joe's attempt to "camouflage" Pog Hill Lane years earlier (85, 92, 346–47). The survival of the village depends on its ability to adapt to a changing world, to become an example of "the transformation of localities themselves," which Tomlinson ranks among the most important of globalization's cultural impacts.[42] Certainly, *Blackberry Wine* is a work of nostalgia, provided, that is, that the concept is understood in the revisionary sense proposed by Jeffrey Richards: "It is a great mistake to see nostalgia as a passive, wishy-washy, rose-tinted yearning for the past. Nostalgia is a vital force, passionate, active, committed to the ideal of reviving and preserving the best of the past."[43]

Readers of an essay devoted to a novelist whose work has been repeatedly presented as both referential and self-referential must have begun to wonder what has happened to her diegetic representative within *Blackberry Wine*. Although a gradual shift in emphasis from "Jay the writer" to "Jay the gardener," no doubt reflected here, is entirely consistent with the character's own evolution within Harris's novel, this change only comes about as the result of a complex, even a somewhat convoluted, process during which Jay's dual identities remain intricately interrelated. Still, although the stories of Lansquenet and of Jay's new manuscript are equally important, periodically intersecting, and unquestionably analogical—notably, in the multiple options, shifting directions, and uncertain futures that shape both narratives—they are not finally interchangeable; one overlays rather than overlaps the other. In my turn, rather than alternating their discussion throughout this essay, as Harris does in her novel, I have preferred to go back to move forward, in what I hope will prove an appropriately nostalgic gesture of my own.

The disorientation generally characteristic of Jay's adult life is reflected in the indecision that marks his career as a writer. During the years that he has futilely struggled to produce a sequel to *Jackapple Joe*, his only "adult book," he has published seven profitable novels under the pseudonym of Jonathan Winesap, his "evil twin," who writes works of science fiction and fantasy (4). The distinction that Jay makes between two kinds of literature goes well beyond dissimilarities of genre, audience, or critical approval to address more fundamental differences of both inspiration and interpretation. Jonathan, "that cynical advocate of Fiction In Its Rightful Place" (35), writes escapist works, meant not only to distance their author, as well as his readers, from daily life but constructed out of the codes, cliches, and conventions of popular culture as well.[44] This redoubled refusal of "reality" produces works that are attractive formally but empty of content—"a parody, like Jay himself, . . . all surface glitter but nothing underneath" (6). On the order of the produce sold in today's Paris markets or the appealingly red and round but tasteless tomatoes that scandalize Joe, Jonathan's books are all interchangeable, both with each other and with others of the same kind (54).

Jay's repeated references to "keeping fiction in its place" and description of his pseudonymous works as "safely fictional" seem curiously contradictory at first reading, given that *Jackapple Joe* unquestionably qualifies as a novel as well (3). The individuality of the latter stems from its origins in Jay's own life rather than in his knowledge of popular culture or genre fiction; the hero of *Jackapple Joe* is based on a person who really existed. Similarly, and as a result, the novel also has an emotional impact—the power to touch its readers' lives—quite unrelated to the temporary distraction held out to Jonathan's audience. Since Jay, Jonathan, and Joe are themselves literary characters, however, products of Harris's own imagination and/or memory, this discussion has already begun to have the somewhat vertiginous effect of an endless series of internal duplications in which words like *real* and *fictional* lose all meaning.[45] Such a crossing of boundaries between "reality" and "fiction" is, of course, a common strategy of postmodern literature, as is that between popular culture and serious fiction, which inevitably coexist in Harris's novel despite her hero's determination to keep them apart. The knowledge, which Jay resists and will only gradually come to understand in and through the process of drafting his new novel, is resumed in the most important lesson, a distinctly postmodern one, that Joe once tried to teach him, that is, "that some things can be both real and imaginary at the same time, that some lies can also be true, that broken faith can be restored" (7).

Ironically, when Jay first meets Joe in Pog Hill Lane, he has difficulty believing in his rituals and charms precisely because the old man's eccentricities seem so ordinary, so unlike the conventions of popular culture that

Jay has already begun to reproduce in his own short stories: "To his adolescent self much of Joe's magic seemed rather *too* commonplace, too natural, like cooking or gardening, stripped of its mysteries. He would have preferred solemn invocations, black robes, midnight ritual. *That* he might have believed. Reared on comic books and trash fiction, that at least would have rung true" (234).[46] But Joe is also a storyteller, yet another version of the artist within the text of *Blackberry Wine*, who gradually seduces Jay with his wonderful tales of world travels, full of detailed descriptions of the exotic places he has visited and the fascinating people he has met. These stories also inspire Jay to write, and the pages of what is already "not quite a diary" will take final form years later in *Jackapple Joe*.

Yet, paradoxically, Jay not only stops believing in Joe, but loses the very capacity to believe in anything or anyone, on the day he discovers that the old man is, in fact, a fabulist, a creator of fictions, and one, moreover, whose method of composition resembles that which Jay later privileges as the path to adult fiction. Although Joe's stories are not generated out of the raw material of his own life, which explains Jay's disillusion and sense of betrayal, they nonetheless originate in a textual source that is factual, not fictional—*National Geographic*: "All his experiences, his anecdotes, his adventures, near-misses, his swashbucklings, his ladies in Haiti, his traveling gypsies—all taken from this pile of old magazines, all as fake as his magic, his layman's alchemy, his precious seeds, no doubt collected from growers or mail-order suppliers while he wove his dreams—his lies—alone . . ." (265).

In *National Geographic* Harris has found a wonderful metaphor for the global literature of postmodernity, Clifford's "new world order of mobility."[47] Within the pages of a single issue, the reader is perpetually uprooted and displaced in a microcosmic tour of a highly diverse geography.[48] For many of us, the magazine was our first introduction to the world of the imagination reproduced in textual form, a magical journey that provided the reader what writing gives Jay: "[our] own version of Joe's maps and traveling" (154). Given its focus on the strange and the exotic, it had (and no doubt has) powers traditionally reserved for fiction: the ability to create a sense of childlike wonder in an audience of adolescents and adults and to allow its readers to lose themselves in a place that temporarily becomes more "real" than their own everyday "reality." Paradoxically, of course, the world depicted in *National Geographic* actually does exist; the magazine's articles and images are therefore truthful, factually accurate, and yet, at the same time, they are frequently implausible in the very foreignness of the cultures and customs they describe. (This might explain why Joe's stories "ring true" to someone, like Jay, steeped in the fantastic codes of popular culture.) Much like the postmodern novel, then, *National Geographic* proves that it is possible to write about "the real" without being in the least bit "realistic." As Joe says, "some things can be both real and imaginary at the same time" (7, see also 350).

As we know, Jay's search for a "real counterpart" to the imaginary worlds of literature, a place where "fiction and flesh could be brought together," brings him to Lansquenet (35). His arrival, however, coincides with what corresponds to a new departure, not just because Jay begins a new book, but because what he describes as "that stranger growing on the reverse of the old manuscript" (173–74) initially expands with such surprising ease that it almost seems to be writing itself, obliging Jay "to follow the story where it lead[s]" (128). In the first stage of what will turn out to be a very circuitous journey, marked by repeated halts, turns, and detours, Jay begins writing a kind of "sequel" to *Jackapple Joe* in which Lansquenet and its citizens substitute for Pog Hill Lane and Joe. Now inspired by Jay's present life rather than the past, the book will paint an even more realistic portrait that did its predecessor. Indeed, it eventually becomes a collaborative project in which the villagers offer him stories, anecdotes, and personal experiences with the hope that he will include them in the book.

Paradoxically, however, the more that Jay learns about Lansquenet, the less possible it is to tell its story. More importantly, he is forced to acknowledge that the existing manuscript, which he conceived as a realistic novel, that is, an accurate, faithful transposition of the lives of real people, is, in fact, a work of pure fiction, carefully crafted to conform to the novelist's personal aesthetic vision. In other words, he has largely invented the world he would have his readers see as representational. Appropriately, the intrusion of unwelcome reality occurs during Jay's visit to the Clairmonts, whose modern ways already clash with his nostalgic fantasies. The Clairmonts' gossip about Marise d'Api—the rumors of an adulterous affair, a mysteriously deaf child, a husband driven to suicide, a vengeful mother-in-law—disrupts the suddenly evident patterns of his fiction: "His book—if there was ever going to be a book—didn't need this. . . . He wanted apple-faced women picking herbs in their gardens. He wanted a French idyll, a *Cider with Rosette* . . . " (151). In the context of *Blackberry Wine*, and speaking metaphorically, it seems fair to say that Jay is mockingly exposed as a would-be "Peter Mayle," who writes romantic, idealized portraits of rural villages and their colorful local characters in order to appease his own nostalgia and to satisfy the naive expectations of his readers. For Jay must now, of course, confront the falseness, artifice, and inaccuracy of his first book as well:

> *Jackapple Joe* never even came close to what really happened. It was a fabrication, a dream of what things should have been like, a naive reenactment of those magical, terrible summers. . . . In his book Joe was the bluff, friendly old man who steered him toward adulthood. Jay was the generic apple-pie boy . . . No wonder everyone loved that book. It was the triumph of deceit, of whimsy over reality, the childhood we all secretly *believe* we had, but which none of us ever did. *Jackapple Joe* was . . . the worst kind of lie; half-true, but lying in what really matters. (131)

The gossip about Marise may or may not be "true," but it is certainly not easily credible; indeed, the rumors that circulate among her neighbors are far more fantastic than any of Jay's naive fantasies. Thus, his new fascination with Marise and his sudden, compelling need to write her story brings about an essentially superficial "translation" of his manuscript, as if he had once again simply reversed the pages. Jay switches fictional categories—the fairy tale romance becomes a melodrama with hints of tragedy (Marise's preferred version) and *roman noir* (his own)—but the novel as a whole distances itself even further, if possible, from a realistic tradition. In fact, Jay's "evil twin," the advocate of "keeping fiction in its place," now seems to have taken the place of "Peter Mayle." Jay is not attracted to Marise's story in spite of its transparently fictional nature, as he professes, but, on the contrary, precisely because of it; he immediately remarks the "curiously pervasive" nature of a narrative he recognizes as "an old story—not even an original story" (151–52). Indeed, this is an archetypal tale—"primitive," "visceral"—that foregrounds its own conventions: "The woman living alone with her secrets, the man dead in the barn, the dark triangle of mother, grandmother, daughter" (153). Moreover, when "the woman" in question finally confides in Jay, she too presents the "truth" as a pre-scripted literary adaptation: "it seemed perfectly unreal. So dramatic—like a film or a novel. It couldn't possible be her life" (339).

Such a parodically conventional story lends itself to a postmodern rewriting, but Jay, as I have already suggested, is not the novelist that Harris is. As he settles into the community, he is struck more and more by the complexity of the people he originally saw "merely as amusing, ready-made characters in his as-yet-unfinished book" (210). Marise proves particularly elusive, and as the distance grows between the dangerous and unpredictable woman who is the heroine of his novel and the devoted mother and dedicated viticulturist whose property borders his, Jay increasingly finds that Marise is "more interesting than any fiction" (277). The activities of gardening and writing, once analogical, complementary, and equal in importance, now compete for Jay's time and attention, and the garden ever more frequently wins. When the village and the book about the village turn out to be incompatible, the success of the latter threatening the survival of the former, Jay chooses reality over realism, destroys the manuscript that he no longer wants to finish, and gives up writing.

It is not uncommon in modern fiction to discover that the novel we have just read and the novel that a character within the text has been writing are one and the same. Indeed, to learn that the two novels are not, at the very least, closely related would already be unusual, and for no doubt obvious reasons, very few texts end, let alone end happily, in their own self-destruction—not even within the disposal culture of postmodernity. Harris needs Jay's story for much the same reasons that he needs Marise's; in both cases, the very structure of the novel is at stake. Despite the many disparities between *Blackberry Wine* and Jay's unfinished manuscript, his description of the form of his work in progress functions as a *mise-en-abyme* for Harris's novel: "Without this central tale, his book was no more than a collection of anecdotes. With Marise's story to bind them together, it might become a rich, absorbing novel. If only he knew where it was leading" (191).

In keeping with the dominant network of imagery within *Blackberry Wine*, the word *bind* itself contains a range of meanings, whose connotations extend from promises of unity and cohesion to simple enclosure to outright constraint. In the geography of Harris's novel, spaces associated with either end of the spectrum are viewed as either negative or unattainable—the mines imprison Joe, his "perimeter ritual" always fails to protect the village. The privileged metaphors of *Blackberry Wine*, what I earlier described as "fruitful contexts," all take the form of relatively open spaces, indeed places of unusually free access with a capacity to contain as loose as their contents are diverse. If Joe's six "Specials," the original and recurrent generative sources of the novel as a whole, might seem to contradict this description, the wine in fact has the expansive power of Aladdin's lamp or of a genie in a bottle to produce a rich world of language and literature. Appropriately no doubt, it explicitly marks both the "opening" and the "closing" of Harris's novel. Just as the first bottle that Jay uncorks releases the raw materials of the fiction to come, the final bottle he consumes metaphorically contains all that has come before: "For a moment he thought he could distinguish all the rest of Joe's wines in that glassful, raspberry and roses and elderflower and blackberry and damson and jackapple all in one" (301).

Importantly, there is nothing obviously appealing about Joe's specials, either in or out of the bottle. A wine meant to be consumed rather than collected has been allowed to "age" for over twenty years, and, by Jay's own admission, it smells disgusting, looks awful, and tastes dreadful. Yet, it is precisely this "sweetish ferment of flowers like a whiff of garbage" that has the evocative power to bring back lost or forgotten memories and emotions and to recreate the past in the present (15).[49] *Blackberry Wine* is itself bound together by a series of comparable objects and especially places in which the apparent absence of all beauty and worth actually conceals an abundance of useful treasures. Nether Edge, the abandoned, stagnant fields on the outskirts of Kirby Monckton, is such a place for the adolescent Jay. Full of years of accumulated garbage, it is "an ugly—perhaps a dangerous—place" but also "a secret place, an old, somehow forbidden place," and there Jay discovers "a spill of exotic, discarded treasures" (22–23). Under Joe's tutelage, Jay learns to recognize the value of what others have abandoned, and in his second summer, he brings Joe the "new glories" he finds on the dump and the "riches" delivered along the railway (72). In Lansquenet, Clairmont, convinced that Jay's skepticism about modernization must stem from a fondness for "le rustique," regularly delivers a truckload of junk, "all the unloved and abandoned detritus of loft and cellars," which Jay fully intends to burn until he discovers, much to his own surprise, that everything can be put to use (163, 169). Jay returns to Pog Hill Lane to find that Joe's garden has been converted into a landfill site, but within this "continent of litter" still lie a number of his belongings, including the six precious bottles, "miraculously unbroken," of his Specials (307–8).[50]

Clearly, Joe's seed chest and Jay's spice cabinet—equally old, dusty, and abandoned in appearance and filled, each in its turn, with dead-looking seeds—are the most important of Harris's metaphors of fertility and regeneration. On the final page of *Blackberry Wine*, Jay, the former writer, offers a modest redefinition of his identity: "I'm just a collector. I have collected a large number of different seeds on my travels around the world" (357). Ultimately, Harris too is "just a collector" and *Blackberry Wine* "no more than a collection of anecdotes." In illustration of Joe's motto that "nothing ever really disappears" (172) and his determination to let nothing go to waste, Harris's novel also constitutes a rather crowded space in which she recycles a plethora of literary possibilities. This postmodern *bricolage*, as we have seen, mixes realism and fantasy, tradition and modernity, romance and tragedy, folktales and popular culture, metafiction and memoir. Unlike Marise's story, which endlessly eludes Jay, Harris does have Jay's story as "central tale," and yet his unfinished manuscript may finally serve as a more appropriate metaphor. Not only doesn't Jay know where his novel "[is] leading," but neither, of course, do we have any idea where it ends up. Despite the apparent incompatibility of the various directions in which it seems at different times to be heading, nothing indicates that Jay either discards or revises any part of it. On the contrary, the pages just keep piling up, eventually without any explanation of what they might contain, and at times to an end that might suggest incoherence.[51] Thus, after explicitly identifying the gossip about Marise as totally inconsistent with what he has written so far, Jay heads home to record this story, and we are told that the ten additional pages, which it inspires that very night, "fit easily with the rest" (191).

By chance, Agnès Varda's two most recent films, as noted earlier, are explorations of the metaphor of "gleaning" seen at once as a reflection of the human condition in the modern world and of her own filmmaking practice. Or perhaps coincidence has nothing to do with chance, since the image of the artist as collector has become a recurrent figure in the recent fiction of literary globalism.[52] This productive form of nostalgia, in which the best of the old is salvaged and recycled into the new, is equally unlikely to result in formal perfection in the case of globalization as in that of a novel whose textual representation of its own process of composition reflects the ongoing construction of a new Europe and a new world. In both instances, the incorporation of heterogeneity and diversity, even when they can't be neatly "contained," inevitably matters more than the appearance of unity and homogeneity; as Joe reminds Jay, "it's not what things look like that matters. It's what's *inside*. The *'art'* of it" (172).[53] Smith's belief that a developing global culture, "this new cosmopolitanism," will lead to "a rich inchoate *mélange*" rather than to "the planned 'unity in diversity' beloved of official Europeanism" strongly echoes Harris's version of the literature of globalization.[54] In the specific case of *Blackberry Wine*, however, the novelist's own interpretation of the critical term "organic fiction," which she is told has been applied, without explanation, to her work, may provide its most appropriate metaphor. On the model of the fruits and vegetables produced by her own heroes, "organic fiction," Harris surmises, "often has irregularities in texture and shape" but also "tends to taste better and to be better for the health," in which case, she concludes, the analogy is "fine" with her.[55]

5
Mosaics of the Might-Have-Been: Metaphor, Migration, and Multiculturalism in Claire Messud's *The Last Life*

TRANSLATED INTO FRANCE AS AN EXCLUSIVELY ENGLISH-LANGUAGE bookstore in the heart of Paris, the Village Voice might be said to embody the linguistic and cultural contradictions of a newly globalized universe. The shop regularly hosts evening readings by writers from throughout the Anglophone world who read from their recent work in the language in which it was written but whose presence in France on that particular day is almost always motivated by the fact that the book in question is about to appear in French translation. Indeed, the translator is usually in attendance as well and sometimes also reads a passage in French to the largely bilingual audience, who can then take advantage of an exceptional opportunity to buy a book that the Village Voice does not normally sell. Such were the circumstances on January 11, 2001, when Claire Messud, in Paris to promote the forthcoming translation of her second novel and accompanied by her translator, Guillemette Belleteste, sat down behind a table displaying copies of *La Vie Après* (2001) to read an excerpt from *The Last Life* (1999).

In the particular case of these two books, however, a juxtaposition that should have been merely circumstantial and gratuitous turns out to be not only appropriate but almost essential. Although the increased income and audience that result from a translation no doubt serve to support the creative process, the translation itself does not normally function as an integral component of literary composition. *The Last Life*, in contrast, not only unfolds in an intermediary and multilingual space, at once in and in between France, America, and colonialist Algeria; but translation from the French already figures both importantly and diversely in the original English-language version of the novel. Simultaneously a metaphor for storytelling and for the temporal and spatial displacement that narration involves—"Now I find myself wanting to translate the world inside," explains Sagesse LaBasse—translation also acts to generate the very language spoken by Messud's first-person narrator.[1] Indeed, *The Last Life* may be the first text whose existence confirms the atavistic nature of "foreign authors" in what Jean-Christophe Bailly and Michel Deutsch have characterized as an era that is "fundamentally already 'translated.'"[2] In the question-and-answer period following her reading at the Village Voice, Messud, whose father is French, revealed that she systematically imagined the dialogue of her French characters in their native language before "translating" it into English, a strategy that made the subsequent translation of *The Last Life* (back) into French "curiously difficult," according to Belleteste, who described the American novel as having "French resounding through the sentence." Messud, in turn, found herself similarly disoriented upon reading *La Vie Après*, whose actual words both recalled and yet almost inevitably differed from those she too had first conceived in French.

Anyone who has ever read the same literary work twice, once in the original and once in translation, knows, of course, that they have really read two different books. In the case of *The Last Life* and *La Vie Après*, this fact is already evident in the space opened up between the two titles. The substitution of an adverb (*après*) for an adjective (*last*), characteristic of the passage between English and French, here results in a further transposition of meaning, which, although equally common, is nonetheless also unusually appropriate in this context. The semantic reversal, which turns our gaze from the past to the future, away from the life left behind and toward the life that came afterward, simultaneously fuses and confuses the American novel and its French translation. In a revelation only made possible by the coexistence of the two versions of the text, the English title most accurately identifies the French upbringing that Sagesse will ultimately reject, while the French title more exactly names the American lifestyle that she will finally embrace. (The *chassé-croisé* also figures prominently among the standard procedures employed by those who translate between French and English.)[3] Moreover, the tension between these variant interpretations and counterpoised orientations works to foreground one of the most important of the novel's recurrent motifs: momentary entrapment between the past and the rest of one's life.

On the model of the somewhat disorienting phenomenon by which the Frenchness of French films now depends on the citizenship of the director rather than on the language of the text, so that the weekly entertainment guide *Pariscope* talks about such curiosities as a "comédie dramatique française (version originale en anglais)" (French dramatic comedy [original English version]) or a "comédie dramatique française (en langue anglaise)" (French dramatic comedy [in English]), one might describe *The Last Life* in similarly postmodern terms of hybridity as either an English-language French novel, or an American novel in the original French, or both.[4] The nationality of Messud's novel thus reflects that of its youthful narrator, whose story also begins in ambivalence: "I am American now, but this wasn't always so" (3). Appropriately, then, journalists have tended to review *The Last Life* not only together with other novels but specifically with those of non-American writers. Brooke Allen, for example, groups Messud with Irish and Czech authors, and Sarah Kerr puts her in a category of "new literary globalists" whose other members are Scandinavian and Korean/Japanese.[5] In keeping with other examples of the specifically Anglo-American novel of globalization, *The Last Life* also qualifies as a "traveling novel," which crosses multiple boundaries, both literal and metaphoric. The experience of Messud's reader corresponds to that attributed by Stuart Hall to the spectator of what he classifies as "traveling films": "We are in the world of movement, of migration, of the dissolution of boundaries, of national borderlines."[6]

Still other reviewers interrogate the generic identity of *The Last Life*. Notably, Michiko Kakutani finds Messud's writing "so vivid" and "so fraught with felt emotion" that she believes "the reader might mistake it for a memoir."[7] Such is indeed the case to judge by the reaction of the audience at the Village Voice, visibly taken aback to hear Messud assert—in response to the first, and clearly pro forma, question she was asked that evening—that the novel was "not autobiographical." As Kakutani suggests, the assumption that the book must be based on the author's life does not stem from knowledge of Messud's biography but rather from the attributes of the writing itself, including, no doubt, the literary convention that encourages readers to equate the coming-of-age story of a first-person narrator with reality.[8] In a self-referential passage, in which the situation of the narrator once again contains the novel as a whole, Messud metaphorically configures the paradoxical suspension of both in a palimpsestic time and space of national, linguistic, and thematic tension, a motif whose recurrence and structural importance must already be evident. Sagesse describes the secret pastime of her adolescence; in the library of her home on the French Riviera, she watches old American cop shows and westerns "dubbed clumsily" for French television: "Ordinarily I spent such times lipreading, trying to pick out the American dialogue beneath the sonorous French voices, gloating that it was my secret language .... Discovering a sentence was a triumph, proof that someday I would escape my sultry palm treed prison for a real life, with my American self . . . in English" (39).

In *The Last Life*, the traditional nineteenth-century bildungsroman merges with what Ella Shohat and Robert Stam qualify as "national allegory" in the sense of "texts which metaphorize the public sphere even when narrating apparently private stories."[9] Framed by the first-person narrator's present-day life in New York, Messud's novel is divided into ten parts throughout which Sagesse LaBasse, now in her early twenties, recounts her life at fourteen and fifteen in the South of France, from the summer of 1989 to the fall of 1991. Born in France of an American mother and a *pied-noir* father, whose family was forced to leave Algeria at the time of independence, Sagesse is bilingual and multicultural from birth. In keeping with this heritage and with the transitional nature of adolescence itself, a period when time seems at once to come to a near standstill and yet, paradoxically, to be constantly interrupted by sudden and dramatic changes of direction, the narrator's chronological account of daily life in the world of the exclusive Bellevue Hotel, owned by her family, is punctuated by a series of earlier revelations that center on colonialist Algeria. What Sagesse discovers about her own past leads simultaneously to the recovery of French national history. Three events, in particular, each in its own way inexplicable and irrevocable, haunt Sagesse and drive her quest for narrative understanding: the birth of Etienne, her severely disabled younger brother; the shooting by her grandfather Jacques at a group of Sagesse's friends; and the suicide of her father Alexandre. The figurative expulsion from paradise, which recurs in each of these events as well as in their Algerian backdrop, is further sustained by Sagesse's ongoing dialogue with Saint Augustine and Albert Camus.

In deciding to speak first of the night of her grandfather's crime—"the beginning as I take it"—Sagesse highlights less the significance of a particular event than the nature of the storytelling process itself: "In this way every story is made up, its shape imposed" (4). Appropriately, in a novel in which the "burden of Original Sin" already weighs down the opening passage of the text, the "genesis" of the narrative plays an especially important role, both literally and metaphorically: "the beginning was not really then, any more than was the day of my brother's birth, or, indeed, of mine" (4). Sagesse's awareness that every story is analogous to a journey, its itinerary dependent in the first place on its point of departure, immediately marks *The Last Life* as a postmodern novel, not simply because it foregrounds the story of its own construction in and through language, but because it also unfolds formally, as well as thematically, in "the new world of mobility," which James Clifford equates with "postmodernity" itself.[10] Coming of age for Sagesse involves above all else a coming to narration, en-gendered in keeping with the LaBasse family tradition in which women mythologize the lives of men: "What is a hero if not a man about whom stories are told" (180). Initially, her grandmother Monique and her mother Carol are rivals for control of the narrative process so that Sagesse must seek understanding of the mystery of her grandfather's and her father's motives and actions in the space opened up in between different versions of the same tale: "It was my grandmother who told the stories, who wove a narrative out of the lives of the LaBasses.... And it was my mother who had more often than not unravelled those stories at her leisure, and put them together again, with a different, darker meaning" (179).

Messud thus identifies her narrator, whose role in relation to her female ancestors also makes Sagesse the representative of the reader within the text, with the origins of narrative itself. Louis Mink, for example, locates the uniqueness of narrative in its ability to mediate among events, to describe their intersections and interrelationships; similarly, Hayden White links narrative to the movement "back and forth," the "running to and fro," inscribed in the etymological roots of discourse.[11] Sagesse's subsequent transformation from representative reader into metaphoric writer is no less symbolic. In keeping with her name, at once accurate and ironic, narration, derived from the Latin word for knowledge, constitutes what Mink calls a "primary cognitive instrument," which functions to make human experience comprehensible.[12] In the context of *The Last Life*, it is not unreasonable to think of Sagesse in this role as a contemporary reflection of the original Eve, for whom knowledge of good and evil will result once again in expulsion from paradise into a life of wandering throughout the world. Indeed, Messud's many references to St. Augustine's doctrine of original sin are appropriately announced "in the beginning," in an epigraph whose explicit but abstract naming of the narrator also prepares us for the allegorical nature of the novel to come: "He who puts on *wisdom*, puts on grief; and a heart that understands cuts like rust in the bones" (my emphasis).[13]

Although Ella Shohat's and Robert Stam's suggestion that beliefs about nations "often crystallize in the form of stories" is based on the study of film,[14] *The Last Life* confirms that their thesis can apply to the postcolonial novel as well. The coincidence between Sagesse's own birth, another possible narrative point of departure, and the fall of Saigon establishes the private story of her family as a metaphor of nation(s) literally from the beginning. Since allegory and metaphor, like translation, also function as forms of displacement, rhetorical and thematic mediation between one place and another operate interdependently to support the metafictional and the sociohistorical dimensions of Messud's postmodern fiction of storytelling.[15] In the case of Vietnam, Carol identifies her own confusion with that of her country, an America "in pain and internally divided as she, in exile, was herself," while Alexandre substitutes his own history, both private and public, for America's tragedy and grieves anew for the loss of his beloved Algeria and the end of French colonialism (9–10). Edmund White's assertion in *The Married Man* that "a love affair between foreigners is always as much about the mutual seduction of two cultures as a meeting between two people"[16] informs the scenario that Sagesse imagines for the "eager young American" and the "gallant young Frenchman" who become her parents, in yet another potential path to the family story: "For that matter, I could have begun with my parents, with their meeting" (9).

But if *The Last Life* initially, albeit superficially, respects the conventions of the classical tale of the American in Paris, the novel's exploration of "nationalist narrative"[17] quickly proves to be both much more complex and much more modern than its many literary and cinematic predecessors. In this self-referential "fiction" of love at first sight (204), Alexandre's appeal to Carol depends not only on "the quintessential Frenchness" of his own appearance but also on his immediate confirmation of its successful replication in hers: " 'I thought you must be French,' was the first full sentence my father uttered to my mother, a compliment, as she took it, after months of attempting that very deception" (202). Ultimately, however, what Carol's marriage to Alexandre subsequently transforms into a lifelong attempt "to impersonate a Frenchwoman" (8) is doomed to failure. The fault lies not only in the quality of the performance and the choice of an audience, issues to which I will return, but in the nature of the role as well, for the "French self," which Carol constructs through careful mimicry of her mother-in-law, turns out not to be French at all but rather a reflection of "the antiquated trivia of an Algerian life," itself still extant "only as a result of virtuosic mimicry all round" (210). The error Carol makes in relation to Alexandre is essentially identical, although the failure to ask " 'Who is he?,' thinking simply, and wrongly, that he was France incarnate, a sort of male Marianne" will in this case cover up a destructive psychological split, as well as a cultural division, within the self (203).

"Stories are made up, after all, as much of what is left out," observes Sagesse, in a statement that functions as a refrain (see, for example, 10 and 180). In the case of the LaBasse dynasty, what has been omitted from the family legend is its Algerian past—not, of course, as historical fact but certainly as meaning and source of identity. If Carol's "Frenchness" is impersonated, that of Alex and his parents is imposed; in both cases, national identity is artificial and inauthentic. In fact, all of the principal characters in *The Last Life* are essentially migrants, emblematic figures of the intermingling of "home and the loss of home" that Aamir Mufti and Shohat describe as the "recurring motif of modernity" in their introduction to *Dangerous Liaisons*, a collection of essays on nation and postcolonialism.[18] The status of the *pied-noir*, the French native whose Algerian birth takes place in a paradoxical space at once both in and outside of France, offers an especially powerful metaphor for a tension also evident in Joanne Harris's novels. Emily Apter, in a recent study that traces the erosion of French national identity in contemporary Europe back to its colonialist origins, uses appropriately geographical language to characterize the expression "French Algeria" as a contradiction in terms: "How can a culture be true to its roots if it has deserted the ancestral domain to set up house in a land of strangers? What does *francité* signify when it is *déracinée*, that is, transplanted to another cultural context?"[19]

Certainly, Sagesse's search for the missing ancestors of her own family history consistently leads to the rediscovery of a series of displaced persons. Long erased from her grandmother's stories of Jacques, his eldest sister Estelle turns out to be a runaway, whose flight at sixteen leads to an increasingly rootless life (54–68). First "lost" in France—ironically, the "original" family homeland where she might instead be "found"—she will finally "disappear" into America. Indeed, in the version (re)told by Sagesse's mother, not even the cemetery in Tangier where Estelle is buried marks a stopping point; Carol imagines her "dug up and thrown in the sea to make room for someone else" (168). If Estelle sees herself as Jacques's "twin"—and her brother will indeed be among the earliest French *colons* to make plans to leave Algeria—Sagesse's own counterpart is her great-great-great-aunt Christine, literally a "*sage-femme*" (midwife), like the distant descendant who might have been named for her. Born the year Algeria is first colonized by the French, Tata Christine is the original emigrant, and yet her story is not the expected one of settlement but rather one of constant movement, first in between metropolitan France and its colony and then within the latter (88–91). After the death of her husband, Christine begins "her travels" back to "the place whence she had set out" only to "set off back, back again" less than two years later. In Algeria, too, her life is one of repeated "disappearances" into the hills in the wake of nomadic tribes, "travels" she does not discuss with her French neighbors. Sagesse remembers the relative she casts as a fellow "solo traveler," in contrast to the "glamorous adventuress" Estelle, as she sets out alone for America after her grandfather's crime, a first trip that is already envisioned as an "escape" (82) and one that will be initially temporary, often repeated, and never entirely over.

In the only story that Jacques narrates directly—shortly, and ironically, just after his own release from prison—he tells Sagesse about Serge LaBasse, a cousin who has been excised from the family history as an unseemly "remnant" of its humble origins (266–72). In 1955, when Jacques is already deputy manager of a glamorous hotel in Algiers, Serge has the bad taste to remain a "peasant," a "farmer," that is, in short, a *colonist*, whose property is destroyed in the first Arab uprisings, because, as one of his own former workers tells him, "The buildings may be yours but the land upon which they stand is ours. Since forever" (270). Serge's violent expulsion foreshadows the imminent fate of the *pied-noir* population as a whole, including that of the LaBasse family, but not even a common experience of forced departure can lead to either narrative or national (re)integration. Constructed in significantly geographic and metaphoric language, the official story of the LaBasse family—of which the patriarch himself takes charge—no doubt reflects that of the postcolonial history of the nation; both are conceived as itineraries, willfully incomplete and artificial, shaped to meet the needs of the teller. Parts of those who, like Serge and Estelle, cannot "truly fit" a narrative tailored for private or public glory have simply been discarded: "Little bits of them had been chipped, like grindings, from the larger stones of their selves, and pressed into the mosaic of my grandparents' path: it was a way simultaneously to remember and to forget those who fell by the wayside, who were lost on the road to the Bellevue and success" (272). ("Stories are made up, after all, as much of what is left out.")

Like his father and his daughter, Alexandre also has a counterpart, a "blood brother" (305), among those members of the family who have "gone missing."[20] In this case, however, Sagesse's "almost uncle," a "shadow-man" without a name, whose disappearance from the LaBasse home predates his birth, returns to haunt the text of *The Last Life* from beginning to end (see, especially, 234–39 and 298–304). The man whom Sagesse arbitrarily decides to call Hamed is the definitive figure of the in-between—the illegitimate (in every sense of the word), mixed-race child of Jacques and an Arab servant—who can never be anything but an eternal stranger, an outcast in Algeria and an outsider in France. Still, as Sagesse insists, "his story . . . limned ours" (298) and especially that of the half brother who will never even know of his existence. Alexandre, who at seventeen refuses to leave Algeria when his parents do and stays until the last possible moment with his dying grandmother, is finally forced to abandon the homeland that could never be a home and is no longer even France. Unlike his fellow *pieds-noirs*, obliged to choose "the suitcase or the coffin" (318), Alex is permanently imprisoned in the space in between the two. Indeed, the luggage with which he attempts to board one of the last departing ships consists only of his grandmother's coffin, which cannot be made to "fit" into the only territory remaining to France; her subsequent burial in the Bay of Algiers no doubt metaphorically reflects both the fear and the desire of the colonialists themselves as well as the fate of their beloved country, forever "lost to them, like Atlantis" (145).[21]

One of the distinctive characteristics of *The Last Life* within the category of travel literature, whether ethnographic or fictional, is Messud's substitution of departures for arrivals as the privileged scenes of the genre, with a corresponding shift from the excitement and joy of discovery to the pain and tragedy of loss. In the LaBasse family, "departure and death become forever mixed up" with the flight of Estelle (61), and Alexandre first tries to kill himself soon after leaving the land of his birth. Every bit as "*dépaysé*" (disoriented, not at home) in France as Hamed would have been and just as much of a "pariah," tormented by his classmates as "a freak, a racist, an African" (217), Alex's failure to die permanently erodes his emotional stability and his sense of self. Although a quarter century will pass between his first and his final suicide attempt, Alex's death is overdetermined; outside of Algeria, he literally cannot breathe, as marked by his recurrent asthma attacks (216). Within a narrative whose present-day story otherwise unfolds chronologically, the death of Sagesse's father is the only event that is at once displaced and repeated. After the suicide is announced at the end of part 6 of the novel, the next two sections of *The Last Life* are structured as a flashback to the last year of his life. The burden of our knowledge of the death to come is further reinforced by an effect of slow motion. A period that begins as Sagesse grows increasingly "sluggish . . . incapable of locomotion" (227) ends with days that "slog" to create "a time so slow . . . so very near to stopping altogether" (277) that it is as if our unbearable wait will never end and yet the inevitable death never stop occurring.

One might say that the very structure of the novel momentarily traps Messud's readers, like Alexandre on his last night in Algiers, "in the moment between the past and the rest of their lives" (218). Such an analogy is highly appropriate embedded in a postmodern fiction in which the conscious construction of the novel consistently serves to reflect and to support its referential and allegorical meaning. Not only narrative but the raw materials out of which stories are created—words, sentences, even grammatical principles—play an unexpectedly visible role in this process. In particular, Messud privileges syntax and tense. Even more than a man without a home, Sagesse's father is a man without a future, doubly imprisoned in a past that is itself unreal. Alexandre is the victim—or villain—of a life that does not exist outside of the stories told about him by his mother and his wife: "Stories, the fragments shored up against his ruin, were merely that: fragments, words. And all the telling . . . did not point, for him, to a future" (297–98). More importantly, he is forever locked in the pluperfect tense of the unspoken condition that would have let him stay in Algeria—the multiple possible variations that must exist of the generic formula "if things had been otherwise"—so that "any future he might have wanted glimmered in that unreachable place, the might-have-been" (291). The Algeria passed on to Sagesse is equally conditional, although what was once contrary to fact has become merely impossible. Even if she could travel to Algiers and look beyond the changes of forty years, she would not find her family's home: "It is that I would seek an imaginary city, a paradise conjured of words and partial recollections, a place that never, on the map, existed" (298).

E. Ann Kaplan notes that the home to which one can never return becomes "purely imaginary" and, in the imagination, "a fixed place."[22] In the case of *The Last Life*, this image is literally realized in the form of a painting, which functions as an objective correlative for Sagesse's view of the world.[23] Appropriately mobile, in keeping with both the reality and the fiction it represents, the watercolor of the Bay of Algiers moves first with Alexandre from Algeria to France and then from France to America with Sagesse. Shortly before her father's suicide, Sagesse recalls her childhood conviction that if you look long and hard enough at a picture, you can enter its frame and live inside its "story":

> At fifteen, I know which picture I would have chosen: it would have been the watercolor of the Bay of Algiers, that sun-filled, gleaming wonder, painted at a time when everything still seemed possible, when the city might just have become— the impossible future of that pluperfect past—in time, Augustine's City of God or Camus's City of Man. I would have willed myself into that picture, and made that world different with the knowledge I brought—of the loss and hate to be averted. I would have altered the course of history. I would have willed Camus's dream of a paradise on earth, of a Mediterranean culture democratic and polyphonous . . .
> But at fifteen, I was no longer a child, and I knew it to be impossible. (273–74)[24]

Long before Alexandre's failed attempt to live in the might-have-been of an Algeria forever French, St. Augustine and Camus, Algeria's most famous progeny and Messud's direct literary ancestors, imagine a similarly ideal but very different society from his. In fact, this vision of a harmonious, multicultural *cosmopolis*, in which Hamed and Alexandre might really have lived as the brothers they were, is far more utopian than her father's, at least—and especially—in the case of Algeria.[25]

"There's no place like home," insists Dorothy, just back from her celebrated trip to Oz, a conclusion that Mufti and Shohat reinterpret at present as desire rather than reality.[26] In the case of *The Last Life*, we might still take Dorothy at her word, indeed, at its very origin, since the ambiguous etymology of *utopia* designates "no place" as well as a perfect place. Certainly, in the contemporary France of Messud's novel, the *pieds-noirs* are repatriated to a country in which the imagined paradise of Algeria quickly comes to resemble a nightmare more than a dream. Anne Donadey, recalling Ernest Renan's conviction that the construction of a national identity requires that certain aspects of the past be forgotten ("Stories are made up, after all, as much of what is left out"), argues that French amnesia about its colonial past has led to the displacement of the Algerian trauma into the present: "The war, rather than being simply relived through memory, is actually being waged again and again on French territory through racially motivated incidents and racist discourses."[27]

One such incident occurs at the very beginning of *The Last Life* and functions as a *mise-en-abyme* for the novel as an allegory of France. Shortly before Sagesse's grandfather puts a violent end to her friends' noisy nighttime swims in the hotel pool, the whole town is distracted by "a local event of sudden national importance" (11). Three young people with ties to the National Front build a bomb to plant in a nightclub frequented by "Arabs," but its premature explosion kills only the would-be terrorists. What matters "in this summer bombing, or, more accurately, in this failure to bomb" is precisely the latter, which identifies the fundamentally self-destructive nature of such a "nationalist cause" (12–13). The reaction of Sagesse's father makes explicit the analogy with the Algerian war, primary source of an Arab presence in contemporary France: "Just like Algiers when he was a boy—it's the first thing he said" (12). The probable cause of the accident also points to the phenomenon of historical displacement; the inept setting of "the timer" and the "frozen watchface" of one of the victims (13) metaphorically condemn racist and xenophobic violence as both "untimely" and retrograde.

The weekly outdoor market, where Sagesse and her mother love to shop, superficially offers a Mediterranean vision of the intermingling of different cultures and classes with its "parade of women" of different racial, ethnic, national, and economic backgrounds (16). In reality, however, the market is a place of hostility, characterized by fundamental incompatibilities and resentments, a space in which Carol is verbally accosted when her ironically successful "emulation of a certain type of Frenchwoman" causes a seller to (mis)take her for a representative of the National Front (17). In the aftermath of the bombing, the degree to which the modern town represents at once a repatriated France of the past and the aftereffects of colonialism becomes evident: "In addition to the regular gamut of French citizenry, there were many, like our family, white refugees from Algeria, some of whom sympathized passionately with the bombers; and many *harkis*, who feared the rekindling of old tensions; and many more recent North African immigrants, suddenly terrorized and enraged" (16).[28]

Sagesse's grandfather, "a nationalist and a Frenchman," is certainly one of those who sympathizes, and although he may not vote for Jean-Marie Le Pen, his colonialist view of Algeria explicitly positions the leader of the Front National as its champion in place of St. Augustine and Camus (21). Jacques does not believe in a multicultural paradise that never existed but in "the earthly city that he had left behind, where people, and races, knew their place" (193). Sagesse comes to understand that her grandfather's curious "Nostalgérie"[29]—his "nostalgic ideal of France, a pure France," paradoxically located in an imaginary space that is neither French nor homogeneous—constitutes a country in which her American mother (if not her *pied-noir* father) would make her every bit as much a "foreigner" as Sami and Lahi, the children of North African immigrants whom she briefly befriends during her grandfather's trial (227).[30] Indeed, Jacques's own definition of "the problems that this nation faces, overrun with immigrants—Arabs, Africans, the English-speakers, all of them—our culture assailed on all sides" makes this connection explicit by grouping the formerly colonized with those who literally no longer "know their place" (23). This fusion of the double threats represented by globalization and immigration, both very real concerns in contemporary France, allows Messud to foreground once again not only the tragically contradictory nature of a national narrative, whose coherence requires denying the very history of the nation, but also its inherent self-destructiveness.[31] Jacques's violence, like that of the local terrorists and of his own son, is directed against himself; he does not shoot at the foreigners he openly condemns but rather at France's own children. His aim, of course, is therefore also entirely accurate.[32]

As a *pied-noir* "by extension" (168) and "the American girl in France" (225), Sagesse occupies from birth the in-between status of both her ancestors and her contemporaries. She is raised in a hotel, the emblematic figure for Clifford of postmodernity's "new world order of mobility."[33] Sagesse, "for whom the hotel was home" (5), traverses the "beautiful but vacant surroundings" of the Bellevue (30) in the company of a constantly changing international clientele. Essentially identical to all the other luxury hotels scattered throughout the world, the Bellevue is equally interchangeable with the house in which Sagesse actually lives. Built for her brother, her parents' villa has "the same marble stillness," "the same capacity for echoes and light," the same ability to convey "absence" (7); alternatively, the house resembles a hospital, yet another contemporary space characterized by passage rather than permanence. In between these places and the airports, the boarding school, or the house of the American aunt that once again equates home and hotel, Sagesse's entire adolescence unfolds in what John Tomlinson calls the new "non-places" of global uniformity and ubiquity that are unique to the cultural landscape of the late twentieth century.[34] Within the specific context of literature, such locations become "unhomely" in the willfully awkward term coined by Homi K. Bhabha to designate "a paradigmatic postcolonial experience": "the sense of the relocation of the home and the world."[35] As one of a growing number of Anglophone novels of an emergent literary globalism, Messud's *The Last Life* and similar texts appear to confirm Bhabha's hypothesis that "transnational histories of migrants" may well replace "the transmission of 'national' traditions" as the major theme of world literature.[36]

"To be unhomed is not to be homeless," insists Bhabha,[37] and indeed Sagesse will find something like the postmodern equivalent of a "home" in America. An expatriate like her mother, Sagesse's experience of national identity is not fundamentally different from Carol's. In the contemporary world, notes Hall, identities can no longer be "occupied" (like former colonies, one might add), but must be actively "produced."[38] Certainly Sagesse's Americanness is freely chosen, but it is nonetheless "a mask" (3), "a simulacrum of real life" (3), a "disguise" (333). If Sagesse succeeds in her determination "to master [her] guise more enchantingly than [her] mother had hers" (337), the differences are not ones of method nor talent nor even of age, although once again the story of adolescence no doubt complements the allegory of nation, but rather of role and of audience. Whereas France is no doubt the Western country in which it is most difficult to pass as native, given the importance of language, appearance, and cultural patrimony,[39] America is surely the easiest. Still, even if the same multicultural background that marks Sagesse's foreignness in France helps identify her as an American in New York, it is nonetheless the playing of the part that makes her indistinguishable from "the Korean saleswoman or the Bangladeshi businessman or the Nigerian student, [from] the Iowan nurse and the Montanan secretary" who surround her (3). Messud hypothesizes that national identity in America is always essentially a performance, a work in progress presented to a public who is more than willing to suspend disbelief. In her short time in America, Sagesse herself has been "most often, French; but also French Canadian, or simply American . . . and upon occasion, Argentinian or Venezuelan, for kicks" (349).

Like Messud herself, I have been careful throughout this chapter to refer whenever possible to the United States as "America," a designation understood to be in quotation marks, whether visibly so or not. One of the merits of Messud's postmodern novel is to make us acutely aware of the constructed nature of national identity and of the imaginary or metaphorical character of nations, widely assumed and extensively explored in historical and cultural studies since the publication of Benedict Anderson's highly influential *Imagined Communities: Reflections on the Origin and Spread of Nationalism*. If Anderson's argument applies to all countries, a metaphorical America has long played a particularly prominent role within the discourse of "imagined communities."[40] The "France incarnate" (203), which Alexandre initially represents for Carol, clearly originates in a highly specific, if stereotypical, set of gestures, codes, and behaviors that she has learned to associate with "Frenchness." In marked contrast, the "salvation" that Carol signifies for Alex is infinitely open-ended and unlimited; in Sagesse's words, "She was, to him, all that America was to me before I went there: a shining idea, without history, without context" (206). The power of this vision and its prevalence among the French can perhaps be most quickly and efficiently demonstrated simply by citing Régis Debray. Best known in recent years for his often virulent anti-Americanism, Debray nonetheless similarly describes "America" as "a metaphor, the repository of the world's dreams, phobias, and fantasies."[41]

Rob Kroes agrees that America has been "turned into a metaphor" in Europe, but where Debray and others, including Alexandre, essentially see a *tabula rasa*, a blank screen on which to project their desires, Kroes posits an America that functions somewhat more concretely to house "a European repertoire of myths and symbols." As the country of "bricolage," however, America also freely disassembles and recombines the materials it has borrowed or inherited from Europe.[42] Messud conceives America in somewhat these same postmodern terms as a space of free expansion and constant mobility into which "France," both as past and as present, will be metaphorically displaced in *The Last Life* in a particularly significant example of literary globalism. Messud alerts her reader to the fact that something is "out of place" even before the novel begins through the juxtaposition of the two epigraphs out of which, as I have already suggested, key elements of the (meta)fiction to come will be generated.

Even the reader who has absolutely no prior knowledge of the novel, who has somehow avoided perusing either the book jacket or the book cover before beginning to read, and who may not therefore automatically connect St. Augustine to Algeria, let alone Camus, even that reader will find the epigraph that follows Augustine's immediately jarring. What initially surprises is less the quotation itself than the source to which it is attributed. *"Is Life Worth Living?"* is a question so strongly associated with Camus and so integral to the existentialist philosophy it essentially summarizes that one first assumes, if only for a second, that its attribution to William Hurrell Mallock must somehow be an error, however improbable. And so one turns back, and not for the last time in this "traveling novel," to reread the epigraph: "It is only for the sake of the dreams that visit it that the world of reality has any certain value for us. Will not the dreams continue, when the reality has passed away?"

For Alexandre, certainly, the dream of Algeria remains long after the reality has disappeared; indeed, it is the unbearable discrepancy between dream and reality that will ultimately lead him to answer "no" to what Camus considered the only question worth asking. Sagesse's own dream—that she might somehow have been able to save her father—would require the impossible realization of her childhood fantasy: "Would I not have had, rather, to enter the watercolor of the Bay of Algiers, to try to change the course of history from long before his birth . . . And even then?" (291). Sagesse cannot, of course, will herself into the picture or the past, but what she can do is travel to the country her father saw as "a shining idea" and "his salvation" (206). Inevitably, America loses its quotation marks and ceases to be "a shining thing in the mind, the imaginary place of [her] future, the way Algeria was the imaginary place of [her] past" from the moment Sagesse steps off the plane (92). But if the reality of America assaults her on her first visit, her father's subsequent suicide reveals not only "the enormous gulf between the imaginary and the real" but also the fundamental impossibility of living in the former (297). Moreover, in the case of America, the gap between reality and image turns out to be less wide than Sagesse initially assumes. The very dream she loses in coming to America turns out to be renewable, which is no doubt an essential part of the dream to begin with, so that ten years later Sagesse lives "like any immigrant," indeed, almost literally so, since she constantly invents and reinvents herself to appear, as she chooses, American or French or, most significantly, "a plausible mid-Atlantic hybrid" (128).

What Sagesse loves most about America even that first summer is the fact that it is "all future" (111). Indeed, Messud not only explicitly portrays America as the *real* place of Sagesse's *future* but she implicitly imagines it as the *real* place of her *past* as well, the only space in which the "might-have-been" is the "still-could-be." The dream of a democratic, cosmopolitan, and multicultural America is surely optimistic; dreamed, however, in relation to a country that stereotypes itself as a nation of immigrants, it is perhaps no longer utopian. If Sagesse is unable fully to meet what she is told is the single requirement for being American—to believe that America is "the best place"—she nonetheless believes "that it is real" (332). This revision of the double etymology of "utopia"—not (yet) a perfect place, it can (begin to) exist—has a counterpart in America's ability to represent "a home of a kind" (348), no doubt the only kind suitable to a postmodern world of "the unhomely," of "travel culture" and "rootless histories," of "roots and routes," of "home and the loss of home."[43] If the simultaneous loss of both home and utopia, as in the case of Sagesse's father, leads to unbearable nostalgia, then she concludes that "the opposite of nostalgia," whatever that might be, "is the answer to the question of whether life is worth living" (246). The response implied by *The Last Life* lies once again in Sagesse's relocation to America, a place of paradox and mediation in which those who are permanently homeless can feel most "at home." Ted Morgan, a former Frenchman whose memoir, *On Becoming American*, intersects in a number of ways with the experience and insight that Messud attributes to her fictional narrator, explicitly argues that attachment to home, on the one hand, and rootlessness, on the other, are the inseparable and complementary characteristics of a permanently unsettled nation of displaced persons (253).[44]

Home is also, affirms Morgan on the basis of research done at the New York Public Library, the most important word in the English language.[45] The same statement might well be made about *The Last Life*; if *home* is not the single most important word in Messud's novel, it is certainly among those that recur most frequently and whose multiple emotional and metaphoric meanings resound most widely throughout the text. It is also a specifically American word with no exact equivalent in French, a fact that inevitably plays a key role in structuring the relationship between the original version of the novel and its French translation. Every time that *The Last Life* reads "home," *La Vie Après* must substitute either *"la maison," "le pays,"* or the appropriate version of *"chez moi."* In comparison, if not in isolation, the French translation at times clearly loses connotative and rhetorical force, as when, for example, "the scent of home" which explicitly emanates from the smell of Etienne's helpless body, becomes simply *"l'odeur de la maison"* (160, 240) or when the insistent "our house, the home" is reduced to *"notre maison, celle"* (7, 19). The most significant loss, however, is that of the range of meanings contained in a single word; this textual equivalent of both the diversity in unity and the mobile network of intersections and interrelationships characteristic of the postmodern world of globalization helps to recreate that universe within the space of Messud's novel.

In this context, Messud's writing also exhibits a characteristic and distinctive syntax that works similarly. The following example occurs at the beginning of a paragraph toward the end of the novel:

> Which is to say that when my father killed himself, the act was not in some absolute way, a surprise; but that its timing—in a valley of apparent quiet, so long after the era of tribulation had settled, and my little life had begun to sprout, seemingly, its own patterns, for the first time not wholly dependent, in submission or reaction, on the patterns of my family—was. (290)

The combination of syntactical strategies—a sentence beginning *in medias res*, which might therefore start elsewhere or again; a main clause whose ending is delayed by an expansion of meaning to create a sense of suspension in time and space; a self-reflective insistence on patterns; a network of conjunctions and prepositional phrases that create complex (inter)relationships— results in what one might call a "traveling" sentence and yet one that also configures the ambivalent space of what Messud understands by "home."

From his own new home in the United States, Ted Morgan begins the story of his journey by describing the compatriots he has freely chosen as "the true existentialists."[46] Camus, displaced from the entry to *The Last Life* to be replaced by the American Mallock, also metaphorically travels from France to reappear in the American space of Messud's text; indeed, in this "traveling novel," the postmodern ability to leave is closely associated with existentialist freedom. The "structural homology" between the United States and France, which Jean-Philippe Mathy has most recently reiterated in *French Resistance: The French-American Culture Wars*,[47] includes the historical importance of the two nations as popular destinations for both immigrants and tourists. On the other hand, comparatively few of the French themselves ever vacation outside the borders of France, let alone choose to emigrate. Initially, Sagesse cannot even imagine leaving the Mediterranean coast for the summer—"who would leave . . . the place where the entire nation sought to come on holiday?" (34)—let alone the country itself and forever.[48] She is, moreover, eager to return to France after her first trip to America. Although her experience is already described in terms strongly reminiscent of the basic tenets of French existentialism, Sagesse's initial experience exposes her only to its philosophical hazards: the burden of freedom and the temptation to abandon the responsibilities it entails. She discovers that her American relatives see in her a series of different girls, all of their own invention, and if she initially welcomes the literal "self-abandonment" that such false freedom entails, she will shortly recognize its limits: "I had thought to have found in my shape-shifting American self, a power unexplored; but my form was, alas, dependent upon other people's vision" (98, 127).

Sagesse's first departure from France, thrust upon her rather than freely chosen, is analogous to her father's imposed exile from Algeria. Alexandre's desire to die and his inability to project himself into the future make him the very antithesis of Camus's existentialist heroes, and his metaphoric suicide appropriately takes place in the space of narrative. As we have already seen, he allows himself to be defined and his life to be reified in the stories constructed by others. In marked contrast to her father, although similarly expressed, once Sagesse recognizes in herself "a person who could choose" (308)—an insight she will later come to understand as "an American realization" (170)[49]—she becomes the narrator of her own life and of Messud's newly transnational existentialist novel: "the beads of the story mine to fashion, the ellipses mine to select" (287).

Since this process originally involves the omission not only of her past history but of the three male members of her immediate family, Sagesse might seem to be reconstructing the story of the LaBasse family, in imitation of her ancestors, on the model of the mosaic—a decorative, carefully contained, permanently secured, varicolored surface of identical geometric forms. In fact, *The Last Life* is patterned after the jigsaw puzzle; stationary, the puzzle can certainly resemble a mosaic, but its pieces are actually of irregular shape, variable in size, and individually multicolored. Most importantly, the puzzle, as conceived by Messud, is mutable, potentially in motion, and therefore always somewhere in between a multitude of different possible images, not unlike the watercolor of the Bay of Algiers and very much like the multicultural and migratory world of postmodernity in which neither individuals, nations, nor narratives can be contained within preestablished and conventionally fixed boundaries of color and kind. Initially, the puzzle image is connected to the creation and recreation of the self, as Sagesse, newly arrived in America, ponders different configurations of identity: "My self seemed like a fistful of puzzle pieces thrown in the air; I was free to rearrange them into any design I chose, adding in new bits, leaving old ones out, and if I didn't like the result, I could simply re-jig it" (104). Later, the analogy to fiction is explicit: "I fabricate, aware as I do of my life's puzzle pieces drifting, mutable in language if not in fact" (349).[50]

"Stories are made up, after all, as much of what is left out." In marked contrast to the narrative form I have just described, it must seem as if my own essay has taken on the shape of the official version of the LaBasse family; I too appear to have erased one of its most important members from these pages. Although there would be nothing unusual about the omission of the problematic existence of Etienne, conspicuous by his absence from reviews of *The Last Life*, in fact he is arguably as omnipresent in my own text as he is in Messud's. The last of the possible beginnings to Sagesse's story, Etienne's birth deprives him forever of an identity of his own to leave him Metaphor Incarnate. His momentary entrapment in the birth canal permanently suspends him in that terrifying instant between the past and the rest of one's life.[51] He is the emblematic missing person, the reincarnation of Hamed, the "shadow-man" who disappears from the family history before he is ever born. Named "Etienne Parfait" when the very thought of perfection was not yet hopelessly utopian, he embodies the "might-have-been" of French Algeria and the *tabula rasa* of a mythic America: "he was *plus-que-parfait*, more than perfect, pluperfect, an irretrievable tense in the language he would never speak" (11).

Etienne—the child who will never come of age and never move away—is both the antithesis of his sister and her invisible but inseparable double. He is the metonymic emblem of his grandfather's and his father's self-destructiveness and of his parents' fundamental incompatibility. The embodiment of the doctrine of original sin and the sign of our expulsion from paradise, he is also the existentialist signifier of humankind's terrible solitude, the incarnation of an absurd universe, and the silent answer to the question of whether life is worth living. Born outside of language, Etienne is "the repository" of all the memories projected and all the stories told by others.[52] Most consistently and significantly, whether in the house built for him at his birth or in the impersonal institution in which he will die, he symbolizes "home" to Sagesse, "in all its lost possibility": "if 'home' had a name, it was his" (161).[53] He is all of this and more, a presence at once essential and superfluous, the puzzle whose pieces can never quite fit together to configure a fully coherent image. "Stories are made up, after all, as much of what is left out."

6
Modernism and Mystery: The Curious Case of the Lost Generation

If you are lucky enough to have lived in Paris as a young man, then wherever you go for the rest of your life, it stays with you, for Paris is a moveable feast.

"It's great, hey? It's a feast, Paris."
"Yes, I said, but it's a sort of moveable feast, isn't it? It leaves you with memories so powerful that you can never really forget them. They stay with you forever."

THE JUXTAPOSITION OF THE TWO PASSAGES ABOVE ENCAPSULATES THE mobility and the potentiality, the "moveability" of the "feast," referenced by a certain literary image of France. Ernest Hemingway's celebrated description of Paris has traveled from the title page of *A Moveable Feast* to settle temporarily into the dialogue of a contemporary detective novel, Walter Satterthwait's *Masquerade*.[1] In the course of the trip, moreover, "Ernest Hemingway" himself has been transformed into a fictional character, whose own words serve merely to prompt the once "original" text now attributed to the novel's female hero. Yet, what initially stands out as a dramatic change of location, both spatial and temporal, will in retrospect prove to be the logical destination of a voyage whose itinerary is arguably not only predictable but even overdetermined. Already, of course, Hemingway's seminal story of Paris in the 1920s was written years later in America and raised immediate and ongoing questions about its accuracy as memoir. Indeed, by the writer's own prefatory admission, *A Moveable Feast* is uneasily contained within traditional literary boundaries: "If the reader prefers, this book may be regarded as fiction. But there is always the chance that such a book of fiction may throw some light on what has been written as fact."[2]

That detective novels and mysteries should constitute one distinctive subcategory of contemporary Anglophone fiction set in France is in no way surprising; even Peter Mayle, whose best-selling nonfictional books about Provence can be assumed to have significantly helped to create an audience for contemporary English-language texts set in France, has since turned his attention to fiction in the form of lighthearted romantic mysteries. The plotlines and characters of what Carolyn Dever and Margaret Cohen qualify as the most popular genre of the twentieth century frequently appear in mainstream fiction about France in the form of textual conventions and models or intertextual references and allusions.[3] Moreover, within postmodern theory, the mystery novel and/or the detective story have come to serve as representative of an international and a hybrid art form, one that transcends both geographic and generic boundaries.[4] Pierre Verdaguer introduces the work of Estelle Monbrun, a French writer who also writes Franco-American detective novels, by stressing the thematic and stylistic flexibility of the form: "Il permet tous les amalgames et peut à l'occasion favoriser la juxtaposition de registres culturels dont on signale d'ordinaire l'incompatibilité" (It allows every kind of mixture and can sometimes support the juxtaposition of cultural registers usually deemed incompatible).[5]

Within the "amalgam" of recent American detective novels about France, which include Cara Black's intriguing new series of murder mysteries set in 1993–94 in different *quartiers* of Paris and Sarah Smith's polished trilogy of historical mysteries set in America and France in the first decade of the twentieth century, I want to focus on another group of three texts whose similarities cannot be attributed to the particular vision of a single author.[6] Written in the 1990s and set in consecutive years of the early 1920s, Satterthwait's *Masquerade* (1998), Howard Engel's *Murder in Montparnasse* (1999), and Tony Hays's *Murder in the Latin Quarter* (1993) all feature a cosmopolitan Paris in which an international community of writers and artists frequents the famous literary salons, bookstores, and cafés of the period, where fictional characters interact with fictionalized versions of Hemingway, James Joyce, Gertrude Stein, and numerous other legendary figures of the era.[7] The pattern established by these three mysteries confirms Verdaguer's conviction that the formal flexibility of the genre encourages the combination of elements conventionally deemed incompatible.

Literary scholars generally concur that the second and third decades of the twentieth century mark both the golden age of the detective novel and the prime of modernism.[8] What might seem easily dismissable as a fortuitous accident of cultural history is transformed into an intriguing paradox by a second and related critical conviction, "difficult to prove" but "taken for granted," in the words of Michael Holquist.[9] Scholars also assume that the two categories of literature appeal primarily to intellectuals, so that in the 1920s and 1930s an identical group of readers simultaneously consumes the products both of modernism and of mystery. Thus the detective novel serves as a kind of antidote to the apparent risk of being poisoned by early modernist fiction; according to Marjorie Nicolson, whose 1929 essay "The Professor and the Detective" is virtually contemporaneous with the literary texts of which it speaks, the detective novel constitutes a "literature of escape" that offers, contrary to our expectations, "escape not from life, but from literature."[10] Such crimes as subjectivity, purposelessness, pessimism, emotionalism, and formlessness, which Nicolson attributes to avant-garde fiction epitomized by James Joyce's *Ulysses*, are avenged by the causal structure, intellectual engagement, purposeful plot and character, and rational order characteristic of the classic detective novel. In an even more radical challenge to conventional genre assumptions than that of Nicolson, Holquist similarly displaces "the world [as] a threatening, unfamiliar place" from its usual location within the detective novel to reposition it within modernist fiction:

> It was during the same period when the upper reaches of literature were dramatizing the limits of reason . . . that the lower reaches of literature were dramatizing the power of reason in such figures as Inspector Poirot . . . . Is it not natural to assume, then, that during this period when rationalism is experiencing some of its most damaging attacks, that intellectuals, who experienced these attacks first and most deeply, would turn for relief and easy reassurance to the detective story, the primary genre of popular literature which they, during the same period, were, in fact, consuming? The same people who spent their days with Joyce were reading Agatha Christie at night.[11]

To read Joyce in the United States in the 1920s was in essence a criminal act, as Tony Hays reminds us. In *Murder in the Latin Quarter*, the projected publication of *Ulysses* in Paris informs a murder investigation in which Joyce himself is the primary suspect until "Hem" and his good friend "Jack Barnett" set about solving the crime. In *Murder in Montparnasse*, Engel's narrator frequents Michaud's until he finally succeeds in spotting Joyce, just as his peaceful family dinner is suddenly interrupted by the arrival of an unruly "redheaded Bohemian" who calls the reigning literary genius of Paris "Jimmy" and whom Mike finally identifies as Ezra Pound (74–76). Although Joyce fails to make an appearance in *Masquerade*, a copy of *Ulysses* is prominently displayed in the apartment of the British writer Sybil Norton, who insists on lending Satterthwait's narrator a copy of her first novel, *The Mysterious Affair at Pyles*, featuring a "clever little French detective who runs around and solves crimes" (42). If it remains true today that academics are equally familiar with modernist novels and detective fiction, then the readers of this chapter will have understood that in the 1990s even Agatha Christie herself is metaphorically "spending her days with Joyce." Modernism has been (re)written into the detective novel so that both can now be read not merely successively or even concurrently but literally at one and the same time.

Once again, however, in keeping with the pattern posited in the opening paragraph of this essay, evident change turns out in a postmodern era to be both less unexpected and less innovative than it initially appears. In an historical overview of the critical study of detective narrative, Heta Pyrhönen argues that the contemporary challenge to modernism's rigid demarcations, both aesthetic and generic, has retrospectively revealed "remarkable similarities" between once dichotomous popular fiction and serious literature :

> Whereas earlier the detective genre was felt to be totally opposed to the literature of high modernism, it is now often aligned with its former opposite: it is said to exhibit many links with the discourse of modernity and have a place *within* its canon as texts that, structurally and thematically, negotiate the same or similar notions, ideas, tendencies, prejudices, and preferences as the literature of modernism.[12]

Thus, far from viewing Joyce and Agatha Christie as polar opposites, Nicholas Birns and Margaret Boe Birns reclaim the latter as herself "aesthetically modernist."[13] Moreover, by focusing in particular on "Christie's formalism, on what her critics have called her 'formulaic' qualities," Birns and Birns simultaneously put to rest the question of literary merit.[14] In this interpretation, Christie's experiments with narrative voice, generic codes, and self-reflexivity constitute less an "escape from literature" than a foregrounding of its very nature in a strategy that also provides a convincing explanation for the tendency of the mystery novel to attract a readership among intellectuals.[15]

Similarly, the contemporary detective novels of interest to us here are postmodern without being in any literal sense post-modernist. Holquist argues that the experimental novelists who came after Joyce logically turned for inspiration from myth to detective fiction precisely because the genre came pre-packaged as antimodernist.[16] Unlike writers such as Alain Robbe-Grillet or Paul Auster, however, who incorporate the conventions of the mystery novel into their fiction in order to undermine not only those very conventions but also, and more importantly, the rational world view they support, Satterthwait, Hays, and Engel allow their readers more traditional pleasures, albeit in unexpected combinations. All three of their novels both recreate the world in which modernism flourished and fully satisfy the demands of formulaic fiction: in every case there is a murder, a victim, a motive, a detective, a criminal, an investigation, and a resolution.[17] Postmodern irony does not consist of subverting either literature or reality but rather of situating the very writers who famously challenged traditional literary and cultural norms, who revolted against standard limits of reason and authority, within the most predictable, normative, ordered, and conventional of generic modes.

Moreover, the literary figures in *Masquerade*, *Murder in Montparnasse*, and *Murder in the Latin Quarter* do not simply make cameo appearances as themselves, but neither are they simply cast in conventional roles within the plot of the detective fiction. Rather, multiple identities coexist in a postmodern bricolage that destabilizes distinctions of genre, aesthetic hierarchy, and, sometimes, common sense. In *Masquerade*, for example, Gertrude Stein hosts her usual Saturday salon, but the keen eye with which she has amassed the remarkable collection of cubist paintings on display also ferrets out an important clue to the identity of a killer; and her massive bulk does not prevent her from throwing her well-aimed umbrella at his armed accomplice at an extremely timely moment. Even behind the wheel of Godiva, en route to save the life of one Pinkerton agent and accompanied by another, she does not abandon her characteristic interest in educating her traveling companion about "her place in English literature. Basically, there was William Shakespeare, and then there was Miss Stein. She explained to [him] why this was so" (308). In *Murder in the Latin Quarter*, Ernest Hemingway puts his standard boasting about his prowess as a boxer to the test when he knocks out an attacker with a single blow; and James Joyce's bad eyesight provides him with an essential alibi in a murder investigation. In *Murder in Montparnasse*, the early manuscripts presumed to have been lost by Hemingway's first wife resurface to become a motive for blackmail and murder as well as for divorce and remarriage.

In contrast to Monbrun's literary mysteries, in which the writing of Proust or Colette informs the development of character, plot, or theme;

Satterthwait, Hays, and Engel are generally far more interested in authors than in their texts. This no doubt corresponds to a revealing Franco-American cultural difference between a reverence for literature and a cult of celebrity. Interestingly, the early twentieth century saw the rise of the modern biography as well as that of the detective novel, an occurrence that Glenn W. Most sees as more than coincidental, surmising that many readers treat detective stories as "installments in the fragmentary biographies of their heroes."[18] *Masquerade, Murder in the Latin Quarter*, and *Murder in Montparnasse* clearly invite such a reading, although the recurrent "heroes" whose lives are of interest are now the literary celebrities of the 1920s rather than the novels' actual detectives. Holquist is surely right to insist that postmodernist writers no longer turn to myth for inspiration in the sense that Joyce once did in crafting *Ulysses*, but myth nonetheless remains a key component of the modernism of mystery.[19] The major figures of what Stein called a "Lost Generation,"[20] as well as the Left Bank expatriate community in general, had already taken on a mythic quality in their own time and much of that myth was of their own making.

In this context, *The Moveable Feast* stands as paradigmatic; its fluid boundaries between "fact" and "fiction," between reality and myth, demarcate the general shape of our knowledge of Paris in the 1920s. So much has been written both by and about the members of the American expatriate community, over such a long period of time and to such different ends, that what emerges might best be conceived in visual terms as a cubist portrait whose fragmented geometric shapes have been superimposed on the vague forms of an impressionist landscape; it is a decidedly postmodern vision. The recent addition of three mystery novels to this particular corpus takes on special interest. Not only has the analogy between detective and either reader or literary critic, or both, become commonplace within narrative theory,[21] an association of unusual significance in the case of texts that focus on writers and their works, but the genre of detective fiction foregrounds an act of repetition that has become an integral part of both postmodern literature and contemporary cultural globalism. As Porter notes in *The Pursuit of Crime*, the tendency of mystery writers to "endlessly repeat the vocabulary, tropes, and topoi not only of predecessors writing in the genre but also of the culture as a whole" confirms the general principle that "writing is in an important sense a form of recycling of the previously written."[22] Such a conviction indeed underlies much of modern textual theory and criticism, as Porter aptly observes; appropriately, moreover, it also identifies, once again, the modernist practice by which *The Odyssey* became *Ulysses*.

Readers of *Masquerade*, *Murder in the Latin Quarter*, and *Murder in Montparnasse* certainly encounter and recognize examples of intertextuality or exact literary reference, such as those reflected, for example, in the epigraphs to this essay, as they travel through each of these fictions of Paris. By the conclusion of the third, however, readers are likely to suspect that they have been set adrift in a distinctively postmodern whirlpool of free-floating bits of literary and cultural information, which have been recycled from so many previously existing texts and contexts that any conventional notion of origin, authorship, originality, or authenticity is not simply meaningless but entirely irrelevant. Hemingway's own writing, of course, already proposes multiple and inconsistent versions of Paris in the early 1920s. On the one hand, the purportedly fictional characters and events of *The Sun Also Rises* (1926) are closely modeled on the actual experiences of the novelist and his friends in 1925–26. On the other hand, the purportedly real people and places of the same period described in *A Moveable Feast* (1964) result from a combination both of willful fabrication and failure of memory on the part of the memorist.[23] Hemingway's textual practice appears eminently straightforward, however, in comparison to the postmodern methods of Howard Engel, who in 1999 transplants elements of both works to the world of formulaic fiction and popular culture, where Hemingway's adventures in Paris in the fall of 1925 collide with the even more dramatically displaced story of "Jack de Paris," a Parisian version of Jack the Ripper.[24]

More pasticcio than pastiche, *Murder in Montparnasse* nonetheless begins with parody. The novel itself, whose opening quotation from one Jason Waddington's *New Wine* so closely echoes the tone and content of *A Moveable Feast* that I am unlikely to be the only reader who attempts to locate the original passage, is preceded by an editor's note, whose various textual references include, but are in no way limited to, Hemingway's memoir. Adopting the conceit of the eighteenth-century epistolary novel, whose notable examples appropriately include the letters in which Montesquieu's Persian prince records the observations of an earlier version of the naive foreigner in France, "William Duff Gaspard" claims to reproduce "a portion of the memoirs and fictional writings" bequeathed to him by his grandfather, who lived in Paris as a young man in the early 1920s. In "an attempt to turn what was simply reportage into a roman à clef," the author of the manuscript in question refers to some characters by their real names (Stein, Joyce, Picasso), makes up seemingly arbitrary names for others (Hemingway = Waddington), and identifies still others by variants of the names they bear in *The Sun Also Rises* (Lady Biz Leighton = Lady Brett

Ashley). What Gaspard calls a "maddening device," is, of course, also a highly vertiginous one, designed to transgress all known boundaries of literary genre, period, and property. In brief, the detective novelist Howard Engel creates the editor William Duff Gaspard, who presents the fictionalized memoir/autobiographical novel of "Mike Ward," who does indeed appear as a friend of Ernest Hemingway's in the equally difficult to classify *A Moveable Feast*,[25] but who surely does not help him capture a mass murderer nor count Duff Gaspard among his descendants.

Aptly subtitled "A Literary Mystery of Paris," *Murder in Montparnasse* also questions the codes and conventions of the detective novel even as it performs them. Indeed, in keeping with postmodern practice, Engel repeatedly foregrounds the process of deconstruction. In one particularly evident example of *mise-en-abyme*, the narrator meets "Georges Sim . . . from Liège"; unlike the Belgian writer of mysteries, Georges Simenon, to whom Engel makes ironic reference, Sim earns a living "writing pot-boilers" because he is "too easily confused by puzzles" even to attempt the genre practiced by his near namesake. His friend Anson Tyler similarly attributes his own failure to complete a detective novel to "the form": "They're trash, a truant occupation. There's no room for literary interest. In fact, it's almost breaking the rules to put in anything but the puzzle" (150). In that event, Mike, i.e., Engel, who puts "*everything* but the puzzle" into *Murder in Montparnasse*, commits the only real crime in a novel in which "literary interest" so quickly and completely crowds out all else that we are surprised by recurrent, if occasional, references to a highly secondary, if not entirely gratuitous, plot of serial murder and its investigation.[26]

Engel's "literary mystery of Paris" is in fact a novel about Ernest Hemingway or, more accurately, *two* novels about Hemingway, since "Wad" appears in *Murder in Montparnasse* both as Hemingway the writer, who is working on his "Spanish novel," and as Hemingway, a.k.a. Jake Barnes, the narrator-hero of *The Sun Also Rises*, who is drinking his way through the bars and cafés of "the Quarter." Moreover, "Hemingway" not only plays a double role, but he also has a textual double in Mike Ward. As author of the text we are reading, Mike is just as guilty as Wad of "trying to make a book out of what went on in Spain this summer" (26). Nor is Mike dependent on what he learns by his persistent questioning; he is also a regular witness to what Lady Biz Leighton (a.k.a. Lady Brett Ashley a.k.a. Lady Duff Twysden) refers to as "encore[s] of one of our Pamplona evenings" (43).

More importantly, Mike is the ironic counterpart of Hemingway, a young journalist who comes to Paris to satisfy his literary ambitions only to learn that he has arrived "five years too late" (100): "I get the feeling—

and I've had it more than once—that I've missed the best years in the Quarter. Today we have only the left-overs from a brilliant era, wondering where the parade went" (153). Trapped in "a time when one day and one hangover blended into the next" (57), Mike epitomizes the wasted bohemian life of Stein's "lost generation." Worse still, when he does retreat temporarily from the life of "the Quarter" to attempt to write, Mike, even more clearly than Anson Tyler, proves beyond a doubt that he is *not* Hemingway.[27] Far from achieving the latter's goal of writing "one true sentence," let alone "one true sentence after the other" (141), and still further from being able to follow Stein's advice "to see things in the new way" (253), Mike exhibits a truly painful lack of talent. Since the willingness to put bad writing on display is surely relatively rare, even in formulaic fiction and in a playful postmodern context, one is tempted to conclude that Howard Engel, and not Mike Ward, is at fault. Yet the examples are so exaggerated, clash so clearly with the surrounding text, and are so obviously set up to be mocked by their own context that I am convinced that they are as deliberately crafted on Engel's part as they are presumably unconsciously conceived on Mike's.

To wit: Once Mike's admiration for no lesser a work than *Ulysses* reminds him of his desire "to become more than a journalist," he buys notebooks at Joseph Gibert and sets out in search of something to write about. When a seemingly endless hour spent in a café on the boulevard St-Michel fails to bring the expected inspiration, Mike tries another of Hemingway's favorite strategies and goes for a walk. Watching children sail boats in the Luxembourg Gardens, Mike is apparently serious when he considers the possibility that he "could write something about them." Fortunately, if fortuitously, he is saved from a fate somewhat beyond mere banality by an encounter with an angry white poodle named Basket and a similarly uncivil "thin, tiny woman with an olive complexion" and "dark, rather Spanish eyes": "Maybe I could write something about them, too, I thought" (64–66). The desire to write about Alice B. Toklas, even in the absence of her companion, is hardly an original idea either; indeed, even Mike seems to foresee rival texts of the future as he rereads his own: "It was very depressing, a description of my encounter in the Luxembourg with the swarthy lady and her poodle. Had I been successful in describing her fussy, correct manner, her studied insolence at my rebuke of her dog? Maybe it required a greater subtlety than I could manage" (86). Although *Murder in Montparnasse* includes subsequent references to Mike's "stories," notably to Stein's dismissal of them, no further details are provided of either their content or their style nor are we made to suffer through any more examples.

A Moveable Feast and *The Sun Also Rises* also provide an intertextual context for Satterthwait and Hays. The suicidal murder victim in *Masquerade* is once again a figure out of Hemingway's fiction. According to some reports, Dickie, an ambulance driver in World War I, never recovered from the war and was busily drinking his way to oblivion, notably with the Fitzgeralds (38–39), at the time of his death. Other characters, however, attribute Richard's despair to the fact that he, like Engel's Tyler, lacked the one thing that mattered most in Paris in the 1920s: "He had everything he wanted. Except talent.... He wanted desperately to be an artist. He tried poetry, he tried painting. He failed at both" (203–4). Although *Murder in the Latin Quarter* is more convincing as a murder mystery than *Murder in Montparnasse*, Hay's novel also tells the parallel story of what happened to Hemingway's friend Jack Barnett in the war and of how Hemingway came to turn this story into that of Jake Barnes in *The Sun Also Rises*. As one illustration of a common practice, note also the correspondence between the following passages, taken respectively from *A Moveable Feast* and *Murder in the Latin Quarter*. "I sat in a corner with the afternoon light coming in over my shoulder and wrote in the notebook.... The story was about coming back from the war but there was no mention of the war in it" (76); "Hem pulled out a pad and pencil and started scribbling.... It's about the war, but, I don't want to mention the war in it" (141).

In the introduction to *Paris in American Literature*, Jean Méral makes the clearly surprising assertion that Paris as a literary motif is of relatively little importance in American writing; and at the end of what is nevertheless a comprehensive and detailed discussion of the subject, informed by some two hundred works of fiction, he concludes that the theme, in steady decline since 1940, has in all probability been definitively exhausted:

> Paris has become a neutral territory where writers can no longer find very fertile soil. It has become a mere literary cliché. Will the capital ever inspire other major works of American literature? All signs point to the end of its role as a creative catalyst for successive generations of writers. It does not seem to offer a challenge any more, eliciting new and fresh responses from authors and shaping the destinies of their heroes.[28]

By chance, Méral reaches this conclusion at precisely the point in time when the metamorphic powers of "the moveable feast" have already begun to inspire a new generation of writers who will in the ensuing decade significantly increase the total number of twentieth-century American novels set in Paris. In fact, Méral's pronouncement can fairly be deemed ironic rather than merely coincidental, since he arguably fails to anticipate the postmodern future of global popular culture, thereby missing something significant about American literary culture as well. Méral, who is French, bases his study on the assumption that the Paris of American literature has "no mythical value of its own" and can only be read as "the echo of another nation's myth, apprehended through a foreign sensibility."[29] But what he therefore dismisses with scorn in its final incarnation as "mere literary cliché" constitutes the very generative material that will produce "new and fresh responses" within the context of postmodernism, courageously, if no doubt controversially, claimed by Frederic Jameson as "the first specifically North American global style."[30]

In the "neutral territory" of the Paris settings of Satterthwait's, Hays's, and Engel's novels, the reality of the city is indeed openly cliched. In *Masquerade*, for example, which unquestionably provides the most detailed and comprehensive visit of the three, Paris is nonetheless playfully reduced to its most famous signifier, whose apparently identical reproductions circulate throughout France and the novel. The same "charming (if not terribly accomplished) print of the Eiffel Tower," whose sight enchants the exuberant Jane Turner as she looks up from "[her] French bed, in [her] French hotel room, in [her] French town, in [her] French France" on the first night of her very first trip to France (4), similarly orients Phil Beaumont, her considerably more worldly and better traveled Pinkerton colleague: "Except for a print above the bed, a painting of the Eiffel Tower, it could have been a room in any decent hotel in Pittsburgh or Portland or Peoria" (16). By the time Beaumont finally gets to examine the scene of the murder, the reappearance of the image in question, now logically described as "a familiar-looking framed print of the Eiffel Tower" (41), has become thoroughly predictable. *Masquerade*'s use of the Eiffel Tower to signify Paris confirms Porter's contention that the "mythic landscapes" of the detective novel habitually rely on the very same cultural references commonly encountered in tourist brochures.[31] Interestingly, Martine Guyot-Bender recently discovered that the magazine distributed to travelers by United Airlines accompanies its many and no doubt inevitable photographs of the Eiffel Tower with numerous and far less expected references to the idealized Paris of the "Lost Generation," complete with several quotations from Gertrude Stein. Guyot-Bender's assumption that the magazine highlights this period as the "most illustrious for many Americans" and therefore the best known by the airline's target audience corresponds to Méral's conviction that "the Parisian theme in American literature is most richly orchestrated" in the 1920s.[32]

Such evidence of readers' knowledge of and ongoing interest in the American expatriate community of the 1920s, consistent with the success of Shakespeare and Company's 2003 literary festival, helps explain why the "Lost Generation" figures in so many contemporary novels set in France. We must explore another aspect of American literary history, however, to help us understand why so much of that fiction should consist of detective novels. "The Murders in the Rue Morgue," first published in 1841, conferred on Edgar Allan Poe the undisputed title of the inventor of detective fiction as a literary genre.[33] This tale and its two sequels, "The Mystery of Marie Roget" and "The Purloined Letter," are all set in Paris and star a Frenchman, C. Auguste Dupin, whose adventures are narrated by an unnamed American friend. Dupin's ability to resolve the most puzzling of crimes by the methodical application of his superior powers of reason logically provides yet another explanation for the consistent positing of intellectuals as the primary audience of detective fiction. Poe's association with France subsequently becomes so strong that Verdaguer claims that the author of a recent critical study begins by reminding his French audience that "Edgar Poe est un écrivain américain" (Edgar Poe is an American writer).[34] If the humor of the comment already depends to some extent on the possibility that such a clarification might actually prove revelatory for some readers, it becomes pointedly ironic when we remember that Poe not only wasn't French but in fact, like Walt Whitman, never even visited France.

The trope of "mysterious Paris," with whose invention Méral also credits Poe, is thus entirely imaginary—or, rather, already literary—from the time of its inception. Poe travels to Paris, as do other readers of popular fiction in the nineteenth century, by turning the pages of novels by Victor Hugo, Honoré de Balzac, and, after 1942, Eugène Sue.[35] The analogy with the detective fiction of Engels, Hays, and Satterthwait, whose readers reach the same geographical destination through the literature of modernism, is clear. Similarly, Poe's short stories, informed by literature rather than life, can be said to include among their many other innovations early examples of such basic strategies of postmodern mystery as multilayered intertextuality, cross-cultural germination, and the conflation of "original" works and their subsequent "translations," both textual and geographical. One of the most recent manifestations of the importance of Poe's stories to both the history of the detective novel and the establishment of Paris as its privileged location took place in a suitably literary setting. During the late fall and winter of 2000–01, the Bibliothèque des Littératures Policières

(BILIPO), a library in the Latin Quarter that houses a special collection of novels and reference works devoted to detective literature and criminology, organized an exposition on "Les Crimes de Paris, lieux et non-lieux du crime à Paris au XIXe siècle," along whose "parcours littéraire" (literary route) manuscripts and illustrations of Poe's short stories figured prominently.[36] In a pertinent example of interior duplication, Dupin and his friend first meet in "Murders in the Rue Morgue" in an "obscure library"[37] and pass much of their time subsequently in the "little back library or book closet" in which Dupin essentially lives.[38]

If Poe's choice of Paris results in part from the city's preestablished reputation as a site of crime and his particular vision of Paris from his reading habits, the connotations of the city no doubt play a role in the creation of the character of Dupin as well. The capital of the nation forever associated with universal Reason after the French Enlightenment would seem to be the only logical birthplace of Poe's supremely adept promoter and practitioner of ratiocination. In the first half of the nineteenth century, moreover, France is also the home of Romanticism, whose influence largely explains the singular appeal that Poe's poetry and macabre tales held for Charles Baudelaire, among others. Even in his detective fiction, however, Poe creates a hero who is as much a proponent of poetry as he is of abstract logic.[39] This early appearance in detective fiction of the amateur detective as at once artist, aesthete, and problem solver, whose methods are both confined by reason and freed by imagination, brings us back, of course, to the increasingly less curious conjunction of modernism and mystery.

Poe is credited, in particular, with establishing the hard-boiled version of the detective novel, the American counterpart to the British whodunit.[40] Despite the predictable presence of some elements of the latter in *Masquerade*, *Murder in Montparnasse*, and *Murder in the Latin Quarter*, the importance of professional detectives and sensational crimes places all three novels prominently within Poe's lineage; moreover, among a wider range of literary descendants of Poe and the American hard-boiled narrative, the work of Hemingway is among the most frequently cited.[41] The influence of Poe's detective fiction is most directly evident in *Masquerade*, even though the single explicit reference within Satterthwait's novel adverts only to the writer's horror tales (121) and despite the fact that Poe inevitably enters postmodern mystery in impure form, his texts overlaid and revised by those of his many successors.

The crime under investigation in *Masquerade* is a variation on the locked-room mystery, whose earliest ancestor is "The Murders in the Rue Morgue," and the American Phil Beaumont teams up with the French

Henri Ledoq to solve a murder that foregrounds the parallelism between detective and criminal essential to the resolution of the crime in "The Purloined Letter." Still, although Ledoq is both amateur detective and aesthete, independently wealthy, and closely connected to some of the most prominent artistic and political figures of Paris, his portrait ultimately owes less to Poe's Dupin than to Agatha Christie's Hercule Poirot.[42] (Anything else would be surprising in a novel that features, as noted earlier, a barely disguised Christie among its cast of characters.) In contrast, Beaumont, who narrates *Masquerade* in the first person, nonetheless bears no further resemblance either to Dupin's American companion or to such British descendants as Christie's Hastings (*The Mysterious Affair at Styles*) or Conan Doyle's Dr. Watson. Indeed, although Ledoq, disguised as Sherlock Holmes, suggests that Phil might like to accompany him to the masquerade ball in the guise of Watson (263), traditional roles are, if anything, reversed, as Ledoq alternately puzzles and marvels over Beaumont's mind, manners, language, and behavior.[43]

The interplay between Ledoq and Beaumont sets *Masquerade* apart from *Murder in Montparnasse* and *Murder in the Latin Quarter*, whose almost exclusive focus on the American expatriate community in Paris reflects the similar insularity evident in the texts written both by and about modernist writers in the early twentieth century: "one of the most common misconceptions about American literature is to imagine that Paris is a major theme for the writers of the Lost Generation."[44] In Satterthwait's novel, in contrast, cross-cultural comparison becomes a source both of insight and of comedy as Ledoq continually revises his assessment of Beaumont's claim to French ancestry. Porter argues that just such an embodiment of national ideals and cultural stereotypes constitutes part of the ongoing appeal of detective fiction:

> The evidence suggests that the international audience which continues to read detective fiction still enjoys its Englishmen upper class and urbane, its Americans lean and tough, and its Frenchmen skeptical, tolerant, and worldly-wise. Such cultural stereotypes seem to confirm that the world may be known once and for all; in the face of apparent change, Englishness, Americanness, and Frenchness go on forever. The attraction of popular literature resides not least in the authority with which it offers the certainties of myth for the confusions of history.[45]

In the case of *Masquerade*, on the one hand, Henri is dismayed by Phil's notable lack of appreciation for the essential components of Frenchness: *cuisine* (Phil refuses to eat "organ meats" [48] and insists on steak "cooked all by itself. No cream sauce. No wine sauce" [185]; Henri accompanies a car chase with his recipe for *soupe à l'oignon* [148–50] and shares recipes for *coq au vin* with a police inspector at the scene of a double murder [169–70]); *couture* (Phil arrives in Paris with a single small suitcase; Henri needs three large ones to go into hiding for two days); and *culture* (Phil suspects Henri's good friend Gertrude Stein of excessive drinking when she informs him that "Rose is a rose is a rose" [218]). On the other hand, Henri is delighted to have his belief in Americans as "invariably straightforward and open" countered by Phil's penchant for irony and duplicity (see, for example, 8, 24) and relieved to see Phil rapidly abandon "that famous American sense of fair play" when their lives are at risk (133).

In terms of location as well, *Masquerade* has far greater geographical reach than its two companion mysteries whose characters never leave the Left Bank unless they have the telling misfortune to be kidnapped. Satterthwait's two Pinkerton agents take us on a charming whirlwind tour of Paris, which includes visits to all three of the literary versions of the city identified by Méral.[46] In Poe's "mysterious Paris," Phil and Henri are chased by car through the narrow streets around Les Halles and escape on foot through the sewers; in a third version of the same self-reflectively circuitous route, someone shoots at Jane in the catacombs, for Méral "the most striking architectural feature of the mysterious city" and one "admirably suited to the twists and turns of the detective novel."[47] In "Bohemian Paris," Jane is propositioned in the afternoon by the very seductive "Virginia Randall" (a.k.a. Nathalie Barney) in the marble temple of her garden on rue Jacob and in the evening by a very boorish Ernest Hemingway in Gertrude Stein's kitchen on rue de Fleurus. Despite Phil's lament—"It would be a good city to investigate, I decided, if I weren't already investigating a murder" (162)—there are even excursions into "Tourist Paris." Jane shops in Coco Chanel's boutique and Phil races through "Bon Marché" in an attempt to shake pursuers as Henri delivers the history of the department store, complete with appropriate literary references to Zola's *Au bonheur des dames*.

In conclusion, I want to recall once more Rob Kroes's provocative suggestion that representations of contemporary popular culture are victims of an essential contradiction that reverses the original intentions of modern literature:

> What is often held against the emerging international mass, or pop, culture is precisely its international, if not cosmopolitan, character. Clearly this is a case of double standards. At the level of high culture, most clearly in its

modernist phase, there has always been this dream of transcending the local, the provincial, and the national, or in social terms, to transgress the narrow bounds of the bourgeois world and to enter a realm that is nothing if not international: the transcendence lay in being truly "European" or "cosmopolitan."[48]

The conjunction of modernism and mystery in recent American detective novels meets this challenge head-on. By revisiting the 1920s through the framework of the 1990s, by both remembering and reinventing the myth of Paris as "a moveable feast," by recreating the expatriate literary community of the turn of one century for the globally literate readers of the beginning of another, Satterthwait, Hays, and Engel, among many other contemporary American cosmopolitan novelists, confirm the many intersections of modernism with postmodernity and of France with the United States, including, most importantly, a shared commitment to the international and to the experimental: "Miss Stein, it seemed, had been right all along: the two countries that instinctively shared in common a love of the modern and a gift for creating it were America and France."[49]

7
Museum, Maze, Madhouse: Sarah Smith's "Theatre du Monde"

DESPITE THE GLOBAL PROMISE OF THE NAME AND OF THE SITE OF DISTRIbution of United Airline's in-flight magazine *Hémisphères*, Martine Guyot-Bender finds that the insistent representation in the April 1999 issue of the idealized Paris of the Lost Generation reduces France to "a static, museum-like place, fixed in an unspoiled and longed for past."[1] It would not be surprising in that event that American tourists, who disembark into the sharply contrasting reality of a modern multicultural city, might well hasten to reenter the Paris of their imaginations, a location they can no longer expect to find outside of actual museums, whether figurative—the guided tour through "Hemingway's Paris," the obligatory scotch at the Closerie des Lilas—or literal. Moreover, the setting of even this final destination has become increasingly difficult to pinpoint. If one predictable stop on almost every itinerary will be the musée d'Orsay, many travelers will need to venture further afield to the Centre Georges Pompidou and the Musée Picasso as well. As Guyot-Bender notes, the turn-of-the-century nostalgia promoted by United Airlines assumes that "the Cubist period—along with the Impressionist period—is probably the most illustrious for many Americans."[2] But if the works of the artists who once attracted expatriate Americans to Gertrude Stein's weekly salon are now on display throughout Paris, modern French painting originally hung in another museum that most visitors to France are equally likely to include on their itineraries today. For in the absence of Manet's "Olympia" and Picasso's "Demoiselles d'Avignon," the Louvre remains the home of what is perhaps the most famous painting in Paris, if not the world: the Mona Lisa.

In Sarah Smith's *The Knowledge of Water* (1996), the second in a trilogy of historical novels that also includes *The Vanished Child* (1992) and

The Citizen of the Country (2000), the Louvre constitutes a much more eclectic space than it does today in which the Mona Lisa and the modern art collection still occupy adjacent rooms off the Grand Gallery.[3] Although Smith's novel, set in 1910, not only recreates yet another version of Stein's Paris but even one in which the Louvre itself occupies a place of privilege, the fictional universe of *The Knowledge of Water* is anything but a "static, museum-like place" meant to enshrine the world of the past. In contrast to the traditional museum, Malcolm Bradbury borrows André Malraux's notion of the "musée imaginaire" to describe the age of postmodernism, a "period of outstanding eclecticism" whose characteristic multiculturalism and pluralism make "most styles of the past and the present, from whatever sources, simultaneously available and usable."[4] In the late twentieth century, concludes Bradbury, "the arts are, as they were at the century's turn, in international intersection."[5] Smith's work actualizes this metaphor of the "imaginary museum" in a fictional series that simultaneously reconstructs and deconstructs a mobile cosmopolitan community of 1905–11 as representative of the globally diverse universe of postmodernity. In particular, Smith's "museum without walls," to cite Malraux in English translation,[6] privileges the postmodern strategy identified by Douglas Crimp in "On the Museum's Ruins." Smith rewrites the original fiction of the museum as a closed, coherent, homogeneous system to disclose the actual site of a "heterogeneity of texts," a pile of "bric-a-brac," essentially organized by random spatial juxtaposition.[7]

The very structure of Smith's three novels introduces us to a sequence of texts whose strict linear chronology belies their geographic and generic diversity. Appropriately, *The Vanished Child*, the first in the series, is to some extent the most uniform in identity. Set almost exclusively in America, the novel can be readily classified as detective fiction; moreover, the central focus on a locked-room mystery equates the national origins of the novel with those of its hero. The Baron Alexander Von Reisden's return from Europe to New England in the summer of 1905 leads to the resolution of a double enigma: the murder of William Knight and the subsequent disappearance of his eight-year-old grandson Richard eighteen years earlier. Still, the first appearance of a museum in the early pages of Smith's trilogy tellingly undermines the seeming stability of traditional categories. The visit of Reisden, a chemist engaged in neuromuscular research, to the Boston Museum of Ethnology might be expected to return us to the origins of the museum, founded in the discipline of natural history and dedicated to the exhibition of objects of scientific, historical, or aesthetic value. In keeping with the semantic range of the word *distraction*, however, what begins as a simple diversion becomes increasingly disturbing as Reisden finds himself alone and disoriented: "he looked for the exit; and then he got lost, it seemed for hours, in the endless corridors of the museum" (36). Moreover, Smith's museum has already evolved into a postmodern space that foregrounds at once its own obsolescence as a still viable institution and its metamorphosis into the self-reflective realm of contemporary art: "There were too many stuffed animals. They were too silent, too very much unlike animals. Preparing them for exhibition had made them much more like each other than any were like the living species they mocked. Louis would say, he thought, Only Reisden is such a fool as to notice everything in a museum is dead" (35).[8] That this particular museum—or mausoleum—much more closely resembles a museum of natural history than a museum of ethnology, despite a few distinctively "American touches," further emphasizes the constructed nature and the artificial imposition of homogeneous boundaries that define the traditional museum.

Smith's work similarly challenges the capacity of conventional distinctions of genre to describe and delimit the space(s) of contemporary narrative. Although the investigation of a murder continues to play a significant structural role in *The Knowledge of Water*, Smith's ostensibly "mainstream" text now literally flows beyond the borders of detective fiction and mystery novels to display a fluidity appropriate to its title and to the events it recounts. The second novel in the trilogy expands into the realms of romance, melodrama, historical fiction, and *roman à clef*. Against the metaphoric background of the 1910 flood that threatened the emergence of modern Paris, Reisden and Perdita, the blind American pianist he met in *The Vanished Child*, cross conventional boundaries of Victorian morality to become lovers. The novel's central focus on Perdita's similarly revolutionary struggle to establish a professional career, initially as a woman but eventually as wife and mother as well, introduces us to both the recently established and the still avant-garde artistic communities of the early twentieth century. On the one hand, Perdita is befriended by Suzanne Mallais, once peasant laundress and now widow of a celebrated Impressionist painter, and, on the other, by the thoroughly modern Milly Xico, recently divorced ex-writer currently employed as an actress and sometime journalist. If the work of Claude Monet, among others, clearly inspires the painting, if not the portrait, of the fictional Claude Mallais, Milly is, of course, just another name for Colette.

Unsurprisingly, given the thematic interest of the novel, the geography of *The Knowledge of Water* features a series of museum-like places, ranging from the salon of Esther Cohen (a.k.a. Gertrude Stein) to the official

Salon d'Hiver in the Grand Palais, embracing both private collections and public galleries, and including such figurative spaces as the historic building owned by Reisden in which the extensive archives of Jouvet's Medical Analyses fill up room after room. But it is the Louvre itself that takes center stage at the midpoint of Smith's trilogy. Indeed, this version of the "imaginary museum" serves as a microcosm of the paradoxical geography of postmodernity inscribed in Smith's fictional world. At once a magnificent monument to high culture and a mere tourist attraction, the Louvre in *The Knowledge of Water*, "one of the few warm places where homeless people and beggars could sleep" (76), is also the haven of vagrants, perhaps the most thoroughly realized form of the emblematic figure of the migrant that Aamir Mufti and Ella Shohat associate with global modernity.[9]

The Louvre we visit with Roy Daughterty, Boston detective and stereotypically naive American tourist, has the same characteristics of the postmodern places we have repeatedly encountered in contemporary English-language fiction set in France. It is a highly eclectic space whose "long corridor[s], chock-a-block with pictures and furniture and statues and every sort of gaud, half a museum, half a warehouse" (173) simultaneously recall the fiction and expose the reality of the museum. Daughterty must use his "guidebook map" to navigate the route to the modern art collection, housed in a room "crowded as Leviathan's stomach, the walls jammed with double and triple rows of gilt-framed paintings," whose casual juxtaposition of heterogeneous styles and influences, some in evident contradiction with their designation as "modern," ultimately appears to be totally random: "Landscape. Naked woman . . . Another naked woman. Man and woman harvesting, . . . Landscape. Three men wearing theatre getup and crossing swords. Another naked woman. Woman in a veil. Two marble statues of Virtue and Purity" (173). A bit further on, beyond the "Crucifixions and Virgin Marys and long dark saints," Daugherty has a chance encounter with the single work that he recognizes: "Well, he thought, now I have seen the Mona Lisa" (176). Somewhere appropriately in the middle of this disparate space hang two paintings by Mallais whose representations of an urban bathhouse and of fields at sunset identify Smith's fictional Impressionist as the key representative of a transitional and mobile age: Mallais's "distinctive style and subject" make him the painter of "the edge between city and country, the landscape of the suburbs," the paradigmatic in-between setting of a postmodern age (175).

Indeed Mallais's fascination with margins and intermediary spaces cannot be contained within the borders of the frame. His work both conceals and reveals a much more precarious intersection that challenges the very nature of representation. The juxtaposition of "Spruce and Shadow" and a photograph of the artist's wife taken in the same place at the same time makes visible the absence of the garden depicted in the painting. What interests the noted collector of modern art who currently owns the work, however, is not the missing "impression" of Suzanne Mallais's flowerbeds but the evidence of their subsequent existence: "She put a garden in that spot afterward, did she? Very handsome of her. Life imitating art. Homage to my painting" (267). In a fascinating, if fortuitous, linguistic parallel, the word *landscape* itself exemplifies just such a paradoxical crossing of boundaries from the real to the artificial. The history of the word shows that people only began to see natural landscapes some years after they had been introduced to them in paintings.[10] Similar landscaping shapes the third novel in Smith's trilogy, which unfolds in just such an ambiguous setting, characterized by intangible, variable, and shifting frontiers between past and present, fact and fiction, reality and representation, realism and self-referentiality.

The Citizen of the Country once again reaches beyond the boundaries of the mystery to add the territories of Gothic fiction and the spy novel to the heterogenous forms previously on display in the first two "stories" of Smith's imaginary museum. Similarly, the America of *The Vanished Child* and the Paris of *The Knowledge of Water*, already predominantly places of passage and of passageways, now become a European, and ultimately a global, space, as vaguely defined, both linguistically and geographically, as the title of Smith's third novel would suggest. Although murder and death pervade the story of Reisden's efforts to save at once his marriage, his business, and the sanity of his friend André, Smith structures *The Citizen of the Country* around "the secret of Montfort" in a superimposition of plot and place that admirably illustrates Franco Moretti's conviction that "geography shapes the narrative structure of the European novel."[11]

The curiously discordant outline of "ridiculous, grandiose" Montfort, André's ancestral home, dominates the landscape of French Flanders. The hilltop on which it stands, "spiky with towers—square ones, round ones, towers with pointed roofs, towers with battlements," is encircled by walls that run "round and round . . . like a maze" and bear disconcerting inscriptions that resemble "art made by the insane" (67). The original medieval castle, still visible in the half-restored main building, has been refurnished in postmodern kitsch with "a wagonload of the Middle Ages" ordered from the postmodern equivalent of the museum, in this case, "the biggest department store in Belgium" (68). Adjacent to stone ramparts in ruins stands the crumbling chalk framework of a "new fancy-work Montfort" (252), whose ongoing and interminable construction is undertaken anew each weekend by an eclectic crew of volunteers; soldiers, ultrapatriots, architecture students, miners, and tenant farmers work side by side (78). Consistent with Bradbury's notion of "the global village assimilativeness of modern consciousness," which results in Malraux's "musée imaginaire," Montfort epitomizes an age characterized by "a vast compendium of styles, jostling each other in threatening and often parodic relation."[12] In Smith's realization of the "disintegration of form" inherent to postmodern architecture, the museum has escaped its walls, even as they multiply, to become both madhouse and maze.[13]

Metaphor for an entire world on the verge of madness as World War I approaches, Montfort itself is a world already gone mad. Not unlike André himself, the disturbing incongruities and asymmetries of the visible exterior of the castle pale in comparison to what lies beneath the surface. Built above the ancient Roman mines that form "an underground maze" throughout the region (55), the multileveled cellars of Montfort consist of cold, dark, terrifying "tunnels leading nowhere . . . , not meant to be lived in, only to be built and built and forever to be built" (113). A gratuitous place of "no visible use," Montfort is "a joke," "an actor's folly" (254), an illusory world of trompe-l'oeil now literally transformed into a movie set, the outdoor stage for the latest production of André's sinister "Theatre du Monde." *The Citizen of the Country*, in short, explicitly takes place in the "paradoxical and labyrinthine" decor of the postmodern novel theorized by Brian McHale in *Constructing Postmodernism*.[14] Smith's fictional French Flanders "crystallizes a 'liminal' or in-between space" of mediation that recalls Charles Jenckes's description of the Chinese garden.[15] Like the tunnels that lie beneath Montfort, the path through such a paradigmatic postmodern space is often "skewed or distorted, subject to abrupt shifts and transformations and ambiguous as to its boundaries."[16]

Within the "liminal" space of Smith's own fiction, our first encounter with madness appropriately takes place at the actual threshold of her trilogy. The opening sentence of *The Vanished Child* introduces its hero as literally out of his mind: "The Baron Alexander von Reisden went mad after his young wife died, and in five years he had not got himself sane" (1). Yet, whatever responsibility a driver may bear for a car accident that kills a passenger and however guilty he may reasonably feel, even Reisden fully understands that his own absolute conviction that he murdered his wife is entirely irrational; it constitutes "his singular and inexplicable and apparently incurable madness" (1). That my initial description of the relative "stability," both generic and geographical, of the first novel in Smith's trilogy explicitly focused on its "identity" as an American detective novel thus proves particularly apt. Reisden's story begins as the liminal response of a "missing person" to the parallel absence of a place to call home and a sense of self.

When we first meet Reisden, he is living "like a dead man" (6) in Switzerland, a nation whose identity has traditionally—and paradoxically—been defined precisely by its determination not to have one. A neutral country, reputed for its refusal to take sides, to choose a position, to stand in one place rather than another, Switzerland's figurative geography makes it an ideal destination—or, rather, a perfect stopover—in a global world of mobility and mediation. Reisden himself stands in a prototypical postmodern place of passage and impermanence; he is waiting on the platform of a train station, equally unwilling to return to Italy and to move to Paris, when he is first recognized as Richard Knight. If an incident openly acknowledged to be "like melodrama" (7) nonetheless suffices to justify his presence at the Knight family home in Boston a few months later—" 'they recognized me,' Reisden said, as if it explained everything" (83)—perhaps this is because *The Vanished Child* also resembles melodrama in its need to repeat one of that genre's most characteristic motifs. The only identity that Reisden has ever known results from an identical experience: his recognition, at the age of ten, by the man who becomes his guardian:

> "the son of my friend Franz von Reisden. That is who you are. You understand that. See, here is the paper that tells who your parents were." *I am Alexander von Reisden*, he had said to himself, a delighted child. . . . It had been that very moment when Reisden had understood that he was unique, himself, because someone else had said so. At that moment he had known exactly who he was, and his sense of himself had been as close to him as the pulse in his neck. (34)

Significantly, within the text of the novel, the passage in which the child is found in Africa is immediately followed by that in which the adult gets lost in a Boston museum; indeed, one might represent Reisden's entire life as an endless game of hide and seek played in the museum-like space of a lost and found. The amnesia that has erased his own memories of everything prior to the first moment of recognition has deprived him of any independent, and therefore any permanent, sense of self. "In general amnesia, the kind so loved by Victorian melodrama, one forgot one's identity completely," observes Reisden, fully aware that miraculous cures (unlike recognition scenes) rarely occur offstage: "General amnesia repaired itself within weeks or not at all" (33). Alternately identified as Richard and Reisden, Smith's hero—one hardly knows by what name to call him—is perpetually trapped in between the two identities. James Clifford has suggested that in "postmodernity, the new world order of mobility, of rootless histories," we can no longer ask "Where are you from?" but only "Where are you between?,"[17] precisely the question, the only question, that Reisden can answer. In a clearly metaphoric passage, once he agrees to accompany Richard's uncle Gilbert to the summer home from which the child long ago vanished, Reisden leases a car in which he envisions "escape" as a state of permanent suspension between flight from one place and arrival at another: "as long as he was moving between here and there, he could really be neither who he was nor what he had got himself into" (87).

Like the travel writers described in Dennis Porter's *Haunted Journeys* who "combine explorations in the world with self-exploration," Reisden undertakes a journey literally haunted by "the ghosts" and the "*deja vu*" that Porter metaphorically associates with all travel.[18] At its outset, Reisden too explicitly equates past, place, and personhood: "What we want from memory is what we want from our own city, a sense of being at home, or at least known, a sense of ourselves" (45). Such a desire is both nostalgia and wishful thinking on the part of a man for whom the old adage that "you can never go home again" is much more than a cliched lament. At the first sight of the Knight family home in Matatonic, Reisden feels "instinctively uneasy": "The house was wrong." Designed to be as "clean and balanced" as "a proportional cube," the exterior in fact reflects the madness once contained within. Less a Victorian mansion than an early prototype of Montfort, everything at Matatonic is slightly askew—the roof too high, the windows too blank, even the principal entrance "pushed to one side, marring all balance" (95). Untouched since the night of William Knight's murder, the house has been preserved as both museum and mausoleum. Reisden opens the front door onto "a vast funeral hall smelling of carpet mold, old fires, old food, old damp wall paper." The patterned diamonds that carpet the oddly angled hallways are "optically the wrong size"; and "little dead-white china plaques" bearing oversized Biblical quotations hang throughout the house "like some skin disease on the walls" (96–97).

Living in a house that can never be a home positions Reisden within what Homi Bhabha calls "the unhomely," permanently suspended between "home and loss of home."[19] "Locating" his identity embodies similar paradox. What Alan Wilde calls "modernism's balanced 'either-or,' " a textual space in which Smith's hero could definitively be *either* Richard *or* Reisden, has been openly displaced in *The Vanished Child* by "postmodernism's more comprehensive 'both-and,' " wherein Smith's hero must always remain *both* Richard *and* Reisden.[20] Moreover, Reisden is equally lost in both identities long before their disorienting fusion so that he not only duplicates the uprooted and rootless characters we have encountered elsewhere in the fictions of globalization but he does so twice over. The Richard he has forgotten seeks to disappear long before he finally succeeds. A frequent runaway, an enthralled reader of adventure stories whose young heroes escape to faraway lands, eventually he must simply "have gone too far, or forgot how to get back" (238). The fragmented memories of the period that follow are those of a "wanderer," consistent with the name of the ship on which Richard is presumed to have fled to Africa. The child identified as Alexander von Reisden is also an orphan; this time he vanishes into Europe.

It is hardly surprising then that Reisden should describe acting as "the passion of his life" (4) nor that he should continue to act on occasion even after his conversion to chemistry. Reisden's own identity can never be anything but a performance, its success determined entirely by his ability to convince the audience of its credibility. If Gilbert and Perdita are ideal spectators, eager to suspend their disbelief, for others, including himself, Reisden will never be anything but an actor, that is, "a fake" and an imposter (104): "this is all acting. All pretense" (174). Deprived of any sense of his own individuality, one would hardly expect Reisden to be a good character actor; and indeed he is typecast as Richard solely by virtue of his extraordinary physical resemblance to the other male members of the Knight family. He is surrounded by his own doubles, both real and represented, in whose reflection he too is ultimately forced to "recognize" himself as Richard.

In what may be the epitome of postmodern paradox and dissolution of boundaries, Reisden acts out the part of the person he actually is—or, at least, once was.[21] In pretending to be Richard, Reisden in fact assumes his own original identity; and he does so, moreover, for the contradictory purpose of disabusing his audience of the conviction that he really *is* Richard: "For three days Reisden had played the role of Reisden unwillingly being Richard Knight. . . . Roles and acting, in the long-ago time when he had done such things, usually had released him and given him his emotions. But not now. . . . Richard was Reisden's madness, working itself out" (63, 65). If the performance represents the real, reality itself, in contrast, increasingly resembles a game of make-believe. The imposter in *The Vanished Child* is none other than Reisden himself, despite all evidence to the contrary: "He was Alexander von Reisden. Baron Alexander Josef Jászai von Reisden. His father was the Baron Franz Eugen Joachim von Reisden;

his mother, Charlotte-Elisabeth Adelaïde von Loewenstein, cousin of the Graf Leo von Loewenstein.... He knew who he was" (154). Regardless of their weight, the words on which Reisden's carefully constructed sense of self depends are finally only empty signifiers. The person he knows himself to be, the person he has spent twenty years becoming, the only person he can ever remember being does not in fact exist. Falsely identified by a fake cousin who imposes a fictional identity, Reisden, not Richard, turns out to have been the victim of a kidnapping.[22]

"Richard was Reisden's madness, working itself out" (65). Indeed, regardless of clinical accuracy, anyone who suffers permanently from the coexistence of disparate identities might reasonably be described as schizophrenic. In "Postmodernism and Consumer Society," Frederic Jameson interprets the disorder as both linguistic and temporal.[23] The schizophrenic experiences a breakdown between the signifier and the signified (the word and what it represents), which, much like Reisden's relationship to the genealogical signs of identity that he recites in the passage quoted above, erodes his sense of who he is. Similar disruption in the persistence of personal identity over time leaves the schizophrenic lost in the present—like Reisden once again, whose alternative past histories are either irretrievable or discredited. Significantly, Jameson identifies this conception of schizophrenia as one of two significant features that make up "the specificity of the postmodernist experience."[24]

That Smith intends Reisden to be a paradigmatic figure of the postmodern world is further confirmed by the reflection of his experience in that of others. His Uncle Gilbert, for example, deliberately uproots himself by refusing both to marry and to join the family business. "Disinherited and forgotten," the only remaining son of the Knights joyfully takes to the road to become "an itinerant used-book seller, of all things" (11). On the morning of Richard's disappearance, his uncle reads to him from *The Coral Island*, which begins: "Roving has always been, and still is, my ruling passion, the joy of my heart, the very sunshine of my existence" (184). But Perdita's example is no doubt the most significant, precisely because it serves not only as metaphor but only as metaphor. The girl whose very name identifies her as a lost child is in reality anything but. Perdita is neither orphaned nor estranged from her parents; yet she is raised by an uncle far away from her home and eagerly looks forward to a future of concert touring. In a passage that functions as *mise-en-abyme*, Reisden reads aloud to Perdita who "had never read *The Winter's Tale*, though she has been named for its heroine" (75). Shakespeare's Perdita, unlike her namesake, is very much a "vanished child." Denied by her father and believed to be dead, found in a distant country by a shepherd who raises her as his own daughter, Perdita's true identity is finally restored years later as a result of her extraordinary resemblance to her mother.

In the reading of the play lies yet another scene of recognition, this one staged by Smith for her readers rather than her characters. Indeed, the text of the novel has become unexpectedly palimpsestic, for if Reisden's story is clearly reflected in that of Shakespeare's Perdita, a far more famous drama just as clearly underlies them both. Oedipus, too, is abandoned at birth, presumed to have died, and raised in a foreign land in total ignorance of his original identity. In fact, the appearance of *Oedipus Rex* in *The Vanished Child* might almost be characterized as predictable, if not inevitable, given the frequency with which those literary historians who take what Porter calls "the long view" substitute Sophocles' tragedy for Poe's tales at the origins of detective fiction.[25] In the final chapters of Smith's novel, Reisden moves from acting to directing. In an attempt to discover "what made Richard run" (243), he restages William Knight's murder on the nineteenth anniversary of his grandfather's death. Although the possibilities for terror, suspense, and shocking revelations are worthy of Poe, whose own detective stories have a hero almost as enigmatic as Smith's, Reisden refuses to tell "ghost stories" and predictably sets his production in the world of theater (242). Once again an interruption in an Elizabethan work —"The play's the thing, wherein I'll catch the conscience—of someone. Perhaps my own" (244)—exposes the ancient Greek text that lies behind: "Not Shakespeare but Sophocles. I do not want to know but I must know" (245).

Reisden's discovery that Richard shot his abusive and tyrannical (grand)-father makes him, like Oedipus, at once detective, victim, and murderer. In theory, thanks to yet another level of textual layering, it could also cure his madness: "If he was Richard, he was sane" (189). Scenes of reenactment and the figure of Oedipus haunt the history of psychoanalysis quite as much as that of the detective novel. In a classic case of Freudian displacement, the joy and relief that Richard feels after he kills William resurface years later to convince Reisden that he is the murderer of his wife. The original crime has been locked away in Reisden's unconscious mind by Richard's refusal to speak at the time of his grandfather's death—"I won't tell, I'll never tell" (13)—until the staged repetition in the "murder room" at Matatonic mirrors the "talking cure" of psychoanalysis. Interestingly, Jameson, following Jacques Lacan, describes schizophrenia not only as a language disorder but specifically as "a linguistic version of the Oedipus complex" in which Oedipal rivalry now focuses on paternal authority:

"schizophrenia emerges from the failure . . . to accede fully into the realm of speech and language."[26]

Although the knowledge restored to Reisden does not drive him, like Oedipus, to literal blindness (perhaps displaced onto Perdita), he does choose a metaphorical equivalent. He has Richard Knight declared dead and both renews his own promise "never to tell" and extends it to Gilbert, Perdita, and Roy Daugherty. If the deliberate decision to repress psychological knowledge and to conceal the identity of a murderer makes him a bad psychiatrist and a corrupt detective, they also remind us that Reisden is very much a hero of our times. The intertextual heterogeneity contained within *The Vanished Child* might seem to suggest a positive response to Roland Barthes's rhetorical question: "Isn't every story a form of the Oedipus story? Isn't all narrative a search for one's origins . . . ?"[27] In fact, Reisden consciously chooses to remain in the "liminal or in-between state" of suspension that has defined his entire life, in keeping with Wilde's description of postmodernism: "paradise, once lost, is now abandoned. . . . nostalgia over origins is replaced by a dismissal of them."[28]

Significantly, Reisden's reconstruction of the murder is all about movement; in the absence of a text he has only stage directions and blocking to use as "scaffolding": "Movements, gestures. The right action creates the play" (245). At the end of the first volume of Smith's trilogy, Reisden is once again in motion, on his way to New York and then to Paris. Curiously, *re*patriation, the discovery of his father, is transformed into *ex*patriation, the renouncing of his native land, in an experience of shifting and unstable signifiers not unlike what Jameson calls schizophrenia. Metaphorically, Reisden is in every sense a fugitive, at once runaway, refugee, and criminal. Most importantly, freed from the displacement that defined his madness, Reisden has become a permanently displaced person, illustrative of "the unhoming" described by William V. Spanos as the central aesthetics of postmodernism: "*dépaysement*, the ejection from one's familial and familiar 'homeland' . . . reveals . . . the primordial not-at-home of the in-between."[29]

Perhaps it is inevitable then that *The Knowledge of Water*, set in Paris in the winter of 1910, finds both Reisden and Perdita living in a country whose language has no word for "home" and in a city described by Priscilla Parkhurst Ferguson as "the cosmopolitan Other, an alien site . . . , the great escape for the women and men whose fortunes we follow in so many novels both French and foreign."[30] Focused on the *belle époque* rather than the "Lost Generation," the second novel in Smith's trilogy takes place a decade earlier than the other contemporary mysteries of modernism we have encountered. If Stein's famous salon is therefore still more French than American, it is also paradoxically far more international. The artists "collected" by Esther Cohen (a.k.a. Stein) feature most prominently "the soon-to-be-world-famous Spanish painter" Juan Gastedon (a.k.a. Picasso) (51) and the "anarchist poet" and "pornographer" (63) George Vittal, clearly modeled on Apollinaire whose mysterious birth, hybrid origins, and rootless youth parallel those of Reisden himself.[31] Their most important French counterparts include Henry de Xico (Willy) and his ex-wife Milly (Colette), both equally worldly and permanently promiscuous, aesthetically as well as sexually.[32] In contrast then to Jean Méral, who concludes at the end of his 1989 study of *Paris in American Literature* that the "global village" of contemporary reality "has put an end to Paris as a privileged meeting place of two continents and two civilizations," *The Knowledge of Water*, like other recent American fiction set in France, suggests not only that the "global village" and the "privileged meeting place" are both located in Paris at the end of the twentieth century but that they already were at its beginning.[33]

Although Smith's second novel has a single setting, its geography is as unsettled as the lives and identities of its residents. In keeping with Clifford's notion of postmodern location as "an itinerary rather than a bounded site," all of the characters in *The Knowledge of Water* spend much of their time moving through Paris, their meandering paths above ground mirrored by the growing labyrinthine network of interconnected subway tunnels under construction below the surface of the city.[34] But if Paris's narrow streets and underground passages have often proven particularly conducive to the atmosphere of the detective novel, Smith's version confirms Méral's conviction that "it is above all the Seine . . . that forms the main axis of mysterious Paris."[35] From the opening scene of the novel, in which Reisden is called to the Paris Morgue to identify a body pulled from the river, to the final episode, in which *le tout Paris* gathers on the Pont-Neuf to watch the flood waters crest, the Seine is omnipresent as sight, sound, and smell. Reisden lives "near the river" (104) and the house he rents in Courbevoie for Perdita lies both "by the Seine" and "on the other side of the Seine" (31), in an especially apt metaphor for the ambiguous borderlands and passageways of globalized postmodernity.[36] In January 1910, moreover, this already fragile and transitory landscape is further destabilized as the Seine overflows its banks and threatens its own bridges.

The museums of Paris, present and future, also lie along the Seine, as one of Reisden's "aimless strolls" through the central city reveals: "He walked back toward the river, past the dark bulk of the Louvre; at the

Point-Royal he crossed the Seine and stood at the end of the bridge, in the lights from the Gare d'Orsay, looking upriver" (102–3). Although neither Reisden nor Perdita ever enter the Louvre, the museum has a structural importance and a thematic influence within Smith's novel that both rival and reinforce those of the Seine. As noted above, the reader's tour of the Louvre coincides with Roy Daugherty's first encounter with Mona Lisa and Mallais in a scene that I now want to revisit. Unlike our observant but uninformed guide, Smith's readers can be—and surely are—expected to recognize the works he can only describe: "a statue of a woman with wings but no head or arms" is, of course, the *Victoire de Samothrace*; in "Man and woman harvesting, looked like they knew what they were doing; late in the day for it, though," we perceive the emotional depth and the distinctive landscape of Millet's *Les Glaneurs*; and the characterization of "Three men wearing theater getup and crossing swords" positions us in front of *Le Serment des Horace*, David's neoclassical study of heroic virtue. Of particular significance is Daugherty's description of a "Naked woman on a couch with a fan in her lap and not a thing on but shoes" (173). This fourth and final example of an identifiable painting confirms a deeper purpose on Smith's part than either the playful mocking of a particularly literal-minded American or the testing of the reader's knowledge.

In fact, our own recognition of Manet's *Olympia* within the text of Smith's novel explicitly functions as a *mise-en-abyme* to duplicate our reading of the painting itself.[37] Crimp locates the origins of modern art in *Olympia* precisely because Manet makes its relationship to Titian's *Venus of Urbino* "shamelessly obvious."[38] By leaving his historical model visible within his own picture of a modern courtesan, Manet "rendered painting's relationship to its sources self-consciously problematic."[39] Interestingly, in light of the importance of the museum to an understanding of Smith's work, Michel Foucault qualifies *Olympia* as the first "museum" painting; its self-reflexivity demonstrates both "the existence of museums" and the "interdependence" of the paintings that hang in them.[40]

As Daugherty continues his tour of the Louvre, he too will experience something of the autonomy and the intertextuality that structure the space of modern art. Just as he is recovering from the shock he feels at the sight of "the actual Mona Lisa" who "looked like you'd think," Daugherty notices a copyist "painting another Mona Lisa" that is "astonishingly like the first." Not only does the American detective like the copy quite as much as the original; he clearly prefers the artisanal task of imitation to the creative act of composition: "It was sort of comfortable seeing a painting being made, like tinkering or a construction site, not like art at all" (176–77). To his surprise, the copyist, who turns out to be the grandson of Claude Mallais, vehemently refuses Daugherty's request that he copy one of his grandfather's paintings that hang nearby. What the detective identifies as the look of "a boy caught stealing" is only erased by an agreeable smile when Daugherty "mechanically" inquires if the boy will make him a Mona Lisa. In fact, Daugherty settles for several of the "little china lockets of the Mona Lisa, pink and green" that street vendors peddle just outside the museum. His lingering lament—"What would he do with a Mona Lisa from Jean-Jacques Mallais?"—further undermines traditional notions of identity and originality, for it seems to imply that a copy produced by someone who happens to be related to the original artist might thereby be authenticated (177–78).

Although Daugherty's visit to the Louvre begins with an allusion to the aesthetic practice that defines Manet as the first modernist artist, his discovery of the Mona Lisa quickly reminds us that Smith herself is a postmodern writer. To clarify the distinction between modernism and postmodernism, Crimp contrasts Manet's duplication of certain details of Titian's painting with "the radically different pictorial logic" that informs Robert Rauschenberg's use of the images he borrows from the works of Velázquez and Rubens.[41] Rauschenberg's art enacts the same move from "techniques of *production* . . . to techniques of *reproduction*" that Daugherty finds so reassuring in the passage described above: "The fiction of the creating subject gives way to the frank confiscation, quotation, excerptation, accumulation and repetition of already existing images. Notions of originality, authenticity and presence, essential to the ordered discourse of the museum, are undermined."[42]

In *The Knowledge of Water*, the plot that threatens to destroy "the ordered discourse of the museum" is hatched within the space of its own galleries. On another visit to the Louvre, George Vittal (Apollinaire), accompanied by Juan (Picasso), Milly (Colette), and Esther (Stein), outlines a plan to steal the Mona Lisa, replace it with a copy, and throw the original into the Seine (76–80). In fact, George's revolutionary spirit and passion for excess lead him to imagine a popular revolt in which twenty-eight copies by twenty-eight different artists would be simultaneously jettisoned from Paris's twenty-eight bridges at noon on January 28 (51–52).[43] Appropriately, in a world in which "confiscation" and "repetition" go hand in hand, the question of whether Leonardo DaVinci's masterpiece—or only its likeness—will be stolen remains open to constant speculation throughout the novel; even in the final scene, the crowd of Parisians who watch George drop the Mona Lisa off the Pont-Neuf openly disagree about whether the cresting Seine carries off the original or a copy (463–64).[44] The meaning of George's protest, in contrast, is perfectly clear. His desire not only to replace "the old Mona Lisa" but also to "crown the new" (218) explicitly identifies "museum art," that is, "Art," as his target and redefines "art"—"the only true art is the death of art" (50)—as its destruction: "I have come to free you from the tyranny of Art. . . . I spit on the rotted corpse of Art and cast her in the Seine" (463).

Significantly, the impetus behind George's plan, the conclusion he reaches at the Louvre that the Mona Lisa "could be replaced by a copy," is not based on the assumption that the tourists gathered around the famous painting would be unable to tell the difference between an original and a reproduction but rather that "they wouldn't care" even if they could (78). On the model of Daugherty himself, visitors to the Louvre are not in search of a remarkable work of art, let alone an entire collection of such works; rather, they come to gape at Paris's perhaps most famous—certainly her most accessible—celebrity:

> The Mona Lisa gleamed in the center of the western wall, a greenish painting in a great gilt frame, which was in turn enclosed in a glass-filled, white-painted, thiefproof box. Around her hung virgins and martyrs, Holy Families glowing with Italian light; but the tourists only looked briefly at the others—check, check, check, now we've seen that—before gathering in a semicircle around the Mona Lisa. (77–78)

In *Becoming Mona Lisa: The Making of a Global Icon*, Donald Sassoon dates the transformation of the work of art into a celebrity, its status no longer determined by aesthetic merit but based solely on fame, and the corresponding conflation of the worlds of art and entertainment from the precise moment when the Mona Lisa literally left the museum.[45] Smith, already immersed in the borderless world of postmodernity, eliminates the logic of cause and effect to make the theft of the Mona Lisa and its metamorphosis into a global icon contemporaneous.

In a postmodern era, the painting whose presence within the Louvre has become integral to the very identity of the museum itself can paradoxically no longer be contained, either spatially or aesthetically, inside its walls. Perhaps it is only fitting that the portrait of a woman, whose mysterious origins and ambiguous smile have elevated her likeness to the stature of enigma incarnate, should have come to exist in a seemingly endless variety of forms. Similarly, a work that is at once critically acclaimed and enormously popular seems particularly well suited to represent the locus at which the products of high and low culture can no longer be distinguished.

In the introduction to *Dangerous Pilgrimages*, Bradbury notes that in a contemporary age of mass culture, "we now take images, icons, for the illusory things they are. They are commodities, identities, not facts but refractions, not realities but simulacra . . . . In short, they are fictions."[46] Although Bradbury's work focuses on novels that predate Smith's, *The Knowledge of Water* offers a particularly apt illustration of his notion of a "transatlantic fiction."[47] One of the most interesting and innovative of the many reproductions of the Mona Lisa that flood the pages of Smith's novel is explicitly fictional in nature.

In a sustained plot, interwoven with the story of Reisden and Perdita, the police seek to solve the murder of the woman whose body Reisden identifies in the opening pages of *The Knowledge of Water*. The "colorful corpse" pulled from the Seine with "waterlogged postcards and parts of postcards, recognizable as Leonardo's painting" (2) pinned to her clothes reads in retrospect like an ironic foreshadowing of the inevitable transformation of "the rotted corpse of Art," whose body, also feminine, George will cast into the river at the end of the novel (463). In this version of art history, rewritten to incorporate the conventions of the detective novel, the Mona Lisa is a street beggar who claims to live in an "imaginary palace" located "at the end of the Seine" (4). Leonard, the man she calls "her artist, Leonardo" (48), does in fact live in the guards' quarters in the basement of the Louvre. What makes Leonard "extraordinary" is the fact that "he would do anything for love" (47) and he "loves the Mona Lisa" (150). One of Mallais's copies hangs above his bed and he treasures the difficult assignment of guarding the original: "The Mona Lisa is worth any amount of trouble, any extreme of service. The more trouble a man has in loving her, the more worthy he is of her" (47–48). In Leonard's case, however, "the trouble" he experiences will rapidly drive him to violence as this paradigmatic citizen of a postmodern world becomes increasingly unable to distinguish the real from the false. The fusion of the woman who loves him and the figure in Da Vinci's portrait is multiplied to the point of madness by the reproductions that haunt and disorient him wherever he goes. All of Paris has become an "imaginary museum," a postmodern marketplace in which the "fictions" of the Mona Lisa are endlessly available; Leonard is lost in a self-referential world of global icons:

> All through Paris he sees her. She appears on *baci*; she is a brand of milk and of cigarettes. The singer Mistinguett dresses as her; she appears in revues; little girls wear her on china lockets. There is a Mona Lisa laundry on the rue Quincompoix, the Mona Lisa café on the rue Léonard-de-Vinci,

a Mona Lisa line of blouses, Mona Lisa matches, a Mona Lisa bath powder. In the Louvre itself, copyists paint her to sell to people who love her. She is everywhere: and wherever she is, Leonard looks at her in longing and pain. (48)

The Mona Lisa also makes an appearance, albeit an interestingly brief one, in Paul Watkins's *The Forger* (2000), yet another example of contemporary American fiction set in France. The hero of the novel, whose title identifies the practice in which he is highly skilled, asserts his ability to "forge almost anything." Asked to clarify the limits of "almost," Watkins's forger locates the boundary of the impossible "at the Mona Lisa's smile. It can never be duplicated. There is something unearthly about it."[48] In fact, although replicas of the Mona Lisa are omnipresent in *The Knowledge of Water*, Smith also distinguishes between two kinds of "duplication": the reproduction of an original work of art that results in a copy and the repetition of the original act of creation that leads to a forgery. In pronouncing the copies of the Mona Lisa made by Mallais's grandson "as good as forgeries" (148), Milly, unlike Jean-Jacques himself, fuses two initially separable plots.

References to forgery are as prevalent in Smith's novel as are replicas of the Mona Lisa, and both are equally variable in form. Questions of authenticity initially focus on a single Mallais painting owned by Reisden's cousin Dotty. From the beginning, genuineness appears to have little to do with the painting itself, a view of the Seine at sunset on whose exceptional beauty everyone agrees. What matters initially is not the painting's originality but rather Dotty's still modernist preoccupation with its origins. The work is a Mallais because it was purchased directly from the dealer who bought it from the artist's widow; the work is a Mallais because it was legally sold as a Mallais and bears his signature; the work is a Mallais because the landscape it depicts exists in reality; the work is a Mallais because it hangs in a retrospective of his paintings. The work is a Mallais because no one has ever noticed that it isn't.

Moreover, even once "a detail that's rather off" (109) becomes visible, authenticity remains a highly problematic concept. Barry Bullard, the expert who spots the forgery, readily acknowledges that "forger = artist" and that so fine a painting was necessarily "done by a remarkable artist" (139). Indeed, he suspects that the forger "might be a known painter" (141), and Juan Gastedon figures far more prominently among the early suspects than does Mallais's own grandson. Paradoxically, the crime of forgery is also a highly creative art. Based on nothing preexistent, in contrast to a copy, the forged painting is by definition original; only the signature is counterfeit. To further complicate matters, notes Bullard, many young painters consciously imitate better-known artists just as the latter frequently sign student work of high quality. Even the restoration of a work of art qualifies as "a form of forgery" (148). If Reisden is right that arthritis forced Mallais to "forge" his own suicide in 1900 and that his "postmortem" paintings are drawn from photographs and memory, does Mallais's inability to "paint from the immediate impression," "to catch the passing moment as it happens" (286), make him a fraud? If his wife helped him complete some of the paintings, do they all become suspect?[49]

The surprising truth is that none of the paintings are forgeries but not because Mallais is alive, although he is, or because he continues to paint, which he doesn't. Neither does the inability to distinguish among "pure Mallais," "Mallais-and-Madame," and Suzanne Mallais's "forgeries" (437–38) reflect negatively on those who view them or positively on those who painted them. As Suzanne Mallais finally admits in a joyful outburst that fuses artist and audience: "I paingted them all, but look at them, aren't they beautiful!" (444). The only real forger is Mallais himself whose fraudulent signature on his wife's work nonetheless paradoxically serves to authenticate it. In the postmodern world of *The Knowledge of Water*, the determination of origin, originality, authenticity, and authorship has become not only difficult and provisional but ultimately irrelevant; what matters, as Suzanne points out, is not who painted the works known as those of Mallais but that they exist. The only authentic "impression" is that made on the viewer, as Smith's epigraph, taken from Mark Jones's *Fake: The Art of Deception*, underscores: "art is mainly fashioned to be appreciated and acquired by others."

Méral adopts a similar vocabulary of authenticity and forgery to challenge the integrity of the American expatriates who, like Stein, chose Paris as their place of residence in the early years of the twentieth century: "If not actual forgers . . . many are fakes." The aphorism he borrows from Hemingway's Jake Barnes to sum up the expatriate's situation also identifies the ongoing crisis of Reisden's life: "You can't get away from yourself by moving from one place to another."[50] The mysteries of identity that were figured by images of the theater and performance in *The Vanished Child* are expressed through the thematics of forgery in the second volume of the trilogy. Fraud is the only option for Reisden and Perdita just as it is for Suzanne Mallais: "A peasant woman does not hold a palette, any more than a blind married woman becomes a touring pianist, or—G——d knows—an eight-year-old murderer matures into a husband and father" (451). In a postmodern world dominated by artifice and imitation, one cannot choose between the real and the counterfeit but only between more or less successful versions of the latter. Unable to forget a second time that his identity as Reisden is "faked," Smith's hero "want[s] to make it at least a good, solid forgery, a compelling forgery, like the Mallais; one that no one will ever spot" (159). Perdita's claim that she can give up the piano for marriage and motherhood similarly echoes the painting: it is "a forgery, like that, very handsome; but a forgery" (137).

No doubt the historical novelist strives to produce a forgery that can be similarly described: good, solid, compelling, very handsome. Reisden's admission that "even the forger want to pretend his work is true" (236) identifies a practice of artistic deception at which Smith proves particularly adept. She at once creates an illusion and exposes it as illusory, in keeping with postmodern playfulness and its reenactment of the original meaning of the word *illusion* (*illudere*, to mock; *in* + *ludere*, to play). Already, in the epilogue to *The Vanished Child*, fictional characters are paradoxically authenticated by virtue of being openly positioned within "a book." In a curious border crossing, just as Reisden and Perdita propose to move "outside" the book into a century where "anything may happen," an unimaginable event that will in fact take place, the bombing of Hiroshima, is relegated to the pages of "another book" (286). If reality is preinscribed as textual, then a text, even fictional, might conceivably open out into the world.

In the pages that take her second novel beyond its evident endpoint, Smith initially appears intent on confirming the reader's fantasies that such movement might be possible. Since Stein, Apollinaire, Colette, and Picasso are immediately recognizable as the historical models for their fictional counterparts in *The Knowledge of Water*, most readers are likely to have at least entertained the suspicion that is seemingly validated by the opening sentence of the afterword: "'The history of "Suzanne Mallais," like that of Marianne Blakelock, is among the most fascinating women's stories in the annals of Impressionist art'" (465). Indeed, the quotation marks that enclose the entire first paragraph, as well as its style, encourage us to believe that Smith is citing a published work, perhaps an entry in an encyclopedia of art. But the ellipses at the end of the passage lead to an abrupt negation, not just of the premise of the preceding paragraph nor even of the novel just read but rather of historical fiction in general and ultimately historical memory itself:

> No.
> Madame Mallais never painted. Esther Cohen has no readers; George Vittal never threw any *Mona Lisa* off the Pont-Neuf; even Milly, whose books ought to be still available in Livre de Poche paperback editions, never wrote a word. The persons in this book are fictional, and any resem-

> blance to actual persons, living or dead or yet to come, is a mere impression, or a forgery.
>
> The flood is a forgery too, a collage of newspaper stories, engineers' reports, eyewitnesses' accounts, and over three thousand photographs. (465–66)

What distinguishes these assertions from the conventional disclaimer they obviously imitate ("any resemblance to actual persons . . .") is less the forger's sudden refusal "to pretend [her] work is true" than her insistence that we acknowledge it isn't. By expressing rather than concealing "the seam along which fact and fiction meet," *The Knowledge of Water* identifies itself with what Linda Hutcheon calls "historiographic metafiction" and what McHale describes more simply as "a historical novel of the postmodern type."[51] In her afterword, Smith reveals that "quotes and misquotes" from the works of Apollinaire, Colette, Picasso, and Stein "are collaged throughout the book, in true forgers' style without attribution" (467). She exposes her characters too, even Reisden, as postmodern ventriloquists who mouth the ideas and the words of others. Although Smith's novel might nonetheless seem to hang back at the mainstream margins of the postmodern text, to the extent that she waits until she has exited the fictional world to undermine it, in fact, by making the afterword an integral part of the novel itself, Smith straddles what Hutcheon calls the "most radical" of boundaries, "those between fiction and non-fiction—and by extension—between art and life."[52]

Moreover, within the text of the novel, Milly figures as Smith's diegetic alter ego in an extended and multilingual *mise-en-abyme* of the novelist's own textual practice. In a passage visible as an imitation of Colette's *La Vagabonde*, itself a barely fictionalized autobiography, Milly (Renée, Colette) learns that after publishing her *Midinette* (*Claudine*) books under his own name, Henry (Adolphe Taillandy, Willy) has now sold the copyrights (53–56). Milly avenges herself by signing Henry's name to her reviews of Perdita's debut concert, reproduced in multiple versions, some of them plagiarized by Smith from George Bernard Shaw (467). At the end of *The Knowledge of Water*, Milly begins to write a new novel on the blank pages of the first published copy of *La Midinette à Paris*, a gift given (back) to her by Henry "as if from himself" (462). Milly's newspaper articles on the flood are similarly reproduced within the pages of Smith's novel as autonomous texts, part of "the collage" of data that makes the flood "a forgery" (465).

Although this vertiginous repetition of a writing practice, which indiscriminately combines plagiarism, forgery, theft, copying, and rewriting,

7 / MUSEUM, MAZE, MADHOUSE   155

might seem to take us back to the analogy with schizophrenia evident in the first novel of Smith's trilogy, in fact it is pastiche, the second of the two significant features that for Jameson determine "the specificity of the postmodernist experience," that predominates in *The Knowledge of Water*.[53] Jameson explicitly defines postmodern pastiche by distinguishing it from the historical novel. Like the former, Smith's text is a mise en scene of certain contemporary ideas about 1910 Paris rather than the integral recreation of that place and period characteristic of the latter. In a self-referential world, argues Jameson, "we are condemned to seek the historical past through our own pop images and stereotypes about that past, which itself remains forever out of reach."[54] Thus, in her reinvention of "the most illustrious" period(s) of the Parisian past,[55] Smith (re)assembles the "dead styles" of cubism and impressionism; and both the novelist and her characters "speak through the words and with the voices of the styles in the imaginary museum."[56] Appropriately, then, *The Knowledge of Water* ends by literally relegating the historical past and its fictionalized characters to the now museum-like space of the novel in order to reenter the present-day reality of its readers, whom Smith exhorts to undertake their own postmodern performance of travel and adventure: "Paris is there now, much better than this pale forgery. Go there. . . . Throw something in the Seine. Throw this book, which is now over. And then try something new . . . It might work, in Paris" (469).

The emphasis that Smith places on the book as a constructed object at the end of the second novel in her trilogy anticipates the direction she will take in the third. *The Citizen of the Country* unfolds in a metaphorical space we might identify as that of the imaginary library, a specifically textual equivalent of Malraux's "museum without walls." Crimp, following Foucault, locates the original counterpart to Manet's " 'museum' paintings" in the work of Flaubert, for whom the library figures both as "the generator of modern literature" and "the dumping grounds of an irredeemable classical culture."[57] McHale similarly describes the spaces of postmodern literature as "literary labyrinths" and the paradigmatic postmodern novel as an explicitly "library labyrinth."[58] In the "library novel" that concludes Smith's trilogy, an intertextual network of interrelated literary works doubles the underground maze whose passageways mine the geography of France to produce a complex representation of the landscape of postmodernity.

In describing the theatricality that gave the *belle époque* its unique flavor, Roger Shattuck notes that Paris itself became "a stage, a vast theater for herself and all the world."[59] Set in the summer of 1911, *The Citizen of the Country* opens with a theatrical performance staged on the steps of

Jouvet's Medical Analyses in which one of the actors plays the role of Reisden himself. Such self-reflexivity is generally characteristic of André de Montfort's "Grand Necropolitan Theatre du Monde," a true "horror show," both literal and metaphoric.[60] Its blatantly silly and repetitious plots —openly farcical, melodramatic, and full of self-referential allusions to the theater—are nonetheless counterbalanced by "special effects" and "magic tricks" so "horribly convincing" that they succeed in thrilling and terrifying the audience (38). In his starring role as "Necrosar, King of Terrors," André specializes in playing "vampires, eviscerators, and ax murderers" in a theater whose enactments of death and murder privilege exaggerated violence and excessive gore (384).

Méral transforms Shattuck's description of turn-of-the-century Paris into a timeless but transparent characteristic of the city itself: "Paris, a city of theaters, is itself a marvelous spectacle, but a spectacle of illusion and artifice."[61] Similarly, despite the Theatre du Monde's reputed ability to deceive its spectators, Smith's readers know from the beginning that it too is a place of magic and trickery. The Jouvet performance is described from the offstage perspective of Maurice Cyron, André's adoptive father, who appears to view the entire world, Jouvet included, as a stage set to be deconstructed: "A business is like a theatre: the fronts are all airy-fairy; it's the back of the house that tells you the tale" (9). Cyron despises the type of plays that André performs and he resents even more the fact that the son he raised to be a military officer performs at all. Yet, although Cyron is a former soldier and war hero, he is also, paradoxically, both theater director and lead actor in his own right. As formulaic as the Theatre du Monde, the repertory of the "Théâtre Cyron" consists of representations of war and heroism in which Cyron leads French soldiers into battle to triumph repeatedly, despite overwhelming odds, over their German enemies. For Cyron these plays depict a reality as ordinary as the lives of the spectators they attract; behind the soldiers and their families seated up front are "rows and rows of the clerks, shop assistants, grocers, cooks, and waiters" who will serve in future wars (47). Cyron's theater too, however, is described from the point of view of a character who is less a spectator than a hostile witness. Reisden hates Cyron's theater of violence and death as much as he does André's, and he recognizes both as equally unrealistic. Cyron substitutes the lies of propaganda and the fictions of myth for his son's special effects and magic tricks.

Consistent with Reisden's conclusion that "André and Cyron were more alike than they thought" (47), father and son collaborate on a film that opens up what McHale calls an "intertextual zone" in *The Citizen of the Country*, "constituted whenever we recognize the relations among two or more texts or between specific texts and larger categories such as genre, school, period."[62] Indeed, in this case, it would be more accurate to say that Smith's novel as a whole takes place in such a zone, since *The Citizen of the Country* is structured around the production of a film based on a highly recognizable text. André directs his father in *Citizen Mabet*, Cyron's adaptation of Shakespeare's *Macbeth*, now set in France in the 1790s and complete with "The Revolution, the Terror, witches, battles, guillotines" (41). Constructed, of course, as "a military film"—"what else would it be with Cyron in it?"—André has been promised "corpses and disembowelments" in the battle scenes; even Reisden acknowledges that "it would be wonderful" (40–41).

The choice of Shakespeare in general and *Macbeth* in particular as intertextual references is highly appropriate. Jameson includes among the features of pastiche "the allusive and elusive plagiarism of older plots,"[63] a postmodern strategy that Shakespeare not only facilitates for others but already practices himself. The Elizabethan dramatist commonly borrowed his stories from multiple sources to produce plays that represent, like *The Knowledge of Water*, both a pastiche and a collage of earlier authors. In the case of *Macbeth*, the published version of the play is presumed to contain passages interpolated from Thomas Middleton's *The Witch* as well as an interpretation of Scottish history drawn from Holinshed's *Chronicles*, in what almost seems to be a foreshadowing of the collaboration between André and Cyron.[64] Not only does Shakespeare's popularity worldwide make him the kind of global icon represented in the world of art by the Mona Lisa, but translation has allowed his work both to escape national boundaries and to be claimed by multiple nations.

No doubt Shakespeare is also the most widely quoted writer in the world. Jim Collins attributes the fact that his work is particularly "ubiquitous" in the detective novel to authorial desire to improve the status of popular fiction by association with "bona fide Serious British Literature."[65] In the case of *Macbeth*, however, Shakespeare's own play already exemplifies the Gothic, often considered a subgenre of detective fiction;[66] its dependence on ghosts, hallucination, bloody murders, betrayal, and madness admirably suits the stage of André's campy Theatre du Monde. Moreover, the tragedy's reputation as accursed has made *Macbeth* an especially popular intertext for detective fiction;[67] in Smith's novel as well, the filmmaking turns into "a disaster" that will result in multiple murders among the cast and crew. Finally, the play within the play in *Hamlet* provides perhaps the most common illustration of *mise-en-abyme*, the preferred strategy of postmodern art for revealing its own fictionality by mirroring itself from within, an act performed in *The Citizen of the Country* by *Macbeth*. Shakespeare's work in general is full of self-referential theater allusions, and one of the best known appears in Macbeth's final speech of disillusionment: "Life's but a walking shadow, a poor player / That struts and frets his hour upon the stage / And then is heard no more."[68]

Although the custom of referring to Macbeth as "the Scottish play" in an attempt to ward off misfortune originates in superstition, the attention that the epithet necessarily draws to questions of nation and nationality is highly appropriate in the case of *The Citizen of the Country* (40). The word *theater*, which identifies the setting of military operations as well as of dramatic works, is itself of similar linguistic significance in Smith's novel. Indeed, alternate meanings are fused in the Théâtre Cyron, a gift of the French army specifically conceived to allow a former war hero "to re-enact his triumphs" (48). Moreover, the latter originally occurred at Montfort, now the site of the filming of *Citizen Mabet*, in a further merging of the different stages on which Cyron performs. Still, although Milly's and Reisden's choral introduction of Cyron as both "an actor" and "a hero. Our French hero" characteristically combines his two identities (18), Cyron himself does not see them as either synonymous or complementary. Rather, the theater serves only as a means to an end, "Cyron's greatest weapon against the enemy" (378), in what he views as an uninterrupted military career. He is horrified to discover that André's scrapbooks have preserved a detailed record of "the wrong life": "I was no actor, boy. I stood for something. I belonged to France" (374). Indeed, the actor is absent from the pictures of "Sergeant Cyron, the hero; the real thing" that cover the walls of his own theater; and even Reisden finds the onstage version of the French hero as convincing as its real-life model: "He was every French drill sergeant who had ever trained a crew of left-footed conscripts; he was every soldier looking out over the fields, toward the enemy's overwhelming guns; he was every ordinary wordless man who had ever wiped a tear away from an old accordion song or a letter; every unexpected hero. He was Cyron; he was France" (46).

In arguing that "beliefs about the origins and evolution of nations often crystallize in the form of stories," Ella Shohat and Robert Stam identify film as the most appropriate genre in which to inscribe such fictions: "The cinema, as the world's storyteller *par excellence*, was ideally suited to relay the projected narratives of nations and empires."[69] Although *The Citizen of the Country* as a whole qualifies as a "narrative of nation," Cyron explicitly adapts *Macbeth* as national "allegory" in the sense of "texts which metaphorize the public sphere even when narrating apparently private stories."[70] In setting *Citizen Mabet* at the time of the Revolution, Cyron literally returns to the original moment of French nationhood to repeat and to rewrite the story of France. Importantly, filming takes place at Montfort. André's family home, transformed by Cyron into "a national monument" ("Montfort is France"), plays a central role in "the myth that was Cyron" (42, 49). The making of the film is intricately tied to Cyron's mysterious rebuilding project. In July 1911, France and Germany once again appear to be on the brink of war; and Germany's need to confirm the rumors that a military fortification is under construction in the cellars and tunnels below the castle is matched only by France's own desire to spread the story. The multiple deaths that occur among members of the cast and crew of *Citizen Mabet* result not from the fabled curse of *Macbeth* but from attempts to discover or to protect "the secret of Montfort."

In a vertiginous example of postmodern border crossing, text and intertext, reality and illusion, fiction and fact keep shifting. Indeed, the French government suspects that Germany has mistaken the battle scenes rehearsed for *Citizen Mabet* for actual military maneuvers. Paradoxically, André never actually films the battles, abandoning the artifice of war as pageantry and adventure—the air "full of banners," the costumes "glittering," the soldiers "shouting and charging"—in favor of the "nothing," the death, which is the reality of war: "Bloody stumps for hands. Bloated faces. Blood-soaked uniforms. . . . André films the dead for two days. They lay in piles in the hot sun, among the ruined fields. . . . Motionlessness, silence, bodies, broken hay" (290). In contrast, Bastille Day, the national holiday whose celebration marks the center of the novel (229–41), is not only pure theater but pure "Théâtre Cyron" complete with army revue, booming canons, patriotic speeches, flag waving, and shouts of "Vive la France! Vive la République!"

The last scene that André shoots for *Citizen Mabet* lies at the most complex intersection of appearance and reality. Announced as factual by the newspaper heading that precedes the novel, the long-awaited episode, narrated in the present tense, resembles the shooting script of a movie when it finally occurs. Indeed, the guillotining of the wife of Citizen Mabet is meant to be the "marvelous illusion" that André initially believes his camera has recorded (313). But when the "severed head" of the actress playing the role turns out not to be a prop, the director stands accused of the murder of his own wife, whose life he has in fact publicly threatened a few days earlier, albeit in an effort to provoke the expression of horror he needs for another scene of the movie. Since Sabine's reaction does not stem from fear of her husband but rather of his discovery that she has murdered three people, her own death could be interpreted as an execution as lawful as that of the character, patterned on Lady Macbeth, whom she portrays in *Citizen Mabet*. In fact, although official France is directly involved, Sabine is killed and André framed for the sole purpose of protecting "the secret of Montfort." As in the story of the Dreyfus Affair, the second most important of the textual references that circulate throughout *The Citizen of the Country*, both André and Sabine are the victims of a military "plot," conceived as fiction as much as conspiracy (see, for example, 388, 392). Ultimately, Cyron the soldier/hero and Cyron the actor/director prove to be indistinguishable and interdependent. The "sense of France" that Cyron claims to be "rebuilding" at Montfort (66) is as illusory as the fortification whose hidden entrance Reisden finally discovers in the lowest cellar of the castle: "Cyron's secret was a tunnel or a fortress. . . . But it doesn't exist. That's all there is to it, an entrance. A stage set. There is no secret of Montfort. . . . Cyron hadn't built a fortress. He'd built a mystery" (365).

In reality, *The Citizen of the Country* does have a secret to reveal, and place remains key to the resolution of the mystery. Like Macbeth, Cyron too is a usurper, less because he adopts André solely to gain possession of Montfort than because he falsely claims to represent France. The internal story of nation tied to the adaptation and production of *Citizen Mabet* is, of course, contained within a larger narrative of nation aptly entitled *The Citizen of the Country*. Smith uses metaphor not only to reflect both the constructed and the imaginary nature of nation and nationality but also to construct an imaginary model of her own better suited to the globalized universe of the twenty-first century. Below the artificial space of theatrical performance and illusion lies the geographical expanse of the contemporary world. Smith's "theatre du monde," her theater of the *world*, unfolds in Flanders, "land fought over since Roman times" (232). A historically independent region made up of parts of France, Belgium, and the Netherlands, Flanders, whose very existence depends upon the erasure of national boundaries, serves admirably to represent a contemporary Europe currently under construction. Similarly, although Cyron still conceives of national politics through a dated scenario whose only characters consist of France and Germany engaged in a "private war" (253), France has in fact joined the world; as a result of her strong alliances with England and Russia, she has recreated herself beyond the nation-state as "the key to Europe" (21). Indeed, in Smith's novel France faces an international conflict whose theater of operation extends well beyond Europe, originating in America (246–47) and reaching into northern Africa (122–23).

Ironically, Cyron's real secret makes him an ideal "citizen of the country," a place that Cyron wrongly limits to the countryside, the *terroir*, of a mythical *France profonde*. Cyron's nostalgia for a home that was never his to return to dismisses the myth of nation he represents as mere propaganda, an ideological fiction. Icon of a France that no longer exists, if it ever did, Cyron is less "national symbol" (377) than postmodern metaphor, an empty signifier, whose life, like that of Macbeth, has become "a tale / Told by an idiot, full of sound and fury / Signifying nothing."[71] The self-referential final shot of *Citizen Mabet* captures Cyron staring silently into the camera, "a puzzled old soldier . . . wondering why he is still onstage" (411). Appropriately, citizenship itself is Cyron's tragic flaw. Born in Alsace, he failed to "declare himself still a French citizen" after Germany annexed the province in 1871 (394). To admit to himself that he is German would force Cyron, "our French hero," to see himself as France's enemy, a spy and a traitor to his country. In the larger context of Smith's novel, however, Alsace, like Flanders, represents a newly conceived sense of citizenship and country more appropriate to the globalized world of postmodernity. As an Alsatian, Cyron is both French and German, already by birth a citizen of an emergent Europe.

That Reisden is the one to guess Cyron's secret should not surprise us. The truth he states to Cyron—"You're German. The way my wife is Austrian, who's American, and I'm Austrian, who am Parisian" (395)—emphasizes at once the arbitrariness and hence the fluidity of national identity within global postmodernity. The man without a homeland, the permanently displaced person perpetually "cast as the foreigner" (66), and who remains "lost between lives" in *The Citizen of the Country* is best placed to redefine the meaning of nationality and nation. In keeping with the quotation from Rainer Maria Rilke, which serves as an epigraph to the novel, Reisden will choose to become a "citizen of the country": "We are born, so to speak, provisionally, it doesn't matter where. It is only gradually that we compose within ourselves our true place of origin." In direct contrast to Cyron's idealized devotion to the place of his birth, resignation and practicality lead Reisden to apply for French citizenship; France is "as good as [he and Perdita] shall have" (231) and, more importantly, it is simply where he lives (132, 413).[72] If, as Reisden suggests, it can also become "[his] country" because he and Perdita have "made" it together (369), in Smith's novel the postmodern world nonetheless becomes home only to those who remain effectively homeless, as Perdita's evolution reminds us. She is "sadly relieved" to discover that she no longer belongs in America: "Now she could go back to Paris homeless, ready to find a home" (93).

Thus, in the final novel of Smith's trilogy, the cosmopolitan space of Paris we encountered in *The Knowledge of Water* has expanded to fill all of France. Virtually every character who merits mention is one or more of the following: orphan, refugee, foreigner, expatriate, adoptee, spy, naturalized citizen, temporary resident.[73] Reisden, whose very name appears to mark him, by design or by chance, as the latter, has been, is, or will be all of these.[74] Wherever he resides, Smith's hero will be John Tomlinson's cosmopolitan "citizen of the world";[75] he has achieved the identity T. S. Eliot once attributed to Henry James, whose own international novels at the turn of the century forged the path for those of contemporary American writers: "It is the final perfection, the consummation of an American to become, not an Englishman, but a European—something to which no born European, no person of any European nationality can become."[76]

In the final chapter of *Dangerous Pilgrimages*, devoted to "transatlantic fictions today," Bradbury moves beyond character and author to describe the contemporary international novel itself as "an instinctively cosmopolitan and wandering form."[77] *The Citizen of the Country* offers one significant example of the structure of such a work. The final novel of Smith's trilogy resembles what Alison Russell calls a "nomadic text," characterized by its reliance on an understanding of space as "an interlocking network of 'lines' or 'ways through' " rather than "a block of land hemmed in by frontiers."[78] The landscape of Flanders, whose borderless geography already subverts traditional notions of national boundaries, is supported underground by "dark mazes" of tunnels whose branches stretch throughout the region (271): "At the center of each, like a spider in its web, were the Arras boves. Outward from them radiated various configurations. . . . Four long, optimistic, Haussmann-straight tunnels in the form of a cross. A tunnel under the Arras road. A tangle of tunnels connecting underground . . . " (345). After Sabine's murder, Reisden and André take refuge in this paradigmatic space in which they remain hopelessly lost for days. They wander back and forth in search of a "way through," much as Smith's own narrative moves between Perdita's travels in America and Reisden's trip to Flanders, consistently adopting a strategy of doubling back before moving forward as the narrative alternates between different places and different perspectives. Reisden's self-reflective commentary on the novel he is in describes the intricate narrative and intertextual maze of *The Citizen of the Country*: "Like pieces of different puzzles mixed together, different stories, each trying to make itself the only puzzle, the only story" (402).

Russell connects the nomadic narrative, in which the description of traveling replaces the portrait of place, to "the process-oriented maneuvers of postmodernism."[79] Smith's narrative is similarly and insistently process-oriented, figured most significantly by the endless and never-ending construction of Montfort but also by a war that "had been going on for a century" with no definitive victories or defeats (20). The tunnels into which Reisden descends at the end of the novel are similarly placeless and timeless. Of unknown origin, they too have been under constant transformation for hundreds of years: mined by the Gauls, the boves contain a pre-Revolutionary ossuary as well as a Holy Well and enigmatic sculptures believed sacred both to pagan religions and to modern witches.[80] In this space, Reisden will relive the murder of his grandfather in a hallucinatory fantasy that combines past, present, and future. Still disoriented, dislocated, out of place, Reisden emerges from this space that is at once museum, maze, and madhouse into the open-ended country of Smith's "theatre du monde." The final pages of *The Citizen of the Country* offer neither happy endings nor permanent answers, but the principal resident of this world has come to terms with the anxiety of contemporary life: "Not live happily ever after, not know all the answers . . . no solution but a dilemma, a house half-finished, something always needing fixing; too big, half-explored; something to live up to, to grow into; home. The place where one lives" (413). Wilde describes such a willingness to live in suspension, indecision, and uncertainty as essential to the representation of postmodernity: "Tolerating the anxiety. It is a reasonable, if not complete, definition of the postmodern sensibility."[81]

8
The Re-Zoning of Gay Paris: Edmund White's *The Married Man*

AT ABOUT THE SAME TIME THAT THE HEROINE OF DIANE JOHNSON'S *LE Mariage* laments the seemingly unrelenting determination of Americans to write books about France,[1] the narrator of yet another, Philippe Tapon's *A Parisian from Kansas* (1998), yearns to join them:

> I look across the table at what I might one day become: the expatriate American writer enjoying a sizeable reputation in Paris, living mildly and elegantly on the Left Bank, writing distinguished scholarly books and essays about literary Frenchmen and America.[2]

Tapon's portrait of "Edward Gray," instantly recognizable as Edmund White, appropriately pays tribute to a contemporary American writer whose fourteen-year stay in Paris (1983-97) provides the background for his most recent novel. Moreover, given the complex set of texts and textual relationships that determine the context for our reading of *The Married Man* (2000), it seems almost inevitable that White should turn up as a fictionalized character in someone else's English-language novel set in Paris even before he becomes the model for the hero of his own.[3] In what might be described as a personal illustration of the broader pattern of recent Anglophone writing about France, White himself offers a number of alternative and interrelated versions of such texts. As he rewrites the narratives of the American in Paris and of cross-cultural romance that we first encountered in Johnson's *Le Divorce*,[4] White tells the same story repeatedly and in different forms and genres. Most fully developed in *The Married Man*, a third-person novel, selected elements or variants of the whole also figure prominently in a memoir, *Our Paris: Sketches from Memory* (1994); the final volume of a first-person "autofictional" trilogy,[5] *The Farewell Sym-*

phony (1997); Stephen Barber's authorized biography, *Edmund White: The Burning World* (1999); and a literary essay, *Le Flâneur: A Stroll through the Paradoxes of Paris* (2001).[6] As a work in which gay characters figure prominently, *The Married Man* is further representative of what has begun to emerge as a distinctive subcategory within Anglophone fiction about France, including, in addition to Tapon's novel, Patricia Duncker's *Hallucinating Foucault* (1996), Matthew Stadler's *Allan Stein* (1999), and Monique Truong's *The Book of Salt* (2003).[7] From the beginning, then, *The Married Man* exists in a peculiarly postmodern space, at once everywhere and nowhere, in and in between a number of different texts.

It is not coincidental in that case that I began this chapter, as I did this book, by invoking the work of Diane Johnson. If the prominence of *Le Divorce*, nominated for a National Book Award in 1997 and released as a major motion picture in the summer of 2003, has been instrumental in focusing attention on the renewed importance of France in contemporary English-language fiction, Johnson's *L'Affaire* (2003) is also the most recent example of the phenomenon to date.[8] Prior to his tour as Edward Gray, White inspires the character of Ames Everett in *Le Divorce*; and *The Married Man*, the title White subsequently chose for his own contribution to the emergent trend, seems clearly designed to evoke and echo that of Johnson's *Le Mariage*.[9] Certainly White and Johnson, personal friends as well as colleagues familiar with each others' work,[10] are interestingly, if superficially, alike in a number of ways. Both were highly respected writers with well-established careers prior to the mid-nineties when each began to write about Paris. *The Married Man*, like Johnson's last three novels, can be described as a relatively traditional comedy of manners; and the recent work of White and Johnson frequently invites comparisons not only between the two writers, but also, significantly, of both novelists to Henry James. Although Johnson still spends at least a few months a year in San Francisco, she has lived the better part of the last eight years in Paris so that she and White together are no doubt best positioned to fulfill Tapon's desire "to maintain the reputation of American expatriate writers living in Paris" (317). *The Married Man* thus offers a particularly suitable context in which to explore the state of contemporary literary globalism a final time; the similarities and differences between White's and Johnson's work suggest patterns of both continuity and change that characterize recent English-language fiction set in France.

Reflecting the composite it forms with its companion texts, *The Married Man* is itself internally eclectic, at once a love story, a portrait of Paris, a social satire, a cross-cultural comparison, an AIDS chronicle, a semiautobiographical portrait of the author, a psychological mystery, and a travelogue. In an elementary plot based on White's own relationship with Hubert Sorin and summarized by one reviewer as "one of the greatest boy-meets-boy stories ever,"[11] Austin Smith, a middle-aged American writer living in Paris, falls in love with Julien, a much younger French architect in the process of divorcing his wife. Although Julien pledges to care for Austin, who has been HIV-positive for at least three years, in fact it is Austin who will nurse Julien through a series of painful and debilitating illnesses until his death from AIDS. Narrated in the third person from Austin's perspective and set in 1989–90, the novel encompasses the brief period of Austin's and Julien's union. Characterized by description far more than action, *The Married Man* essentially paints a detailed picture of the daily life of a couple.

Curiously, despite the desperate march toward death that determines the structure of the novel as a whole, *The Married Man* is far less concerned with the passing of time than with the passage through space. Indeed, as any possibility of a future recedes into the distance, White's characters travel ever farther and faster. In the course of the novel, Austin and Julien visit six countries (France, Mexico, Italy, Canada, Morocco, and the United States) on three different continents; and in each geographical location they inhabit so many different abodes that the couple appears to be constantly moving as well as on the move. Although the multiple settings of the novel suffice to make clear the general importance of spatiality, we are alerted to the specific significance of place in *The Married Man*, the dynamics of interior and exterior, by an unusually consistent pattern of professional training and expertise that unexpectedly links the novel's characters. No doubt there is nothing remarkable in the fact that Austin, an art historian who is writing the definitive book on eighteenth-century French furniture, should fall in love with Julien, an architect, even if they meet by chance in a gym. But Peter, Austin's former partner, is an interior designer who also has a degree in the history of furniture, and "Little Julien," the current Julien's most immediate predecessor, is a law clerk to whom the French government nonetheless grants "a paid year's leave of absence to study furniture making" (15). That even marginal characters whose professional interests are otherwise irrelevant also fit the pattern confirms it to be a deliberate choice rather than coincidence or lack of imagination. We learn, for example, that two of Austin's friends, secondary characters in their own right, have affairs with a furniture designer and an architectural student respectively. Like Henry McVay, the wealthy collector who is the "leader of the American expatriate colony" in Paris (12), those characters who don't design, make, or arrange either buildings or what they contain tend to be the clients of those who do: "Most important, we were both connoisseurs, even if Henry *owned* the paintings and chairs he admired and Austin merely wrote about them" (28).

Clearly there are multiple ironies in this insistence on interior space in a novel that is, as we will see, centrally concerned with (re)mapping the external geography of the contemporary world. Notably, despite the growing intimacy of the couple formed by Austin and Julien, their lives are anything but "domestic" in any conventional sense of the term: they have no traditional notion of home or household nor do their interests coincide with those of a specific country—quite the opposite, in fact. The emphasis White places on training and occupation is similarly puzzling initially, given that almost no one in the novel, and especially not the two main characters, ever really practices a profession. Julien can no longer work, and Austin, essentially a dilettante who introduces himself to us as "lethargic" and "lazy, creaturely" even though he loves walking through the streets of Paris, doesn't want to (10). The hero of *The Married Man* thus identifies himself from the beginning of the novel as a *flâneur*, both a person who likes inactivity and one who likes to stroll about without purpose or destination. In keeping with a word that has no equivalent in English and is difficult to translate accurately, the *flâneur* exhibits behavior that is eminently French and, more importantly, distinctively Parisian, as White reminds us in *The Flâneur*: "more than any other city Paris is still constructed to tempt someone out for an aimless stroll" (38).[12]

Seen as a "companion piece" to *The Married Man* not only by booksellers[13] but also by White himself, who includes his own novel, described as "a paean to contemporary Paris," in the reading guide that accompanies *Le Flâneur*,[14] the two texts open up an intertextual space in which we can begin to clarify the dynamics of interior and exterior that make up one of the key "paradoxes of Paris" announced in the subtitle to *Le Flâneur*, the first volume of Bloomsbury's new series on "The Writer and the City." In his essay, itself a walking tour of contemporary Paris, White strolls through a landscape whose appearance of "superficial uniformity" and "seamless unity" create the impression of a city "without barriers" in which one finds oneself "gliding along from one area to another" as if in a dream.[15] At the same time, however, White's essay focuses extensively on the distinctive identities of particular *quartiers* of the city such as the Jewish community in the Marais and the racially mixed neighborhoods of Belleville and Barbès to the north. What White calls "this inside/outside dichotomy" of the city produces the paradox repeatedly noted by Walter Benjamin, the celebrated nineteenth-century essayist of the Parisian *flâneur*: "Just as *'flânerie'* can make an interior of Paris, an apartment in which the neighbourhoods are the rooms, so neatly marked off with thresholds, in an opposite way the city can present itself to the stroller from all sides as a landscape stripped of all thresholds."[16]

Julien and Austin experience this contradiction most intensely in *The Married Man* when their unexpected return to Paris four days after they move away temporarily positions them outside real time and space. Once residents, now "ghosts who'd come back to haunt their former lives," they abandon their "ghostly" apartment to live outdoors in an equally "ghostly" city, whose phantom landscape reinforces its metaphoric importance. Austin and Julien "just wal[k] and wal[k], visiting all their favorite places," moving effortlessly and immediately from one to another. In this fantasy decor, the paths of the Jardin des Plantes appear to lead directly beneath the Louvre's pyramid, into the Sainte Chapelle, and along the Rue de Rivoli, as if these sites were paradoxically situated in a continuous path, contained within a common surface area, or both at once. Under the Rivoli arcades, once again they "wal[k] and wal[k]," passing through a space of diversity—past "rich Arabs, "old tourists from the provinces," "gypsy girls," waitresses, tailors, and English booksellers—to emerge into "the immensity of the Place de la Concorde," whose surrounding circle of statues appropriately encloses "the cities of France" within Paris itself (132–34). Moreover, Austin's concluding observation that "the eye was led up . . . to the gray skies" suggests that the central square of Paris also opens on to a much larger world.

In "The World and the Home," Homi K. Bhabha notes that "the image of the house has always been used to talk about the expansive, mimetic nature of the novel," even as he proposes that this interior, domestic metaphor may no longer suit the mobile, multicultural fictions of the postmodern world of "the unhomely."[17] Like Johnson and other mainstream novelists of contemporary globalization, part of White's originality lies in the ability to adapt the traditional novel of plot, place, and character to the expression of a changing reality. Although the overall structure of *The Married Man* is rigorously chronological, individual chapters are not internally sequenced in strictly linear fashion; as a result we not only become aware of the text as a formal construct but also of its construction as a specifically spatial entity. In White's "house of fiction,"[18] each chapter corresponds to a room filled with eclectic contents, including both a mixture of narration, description, dialogue, cultural observation, and self-reflective commentary and a diversity of people and places of varying importance.

Passing through this textual space, the experience of the reader strongly resembles that of the Parisian *flâneur*. Indeed, chapters often begin with a change of location and almost every chapter includes the description of an interior space that serves as a *mise-en-abyme* for both the fictional and the referential world. The first of these, Austin's tiny Paris apartment with its ancient stone tablets from North Africa, its curtains of "a very 1960s pattern," the Austrian landlady's collages, and its jerry-built appliances, is openly metaphoric: "scaled more for a doll's house than human habitation" (10). Similarly, the *dacha* Austin takes Julien to visit in Deauville "look[s] authentic from the outside," much like the ostensibly conventional novel we are reading, "but inside it was a charming hodgepodge of stained-glass windows from Morocco, low settees from Edwardian America, stag's antlers on the wall, a white porcelain stove from Sweden and, scattered on every table surface, hundreds of framed turn-of-the century photographs of Slavic aristocrats."[19]

In both of these cases, the geographical expansion figured by the diverse national origins of each dwelling's furnishings is enclosed within a self-contained interior space representative of both the novel and the contemporary globalized reality to which it refers, in a pattern we have consistently encountered in Anglophone novels set in France. In the particular dialectics of "world and home" that characterize White's work, the privileged figure of the island repositions the autonomous space of the house within the world itself. In Paris, Austin lives on île Saint-Louis, viewed simultaneously as an expatriate haven—"Americans always gravitated to the île Saint-Louis"—and his own private property, "his poetic island" (8). When he leaves the île Saint-Louis, the island within the city, Austin favors two parallel locations: Venice, the city that is itself an island, and Key West, the city on an island of the same name.[20] In contrast to other novelists of globalization who emphasize the crossing of boundaries, White foregrounds a space in which territorial borders are entirely eliminated and, with them, the stability of nation and national identity that frontiers exist to define. Venice, notably, is both "the drawing room of Europe" and "a crowded museum" full of English aristocrats, French decorators, and Milanese businessmen (102–3); the island's "mysterious topography" is typified by street signs that direct you at once right and left to reach a single destination (98). Moreover, in *The Married Man*, a novel that centers on travel, White transforms the world into a succession of insular places, appropriately reminding us that "island" is also a transitive verb.

John Tomlinson borrows the term *deterritorialization* from the French anthropologist Marc Auget to describe the way in which globalized modernity replaces "real localities" or "anthropological places" with "non-places."[21] In *The Married Man* Austin and Julien spend their entire lives in and in between the anonymous, transient, interchangeable islands of postmodernity. The novel opens among strangers in an urban health club and ends on a plane in mid-air, literally in a state of suspension. In the interim, Austin and Julien pass through a series of nameless hotels and hospitals, pausing only briefly in the equally impersonal setting of the furnished apartments and houses they temporarily rent or borrow. Ultimately, they spend as much time in cars, trains, and airplanes as they do in fixed locales; and the hotels where they stop, characteristically isolated from the local population, might be anywhere and yet, at the same time, are nowhere at all. In a trip through Mexico, for example, they stay in a brand new hotel, whose dark, empty rooms are sparsely populated by tourists "speaking French Canadian" (155). Farther down the coast, they pass massive hotels that stand out against their surroundings like "battle stations that had just landed from alien solar systems" (155). Finally, they arrive at a luxurious rented house in a gated compound whose well-lit suburban streets are all "named in English after North American birds (Robin, Bluebird, Oriole)" (156). The Mayans who inhabit the region are nowhere to be seen, but neither do White's characters dwell in any recognizably North American space.

Not surprisingly, airports, and particularly their departure lounges, figure prominently in Auget's conception of non-places as "places of solitude (even in the presence of others), silence, anonymity, alienation, and impermanence," "places where interaction is instrumental and 'contractual' . . . lifted out of any organic relation with a community."[22] *The Married Man* contains a paradigmatic example of such a place in which the waiting room has expanded to fill the entire airport (114–24). Justin, having "given up his wife, his apartment, his country and his language" to emigrate to America (124), never gets out of the Boston airport. In a country where "we're all immigrants" according to Austin (114), he and Julien are promptly separated at the Immigration desk. Unable to extract any information from the mysterious American official who insists on speaking to him in French—"It seemed grotesque that two Americans in America were speaking French to each other" (122)—Austin is left in a kind of limbo; paradoxically, having finally returned "home," he spends his first day at the airport as if he were about to depart. When he is finally led through back corridors and deserted hallways to the guarded room where Julien has been sequestered, Austin discovers that the same customs official, now surmised to be French, has forced Julien to speak to him for hours in English only "at the end to say something in perfect French" (124). In a bizarre confusion of direction, even within a place of passage, Julien is sent back to Paris on the same plane on which he left; at the end of the day, we are back at its beginning. This Kafkaesque scenario, in which conventional distinctions between native and foreign break down and arrivals and departures become indistinguishable, serves as an apt metaphor for the ambiguous spaces of globalized postmodernity.

Similarly ambiguous, Austin's and Julien's final trip together functions both as a *mise-en-abyme* for the novel as a whole and a microcosm of postmodern experience. In the final chapters of *The Married Man*, White's version of what James Clifford calls the "new world order of mobility" is at once condensed, inverted, and exaggerated to produce a miniature mirror image of all that has come before.[23] In an increasingly ironic imitation of their previous vacations, Austin and a dying Julien set out to tour Morocco. Their off-season trip takes them once again to a series of new, modern, largely empty hotels with walled-in grounds that isolate them within and from Morocco itself, whose own streets are in any event left strangely quiet and empty by the monthlong celebration of Ramadan. The couple's single attempt to visit a local village, which is not on the "elaborate itinerary" Austin has prepared in advance (266), ends in failure when the dirt road proves impassable; and Austin's and Julien's access to Morocco is finally reduced to local television whose single channel relentlessly broadcasts the same image: "the inevitable king sitting cross-legged in the mosque" (283). Julien himself, whose illness gives him the altered appearance of "an ethnic" (264) and forces him to clothe his fleshless body in a loose-fitting caftan, and who spends more and more of his time thumbing through the "incomprehensible pages" of a used Koran (277), becomes a kind of parodic stand-in for the local population.

On the rare occasions when Austin and Julien are not the only guests in hotels and restaurants, they find themselves "self-quarantined" by the hostile gazes and "appalled silence" with which European tourists greet the sight of Julien's decaying body (273). Despite their modern facilities, the "oasis towns" through which Austin and Julien pass thus provide anything but the promised refuge from their harrowing daily drives through "hundreds of hairpin turns" toward increasingly remote locations (269). Theoretically parallel to White's preferred geographical space, in reality the oasis turns out to be the negation rather than the counterpart of the island. Despite Austin's optimistic conviction that Julien still "want[s] to go places and see things" (275), they are not only unable to complete their journey as planned but must, in fact, retrace their steps in a pattern of temporal and spatial erasure that we have seen before.[24] On the return journey, by ambulance rather than car, the former travelers have become mere passengers; and although Austin and Julien spent their final night together in yet another "bright, modern room," this one is located in the "reassuringly institutional" space of a local hospital rather than the luxurious interior of a French hotel (296). The couple's isolation from others ultimately invades their own relationship; in the hours before his death, Julien is transformed into a hostile stranger who refuses to speak to Austin. Not even death provides a definitive end to the "passages" of postmodernity. Typically, Austin misses his scheduled return flight to Paris and spends hours in the Marrakesh airport waiting for another; ten days pass before he can arrange the repatriation of Julien's body.

In contrast to the many theorists, including Auget, who are openly critical of the mobility and the transience they ascribe to the postmodern world, Tomlinson insists that the contemporary experience of displacement is characterized by ambivalence rather than alienation; postmodernity can be lived positively as well as negatively.[25] Significantly, Julien's horrible death marks neither the end of the novel nor the last episode of Austin's travels. Despite the attention paid in *The Married Man* to the uncertainties and ambiguities that clearly accompany life on the move, Austin, like White himself, is fundamentally at home—and only at home—in the postmodern space of the "not-at-home";[26] on an island, one is metaphorically both rooted and still at sea.[27] In keeping with the borderlessness and the placelessness of the geography of *The Married Man*, Austin also lacks any notion of citizenship; his self-defined sense of identity as "the foreigner in France, the expatriate in America" displays a crucial duality that positions him always beyond the boundaries of nation (130). Austin is essentially comfortable anywhere and everywhere—as comfortable, that is as anyone can be in the postmodern world of mobility.

As a result, Austin is able to lead the reader of *The Married Man* on a stroll through a fictional version of the contemporary world that repeats his walks through Paris on an international scale. "*Text* and *space* are parallel terms," notes Alison Russell, in a recent discussion of the postmodern confluence of geography and literature, and "travel narratives" construct "verbal maps" to shape the world.[28] In the fictional topography of White's self-proclaimed "novel about Paris,"[29] the city of that name functions most importantly as metaphor and metonym in keeping with the novelist's stated desire "to turn 'France' into a region of my mind."[30] In *The Married Man* White indeed transforms the "Paris" that he personally experienced as the site of "intersecting cultures" and "the dissolution of national identity"[31] into what Brian McHale calls a "zone," a distinctively postmodern textual space characterized by the juxtaposition of geographical locations that are in reality noncontiguous and unrelated.[32] Austin roams freely through the cosmopolitan setting of *The Married Man*, guided by a "verbal map" that associates Paris and Providence, connects Venice and Quebec, and juxtaposes Key West and Marrakesh, much like an earlier writer who shared White's fondness for both Paris and *la flânerie*. In the poem titled "Zone," Apollinaire creates a *flâneur* whose stroll through the neighborhoods of Paris becomes a tour of modern Europe:

> Te voici à Marseille au milieu des pastèques
> Te voici à Coblence à l'hôtel du Géant
> Te voici à Rome assis sous un néflier du Japon
> Te voici à Amsterdam avec une jeune fille . . .
> . . . .
> Tu es à Paris . . . .

(You're back at Marseille among the watermelons / Back in Coblenz at the Hôtel du Géant / You're in Rome sitting under a Japanese medlar / You're in Amsterdam with a girl . . . / You're in Paris. . . .)[33] / "Zone," derived from the Greek word for *girdle*, also specifically identifies an area that encircles or surrounds, recalling, of course, the island settings most favored by White.

Since Disney specializes in the worldwide construction of autonomous "zones" or "islands" of fantasy, we might reasonably expect Austin's reaction to Disney World to resemble Isabel's response to EuroDisney in Johnson's *Le Divorce*. Fearful of encountering an embarrassing imitation of the real-world decor of Europe, "an American dream of old-world splendor," Isabel is pleasantly surprised to rediscover America, albeit in idealized form: "I had to admit that it was nice to be back in America, especially America refined to its ideal essence." For Isabel, France itself constitutes "the make-believe world" (262–63). In contrast, from the moment Austin arrives in Providence, "an outpost of an alien culture" inhabited by "Americans," he finds it profoundly disagreeable to be "back 'home,' " a possibility immediately undermined by quotation marks within the text of *The Married Man* itself (128–30). For Austin, too, however, Disney World functions as the "essence" of America, although the "ideal" it embodies is now deeply dystopian and entirely too real.

Although Austin is initially unsure exactly where or what Disney World might be, there is never any doubt that it is somewhere in America. Indeed, Peter responds to Austin's ignorance with the accusation that he is "not even a real American" (187). Peter is, of course, and Julien, who isn't, is pointedly not invited to go along. Moreover, Peter chooses Disney World in answer to Austin's offer to take him "anywhere . . . to Paris or San Francisco or Rome or London" precisely because the resort isn't just *located* in America, it *is* America.[34] Indeed, the amusement park begins to metamorphose into the paradoxically named "fun house" when Austin encounters the signature ride whose "small world" theme explicitly identifies it as a *microcosm*—literally a "small world," from the Greek *mikros cosmos*—of America. This display, in which rows of identical mechanical dolls in different national costumes and with a variety of ethnic accents all sing the same "high wailing song about a small, small world," offers a relatively anodyne but fully paradigmatic version of the world according to Disney (189–90).

Epcot Center confirms that Peter's choice of Disney World is not a rejection but rather the fullest realization he can imagine of Austin's proposal to take him "anywhere": "It's like traveling to Asia and Africa and Europe without ever leaving America" (188). Although Peter's assertion might almost seem to describe the experience of reading *The Married Man* and other English-language novels of globalization, White in fact portrays Epcot Center as a travesty of postmodernity and its cosmopolitan narrations. In contrast to the international zone figuratively constructed within the textual space of White's novel, Epcot Center pretends to substitute America for the entire world. Similarity, a stultifying and "standardized" sameness, replaces all difference, and yet, paradoxically, simultaneously eliminates any reason to travel; stasis brings an abrupt halt to the movement that crucially defines Austin's life. He can't even drive to and from the park but must be "ferried" in "Disney buses" that make even temporary escape impossible (189). The postmodern spaces of passage that White's novel opens up beyond and in between borders have been reduced to a miniature facsimile carefully contained within the boundaries of a much too small "small world." Metaphor becomes parody at best, mimicry or mockery at worst, and the imaginary merely artificial, as crude cultural stereotyping eliminates authenticity and transforms real world spaces into a single "unreal place . . . a place that was just a hot, sunny void in central Florida" (190). Austin is understandably horrified by Peter's evident preference for "this county fair, this vile fake" over the historical reality of "the world's most civilized city":

> There they were, in "Paris," and part of "Paris" was "the île Saint-Louis," and Austin had a snobbish reaction to this silly simulacrum—the ridiculous berets and baguettes and the Edith Piaf sound track, the beveled windows

and lacquered walls containing half a café, cut open in a longitudinal section ten feet away from a baby Eiffel Tower. Austin was also frightened by it, as if it meant to suggest he'd never gotten out of America, never lived on the real île Saint-Louis for eight years.... (191)

White reminds us that the word *expatriate* refers not only to someone who resides in a foreign land but also to a person who renounces his or her native country; certainly the notion of a "homeland" would be highly antithetical to the mobility and expansiveness of Austin's postmodern identity. Johnson's relatively indulgent description of the spaces of American pop culture is consistent with her sense of herself as a fundamentally American novelist, who writes for an American audience, albeit from France.[35] In contrast, White's official biographer reports that his move to Paris marked the moment at which he began "to view himself as a European rather than American writer, both in terms of his audience and his creative preoccupations."[36] Even before White left the United States, he typically described his "ideal reader" as "an imaginary European" who understood English but did not live in America, thereby serving as "a filter, a corrective" to any narrowly American view of the world.[37] Since 1985, all of White's work, including *The Married Man*, has been published in Britain prior to appearing in the United States. The profound discomfort, which White uncharacteristically attributes to Austin while he is in "America," may also have something to do with the decision to set the novel in a period when the conformity imposed by "political correctness" has introduced the standardization of Disney World into the "small world" of the university itself. Even the benign lectures on eighteenth-century French furniture-making, which Austin has been invited to give at the New England School of Fine Arts, immediately result in official student complaints about "his sexist reading of history" and his "insensitivity to feminist issues" (136–37).[38]

Although the overall topography of *The Married Man* clearly seems ideally suited to illustrate what Emily Apter calls "postnational borderlessness," White nonetheless does not abandon the cross-cultural comparison that Apter deems distinctive of earlier "transnational paradigms" in which neither nations nor their boundaries are eliminated.[39] For White, however, people, not places, embody cultural specificity and difference so that personal relationships rather than geographical locations provide the essential context for comparison in *The Married Man*.[40] In a particularly concise and forceful expression of a principle that might well be considered axiomatic within recent American fiction set in France—and which I have therefore already quoted more than once, notably in relation to Johnson's novels—Austin asserts that "a love affair between foreigners is always as much the mutual seduction of two cultures as a meeting place between two people" (70). Initially attracted to Julien largely because "knowing him represented a total immersion into France" (68), Austin is subsequently undeterred by his own growing awareness that Julien (like any individual, Austin himself might add) is in many ways neither traditionally nor even idiosyncratically French: "Julien was an exception to the normal French way of doing things (even the assumption that such a norm existed), but with every eccentricity he confirmed or revised Austin's sense of the national character" (70).

White's focus on character and behavior, far from distancing him from the outside world, in fact provides yet another means to illustrate the paradoxical "inside/outside dichotomy" of a metaphoric Parisian landscape.[41] Indeed, the revised representation of Julien's native country, which Austin quickly substitutes for any potential challenge to Julien's "Frenchness," explicitly takes the form of the transformation of external space. Austin's relationship with Julien alters less the gender of France, already perceived as a physical terrain, than his understanding of its construction. Initially, Austin's relatively conventional view of "France as female"—tellingly configured as "the soft valley of Paris itself, lying, inviting and seductive, below the stiff male lingam of the Eiffel Tower"—reflects a human world in which men play "the duller role." Only after meeting Julien can Austin finally see the creative movement of "male hands" working behind the scenes "like landscape architects in a formal French garden" (68–69). Upon Julien's death, Austin inevitably finds that France has once again become a foreign country: "And Austin did feel less integrated into French life without Julien. . . . without Julien he was a tourist again" (309).

Bhabha too directly connects his theory of spatial reorganization, in which "the unhomely," an "estranging sense of the relocation of the home and the world," has invaded the contemporary "house of fiction," to a reading of the construction of character and the crafting of interpersonal relationships in the novels of Henry James, whose work necessarily informs the fiction of contemporary Anglophone literary globalists.[42] White and Johnson, in particular, are openly and frequently compared to James, who thus serves to bridge the textual space between them as well.[43] Bhabha singles out *The Portrait of a Lady*, the novel that provides much of the intertextual scaffolding for Johnson's *Le Divorce*, to illustrate his argument: "As Isabel [Archer] struggles to survive . . . , James introduces us to the 'unhomeliness' inherent in that rite of 'extra-territorial' initiation—the relations between the innocent American, the deep, dissembling European, the masked emigré—that a generation of critics have named his 'international theme.' "[44] White's own statement of intentions reveals an identical understanding of James's subject matter as well as the specific desire to reproduce it once again: "I wanted to give the experience of what it's like for a very open American to live with a very enigmatic French man, which is a theme Americans have been writing about since Henry James."⁴⁵

The lexical changes evident here—from "innocent" to "open" and "dissembling" to "enigmatic"—rightly suggest a somewhat less consequential version of James's "international theme," once again positioning *The Married Man* and its characters in an intermediary space, in between *The Portrait of a Lady* and *Le Divorce*. Certainly, Austin considers "his kindness" one of his most appealing cultural traits—the complement, in fact to his American accent—and he is a remarkably generous friend, even if his liberality is fundamentally motivated by his own, perhaps not entirely un-American, need for "constant transfusions of interest and affection" (3–4). Similarly, prior to becoming Julien's "primary caregiver," Austin has lived the "unbelievably carefree" life of "a kid." Leading such a life in Paris, however, has also magically conferred "the weight of an artistic pursuit or a proof of civilized elegance" on his irresponsible American "boyishness" (236). In general, Austin's years of living in between have brought him some understanding of how his own national characteristics appear to others:

> Since moving to Europe he'd come to doubt his democratic frankness, his "transparence," as the French called it as though it was no more interesting than a clear pane of glass. He'd learned not to blurt out whatever happened to be passing through his mind.... If another American called out anything in a loud, unironic voice, he'd exchange amused but slightly alarmed glances with his French friends—can humankind bear so much candor? he seemed to be asking. (38)

Austin, then, unlike either Isabel Archer or Isabel Walker, has learned not only to identify but, more importantly, to control certain behaviors of the "innocent American" prior to his unsettling encounter with the "dissembling European."

Since Julien does indeed dissemble, White's choice of the term *enigmatic* to describe him is of special interest. The model and motifs of the mystery novel may be far less visible in *The Married Man* than in the recent work of Johnson and Tremain, for example, but neither are they entirely absent; in particular, they inform the character of Julien and structure his relationship with Austin. Almost nothing that Julien says about his past is true, and yet, in keeping with both the self-reflexivity and the ambiguity of many postmodern detective novels, he is characterized less as a liar than as a creator of fictions. This man, who proclaims a love for "artifice" reminiscent of the excesses of Joris-Karl Huysmans's Des Esseintes (30),[46] invents a false "family chronicle" that he continually embellishes: "Day after day Julien told Austin the story of his family" (76). Although a story can, of course, be true, Austin clearly suspects—and, more importantly, allows us to realize—that Julien's memories are largely autogenerative fabrications, more faithful to a narrative tradition than to the facts of a particular life. When Austin first hears Julien's favorite tale of his mother's suicide, he immediately dismisses the possibility that Julien might be "a reliable narrator." Unlike "an impartial, objective American, respectful of the truth," Austin describes the Frenchman as "a passionate Latin male . . . whose voice hypnotized his mind into believing whatever it had proposed and was elaborating " (44–45). Austin, in contrast, identifies Julien's narration as melodramatic cliche: "Austin thought he'd heard the same story all his life, about the young mother" (45).

Yet, despite this moment of insight and occasional impatience with "all the mystery" that surrounds Julien (81), the cross-cultural distinction that Austin introduces between narrators of different nationalities does not finally extend to their audience. In general, Austin so willingly practices the suspension of his disbelief that he is the ideal reader of the text authored by Julien, even if Austin's tendency to ignore or dismiss a number of clues that Julien is not who he pretends to be simultaneously undermines him as a detective. Just as Julien's thin, pale, acned appearance on first meeting belies his implausible accusation to have contracted AIDS from Austin, so such behavioral inconsistencies as "his sudden, utterly fake booming laugh, so out of character" paradoxically expose Julien as a fraud at the very moment when he may actually be most natural (41). Linguistic signs accompany the physical evidence; Austin himself favors such expressions as "looked like" and "resembles" in attempting to ascribe to Julien the noble heritage to which he lays claim.[47] Austin even manages to overlook what his own eyes tell him is patently false. Christine, Julien's ex-wife, may be sporting an "unexpected punky look" when Austin meets her (64), but she is anything but the "grotesquely fat and vulgar" woman described by Julien (30). Like any knowledgeable reader, Austin authenticates Julien's story, despite its evident discrepancies and omissions, by citing a plausible parallel in classical French literature: "it was Baudelaire . . . who was speaking through his lips . . . he was echoing (at least to Austin's ears) Balzac's Lucien de Rubempré" (70). Only after Julien's death does Austin finally confront the fact that "everything Julien had said about his family had been compounded of lies" (306). Even then Austin resents the deception far less than he regrets the loss of the illusion "as if the only thing that had raised them all above the ordinary was existing in Julien's consciousness, exactly as if his mind had been a stage ... and they'd been allowed to appear on it only as figments of Julien's imagination" (309).

In *The Farewell Symphony*, the unfinished account of the same relationship that is fully examined in *The Married Man*, White's narrator notes the linguistic fusion that the French language introduces between loving (*avoir une histoire*) and narrating (*raconter une histoire*): "The French call a love affair a 'story,' *une histoire*, and I see getting to it, putting it down, exploring it, *narrating* it as a challenge I may well fail."[48] In a reflection of this idea in *The Married Man*, Austin hypothesizes shortly after meeting Julien that his continued attentiveness to a narrative he has already heard a number of times must mean that "he's a little bit in love with Julien; how else could he concentrate on all these stories?" (76). Similarly, Austin ultimately justifies their fictionality as proof of Julien's love for him: "Poor Julien, Austin thought. He felt he had to lie in order to appear worthy of me" (306). If reciprocal affection no doubt influences both Austin and Julien, the behavior of the two men nonetheless continues to unfold in a national, rather than an individual, context, in keeping with White's conviction that "a love affair between foreigners is always as much the mutual seduction of two cultures as a meeting place between two people" (70). That Julien must dissemble to be acceptably French and that Austin will be a willing collaborator in this deception, "constantly applying more and more layers of mythic lacquer to his idea of Julien" (70), is clear from the beginning of their relationship. When Julien mistakenly identifies the *blanquette de veau* that Austin has spent all afternoon preparing as pike in a *beurre nantais*, he decides not to correct his new friend: "that would destroy the illusion they both fostered that Julien, as a Frenchman, knew everything about food, wine and fashion" (51).

Originally the word *seduction* had specifically spatial connotations (derived from the Latin *seducere*, to lead away or "astray"), and Austin, who has lived in France for years, is nonetheless "unhomed" by the particular version of a Frenchman that Julien chooses to impersonate. Although Austin claims to have "learned to sneer at his American infatuation with titles," his failure to verify Julien's assertion that his family belongs to "Minor nobility. *La petite noblesse*" clearly has far less to do with his habitual laziness that with his continued fascination with aristocratic origins (80). That this obsession with "old France" (*la vieille France*) is indeed a specifically American idea of authentic Frenchness is confirmed by his friend Joséphine's incomprehension: "God, Joséphine, sometimes I have the feeling *I'm* the Frenchman and *you're* the American. You know, Old France, proper, stuffy, *comme il faut*" (35). Although—or perhaps *because* —Austin, as we know, is fundamentally a traveler, fully at ease in the indistinguishable mass-reproduced "non-places" of postmodernity, he seeks the incarnation in Julien of exactly the opposite: the *terroir* (both *soil* and *region* in English), *la France profonde*, the static, rooted, traditional, agricultural heartland of the nation. Austin decides that all of Julien's tics and habits are "rooted in the soil of *'la douce France*,' a soil he so cherished that he . . . could still go misty-eyed once *la campagne* and *les paysans* entered into the conversation" (69). On this occasion, Austin appropriately cites a novelist reputed for her lyrical descriptions of rural France to position Julien within an ongoing tradition: "Austin was reminded of Colette's Julie de Carneilhan . . ." (69).

In keeping with Benedict Anderson's highly influential notion of "imagined communities," the relationship between Julien and Austin provides an extended fictional illustration of the constructed nature of national identity and of the imaginary or metaphorical character of nations.[49] In contrast to Anderson, however, *The Married Man* emphasizes that nation and national identity at the turn of the twenty-first century are no longer either the sole creation or the private possession of the citizens of a given country; neither are they developed in isolation from and without the participation of other nations. Consistent with the displacement and "deterritorialization" that distinguish the postmodern world, White suggests that traditional notions of national character may be perpetuated less as relics of domestic nostalgia than as stereotypes that spring up in an in-between space of "mutual seduction between two cultures." Once Julien moves to Providence, he adopts a new public role, one better suited to appeal to Americans whose only trip to "France" has taken place at Disney World. Without ever having been to Epcot Center himself and prior to Austin's visit, Julien recreates its semblance in Providence. Having located "something that resembled a café," Julien sets out after "an elaborate toilette" to spend every afternoon "sipping his coffee" or "reading a two-day-old copy of *Le Monde*" (165). Initially unnerved because no one in the café ever looks at him, he finally meets Lucy, who falls for his "French allure" and begins to say " '*oui, oui*,' in the midst of an English sentence" in the belief that she has learned French from Julien (181). As Austin notes, "Americans had lost interest in the game of high culture. Europe concerned them not at all except as an optional but fun theme park" (180).[50]

Julien's silences, in contrast to his lies, concern his sexuality rather than his nationality, but the two function similarly in *The Married Man* to keep

White's characters both on the move and within the intermediary spaces of postmodernity. Indeed, the French language uses an explicit metaphor of travel to refer to Julien's ambiguous sexual orientation: "'And do you really like to travel both by sail and steam?' (*voyager à voile et à vapeur*)," a stranger asks him at a party, using "the French way of referring to bisexuality" (90). In an exploration of the cultural history of the discourse of AIDS in France and the United States, David Caron observes that the modern gay man "has been constructed as essentially cosmopolitan and an unstoppable border crosser" (106), and he concludes that "the 'gay lifestyle' is emblematic of *mondalisation*."[51] It would obviously be difficult to imagine more exact descriptions of Austin Smith and *The Married Man* than those fortuitously provided by Caron. Moreover, White's novel also offers a fictional corrective to the real-world consequences that Caron envisions. He argues that the attribution of the AIDS epidemic to "the unprecedented mobility of the world's populations in the late twentieth century" and, more specifically, to "the alleged cosmopolitanism of gay men," has undermined the very notion of mobility and resulted in the worldwide reinforcement of national borders.[52]

In *The Married Man*, in contrast, AIDS, already a specifically modern disease, becomes a postmodern one as well. "AIDS-restlessness" (226), as we have seen, turns Austin into a multidimensional representative of the contemporary world: at once *flâneur*, expatriate, traveler, stranger, tourist, and homeless person, Austin has become a citizen of a universe whose interconnectedness has erased both internal and external boundaries, metaphorically transforming global geography into an accessible island. For Austin, moreover, who has been HIV-positive for years, living and dying are essentially indistinguishable. By definition, his life unfolds in a permanent state of waiting, located in the in-between space of existence itself. If Alan Wilde is right that "tolerating the anxiety" constitutes "a reasonable, if not complete, definition of the postmodern sensibility," then Austin's remarkable ability to cope with constant uncertainty once again identifies him as the ideal representative of postmodernity.[53] So too does McHale's contention that postmodern fiction is "*about* death" in a way that differs from other novels and that "it is *always* about death" to the extent that such fiction makes ontological boundaries visible.[54] Julien's death functions traditionally to bring *The Married Man* to a close, but Austin's ongoing suspension in a "passage," once a synonym for death that now leads to it, clearly foregrounds "the one ontological boundary that we are all certain to experience, the one we shall all inevitably have to cross," even in White's otherwise borderless world.[55]

Toward the end of *A Parisian from Kansas*, the eponymous hero of Tapon's novel takes a cab to Notre Dame, hoping to die "at the point from which all Paris shoots out" (325). In actuality, all of France emanates from the square in front of the cathedral, which marks the *kilomètre zéro* (zero point) of every national road in the country. The limits imposed on the boundaries of the surrounding area matter little, however, in comparison to the image of the city itself as geographical origin and engenderer. Clifford, in the aptly titled *Routes*, also chooses Paris, the hybridic locus of "dwelling/traveling" and "a place of departures, arrivals, transits," to represent the metropolitan center as a powerful "site of cultural creation" nourished by the comings and goings of a varied group of international artists.[56] Appropriately, this is the same site celebrated by Shakespeare and Company's 2003 literary festival, held directly across from *kilomètre zéro*, and the very place from which we first set out to explore the contemporary novel of globalization.

Although Clifford draws on the experience of the Surrealists, who lived in "hotel-like transient digs" and were constantly "moving in and out of Paris" years before Austin and Julien exhibit the same behavior in *The Married Man*, White's and Clifford's metaphoric cities clearly resemble each other.[57] Nor is it surprising that other contemporary English-language novels in which gay characters play a role should have a similar setting, since Paris has been linked throughout the twentieth century to fictional explorations of homosexuality in both British and American literature.[58] Just as White transforms his imaginary Paris into the space of global postmodernity in *The Married Man*, the novel itself can stand at the figurative center of a larger textual zone, which brings together three other examples of literary globalism representative of what Clifford calls "different routes in an interconnected but not homogenous modernity."[59] In keeping with White's own fondness for *la flânerie*, I want to exit this chapter and this book by venturing briefly into an intertextual space that is no doubt still under construction.

In *The Poetics of Postmodernism* Linda Hutcheon argues that "the most radical boundaries crossed" in contemporary fiction "have been those between fiction and non-fiction and—by extension—between art and life."[60] In the case of White's most recent novel, the reader must literally cross the boundaries between fictional and nonfictional versions of the novelist's personal life, ostensibly contained in separate texts, to confirm that *The Married Man* is no exception to White's admission that he always writes "autobiographical fiction."[61] If the metamorphosis of Hubert Sorin (Barber) into "Hubert" (*Our Paris*) and "Brice" (*The Farewell Symphony*) and "Julien" (*The Married Man*) can seem a bit hallucinatory, any such impression is insignificant in comparison to the singularly unnerving experience of reading *Hallucinating Foucault*. Duncker's novel, like White's, centers on a cross-cultural love affair between two men of different ages and nationalities, one of whom dies in the end. This time the "mutual seduction of two cultures" takes place between Duncker's first-person narrator, an unnamed Cambridge graduate student, and Paul Michel, the established French novelist on whom the Englishman is writing his dissertation. From the beginning, the description of Michel, both his work and his life, is so plausible, indeed, somehow so *familiar*, that the narrator's affirmation that "everyone has heard of Paul Michel with a little prompting" is immediately more reassuring than puzzling (5). Not only does Michel's reputation as "the wild boy of his generation" correspond to a longstanding myth of the artist that has particular resonance in France (5), but his career also clearly echoes those of specific modern gay writers: Rimbaud, Genet, Artaud, in particular. Throughout *Hallucinating Foucault*, Duncker herself foregrounds the "uncanny links" between Paul Michel and Michel Foucault, already evident in the juxtaposition of their names and in the title of the novel (6).[62] It is hardly surprising in that event that Ralph Sarkonak, in the first substantive critical essay devoted to Duncker's first novel, should argue that her "metatextual homage to another writer's work" extends beyond that of both Paul Michel and Michel Foucault to embrace the texts of novelist and photographer Hervé Guibert as well; Guibert's photos do in fact appear on the cover of Duncker's novel.[63]

Nor was I immune from the fascination that *Hallucinating Foucault* exercises over its reader, what Sarkonak justifiably calls "a haunting reading experience."[64] Despite the fact that the novel is openly self-referential and entirely self-contained, despite years of training and experience as a highly critical reader, at some point I nonetheless began to doubt my own knowledge of twentieth-century French literature. Perhaps Michel had won the 1976 Prix Goncourt, since neither I—nor, I suspect, almost anyone else— now remembers who did.[65] To satisfy my curiosity, I eventually did a Web search to verify that Paul Michel was indeed a fictional creation. The story should have ended as I expected it to when no one by that name figured in the catalogs of any local or state library system. Even when a final nationwide search revealed a listing for one "Michel, Paul," I was at first simply surprised to discover that what I had presumed to be a rather common French name apparently wasn't. The author of only a single book—one published, moreover, in Germany in 1924 and therefore in the wrong place at the wrong time—the existence of this Paul Michel would clearly have been irrelevant had it not been for one extraordinary detail. Although Patricia Duncker unquestionably invented a fictional French novelist named "Paul Michel," by an eerie coincidence the only real writer of that name just happens to have written a book entitled *August Duncker*.[66] I couldn't resist requesting the book, but I was also deeply satisfied to learn that it was unavailable; only the New York Public Library owns *August Duncker* and its copy does not circulate. I have never been tempted to pursue the matter further.

Certainly I know that the mysterious connection I choose to leave unexplored is entirely the result of coincidence. Chance occurrences, however, as the Surrealists taught us, are sometimes peculiarly revealing; and in this case it is difficult to imagine a more appropriate response to *Hallucinating Foucault* than my own encounter with the "uncanny," a word that noticeably recurs in Duncker's novel. The radicalness of her challenge to the boundaries between art and life ultimately centers neither on the plausibility of the existence of Paul Michel nor on the inclusion of an imaginative portrait of Michel Foucault, although certain similarities to White's own fictional depiction of the philosopher reinforce my hypothesis of an undeclared zone of intertextual commonality. Notably, Foucault's declaration that the narrator of *The Final Symphony* is "'a real writer,' unlike him"[67] echoes the revelation in Duncker's novel that Foucault, who "wanted to write fiction," lived vicariously through the novelist Paul Michel (149). In this literal example of spatial "coincidence," White's and Duncker's characters suddenly appear to occupy the same textual space. Of far greater relevance, however, are White's descriptions of his ideal reader. The encounters for which the narrator of *The Farewell Symphony* can only yearn, "These secret meetings—unpredictable, subversive—of reader and writer were all I lived for," become the primary subject matter of *Hallucinating Foucault*.[68]

The intimate affair at the heart of Duncker's novel celebrates "the love affair between a writer and a reader" (149). If Paul Michel's attachment to Foucault—"he was the man I loved most. He was the reader for whom I wrote" (149)—provides the model for this relationship, Duncker explores it on a number of different levels, both literal and metaphoric. The narrator of *Hallucinating Foucault* introduces himself to Michel as "your English reader" (96), but his anonymous first-person voice and his fusion with his female lover, who "had read every single one of Paul Michel's books" (9), in fact allows him to represent any and all readers, including, of course, Duncker's own. In keeping with McHale's discussion of the treatment of love in postmodern fiction, the actual love affair between Michel and his reader(s) thus both renews the convention that "we 'love' the books we read" and "restores to it its full erotic connotations."[69] Moreover, even as Duncker erases the boundaries between fiction and reality to confirm the status of the postmodern novel as "an illusion-breaking art"[70]—"Writing," notes Paul Michel, "is, in itself, an act of violence perpetrated against reality" (120)—she also transforms both reader and writer into representative figures of globalization.[71]

From the very beginning, Duncker's narrator imagines his encounter with Paul Michel as "an adventure," "a voyage" (34–35), and indeed his search for the author, who has spent the last nine years in hospitals for the insane, takes him on a journey that is structured textually and geographically by his travels from England to Paris to the south of France.[72] Paul Michel himself pushes the rootlessness of an Austin Smith—or even an Edmund White—to the extreme. Although Michel theoretically inhabits a succession of "small rooms"—"He moved on, from room to room, a ceaseless, unending stream of different addresses"—he actually lives only out of doors in "the streets, the cafes, the bars, the gardens of Paris: along the canals, beneath the motorways, by the rivers" (53). Indeed, he has never been photographed indoors (111). Michel suffers, in fact, from severe claustrophobia, perhaps the postmodern disease *par excellence*, and, in keeping with the suggestive titles of his own novels, *L'Evadé* (The Escapee) and *La Fuite* (Escape), stories of men on the run, he is expert at escaping from the institutions in which he is interred: "He got out. He always does. It's one of his specialities" (89). Even at the hospital where the narrator finally tracks him down, their daily meetings always take place in the outdoor gardens. Asleep, Michel's dreams transport him to "the oceans, the deserts, endless spaces"; only "the nightmares" of his books unfold in enclosed areas (111). Most importantly of all, Michel invites us along on his travels. He casts the beloved reader in the role of "a traveling companion" who metaphorically accompanies the writer on "his long, painful journey" of creation (58), just as the narrator of *Hallucinating Foucault* literally follows Michel down the final road that leads to his death. Thus, even though Paul Michel figures at once as postmodern hero and postmodern writer, the most original aspect of Duncker's novel lies in moving beyond both creator and character to turn the reader him or herself into the perfect incarnation of the mobile world of postmodernity.

The first-person narrator of *Allan Stein* also falls in love with a text whose passionate pursuit takes him from America to Paris and then, once again, on a final desperate journey to the south of France. Only in the final pages of Matthew Stadler's novel do we learn that author and character share the same first name (248).[73] Like Stadler himself, "Matthew" is a creator of fictions—"The story in my head was not a lie but a kind of reality-in-progress" (52)—who travels to France under the assumed name and identity of his friend Herbert Widener. This superimposition of writer, narrator, and character, which turns a geographical voyage into an existential one as well, leads to further duplications within the novel. Matthew ostensibly goes to Paris in search of Picasso's sketches of Gertrude Stein's nephew, presumed to have posed in 1905 for the painter's *Boy Leading a Horse*. But the true object of Matthew's fascination is the lost child identified in the novel's title, whose metaphorical disappearance behind the painting Stadler explains by quoting the author of *The Married Man*: "His life was erased by what Edmund White calls 'the tyranny of art.'"[74] In recovering that life, moreover, Matthew's obsession for Allan Stein will fuse not only with his passion for Stéphane, the fifteen-year-old son of his Parisian hosts, but also with his own adolescent self in an example of what White, who reviewed Stadler's novel for the *New York Times Book Review*, calls "the pedophilia of autobiography."[75]

Matthew's habitual inability to resist becoming someone else repeatedly sets him "adrift in [his] chameleon instabilities" (15; see also 11, 168). Interestingly, given the importance in the fiction of globalization of spatial structures and movement through space, Matthew attributes his transformations of self to his physical surroundings; the decor determines the role to be played and provides the scenario. Appropriately, then, Matthew comes to inhabit the "big, bare room" that he discovers in "the name Herbert" (128–29) by passing through a now thoroughly familiar postmodern geography of "non-places." As if White's Disney World and its Orlando setting had somehow fused, Matthew lives in an unidentified American city whose "grand theatricality" masks particularities of time and place behind an artificial facade of "scrims and screens," which give the nocturnal skyline the appearance of "a grand, jumbled stage set for all the dramas of Western history" (14–15).[76] The Hotel Grand, where Matthew plots his escape to Paris, resembles "a staging area for some kind of theme-park ride" (28). He departs from a "torn-up and confusing" airport (58) that proves once again to be a paradigmatic postmodern place of passage, marked by "silence, anonymity, alienation, and impermanence."[77] Missing signs and even walls make the terminal difficult to locate and dangerous to navigate; noise drowns out all attempts at inquiry or conversation. Finally led to his gate by a silent woman with a "hard and expressionless" face, Matthew discovers that "everything about [his] flight had been changed." After a nightmarish trip that seems to last for "days," he arrives in Paris only to head for a hotel rather than the home of his host family; he spends the afternoon wandering through a public park and sitting alone at an outdoor cafe. This prolonged journey through an unending passageway, in which the same fusion of departure and arrival practiced by White creates a permanent space of transience—"the airport, the plane, the car, my hotel room, even the pleasant café, were in between"—ends in a "breakdown"; Matthew collapses in tears when he finally reaches his destination (58–67).

In general, the fictional typography of *Allan Stein* is characterized by a degree of abstraction that coincidentally recalls Gertrude Stein's famous description of Oakland, California: "There's no there there." Once asked "what separates one place from another," Matthew responds "other places" (8). To some extent, Paris initially seems to constitute an exception to this pervasive "placelessness" of the postmodern world. Stadler's novel is one of only four works of fiction that White includes, along with his own *The Married Man*, in the list of recommended "guidebooks about Paris" that follows *Le Flâneur: A Stroll Through the Paradoxes of Paris*;[78] and Stadler's own novel concludes with a bibliography in which guidebooks to Paris and France outnumber reference works about the Stein family. "City" also figures prominently in the title of White's review of *Allan Stein*. If White accurately attributes the narrator's "aleatory" discovery of Paris to his triple obsession with Allan, Stéphane, and his own adolescent self,[79] Matthew is nonetheless a dedicated *flâneur* who provides us with precise, detailed verbal maps of the areas of the city through which he walks or cycles. Still, a friend's account of the visit that Allan himself arranged to introduce her to Paris may provide the best illustration of the city's unique ability to function more as a metaphor of place, a site of promise, than as an actual place in its own right: "Allan took me to see Paris. We did not walk, we ran, just everywhere and through everything. . . . His chief object was not to have me see anything definitely, but just to kind of get an impression . . . just to get an idea of the possibilities of Paris" (135).

Unlike White's Paris, however, which expands in *The Married Man* to contain an entire world, Stadler's will inevitably shrink to the dimensions of a real city. The very fragility of Paris's initial appeal to the visitor's imagination paradoxically ends up forcing him or her back into "postmodernity, the new world order of mobility."[80] Stadler's characters are ultimately *errants* (world wanderers), not *flâneurs* (urban strollers):[81]

[We talked] about geography and the peculiar way in which a new place . . . is unable to resist the power of one's imagination—there is too little reality gathered there—which makes it malleable and transporting like a dream or a thinskinned fantasy that both enchants and is completely misleading to the traveler, who falls in love with it and stays, only to discover that every place is real, its intransigent bulk hidden, the airy island drift of its first appearance an illusion, and that unless he keeps moving he is trapped in a world of stubborn realities, of actual places. (132–33)[82]

The readers of *Allan Stein* travel through a universe of "sights/sites/cites" in a postmodern version of what Joanne P. Sharp identifies as the traditional destinations of Western travel writing: "The three interdependent terms of sight, site, and cite are key to the experience of travel: the privileging of the visual, the location of the traveler in key historical locations, and the intertextuality of places on the tourist trail."[83] Stadler immediately establishes the centrality of "sight/site/cite" to the experience of reading and writing about travel as well. The text of *Allan Stein* is contained between two versions of a passage that connects the view (sight) of a French landscape (site) to the words that describe it (cite). The final "vista" that Matthew sees in France becomes a "constantly returning spectacle" that at every recurrence momentarily supplants present reality: "In that breathless gap, marked by my reverie, space collapses into nothing and at the same time enlarges to monstrous, devouring proportions—rather like the panoramic view of a reader whose nose is buried in a book" (3). In the case of *Allan Stein*, panoramas of France and especially of Paris pass before us like the "sequences of pretty pictures" that Matthew traverses on his first walk through the city: "I went on through this picture book" (75–76).

In contrast to White, who juxtaposes different places to construct a textual space within *The Married Man*, Stadler combines different texts to create a portrait of a place. Despite the role played by visual art in *Allan Stein*, the fictional landscape of the novel is far less a result of déjà vu than of *déjà lu*. Given the mythic stature of the capital of France, notes Crystel Pinçonnat, any writer who chooses to describe Paris must necessarily work with or against the idealized image of the city fashioned by a long literary tradition.[84] Stadler's postmodern strategy consists of directly borrowing the prefabricated—and often unattributed—representations of others.[85] Matthew's first-person tour of present-day Paris is intercut not only with his own third-person reconstruction of Allan Stein's life in Paris but also with portions of authentic letters written by friends and servants of the Stein family. Most frequently of all, Matthew quotes lengthy passages from what we can presume to be the early twentieth-century Paris guidebooks included in the bibliography that follows the novel: "Excerpts from the following works have been quoted in the text" (255). Within the diegetic space of the novel itself, however, we have no way of knowing who or what is being quoted; the punctuation marks that define the boundaries of these passages identify only the generic presence of foreign words. Stadler not only crosses the frontier between fiction and fact, like Duncker and White, but he ultimately erases it; if "text" and "space" are already "parallel terms" in *The Married Man*,[86] reading and traveling become identical activities in *Allan Stein*.

"Books," notes Matthew, function "as portals into other worlds" (94). He boards the plane to Paris carrying at least eight of them, including, in addition to "some Henry James," no fewer than five guidebooks dating from 1900 to the present (59). The distance between the Paris airport and the city itself is not measured by anything Matthew actually sees along the highway but rather by the length of the quotation we read; moreover, this description offers a panoramic view of a perfectly symmetrical—and highly figurative—space visible only to the imagination: "'Paris is like a fruit divided into two halves by the glowing steel of the river,' [this from one of my books] 'and over each half on either side rises a height which augments the impression of immensity . . .'" (61). Gradually, texts lead to other texts rather than back to the city in which the novel is set: "'The spring in Paris, since it has fairly begun, has been enchanting.' [This from another book.] 'The sun and the moon have been blazing in emulation . . .'" (108). By the end of *Allan Stein*, during Matthew and Stéphane's flight south, reading a text, any text, definitively triumphs not only over experience but even its representation. As quotations increasingly interrupt Matthew's story at impossible moments (239, 240–41) and as he quotes from more and more different sources in ever longer sequences (242–43), we are led into an intertextual labyrinth whose undisclosed origins and arbitrarily defined borders foreground at once the postmodern autonomy of the text and the essentially textual construction of "France."

The Book of Salt focuses once again on a marginal member of Gertrude Stein's household. Binh, Monique Truong's first-person narrator, originates in the brief portrait in *The Alice B. Toklas Cookbook* of a Vietnamese man who cooked for Gertrude and Alice during their final years in Paris. Truong's novel not only resembles in many ways those of White, Duncker, and Stadler, but it also repeats the patterns we have discovered in a number of other contemporary American and British novels set in France—notably, it is a homosexual love story between men of different nationalities, a self-reflexive narrative of travel that takes place in the intermediary and impersonal spaces of postmodernity, and an allegory of nation that crosses the boundaries between fiction and reality. What I will concentrate on here, however, is the one key difference that to some extent distinguishes this novel from all those previously discussed. Whether or not Truong's new preoccupation with going home announces a more general shift of focus within the fiction of globalization, it certainly provides a fitting end to the final chapter of this book. Even Edmund White, the committed "European" expatriate whose biographer describes him as "essentially itinerant and rootless, incessantly on the move," very much like his fictional counterpart in *The Married Man*, returned to New York in 1997 and now holds a permanent teaching position at an American university.[87]

The Book of Salt begins and ends on the day on which Alice B. Toklas and Gertrude Stein, whose Parisian salon was home to American expatriate writers at the beginning of the twentieth century and whose presence continues to echo throughout contemporary Anglophone fiction set in France, finally begin their journey back to America. "They had lost their wanderlust" (4), notes the narrator, who on the same day he learns of the planned departure of his "Mesdames," receives a letter from his brother telling him too that "it is time to come home to Viêt-Nam" (8). Already Binh and Stein have in some sense delayed their return: Binh's brother responds to a letter written five years earlier, in December of 1929, when "the talk everywhere was the same: 'The Americans are going home'" (6). Even before we enter the diegetic space of the novel to find ourselves at the Gare du Nord, we discover that Truong, who was born in Vietnam, has dedicated her first novel to her father, "a traveler who has finally come home," and included a prefatory note in which she first introduces the dominant motif of the novel, the journey as a metaphor for storytelling, in her own voice: "This book was written on two islands, in two countries, three states, and five cities. It has been a trying, scary, but above all an amazing journey.... But in the end the metaphor of a journey is empty, utterly meaningless, without someplace and someone to come back home to."[88]

Binh himself, who learns from his mother that stories are "free to roam, to consider alternative routes, to invent their own ways home" (81), lives a life of forced exile in a series of places he can only temporarily consider familiar. The ships on which he spends years in limbo, metaphorically as well as literally "at sea," contrast sharply with the equally borderless but anchored settings of White's islands. Even on land, cooking paradoxically allows—and forces—Binh to continue living "like a migrating bird, a fish in a borderless sea. A blessing that is also a curse" (189). If "every kitchen is a homecoming, a respite" (19), every cook "will always be a traveler. He will always cook from all the places where he has been. It is his way of remembering the world" (99). In general, food provides one of the more optimistic contexts in which Truong explores the ambiguities of national identity. On Sundays, Toklas and Stein always heap "their memories of their America" onto their plates, apparently without noticing that Toklas's menus have come to "map the world," that her "apple pie" oozes with French custard and her "meat loaf" bathes in white wine (27).

Race, in contrast, reveals the intransigence as well as the ambivalence of national identity. Although many of Binh's French employers are "collectors" of outcasts, who revel in the story of his travels—"I grudgingly reveal the names, one by one, of the cities that have carved their names into me (16)"—and gratefully taste "a nostalgia for places they have never been" in the food he prepares, he is nonetheless disposable, easily replaceable by any other in the "long line" of former colonial subjects in exile in France: "The Algerian . . . , the Moroccan . . . , the Madagascan . . . , these are the wounded trophies who have preceded me" (19). Nor will Stein and Toklas be able to resist asking if Binh's American lover, whose mixed blood makes him an exile in the land of his birth, is a Negro: "All these years in France . . . and Lovey and Pussy are still Americans, after all. Of course, they are. . . . Of course, they are" (189).

For Binh, equally at a loss for words in French and English, language itself is "a house with a host of doors" in which he finds himself "too often uninvited and without the keys" (155). In keeping with this dynamics of interior and exterior and the construction of the text as a specifically spatial entity, techniques that also characterize *The Married Man*, Binh's narrative is structured to take the reader on a journey through a dense textual space that reflects both his travels through the world and his desire to go home. In yet another version of postmodern *flânerie*, *The Book of Salt* self-consciously meanders, continually traveling between past and present and from place to place. The use of flashback and repetition creates the paradoxical impression that we are simultaneously both moving forward and left standing still, until finally the circular structure of the novel as a whole brings us back to the quai of the Gare du Nord in a kind of "homecoming." In one of the many passages of *mise-en-abyme* that reflect at once the landscape of the narrator's life and his storytelling strategies, Binh foregrounds the primacy of space, generally characteristic of contemporary novels of literary globalism: "Time can also be measured in terms of water, in terms of the distance traveled while drifting on it. . . . When measured in this way, time loops and curlicues, and at any given moment it can spiral me away and then bring me rushing home again" (190). Not surprisingly, Binh's invented language, in which negatives and repetitions substitute for the "impromptu absences" of French words (a pineapple becomes "a pear . . . not a pear" and Basket "a-dog-not-a-dog"), functions similarly (35–36).

Only once in the space of Paris does a chance encounter with a fellow traveler from his lost homeland allow Binh to speak Vietnamese. The most important scene in *The Book of Salt*—and the narrator's most haunting memory—takes place on a bridge, in the in-between space of postmodernity: "two men on a bridge that connected us to neither here nor there" (92). Although Binh never stops searching for the man with whom he spends a single night, he does not learn the identity of his double, who calls himself "Nguyễn Ái Quốc," until the final pages of the novel. If "Nguyễn" is the surname of "almost everyone" in Vietnam, including Binh, he recognizes the combination "Ái Quốc" as clearly metaphoric of the postmodern condition: "By itself, the words mean 'love' and 'country' in that order but when conjoined they mean 'patriot.' Certainly a fine name for a traveler to adopt, I thought, a traveler whose heart has wisely never left home" (247).[89] At the end of *The Book of Salt*, Binh's own destination remains unknown: " 'What keeps you here?' I hear a voice asking. . . . as if someone has called out my name" (261). And yet, since the original meeting with the man on the bridge has transformed Paris once already into the city of "promise" in which so many other contemporary English-language novels are set, one might reasonably assume it will be able to do so again: "For a traveler, it is sometimes necessary to make the world small on purpose. It is the only way to stop migrating and find a new home" (258). In that event, Truong's vision of the global world of postmodernity may not, after all, be distinctively different from all those that have preceded.

Conclusion:
Diane Johnson's *L'Affaire*

"'I BELIEVE AMERICANS ALWAYS DO RETURN TO AMERICA,'" AFFIRMS THE French lawyer Antoine de Persand in Diane Johnson's *L'Affaire*, only to be immediately corrected by his British colleague Trevor Osworthy: "'On the contrary, They never seem to, once they taste expatriation.'"[1] Although the most recent of the three novels that Johnson has set in France since 1997 does indeed conclude with the imminent departure of its heroine, Amy Hawkins's decision to go home, far from being the inevitable consequence of national identity, fully reflects the ambiguity, complexity, and cultural confusion that is not only characteristic of the conversation cited above but also of the legal entanglements that similarly divide the two men throughout the novel. *L'Affaire* was published in the summer of 2003 at a time when at least some readers of *Le Divorce* and *Le Mariage*, in which Persand also appeared, presumably joined the many Americans who chose never to leave home to begin with as a result of the latest skirmish in "the well-known lovers' quarrel between America and France,"[2] the metaphoric fault line along which all three of Johnson's Franco-American novels are constructed. In the case of the third, however, the parallels between fiction and reality are at once explicit, literal, and unusually timely, making *L'Affaire* the particularly appropriate "final installment" in a series of essays devoted to English-language literary globalism if not necessarily to Johnson's own "trilogy" of texts set in France.[3]

In the case of *L'Affaire*, human and geological shifts combine to produce a series of cataclysms, at once natural and cultural, comic and tragic, and literal as well as figurative. Amy, a newly rich dotcom executive from Palo Alto, initially joins the "mysteriously alien" European clientele of the Hôtel Croix St. Bernard in the French Alps as part of "a personal program of self-perfection," designed not only to improve her skiing but also to introduce her to a wide range of such "deferred skills" (2–3) as cooking, speaking French, and even stain removal: "Linen had been part of her agenda from the beginning" (64). These plans, more ambitiously expressed as the resolve to acquire "culture, in its broadest sense" (31), are quickly complicated by an avalanche, attributed in the distinctively "old Europe" setting of Valméri to "vibrations from low-flying American warplanes" (7), which leaves two hotel guests—Adrian and Kerry Venn, a British publisher living in France and his young American wife—in a coma. Amy soon finds herself at the center of the personal, political, and especially cultural storm that ensues. Her friendship for fellow American Kip, Kerry's younger brother and default caretaker of his sister's baby, pits her against other Venn children—the recently arrived Posy and Rupert and the newly discovered Victoire—in the legal and medical controversy that surrounds Adrian Venn's death and the disposition of his property. At the same time, Amy's solitary status as representative American simultaneously designates her as the defender of America and as the target of growing anger at "the surly superpower" (7). When Victoire's estranged husband Emile Abboud—rising French intellectual, exceedingly attractive philanderer, and the very personification of anti-Americanism—appears on the scene, he provokes a series of new peripeteias whose consequences take the characters back to Paris where everyone's life is altered and Amy's plans undergo serious revision.

Given what one journalist calls the "relationship-flavored titles" of *Le Divorce* and *Le Mariage* and another describes as "titles that toggle easily between English and French,"[4] perhaps it was inevitable that virtually all of the early reviewers of *L'Affaire* would interpret the title of Johnson's third novel as not only similar but also similarly transparent, both in meaning and in reference, to the titles of the first two.[5] Four extramarital affairs do after all take place in *L'Affaire*, although the fact that three of them are cross-cultural, pairing lovers of different nationalities (English/French, American/German, and American/French as well as English/English), without any of them being bilingual might also serve to alert readers to the linguistic paradoxes of a globalized world in which, as Amy notes, there are a "high proportion of people who could speak English, even though they chose not to much of the time, and it wasn't conducive to her learning French" (151). Robin Crumley, a British poet irritated by the lack of interest the literature of his own country typically inspires in France, offers Amy unexpected solace in a passage that also serves as a *mise-en-abyme* of Johnson's own lexical strategy: "'They [the French] are so preoccupied by their own language, limited as it is. . . . A relatively small vocabulary, so they have to use the same word for a number of things, another sort of problem'" (138).

As no doubt befits a novel about an avalanche, the topography characteristic of *Le Divorce* and *Le Mariage* has shifted in *L'Affaire* so that Johnson's trademark spatial image of diversity within unity, most memorable in her depictions of the Paris flea market, is now subject to both expansion and contraction. In keeping with the greater abstraction evident in the vocabulary of French in comparison to that of English, accurately described by Robin above, the single-word title of Johnson's third novel encloses the highly varied contents of the fictional world as a whole.[6] In this instance, a contemporary American novel is not only set in France, but it has in some sense apparently become a French novel as well, one content to "use the same word for a number of things." The French word *affaire* refers at one and the same time to the following: something to be done (*à + faire*), a personal problem, a public scandal or controversy, a legal case, a military conflict, a business deal, a commercial enterprise, a social function, and the list goes on. In short, in the case of *l'affaire*, the word itself provides a summary of the essential concerns of the novel of the same name, ranging from Amy's program of self-improvement to her plan to fund a charitable foundation, from the recurrent cocktail parties that punctuate the plot to public outrage at America's acts of aggression, from the legal battle over Adrian Venn's will to the media attention accorded to a reported sighting of Joan of Arc, from Amy's dotcom past to Rupert's desire to start a new business.

In other words, a phrase obviously meant to be taken literally here, the title of Johnson's novel refers to almost anything and everything—with the single exception, that is, of the one thing that most readers will assume that it designates. This is not to suggest that *une affaire* is totally unrelated to romantic or sexual relationships, but the word requires qualification to embrace them in the compound nouns *une affaire de coeur* or *une affaire d'amour*, expressions, moreover, which strongly privilege emotional attachment over physical pleasure. Even in a world in which native speakers of French have to be officially instructed to say *courriel* rather than *e-mail* or *fin de semaine* rather than *weekend*, the only correct translations of the English word *affair* remain *une aventure, une intrigue, une liaison,* or *une passade*. It is a matter of considerable cultural curiosity (what we might call *une affaire*) that the English cognate, which in fact retains the multiple meanings present in its French relative, should nonetheless have come to have illicit sex as its primary association in—and only in—the language of a people characterized by Amy herself as "so uptight and prudish, so unequal to the French mood, so American" (171). But perhaps I too have been misled by the titles of Johnson's two previous novels to reach the false conclusion that *L'Affaire* once again identifies a French word. In fact, "affaire d'amour" and "affaire de coeur" figure without italicisation in between "affair" and "affect" in the third edition of *The American Heritage Dictionary of the English Language*. Moreover, Amy herself ultimately abandons all of the personal, political, financial, and cultural projects that she originally comes to France *à faire* in favor of an *affair* with Emile that gives her "after all, maybe, what she had come for" (332).[7]

Inside a novel self-generated from the postmodern avalanche of associations triggered by a single word, Amy serves as another container whose culturally eclectic contents will eventually both replicate and rival those of the novel as a whole. Initially, however, Géraldine Chastine, her "worldly" Parisian advisor (34), immediately senses that Amy's "somewhat unfilled mind" makes "a remarkable tabula rasa ripe for European impressions" (37). Nor does Amy's own view of herself appear to be distinctively different. She has in fact come to Europe in search of just such a state of mental "blankness"—"An emptiness to fill with a headier, more concentrated program of new ingredients. Haydn, French literature, antiques correctly patinated, geopolitics"— in the hope of creating "a new soup of limitless scope" (110). Although this particular list appears to reflect a traditional understanding of the acquisition of culture—or Culture—as a primarily intellectual and aesthetic endeavor eventually resulting in a fluid blend of knowledge, Amy more often imagines what she is missing as a far less coherent mixture of the theoretical and the practical, the abstract and the concrete, the *mondain* and the mundane, the specifically French and the widely global:

> What did she know about poetry, about meter and stanza form, music, tradition, masterpieces? About world religion, Hinduism, Buddhism? The white-wine glass, the red-wine glass? What was a *godet*? What was the line between despair and cynicism, between taste and vulgarity.... How to make a soufflé such as the remarkable soufflé of cheese and anchovy they had been served at dinner? (71)

In fact, the vague dissatisfaction that Amy soon experiences in France, her discovery that "culture as she had imagined it—a rich concoction of art and music discussed in old languages with assured taste—wasn't here exactly" (70), has much to do with the specifically American nature of her project to begin with. Interest in the proper restoration of antique furniture, incongruous in the conversation above, originates in a chance conversation in Seattle where Amy overhears a shopkeeper justify the sale of "stuff so overvarnished, it's ruined" by the ignorance and bad taste of "the dotcommers" who "think it ought to be shiny" (31). Paradoxically, Amy's European quest is not motivated by perceived gaps in her formal education —although there are quite enough of these to raise serious questions in the reader's mind about Stanford's commitment to the liberal arts—but rather by a curious surge of nostalgia for the lost domestic arts of housekeeping and hostessing, once passed down from mother to daughter and now the celebrated mission of a single would-be savior: "If it wasn't for Martha Stewart the whole culture would be down the drain" (3). Forced to acknowledge that she "doesn't know ironing, or how to set a table," Amy sets off to acquire this "wider store of lore usually purveyed by mothers, equated with culture itself, endangered at that" (31–32).

To arrive at a precise understanding of the notion of culture is no doubt as daunting a task as that of limiting the word *affair(e)* to a single meaning; and in this case too Franco-American differences clearly play a highly significant role. To the extent that Amy makes any progress in France, she essentially pursues an American program of self-improvement that focuses on the acquisition of skills rather that the pursuit of knowledge. "Culture" is, of course, embedded by definition in the beliefs and institutions of a particular society, and however much Amy may look like an empty vessel to European eyes, Johnson's heroine is in fact a virtual compendium of Americanness. At once ambitious, successful, earnest, sociable, spontaneous, and generous, even Amy's physical appearance seems "peculiarly American," as if her "optimist's temperament" is visibly reflected in her facial features (4). Her understandable "enthusiasm for the kind of American capitalism that had rewarded her" leads Amy to conclude that America is "the best country, hands down" (32), the core conviction that the newly American narrator of Claire Messud's *The Last Life* defines as a necessary and sufficient requirement for "being American."[8] More crassly and less consciously, though perhaps just as characteristically, Amy behaves as if money can buy anything, even as she increasingly fears, like many an American literary heroine before her, that people are attracted to her fortune rather than her person.

In keeping, however, with yet another of Amy's national beliefs—that "she would profit from making her own mistakes"—she learns that money can't buy culture (127). No matter how many specialists she hires or how many lessons she takes, French cooking is the only skill that Amy finds, at least potentially, "within her level of competence" (252). French itself, whatever its lexical deficiencies, proves to be an entirely different matter; no amount of effort will ever make Amy "sound French," let alone allow her "to assimilate mysteriously the core of cultural assumptions that went with the language" (252–53). Theoretically Johnson's protagonist, like any American, also knows that money can't buy happiness, even if Amy's encounter with this truism paradoxically results from her momentary identification with the unhappy heroine of Stendhal's *The Red and the Black*, the "seminal" French literary text she struggles to read throughout the novel (309). On the other hand, money, it turns out, can, at least indirectly, buy *un*happiness; and Amy makes the curious discovery that a hopeless love affair, promising years of future suffering, is precisely the cultural experience that will make her if not really French then at least less American. In providing an opportunity for Amy "to indulge the potentiality for emotion and passion that she knew must lie somewhere beneath her practical common sense surface," Emile allays "her greatest fear," the possibility that "she really was just a stable, contented, commonsensical person with no depths at all," that she "really was," in short, (just) an American (70).

Still, despite—or at least until—this transformative experience, Amy seems unlikely to satisfy what she considers "her patriotic duty to refute by her own example the things people were always saying about Americans" (32).[9] In *L'Affaire* Johnson offers us an essentially comic, if at times also poignant, version of the allegories of nation and national identity we have frequently encountered in other contemporary Anglo-American novels set in France. Successive European accusations that the American government has caused an avalanche, denied its responsibility, and attempted to cover up its actions are consistently met with outrage and disbelief by all of the Americans at the Hôtel Croix St. Bernard. Moreover, their position is supported by a host of alternative theories and contradictory evidence, which suggest, for example, that no American airplanes were ever near the site of the accident, although French and English ones may well have been, and that, in any event, plane vibrations, regardless of nationality, cannot trigger an avalanche. Yet, in an astonishing demonstration of American individualism and capacity for self-reproach, every single American in Valméri also comes to fear that he or she may be personally responsible.[10]

Indeed, in Johnson's third Franco-American fiction, the avalanche becomes the focus of the mystery-novel motifs evident throughout *Le Divorce* and *Le Mariage*, as the political drama of national (though certainly not cultural) accountability is absorbed into the question of "Who killed Adrian Venn?" Kip, who let out an "enormous shout" of pleasure while snowboarding above Adrian and Kerry, dreads the inevitable moment when everyone will realize "he had killed his sister and her husband" (134). Amy, who was also skiing in the area, has additional reasons, to which I shall return, for feeling culpable; indeed, if Kip merely waits for the police to arrive, Amy actively seeks to destroy the evidence of her presumed guilt. Even the mysterious Europeanized American Joe Daggert eventually admits that he was part of a party of American snowmobilers who watched the avalanche occur from "the ridge above the place the Venns had been swept away" and yet neither phoned for help nor attempted to search for survivors (338). Finally, even if Joe is right that most avalanches are set off by their own victims, that simply leaves yet another American skier, Kerry Venn, metaphorically accused of her husband's murder.

Thus, Amy's defensiveness when a Valméri cashier holds her personally responsible for the still unproven actions of her native country is obviously meant to be seen as more than a bit disingenuous and self-serving, given her customary eagerness both to defend and even to personify the country she considers "the best, hands down" (32): "As at other times, Amy felt she was being made to stand for all Americans. . . . It was stereotyping, it was profiling. . . . Not that she wasn't an American, but she was she, herself, not just a representative specimen of her countrymen. She hadn't even voted for the present president, certainly not" (139). Here, as elsewhere, Johnson explicitly identifies the story of the avalanche as a metaphor for European hostility to the war in Iraq—it is certainly not by chance that many of the guests in Valméri are Russian and German as well as French and English.[11] In this context, however, Amy's outburst much more accurately reflects the 2002–03 Franco-American conflict than does the chance remark that provokes it. As Justin Vaïsse notes, "Europhobia," and particularly "Francophobia," have recently become systematic and widespread in America, and "French-bashing" targets both the French nation as a whole and all of its citizens. In France, in contrast, as Amy's insistent defense of her voting record implicitly acknowledges, opposition has consistently focused on a particular president and his policies: "Americans have been anti-French, not anti-Chirac, whereas French have mostly been anti-Bush, not anti-American, in this latest dispute."[12]

Appropriately, and not simply because he is French anti-Americanism incarnate, it is Emile who paradoxically both imitates and exposes the readiness, however unreflective, of individual Americans to model their private behavior on their country's public policy, visible throughout *L'Affaire*. Like an ironic mirror image of anti-French Americans, Emile's persistent rudeness to Amy springs from his very identity as "a certified French intellectual" whose "dogmatic" and "unwavering" belief in "the unregenerate wickedness of America . . . naturally extended to Americans themselves" (118). Although Johnson's parody clearly recalls any number of outspoken French media personalities, from Bernard-Henri Lévy to Régis Debray, one in particular stands out as the object of American hostility. In September 2003 both Elaine Sciolino of the *New York Times* and Michael Eliott of *Time* attributed the latest round of postwar Paris bashing to American antipathy to the very person of France's foreign minister.[13] Like Amy's equally despised but also irresistible Emile, Dominique de Villepin looks "arrogant and impetuous" to American eyes;[14] far worse, however, Villepin exhibits the same physical attractiveness, articulate defense of French reason, serene self-confidence, and broad culture characteristic of Emile, who has himself risen to a position in the French government by the end of *L'Affaire*: "There is something about Dominique de Villepin, the oleaginous French minister—with his dashing good looks, his volumes of poetry, his love of the word logic—that just gets under American skins."[15] Apparently Jean-David Levitte, France's ambassador to the United States, has proven similarly irritating to at least one prominent American. Secretary of Defense Donald Rumsfield no longer accepts invitations to dine at the home of his Washington neighbor.[16]

The strongest parallel between the behavior of a fictional character and the real world actions of an international superpower originates in what also makes Amy most American. Emile momentarily seems to mistake Amy (of all people) for French when he assumes that her defense of self-improvement as "a gesture of cooperation to the world" must be "ironic," in what is certainly an example of Johnson's own irony (267).[17] On the contrary, Amy's quest for "personal roundedness" is directly linked to her determination to turn the promotion of her long-term passion, Prince Kropotkin's philosophy of Mutual Aid, into her lifelong goal (33). For Amy, moreover, nothing could be more American than a Russian prince's anti-Darwinist conviction that the survival of the human species depends upon cooperation rather than competition. Although she acknowledges Kropotkin's surprising failure to use the barn raisings and sewing bees of early American pioneers to illustrate his theory, they nonetheless constitute in her mind "superb American examples" of "a rooted behavior" whose roots Amy clearly locates in America (32).

Thus, when Amy realizes that her money will allow her to pay for a medevac plane to transport Adrian Venn to the London hospital where his English lawyer has told her he can be saved, she naturally leaps at this chance to perform "a Karmic gesture in the service of mutual aid" (126). Much like Henry James's Isabel Archer, whose textual presence was already evident in *Le Divorce*, Amy too wants to be "of use." As naive as

Isabel is innocent and equally idealistic, Amy is also "a young person of many theories" and almost no experience of the world, a combination that will once again lead a wealthy American literary heroine to make a mistake she will come to understand only when it is too late to correct it.[18] However good Amy's intentions in arranging what Emile calls "a kidnapping of a corpse," she acts in willful ignorance of medical ethics, inheritance laws, and the contradictory wishes of Venn's children and potential heirs (131). To no one's surprise but her own, Amy's gesture of goodwill inevitably leads to resentment rather than gratitude, an outcome clearly meant to recall that of a larger American venture involving the similarly misguided use of planes and power. Indeed, Emile explicitly describes Amy's interference as "another example of unilateral American meddling, with no regard for the consequences to others" (164).

This accusation, which finally alerts Amy to the possibility that she may have been "at fault" (165), is made during a restaurant lunch that concludes with what at the time seems to be an unrelated and even incidental event. Amy ends up paying the bill for Posy, Rupert, Kip, and Emile, all potential Venn heirs, ostensibly because no one else offers to contribute. The next day, however, at a memorial service for the victims of the avalanche, who now include Adrian Venn, Amy finds herself surrounded by the sound of people repeating "pay, pay, pay" in what she interprets as "a stark litany, but not an unrealistic analysis, of life's guilty feelings of obligation" (217). Despite her subsequent embarrassment when she realizes she has mistaken *paix*, the French word meaning "peace," for the English word *pay*, Amy's misunderstanding has a solid linguistic rationale, albeit a highly surprising one. Even *The American Heritage Dictionary of the English Language* pronounces the derivation of *pay* from *pax*, the Latin word for peace, "difficult to believe." Although a particularly complicated word history now replaces the complexity of meaning characteristic of the confusion between *l'affaire* and *affair*, this new example of the cross-cultural interrelatedness of words confirms a playfully postmodern interest on Johnson's part in the visible exploration of the relationship between signifier, signified, and referent in her third Franco-American fiction. In the journey from Latin to French to English, a noun (*pax*), whose original meaning already included "a settlement of hostilities" as well as "peace," subsequently evolved into a verb, whose expanded sense comprehended, first, "to appease" (Late Latin *pacare*) and then also, "to pacify" (Old French *paiier*), all of which carried over into English. This intricate etymology also determines the progression of Johnson's novel. The demand that the victims of the avalanche "be compensated at least," first addressed to Amy by the cashier who sees her as American guilt personified, is satisfied at the end of *L'Affaire* in what is clearly an attempt to *pay*, that is, to pacify and to appease: "In the midst of escalating tensions between the U.S. and France, the United States had officially denied its role in causing an avalanche in the French Alps, but was compensating certain of the victims nonetheless" (338).

Amy, on the other hand, actually manages to overcome her own "guilty feelings of obligation" (217). She may pay for lunch, but she does not finally buy the chateau owned by Adrian Venn in the south of France, even though its purchase would not only instantly appease Venn's quarreling heirs in "a textbook example of mutual aid" (304) but also put her in possession of a property ideally suited to "become the seat of the Mutual Aid Foundation" (317). Importantly, Amy's change of heart is directly linked to her decision to go home: "She was not a châtelaine, and not even a European, . . . like it or not, she was an American person from Palo Alto, there was no getting around this" (328). Prince Kropotkin, in contrast, was an emblematic citizen of Europe, a Russian who lived successively in the United Kingdom, Switzerland, France, and then again in Britain, before finally returning to Moscow at the end of his life. Moreover, despite Amy's determination to set aside his "totally ridiculous political philosophy," Kropotkin was also, of course, an anarchist (138). In what Johnson clearly intends as an ironic contradiction, Amy chooses as her role model a figure who is at once her direct opposite and the very epitome of the postmodern hero we have seen elsewhere in English-language novels of globalization, including, to some extent, Johnson's own. A constant traveler and a citizen of the world who refused allegiance to any particular nation, Kropotkin was also a renowned geologist and geographer, making him, by chance, a specialist on avalanches as well. Appropriately, then, it is precisely along the fault line of Franco-Anglo-American discord over conflicting national laws and interests that a novel dedicated to the person who introduced its author to Prince Kropotkin and his book *Mutual Aid* disrupts in disorder and confusion to challenge any possibility that cooperation controls human behavior, at least in the world of Johnson's fiction.

If Kropotkin's influence, evident throughout *L'Affaire*, constantly positions Johnson's seemingly very American heroine against a curiously contrasting background of expatriation and antinationalism, it is only with the unexpected (re)appearance over halfway through the novel of the most French of icons imaginable—barring the sudden animation of Marianne herself[19]—that national identity becomes truly anarchic. When Kerry Venn finally awakens from her coma, she reports having seen the figure of a woman, who "glittered all silvery in a beam of light, as though she was wearing armor," materialize on the ridge above her just before the avalanche (196). Instantly recognized by the hospital staff as Jeanne d'Arc, Kerry's vision undergoes rapid embellishment as local reporters, national journalists, and soon the international news media descend on Valméri. Emile quickly becomes a regular on CNN when he finds in the conditions of postmodernity an ingenious solution to the oddity of "The Maid of Orleans so strangely transported to the Alps" (209): "The fact that she now turns up here—I suppose it is globalization" (206). As "a powerful symbol," moreover, St. Joan "is mutable and can signify for the times, any times"; and in 2003 her eternal ability to express "fear of the alien invader" is clearly most urgently required in the French Alps (232). The "warlike saint" (205) obviously appears in response to the presence of foreign military planes in the region to strike back once again at France's enemies: "That the victim was English is perfectly consistent with tradition . . . . What could be more suitable for Jeanne to do to the English and their avatars, the Americans, then to remove them?" (206).[20]

Even Emile, however, can't quite explain how an American came to gain access to the presumably French "collective unconscious" that inspired Kerry's vision (205–6), let alone why one should subsequently become, as Kerry does, the contemporary "goddess"—even the substitute "saint"—of the votaries of Jeanne d'Arc (336). This apparent case of cross-cultural contradiction and confusion receives further support when Europeans begin to denounce Kerry as the agent of "an American plot" designed to divert attention from America's own guilt.[21] But neither Kerry's transformation into a modern day patron of a French saint nor the United States government's supposed interest in exploiting Joan's legend can begin to compare with the total reversal of national identity involved in our gradual recognition that the "real" Jeanne d'Arc is none other than Amy herself. Although the recently arisen Kerry believes that the woman who appeared to her came in warning, others, more mystically skeptical, immediately assume that the person Kerry saw caused the avalanche, and the police begin to search for an unreported victim.

The color of Amy's "pale silver-grey" ski clothes is virtually the first detail Johnson reveals to her readers (6), but only when Euronews begins to broadcast images of statues and engravings of Joan of Arc does Amy herself remember where she was and what she was wearing on the afternoon of the avalanche—and even then only because a chance occurrence interrupts her usual state of self-absorption: "A ray of light from the window, striking her reflection in the mirror, had startled her. What she saw was an image of glittering silver, now seeming, to her mind looking back, almost like a suit of armor, as if she herself could have been mistaken for Joan of Arc" (209). A similar experience at the conclusion of the candlelight memorial service leads to public exposure and general condemnation of Amy's "silvery guilt" (217). Sensing her own person to be the unique target of "European anger" (217), Amy flees not only the church but Valméri as well, though not before she throws "her silver Boegner *combinaison*" into a public trash container in the middle of the night, "feeling like a criminal" (232).

Johnson's satirical assault on the inviolability of national frontiers and the sovereignty of nations goes much deeper, however, than surface appearance. Even as she creates the most resolutely American of her recent fictional heroines, Johnson simultaneously constructs Joan of Arc as an objective correlative for a much more characteristically postmodern siege on national identity.[22] In the twenty-first century, the legend of Joan of Arc may well have greater importance as a source of literary rather than religious inspiration, and Johnson draws on a rich intertextual tradition to add *L'Affaire* to a long, international list of dramatic and aesthetic works informed by St. Joan.[23] In contrast to Prince Kropotkin, who serves as Amy's cosmopolitan opposite, Jeanne d'Arc paradoxically functions as her French twin in an ironic superimposition of their curiously parallel stories. This mystery, designed by the novelist for the pleasure of her readers in a gesture of postmodern self-reflection also evident in Rose Tremain's *The Way I Found Her* and Sarah Smith's *The Knowledge of Water*, constitutes the palimpsestic subtext of *L'Affaire*.

Unlike "la Pucelle d'Orléans" (literally, "the Virgin," not "the Maid," of Orléans), her contemporary counterpart has had sex, if not a serious relationship. On the other hand, Amy certainly remains maiden-like, not only because she is unmarried but especially because her cultural ignorance leaves her in a pure, that is natural, and even native, state of Americanness. Directed by visions of early Christian martyrs, Joan forms an army that temporarily drives the English out of France. Amy is inspired by the arguably equally mystical message of a man who martyred himself for his beliefs to practice a form of Mutual Aid that results in an Englishman being forced to leave France without his consent and against his family's wishes. In the only moment of overt interpretive assistance Johnson offers her readers, Géraldine complains that Amy "sees herself as a sort of savior, Joan of Arc or something . . . " (315). Although Joan and Amy enjoy considerable success in the provinces, both their adventures flounder in Paris, where each is betrayed by an ally. Joan is abandoned by her own army and perhaps even Charles VII, the king she crowned; Amy is sued for thirty million dollars by Kerry, her fellow American and the one person who would have benefitted from her husband's dying in England.[24] True, Joan is burned alive as a heretic by the English, a fate considerably worse than being humiliated and hated by anti-American citizens of contemporary France. Still, some of the aura of Joan's sainthood nonetheless appears to surround Amy at the end of *L'Affaire*, where even Emile, still her worst enemy, finds himself "a bit dazzled" by her metamorphosis into a "mondaine creature" who seems "aglow, radiant in a way he had not noticed before" and to "shine with beauty, even glamour" (265–66). Admiration for Joan's courageous death extended even to her enemies, and her martyrdom sparked a resurgence of patriotism among her contemporaries. Amy must settle for the conversion of Emile and the realization that America, if not the object of her unqualified devotion, is nonetheless the only place she belongs.[25]

The process by which Amy paradoxically becomes the most French of French heroines even as she remains the most American of fictional characters is only the most striking example of an abundance of cultural discrepancies, disjunctions, and reversals evident throughout *L'Affaire*. For example, Amy runs into Posy at Napoleon's tomb where the Englishwoman is fulfilling her oath to "perform a reverence" to the Frenchman who, although "second only to Hitler in the list of tyrants who had attempted to conquer their sacred isle" (225), is also the "wise author" of the law that allows her to inherit against her English father's wishes (296). Indeed, Posy suddenly perceives a strong resemblance between her father and Napoleon and ponders the suitability of sprinkling Adrian Venn's ashes on the emperor's tomb. In her half sister Victoire, Posy instantly identifies an only slightly culturally distorted image of her own reflection: she was a "more ineffably French version of Posy herself—it was *herself* Posy recognized" (135). Their mothers bond equally quickly, despite significant differences in social class that make Pamela Venn, "so sturdy and English," the epitome of British dowdiness and Géraldine the very incarnation of French elegance (261).

Curiously, given Amy's professed ignorance of maternal lore and decided lack of polish and sophistication, it is nonetheless she and not Victoire whom Géraldine repeatedly qualifies as "the ideal daughter" in a paradox that is, of course, only apparent (12; see also 255). Despite "standing as she did for everything French and right-thinking" (90), Victoire is actually "three quarters an Anglo-Saxon," a "secret taint" that has ironic consequences (91). For Victoire—born in France, raised as French, lifelong resident of France, holder of a French passport, and who has "never in her own mind thought of herself as anything but French"—is, if possible, a more recognizable American type than Amy herself, a contrast that reveals further aspects of Amy's own potential "Frenchness." To her mother's despair, Victoire, unlike Amy, has no interest in "being stylish, *maquillée*, a hostess" (92). Having made the mistake of choosing marriage, so "out of fashion among French young people" and an institution Amy finds incomprehensible, Victoire, more in keeping with the morality of the British queen for whom she is named than with the mores of her own country, actually dares to view infidelity as cause for divorce rather than an inevitable flaw of French husbands to be dutifully overlooked. Beloved by everyone for her charm, energy, sweet disposition, and multiple talents, Victoire is, above all, relentlessly optimistic and "her tendencies to happiness" increasingly evident as Amy sinks into melancholy and misery (183). Indeed, as the only Venn sibling not only content to sit by the dying father who never acknowledged her existence but also to attend to his new wife and son, Victoire has no small claim of her own on sainthood.

In *L'Affaire*, in contrast to *Le Divorce* and *Le Mariage*, Johnson's cast of characters is made up of a significant number of English as well as American citizens, an innovation that supports my own decision to include both English and American examples of contemporary fiction set in France in this book. Although Johnson certainly signals the parallelism of anti-French feelings on both sides of the Atlantic as well as that of Anglophobia and anti-Americanism in France, a country where Amy notes that the English often appear to be "even less beloved than Americans" (264), *L'Affaire* also systematically undermines such sentiments as formulaic, arbitrary, and frequently perfunctory. Thus, on Posy and Rupert's first night in Valméri, when she confesses the fondness for France her brother fully shares, he nonetheless immediately responds with "an Englishman's obligatory rejoinder": " 'Except for the French,' Rupert said" (56). Anti-Americanism, as we know, is simply a job requirement for Emile. Moreover, on those occasions when a character's personal ill humor overflows in an avalanche of negative cultural stereotypes, Johnson ironically reverses conventional premises. The English poet Robin, for example, accuses the French—"A people who bestowed their Légion d'Honneur on English romance novelists, a people for whom Barbara Cartland was as good as Elizabeth Bowes, or Jerry Lewis as good as Olivier" (177)—of the very same lack of high standards and good taste, the very same confusion of Culture and mass entertainment, for which the French customarily fault Americans. Similarly, when the usually tolerant Victoire turns on "Perfidious Albion," her list of England's failings in the areas of cleanliness, ethics, commerce, and modernization bears more than a passing resemblance to perennial attacks on her fellow citizens of France: "This was what the English were like, the horrible English with their poor personal hygiene, slippery morals, sleazy business practices, hopeless engineering" (213).

In yet another indication of the mobility and the unpredictability of cultural assumptions, the English characters in *L'Affaire* occasionally prove to be as anti-American as the French, although they are no doubt quicker to add "not you, Amy, of course" (161). Nor are Americans themselves necessarily free of anti-Americanism nor the French innocent of discriminating against their own. Crossing the street in Paris, Amy is horrified to discover that the strange word "bunjer" that someone has addressed to her comes from "embarrassingly dressed people, their fat bodies, plaid pants, and sneakers marking them unmistakably as Americans"; ironically, her refusal to respond simply confirms the tourists' preconceptions of the French as an "arrogant and rude" people who "hate Americans" (299). Although Emile is French-born and Catholic, his Tunisian heritage makes him a permanent stranger in his own country. Even Posy counters his conventional assertion that Frenchmen adore "beautiful English girls" with the unspoken thought "that the opposite was also true, she was drawn to the idea of sheiks and pashas" (77); when Emile's lovemaking proves conventionally, if brilliantly, French, however, Posy decides that *The Arab Art of Love* must after all be the fictional creation of one of her own countrymen (78). Finally, by the end of *L'Affaire*, a novel set entirely in France and primarily among Europeans, America seems to have insidiously succeeded in realizing Europe's worst fears, both literary and literal, albeit with a good deal of help from the French themselves. At once the source of the avalanche, its cover-up, and its reparation, and simultaneously victim and criminal, savior and murderer, and defendant and prosecutor, Americans have metaphorically invaded France, removed the French, and turned Europe into an overseas extension of America itself.[26]

L'Affaire is the first of Johnson's three Franco-American fictions to take place entirely in the nationally and culturally ambiguous spaces of postmodernity through which we also travel in Edmund White's *The Married Man* and Joanne Harris's *Chocolat*, among other contemporary English-language novels set in France. In going to Paris, Amy never really leaves the Hôtel Croix St. Bernard whose "kitschy pseudo-Swiss decor" (5) and perplexing musical taste "for old American show tunes and Russian folk music" (72) are the visible and audible reflections of the cultural contradictions, inconsistent behaviors, and artificial national distinctions that ultimately make Valméri's international and cosmopolitan clientele globally interchangeable. Certainly, even late in Amy's stay in the Alps, Johnson's unworldly heroine remains "entranced by the national diversity" she perceives in those around her in such sharp contrast to the "sameness" of her friends and colleagues in America (160). Tellingly, however, weeks later, she indulges a fantasy of being like the beautiful and elegant French diners who sit near her in a Paris restaurant "effortlessly speaking" their native language. Alas, just as Amy congratulates herself on noticing "such subtle cultural differences as collars," evidence that "she might be making progress in the awareness department," everyone at the neighboring table switches, to Amy's utter astonishment, into heavily accented Texan English (257).

Even Amy, however, experiences what James Clifford calls "the hotel as figure of the postmodern,"[27] the principal example of the solitary, anonymous, transient, impersonal, and intermediary "non-places" of the globalized world):[28]

> The whole time she had been here, she had been feeling like a spy, or someone in disguise, unable to talk about her real situation in life, her conversations limited to empty social exchanges and one sexual interlude. Of course, wasn't that the situation of any hotel guest? In a hotel, all were devoid of pasts, of contexts, everybody interacting in the present, putting forward only as much of themselves as necessary. Being a hotel guest was somewhat lonely, was the truth of it. (190)

Nor do things improve once Amy takes up temporary residence in the urban apartment that she has hired strangers to rent, furnish, and decorate for her as a showplace, not a home.[29] Indeed, a few weeks after her arrival in Paris, Amy begins to identify with the literally homeless who live in the metro tunnels beneath the city: "it was these outcasts Amy had the most fellow feeling for, as lonesome and without direction as herself" (239). Simply by virtue of leaving home, Amy has entered the world of postmodernity to find that "she had in some way become homeless, fitting neither here, nor, she had a suspicion, there, if ever she had" (337).

Thus, in the conclusion to *L'Affaire*, qualified by Amy herself as "almost a metaphor of her French experience," she chooses to hold her farewell party, an example of "mutual aid at its sweetest," in a place of exile (333–34). She hires the suggestively named *Elba* to take her guests on a dinner cruise in the Seine whose fixed "circuit" inevitably marks the starting point of Amy's journey as also her final destination. In a last chapter reminiscent of the fifth act of a Molière play, Amy reconvenes everyone she has met since her arrival in France, most of whom she barely knows, to recreate the internationally diverse group of strangers who figuratively represent "Europe." Amy serves them a "moveable feast" of "caviar tacos," "lobster enchiladas," and "rare roast beef chili" whose cultural eclecticism connects North America to Europe in a postmodern fusion of the *haute cuisine* of France and the already ethnically diverse crossover cooking of California. Although Amy acknowledges a certain incompatibility between the sound of the mariachi music she has ordered and the sight of the Old World splendor of the passing city, even this disjunction accurately reflects postmodern performance, ambivalence, and paradox: "[The mariachis] certainly accomplished the mood of New World ebulliance [*sic*] with which Amy had hoped to signify her mood at leaving. Of course it was a lie" (337).

Amy's discovery that the skills she came to France to acquire "were turning out to be nothing she couldn't learn at home" should not be taken as a dismissal of the fundamental premises of this book (295). What Amy articulates is much less a rejection of cultural diversity than a recognition of the growing internationalism of the entire world that allows all of us "to become better at being where [we are]" (330). The final location of Johnson's heroine positions her "on a cusp," metaphorically suspended in the same space of transition and intersection that is not only reinscribed within every novel discussed in these pages but also figures the literary landscape of globalized postmodernity (329). The bilingual titles of Johnson's fictions, at once true cognates and what the French call "false friends" (*faux amis*), foreground the ambiguous nationality, the cosmopolitanism, the border crossing, the cultural complexity, and the self- reflexivity that also characterize other contemporary English-language novels set in France. *L'Affaire* represents only the most recent example of a metaphoric avalanche that even the recent renewal of hostile relations between France, England and the United States seems more likely to speed up than to halt. In an essay appropriately focused on the language used by Americans and the English to describe the French, Geoffrey Nunberg notes that France-bashing, which implies "a cosmopolitan familiarity with the place," is "also a tribute to the continuing cachet of French culture." Moreover, America's apparent eagerness to make Francophobia the same essential trait of American national identity that it has always been for the British paradoxically marks America as every bit as European as France: "In the end, it's hard to think of anything that is more old Europe that those appeals to national stereotypes."[30]

Notes

INTRODUCTION

1. Stein is variously reported to have said that "America is my country but France is my home" and/or "America is my country and Paris is my home town." I have combined statements that may well be apocryphal in any case, although both no doubt reflect Stein's sentiments with equal accuracy. See, for example, Noel Riley Fitch, *Sylvia Beach and the Lost Generation: A History of Literary Paris in the Twenties and Thirties* (New York: W.W. Norton, 1983), 56; and J. Gerald Kennedy, *Imagining Paris: Exile, Writing, and American Identity* (New Haven, CT: Yale University Press, 1993), 40.

2. Sylvia Whitman, *Lost, Beat and New: Three Generations of Parisian Literary Tradition* (Paris: Shakespeare and Company, Dec. 2002).

3. Fitch, *Sylvia Beach*, 42.

4. Lawrence Ferlinghetti subsequently opened City Lights, a bookstore modeled on Shakespeare and Company and equally legendary, in San Francisco.

5. Fitch, *Sylvia Beach*, 232.

6. In 1951, George Whitman opened Le Mistral at the present location of Shakespeare and Company. Following Sylvia Beach's death in 1962, he renamed his bookshop in her honor, although his claim to have done so with her permission remains unverified. Similarly, little visible effort is made to distinguish the present store from the one owned by Beach, and some believe that Whitman himself is the primary source of the rumors concerning his relationship to Walt Whitman. In the pamphlet he sells in the bookstore (*The Rag and Bone Shop of the Heart* [Paris: Shakespeare and Company, 2000]), however, the current owner of Shakespeare and Company identifies a different kind of affinity: "I like to think there is a trace of genius in all of us and in my case there might be a vague resemblance to Walt Whitman who also ran a bookstore and printing-press in Brooklyn over a century ago. I feel a kinship with Walt Whitman and believe the bookstore had the faults and virtues it might have if he were the proprietor. It has been said that perhaps no man liked so many things and disliked so few as Walt Whitman and I at least aspire to the same modest attainment." Sylvia Beach Whitman organized the 2003 literary festival and appears ready to take over the family business. For the history of Shakespeare and Company, see, for example, Sylvia Beach, *Shakespeare and Company* (New York: Harcourt, Brace, 1956); Fitch, *Sylvia Beach*; and John Affleck, "Ernest Hemingway's Places," http://www.literarytraveler.com/hemingway/ shakespeare.htm; as well as the bookstore's own Web site.

7. Over the years Whitman has combined three stores and three apartments into the current bookstore, spread out over three floors. Whitman, who celebrated his ninetieth birthday

in 2003, reports that he still hopes to acquire three additional floors on the opposite side of the building and add on the adjoining hotel. The sleeping spaces located in the library are called the "Tumbleweed Hotel" (G. Whitman, *Rag and Bone Shop*).

8. Fitch, *Sylvia Beach*, 43.

9. Shakespeare and Company in fact belongs to the patrimony of France, having been designated a historical monument by the French Ministry of Culture (G. Whitman, *Rag and Bone Shop*).

10. Ethan Gilsdorf, "The Expatriate Writer in Paris: Revising the Myth," *Poets and Writers Magazine* (May/June 2001): 14.

11. Harry Mathews, Mark Ford, C. K. Williams, Wyatt Prunty, Susan Fox, Pansy Maurer-Alvarez, and Margo Berdeshevsky.

12. Victor Erofeyev, Jung Chang, and Viken Berberian. According to Gilsdorf ("Expatriate Writer," 15), a writer at the *L.A. Times* coined the term "the Third Wave" to describe the influx of Americans in Paris in the 1980s.

13. In the past, Anglophone novelists who migrated to France tended, like Hemingway, to write about their homeland rather than their host country. In contrast, the novelists of interest here write about France, although they are not necessarily expatriates or even unusually frequent visitors. Most spend some time in France and may well have French relatives but they maintain residency in the United States or England. In general, not they but their characters live in or travel to France.

14. See, in order, Dean MacCannell, *The Tourist: A New Theory of the Leisure Class* (Berkeley: University of California Press, 1976), 76; Patricia Parkhurst Ferguson, "Is Paris France?," *French Review* 73 (May 2000): 1052; Jean Méral, *Paris in American Literature*, trans. Laurette Long (Chapel Hill: University of North Carolina Press, 1989), 239.

15. James Clifford, *Routes: Travel and Translation in the Late Twentieth Century* (Cambridge, MA: Harvard University Press, 1997), 30.

16. Gilsdorf, "Expatriate Writer," 16.

17. Ibid.

18. Clifford, *Routes*, 1.

19. John Tomlinson, *Globalization and Culture* (Chicago: University of Chicago Press, 1999), 1.

20. Affleck, "Ernest Hemingway's Places."

21. Although I fundamentally disagree with Joseph McMahon's contention that the experience of being an American in Paris "has generally been less a Parisian experience than a human one which might conceivably have been had elsewhere" and that "almost without exception" Paris is "principally a backdrop" in American writing ("City for Expatriate," *Yale French Studies*, no. 32 [1964]: 144–45), some of the contemporary English-language novels set in France, including several of the most popular, fit this description. Notably, Sebastian Faulks's trilogy of historical novels, set in France during World War II—*The Girl at the Lion d'Or*, *Birdsong*, and *Charlotte Gray*—are essentially love stories whose cultural, geographical, and even historical location is immaterial.

22. See, for example, Brian McHale's *Postmodernist Fiction* (New York: Routledge, 1987). McHale's corpus of postmodern novelists has metafictional roots in Latin American magic realism and the French New New Novel; its practitioners include Samuel Beckett, Alain Robbe-Grillet, Carlos Fuentes, Thomas Pynchon, and Robert Coover.

23. Francofil: French Studies Discussion List, "Call for Papers—Voyages," http://www.bristol.ac.ukfrancofil.

24. Stuart Hall, "European Cinema on the Verge of a Nervous Breakdown," in *Screening Europe: Image and Identity in Contemporary European Cinema*, ed. Duncan Petrie (Lon-

don: British Film Institute, 1992): 47; Alison Russell, *Crossing Boundaries: Postmodern Travel Literature* (New York: Palgrave, 2000), 7.

25. This information was offered by one of the principal organizers of the festival. First scheduled to read, Johnson's ultimate choice to invite the writers who had participated in the festival to her large apartment on the rue Bonaparte recalls the role of Stein's literary salon.

26. Benedict Anderson, *Imagined Communities: Reflections on the Origin and Spread of Nationalism*, rev. ed (London: Verso, 1991).

27. Edmund White, *The Married Man* (New York: Alfred A. Knopf, 2000), 70.

28. Margo Jefferson, writing in the fall of 2003, notes that "of all the books translated worldwide, only 6 percent (maybe less) are translated from other languages into English" ("The Fortress of Monoglot Nation, *New York Times*, Oct. 26, 2003, sec. 7:31.)

29. Kristin Hohendel, "European Films Learn to Speak English," *New York Times*, Jan. 20, 2000, sec. 2:15.

30. Shakespeare and Company has been joined in recent years by the Village Voice, a particularly frequent sponsor of readings in English by writers either living in Paris or simply passing through. In the summer of 2003, "San Francisco and Company," which sells used books, was opened on rue du Monsieur-le-Prince, not far from where Beach's original bookshop was located.

Chapter 1:
The New International Novel

1. Diane Johnson, *Le Mariage* (New York: Dutton, 2000), 11. Subsequent references to both this novel and to Johnson's *Le Divorce* (New York, Dutton, 1997) appear in parentheses in the text.

2. Thomas Friedman, *The Lexus and the Olive Tree* (New York: Anchor Books, 2000); John Tomlinson, *Globalization and Culture* (Chicago: University of Chicago Press, 1999).

3. Tomlinson, *Globalization and Culture*, 19.

4. Ibid., 1–2.

5. Rob Kroes, *If You've Seen One, You've Seen the Mall: Europeans and American Mass Culture* (Urbana: University of Illinois Press, 1996), 126. My use of the terms "high," "low," "elite," or "popular" in relation to culture is purely conventional and should not be taken to imply any hierarchy of my own in terms of literary value.

6. I do not mean to suggest that globalization itself is new; the phenomenon, however, does appear to be cyclical and to take on different forms in different historical periods.

7. *Une Américaine à Paris* (Paris: NiL éditions), the French translation of *Le Divorce*, appeared in the fall of 2001; and a film version of Johnson's first novel, directed by James Ivory, was released in August, 2003. Johnson's *L'Affaire* (New York: Dutton), a third novel set in France, was also published in the fall of 2003. As we will see, a similar pattern is evident in the work of other novelists of globalization. Some of the characters who first appeared in Joanne Harris's *Chocolat* (New York: Viking, 1999) reappear in *Blackberry Wine* (New York: HarperCollins, 2000) and both novels take place in the same French village; *Five Quarters of the Orange* (New York: HarperCollins, 2001) completes what Harris qualifies as a trilogy. In addition, a film version of *Chocolat*, directed by Lasse Hallström, was released in December, 2000. Edmund White also remakes his memoir, *Our Paris: Sketches from Memory* (New York: Alfred A. Knopf, 1995) in the form of a novel in *The Married Man* (New York: Alfred A. Knopf, 2000).

8. Bill Goldstein, "An American In . . . ," *New York Times*, Apr. 16, 2000, sec. 7:10.

9. Ella Shohat and Robert Stam, *Unthinking Eurocentrism: Multiculturalism and the Media* (London: Routledge, 1994), 101; Friedman, *Lexus and the Olive Tree*, 22.

10. Louis Mink, "Narrative Form as a Cognitive Instrument," in *The Writing of History*, ed. Robert H. Canary and Henry Kozicki (Madison: University of Wisconsin Press, 1978), 133. Isabel Walker, the narrator of *Le Divorce*, is well aware that narratives have nationalities: "If I were telling an American story, to mention nail polish would be to signal that it was not a serious story, was meant to be read under the hair dryer. But in a French story it is a revealing, spiritual detail" (119). In *Le Mariage*, Anne-Sophie is concerned about the differences between French farce and American melodrama: "So would you rather be the wife in a French play or an American one? Should an American man and a French wife settle beforehand which kind of play they were in?" (208).

11. White, *Married Man*, 70.

12. Tom Bishop, "I Love You, Moi Non Plus," in "France's Identity Crisis," ed. Tom Bishop, special issue, *SubStance* 76/77 (1985): 21. Among recent novels, see, for example, Lily King, *The Pleasing Hour* (New York: Atlantic Monthly, 1999); and White, *Married Man*. The Franco-American couple also figures importantly in nonfictional works; see, for example, Raymonde Carroll, *Evidences invisibles: Américains et Français au quotidien* (Paris: Seuil, 1987); and Harriet Welty Rochefort, *French Toast: An American in Paris Celebrates the Maddening Mysteries of the French* (New York: St. Martin's Press, 1999).

13. See also Patricia Ferguson, "Is Paris France?," *French Review* 73 (May 2000): 1052: "Is Paris France? Or is it the cosmopolitan Other, an alien site . . . the great escape for the women and men whose fortunes we follow in so many novels both French and foreign?"

14. Ethan Gilsdorf, an American poet who resides in Paris, concurs that "writers who move to Paris today are haunted by the legacy of those who have previously made the pilgrimage" ("The Expatriate Writer in Paris: Revising the Myth," *Poets and Writers Magazine* [May/June 2001]: 14).

15. Ironically, of course, Isabel's very desire to "divorce" herself from her background and define herself in her own terms might well be considered a clear sign of her Americanness. Johnson notes in a recent interview that she writes about the "tension between people trying to be themselves once they're out of their native context versus the obligation that is laid on every American to be an American, with all the flaws imputed to America by other countries" (Goldstein, "An American"). Isabel herself is aware that as an "American, a member of a nation," she can't "help but be afflicted by all those limitations other people saw as 'American'" (196).

16. Aamir Mufti and Ella Shohat, introduction to *Dangerous Liaisons: Gender, Nation, and Postcolonial Perspectives*, ed. Anne McClintock, Aamir Mufti, and Ella Shohat (Minneapolis: University of Minnesota Press, 1997), 2.

17. In *Le Mariage*, a painting also functions as *mise-en-abyme*. The copy of Rubens's painting of a nude Diana surrounded by leering satyrs, which hangs in the mayor's office, duplicates Clara's own discomfort at being alone in a room with a dozen male hunters. Moreover, the picture subsequently "comes to life" in the attack on Clara at the post office, an event that is itself recorded in a photograph in *Paris Match*. In having an affair with the man who identifies the painting for her, Clara will also act on the double meaning of "venery" that it represents: "How odd that this picture, pointedly associating hunting and sex, should depict the goddess of chastity. What did the word *vénerie* mean to the French?" (60).

18. Tomlinson, *Globalization*, 1–2.

19. Antoine Compagnon, *La Seconde Main ou le travail de la citation* (Paris: Seuil, 1979), 337. All translations from the French are my own, unless otherwise indicated.

20. To take just two examples, chapter 2, in which Isabel is first introduced to the American community in Paris, is prefaced by a quotation from Benjamin Constant's *Adolphe* (Paris: Flammarion, 1989), 9: "I was welcomed at this court with the curiosity naturally inspired by any stranger who comes and breaks into the restricted circle of monotonous etiquette." In chapter 23, another quote from *Adolphe* prepares us for Roxy's suicide attempt: " 'Yonder,' I said to myself, 'some poor wretch may be struggling on in grief, or wrestling with death . . . the certain end which brings neither consolation nor peace' " (160).

21. In fact, "Anglophone books about France," might well be divided into two subgroups, differently "cultured" as European or American and differently "gendered" as "feminine/feminist" or "masculine/masculinist"on the basis of a primary alliance either with Henry James or with Ernest Hemingway.

22. Emily Apter, "From Literary Channel to Narrative Chunnel," in *The Literary Channel: The Inter-national Invention of the Novel*, ed. Margaret Cohen and Carolyn Dever (Princeton, NJ: Princeton University Press, 2002), 292.

23. *Le Petit Robert 2: Dictionnaire universel des noms propres* (Paris: S.E.P.R.E.T., 1975), s.v. "Constant, Benjamin."

24. That Tim suddenly begins to feel that he "belong[s] in America" (284) as a result of *being* in America offers further evidence of the importance of place in Johnson's work.

25. Take, for example, the situation of the two Americans who find the body of a murder victim in the Paris flea market: "He was thinking this could be a story either for CNN (Dream Trip to Paris Turns into Nightmare) or for *Reliance* (American citizen, deprived of passport, held without charges on flimsy grounds)" (46).

26. Kroes, *If You've Seen One*, 126.

27. Isabel also finds film, with "its fitful changefulness, its arbitrary notions of coherence" to be not only "a more appropriate medium" for telling her own story but one that is "emblematic" of "the nature of the two societies, American and French" (*Divorce*, 4). Johnson wrote the screenplay for *The Shining*, and she has acknowledged that the character of Serge Cray is modeled in some ways on that of Stanley Kubrick; notably, Cray, like Kubrick prior to *Eyes Wide Shut*, has been working on the same film for years, and he too is an expatriate American director—with labradors.

28. In *Le Divorce*, the American writer Olivia Pace, owner of a fine collection of faience from which a tureen is stolen and offered for resale to Isabel in *le marché aux puces*, characterizes theft at this level as both nationally specific and synonymous with collecting itself: "Burgling seems such a French crime. . . . Domestic, focused on material objects, requiring a certain power of discrimination, and non-violent" (259).

29. Tomlinson, *Globalization*, 1–2.

30. This description, taken from *Le Divorce*, announces the crime of which Clara will be accused in *Le Mariage*.

31. The protagonist of White's *Married Man* feels rather differently about the "silly simulacrum of Paris" that he encounters at the Epcot Center in Florida; "this county fair, this vile fake" also frightens him, "as if it meant to suggest he'd never gotten out of America, never lived in the real île Saint-Louis for eight years" (191). The actual American heartland of Ron Howard's *Ain't It Romantic?: An Entertainment* (New York: HarperCollins, 2003) provides a curious cross-cultural reversal fully in keeping with the novel's subtitle. French tourists stranded in Seldom, Nebraska, find themselves portraying Marie Antoinette and Louis XIV at "The Revels," an annual celebration held in honor of Bernard LeBoeuf, the town's Québecois founder, in which geographical confusion rivals historical inaccuracy. Surrounded by "the citizens of Seldom milling about like *Les Miserables* in the costumes of French chambermaids, urchins, revolutionaries, street walkers, and Parisian apaches," Na-

talie delivers queenly waves to children on the Tilt-a-Whirl and Pierre fires the starter's pistol for the demolition derby (59–61).

32. I will follow Johnson's own example in assuming that my readers, like hers, are generally familiar with Renoir's film.

33. Terrence Rafferty, "A Critic at Large: The Essence of the Landscape," *New Yorker*, June 25, 1990, 83. To be exact, Truffaut cites *La Règle du jeu* and *Citizen Kane* as equally influential.

34. Richard F. Kuisel, *Seducing the French: The Dilemma of Americanization* (Berkeley: University of California Press, 1993), 230.

35. Kroes, *If You've Seen One*, xiv, 40.

36. Kroes, ibid., 21, also remarks on American anti-Americanism: "In general it is safe to say that Americans are second to none in their anti-Americanism. It is almost a constant of American culture, although this tends to escape European critics. At regular intervals American intellectuals indulge in self-criticism and self-rejection that do not differ greatly from European critiques either in sharpness or in use of metaphors." See also Jean-Philippe Mathy, "The Popularity of American Culture," *Sites* 1 (Spring 1997): 141–56.

37. In addition to titling her novels in French, Johnson uses language creatively within the text as well. Notably, Anne-Sophie employs expressions that the Americans in *Le Mariage* fail to understand and which are, in fact, literal translations of French idioms: e.g., "I felt a little that she has breathed on my star" (*souffler la vedette à quelqu'un*) or "he pointed the gun, and Antoine de Persand jumped, and the thing was sewn with a white thread" (*cousu du fil blanc*) (308–9). It is also evident that in the course of the novel Johnson begins to substitute words with a clear French origin for their more usual synonyms in English—e.g., inquietude, ravished, uxorious, grandeur, interdicting, uriniferous, and so on.

38. Kroes, *If You've Seen One*, 39.

Chapter 2:
Intertextual Travel and Translation

1. Rose Tremain, *The Way I Found Her* (New York: Farrar, Straus and Giroux, 1997), 61. Subsequent references appear in parentheses in the text.

2. The "jardin à la française" (formal garden) would be an artificial space, by definition, but the Jardin du Luxembourg is an "English garden," in which vegetation is theoretically left to grow in its "natural" state.

3. The term *narrateur-témoin* refers to a first-person narrator who witnesses and records the adventures of another, usually the main character. The classic example in English literature is Dr. Watson in Conan Doyle's stories of Sherlock Holmes.

4. Alain-Fournier, *Le Grand Meaulnes* (1913; repr., Paris: Librairie Fayard, 1971).

5. Karlheinz Stierle, "The Reading of Fictional Texts," in *The Reader in the Text: Essays on Audience and Interpretation*, ed. Susan R. Suleiman and Inge Crosman (Princeton, NJ: Princeton University Press, 1980), 87.

6. John Tomlinson, *Globalization and Culture* (Chicago: University of Chicago Press, 1999), 1–2.

7. "Master tropes" are the subject of Hayden White's *Metahistory: The Historical Imagination in Nineteenth-Century Europe* (Baltimore: Johns Hopkins University Press, 1973).

8. John Fowles, afterword to *The Wanderer or The End of Youth*, by Alain-Fournier (New York: New American Library, 1971), 223.

9. Ibid.

10. Julia Kristeva, *Révolution du langage poétique* (Paris: Seuil, 1974), 59–60.

11. Karen D. Levy, "*Le Grand Meaulnes* and *Le Roi des aulnes*: Counterpointed Echoes from a Distant Past," *Romance Notes* 29 (Winter 1988): 116. Levy's comments are made in a context similar to my own; she explores the intertextual relationship, both acknowledged and unacknowledged, between *Le Grand Meaulnes* and Michel Tournier's *Le Roi des aulnes*.

12. The parallel passage in *Le Grand Meaulnes* reads as follows: "il se rappela un rêve—une vision plutôt, qu'il avait eue tout enfant, et dont il n'avait jamais parlé à personne: un matin, . . . il s'était trouvé dans une longue pièce verte, aux tentures pareilles à des feuillages. En ce lieu coulait une lumière si douce qu'on eût cru pouvoir la goûter. Près de la première fenêtre, une jeune fille cousait, le dos tourné, semblant attendre son réveil . . . " (69; cf. 91) ("he recalled a dream, a vision, rather, which he had had as a small child, and of which he had never spoken to anyone: one morning, . . . he had found himself in a long green room with tapestries that looked so soft that it seemed as if one could taste it. He had seen a young girl sewing near the first window, apparently waiting for him to awake" [Lowell Bair, trans., *The Wanderer or The End of Youth*, (New York: New American Library, 1971), 48–49]).

13. No doubt the relationship between writer and reader, who are also represented by Valentina and Lewis, is always potentially erotic as well, a possibility that Patricia Duncker explores in depth in *Hallucinating Foucault* (New York: Vintage, 1996).

14. Kristeva, "Pour une sémiologie des paragrammes," *Tel Quel* 29 (1967): 53–85.

15. "Prisunic" identifies a popular chain of discount stores in France, the equivalent of K-Mart or Target in the United States.

16. See, for example, Jim Collins, *Uncommon Cultures: Popular Culture and Post-Modernism* (New York: Routledge, 1989); and Linda Hutcheon, *A Poetics of Postmodernism: History, Theory, Fiction* (New York: Routledge, 1988), 31–32.

17. Pierre Verdaguer, "Introduction: Estelle Monbrun," *Sites* 1 (Spring 1997): 369. In Monbrun's case, *Meurtre chez tante Léonie* (Paris: Viviane Hamy, 1994), *Meurtre à Petite Plaisance* (Paris: Viviane Hamy, 1998), and *Meurtre Chez Colette* (Paris: Viviane Hamy, 2001) combine the conventions of the detective novel with literary mysteries involving Marcel Proust, Marguerite Yourcenar, and Colette respectively; the settings and characters of her novels also link France and the United States.

18. Alexis, who plans the kidnapping, appears to be modeled in part on Frantz in *Le Grand Meaulnes*. Valentina tells Lewis: "You see, he's never really got beyond adolescence. He dreams stupid dreams and deludes himself about what he can or cannot do" (303).

19. Collins, *Uncommon Cultures*, 60.

20. Hutcheon, *Poetics*, 10.

21. Lewis Carroll, *Alice in Wonderland*, 2nd ed., ed. Donald J. Gray (1865, 1872; repr., New York: W.W. Norton, 1992, 1971). Indeed, Alice expresses the endlessness of her fall by a comparison whose analogy with Tremain's novel will be clear: " 'After such a fall as this, I shall think nothing of tumbling down-stairs! . . . Why, I wouldn't say anything about it, even if I fell off the top of the house!'" (8).

22. Lewis is so emotionally damaged by Valentina's death that at the end of the novel he has taken refuge in the abstract world of pure mathematics: "In the flickering paraffin light, which reminds me of the light in the attic room of François Seurel, I do my mathematical calculations and the numbers go forwards and onwards, taking me with them through time" (359).

23. Hutcheon notes that the chess game is a familiar metaphor in postmodern metafiction in *Narcissistic Narrative: The Metafictional Paradox* (New York: Methuen, 1980), 83.

24. In an intriguing fusion of intertextual interests, Georges Jacques ("*Le Grand Meaulnes*: Où une magie en cache une autre," *Lettres romanes* 1–2 [Feb.–May 1989]: 30) believes that Alain-Fournier "borrowed" the following passage from Lewis Carroll's *Alice's Adventures in Wonderland*: "un extraordinaire petit jeune homme sortit du bâtiment voisin. . . . Il avait un chapeau haut de forme très cintré qui brillait dans la nuit comme s'il eût été d'argent; un habit dont le col lui montait dans les cheveux, un gilet trés ouvert, un pantalon à sous-pieds . . . Cet élégant, qui pouvait avoir quinze ans, marchait sur la pointe des pieds comme s'il eût été soulevé par les élastiques de son pantalon, mais avec une rapidité extraordinaire. Il salua Meaulnes au passage sans s'arrêter, profondément, automatiquement, et disparut dans l'obscurité, . . . Apres un instant d'hésitation, notre héros emboîta le pas au curieux petit personnage. . . . L'élégant s'y engouffra, Meaules le suivit. . . ." (Alain-Fournier, *Grand Meaulnes*, 82–83). ("an extraordinary little young man came out of a nearby . . . building. He was wearing a sharply curved top hat that gleamed in the night as if it were made of silver, a dress coat with a collar that came up into his hair, a low-cut vest, and trousers with straps that fitted under his shoes. This coxcomb, who might have been fifteen, was walking on tiptoe, as though lifted by the elastic straps of his trousers, but with startling speed. He bowed deeply and mechanically to Meaulnes, without stopping, and disappeared into the darkness, . . . After a moment of hesitation, our hero set off behind this odd little personage. . . . The coxcomb went inside. Meaulnes followed him" [Bair, *Wanderer*, 57]).

25. Carroll, *Alice*, 163.

26. This fusion of reading and translation reproduces, no doubt unintentionally, the reading experience of many non-French adolescents and young adults for whom *Le Grand Meaulnes* is often the first full-length text they encounter in intermediate-level language courses at a time when they cannot yet read French with ease and without frequent recourse to a bilingual dictionary.

27. The version that Lewis finally prefers is different still: " 'I will now attempt a perfect but fluid translation of this sentence by Alain-Fournier, the Lewis Little Version! 'I was fifteen. It was a Sunday in November, very cold. It was the first day of that autumn which made you remember that winter was just around the corner . . . ' " (23). There are two errors in Tremain's citation of the original sentence from Alain-Fournier: "novembre" should not be capitalized; and the verb *fit* should have a circonflex accent mark.

28. The analogies between Lewis and François bring to realization a motif that has been insufficiently studied in *Le Grand Meaulnes*: François's role as the writer, as well as the narrator, of the story.

29. Claire Messud, "Looking for Love," *New York Times*, Aug. 2, 1998, late ed., sec. 7:7.

30. Fowles, afterword, 221.

31. Qtd. in Emily Apter, *Continental Drift: From National Characters to Virtual Subjects* (Chicago: University of Chicago Press, 1999), 4.

32. Both the United States and England have a long history of defining their national and cultural identities in opposition to that of France, which no doubt helps to explain the frequent choice of France as stand-in for Europe in English-language novels. See, for example, Jeffrey Richards, *Films and British National Identity: From Dickens to* Dad's Army (Manchester, England: Manchester University Press, 1997), 1–28.

33. Kristin Hohendel, "European Films Learn to Speak English," *New York Times*, Jan. 20, 2000, sec. 2:15.

Chapter 3:
Routes and Roots

1. Joanne Harris, *Blackberry Wine* (New York: HarperCollins, 2000) and *Chocolat* (New York: Viking, 1999). Subsequent references to both novels appear in the text. Harris is in fact the author of two earlier books, *Sleep, Pale Sister* and *The Evil Seed*, now out-of-print, which she identifies as "category fiction" of "a kind of literary horror/gothic genre." Difficult to market and described by the author herself as "largely unread," Harris essentially portrays them as an exercise in writing from which she "learned a lot" (Marla Addison, interview with Joanne Harris, http://www.countrybookshop.co.uk).

2. James Clifford, *Routes: Travel and Translation in the Late Twentieth Century* (Cambridge, MA: Harvard University Press, 1997), 1. The title of this essay is influenced by Clifford's *Routes* as well as by its discussion in John Tomlinson, *Globalization and Culture* (Chicago: University of Chicago Press, 1999).

3. Tomlinson, *Globalization*, 29.

4. Jeffrey Richards, *Films and British National Identity: From Dickens to* Dad's Army (Manchester, England: Manchester University Press, 1997), 1, 351.

5. Theodore Zeldin, *The French* (New York: Vintage, 1984). See also, for example, Richard Bernstein, *Fragile Glory: A Portrait of France and the French* (New York: Alfred A. Knopf, 1990); Robert Daly, *Portraits of France* (New York: Little, Brown, 1991); Richard F. Kuisel, *Seducing the French: The Dilemma of Americanization* (Berkeley: University of California Press, 1993); Alice Kaplan, *French Lessons: A Memoir* (Chicago: University of Chicago Press, 1993); Raymonde Carroll, *Evidences invisibles: Américains et Français au quotidien* (Paris: Seuil, 1987); and Adam Gopnik, *Paris to the Moon* (New York: Random House, 2000); among many others.

6. Harris published *Five Quarters of the Orange* (New York: HarperCollins), a third novel set elsewhere in rural France, in 2001; *The Coastliners* (New York: William Morrow), which takes place on a French island in between France and England, appeared in 2003.

7. Although the year is never indicated in the text of the novel, the date of Easter Sunday alone suffices to inform the interested reader that *Chocolat* is set in 1997, a fact explicitly verified in *Blackberry Wine*. Despite a sense on the part of reviewers that Vianne's story either belongs to a vaguely distant past or is somehow "timeless," Harris clearly means us to associate the novel with contemporary reality. Hallström's film adaptation, in contrast, sets the events in a nostalgic 1959.

8. Tomlinson, *Globalization*, 29.

9. Web sites such as Amazon.com now provide ready access to readers' comments as well as to editorial reviews.

10. Nancy Willard, "Let Them Eat Candy," *New York Times*, Mar. 7, 1999, sec. 7:14.

11. In fact, the opening scene of *Chocolat* arguably functions as the generative matrix of the novel as a whole; we are introduced not only to Reynaud but to most of the important secondary characters in the novel—e.g., Joséphine, Muscat, Guillaume—whose association with the carnival parade already announces their "doubleness," whether dangerous or defensive. My discussion of postmodernism here and throughout this book is indebted to a number of critical and theoretical works. See, in particular, Jim Collins, *Uncommon Cultures: Popular Culture and Post-Modernism* (New York: Routledge, 1989); Linda Hutcheon, *A Poetics of Postmodernism: History, Theory, Fiction* (New York: Routledge, 1988); and Brian McHale, *Postmodernist Fiction* (New York: Routledge, 1987) and *Constructing Postmodernism* (New York: Routledge, 1992).

12. Ella Shohat and Robert Stam, *Unthinking Eurocentrism: Multiculturalism and the Media* (London: Routledge, 1994), 101; Thomas L. Friedman, *The Lexus and the Olive Tree* (New York: Anchor, 2000), 22.

13. Tomlinson, *Globalization*, 1–2.

14. Louis Mink made a slightly different point over twenty-five years ago in "Narrative Form as a Cognitive Instrument," in *The Writing of History*, ed Robert H. Canary and Henry Kozicki (Madison: University of Wisconsin Press, 1978), 133. Describing storytelling as a "ubiquitous human activity," he nonetheless argued that the kinds of stories that get told vary from culture to culture, just as those that get repeated within a particular culture significantly shape its national consciousness.

15. See Rob Kroes, *If You've Seen One, You've Seen the Mall: Europeans and American Mass Culture* (Urbana: University of Illinois Press, 1996), 126; and my discussion of Diane Johnson in chapter 1.

16. See, for example, "Questionnaire: Popular Culture at the End of the Second Millennium," *Sites* 1 (Spring 1997): 349–53.

17. Anthony D. Smith, *National Identity* (London: Penguin Books, 1991), 157.

18. Ibid., 158–59.

19. Ibid., 174. Other novels of literary globalism, however—notably those of Johnson—do propose fictional versions of what Smith refers to as "unity in diversity." Smith also makes the provocative suggestion that French and English might together serve the function of a single European *lingua franca* (174).

20. Aamir Mufti and Ella Shohat, introduction to *Dangerous Liaisons: Gender, Nation, and Postcolonial Perspectives*, ed. Anne McClintock, Aamir Mufti, and Ella Shohat (Minneapolis: University of Minnesota Press, 1997), 2; Emily Apter, *Continental Drift: From National Characters to Virtual Subjects* (Chicago: University of Chicago Press, 1999); Homi K. Bhabha, "The World and the Home," in *Dangerous Liaisons*, 445–55.

21. Clifford, *Routes*, 31.

22. Ibid.

23. Ibid., 17.

24. Robert Darnton, *The Great Cat Massacre and Other Episodes in French Cultural History* (New York: Vintage, 1985), 64.

25. Female writers of fairy tales included, for example, the Comtesse de Ségur, Mme Leprince de Beaumont, Mme d'Aulnoy, Mlle L'héritier, Mlle de Lubert, and Mme de Murat. The aristocratic origins of such women suggest that they shared a certain cosmopolitanism as well.

26. The Eugène Atget photos of Pontoise, which figure on the jacket of the hardback edition of *Chocolat*, convey the photographic perfection of the typical French village square.

27. In keeping with Darnton's discussion (*Great Cat Massacre*, 53–56), Reynaud describes Vianne as "wily" (62) and accuses her of using "ruse" to thwart his plans (96). The questioning of authority is, of course, also a prototypical postmodern stance.

28. See, for example, Mort Rosenblum, *A Goose in Toulouse and Other Culinary Adventures in France* (New York: Hyperion, 2000), 40.

29. The Front National is an extreme-right political party founded by Le Pen in 1972. Beginning in the mid-eighties and continuing into the 1990s, the party's opposition to immigration, judged responsible for unemployment and increased crime, attracted as many as 10–15 percent of French voters. The party's influence appeared to have significantly declined until Le Pen's highly unexpected—and very upsetting—second-place finish in the first round of the 2002 presidential election put him in a run-off election with Jacques Chirac.

30. See, for example, Laurence Wylie and Jean-François Brière, *Les Français*, 2nd ed. (Englewood Cliffs, NJ: Prentice Hall, 1995), 47–48.

31. See Lewis Carroll, *Alice in Wonderland*, 2nd ed., ed. Donald J. Gray (1865, 1872; New York: W.W. Norton, 1992, 1971), 127.

32. Clifford, *Routes*, 11.

33. See John Lanchester's *The Debt to Pleasure* (New York: Henry Holt, 1996), also an English novel set in France, for another version of the intricate relationship between literary and culinary discourses.

34. Tomlinson, *Globalization*, 1.

35. Ibid., 1–2.

36. R. Carroll, *Evidences invisibles*, 212.

37. Tomlinson, *Globalization*, 29.

38. The Hollywood-style ending of Lasse Hallström's film adaptation of *Chocolat* (2000) totally revises the essential premises of Harris's novel; Roux returns to Lansquenet to live "happily ever after" with Vianne in what really is a "fairy tale for adults."

39. Obviously the real Notre Dame is considerably larger, but the juxtaposition of photographs of the cathedral and of its chocolate reproduction produces more ambiguous results; were it not for the absence of cars and pedestrians on the *parvis*, a casual glance might well be misleading.

40. Claude Chabrol's *Merci pour le chocolat* appeared on Paris screens on Oct. 25, 2000; although the timing was presumably coincidental, since the film had a standard two-year production schedule, its release at the time of the Salon du Chocolat is nicely illustrative of the ill-defined boundaries and the eclectic pleasures of postmodernism.

41. *Revue du chocolat* 2 (Fall 2000): Spécial Salon du chocolat, 14, my emphasis.

Chapter 4:
Back to the Future

1. Joanne Harris, *Blackberry Wine* (New York: HarperCollins, 2000), 3, 154. Subsequent references appear in parentheses in the text.

2. *Jackapple Joe*, displaced from the British countryside to the American Midwest, stars Corey Feldman (2). Lasse Hallström's film version of *Chocolat* still takes place in France, but, by chance, he turns the novel into a nostalgia film set in the 1950s.

3. Similarly, the inside jacket of the hardcover edition of *Chocolat* announces that the novel "lingers in the memory like the taste of a splendidly aged Burgundy." Within *Blackberry Wine*, Kerry, Jay's girlfriend, is writing "a lighthearted book entitled *Chocolate—A Feminist Outlook*" (4).

4. Anthony D. Smith, *National Identity* (London: Penguin Books, 1991), 173.

5. John Tomlinson, *Globalization and Culture* (Chicago: University of Chicago Press, 1999), 17–20.

6. Smith, *National Identity*, 173.

7. As we will see, Claire Messud's *The Last Life* (New York: Harcourt, Brace, 1999) also fits this pattern. Both Messud and Harris have a French parent and speak French as well as English; Harris, whose mother is French, is fully bilingual, and she has taught French at the university level.

8. Smith, *National Identity*, 158.

9. See chapter 1 for a discussion of the similar pattern evident in the American novelist Diane Johnson's *Le Divorce* (New York: Dutton, 1997) and *Le Mariage* (New York: Dutton, 2000).

10. Harris, *Chocolat* (New York: Viking, 1999), 241.

11. Richard F. Kuisel, "The France We Have Lost: Social, Economic, and Cultural Discontinuities," in *Remaking the Hexagon: The New France in the New Europe*, ed. Gregory Flynn (San Francisco: Westview Press, 1995), 45.

12. James Clifford, *Routes: Travel and Translation in the Late Twentieth Century* (Cambridge, MA: Harvard University Press, 1997), 1.

13. See, in particular, Johnson's *Divorce*, whose heroine is loosely based on James's Isabel Archer. In her *Mariage*, one of the main characters periodically reads and reports on works by James, Hemingway, and Miller. Johnson, who spends at least six months in Paris every year, is something of an "expatriate" writer herself. See also the discussion of the recent festival held by Shakespeare and Company, the American bookstore in Paris, in the introduction and the analysis of the new "mysteries of modernism" in chapter 6.

14. Peter Mayle, *A Year in Provence* (New York: Knopf, 1990); *Toujours Provence* (New York: Knopf, 1991); *Hotel Pastis: A Novel of Provence* (New York: Vintage, 1993.)

15. Jean-Philippe Mathy, *French Resistance: The French-Culture Wars.* (Minneapolis: University of Minnesota, 2000), 55. Mayle's neighbors were sufficiently distressed by his books that he was forced to sell his property and move to New York, although he has since resettled in the south of France. Both Alan Aldridge ("The English as they see others: England revealed in Provence," *Sociological Review* 43 [1995]: 415–34) and Joanne P. Sharp ("Writing Over the Map of Provence: The touristic therapy of *A Year in Provence*," in *Writes of Passage: Reading Travel Writing*, ed. James Duncan and Derek Gregory [New York: Routledge, 1999], 200–18) argue that Mayle's books are only ostensibly about Provence and must, in fact, be understood as metaphoric explorations of England and of the English themselves.

16. Gian-Paolo Biasin, *The Flavors of Modernity: Food and the Novel* (Princeton, NJ: Princeton University Press, 1993), 3.

17. Ibid., 27–28. Postmodern literary theory posits a similar duality. If, for example, the postmodern novel foregrounds the story of its own construction, it nonetheless remains grounded in sociohistorical reality.

18. "The destiny of nations depends upon how they feed themselves" (epigraph to Mort Rosenblum, *A Goose in Toulouse and Other Culinary Adventures in France* [New York: Hyperion, 2000]).

19. Roland Barthes, *Mythologies* (Paris: Seuil, 1957), 74–77.

20. Biasin, *Flavors of Modernity*, 27.

21. Charles Baudelaire, *Les Fleurs du mal* (1857; repr., Paris: Garnier, 1963).

22. Tomlinson, *Globalization and Culture*, 1–2.

23. Kuisel, "France We Have Lost," 33.

24. Ibid., 34.

25. Aamir Mufti and Ella Shohat, introduction to *Dangerous Liaisons: Gender, Nation, and Postcolonial Perspectives*, ed. Anne McClintock, Aamir Mufti, and Ella Shohat (Minneapolis: University of Minnesota Press, 1997), 2.

26. Alan Riding, "Where are the Beret Factories of Yesterday?," *New York Times*, Aug. 1, 1999, sec. 7:6.

27. Richard Bernstein, *Fragile Glory: A Portrait of France and the French* (New York: Alfred A. Knopf, 1990), 328–32; Kuisel, "France We Have Lost"; Jonathan Fenby, *France on the Brink* (New York: Arcade, 1999).

28. It is certainly not my intention to suggest that xenophobia, racism, and fear of multiculturalism have disappeared in France, but the focus of the national media has clearly shifted in recent years.

29. See, for example, Jeffrey Richards, *Films and British National Identity: From Dickens to* Dad's Army (Manchester, England: Manchester University Press, 1997); and Smith, *National Identity*.

30. Rosenblum, *Goose in Toulouse*, 72.

31. Kuisel, "France We Have Lost," 73.

32. Such protests, in England as well as in France, have focused, for example, on new restrictions on hunters, genetically modified foods, threats to ban raw milk cheeses, and so on. See, for example, Roger Cohen, "Fearful Over the Future, Europe Seizes on Food," *New York Times*, Aug. 29, 1999, sec. 4:1, 3; and Jeffrey Kluger, "Food Fight," *Time*, Sept. 13, 1999, 43–44.

33. Rosenblum, *Goose in Toulouse*. Urban residents of France, including Parisians, have consistently supported strikes and protests by farmers, despite the turmoil they cause; and José Bové, head of *La Conféderation paysanne* has become a national hero (see, for example, Kuisel, "France We Have Lost").

34. See Cohen, "Fearful Over the Future"; and Rosemblum, *Goose in Toulouse*, 73–75.

35. Bové is a well-educated ex-Parisian who transformed himself into a sheep farmer in the French Southwest (see, for example, Rosenblum, ibid.). Joe is also not quite what he seems; Jay notes that "he would occasionally come out with a quote or a literary reference which could only have come from extensive, if secret, study" (225).

36. Adam Gopnick, *Paris to the Moon* (New York: Random House, 2000), 244.

37. Ibid., 239–42.

38. Linda Hutcheon, *A Poetics of Postmodernism: History, Theory, Fiction* (New York: Routledge, 1988), 42.

39. See Smith, *National Identity*, 158–59.

40. Rosenblum, *Goose in Toulouse*, 207

41. Ibid., 9.

42. Tomlinson, *Globalization and Culture*, 29.

43. Richards, *Films and British National Identity*, 365.

44. Jonathan appears to write the same kind of "category fiction" that Harris did at the beginning of her career. The names of his novels, however, also suggest a fondness for postmodern word play: e.g., *The G——sus Gene, Psy-Wrens of Mars, A Date with d'Eath* (3).

45. The relationship between reality and fiction is further complicated by Harris's own methods of composition: "Nearly all my characters contain elements of people I know. Joe is the most obvious; he is based very strongly on my grandfather . . . Jay is an amalgam of several people (including myself) but is loosely based on my friend Paul" (Marla Addison, interview with Joanne Harris, http://www.countrybookshop.co.uk). The similarity of the names of four people who are all storytellers—Joanne, Jon(athan), Joe, and Jay—is surely not accidental.

46. Just before he leaves London, Jay, at his most cynical, mocks the students in his writing class, who produce stories about single mothers and dope addicts, albeit (as they point out) in response to the assignment he gave: " 'Where's the magic?' he asked. 'That's what I want to know. Where are the magic carpets and Haitian voodoo and lone gunslingers and naked ladies tied to railway lines? Where are the Indian trackers and the four-armed goddesses and the pirates and the giant apes? *Where are the fucking space aliens?*' " (48–49).

47. Clifford, *Routes*, 1.

48. Today, of course, *National Geographic* is also published in a number of different languages and sold throughout Europe.

49. The paradox of wine, in general, is that of "the *pourriture noble*, the rot which gives the wine its sweetness and its flavor" (276); the proximity of Marise's vineyards to marsh-

lands is particularly conducive to its formation.

50. Jay's house in Lansquenet is also such a place (129–30), as are Lansquenet and Kirby Monckton themselves on a larger scale.

51. We know only that Jay's agent loves the new book and that Kerry finds it "actually better than *Jackapple Joe*. The way you depict this place—you make everything so *real*" (319). He signs a contract for its publication with "WorldWide, a large international publisher" (286).

52. See, in particular, Johnson, *Divorce* and *Mariage*.

53. Throughout the novel, Joe's pronunciation of *heart* as *'art* seems to suggest a play on words. In Lansquenet, just before his apparition definitively fades, he shows up on successive days wearing t-shirts that read, first, "CAMPAIGN FOR REAL FICTION" and then, "ART FOR ART'S SAKE," perhaps in ironic reflection of Jay's own confusion about the function of literature (278, 295).

54. Smith, *National Identity*, 174.

55. Addison, interview.

Chapter 5:
Mosaics of the Might-Have-Been

1. Claire Messud, *The Last Life* (New York: Harcourt, Brace, 1999), 3. Subsequent references, both to the novel and to the translation (*La Vie après*, trans. Guillemette Belleteste [Paris: Gallimard, 2001]) appear in parentheses in the text.

2. Qtd. in Emily Apter, *Continental Drift: From National Characters to Virtual Subjects* (Chicago: University of Chicago Press, 1999), 4.

3. See, for example, J. P. Vinay and J. Darbelnet, *Stylistique comparée du français et de l'anglais* (Paris: Didier, 1973), 105–7.

4. The two films so described are, respectively, Arnaud Desplechin's *Esther Kahn* (1999) and Patrice Chéreau's *Intimité* (2000).

5. Brooke Allen, "Silence, Exile, Cunning," *New Criterion*, Nov. 1999, 60–65; Sarah Kerr, "People are Talking about Books," *Vogue*, Sept. 1999, 478, 487.

6. Stuart Hall, "European Cinema on the Verge of a Nervous Breakdown," in *Screening Europe: Image and Identity in Contemporary European Cinema*, ed. Duncan Petrie (London: British Film Institute, 1992), 47.

7. Michiko Kakutani, "A Girl's Life, in a Family Unhappy in its Own Way," *New York Times*, Aug. 10, 1999, late ed., E8.

8. The autobiographical nature of the novel is clearly in part a question of interpretation, since Messud's father and paternal grandparents were of *pied-noir* origin; she also spent the summers of her childhood and adolescence in the South of France, although she was essentially raised in Canada and Australia. If Messud readily acknowledges her interest in "the *pied-noir* history and its legacy of displacement and uprootedness," she also insists on the fictionality of the story through which she explores that legacy in *The Last Life*: "None of the things that happen to Sagesse LaBasse has happened to me or to anyone in my family. Sagesse is invented, her brother is invented, her parents and grandparents are invented" (personal communication).

9. Ella Shohat and Robert Stam, *Unthinking Eurocentrism: Multiculturalism and the Media* (London: Routledge, 1994), 230.

10. James Clifford, *Routes: Travel and Translation in the Late Twentieth Century* (Cambridge, MA: Harvard University Press, 1997), 1.

11. Louis Mink, "Narrative Form as a Cognitive Instrument," in *The Writing of History*, ed. Robert H. Canary and Henry Kozicki (Madison: University of Wisconsin Press, 1978), 132; Hayden White, "The Value of Narrativity in the Representation of Reality," in *On Narrative*, ed. W. J. T. Mitchell (Chicago: University of Chicago Press, 1980), 3.

12. Mink, "Narrative Form," 132.

13. The naming of Sagesse is, of course, highly ironic: "[Carol] scanned books and magazines for elegant French names, exclaiming over obscure saints and pursuing their histories, only, too often, to find their martyrdoms sinister and bloody. (Marie, which is my first name, taken from my aunt and from the Madonna herself, was not hard to find; but Sagesse, a fantasy, [my parents] came to on their own, finding it euphonious and thinking, perhaps, and wrongly, that I was the child of their wisdom)" (213).

14. Shohat and Stam, *Unthinking Eurocentrism*, 101.

15. See Linda Hutcheon, *A Poetics of Postmodernism: History, Theory, Fiction* (New York: Routledge, 1988).

16. Edmund White, *The Married Man* (New York: Alfred A. Knopf, 2000), 70.

17. Shohat and Stam, *Unthinking Eurocentrism*, 101.

18. Aamir Mufti and Ella Shohat, introduction to *Dangerous Liaisons: Gender, Nation, and Postcolonial Perspectives*, ed. Anne McClintock, Aamir Mufti, and Ella Shohat (Minneapolis: University of Minnesota Press, 1997), 2.

19. Apter, *Continental Drift*, 37.

20. A character in Rose Tremain's *The Way I Found Her* (New York: Farrar, Straus and Giroux, 1997), 147, describes "to go missing" as the paradigmatic experience of the contemporary world. By chance, Messud reviewed Tremain's novel for the *New York Times* prior to the publication of her own Anglophone novel set in France ("Looking for Love," *New York Times*, Aug. 2, 1998, late ed., sec. 7:7).

21. The exceptionally timely death of Alexandre's grandmother on the very morning of his departure is almost certainly either an assisted "suicide" or a metaphoric "murder" (see 140).

22. E. Ann Kaplan, *Looking for the Other: Feminism, Film, and the Imperial Gaze* (London: Routledge, 1997), 173.

23. See chapter 1 for a discussion of the use of a similar strategy in Diane Johnson's *Le Divorce* (New York: Dutton, 1997) and *Le Mariage* (New York: Dutton, 2000).

24. If one possible way to enter the frame of a picture and live inside its "story" is represented by the cover of a book, those of *The Last Life* and *La Vie Après* support their alternative titles. The English-language novel depicts an isolated rock off the coast of the sea, suggestive of the site of Alexandre's suicide; the French version, on the other hand, uses a photograph of Algeria in the 1950s. Although the photo is not taken at the waterfront, it shows the same juxtaposition of "tiny people in dejellabas and Victorian suits" as does the watercolor of the Bay of Algiers (192).

25. Messud notes that St. Augustine was the half-cast child of a Berber and a Roman and Camus, though French, was Spanish by descent (304).

26. Mufti and Shohat, introduction to *Dangerous Liaisons*, 1–2.

27. Anne Donadey, " 'Une Certaine Idée de la France': The Algeria Syndrome and Struggles over 'French' Identity," in *Identity Papers: Contested Nationhood in Twentieth-Century France*, ed. Steven Ungar and Tom Conley (Minneapolis: University of Minnesota Press, 1996), 219.

28. Jean-Marie Le Pen, the founder of the Front national, served as a paratrooper during the Algerian War. Beginning in the mid-eighties and continuing into the 1990s the party became increasingly influential, attracting 10–15 percent of voters with its opposition to

immigration, judged responsible for unemployment and increased crime. The *harkis* are Algerians who fought with the French in the Algerian War.

29. Donadey, "'Certaine Idée de la France,'" 222.

30. On the one occasion that Sagesse invites Sami to her home, his attention focuses immediately on the watercolor of the Bay of Algiers; under his gaze significant details of the painting become newly visible to her: "A statue on horseback could be made out near the sea . . . the Duc d'Orléans in the Place du Gouvernement, facing, as French national pride demanded, the conquerable interior" (192). Subsequent to Sami's visit, Sagesse begins to read the newspapers and discovers that his outrage is shared by the vast majority of the French: "They found our history ghastly too, an insidious pollutant in the aquarium of French honor. France's error made flesh, the *pieds-noir*, and with them, the *harkis*, were guilty simply for existing. In the national narrative, my father's family was a distasteful emblem, linked, by circumstance, not only to the vicious undeclared war of their homeland, but in dark historical shame to the collaborationists of Vichy and, further back still, to the ugliest excesses of the Dreyfus affair" (227).

31. Donadey argues that the memory of the Algerian War has been displaced by a perceived threat to French identity from *métissage* ("'Certaine Idée de la France,'" 227); Apter similarly attributes France's reluctance to confront its colonialist past to a more immediate obsession with preserving French cultural identity (*Continental Drift*, 66).

32. A *pied-noir* friend, invited to celebrate Jacques's release from prison, calls him "a hero" and assures him that she would have "done exactly as [he] did." The anecdote she then tells to support her view of the necessity of protecting oneself against the actions of "young people today" clearly indicates a curious and no doubt unconscious displacement onto French youth of her own xenophobic fears. The group of teenagers who surround her car "were—I hate to say it, but of course—they were Arabs" (259). When Sagesse later prompts her reflective grandfather to tell her what he is thinking, she does not expect to hear the story of Serge LaBasse: "I projected remorse, and a quiet tide of grief, a recognition that, Kronos-like, he had been engaged heretofore in the voracious consumption of his children, rather than in their nurturing" (266).

33. Clifford, *Routes*, 1, 17.

34. John Tomlinson, *Globalization and Culture* (Chicago: University of Chicago Press, 1999), 111.

35. Homi K. Bhabha, "The World and the Home," in *Dangerous Liaisons* (see note 18), 445–46.

36. Ibid., 449.

37. Ibid.

38. Hall, "The Local and the Global: Globalization and Ethnicity," in *Dangerous Liaisons* (see note 18), 178.

39. See, for example, Richard Bernstein, *Fragile Glory: A Portrait of France and the French* (New York: Alfred A. Knopf, 1990).

40. Benedict Anderson, *Imagined Communities: Reflections on the Origin and Spread of Nationalism*, rev. ed. (London: Verso, 1991).

41. Qtd. in Jean-Philippe Mathy, "The Popularity of American Culture," *Sites* 1 (Spring 1997): 151.

42. Rob Kroes, *If You've Seen One, You've Seen the Mall: Europeans and American Mass Culture* (Urbana: University of Illinois Press, 1996), xiii.

43. The terms I cite originate, in turn, in the following: Bhabha, "World and the Home," 445–46; Clifford, *Routes*, 1; Tomlinson, *Globalization and Culture*, 29; Mufti and Shohat, introduction to *Dangerous Liaisons*, 2.

44. Ted Morgan, *On Becoming American* (1978; repr., New York: Paragon House, 1988), 253. Before Ted Morgan changed his name and his nationality, he was Sanche de Gramont, a Frenchman who wrote cultural studies in English about France and the French; one of the very earliest examples of a modern trend of Anglophone books about France thus actually exists in multiple volumes, written by a man whose bicultural upbringing literally turned him into two different people.

45. Morgan, *On Becoming American*, 253.

46. Ibid., 4.

47. Mathy, *French Resistance: The French-Culture Wars* (Minneapolis: University of Minnesota, 2000), 17.

48. Catherine Hermary-Vieille and Michèle Sarde note that expatriation is perceived by the French as "une désertion" in *Le Salon de conversation* (Paris: JC Lattès, 1997), an example of a complementary pattern of recent Francophone novels about the United States (245).

49. Indeed, the only other character who becomes "a person who could choose" and also alters her life after Alexandre's death is Sagesse's American mother. Much like Roxy in Johnson's *Divorce*, however, Carol stays in France and remakes her future with another Frenchman.

50. At the same time, of course, both Messud's narrative as a whole and the syntax of her characteristic sentence do contain language within a "frame." As Sagesse also states: "It is a terrible thing to be free. Nations know this; churches know this. People, however, seek to skirt the knowledge. They elevate freedom to a Holy Grail, disregarding the truth that *constraints are what define us, in life and in language alike: we yearn to be sentenced*" (328, my emphasis). Similarly, Messud herself has noted her particular interest, in writing *The Last Life*, in the sentence: "In exploring its parameters, its flexibility, its limitations. As Sagesse discovers and articulates, stories are always partial, in both senses of the word; so too are sentences. Expression is always incomplete. But it doesn't stop us from trying. We are sentenced by grammar, just as we are sentenced by narrative form, but these constraints can (one hopes) be our inspiration and our liberation as well as our limitation" (personal communication).

51. In one of the most emotionally powerful as well as clearly metaphoric passages of the novel, Sagesse returns home unexpectedly to find that her father has left her brother enclosed in the dark in his elevator shaft. Although Alexandre's marital infidelity will be revealed as a result of this incident, it is not, in Sagesse's view, "the day's most damaging event": "Far more important to my understanding of my father, or to its failure, are Etienne and his hours in the elevator.... And to my understanding of myself, the fact that I left Etienne there, and shut the door again upon him" (195, 197).

52. At the same time, however, Etienne, who is fundamentally unknowable and untranslatable, defines the limits of Sagesse's desire "to translate the world inside" (3) and to bridge the "gulf between the imaginary and the real" (297).

53. As the essence of "home ... in all its lost possibility" (161), Etienne's metaphoric perfection clearly extends beyond the boundaries of *The Last Life*; on a broader scale, he symbolizes the fundamental paradox of the postmodern condition in which "home" has become "unhomely."

Chapter 6:
Modernism and Mystery

1. Walter Satterthwait, *Masquerade* (New York: St. Martin's Press, 1998), 242. Subsequent references appear in parentheses in the text. A *Moveable Feast* (New York: Simon

and Schuster, 1964) documents Ernest Hemingway's Paris experience during the years 1922–1926. Written in Cuba and Idaho between 1957 and 1960, it was published posthumously in 1964.

2. Hemingway, preface to *Moveable Feast*.

3. Carolyn Dever and Margaret Cohen, introduction to *The Literary Channel: The Inter-National Invention of the Novel*, ed. Margaret Cohen and Carolyn Dever (Princeton, NJ: Princeton University Press, 2002), 23–24. See, in particular, Diane Johnson's *Le Divorce* (New York: Dutton, 1997) and *Le Mariage* (New York: Dutton, 2000) and Rose Tremain's *The Way I Found Her* (New York: Farrar, Straus and Giroux, 1997).

4. See, for example, Jim Collins, *Uncommon Cultures: Popular Culture and Post-Modernism* (New York: Routledge, 1989); Linda Hutcheon, *A Poetics of Postmodernism: History, Theory, Fiction* (New York: Routledge, 1988); and Brian McHale, *Postmodernist Fiction* (New York: Routledge, 1987) and *Constructing Postmodernism* (New York: Routledge, 1992).

5. Pierre Verdaguer, "Introduction: Estelle Monbrun," *Sites* 1 (Spring 1997): 369.

6. The significant number of contemporary Anglophone mysteries set in France, in addition to those discussed or mentioned throughout this chapter, includes the following, all set in Paris: Cara Black's *Murder in the Marais* (New York: Soho Press, 1998), *Murder in Belleville* (New York: Soho Press, 2000), *Murder in the Sentier* (New York: Soho Press, 2002), and *Murder in the Bastille* (New York: Soho Press, 2003); Carole Nelson Douglas's *Chapel Noir: An Irene Adler Novel* (New York: Tom Doherty, 2001); R. Robert Janes's *Sandman* (New York: Soho Press, 1996), *Mannequin* (New York: Soho Press, 1994), and other novels in the St.-Cyr-Kohler series (1990s); Ruth Walker's *The Bathsheba Connection* (New York: Writers Club Press, 2000); Hannah Blank's *A Murder of Convenience* (New York: Hightrees Books, 1999); and Barbara Sohmers's *The Fox and the Pussycat* (Glendora, CA: Sodef Press, 1998).

7. Howard Engels, *Murder in Montparnasse* (Woodstock, NY: Overlook Press, 1999); Tony Hays, *Murder in the Latin Quarter* (Bell Buckle, TN: Iris Press, 1993). Subsequent references to both novels appear in parentheses in the text. Sam McCarver's *The Case of the Uninvited Guest* (New York: Signet, 2002) suggests that the trend will continue into the twenty-first century. Set in the final weeks of 1918, McCarver's novel features Hemingway as a wounded war hero and a novice journalist whose decision to vacation in Paris on his way home to America allows him to help solve a murder. Although the crime takes place in an international hotel at a party attended by a multinational corps of writers—"French, English, American, Dutch. Even Spanish. A normal mixture for Paris, and Le Grand"—in what is clearly already "a cosmopolitan city" (11), the period of *A Moveable Feast* and the future Shakespeare and Company are as yet only a topic of conversation between Hemingway and Sylvia Beach:

> "But later, well, I want to walk these streets with good legs, and write about Paris. There's a beautiful, wistful, elegant sadness about this city. I want to write about the love that's here. And I want to write about the war, too, and how it destroyed the moral standards of my generation, of those who managed to stay alive—the lost generation."
>
> Sylvia nodded. *"Une génération perdue.* . . . And now the war is over, romantics of the world will come here and the intellectuals will meet in salons and they'll all write about life. . . . I'll sell the books they write from my own little bookstore."

8. See, for example, Michael Holquist, "Whodunit and Other Questions: Metaphysical Detective Stories in Postwar Fiction," in *The Poetics of Murder: Detective Fiction and Lit-*

erary Theory, ed. Glenn W. Most and William W. Stowe (New York: Harcourt Brace Jovanovich, 1983), 149–74; Marjorie Nicolson, "The Professor and the Detective," in *The Art of the Mystery Story: A Collection of Critical Essays*, ed. Howard Haycraft (New York: Simon and Schuster, 1946), 110–27; Dennis Porter, *The Pursuit of Crime: Art and Ideology in Detective Fiction* (New Haven, CT: Yale University Press, 1981).

9. Holquist, "Whodunit and Other Questions," 159.
10. Nicolson, "Professor and the Detective," 112–13.
11. Holquist, "Whodunit and Other Questions," 163–64.
12. Heta Pyrhönen, *Murder from an Academic Angle: An Introduction to the Study of the Detective Narrative* (Columbia, SC: Camden House, 1994), 43.
13. Nicholas Birns and Margaret Boe Birns, "Agatha Christie: Modern and Modernist," in *The Cunning Craft: Original Essays on Detective Fiction and Contemporary Literary Theory* (Macomb: Western Illinois University Press, 1990), 120.
14. Birns and Birns, "Agatha Christie," 133.
15. See, for example, S. E. Sweeney, "Locked Rooms: Detective Fiction, Narrative Theory, and Self-Reflexivity," in *The Cunning Craft* (see note 13), 123.
16. Holquist, "Whodunit and Other Questions," 165.
17. Satterthwait, Engel, and Hays have an interesting predecessor in Elliot Paul, who wrote a series of detective novels in the late 1930s set in Montparnasse. Although Jean Méral (*Paris in American Literature*, trans. Laurette Long [Chapel Hill: University of North Carolina Press], 210) describes his work in terms that certainly apply to that of his successors—"Paul makes capital out of the Lost Generation . . . and freely mixes popular detective archetypes with asides to the initiated," the writers of the period appear only as background to Paul's hero, Homer Evans, himself an American expatriate artist as well as an amateur detective. The following example, quoted from Paul's "international mystery," *The Mysterious Mickey Finn or Murder at the Café du Dôme* (New York: Modern Age, 1939), is the only passage in the novel in which members of the Lost Generation appear, complete with a tongue-in-cheek capsule characterization:

> James Joyce was making the sixth revision of page two thousand and forty of his *magnum opus* called "Work in Progress"; Harold Stearns was sitting at the Select bar, murmuring that murders were unusual, therefore banal, consequently uninteresting; Gertrude Stein and Alice Toklas were drinking brandy and soda, Gertrude the brandy and Alice the soda; Ernest Hemingway was in the Bois thinking about what he would do if the Bois was Wyoming, the swans were wild ducks, and he had a gun. (93)

18. Glenn W. Most, "The Hippocratic Smile: John Le Carré and the Traditions of the Detective Novel," in *The Poetics of Murder* (see note 8), 345.
19. Holquist, "Whodunit and Other Questions," 165.
20. Hemingway, *Moveable Feast*, 29.
21. See, for example, Peter Brooks, *Reading for the Plot: Design and Intention in Narrative* (New York: Alfred A. Knopf, 1984) as well as Porter, *Pursuit of Crime* and Holquist, "Whodunit and Other Questions."
22. Porter, *Pursuit of Crime*, 189. Hemingway also recycles materials from his own past—sketches, notes, and artifacts of his stay in Paris found years later—in *The Moveable Feast*, a work that is in many ways more postmodern than modernist, notably in the conscious and overt manipulation of fictional and nonfictional forms and in the use of parody.
23. See, for example, Jacqueline Tavernier-Courbin, *Ernest Hemingway's* A Moveable Feast: *The Making of Myth* (Boston: Northeastern University Press, 1991).

24. Yet, as is frequently the case in these novels, something that seems innovative at first sight, at least in terms of how the preexistent is (re)combined, turns out to have a possible origin in a place at once predictable and unexpected. In *A Moveable Feast*, Stein lends Hemingway what he calls "that marvelous story of Jack the Ripper"; and he cites the mysteries of Simenon as his favorite "after-work books" (27). In what could be an allusion to Poe's Dupin as well as a foreshadowing of *Murder in Montparnasse*, Hemingway also reports on the special pleasures of café reading in Paris: "There are always some splendid crimes in the newspapers that you follow from day to day, when you live in France. These crimes read like continued stories" (167). Jack the Ripper also turns up in Paris in Douglas's *Chapel Noir*, set, however, in the more plausible period of the late 1880s.

25. Hemingway, *Moveable Feast*, 62–64.

26. Satterthwait's *Masquerade* is in fact an epistolary novel in which the letters sent by Jane Turner to a friend in England alternate with Phil Beaumont's first-person account. Satterthwait uses the device to similarly self-referential ends, although in this case his diegetic persona, unlike Engel's, reveals herself to be highly conscious of the proper construction of a mystery story. Jane's letters are structured throughout to create suspense; even at the end of the novel she refuses to reveal the identity of the murderer to her correspondent: "I know that you are the sort of person who, whenever she picks up a crime novel, immediately opens it at the last page, to determine the identity of the killer" (322).

27. Tyler's envy, which leads to the theft of the manuscripts that Waddington believes to have been lost, appears to be based on a confusion between Hemingway the writer and Jake Barnes the bohemian: "He was so jealous of your apparent ease with words that he had to try to destroy your work.... He doesn't know the blood it's cost you; he only sees the sentences one after another put down with precision and simplicity....To him, with your talent for friendship, your sloppy manner around the Quarter—maybe he thought you were unworthy of your genius" (288–89).

28. Méral, *Paris in American Literature*, 244.

29. Ibid., 2.

30. Qtd. in Malcolm Bradbury, *Dangerous Pilgrimages: Transatlantic Mythologies and the Novel* (New York: Viking, 1995), 471n10.

31. Porter, *Pursuit of Crime*, 217–18.

32. Martine Guyot-Bender, "Fiction at Twenty Thousand Leagues Above the Sea. *Hemisphere*'s Fantasies of France," *Sites* 5 (Spring 2001): 147; Méral, *Paris in American Literature*, 244.

33. The Edgar Allan Poe Award continues to honor the best American crime novel published each year. A certain number of critics and theorists nonetheless prefer what Porter calls "the long view" of the subject and trace the origins of detective fiction back to Greek tragedy (*Pursuit of Crime*, 11).

34. Verdaguer, *La Séduction policière* (Birmingham, AL: Summa Publications, 1999), 294n8.

35. Méral, *Paris in American Literature*, 4–6.

36. Dominique Kalifa, *Les Crimes de Paris: Lieux et non-lieux du crime à Paris au XIX$_e$ Siècle* (Paris: BILIPO, 2001), 3. A play on the words *lieux* (places, scenes) and *non-lieux* (case dismissals for lack of evidence) makes the title of the exposition impossible to translate accurately into English.

37. Edgar Allan Poe, "Murders in the Rue Morgue," in *The Unabridged Edgar Allan Poe* (Philadelphia: Running Press, 1983), 658.

38. Poe, "The Purloined Letter," in *Unabridged Edgar Allan Poe* (see note 37), 917.

39. See, for example, ibid., 927.

40. Porter, *Pursuit of Crime*, 128.

41. See, for example, Pyrhönen, *Murder from an Academic Angle*, 59–60; and Stefano Tani, *The Doomed Detective: The Contribution of the Detective Novel to Postmodern American and Italian Fiction* (Carbondale: Southern Illinois University Press, 1984), xiv.

42. The only overt reference to Poe's detective stories occurs in *Murder in the Latin Quarter* in the following brief exchange between Jack Barnett and Hemingway (12):

—You need Auguste Dupin.
—Leave Poe out of this.

In Hays's novel, Police Inspector Duvall, with whom Jack has already worked on a previous case, is another variation on Dupin by way of Hercule Poirot.

43. Beaumont himself clearly prefers the role of Poirot to that of Hastings. After flipping through a copy of Sybil Norton's *The Mysterious Affair at Pyles* about "the famous French private detective Pierre Reynard" and "his buddy, Kippers, the narrator, [who] follows him around and admires his technique" (104), Phil on occasion pointedly compares his own behavior to that of Reynard: "he was a peach" (130). Christie's Poirot is, of course, Belgian.

44. Méral, *Paris in American Literature*, 137.

45. Porter, *Pursuit of Crime*, 217.

46. Méral, *Paris in American Literature*, 4–40.

47. Méral, *Paris in American Literature*, 10–11.

48. Rob Kroes, *If You've Seen One, You've Seen the Mall: Europeans and American Mass Culture* (Urbana: University of Illinois Press, 1996), 126.

49. Bradbury, *Dangerous Pilgrimages*, 305. In this sense as well, *Masquerade*, *Murder in the Latin Quarter*, and *Murder in Montparnasse* are representative of the larger body of contemporary American fiction set in Paris, mainstream novels as well as mysteries. For example, the characters in Smith's *The Knowledge of Water* (New York: Ballantine, 1996), who include "Milly Xico" (a.k.a. Colette) as the heroine's closest friend, attend Stein's salon in 1910. Margaret Vandenburg's *An American in Paris* (San Francisco: Cleis Press, 2000) is no doubt subtitled "a novel" to distinguish her book from that of Janet Flanner. Like Flanner, who is a character in Vandenburg's novel, "Henrietta Adams," the heroine of this *American in Paris*, is also a journalist who covers the avant-garde scene from Paris; this time Stein appears as criminal rather than detective, the co-conspirator of Picasso and Juan Gris in an art forgery fraud. Matthew Stadler's *Allan Stein* (New York: Grove Press, 1999) is set in the present but the story of Stein's nephew and a portrait painted of him by Picasso play a key role in the narrative. In Charlotte Carter's *Coq au vin* (New York: Warner Books, 1999) and Shay Youngblood's *Black Girl in Paris* (New York: Riverhead Books, 2000), historical fascination with the Black American expatriate community of musicians and writers of the 1940s prompts their contemporary heroines to travel to Paris.

Chapter 7:
Museum, Maze, Madhouse

1. Martine Guyot-Bender, "Fiction at Twenty Thousand Leagues Above the Sea. *Hemisphere*'s Fantasies of France," *Sites* 5 (Spring 2001): 150.

2. Ibid., 147.

3. Sarah Smith, *The Vanished Child* (New York: Ballantine, 1992); *The Knowledge of Water* (New York: Ballantine, 1996); *The Citizen of the Country* (New York: Ballantine, 2000. Subsequent references to all three novels appear in parentheses in the text.

4. Malcolm Bradbury, "Modernisms/Postmodernisms," in *Innovation/Renovation: New Perspectives on the Humanities*, ed. Ihab Hassan (Madison: University of Wisconsin Press, 1983), 324–25.

5. Ibid., 327.

6. André Malraux's own life and career offer an early model of globalism and migratory postmodernism.

7. Douglas Crimp, "On the Museum's Ruins," in *The Anti-Aesthetic: Essays on Postmodern Culture*, ed. Hal Foster (Port Townsend, WA: Bay Press, 1983), 49: "Founded on the disciplines of archeology and natural history, both inherited from the classical age, the museum was a discredited institution from its very inception. And the history of museology is a history of all the various attempts to deny the heterogeneity of the museum, to reduce it to a homogeneous system or series. The faith in the possibility of ordering the museum's 'bric-a-brac,' . . . persists until today."

8. On the connotations of the word *museum*, note the comment of Theodor W. Adorno, qtd. in Crimp, ibid., 42: "The German word *museal* [museum-like] has unpleasant overtones. It describes objects to which the observer no longer has a vital relationship and which are in the process of dying. They owe their preservation more to historical respect than to the needs of the present. Museum and mausoleum are connected by more than phonetic association. Museums are the family sepulchres of works of art."

9. Aamir Mufti and Ella Shohat, introduction to *Dangerous Liaisons: Gender, Nation, and Postcolonial Perspectives*, ed. Anne McClintock, Aamir Mufti, and Ella Shohat (Minneapolis: University of Minnesota Press, 1997), 2.

10. According to *The American Heritage Dictionary of the English Language*, 3rd ed. (New York: Houghton Mifflin, 1992), the word *landscape* crosses back and forth over the frontier between reality and art. The original Dutch term referring to "a tract of land" was borrowed in 1598 as a painter's term for a "picture depicting scenery on land." The first use of the English word to designate a view of natural scenery was not recorded until thirty-four years later.

11. Franco Moretti, *Atlas of the European Novel, 1800–1900* (London: Verso, 1998), 8. Moretti seeks to map the space of the nineteenth-century novel, suggesting that the cosmopolitan novel of the late twentieth century has important precursors.

12. Bradbury, "Modernisms/Postmodernisms," 324.

13. Eric Kahler, qtd. in Alan Wilde, "Modernism and the Aesthetics of Crisis," in *Postmodernism: A Reader*, ed. Patricia Waugh (London: Edward Arnold, 1992), 16.

14. Brian McHale, *Constructing Postmodernism* (New York: Routledge, 1992), 157.

15. Ibid., 158.

16. Ibid., 157–58.

17. James Clifford, *Routes: Travel and Translation in the Late Twentieth Century* (Cambridge, MA: Harvard University Press, 1997), 1, 37.

18. Dennis Porter, *Haunted Journeys: Desire and Transgression in European Travel Writing* (Princeton, NJ: Princeton University Press, 1991), 5, 12.

19. Homi K. Bhabha, "The World and the Home," in *Dangerous Liaisons* (see note 9), 445–55; Mufti and Shohat, introduction to *Dangerous Liaisons*, 2.

20. Wilde, "Modernism and the Aesthetics," 19–20.

21. Erika Fisher-Lichte, among others, cites "the dissolution of the self and its boundaries" as a distinctive feature of characterization in postmodern theater in *The Show and the Gaze of Theatre: A European Perspective* (Iowa City: University of Iowa Press, 1997), 262. Like Reisden, the postmodern character experiences what Ihab Hassan calls a sense of "self-less-ness" in which "the self impersonates its absence" ("Pluralism in Postmodern

Perspective," in *Exploring Postmodernism*, ed. Matei Calinescu and Douwe Fokkema [Amsterdam: John Benjamins, 1986], 19).

22. Even though Richard is not in fact a victim, kidnapping may be a curiously American obsession, as the reference to the case of Charley Ross that serves as epigraph to the novel might suggest. Our national sense of identity leads to the following paradox: if, on the one hand, becoming something other than what you are (what you were raised to be) is no doubt the American dream, on the other hand, becoming (being raised as) something other than what you are is also the American nightmare. Change must be self-instigated, not imposed.

23. Frederic Jameson, "Postmodernism and Consumer Society," in *The Anti-Aesthetic* (see note 7), 111–25.

24. Ibid., 113.

25. Dennis Porter, *The Pursuit of Crime: Art and Ideology in Detective Fiction* (New Haven, CT: Yale University Press, 1981), 11; for an example of a critic who takes "the long view," see David I. Grossvogel, *Mystery and its Fictions: From Oedipus to Agatha Christie* (Baltimore: Johns Hopkins University Press, 1979), 23–28.

26. Jameson, "Postmodernism and Consumer Society," 118.

27. Roland Barthes, qtd. in Porter, *Pursuit of Crime*, 253.

28. Wilde, "Modernism and the Aesthetics," 16.

29. William V. Spanos, *Repetitions: The Postmodern Occasion in Literature and Culture* (Baton Rouge: Louisiana State University Press, 1987), 28.

30. Patricia Parkhurst Ferguson, "Is Paris France?," *The French Review* 73 (May 2000): 1052.

31. Roger Shattuck's depiction of Paris in *The Banquet Years: The Origins of the Avant Garde in France, 1885 to World War I*, rev. ed. (New York: Vintage, 1968), 253–57—and especially his portrait of Apollinaire—are similar to those of Smith. Notably Apollinaire is at once performer, impresario, cosmopolitan, avid walker, and citizen of Europe.

32. Or, as "Stein" (Esther Cohen) characteristically puts it: "'They have been divorcing for years, they are always divorcing, they are almost always divorced, but they are not divorced yet'" (77).

33. Jean Méral, *Paris in American Literature*, trans. Laurette Long (Chapel Hill: University of North Carolina Press, 1989), 328. Smith describes Paris in the unpaginated "Reader's Guide" that follows the novel: "Paris was a very cosmopolitan city, and the French firmly believed that any sensible person would want to live in Paris. In fact, a large percentage of the Parisian intelligentsia of the period were foreigners, as are most of the characters in *The Knowledge of Water*."

34. Clifford, *Routes*, 11.

35. Méral, *Paris in American Literature*, 9.

36. In fact, Clifford's sense of the "border" as "a specific place of hybridity and struggle, policing and transgression" (*Routes*, 37) is realized in Courbevoie, where Roy Daugherty, the Boston detective sent by Gilbert, turns up unexpectedly to discover Perdita's and Reisden's illicit love affair and where the lovers struggle to overcome their differences.

37. Manet's Olympia does not have a fan in her lap although she is holding a feather that memory might mistake for one. An informal survey, which included several art historians, confirms that this is nonetheless the painting that Daugherty's description immediately brings to mind.

38. Crimp, "On the Museum's Ruins," 48.

39. Ibid., 45.

40. Michel Foucault, qtd. in Crimp, ibid., 47.

41. Crimp, ibid., 46–47.

42. Ibid., 53.

43. Shattuck (*Banquet Years*, 257) notes that in his own work Apollinaire borrowed with impunity: "the borderline in his mind between originality and imitation is truly difficult to ascertain." Milly proposes that the Mona Lisa be thrown into the Seine on January 28, her birthday.

44. In fact, at the end of the novel Milly appears to be in possession of the "real" Mona Lisa stolen by Leonard and to have given George a copy (461).

45. Donald Sassoon, *Becoming Mona Lisa: The Making of a Global Icon* (New York: Harcourt, 2001). Smith could not have known Sassoon's work given its date of publication. As she notes in her afterword, the theft actually occurred in 1911. As a result of their well-known objections to "museum art," Picasso was questioned by the police and Apollinaire spent a few days in prison.

46. Malcolm Bradbury, *Dangerous Pilgrimages: Transatlantic Mythologies and the Novel* (New York: Viking, 1995), 11.

47. Ibid., 481.

48. Paul Watkins, *The Forger* (New York: Picador USA, 2000), 162. Watkins's novel, set during the German Occupation, is deeply concerned with the preservation of "museum art." Dan Brown's *The Da Vinci Code* (New York: Doubleday, 2003), whose bestseller status confirms the popularity of American novels set in France, opens in the Louvre, and the Mona Lisa plays a key role in the resolution of the murder of the curator.

49. See chapter 2 for a parallel discussion of the paradox posed by the postmodern acts of plagiarism and translation in Rose Tremain's *The Way I Found Her* (New York: Farrar, Straus and Giroux, 1997).

50. Méral, *Paris in American Literature*, 169.

51. Linda Hutcheon, *A Poetics of Postmodernism: History, Theory, Fiction* (New York: Routledge, 1988), ix; McHale, *Constructing Postmodernism*, 152.

52. Hutcheon, *Poetics of Postmodernism*, 10.

53. Jameson, "Postmodernism and Consumer Society," 113.

54. Ibid., 118.

55. Guyot-Bender, "Fiction at Twenty Thousand Leagues," 147.

56. Jameson, "Postmodernism and Consumer Society," 115. Smith's literary style also combines impressionism and cubism: subjective voices are juxtaposed in a collage that simulates the simultaneous representation of multiple and contradictory points of view. In the "Reader's Guide" that follows the novel, Smith attributes the title of *The Knowledge of Water* to a critical comment made by Apollinaire about the Impressionists: "One knows reality as one knows water." This understanding of the changing nature of reality informs the Cubists' and Smith's use of multiple perspective.

57. Crimp, "On the Museum's Ruins," 47.

58. McHale, *Constructing Postmodernism*, 158.

59. Shattuck, *Banquet Years*, 5–6. Steven Connor argues in *Postmodernist Culture: An Introduction to Theories of the Contemporary*, 2nd ed. (Cambridge: Blackwell, 1997) that "theatricality itself connects with many of the most important preoccupations of the postmodern debate" (142).

60. Smith's use of accents on the French word *théâtre* is inconsistent; she writes "theatre du monde" but "Théâtre Cyron." I have respected her usage.

61. Méral, *Paris in American Literature*, 40.

62. McHale, *Postmodernist Fiction* (New York: Routledge, 1987), 57.

63. Jameson, "Postmodernism and Consumer Society," 117.

64. William Allan Neilson and Charles Jarvis Hill, introduction to *The Complete Plays and Poems of William Shakespeare*, ed. William Allan Neilson and Charles Jarvis Hill (New York: Houghton Mifflin, 1942), 1180.

65. Jim Collins, *Uncommon Cultures: Popular Culture and Post-Modernism* (New York: Routledge, 1989), 49.

66. See Peter Hühn, "The Detective as Reader: Narrativity and Reading Concepts in Detective Fiction," *Modern Fiction Studies* 33 (Autumn 1987): 461.

67. Simon Brett's *What Bloody Man is That?* (New York: toExcel, 2000) is a recent example. In *Chasing Shakespeares: A Novel* (New York: Astria Books, 2003), the first work Smith has published since completing the trilogy, the discovery of a new document calls into question Shakespeare's authorship of his own canon.

68. William Shakespeare, *Macbeth*, in *Complete Plays*, 5.5.24–28. Shakespeare also repeats himself, using variations of the same characters and plot devices in different plays. Similarly, the story of the "Vanished Child" is largely repeated in *The Citizen of the Country* where Reisden acts as psychoanalyst to unlock the secret of the death of André's parents. The specific use that Smith makes of *Macbeth* as *mise-en-abyme* focuses on the substitution of the father and son relationship between Mabet and Méduc for the original friendship between Macbeth and Macduff.

69. Ella Shohat and Robert Stam, *Unthinking Eurocentrism: Multiculturalism and the Media* (London: Routledge, 1994), 101.

70. Shohat and Stam, ibid., 230.

71. Shakespeare, *Macbeth*, 5.5.26–28. The period of the Revolution was already a time of uneasy tension between the emergence of nationalism and the universal values promoted by the eighteenth-century *philosophes*; Dreyfus similarly divided France into two groups: his adversaries formed "La Ligue de la Patrie française" and his partisans united in favor of the "Droits de l'homme." The War of 1870 resulted in the third crisis of national identity referenced by Smith.

72. Reisden and Perdita "can't have America. Not together" (231). Still, the mobility of the American characters in the novel suggests a restlessness and a cosmopolitanism particularly consistent with postmodern identity. Daugherty has also settled—for the moment—in Paris and even fearful Gilbert has returned to his itinerant roots at the end of the novel: "I have even thought of traveling. Even—Italy" (404). At the same time, only Americans in the novel also struggle with the loss of "home."

73. For example, Jules and Ruthie, the two most important of the supporting characters, are orphans, Lebanese refugees, and naturalized French citizens; Blantire, the first murder victim, was born in Russia, raised in the United States, and suspected of spying for Germany. The few characters who are native French citizens—Cyron, General Pétiot, and Sabine—are those responsible for the murders that occur in the novel. Smith has commented on her Web site (http://www.sarahsmith.com/conversation_abt_cotc.htm#is_this_the_end) on the two meanings of "country" in the title of the novel: "It's a book about the countryside and country people—nobody's more country than Sabine!—but also about where you live and how you live there, how you take responsibility for creating a part of your world."

74. Unlike a citizen, a resident does not owe allegiance to any country. Curiously, the three subcategories of "one who resides" in the third edition of the *American Heritage Dictionary of the English Language*—a diplomatic official, a colonial officer, and a member of an intelligence-gathering agency—might all apply to Reisden, who was trained to be a diplomat and briefly spied for Austria; Leo claims that his parents were white colonialists in

South Africa. More importantly, Residen's name is German, a language in which there is no word for "resident"; significantly, *Reisender*, the word from which his name would appear to derive, means "traveler" (*reisen*, to travel; *die Reisen*, travels).

75. Tomlinson, *Globalization and Culture*, 184.

76. T. S. Eliott, qtd. in Rob Kroes, *If You've Seen One, You've Seen the Mall: Europeans and American Mass Culture* (Urbana: University of Illinois Press, 1996), 183.

77. Bradbury, *Dangerous Pilgrimages*, 481.

78. Alison Russell, *Crossing Boundaries: Postmodern Travel Literature* (New York: Palgrave, 2000), 88. Russell develops the concept to describe Bruce Chatwin's *The Songlines*, an experimental ethnography of Australian Aborigines.

79. Ibid., 88–89.

80. The dark, narrow tunnels of the boves also contain mounds of skulls and bones (191) like the catacombs, which Méral describes as "admirably suited to the twists and turns of the detective novel" (*Paris in American Literature*, 8). The boves also evoke the original labyrinth of Greek mythology; like Ariane, Ruthie unrolls a ball of string when Reisden and André first descend into the cellars below Montfort (190). The word *clue* is a variant of *clew*, derived from Theseus's use of the ball of thread to guide his way through the Cretan labyrinth.

81. Wilde, "Modernism and the Aesthetics of Crisis, 17.

CHAPTER 8:
THE RE-ZONING OF GAY PARIS

1. Diane Johnson, *Le Mariage* (New York: Dutton, 2000), 11.

2. Philippe Tapon, *A Parisian from Kansas* (New York: Plume, 1997), 257.

3. Edmund White, *The Married Man* (New York: Alfred A. Knopf, 2000). Subsequent references appear in parentheses in the text.

4. Johnson, *Le Divorce* (New York: Dutton, 1997). Subsequent references appear in parentheses in the text.

5. Richard Canning uses this term in "Edmund White," in *Gay Fiction Speaks: Conversations with Gay Novelists* (New York: Columbia University Press, 2000), 77.

6. White, *Our Paris: Sketches from Memory*, with drawings by Hubert Sorin (New York: Alfred A. Knopf, 1995); *The Farewell Symphony* (New York: Alfred A. Knopf, 1997); *The Flâneur: A Stroll through the Paradoxes of Paris* (London: Bloomsbury, 2001). Stephen Barber, *Edmund White: The Burning World* (New York: St. Martin's Press, 1999).

7. Patricia Duncker, *Hallucinating Foucault* (New York: Vintage, 1996); Matthew Stadler, *Allan Stein* (New York: Grove Press, 1999); Monique Truong, *The Book of Salt* (New York: Houghton Mifflin, 2003). Subsequent references to all three novels appear in parentheses in the text.

8. Johnson, *L'Affaire* (New York: Dutton, 2003).

9. The title of *The Married Man* is no doubt also intended to recall Christopher Isherwood's *The Single Man* (New York: Methuen, 1964). The hero of Isherwood's semiautobiographical novel is a sixty-year-old British professor, living in the United States, whose male companion has recently died.

10. Personal communication, 2003.

11. Brian Kenney, rev. of *The Married Man*, *Library Journal*, May 15, 2000, 127–28.

12. White, *Flâneur*, 38. The words *flâner* and *flâneur* have no exact equivalents in English, and most standard translations inaccurately characterize the individual (idler, loiterer)

and the activity (to loiter, idle about) in pejorative terms. As White notes, agenda-driven Americans "are particularly ill-suited to be *flâneurs* (*Flâneur* 40).

13. Barnesandnoble.com, http://www.barnesandnoble.com.

14. White, *Flâneur*, 210.

15. Ibid., 48–49. This cityscape is reminiscent of a sequence in Jean Cocteau's *Orphée*; Maria Cassares leads Jean Marais through an impossible Paris landscape in which different areas of the city appear to lie in immediate proximity to each other. White frequently compares his narrative strategies to film editing techniques, and he includes references to the Paris of the Surrealists in *The Flâneur*.

16. Walter Benjamin, qtd. in White, *Flâneur*, 48–49.

17. Homi K. Bhabha, "The World and the Home," in *Dangerous Liaisons: Gender, Nation, and Postcolonial Perspectives*, ed. Anne McClintock, Aamir Mufti, and Ella Shohat (Minneapolis: University of Minnesota Press, 1997), 446.

18. Ibid., 445.

19. One is reminded, of course, of the descriptions of the flea market in Johnson's novels.

20. Barber (*Edmund White*, 5) notes that White "transforms his cities . . . into the form of an island" to inhabit both simultaneously.

21. John Tomlinson, *Globalization and Culture* (Chicago: University of Chicago Press, 1999), 108.

22. Ibid., 109–10.

23. James Clifford, *Routes: Travel and Translation in the Late Twentieth Century* (Cambridge, MA: Harvard University Press, 1997), 1.

24. Austin's and Julien's final trip is an ironic reversal not only of their own prior vacations but of two other literary journeys as well. On the first of the two trips to northern Africa that frame André Gide's *L'Immoraliste* (Paris: Livre de poche, 1963), Michel is increasingly drawn to the beautiful local boys who shy away from White's characters, and the warmth and sunshine he finds in the desert restore his threatened health. On Michel's final voyage, on the other hand, which has the breathless pace of Austin's and Julien's, he quite literally drags his wife Madeleine to her death. The narrator of Jean Genet's *Le Journal du Voleur* (Paris: Gallimard, 1949) also travels ceaselessly through a borderless postmodern world in Europe and Africa, but Genet's familiar association of travel and sex has obviously disappeared by the end of *The Married Man*.

25. Tomlinson, *Globalization and Culture*, 107.

26. William V. Spanos, *Repetitions: The Postmodern Occasion in Literature and Culture* (Baton Rouge: Louisiana State University Press, 1987), 28.

27. The British writer Neil Bartlett describes White himself as "essentially itinerant and rootless, incessantly on the move within Paris itself, always planning journeys to other cities and islands, and never at home except in the sensations of the present moment" (qtd. in Barber, *Edmund White*, 129). In "Frequent Flyers: Transatlantic fictions today," the final chapter of *Dangerous Pilgrimages: Transatlantic Mythologies and the Novel* (New York: Viking, 1995), Malcolm Bradbury includes White among those writers he characterizes as "migrants wandering the world exchanging their fictions" (482).

28. Alison Russell, *Crossing Boundaries: Postmodern Travel Literature* (New York: Palgrave, 2000), 13.

29. Canning, "Edmund White," 81.

30. Barber, *Edmund White*, 254.

31. Ibid., 253.

32. Brian McHale, *Postmodernist Fiction* (New York: Routledge, 1987), 45.

33. Apollinaire, "Zone," in *Alcools: poèmes, 1989–1913* (Paris: Gallimard, 1920) and *An Anthology of French Poetry from Nerval to Valéry in English Translation*, rev. ed., ed. Angel Flores, trans. Dudley Fitts (Garden City, NY: Doubleday Anchor Books, 1958). See also McHale, *Postmodernist Fiction*, 44.

34. Peter, "a super patriot who'd never condescended to learn any French beyond the most approximate bar-room gabbling," never settles into Paris during the year he spends in France with Austin (37).

35. See Alan Riding, "Siren Paris: Still Luring the Literati," *New York Times*, Apr. 16, 1997, B1–2.

36. Barber, *Edmund White*, 135.

37. White, *The Burning Library: Essays*, ed. David Bergman (New York: Alfred A. Knopf, 1994), 372; and *Farewell Symphony*, 406. In fact, White's ideal European reader was also older, heterosexual, and female. The decision he made while living in Europe to write for a sophisticated gay reader suggests an ongoing interest in reaching a cosmopolitan public.

38. This incident is based on White's experience at Brown University where he taught for a year in 1990–91 (see Barber, *Edmund White*, 189–94).

39. Emily Apter, "From Literary Channel to Narrative Chunnel," in *The Literary Channel: The Inter-National Invention of the Novel*, ed. Margaret Cohen and Carolyn Dever (Princeton, NJ: Princeton University Press, 2002), 286–87.

40. Thus, in the "unreal" space of Disney World, "Morocco" alone retains "its authenticity," despite its equally artificial and stereotypical decor, thanks to the flirtatious behavior, "which would happen in exactly the same way in the real Morocco, the real Marrakech," of the dark-skinned, French-speaking waiter (191–92).

41. White, *Flâneur*, 48.

42. Bhabha, "World and the Home," 445.

43. White himself notes: "I like Henry James' 'international theme,' which still strikes me as fertile material" (qtd. In John Banville, "Coupling," *New York Review of Books*, Aug. 10, 2000, 42). Amazon.com (http://www.amazon.com) calls *The Married Man* "White's Henry James novel" and cites Tom Holland of the London *Daily Telegraph*: "White is a worthy heir of that earlier anatomist of the transatlantic relationship, Henry James."

44. Bhabha, "World and the Home," 445.

45. David Bahr, "French Lessons," *Advocate*, June 20, 2000, 137.

46. Joris-Karl Huysmans, *A Rebours* (1884; repr., Paris: Bibliothèque-Charpentier, 1903). Julien substitutes aesthetic distinctions among women, with cross-cultural consequences, for Des Esseintes's taste in flowers. Julien likes his women "entirely artificial": "If there's one thing I despise it's a healthy, tanned, big-toothed American girl. No, what I admire is a pale Parisian woman, frail, a hot-house flower, expertly painted" (30).

47. Austin never provides a last name for Julien, thus omitting what might constitute definitive proof of the latter's claim to descend from the *ancienne noblesse*.

48. White, *Farewell Symphony*, 4.

49. Benedict Anderson, *Imagined Communities: Reflections on the Origin and Spread of Nationalism*, rev. ed (London: Verso, 1991).

50. Henry McVay, the American counterpart to Julien, incarnates French preconceptions of America for sophisticated Parisians: "[McVay] arrived in Paris at the end of the war as everything the French wanted an American to be—handsome, wealthy, French-speaking and humbled before the monument of French culture" (61).

51. David Caron, *AIDS in French Culture: Social Ills, Literary Cures* (Madison: University of Wisconsin Press, 2001), 106, 156.

52. Ibid., 103.
53. Alan Wilde, "Modernism and the Aesthetics of Crisis," in *Postmodernism: A Reader*, ed. Patricia Waugh (London: Edward Arnold, 1992), 17.
54. McHale, *Postmodernist Fiction*, 231.
55. Ibid.
56. Clifford, *Routes*, 30.
57. Ibid.
58. See, for example, Jean Méral, *Paris in American Literature*, trans. Laurette Long (Chapel Hill: University of North Carolina Press, 1989), 223.
59. Clifford, *Routes*, 13.
60. Linda Hutcheon, *A Poetics of Postmodernism: History, Theory, Fiction* (New York: Routledge, 1988), 10.
61. Banville, "Coupling," 43.
62. Michel Foucault's full name was Paul-Michel Foucault. The convention by which literary critics refer to a writer by his last name alone constantly reminds us that the schizophrenia from which Paul Michel suffers after Foucault's death may well be a displacement of Michel's role as the philosopher's double during his lifetime.
63. Ralph Sarkonak, "Ghost Writing," in *Angelic Echoes: Hervé Guibert and Company* (Toronto: University of Toronto Press, 2000), 258.
64. Ibid., 283.
65. In fact, Patrick Grainville's *Les Flamboyants* (repr., Paris: Seuil, 1997) won the 1976 Prix Goncourt. Although the novel, named for a tropical tree, does concern the friendship between two men who travel through an imaginary but metaphorical Africa in search of a madman, in this case any resemblance to *Hallucinating Foucault* really would appear to be coincidental.
66. There are many further complexities and coincidences. For example, the narrator's lover, who also functions both as his own double and as that of Foucault, is an androgynous woman referred to only as "the Germanist." She is completing a doctoral dissertation on Friedrich Schiller, to whom she writes love letters; like Schiller, "August Duncker," if he existed, was a German dramatist of the late eighteenth and early nineteenth centuries.
67. Michel Foucault, qtd. in White, *Farewell Symphony*, 371.
68. White, *Farewell Symphony*, 406. In "The American Sublime: Living and Dying as an Artist," introd. to *Loss within Loss: Artists in the Age of AIDS*, ed. Edmund White (Madison: University of Wisconsin Press, 2001), White laments what he sees as the consequences of the lack of media attention accorded to the winners of America's literary prizes: "In America we have many great writers but few great readers. (France has the opposite problem)" (10).
69. McHale, *Postmodernist Fiction*, 227.
70. Ibid., 221.
71. The full quotation reads as follows: "'All writers are, somewhere or other, mad. Not les grands fous, like Rimbaud, but mad, yes, mad. Because we do not believe in the stability of reality. We know that it can fragment, like a sheet of glass or a car's windscreen. But we also know that reality can be invented, reordered, constructed, remade. Writing is, in itself, an act of violence perpetrated against reality'" (120).
72. The novel is divided into four sections: "Cambridge," "Paris," "Clermont," and "The Midi."
73. Asked in an interview with David Bergman ("You Can Lead a Boy to Culture," *Lamda Book Report*, Jan. 1999, 8) whether it is peculiar to gay writers to "blur borders" between their "real" selves and their fictional creations by "hiding behind theatrical screens,"

Stadler notes that he has been "performing [him]self" since childhood and that "the dynamics of authorship, wherein the writer makes him or herself present only through the mask of words on the page and of a character, the narrator" is surely present in all writing.

74. Bergman, "You Can Lead," 7.
75. Edmund White, "Sex and the City," *New York Times*, Feb. 21, 1999, sec. 7:34.
76. The unnamed city is modeled on Seattle, where Stadler lives.
77. Tomlinson, *Globalization and Culture*, 110.
78. White, *Flâneur*, 211.
79. White, "Sex and the City."
80. Clifford, *Routes*, 1.
81. In an essay on American expatriate writers, "Paris and the 'New Lost Generation,'" *French Review* 73 (May 2000), Crystel Pinçonnat uses the difference between these two postures to distinguish between two generations, both celebrated in Shakespeare and Company's 2003 literary festival. If the writing of James and Hemingway still portrays *flâneurs*, this is no longer true of the typical Parisian of James Baldwin and Richard Wright: "On ne trouve plus rien chez lui du tourist flâneur qui butine les plaisirs artistiques de la capitale.... Le personnage de l'errant, son isolement et son angoisse prennent l'exact contre-pied de la position du flâneur" ("He no longer resembles in any way the strolling tourist who gleans the artistic pleasures of the capital.... The figure of the wanderer, his isolation and his anguish, are the exact opposite of the situation of the *flâneur*") (1068–69). To some extent, White's identification with *la flânerie* differentiates his Paris novel from those of Duncker, Stadler, and Truong.
82. Stadler's syntax reflects his thematic concerns. At times, for example, his sentences are visibly constructed as spatial entities by the exaggerated use of parentheses and brackets (29). At other times, the use of multiple qualifiers and the addition of new details produces a sentence that imitates on a smaller scale the motion of travel (162).
83. Joanne P. Sharp, "Writing Over the Map of Provence: The touristic therapy of *A Year in Provence*," in *Writes of Passage: Reading Travel Writing*, ed. James Duncan and Derek Gregory (New York: Routledge, 1999), 203; 206n1.
84. Pinçonnat, "Paris and the 'New Lost Generation,'" 1068.
85. White also points out in "Sex and the City" that "*Allan Stein* belongs to a very old literary tradition."
86. Russell, *Crossing Boundaries*, 13.
87. Barber, *Edmund White*, 129.
88. Duncker, too, transgresses the boundaries of fiction even before entering its space. In her opening acknowledgments, she thanks "the real Pascal Vaury" and recognizes "Jacqueline Martel," each of whom will have changed sex (Pascale Vaury, Jacques Martel) by the time we meet their fictional counterparts in *Hallucinating Foucault*.
89. The character of the man on the bridge provides a fictional portrait of Ho Chi Minh as does Binh's American lover of Paul Robeson.

Conclusion:
Diane Johnson's *L'Affaire*

1. Diane Johnson, *L'Affaire* (New York: Dutton, 2003), 284. Subsequent references appear in parentheses in the text.
2. Edward C. Knox, "Déjà Views, How Americans Look at France: Introduction," in "Déjà Views, How Americans Look at France," ed. Edward C. Knox, special issue, *French Politics, Culture and Society* 21 (Summer 2003): 1.

3. Joanne Smith Rakoff, "A Sentimental Education," *New York Newsday*, Sept. 21, 2003, http://www.newsday. Rakoff calls *L'Affaire* "the final installment of Johnson's trilogy about Americans in France" but cites no evidence to support this description. In June 2003, Johnson told me that she had no idea what her next novel would address (personal communication). Given her tendency to write about the places where she is living and her plans to spend more time in Paris, we might well expect more Franco-American fictions. Certainly the critical acclaim already garnered by Johnson's third novel and the ability of Dan Brown's *The Da Vinci Code* (New York: Doubleday, 2003) to dominate bestseller lists throughout the summer of 2003 suggest that English-language novels set in France will continue to appear for the foreseeable future.

4. Regan McMahon, "Diane Johnson Whips up an Avalanche of Greed and Sex," *San Francisco Chronicle*, Sept. 28, 2003, M1; Caryn James, "An American in Valméri," *New York Times*, Oct. 12, 2003, sec. 7:9.

5. McMahon also limits the meaning of the title, albeit to a legal case rather than a relationship. Only Michael Dirda, "'L'Affaire' by Diane Johnson," *Washington Post*, Sept. 28, 2003, BW15, notes that the French word "can refer to a number of things." This chapter was written several weeks after the release of *L'Affaire* and pertains primarily to those reviews that had appeared by late October 2003.

6. On the greater abstraction of French, see also J. P. Vinay and J. Darbelnet, *Stylistique comparée du français et de l'anglais* (Paris: Didier, 1973), 58–62.

7. The word *affair* appears five times in the novel, twice in specific reference to a sexual relationship (see 29, 30, 57, 131, and 192). In keeping with the metaphors frequently used to describe Franco-American relations, Emile describes the current state of "the friendship" by noting that "France has been unfaithful recently, perhaps" (211).

8. Claire Messud, *The Last Life* (New York: Harcourt, Brace, 1999), 322.

9. This is particularly true given what Amy cites as examples: Americans "were too self-absorbed and had no head for history, nor any culture to speak of" (32). Amy has already conceded the last point in her Seattle epiphany and her quest for perfection clearly points to a certain degree of self-absorption. Moreover, Amy's ignorance of history is rivaled only by Emile's exaggerated anti-Americanism. She is unable to respond to his astonishing assertion that the Algerian War "was really the Americans' fault": "Amy would have liked to stick up for America, but she didn't know anything about the Algerian War; had never heard of one" (261–62).

10. Like the characteristics of languages, national character traits are best revealed by cross-cultural comparison, which also often plays a role in their construction. The French tendency to insist "*ce n'est pas ma faute*," even when it is, directly counters the tendency of Americans to confess, "it's my fault," even when it isn't. What Emile chalks up to "the mysteries of culture, *alors*" (276–77) also merits a chapter in Raymonde Carroll's *Evidences invisibles: Américains et Français au quotidien* (Paris: Seuil, 1987).

11. The British prime minister whom Emile dismisses as "so sycophantic in his pro-American effusions" and "a lackey to the American president, a bully and a liar" is obviously Tony Blair, in thrall to George W. Bush (74). Emile also diagnoses the problem feared by American tourists who cancelled trips to France in 2003 and faced by Johnson's representative American in *L'Affaire*: "Great Powers are more effective as an absence. Personified, a powerful institution is just some . . . individuals on a snowmobile" (162).

12. Justin Vaïsse, "American Francophobia Takes a New Turn," in "Déjà Views, How Americans Look at France," ed. Edward C. Knox, special issue, *French Politics, Culture and Society* 21 (Summer 2003): 43.

13. Elaine Sciolino, "The Great French-American Mystery," *New York Times*, Sept. 28, 2003, sec. 4:5; Michael Eliott, "The Real Reason Americans Bash the French," *Time*, Sept. 29, 2003, 43.

14. Sciolino, "Great French-American Mystery."

15. Eliott, "Real Reason Americans Bash." In *Le Mariage*, Clara's opposition to hunting and its consequences are modeled in part on the experience of Dominique Voynet, Ministre de l'Environnement in Lionel Jospin's administration.

16. Sciolino, "Great French-American Mystery."

17. Johnson's irony is evident elsewhere as well. Amy's passion dates from her high school membership in The Mutual Aid Club, "an extracurricular activity frankly designed to embellish the chances of getting into colleges" (8). Amy considers parties to be the last and ultimately perhaps the only way to promote Kropotkin's philosophy: "Parties were mutual aid at its sweetest, proffering pleasure, each guest acceding by his presence to the principle of human sociability" (334).

18. Henry James, *The Portrait of a Lady* (1881; repr., London: Penguin Books, 1972), 49. Amy's growing irritation at "being called an heiress, since she had earned her money herself" obviously owes much to literary history (259). Although Amy's mistakes do not include marriage, a "peculiar institution" she doesn't understand (272), she does recognize in Emile "exactly the kind of bad-news man" that a long literary tradition warns rich girls to avoid (294), and he is far from indifferent to her "big fortune" (325).

19. This possibility is explicitly entertained: "Might it also have been Marianne? . . . Symbol of France?" (205). Ironically, Kerry will eventually be relocated to the "Clinique Marianne" outside Paris.

20. Kerry's long coma adds a new dimension to the paradigmatic in-between representations of global postmodernity we have repeatedly encountered in the English-language texts of literary globalism.

21. Despite Kerry's initial determination to stay in France, she is in fact barred from returning to Adrian Venn's château by French property laws. A legal error, however, allows her, in a "warlike" act of her own, to claim the house in England in which Adrian's first wife has lived for years.

22. Paintings serve this function in *Le Divorce* and *Le Mariage*. Although a painting owned by Adrian Venn does play a role in the inheritance dispute in *L'Affaire*, it does not appear to have any metaphoric significance.

23. This list would include works by Friedrich Schiller, Charles Péguy, George Bernard Shaw, Jean Anouilh, and Paul Claudel, among others.

24. Contrary to what everyone in the novel appears to believe, it is not because Adrian Venn dies in France but because that is where most of his property is located that his estate is subject to French inheritance laws. Venn is actually declared dead in England, although he never regains consciousness after the accident and has been kept alive on respirators in France.

25. Amy does experience a personal "surge of patriotism" at a display of American Revolutionary artifacts in Paris. Paradoxically, she spends her last days in France visiting Lafayette's grave, the Statue of Liberty, and "American museums" (299).

26. In a final peripetia we learn that the mysterious, undiscoverable woman who made the phone call that led to the Venn's rescue was not, of course, St. Joan, as Kerry believes, but yet another American (338).

27. James Clifford, *Routes: Travel and Translation in the Late Twentieth Century* (Cambridge, MA: Harvard University Press, 1997), 17.

28. John Tomlinson, *Globalization and Culture* (Chicago: University of Chicago Press, 1999), 108. Thomas Mann's *The Magic Mountain* (New York: Alfred A. Knopf, 1927) provides another intertextual reference for *L'Affaire*. Within Johnson's novel, Posy is "reading all Mann's books," although she finds his theme of "fraternal rivalry" depressing even before she and her own siblings begin to quarrel over their father's will (84).

29. Kerry too is suspended in a non-place of postmodernity; in the hospital in Valméri, she is not only in a coma but surrounded by visitors waiting to see if she will die or reawaken. After her release, she is taken to a clinic in Paris that is "halfway between a madhouse and a luxurious spa" (306).

30. Geoffrey Nunberg, "The French, There is a Word for Them," *New York Times*, Feb. 9, 2003, sec. 4:5.

Bibliography

Addison, Marla. Interview with Joanne Harris. http://www.countrybookshop.co.uk.

Affleck, John. "Ernest Hemingway's Places." http://www.literarytraveler.com/ hemingway/shakespeare.htm.

Alain-Fournier. *Le Grand Meaulnes*. 1913. Reprint, Paris: Librairie Fayard, 1971.

———. *The Wanderer or The End of Youth*. Translated by Lowell Bair. Afterword by John Fowles. New York: New American Library, 1971.

Aldridge, Alan. "The English as They See Others: England Revealed in Provence." *The Sociological Review* 43 (1995): 415–34.

Allen, Brooke. "Silence, Exile, Cunning." *The New Criterion,* Nov. 1999, 60–65.

Amazon.com. http://www.amazon.com.

The American Heritage Dictionary of the English Language. 3rd ed. New York: Houghton Mifflin, 1992.

Anderson, Benedict. *Imagined Communities: Reflections on the Origin and Spread of Nationalism*. Rev. ed. London: Verso, 1991.

Apollinaire, Guillaume. "Zone." In *Alcools: poèmes, 1989–1913*. Paris: Gallimard, 1920.

———. "Zone." In *An Anthology of French Poetry from Nerval to Valéry in English Translation*. New revised edition by Angel Flores. Translated by Dudley Fitts. Garden City, NY: Doubleday Anchor Books, 229–34.

Apter, Emily. *Continental Drift: From National Characters to Virtual Subjects*. Chicago: University of Chicago Press, 1999.

———. "From Literary Channel to Narrative Chunnel." In *The Literary Channel: The Inter-National Invention of the Novel*, edited by Margaret Cohen and Carolyn Dever, 286–93. Princeton, NJ: Princeton University Press, 2002.

Ashour, Linda. *Speaking in Tongues*. New York: Simon and Schuster, 1988.

Bahr, David. "French Lessons." *The Advocate*, June 20, 2000, 137.

Bair, Lowell, trans. *The Wanderer or The End of Youth*. By Alain-Fournier. New York: New American Library, 1971.

Banville, John. "Coupling," *New York Review of Books*, Aug. 10, 2000, 42–44.

Barber, Stephen. *Edmund White: The Burning World*. New York: St. Martin's Press, 1999.

Barnesandnoble.com. http://www.barnesandnoble.com.

Barthes, Roland. *Mythologies*. Paris: Seuil, 1957.

Baudelaire, Charles. *Les Fleurs du mal*. 1857. Reprint, Paris: Editions Garnier, 1963.

Beach, Sylvia. *Shakespeare and Company*. New York: Harcourt, Brace, 1956.

Bergman, David. "You Can Lead a Boy to Culture." *Lamda Book Report*, Jan. 1999, 7–9.

Bernstein, Richard. *Fragile Glory: A Portrait of France and the French*. New York: Knopf, 1990.

Bhabha, Homi K. "The World and the Home." In *Dangerous Liaisons: Gender, Nation, and Postcolonial Perspectives*, edited by Anne McClintock, Aamir Mufti, and Ella Shohat, 445–55. Minneapolis: University of Minnesota Press, 1997.

Biasan, Gian-Paolo. *The Flavors of Modernity: Food and the Novel*. Princeton, NJ: Princeton University Press, 1993.

Birns, Nicholas and Margaret Boe Birns. "Agatha Christie: Modern and Modernist." In *The Cunning Craft: Original Essays on Detective Fiction and Contemporary Literary Theory*, edited by Ronald G. Walker and June M. Frazer, 120–34. Macomb: Western Illinois University, 1990.

Bishop, Tom. "I Love You, Moi Non Plus." Special Issue: France's Identity Crises. *SubStance* 76/77 (1985): 21–29.

Black, Cara. *Murder in the Bastille*. New York: Soho Press, 2003.

———. *Murder in Belleville*. New York: Soho Press, 2000.

———. *Murder in the Marais*. New York: Soho Press, 1998.

———. *Murder in the Sentier*. New York: Soho Press, 2002.

Blank, Hannah. *A Murder of Convenience*. New York: Hightrees Books, 1999.

Bradbury, Malcolm. *Dangerous Pilgrimages: Transatlantic Mythologies and the Novel*. New York: Viking, 1995.

———. "Modernisms/Postmodernisms." In *Innovation/Renovation: New Perspectives on the Humanities*, edited by Ihab Hassan, 311–27. Madison: University of Wisconsin Press, 1983.

Brett, Simon. *What Bloody Man Is That?* New York: toExcel, 2000.

Brooks, Peter. *Reading for the Plot: Design and Intention in Narrative*. New York: Knopf, 1984.

Brown, Dan. *The Da Vinci Code*. New York: Doubleday, 2003.

Buchwald, Art. *I'll Always Have Paris: A Memoir*. New York: Fawcett Columbine, 1996.

Canning, Richard. "Edmund White." In *Gay Fiction Speaks: Conversations with Gay Novelists*, 75–112. New York: Columbia University Press, 2000.

Caron, David. *AIDS in French Culture: Social Ills, Literary Cures*. Madison: University of Wisconsin Press, 2001.

Carroll, Lewis. *Alice in Wonderland*. 2nd ed. Edited by Donald J. Gray. 1865, 1872. Reprint, New York: Norton, 1992, 1971.

Carroll, Raymonde. *Evidences Invisibles: Américains et Français au quotidien*. Paris: Seuil, 1987.

Carter, Charlotte, *Coq au vin*. New York: Warner Books, 1999.

Chocolat. Screenplay by Robert Nelson Jacobs (based on the novel by Joanne Harris). Directed by Lasse Hallström. Miramax Films, 2000.

Clifford, James. *Routes: Travel and Translation in the Late Twentieth Century*. Cambridge, MA: Harvard University Press, 1997.

Colette. *La Vagabonde*. 1910. Reprint, Paris: Albin Michel, 1990.

Collins, Jim. *Uncommon Cultures: Popular Culture and Post-Modernism*. New York: Routledge, 1989.

Compagnon, Antoine. *La Seconde Main ou le travail de la citation*. Paris: Seuil, 1979.

Connor, Steven. *Postmodernist Culture: An Introduction to Theories of the Contemporary*. 2nd ed. Cambridge: Blackwell, 1997.

Constant, Benjamin. *Adolphe*. 1839. Reprint, Paris: Flammarion, 1989.

Crimp, Douglas. "On the Museum's Ruins." *The Anti-Aesthetic: Essays on Postmodern Culture*, edited by Hal Foster, 43–56. Port Townsend, WA: Bay Press, 1983.

Daley, Robert. *Portraits of France*. New York: Little, Brown, 1991.

Darnton, Robert. *The Great Cat Massacre and Other Episodes in French Cultural History*. New York: Vintage, 1985.

Delbanco, Nicholas. *Running in Place: Scenes from the South of France*. New York: Atlantic Monthly Press, 1989.

Dever, Carolyn, and Margaret Cohen. "Introduction." In *The Literary Channel: The International Invention of the Novel*, edited by Margaret Cohen and Carolyn Dever, 1–34. Princeton, NJ: Princeton University Press, 2002.

Le Divorce. Screenplay by James Ivory and Ruth Prawer Jhabvala (adapted from the novel by Diane Johnson). Directed by James Ivory. Merchant Ivory/Radar Pictures Production, 2003.

Donadey, Anne. " 'Une Certain Idée de la France': The Algeria Syndrome and Struggles over 'French' Identity." In *Identity Papers: Contested Nationhood in Twentieth-Century France*, edited by Steven Ungar and Tom Conley, 215–31. Minneapolis: University of Minnesota Press, 1996.

Dostoevsky, Fyodor. *Crime and Punishment*. Translated by Constance Garnett. 1866. Reprint, New York: Modern Library, 1978.

Douglas, Carole Nelson. *Chapel noir*. New York: Tom Doherty, 2001.

Dulles, Foster Rhea. *America Learns to Play: A History of Popular Recreation*. New York: D. Appleton-Century, 1940.

———. *Americans Abroad: Two Centuries of European Travel*. Ann Arbor: University of Michigan Press, 1964.

Duncker, Patricia. *Hallucinating Foucault*. New York: Vintage, 1996.

Elliot, Paul. *The Mysterious Mickey Finn or Murder at the Café du Dôme*. New York: Modern Age Books, 1939.

Eliott, Michael. "The Real Reason Americans Bash the French." *Time*, Sept. 29, 2003, 43.

Engel, Howard. *Murder in Montparnasse*. Woodstock, NY: Overlook Press, 1999.

Faulks, Sebastien. *Birdsong*. New York: Vintage, 1993.

———. *Charlotte Gray*. New York: Random House, 1998.

———. *The Girl at the Lion d'or*. New York: Vintage, 1989.

Fenby, Jonathan. *France on the Brink*. New York: Arcade, 1999.

Ferguson, Patricia Parkhurst. "Is Paris France?" *The French Review* 73 (May 2000): 1052–64.

Fischer-Lichte, Erika. *The Show and the Gaze of Theatre: A European Perspective*. Iowa City: University of Iowa Press, 1997.

Fitch, Noel Riley. *Sylvia Beach and the Lost Generation: A History of Literary Paris in the Twenties and Thirties*. New York: Norton, 1983.

Fowles, John. "Afterword." In *The Wanderer or The End of Youth*, by Alain-Fournier, 208–23. New York: New American Library, 1971.
Francofil: French Studies Discussion List. "Call for Papers–Voyages." http://www.bristol.ac.ukfrancofil/.
Friedman, Thomas L. *The Lexus and the Olive Tree*. New York: Anchor Books, 2000.
Genet, Jean. *Le Journal du Voleur*. Paris: Gallimard, 1949.
Gide, André. *L'Immoraliste*. 1902. Reprint, Paris: Livre de poche, 1963.
Gilsdorf, Ethan. "The Expatriate Writer in Paris: Revising the Myth." *Poets and Writers Magazine,* May/June 2001, 14–19.
Les Glaneurs et la glaneuse. Screenplay by Agnès Varda. Directed by Agnès Varda. Ciné Tamaris, 2000.
Les Glaneurs et la glaneuse . . . deux ans après. Screenplay by Agnès Varda. Directed by Agnès Varda. C.N.D.F./Canal +/CNC/Ciné Tamaris, 2002.
Gopnik, Adam. *Paris to the Moon*. New York: Random House, 2000.
Grainville, Patrick. *Les Flamboyants*. 1976. Reprint, Paris: Seuil, 1992.
Grossvogel, David I. *Mystery and its Fictions: From Oedipus to Agatha Christie*. Baltimore: John Hopkins University Press, 1979.
Guyot-Bender, Martine. "Fiction at Twenty Thousand Leagues Above the Sea. *Hemisphere*'s Fantasies of France." *Sites* 5 (Spring 2001): 139–55.
Hall, Stuart. "European Cinema on the Verge of a Nervous Breakdown." In *Screening Europe: Image and Identity in Contemporary European Cinema*, edited by Duncan Petrie, 45–53. London: British Film Institute, 1992.
———. "The Local and the Global: Globalization and Ethnicity." In *Dangerous Liaisons: Gender, Nation, and Postcolonial Perspectives*, edited by Anne McClintock, Aamir Mufti, and Ella Shohat, 173–87. Minneapolis: University of Minnesota Press, 1997.
Harris, Joanne. *Blackberry Wine*. New York: HarperCollins, 2000.
———. *Chocolat*. New York: Viking, 1999.
———. *The Coastliners*. New York: William Morrow, 2003.
———. *Five Quarters of the Orange*. New York: HarperCollins, 2001.
Hassan, Ihab. "Pluralism in Postmodern Perspective." In *Exploring Postmodernism*, edited by Matei Calinescu and Douwe Fokkema, 17–39. Amsterdam: John Benjamins, 1987.
Hays, Tony. *Murder in the Latin Quarter*. Bell Buckle, TN: Iris Press, 1993.
Hemingway, Ernest. *A Moveable Feast*. New York: Simon and Schuster, 1964.
———. *The Sun Also Rises*. New York: Charles Scribner's Sons, 1926.
Hermary-Vieille, Catherine, and Michèle Sarde. *Le Salon de conversation*. Paris: JC Lattès, 1997.
"History of Shakespeare and Co. Bookshop." http://www.shakespeareco.org/history/htm.
Holquist, Michael. "Whodunit and Other Questions: Metaphysical Detective Stories in Postwar Fiction." In *The Poetics of Murder: Detective Fiction and Literary Theory*, edited by Glenn W. Most and William W. Stowe, 149–74. New York: Harcourt Brace Jovanovich, 1983.
Howard, Ron. *Ain't It Romantic?: An Entertainment*. New York: HarperCollins, 2003.
Hühn, Peter. "The Detective as Reader: Narrativity and Reading Concepts in Detective Fiction." *Modern Fiction Studies* 33 (Autumn 1987): 451–66.

Hutcheon, Linda. *A Poetics of Postmodernism: History, Theory, Fiction*. New York: Routledge,1988.

———. *Narcissistic Narrative: The Metafictional Paradox*. New York: Methuen,1980.

Huysmans, Joris-Karl. *A Rebours*. 1884. Reprint, Paris: Bibliothèque-Charpentier, 1903.

Isherwood, Christopher. *The Single Man*. New York: Methuen, 1964.

Jacques, Georges. "*Le Grand Meaulnes*: Où une magie en cache une autre." *Les Lettres romanes* 1–2 (Feb.–May 1989): 23–41.

James, Henry. *The Portrait of a Lady*. 1881. Reprint, London: Penguin Books, 1972.

Jameson, Frederic. "Postmodernism and Consumer Society." In *The Anti-Aesthetic: Essays on Postmodern Culture*, edited by Hal Foster, 111–15. Port Townsend, WA: Bay Press, 1983.

Janes, J. Robert. *Mannequin*. New York: Soho Press, 1994.

———. *Sandman*. New York: Soho Press, 1996.

Jeantet, Robert Fields. "Shakespeare & Company: Virtual Tour." http://www.sav.org/shco/.

Johnson, Diane. *L'Affaire*. New York: Dutton, 2003.

———. *Une Américaine à Paris*, translated by Marie-Claude Peugeot. Paris: NiL éditions, 2000.

———. *Le Divorce*. New York: Dutton, 1997.

———. *Le Mariage*. New York: Dutton, 2000.

Kalifa, Dominique. *Les Crimes de Paris: Lieux et non-lieux du crime à Paris au XIXe Siècle*. Paris: BILIPO, 2001.

Kaplan, Alice. *French Lessons: A Memoir*. Chicago: University of Chicago Press, 1993.

Kaplan, E. Ann. *Looking for the Other: Feminism, Film, and the Imperial Gaze*. London: Routledge, 1997.

Kennedy, J. Gerald. *Imagining Paris: Exile, Writing, and American Identity*. New Haven, CT: Yale University Press, 1993.

Kenney, Brian. "Review of *The Married Man*." *Library Journal*, May 15, 2000, 127–28.

Kerr, Sarah. "People are Talking about Books." *Vogue*, Sept. 1999, 478, 487.

"The Kilometer Zero Story." http://www.kmzero.org.

King, Lily. *The Pleasing Hour*. New York: Atlantic Monthly, 1999.

Kluger, Jeffrey. "Food Fight." *Time*, Sept. 13, 1999, 43–44.

Knox, Edward C. "Déjà Views, How Americans Look at France: Introduction." In "Déjà Views, How Americans Look at France," ed. Edward C. Knox. Special issue, *French Politics, Culture & Society* 21 (Summer 2003): 1–6.

Kristeva, Julia. "Pour une sémiologie des paragrammes." *Tel Quel* 29 (1967): 53–85.

———. *Révolution du langage poétique*. Paris: Seuil, 1974.

Kroes, Rob. *If You've Seen One, You've Seen the Mall: Europeans and American Mass Culture*. Urbana: University of Illinois Press, 1996.

Kuisel, Richard F. "The France We Have Lost: Social, Economic, and Cultural Discontinuities." In *Remaking the Hexagon: The New France in the New Europe*, edited by Gregory Flynn, 31–48. San Francisco: Westview Press, 1995.

———. *Seducing the French: The Dilemma of Americanization*. Berkeley: University of California Press, 1993.

Lanchester, John. *The Debt to Pleasure*. New York: Holt, 1996.

Levy, Karen D. "*Le Grand Meaulnes* and *Le Roi des Aulnes*: Counterpointed Echoes from a Distant Past." *Romance Notes* 29 (Winter 1988): 107–18.

Mann, Thomas. *The Magic Mountain*. New York: Knopf, 1927.

Mathy, Jean-Philippe. *French Resistance: The French-American Culture Wars*. Minneapolis: University of Minnesota Press, 2000.

———. "The Popularity of American Culture." *Sites* 1 (Spring 1997): 141–56.

Mayle, Peter. *A Year in Provence*. New York: Knopf, 1990.

———. *Anything Considered*. New York: Vintage, 1997.

———. *Chasing Cézanne*. New York: Knopf, 1997.

———. *French Lessons: Adventure with Knife, Fort, and Corkscrew*. New York: Knopf, 2001.

———. *Hotel Pastis: A Novel of Provence*. New York: Vintage, 1993.

———. *Toujours Provence*. New York: Knopf, 1991.

MacCannell, Dean. *The Tourist: A New Theory of the Leisure Class*. Berkeley: University of California Press, 1976.

McCarver, Sam. *The Case of the Uninvited Guest*. New York: Signet, 2002.

McClintock, Anne, Aamir Mufti, and Ella Shohat, eds. *Dangerous Liaisons: Gender, Nation, and Postcolonial Perspectives*. Minneapolis: University of Minnesota Press, 1997.

McHale, Brian. *Constructing Postmodernism*. New York: Routledge, 1992.

———. *Postmodernist Fiction*. New York: Routledge, 1987.

McMahon, Joseph. "City for Expatriates." *Yale French Studies*, no. 32 (1964): 144–58.

Méral, Jean. *Paris in American Literature*. Translated by Laurette Long. Chapel Hill: University of North Carolina Press, 1989.

Messud, Claire. *The Last Life*. New York: Harcourt, Brace, 1999.

———. *La Vie Après*. Translated by Guillemette Belleteste. Paris: Editions Gallimard, 2001.

Mink, Louis. "Narrative Form as a Cognitive Instrument." In *The Writing of History*, edited by Robert H. Canary and Henry Kozicki, 129–49. Madison: University of Wisconsin Press, 1978.

Monbrun, Estelle. *Meurtre à Petite Plaisance*. Paris: Viviane Hamy, 1998.

———. *Meurtre chez Tante Léonie*. Paris: Viviane Hamy, 1994.

Monbrun, Estelle, and Anaïs Coste. *Meurtre chez Colette*. Paris: Viviane Hamy, 2001.

Moretti, Franco. *Atlas of the European Novel, 1800–1900*. London: Verso, 1998.

Morgan, Ted. *On Becoming American*. New York: Paragon House, 1988.

Most, Glenn W. "The Hippocratic Smile: John le Carré and the Traditions of the Detective Novel." In *The Poetics of Murder: Detective Fiction and Literary Theory*, edited by Glenn W. Most and William W. Stowe, 340–65. New York: Harcourt Brace Jovanovich, 1983.

Mufti, Aamir, and Ella Shohat. "Introduction." In *Dangerous Liaisons: Gender, Nation, and Postcolonial Perspectives*, edited by Anne McClintock, Aamir Mufti, and Ella Shohat, 1–12. Minneapolis: University of Minnesota Press, 1997.

Neilson, William Allan, and Charles Jarvis Hill. "Introduction." In *The Complete Plays and Poems of William Shakespeare*, edited by William Allan Neilson and Charles Jarvis Hill, ix–xvii. New York: Houghton Mifflin, 1942.

Nicolson, Marjorie. "The Professor and the Detective." In *The Art of the Mystery Story: A Collection of Critical Essays*, edited by Howard Haycraft, 110–27. New York: Simon and Schuster, 1946.

Orphée. Screenplay by Jean Cocteau. Directed by Jean Cocteau. André Paulue Film, 1949.

Paul, Elliot. *The Mysterious Mickey Finn or Murder at the Café du Dôme*. New York: Modern Age, 1939.

Le Petit Robert 2: Dictionnaire universel des noms propres. Paris: S.E.P.R.E.T., 1975.

Pinçonnat, Crystel. "Paris and the 'New Lost Generation.'" *The French Review* 73 (May 2000): 1065–75.

Poe, Edgar Allan. *The Unabridged Edgar Allan Poe*. Philadelphia: Running Press, 1983.

Porter, Dennis. *Haunted Journeys: Desire and Transgression in European Travel Writing*. Princeton, NJ: Princeton University Press, 1991.

———. *The Pursuit of Crime: Art and Ideology in Detective Fiction*. New Haven, CT: Yale University Press, 1981.

Pyrhönen, Heta. *Murder from an Academic Angle: An Introduction to the Study of the Detective Narrative*. Columbia, SC: Camden House, 1994.

"Questionnaire: Popular Culture at the End of the Second Millennium." *Sites* 1 (Spring 1997): 349–53.

Rafferty, Terrence. "A Critic at Large: The Essence of the Landscape." *The New Yorker*, June 25, 1990, 80–92.

La Règle du jeu. Screenplay by Henry Cartier, Camille François, Carl Koch, Jean Renoir, André Zwoboda. Directed by Jean Renoir. Nouvelle édition française, 1939.

La Revue du chocolat 2 (Fall 2000): Spécial Salon du chocolat.

Richards, Jeffrey. *Films and British National Identity: From Dickens to* Dad's Army. Manchester, England: Manchester University Press, 1997.

Rochefort, Harriet Welty. *French Fried: The Culinary Capers of an American in Paris*. New York: St. Martin's Press, 2001.

———. *French Toast: An American in Paris Celebrates the Maddening Mysteries of the French*. New York: St. Martin's Press, 1999.

Rosenblum, Mort. *A Goose in Toulouse and Other Culinary Adventures in France*. New York: Hyperion, 2000.

Russell, Allison. *Crossing Boundaries: Postmodern Travel Literature*. New York: Palgrave, 2000.

Sarkanak, Ralph. "Ghost Writing." In *Angelic Echoes: Hervé Guibert and Company*, Ralph Sarkanak, 256–83. Toronto: University of Toronto Press, 2000.

Sassoon, Donald. *Becoming Mona Lisa: The Making of a Global Icon*. New York: Harcourt, 2001.

Satterthwait, Walter. *Masquerade*. New York: St. Martin's Press, 1998.

Sedaris, David. *Me Talk Pretty One Day*. New York: Little, Brown, 2000.

Shakespeare William. *Macbeth*. In *The Complete Plays and Poems of William Shakespeare*, edited by William Allan Neilson and Charles Jarvis Hill, 1180–212. New York: Houghton Mifflin, 1942.

———. *The Winter's Tale*. In *The Complete Plays and Poems of William Shakespeare*, edited by William Allan Neilson and Charles Jarvis Hill, 500–537. New York: Houghton Mifflin, 1942.

Sharp, Joanne P. "Writing Over the Map of Provence: The touristic therapy of *A Year in Provence*." In *Writes of Passage: Reading Travel Writing*, edited by James Duncan and Derek Gregory, 200–18. New York: Routledge, 1999.

Shattuck, Roger. *The Banquet Years: The Origins of the Avant Garde in France, 1885 to World War I*. Rev. ed. New York: Vintage, 1968.

Shohat, Ella, and Robert Stam. *Unthinking Eurocentrism: Multiculturalism and the Media*. London: Routledge, 1994.

Smith, Anthony D. *National Identity*. London: Penguin Books, 1991.

Smith, Sarah. *A Citizen of the Country*. New York: Ballantine, 2000.

———. *Chasing Shakespeares: A Novel*. New York: Astria Books, 2003.

———. http://www.sarahsmith.com/conversation_abt_cotc.htm#is_this_the_end.

———. *The Knowledge of Water*. New York: Ballantine, 1996.

———. *The Vanished Child*. New York: Ballantine, 1992.

Sohmers, Barbara. *The Fox and the Pussycat*. Glendora, CA: Sodef Press, 1998.

Spanos, William V. *Repetitions: The Postmodern Occasion in Literature and Culture*. Baton Rouge: Louisiana State University Press, 1987.

Stadler, Matthew. *Allan Stein*. New York: Grove Press, 1999.

Stierle, Karlheinz. "The Reading of Fictional Texts." In *The Reader in the Text: Essays on Audience and Interpretation*, edited by Susan R. Suleiman and Inge Crosman, 83–105. Princeton, NJ: Princeton University Press, 1980.

Sweeney, S. E. "Locked Rooms: Detective Fiction, Narrative Theory, and Self-Reflexivity." In *The Cunning Craft: Original Essays on Detective Fiction and Contemporary Literary Theory*, edited by Ronald G. Walker and June M. Frazer, 120–34. Macomb: Western Illinois University Press, 1990.

Tani, Stefano. *The Doomed Detective: The Contribution of the Detective Novel to Postmodern American and Italian Fiction*. Carbondale: Southern Illinois University Press, 1984.

Tapon, Philippe. *A Parisian from Kansas*. New York: Plume, 1997.

Tavernier-Courbin, Jacqueline. *Ernest Hemingway's* A Moveable Feast: *The Making of Myth*. Boston: Northeastern University Press, 1991.

Toklas, Alice B. *The Alice B. Toklas Cookbook*. 1954. Reprint, London: The Folio Society, 1993.

Tomlinson, John. *Globalization and Culture*. Chicago: University of Chicago Press, 1999.

Tournier, Michel. *Le Roi des aulnes*. Paris: Gallimard, 1970.

Tremain, Rose. *The Way I Found Her*. New York: Farrar, Straus and Giroux, 1997.

Truong, Monique. *The Book of Salt*. New York: Houghton Mifflin, 2003.

Urry, John. *The Tourist Gaze*. London: Sage, 1990.

Vaïsse, Justin. "American Francophobia Takes a New Turn" in "Déjà Views, How Americans Look at France," ed. Edward C. Knox. Special issue, *French Politics, Culture and Society* 21 (Summer 2003): 33–49.

Vandenburg, Margaret. *An American in Paris*. San Francisco: Cleis Press, 2000.

Verdaguer, Pierre. "Introduction: Estelle Monbrun." *Sites* 1 (Spring 1997): 355–56.

———. *La Séduction policière*. Birmingham, AL: Summa Publications, 1999.

Vinay, J. P., and J. Darbelnet. *Stylistique comparée du français et de l'anglais*. Paris: Didier, 1973.

Walter, Ruth. *The Bathsheba Connection*. New York: Writers Club Press, 2000.

Watkins, Paul. *The Forger*. New York: Picador USA, 2000.

White, Edmund. "The American Sublime: Living and Dying as an Artist." In *Loss Within Loss: Artists in the Age of AIDS*, edited by Edmund White, 3–12. Madison: University of Wisconsin Press, 2001.

———. *The Burning Library: Essays*. Edited by David Bergman. New York: Knopf, 1994.

———. *The Farewell Symphony*. New York: Knopf, 1997.

———. *Le Flâneur: A Stroll Through the Paradoxes of Paris*. London: Bloomsbury, 2001.

———. *The Married Man*. New York: Knopf, 2000.

———. *Our Paris: Sketches from Memory*. With drawings by Hubert Sorin. New York: Knopf, 1995.

White, Hayden. *Metahistory: The Historical Imagination in Nineteenth-Century Europe*. Baltimore: Johns Hopkins University Press, 1973.

———. "The Value of Narrativity in the Representation of Reality." In *On Narrative*, edited by W. J. T. Mitchell, 1–23. Chicago: University of Chicago Press, 1980.

Whitman, George. *The Rag and Bone Shop of the Heart*. Paris: Shakespeare and Company, 2000.

Whitman, Sylvia. *Lost, Beat & New: Three Generations of Parisian Literary Tradition*. Paris: Shakespeare and Company, Dec. 2002.

Wilde, Alan. "Modernism and the Aesthetics of Crisis." In *Postmodernism: A Reader*, edited by Patricia Waugh, 14–21. London: Edward Arnold, 1992.

Wylie, Laurence, and Jean-François Brière. *Les Français*. 2nd ed. Englewood Cliffs, NJ: Prentice Hall, 1995.

Youngblood, Shay. *Black Girl in Paris*. New York: Riverhead Books, 2000.

Zeldin, Theodore. *The French*. New York: Vintage Books, 1984.

Zola, Emile. *L'Assommoir*. 1877. Reprint, Paris: Garnier-Flammarion, 1969.

Further Reading: Additional Anglo-American Novels Set in France, 1994-2004

Alther, Lisa. *Five Minutes in Heaven*. New York: Plume, 1996.

Armstrong, Alan. *Regards, Rodeo: The Mariner Dog of Cassis*. Exeter, NH: Townsend, 1999.

Ball, Terence. *Rousseau's Ghost*. Albany: State University of New York Press, 1998.

Barnes, Julien. *Cross Channel: Stories*. New York: Vintage, 1966.

Bogner, Norman. *To Die in Provence*. New York: Doherty, 1988.

Chevalier, Tracy. *The Virgin Blue*. New York: Plume, 1997.

Daley, Robert. *Nowhere to Run*. New York: Warner Books, 1996.

Davis, Kathryn. *Versailles: a novel*. Boston: Back Bay Books, 2002.

DeWitt, Abigail. *Lili*. Evanston, IL: Northwestern University Press, 2000.

Dunn, Samantha. *Failing Paris*. London: Toby Press, 1999.

Dyer, Geoff. *Paris Trance*. New York: Farrar, Straus and Giroux, 1998.

Gadol, Peter. *Light at Dusk*. New York: Picador/St. Martin's Press, 2000.

Hull, Jonathan. *Losing Julia*. New York: Delacorte, 2000.

Just, Ward. *The Translator*. New York: Houghton Mifflin/Mariner, 1991.

Moore, Brian. *The Statement*. New York: Plume, 1997.

Kretser, Michelle de. *The Rose Grower*. New York: Carroll and Graf, 2000.

LaFarge, Paul. *Haussmann, or the Distinction*. New York: Farrar, Straus and Giroux, 2001.

Lenard, Yvonne. *Love in Provence: Romantic Adventures in the South of France*. Princeton, NJ: Elysian Editions, 2001.

Maso, Carole. *The American Woman in the Chinese Hat*. New York: Plume, 1994.

Moore, Brian. *The Magician's Wife*. New York: Plume, 1997.

Pascal, Francine. *If Wishes Were Horses*. New York: Harcourt, Brace, 1999.

Simmonds, Posy. *Gemma Bovary*. London: Jonathon Cape, 2000.

Sisman, Robyn. *Weekend in Paris*. New York: Plume, 2003.

Smith, Jane S. *Fool's Gold*. Cambridge, MA: Zoland, 2000.

Sobin, Gustaf. *The Fly-Truffler*. New York: Norton, 2000.
Tapon, Philippe. *The Mistress*. New York: Plume, 1999.
Teleky, Richard. *The Paris Years of Rosie Kamin*. South Royalton, VT: Steerforth Press, 1998.

Index

Adolphe (Constant), 20, 33, 215 n. 20
Affaire, L' (Johnson), 19, 165, 213 n 7, 214 n. 10, 241 n. 3, 241 n. 5, 241 n. 7, 241 nn. 9–11, 242 n. 17, 242 nn. 18–22, 242 nn. 24–26, 243 nn. 28–29; cross-cultural romance in, 194, 195, 196; as new international novel, 193–209
AIDS, 181
Ain't It Romantic?: An Entertainment (Howard), 215 n. 31
Alain-Fournier: *Le Grand Meaulnes* by, 20, 43, 44, 47, 48, 49, 50, 57, 59, 217 n. 18, 217 nn. 12–13, 218 n. 24, 218 nn. 26–28
Alice's Adventures in Wonderland (Carroll), 55, 56, 72, 217 n. 21, 218 n. 24
Alice B. Toklas Cookbook, The, 189
Allan Stein (Stadler), 23, 165, 185, 186, 187, 188, 189, 231 n. 49, 239 n. 73, 240 n. 85, 240 nn. 81–82
Ambassadors, The, 33
America: anti-Americanism and, 30, 39, 205, 207, 216 n. 36; as metaphor, 111, 112, 113, 115, 116, 173, 174
American in Paris, An (Vandenburg), 231 n. 49
Anderson, Benedict: *Imagined Communities: Reflections on the Origin and Spread of Nationalism* by, 111
Anglophone literati, 13
anti-Americanism, 30, 39, 205, 207, 216 n. 36
Apollinaire, Guillaume, 22, 145, 146, 148, 154, 233 n. 31, 234 n. 43

Apter, Emily: *Continental Drift* by, 67
Arthus-Bertrand, Yann: *"La Terre vue du ciel"* ("Earth From Above") by, 41–42, 60
artists, expatriate, 16, 133
Ashour, Linda: *Speaking in Tongues* by, 26
Assommoir, L' (Zola), 55
Auster, Paul, 122
auterism, 34, 35

Bailly, Jean-Christophe, 60
Baldwin, James, 14, 30
Balkans, 31
Balzac, Honoré de, 129, 178
Barber, Stephen: *Edmund White: The Burning World* by, 165, 175, 182
Baudelaire, Charles, 84, 130, 178
Baum, L. Frank: *The Wizard of Oz* by, 54, 55, 67, 108
Beach, Sylvia, 13, 14, 16, 211 n. 6, 228 n. 7
"Beat Generation," 15
Beat poets, 14
Becoming Mona Lisa: The Making of a Global Icon (Sassoon), 149, 234 n. 45
Bernstein, Richard: *Fragile Glory: A Portrait of France and the French* by, 26, 85
Bhabha, K. Homi, 18, 67–68, 110, 141, 168
Biasin, Gian-Paolo: *The Flavors of Modernity* by, 83
Birns, Nicholas and Margaret Boe, 121
Black, Cara, 119

257

Blackberry Wine (Harris), 62, 63, 64, 71, 72, 75, 91, 95–97, 213 n. 7, 221 n. 7, 223 n. 35, 223 n. 45, 223 n. 49, 224 n. 51, 224 n. 53; as fairy/folk tales, 63–64, 88, 92, 93, 94, 96, 223 n. 46; intertextual references in, 81, 221 n. 3; nation themes in, 78, 79, 83, 84, 85, 86, 89, 90; nostalgia themes in, 80, 82, 85, 87, 90, 223 n. 32; postmodern paradox in, 20, 61

Book of Salt, The (Truong), 23, 165, 189, 190, 191, 192, 240 n. 81, 240 n. 89

Bradbury, Malcolm, 18, 135, 138; *Dangerous Pilgrimages* by, 150, 162, 231 n. 49

Buchwald, Art, 26

Burroughs, William S., 14

Camus, 112, 114, 115

Carroll, Lewis: *Alice's Adventures in Wonderland* by, 55, 56, 72, 217 n. 21, 218 n. 24; *Through the Looking Glass* by, 55, 56, 57, 218 n. 23

Carroll, Raymonde: *Evidences Invisibles* by, 74

Case of the Uninvited Guest, The (McCarver), 228 n. 7

Chasing Shakespeares: A Novel (Smith), 235 n. 67

Chocolat (Harris), 78, 79, 80, 84, 86, 213 n. 7, 219 n. 11, 220 n. 26, 220 n. 29, 221 n. 7; fairy/folk tales and, 63–67, 68, 69, 88, 220 n. 27, 221 n. 38; Hallström, Lasse, and, 62, 219 n. 7, 221 n. 2, 221 n. 38; postmodern paradox in, 20, 61–77, 207, 221 n. 39, 221 n. 40

Christie, Agatha, 120, 121, 231 n. 43

Citizen of the Country, The (Smith), 22, 135, 138; intertextual references in, 157, 158, 159, 160, 161, 235 n. 68; as new international novel, 161, 162, 235 n. 73, 235 n. 74; postmodernism in, 139, 155, 156, 161, 162, 163, 235 nn. 71–74

Clifford, James, 18, 19, 68, 73, 80, 102, 140, 146, 171, 208; *Routes: Travel and Translation in the Late Twentieth Century* by, 61, 62, 182, 233 n. 36

Cohen, Margaret, 119

Colette, 22, 122, 146, 148, 154, 217 n. 17

Compagnon, Antoine, 31, 32

Constant, Benjamin: *Adolphe* by, 20, 33, 215 n. 20

Constructing Postmodernism (McHale), 139

Continental Drift (Apter), 67

Crime and Punishment (Dostoevsky), 51, 52, 53, 54, 55, 57

Crimp, Douglas, 148; "On the Museum's Ruins" by, 135

cross-cultural romance, 28, 29; of Johnson, Diane, 194, 195, 196; in *L'Affaire,* 193, 195, 196; of White, Edmund, 164, 165, 167, 168, 170, 175–81, 183, 238 n. 43, 238 n. 46

Daly, Robert: *Portraits of France* by, 26

Dangerous Liaisons (Mufti and Shohat), 67, 162

Dangerous Pilgrimages (Bradbury), 150, 231 n. 49

Darnton, Robert: *The Great Cat Massacre* by, 69, 220 n. 27

da Vinci, Leonardo: Mona Lisa of, 147, 148, 149, 150, 151, 153, 157, 234 n. 48, 234 nn. 43–45

Debray, Régis, 111

Debt to Pleasure, The (Lanchester), 221 n. 33

Delbanco, Nicholas: *Running in Place: Scenes from the South of France* by, 26

Desplechin, Arnaud: *Esther Kahn* by, 79

detective novels, 230 n. 33. *See also* mysteries and detective novels, Anglophone

Deutsch, Michel, 60

Dever, Carolyn, 119

Disney World, 173, 174, 175, 180, 186, 238 n. 40

Divorce, Le (Johnson), 165, 193–95, 198, 213 n. 7, 214 n. 10, 214 n. 15, 215 nn. 27–28, 242 n. 22; French texts within, 20, 200, 222 n. 13; as new international novel, 19, 25, 27–40, 42, 176, 177

Dostoevsky, Fyodor: *Crime and Punishment* by, 51, 53, 54

Doyle, Sir Arthur Conan, 131

Dreyfus Affair, 160, 226 n. 30

Dulles, Foster Rhea, 19

INDEX

Duncker, Patricia, 189, 239 n. 71, 240 n. 81; gay themes of, 183; *Hallucinating Foucault* by, 23, 165, 183–85, 217 n. 13, 239 n. 62, 239 nn. 65–66, 240 n. 88; intertextual references of, 183, 184, 185

Edmund White: The Burning World (Barber), 165, 175
Eliot, T.S., 162
Engel, Howard: intertextual references of, 119–27, 230 nn. 26–27, 231 n. 49; modernism and, 122, 123, 129, 131, 133, 231 n. 49; *Murder in Montparnasse* by, 21, 119–28, 130, 131, 231 n. 49
Esther Kahn (Desplechin), 79
EuroDisney, 37, 39
Evidences Invisibles (Carroll), 74
expatriates, writers, 17, 133, 190, 214 n. 14, 231 n. 49, 240 n. 81. *See also* Lost Generation

fairy and folk tales, 20, 220 n. 14, 220 n. 25; *Blackberry Wine* and, 63–64, 88, 92, 93, 94, 96; *Chocolat* and, 63–67, 68, 69, 88, 220 n. 27
Fake: The Art of Deception (Jones), 152
Farewell Symphony, The (White), 164–65, 179, 182, 184
Fenby, Jonathan: *France on the Brink* by, 85
Ferlinghetti, Lawrence, 14, 16
fiction: contemporary Anglo-American, 18; popular *vs.* mainstream, 21, 27; postmodernist, 212 n. 22
fiction, Anglophone: France in, 17, 18, 19, 23, 27, 28, 32, 38, 60, 80, 119, 133, 137, 165, 167, 168, 169, 190, 212 n. 13, 212 n. 21, 215 n. 21, 228 n. 6, 231 n. 49; French texts within, 20
Films and British National Identity (Richards), 62
Fitzgerald, F. Scott, 30
Flâneur: A Stroll through the Paradoxes of Paris, Le (White), 165, 167, 236 n. 12, 237 n. 15
Flanner, Janet, 30, 231 n. 49
Flaubert, Gustave, 155
Flavors of Modernity, The (Biasin), 83

folk culture, 66
folk tales. *See* fairy and folk tales
Fowles, John, 47, 48, 59
Fragile Glory: A Portrait of France and the French (Bernstein), 26
France, 214 n. 13; America and Britain's relations with, 18; in Anglophone fiction, 17, 18, 19, 23, 27, 28, 32, 38, 60, 80, 119, 133, 137, 165, 167, 168, 169, 175, 176, 182, 187, 188, 189, 218 n. 32; mysteries and detective novels set in, 21, 119, 133. *See also* Paris
Franklin, Benjamin, 39, 85
French Lessons: A Memoir (Kaplan), 26
French Resistance: The French-American Culture Wars (Mathy), 81, 82, 114
French, The (Zeldin), 26, 62
Friedman, Thomas, 28; *The Lexus and the Olive Tree* by, 26
Front National (Le Pen), 70, 220 n. 29, 225 n. 28

gay Paris, 182
gay themes: in *Allan Stein*, 186, 239 n. 73; in *The Book of Salt*, 189; in *Hallucinating Foucault*, 183; *in The Married Man*, 23, 134, 165–68, 176, 177, 181, 182, 238 n. 37
Genet, Jean, 23, 183, 237 n. 24
Gide, André, 23, 237 n. 24
Gilsdorf, Ethan, 15, 16, 17
Ginsberg, Allen, 14
Giono, Jean, 20
globalization, 18, 22, 39, 66, 74, 78, 79, 86, 97, 98, 213 n. 6, 222 n. 28, 223 n. 32; literature of, 19, 22, 23, 26–28, 31, 35, 42, 45, 56, 62, 90, 114, 141, 168–76, 181, 182, 185, 186, 189, 190, 193–209, 213 n. 7, 220 n. 19. *See also* nation, themes of; novel, traveling.
Globalization and Culture (Tomlinson), 26, 45, 62, 79
globalization, cultural, 26, 45, 54, 60, 62, 79
Goose in Toulouse and Other Culinary Adventures, A (Rosenblum), 87, 88, 223 n. 33
Gopnik, Adam, 26; *Paris to the Moon* by, 89

Grand Meaulnes, Le (Alain-Fournier), 20, 43, 44, 45, 46, 218 n. 24, 218 n. 26; *The Way I Found Her* and, 20, 43–53, 55, 57–59, 217 n. 18, 217 nn. 12–13, 218 n. 27, 218 n. 28
Great Cat Massacre, The (Darnton), 69, 220 n. 27
Guyot-Bender, Martine, 128, 134

Hall, Stuart, 19
Hallström, Lasse: *Chocolat* of, 62, 219 n. 7, 221 n. 2, 221 n. 38
Hallucinating Foucault (Duncker), 23, 165, 183–85, 217 n. 13, 239 n. 62, 239 n. 71, 239 nn. 65–66, 240 n. 81, 240 n. 88
Hamlet (Shakespeare), 157
Harris, Joanne, 21, 23, 219 n. 1, 220 n. 29, 221 n. 7; *Blackberry Wine* by, 20, 61–64, 71, 72, 75, 78–97, 213 n. 7, 221 n. 3, 223 n. 35, 223 n. 49, 223 nn. 45–46, 224 n. 51, 224 n. 53; *Chocolat* by, 20, 61–80, 84, 86, 207, 213 n. 7, 219 n. 7, 219 n. 11, 220 nn. 26–27, 221 n. 2, 221 n. 38; fairy/folk tales and, 63–69, 88, 92–94, 96, 220 n. 14, 220 n. 25, 220 n. 27, 221 n. 38, 223 n. 46; nation, themes of, 78, 79, 83–86, 89, 90, 220 n. 19; nostalgia, themes of, 80, 82, 85, 87, 90; postmodern paradox of, 20, 61–77, 207, 221 nn. 39–40
Haunted Journeys (Porter), 141
Hays, Tony: intertextual references of, 119, 120, 122, 123, 124, 127, 231 n. 42, 231 n. 49; modernism and, 122, 123, 129, 131, 133, 231 n. 49; *Murder in the Latin Quarter* by, 21, 119, 120, 122–24, 127, 128, 130, 131, 231 n. 42, 231 n. 49
Hemingway, Ernest, 14, 16, 21, 30, 80, 119, 122, 126, 132, 134, 152, 215 n. 21, 222 n. 13, 229 n. 17, 231 n. 42, 240 n. 81; *A Moveable Feast*, 118, 123, 124, 125, 127, 227 n. 1, 228 n. 7, 229 n. 22, 230 n. 24; *The Sun Also Rises*, 33, 124, 125, 127
Himes, Chester, 14
Hobbit, The (Tolkien), 67
Hohendel, Kristin, 23

Holquist, Michael, 120, 121, 122
Hotel Pastis: A Novel of Provence (Mayle), 81, 82
Howard, Ron: *Ain't It Romantic?: An Entertainment* by, 215 n. 31
Hugo, Victor, 129
Hutcheon, Linda, 18; *The Poetics of Postmodernism*, 182

Imagined Communities: Reflections on the Origin and Spread of Nationalism (Anderson), 111
intertextual references, 20; in *Blackberry Wine*, 81, 221 n. 3; in *The Citizen of the Country*, 157, 158, 159, 160, 161, 235 n. 68; of *Le Grand Meaulnes*, 20, 43–53, 55, 57–59, 217 n. 18, 217 n. 22, 217 nn. 12–13, 218 nn. 23–24, 218 nn. 26–27; in *Hallucinating Foucault*, 183, 184, 185; of *The Married Man*, 164, 165, 182, 183, 186; in *Masquerade*, 119, 121, 122, 123, 127, 130, 131, 132; in *Murder in Montparnasse*, 119, 120, 121, 122, 123, 125, 126, 127; in *Murder in the Latin Quarter*, 119, 120, 122, 123, 127; in mysteries and detective novels, 119, 120, 121, 122, 123, 125, 126, 127, 129; of Tremain, Rose, 41–60; in *The Way I Found Her*, 41–60, 217 n. 18, 217 n. 22, 217 nn. 12–13, 218 n. 23, 218 n. 27

James, Henry, 18, 22, 23, 33, 80, 162, 165, 189, 200, 215 n. 21, 222 n. 13, 238 n. 43, 240 n. 81; *Portrait of a Lady* by, 20, 32, 176, 177
Jameson, Frederic: "Postmodernism and Consumer Society" by, 143
Jardin du Luxembourg, 41–42, 56, 60
Joan of Arc, 203, 204
Johnson, Diane, 16, 21, 22, 23, 62, 175, 213 n. 25; cross-cultural romance of, 194, 195, 196; *L'Affaire* by, 19, 165, 193–209, 213 n. 7, 241 n. 3, 241 n. 5, 241 n. 7, 241 nn. 9–11, 242 nn. 17–22, 242 nn. 24–26, 243 nn. 28–29; *Le Divorce* by, 19, 20, 27–40, 42, 165, 176, 177, 193, 194, 195, 198, 200, 213 n. 7, 214 n. 10, 214 n. 15, 215 n. 20, 215 n. 30,

215 nn. 27–28, 222 n. 13, 242 n. 22; *Le Mariage* by, 19, 27–40, 42, 164, 193, 194, 195, 198, 214 n. 10, 214 n. 17, 215 n. 30, 215 nn. 24–25, 216 n. 37, 242 n. 15, 242 n. 22; new international novel of, 19, 25, 27–40, 42, 165, 176, 177, 193–209, 220 n. 19; spatial metaphors and configuration of, 20, 30, 33, 34, 35, 39, 40, 195, 199; White, Edmund and, 164, 165

Jones, James, 30

Jones, Mark: *Fake: The Art of Deception* by, 152

Joyce, James, 14, 16, 21, 119, 122, 229 n. 17; *Ulysses* by, 120, 121, 123, 126

Kaplan, Alice, 107; *French Lessons: A Memoir* by, 26

Kilometer Zero, 17

kitsch, post-modern, 16

Knowledge of Water, The (Smith), 22, 134, 135, 136, 137, 138, 145, 162, 232 n. 7, 232 n. 8, 232 n. 10; intertextual references in, 146, 157, 231 n. 49, 233 n. 31; postmodernism in, 146–55, 204, 231 n. 49, 232 n. 21, 233 n. 22, 233 n. 33, 233 nn. 36–37, 234 n. 48, 234 n. 56, 234 n. 59, 234 nn. 43–45

Kristéva, Julia, 50, 51

Kroes, Rob, 27, 111, 132, 216 n. 36

Kuisel, Richard F., 85, 87; *Seducing the French: The Dilemma of Americanization* by, 26

La Fontaine, 64

Lanchester, John: *The Debt to Pleasure*, 221 n. 33

Last Life, The (Messud), 16, 197, 224 n. 8, 225 n. 13, 225 n. 20, 225 n. 24, 227 n. 50; metaphor in, 98–102, 105, 106, 108, 111–13, 115–17, 225 n. 21, 227 nn. 51–53; migration themes in, 21, 102–8, 110, 111, 113–16, 227 nn. 48–49; multicultural themes in, 21, 98, 105, 108, 109, 111, 116, 225 n. 25, 225 n. 28, 226 nn. 30–32, 227 n. 44; translation of, 98, 99, 100, 114, 221 n. 7

Le Pen, Jean-Marie: *Front National* by, 70, 220 n. 29, 225 n. 28

Levitte, Jean-David, 200

Levy, Karen D., 50

Lexus and the Olive Tree, The (Friedman), 26

literary festival, 2003, "Lost, Beat and New," 13, 15, 16

literary globalism, 67, 86, 165, 220 n. 19. *See also* globalization, literature of

Lost Generation, 15, 123, 240 n. 81; in France and Paris, 14, 128, 134; modernism and, 118, 131, 133; mysteries and detective novels and, 21, 126, 129, 131, 132, 133, 229 n. 17

Louvre, 134, 135, 137, 146, 147, 148, 149

Macbeth (Shakespeare), 157, 158, 159, 160, 161, 235 n. 68

MacCannell, Dean, 19

Malraux, André, 135

Manet, Édouard, 147, 148, 155, 233 n. 37

Mariage, Le (Johnson), 164, 165, 194, 195, 198, 214 n. 10, 216 n. 37, 242 n. 15, 242 n. 22; French texts within, 20, 222 n. 13; as new international novel, 19, 25, 27–40, 42, 193, 215 nn. 24–25

Married Man, The (White), 22, 28, 103, 187, 188, 189, 213 n. 7, 215 n. 31, 238 n. 47, 238 n. 50; as cross-cultural romance, 164, 165, 167, 168, 170, 175–81, 183, 238 n. 46; gay themes in, 23, 134, 165–68, 176, 177, 181, 182, 238 n. 37; intertextual references of, 164, 165, 182, 183, 186, 236 n. 9; as new international novel, 176, 177; postmodernism of, 165, 170–75, 180–82, 191, 207, 238 n. 40; as traveling novel, 21, 166–76, 181, 190, 237 n. 24, 238 n. 34

Masquerade (Satterthwaite), 21, 128, 131, 132; intertextual references in, 119, 121–24, 127, 130, 131, 132, 231 n. 43, 231 n. 49; modernism and, 122, 123, 129, 133, 231 n. 49

Mathy, Jean-Phillipe: *French Resistance: The French-American Culture Wars* by, 81, 82, 114

Mayle, Peter, 20, 26, 85, 119, 222 n. 15; *Hotel Pastis: A Novel of Provence* by,

81, 82; *Toujours Provence* by, 81; *A Year in Provence* by, 81
McCarver, Sam: *The Case of the Uninvited Guest* by, 228 n. 7
McHale, Brian, 18, 155; *Constructing Postmodernism* by, 139
Méral, Jean: *Paris in American Literature* by, 127, 128, 129, 132, 146, 152, 156
Messud, Claire, 16, 22, 23, 224 n. 8, 225 n. 13, 225 n. 20, 225 n. 24, 227 n. 50; *The Last Life* by, 21, 98–117, 197, 221 n. 7; metaphor and, 98–102, 105, 106, 108, 111–13, 115–17, 225 n. 21, 227 nn. 51–53; migration themes of, 102–8, 110, 111, 113–16, 227 nn. 48–49; multicultural themes of, 98, 105, 108, 109, 111, 116, 225 n. 25, 225 n. 28, 226 nn. 30–32, 227 n. 44; translations of, 98, 99, 100, 114; *La Vie Après* by, 98, 99
metaphor: America as, 111, 112, 113, 115, 116; in *The Last Life*, 98–102, 105, 108, 111–13, 115–17
Michel, Paul, 184, 185, 239 n. 71
migrant, metaphor of, 31, 137
Miller, Henry, 80, 222 n. 13
Mink, Louis, 28
modernism, 15, 22; detective novels, mysteries and, 51–52, 119, 120, 121, 122, 123, 129, 130, 131, 133; Lost Generation and, 118, 131, 133
Mona Lisa (da Vinci), 147–51, 153, 157, 234 n. 48, 234 nn. 43–45
Mona Lisa: The Making of a Global Icon (Sassoon), 149
Monbrun, Estelle, 52, 119, 122, 217 n. 17
Morgan, Ted: *On Becoming American* by, 113, 114
Moveable Feast, A (Hemingway), 118, 123, 124, 125, 127, 227 n. 1, 228 n. 7, 229 n. 22, 230 n. 24
Mufti, Aamir, 85, 108, 137; *Dangerous Liaisons* by, 67, 104
Murder in Montparnasse (Engel), 21, 128, 130; intertextual references in, 119–27, 230 nn. 26–27, 231 n. 49; modernism and, 122, 123, 129, 131, 133, 231 n. 49
Murder in the Latin Quarter (Hays), 21, 128, 130; intertextual references in, 119, 120, 122–24, 127, 231 n. 42, 231 n. 49; modernism and, 122, 123, 129, 131, 133, 231 n. 49
Murders in the Rue Morgue, The (Poe), 129, 130
museum, imaginary, 135, 137
mysteries and detective novels, Anglophone: France and Paris in, 21, 22, 119, 125, 126, 127, 128, 129, 130, 132, 133, 228 n. 6; intertextual references in, 119, 120, 121, 122, 123, 124, 125, 126, 127, 130, 131, 132, 217 n. 13; Lost Generation and, 118, 126, 129, 131, 133; modernism and, 51–52, 119, 120, 122, 123, 129, 130, 131, 132, 133, 231 n. 49; modernist novels *vs*., 120, 121
Mysterious Mickey Finn or Murder at the Café du Dôme, The (Paul), 229 n. 17
Mystery of Marie Roget, The (Poe), 129

nation, themes of, 26, 62; in *Blackberry Wine*, 78, 79, 83, 84, 85, 86, 89, 90. See also globalization
National Book Award, 28, 165
National Geographic, 92, 93
national identity, 23–24, 25, 26, 34, 54, 60, 62, 66–67, 71, 110, 111, 180
National Identity (Smith), 66–67, 78
"New Generation," 15, 16
Nicolson, Marjorie: "The Professor and the Detective" by, 120
nostalgia, themes of: in *Blackberry Wine*, 80, 85, 90
novel: mainstream, 19; mainstream *vs*. popular, 21, 27; as spatial entity, 17–18
novel, new international, 26; *The Citizen of the Country* as, 161, 162; of Johnson, Diane, 25, 27–40, 176, 177, 193–209; of Smith, Sarah, 161, 162; White, Edmund and, 176, 177, 240 n. 81
novel, traveling, 21, 186, 187, 189, 190, 191, 192; *The Married Man* as, 21, 166–76, 181, 190, 237 n. 24, 237 n. 27, 238 n. 34, 238 n. 43. See also globalization
novelists, travel, 19

Oedipus Rex (Sophocles), 144, 145
Olympia (Manet), 147, 233 n. 37

On Becoming American (Morgan), 113
Our Paris: Sketches from Memory (White), 164, 182, 213 n. 7

Pagnol, Marcel, 20
Paris, 13, 14, 156, 214 n. 13; descriptions of, 17, 134; literary tradition of, 15; in mysteries and detective novels, 22, 119, 125, 126, 127, 128, 129, 130, 132. *See also* France; gay Paris
Paris in American Literature (Méral), 127, 128, 129, 132, 152
Paris to the Moon (Gopnik), 89
Pariscope, 79
Parisian from Kansas, A (Tapon), 23, 164, 182
Paul, Elliot: *The Mysterious Mickey Finn or Murder at the Café du Dôme* by, 229 n. 17
Picasso, Pablo, 22, 146, 148, 154, 186, 231 n. 49
Poe, Edgar Allan: detective novel and, 22, 129, 130, 144, 230 n. 24, 230 n. 33, 231 n. 42; *The Murders in the Rue Morgue* by, 129, 130; *The Purloined Letter* by, 129, 131
Poetics of Postmodernism, The (Hutcheon), 182
poets, 16
popular culture, 16
Porter, Dennis: *Haunted Journeys* by, 141; *The Pursuit of Crime* by, 123, 144, 230 n. 33
Portrait of a Lady (James), 20
Portraits of France (Daly), 26
postmodern paradox: in *Chocolat,* 61–77; Harris, Joanne, and, 20, 61–77
of Smith, Sarah, 142; in *The Way I Found Her,* 44, 59
postmodernism, 18, 22, 27, 35, 56, 61, 62, 68, 71, 82, 95, 101, 102, 128, 133, 135, 137; in Anglophone fiction set in France, 123, 137, 138, 139, 140, 141, 142, 185, 186, 187, 188, 189, 192; in fiction, 19, 191, 212 n. 22, 222 n. 17; in mysteries and detective novels, 120–23, 129, 132; of Smith, Sarah, 139–43, 145–56, 161–63, 231 n. 49, 232 n. 21, 233 n. 22, 233 n. 33, 233 nn. 36–37, 234 n. 48, 234 n. 56, 234 n. 59, 234 nn. 43–45, 235 nn. 71–74; of White, Edmund, 165, 170, 171, 172, 173, 174, 175, 180, 181, 182, 238 n. 40
Pound, Ezra, 121
"Professor and the Detective, The" (Nicolson), 120
Proust, Marcel, 84, 122, 217 n. 17
Purloined Letter, The (Poe), 129, 131
Pursuit of Crime, The (Porter), 123, 230 n. 33
Pyrhönen, Heta, 121

Red and the Black, The (Stendhal), 197
Renoir, Jean: *Rules of the Game (La Règle du jeu)* by, 20, 37, 38
Richards, Jeffrey: *Films and British National Identity* by, 62
Riding, Alan, 85
Rimbaud, Arthur, 183
Robbe-Grillet, Alain, 57, 122
Rochefort, Harriet Welty, 21
Rosenblum, Mort, 20, 87; *A Goose in Toulouse and Other Culinary Adventures* by, 87, 88, 223 n. 33
Roussel, Raymond, 58
Routes: Travel and Translation in the Late Twentieth Century (Clifford), 61, 182, 233 n. 36
Rules of the Game (Renoir), 20
Running in Place: Scenes from the South of France (Delbanco), 26
Russell, Alison, 19

Said, Edward, 19
Sassoon, Donald: *Becoming Mona Lisa: The Making of a Global Icon* by, 149, 234 n. 45
Satterthwaite, Walter: intertextual references of, 119, 121–24, 127, 130–32, 231 n. 43, 231 n. 49; *Masquerade* by, 21, 118, 119, 121–24, 127, 128, 130–32, 231 n. 43, 231 n. 49; modernism and, 122, 123, 129, 133, 231 n. 49
Sedaris, David, 26
Seducing the French: The Dilemma of Americanization (Kuisel), 26
Shakespeare and Company, 14, 17, 18, 20, 22, 23, 211 n. 6, 211 n. 7, 212 n. 9,

213n. 25, 213n. 30, 228n. 7; 2003 literary festival of, 13, 15, 19, 21, 129, 182, 240n. 81
Shakespeare, William, 13, 14, 122, 235n. 67; *Hamlet* by, 157; *Macbeth* by, 157, 158, 159, 160, 161, 235n. 68; *A Winter's Tale* by, 143, 144
Shaw, George Bernard, 154
Shohat, Ella, 28, 85, 108, 137, 158; *Dangerous Liaisons* by, 67, 104
Simenon, George, 125
Smith, Anthony D.: *National Identity* by, 66–67, 78, 220n. 19
Smith, Sarah: *Chasing Shakespeares: A Novel* by, 235n. 67; *The Citizen of the Country* by, 22, 135, 138, 155–61, 235n. 68, 235nn. 71–74; intertextual references of, 146, 157–61, 231n. 49, 233n. 31, 235n. 68; *The Knowledge of Water* by, 22, 134–38, 145–55, 204, 231n. 49, 232n. 10, 232nn. 7–8, 233nn. 36–37, 234n. 48, 234n. 56, 234n. 59, 234nn. 43–45; new international novel of, 161, 162, 235n. 73, 235n. 74; postmodernism of, 139–43, 145–56, 161–63, 231n. 49, 232n. 21, 233n. 22, 233n. 33, 233nn. 36–37, 234n. 48, 234n. 56, 234n. 59, 234nn. 43–45, 235nn. 71–74; "Theatre du Monde" of, 139, 156, 157, 160, 163, 236n. 80; *The Vanished Child* by, 22, 134–36, 138–45, 152, 153
Sophocles: *Oedipus Rex* by, 144, 145
Speaking in Tongues (Ashour), 26
Stadler, Matthew: *Allan Stein* by, 23, 165, 185–89, 231n. 49, 239n. 73, 240n. 85, 240nn. 81–82
Stam, Robert, 28, 158
Stein, Gertrude, 13, 14, 18, 19, 21, 22, 30, 119, 122, 123, 126, 128, 132, 133, 134, 135, 137, 146, 148, 154, 186, 187, 189, 190, 191, 211n. 1, 213n. 25, 229n. 17, 230n. 24, 231n. 49, 233n. 32
Stendhal: *The Red and the Black* by, 197
Sue, Eugène, 129
Sun Also Rises, The (Hemingway), 33, 124, 125, 127

Tapon, Philippe: *A Parisian from Kansas* by, 23, 164, 165, 182
"Terre vue du ciel, La" ("Earth From Above") (Arthus-Bertrand), 41, 60
"Third Wave," 16
Through the Looking Glass (Carroll), 55, 56, 57, 72, 218n. 23
Toklas, Alice B., 126, 189, 190, 191, 229n. 17
Tolkien, J.R.R.: *The Hobbit* by, 67
Tomlinson, John, 18, 84, 162, 169, 172; *Globalization and Culture* by, 26, 27, 45, 62, 79
Toujours Provence (Mayle), 81
translation: of *The Last Life*, 98, 99, 100, 114; in *The Way I Found Her*, 57–60
traveling cultures, 19
Tremain, Rose, 23, 62, 225n. 20; *Le Grand Meaulnes* and, 20, 43–53, 55, 57–59, 217n. 18, 217nn. 12–13, 218n. 28; intertextual references of, 41–60, 72, 217n. 18, 217nn. 12–13, 217nn. 22–23, 218n. 28; *The Way I Found Her* by, 20, 21, 41–60, 204, 217n. 12, 217n. 22, 218n. 23, 218n. 28, 218n. 32
Truffaut, François, 38
Truong, Monique: *The Book of Salt* by, 23, 165, 189, 190, 191, 192, 240n. 81, 240n. 89

Ulysses (Joyce), 120, 121, 123, 126
Urry, John, 19

Vandenburg, Margaret: *An American in Paris* by, 231n. 49
Vanished Child, The (Smith), 22, 134, 135, 136, 138, 152; madness in, 139, 140, 142, 143, 144, 145; postmodernism in, 139, 140, 141, 143, 145, 153
Varda, Agnès, 97; *Deux Ans après* by, 35; *Les Glaneurs et la Glaneuse* by, 35
Verdaguer, Pierre, 52, 119, 129, 217n. 17
Vie Après, La (Messud), 98, 99
Village in the Vaucluse, 87
Village Voice, 98, 100, 213n. 30
Villepin, Dominique de, 200

INDEX

Way I Found Her, The (Tremain), 21, 204, 218 n. 32, 225 n. 20; *Le Grand Meaulnes* and, 20, 43–53, 55, 57–59, 217 n. 12, 217 n. 13, 217 n. 18, 218 n. 27, 218 n. 28; intertextual references in, 41–60, 72, 217 n. 12, 217 n. 13, 217 n. 18, 217 n. 22, 218 n. 23, 218 nn. 27–28; postmodern paradox in, 44, 59; translation in, 57–60, 218 n. 28

Wells, Patricia, 20

Wharton, Edith, 30

White, Edmund, 16, 26, 187, 188, 189, 238 n. 50, 239 n. 68; cross-cultural romance of, 164, 165, 167, 168, 170, 175–81, 183, 238 n. 43, 238 n. 46; *The Farewell Symphony*, 164–65, 179, 182, 184; *Le Flâneur: A Stroll through the Paradoxes of Paris* by, 165, 167, 236 n. 12, 237 n. 15; gay themes of, 23, 134, 165–68, 176, 177, 181, 182, 238 n. 37; intertextual references and, 164, 165, 182, 183, 186, 236 n. 9; Johnson, Diane and, 164, 165; *The Married Man* by, 21, 22, 23, 103, 164–84, 186–91, 213 n. 7, 215 n. 31, 236 n. 9, 237 n. 24, 238 n. 34, 238 nn. 46–47; new international novel of, 176, 177, 238 n. 43; *Our Paris: Sketches from Memory* by, 164, 182, 213 n. 7; postmodernism of, 165, 170–75, 180–82, 191, 207, 238 n. 40; traveling novel of, 21, 166–76, 181, 190, 237 n. 24, 237 n. 27, 238 n. 34, 238 n. 43, 240 n. 81

Whitman, George, 13, 14, 16, 17, 211 n. 6, 211 n. 7

Whitman, Sylvia Beach, 14, 211 n. 6

Whitman, Walt, 14, 129, 211 n. 6

Winter's Tale, A (Shakespeare), 143, 144

Wizard of Oz, The (Baum), 54, 55, 67, 108

Wright, Richard, 14

writers, Anglophone, 16; expatriate, 14, 18, 212 n. 13

writers, expatriate American, 13, 16

writers, expatriate British, 13, 16

Wylie, Laurence, 87

Year in Provence, A (Mayle), 81

Zeldin, Theodore: *The French* by, 26, 62

Zola, Emile: *L'Assommoir* by, 55

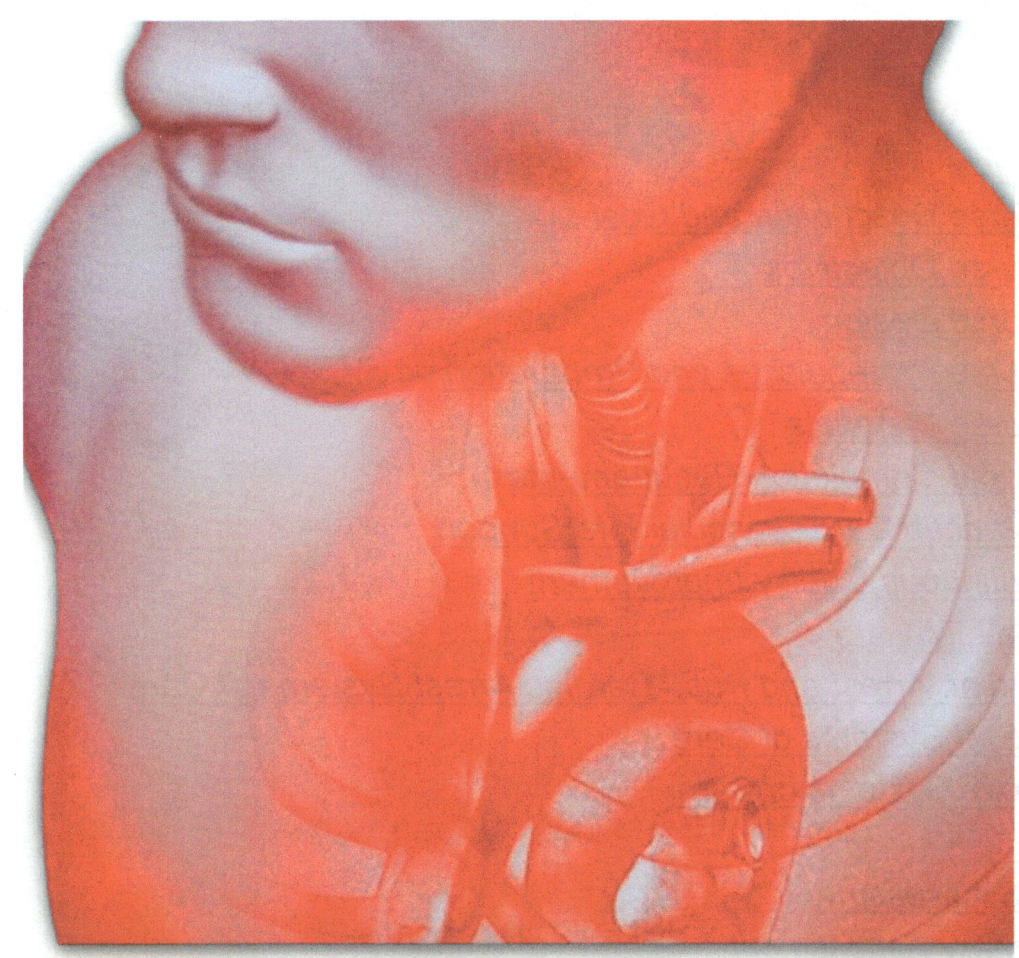

ACLS
Advanced Cardiovascular Life Support

Contents

Part 1: Overview of ACLS

Introduction
- *Course Description and Goal*
- *Course Objectives*
- *Course Design*
- *Course Prerequisites and Preparation*
- *Course Materials*
- *Course Completion Requirements*
- *Advanced Cardiovascular Life Support*
- *Continuous Quality Improvement*

Systems of Care
- *Cardiac Arrest and Post–Cardiac Arrest Systems of Care*
- *STEMI Systems of Care*
- *Stroke Systems of Care*

Systematic Approach
- *BLS Assessment*
- *Primary Assessment*
- *Secondary Assessment*
- *References*

Part 2: Preventing Arrest

Recognition: Signs of Clinical Deterioration
- *Rapid Response*
- *Implementing a Rapid Response System*

Acute Coronary Syndromes
- *Goals for ACS Patients*
- *OHCA Response*
- *Pathophysiology of ACS*
- *Managing ACS: The Acute Coronary Syndromes Algorithm*
- *Symptoms Suggestive of Ischemia or Infarction*
- *EMS Assessment, Care, and Hospital Preparation*

- *Immediate ED Assessment and Treatment*
- *Classifying Patients by ST-Segment Deviation*
- *STEMI*

Acute Stroke

- *Overview*
- *Major Types of Stroke*
- *Approach to Stroke Care*
- *Goals of Stroke Care*
- *Critical Time Periods*
- *Application of the Adult Suspected Stroke Algorithm*
- *Stroke Centers and Stroke Units*
- *Immediate General and Neurologic Assessment*
- *Fibrinolytic Therapy*
- *Endovascular Therapy*
- *Begin General Stroke Care*

Bradycardia

- *Overview*
- *Symptomatic Bradycardia*
- *Managing Bradycardia: The Bradycardia Algorithm*

Tachycardia: Stable and Unstable

- *Overview*
- *Approach to Unstable Tachycardia*
- *Managing Unstable Tachycardia: The Adult Tachycardia With a Pulse Algorithm*
- *Applying the Adult Tachycardia With a Pulse Algorithm to Unstable Patients*
- *Cardioversion*
- *Synchronized Cardioversion*
- *Stable Tachycardias*
- *Approach to Stable Tachycardia*
- *Managing Stable Tachycardia: The Adult Tachycardia With a Pulse Algorithm*

- *Applying the Adult Tachycardia With a Pulse Algorithm to Stable Patients*
- *References*

Part 3: High-Performance Teams

High-Performance Team Roles and Dynamics
- *Roles in a High-Performance Team*
- *Elements of Effective Team Dynamics as Part of a High-Performance Team*

Respiratory Arrest
- *Overview*
- *Normal and Abnormal Breathing*
- *Identifying Respiratory Problems by Severity*
- *BLS Assessment*
- *Primary Assessment*
- *Managing Respiratory Arrest*
- *Giving Supplemental Oxygen*
- *Opening the Airway*
- *Providing Basic Ventilation*
- *Basic Airway Adjuncts: OPA*
- *Basic Airway Adjuncts: NPA*
- *Suctioning*
- *Using Quantitative Waveform Capnography With a Bag-Mask Device*
- *Pulse Oximetry*
- *Providing Ventilation With an Advanced Airway*
- *Precautions for Trauma Patients*

Cardiac Arrest: VF/pVT
- *Overview*
- *Managing VF/pVT: The Adult Cardiac Arrest Algorithm*
- *Applying the Adult Cardiac Arrest Algorithm: VF/pVT Pathway*
- *Physiologic Monitoring During CPR*
- *Routes of Access for Drugs*
- *Ultrasound for VF/pVT/Asystole/PEA*
- *Return of Spontaneous Circulation*

Cardiac Arrest: PEA and Asystole
- *Overview*
- *Description of PEA*
- *Approach to Asystole*
- *Managing Asystole/PEA: The Adult Cardiac Arrest Algorithm*
- *Patients With DNAR Orders*
- *Terminating Resuscitative Efforts*

Cardiac Arrest: Selected Special Situations
- *Treating VF/pVT in Accidental Hypothermia*
- *Respiratory or Cardiac Arrest Associated With Opioid Overdose*
- *ECPR (for VF/pVT/Asystole/PEA)*
- *Ventricular Assist Devices*
- *Cardiac Arrest Associated With Pregnancy*

Post–Cardiac Arrest Care
- *Overview*
- *Multiple System Approach to Post–Cardiac Arrest Care*
- *Managing Post–Cardiac Arrest Care: The Adult Post-Cardiac Arrest Care Algorithm*
- *Application of the Adult Post–Cardiac Arrest Care Algorithm*
- *Other Postresuscitation Care*
- *Neuroprognostication*
- *References*

Appendix
- Testing Checklists and Learning Station Checklists
  - *Adult High-Quality BLS Skills Testing Checklist*
  - *Airway Management Skills Testing Checklist*
  - *Megacode Testing Checklist: Scenarios 1/3/8*
  - *Megacode Testing Checklist: Scenarios 2/5*
  - *Megacode Testing Checklist: Scenarios 4/7/10*
  - *Megacode Testing Checklist: Scenarios 6/11*
  - *Megacode Testing Checklist: Scenario 9*
  - *Megacode Testing Checklist: Scenario 12*

- *Adult Cardiac Arrest Learning Station Checklist (VF/pVT)*
- *Adult Cardiac Arrest Learning Station Checklist (Asystole/PEA)*
- *Adult Bradycardia Learning Station Checklist*
- *Adult Tachycardia With a Pulse Learning Station*
- *Adult Post–Cardiac Arrest Care Learning Station Checklist*
- *Adult Cardiac Arrest Learning Station Checklist (VF/pVT/Asystole/PEA)*
- *Cardiac Arrest in Pregnancy In-Hospital ACLS Learning Station Checklist*
- *Adult Ventricular Assist Device Learning Station Checklist*

ACLS Pharmacology Summary Table

Science Summary Table

Glossary

Part 1: Overview of ACLS

Introduction

Course Description and Goal

The Advanced Cardiovascular Life Support (ACLS) Provider Course is designed for healthcare providers who either direct or participate in the management of cardiopulmonary arrest or other cardiovascular emergencies. Through didactic instruction and active participation in simulated cases, students will enhance their skills in the recognition and intervention of cardiopulmonary arrest, immediate post–cardiac arrest, acute dysrhythmia, stroke, and acute coronary syndromes (ACS). The goal of this course is to improve outcomes for adult patients of cardiopulmonary arrest and other cardiovascular emergencies through early recognition and interventions by high-performance teams.

Course Objectives

After successfully completing this course, you should be able to
- Define *systems of care*
- Apply the Basic Life Support (BLS) Assessment, Primary Assessment, and Secondary Assessment sequences for systematic evaluation of adult patients
- Discuss how using rapid response teams (RRTs) or medical emergency teams (METs) may improve patient outcomes
- Discuss early recognition and management of ACS, including appropriate disposition
- Discuss early recognition and management of stroke, including appropriate disposition
- Recognize bradycardia and tachycardia that may result in cardiac arrest or complicate resuscitation outcome
- Perform early management of bradycardia and tachycardia that may result in cardiac arrest or complicate resuscitation outcome
- Model effective communication as a member or leader of a high-performance team

- Recognize the impact of team dynamics on overall team performance
- Recognize respiratory arrest
- Perform early management of respiratory arrest
- Recognize cardiac arrest
- Perform prompt, high-quality BLS, which includes prioritizing early chest compressions and integrating early automated external defibrillator (AED) use
- Perform early management of cardiac arrest until termination of resuscitation or transfer of care, including immediate post–cardiac arrest care
- Evaluate resuscitative efforts during cardiac arrest by continually assessing cardiopulmonary resuscitation (CPR) quality, monitoring the patient's physiologic response, and delivering real-time feedback to the team

Course Design

To help you achieve these objectives, the ACLS Provider Course includes learning stations and a Megacode evaluation station. The learning stations provide activities such as
- Simulated clinical scenarios
- Video or instructor demonstrations
- Discussion and role-playing
- Group practice to achieve effective high-performance teams

In these learning stations, you will practice essential skills both individually and as part of a team. Because this course emphasizes effective team skills as a vital part of the resuscitative effort, you'll practice as both a team member and as Team Leader.

In the Megacode evaluation station at the end of the class, you will participate in a simulated cardiac arrest scenario to evaluate your
- Integration of core material and skills
- Application of algorithms
- Interpretation of arrhythmias
- Use of appropriate ACLS drug therapy
- Performance as an effective leader and member of a high-performance team
- Achieving objective measures such as chest compression fraction (CCF)

Course Prerequisites and Preparation

The American Heart Association (AHA) limits enrollment in this course to healthcare providers who
- Direct or participate in the resuscitation of patients in or out of hospital
- Have the basic knowledge and skills to participate actively with the instructor and other students

Before class, read the *ACLS Provider Manual*, complete the mandatory precourse work in ACLS Student Resources (accessed via **eLearning.heart.org**), identify any gaps in your knowledge, and remediate those gaps by studying the applicable content in the *ACLS Provider Manual* or other supplementary resources, including the ACLS Student Resources. You must pass the Precourse Self-Assessment with a minimum score of **70%**. You may retake the self-assessment as often as needed to pass. **Print your certificate of completion and bring it with you to the course.**

You will need the following knowledge and skills to successfully complete the course:
- BLS skills
- Electrocardiogram (ECG) rhythm interpretation for core ACLS rhythms
- Knowledge of airway management and adjuncts
- Basic ACLS drug and pharmacology knowledge
- Practical application of ACLS rhythms and drugs
- Effective high-performance team skills

BLS Skills

Strong BLS skills form the foundation of ACLS, so you must pass the high-quality BLS Testing Station to complete this course. *Make sure that you are proficient in BLS skills before attending the class.*

ECG Rhythm Interpretation for Core ACLS Rhythms

The basic cardiac arrest and periarrest algorithms require students to recognize these ECG rhythms:
- Sinus rhythm
- Atrial fibrillation and flutter
- Sinus bradycardia
- Sinus tachycardia

- Supraventricular tachycardia
- Atrioventricular blocks
- Asystole
- Pulseless electrical activity (PEA)
- Ventricular tachycardias (VTs)
- Ventricular fibrillation (VF)

The ACLS Precourse Self-Assessment contains an ECG rhythm identification section. Use your self-assessment score and feedback to help you identify your areas of strength and weakness before attending the class. You must be able to identify and interpret rhythms during course practice sessions and the final Megacode evaluation station.

Basic ACLS Drug and Pharmacology Knowledge

You must know the drugs and doses used in the ACLS algorithms. You will also need to know when to use which drug based on the clinical situation.

The ACLS Precourse Self-Assessment contains pharmacology questions. Use your self-assessment score and feedback to help you identify areas of strength and weakness before attending the class.

Course Materials

Course materials consist of the *ACLS Provider Manual*, in the ACLS Student Resources, and 3 reference cards.

The computer icon directs you to additional supplementary information ACLS Student Resources (accessed via **eLearning.heart.org**).

ACLS Provider Manual

The *ACLS Provider Manual* contains the basic information you will need to participate in the course, including the systematic approach to a cardiopulmonary emergency, information about effective high-performance team communication, and the ACLS cases and algorithms. **Review this manual before attending the class, and bring it with you to the class.** Students using the eBook version should download the manual to their device's eReader app and bring it with them, in case there is no internet connection.

The *ACLS Provider Manual* also contains important information presented in *Critical Concepts* and *Caution* callout boxes that require your attention:

Critical Concepts
These boxes contain the most important information you must know, including specific risks associated with certain interventions and additional background on key topics this course covers.

Caution
Caution boxes emphasize specific risks associated with interventions.

ACLS Student Resources

The ACLS Student Resources (accessed via **eLearning.heart.org**) contain mandatory precourse preparation and supplementary materials.
- Precourse Self-Assessment (passing score 70% or greater)
- Precourse work (complete interactive video lessons)

Use the following website resources to supplement basic concepts in the ACLS Course. Some information is supplementary; other areas provide additional information for interested students or advanced providers.
- Precourse Preparation Checklist (used to ensure that students are ready to attend the class).
- ACLS Supplementary Material
  - –Basic Airway Management
  - –Advanced Airway Management
  - –ACLS Core Rhythms
  - –Defibrillation
  - –Access for Medications
  - –Acute Coronary Syndromes
  - –Human, Ethical, and Legal Dimensions of ECC and ACLS
- Optional Videos
  - –Intraosseous Access
  - –Coping With Death

Reference Cards

The 3 stand-alone reference cards included with the *ACLS Provider Manual* (and sold individually packaged) provide quick reference for training in real emergencies on the following topics:

- Cardiac arrest, arrhythmias, and their treatment
    - –Adult Cardiac Arrest Algorithms
    - –Table with drugs and dosage reminders
    - –Adult Post–Cardiac Arrest Care Algorithm
    - –Adult Bradycardia Algorithm
    - –Adult Tachycardia With a Pulse Algorithm
- ACS and stroke
    - –Acute Coronary Syndromes Algorithm
    - –Fibrinolytic Contraindications for STEMI
    - –Adult Suspected Stroke Algorithm
    - –Emergency Medical Services Acute Stroke Routing Algorithm
    - –Hypertension Management in Acute Ischemic Stroke
- Cardiac arrest in select special situations and neuroprognostication
    - –Opioid-Associated Emergency for Healthcare Providers Algorithm
    - –Adult Ventricular Assist Device Algorithm
    - –Cardiac Arrest in Pregnancy In-Hospital ACLS Algorithm
    - –Neuroprognostication diagram

Use these cards as a reference when you are preparing for class, during the learning stations, and during real emergencies. You may refer to them during the Megacode and the cognitive exam.

Course Completion Requirements

To successfully complete the ACLS Provider Course and obtain your course completion card, you must
- Pass the Adult High-Quality BLS Skills Test
- Pass the Airway Management Skills Test, including oropharyngeal airway/nasopharyngeal airway insertion
- Demonstrate competency in learning station skills
- Pass the High-Performance Teams: Megacode Test
- Pass the open-resource exam with a minimum score of 84%

Advanced Cardiovascular Life Support

ACLS providers face an important challenge: functioning as a team that implements basic and advanced life support to save a person's life. The *2020 AHA Guidelines for Cardiopulmonary Resuscitation and Emergency Cardiovascular Care* reviewed evidence that in both in-hospital and out-of-hospital settings, many cardiac arrest patients do not receive high-quality CPR, and most do not survive. One study of in-hospital cardiac arrest (IHCA) showed that CPR quality was inconsistent and did not always meet guidelines recommendations.[1] Over the years, however, patient outcomes after cardiac arrest have improved. Table 1 shows the recent survival trends in both IHCA and out-of-hospital cardiac arrest (OHCA) in the United States.[2]

Table 1. Recent Cardiac Arrest Survival Data

Statistical update	OHCA incidence, n	OHCA bystander CPR (overall), %	OHCA survival rate* (overall), %	IHCA incidence,† n	IHCA survival rate* (Adults), %
2020	356 461	41.6	10.4	209 000	25.8
2019	356 461	46.1	10.4	209 000	25.6
2018	347 322	46.1	11.4	209 000	25.8
2017	356 500	45.7	11.4	209 000	23.8
2016	356 500	46.1	12.0	209 000	24.8
2015	326 200	45.9	10.6	209 000	25.5
2014	424 000	40.8	10.4	209 000	22.7
2013	359 400	40.1	9.5	209 000	23.9
2012	382 800	41.0	11.4	209 000	23.1
Baseline		31.0	7.9		19.0

*Survival to hospital discharge.
†Extrapolated incidence based on the same 2011 Get With The Guidelines®-Resuscitation study.

Multiple evidence reviews have focused on the essentials of CPR, the links in the Chain of Survival, and the integration of BLS with ACLS. Minimizing the interval between stopping chest compressions and delivering a shock (ie, minimizing the preshock pause) improves the chances of shock success[3] and patient survival.[4] Experts believe that high survival rates from both in-hospital and out-of-hospital sudden cardiac death are possible with strong systems of care.

Several factors have been associated with improved survival in patients with cardiac arrest:
- Training healthcare providers to become more knowledgeable about what improves survival rates
- Proactive planning and simulation of cardiac arrest to provide the opportunity for a healthcare provider to practice and improve responding to cardiac arrest
- Rapidly recognizing sudden cardiac arrest
- Immediately providing high-quality CPR
- Defibrillating immediately, as soon as a defibrillator is available
- Providing goal-directed, time-sensitive post–cardiac arrest care

Rapid intervention by skilled people working within a strong system of care leads to the best outcomes.

Critical Concepts: Optimizing ACLS
Team Leaders can optimize ACLS by integrating high-quality CPR and minimal interruption of chest compressions with advanced life support strategies (eg, defibrillation, medications, advanced airway).
Studies have shown that reducing the interval between compressions and shock delivery can increase predicted shock success. Limit the number of interruptions in compressions to critical interventions (rhythm analysis, shock delivery, intubation, etc), and minimize the duration of necessary interruptions to 10 seconds or less.

Continuous Quality Improvement

Every emergency medical services (EMS) system and hospital system should assess its resuscitation interventions and outcomes through continuous quality improvement (CQI) with a defined process of data collection and review. The current consensus on the best way to improve both in-hospital and out-of-hospital survival after sudden cardiac arrest is to modify the standard quality improvement model according to the Chain of Survival metaphor. Each link in the chain comprises structural, process, and outcome variables that systems can examine, measure, and record. System managers can quickly identify gaps between observed processes and outcomes and local expectations or published standards. Individuals and teams who regularly review their performance in actual resuscitations will, on average, improve their performance in subsequent resuscitation events. Therefore, it is important for resuscitation teams to find the time to debrief themselves at some time after every resuscitation, either immediately or later.

Systems of Care

A *system* is a group of interdependent components that regularly interact to form a whole. The system
- Provides the links for the Chain of Survival
- Determines the strength of each link and of the chain
- Determines the ultimate outcome
- Provides collective support and organization

Healthcare delivery requires **structure** (eg, people, equipment, education) and **processes** (eg, policies, protocols, procedures) that when integrated produce a **system** (eg, programs, organizations, cultures) leading to **outcomes** (eg, patient safety, quality, satisfaction). This integrated response, known as a *system of care*, comprises all of these elements—structure, process, system, and patient outcome—in a framework of CQI (Figure 1).

Structure Process System Outcome

Structure	Process	System	Patient Outcome
People Education Equipment	Protocols Policies Procedures	Programs Organization Culture	Satisfaction Quality Safety

Continuous Quality Improvement
Integration, Collaboration, Measurement, Benchmarking, Feedback

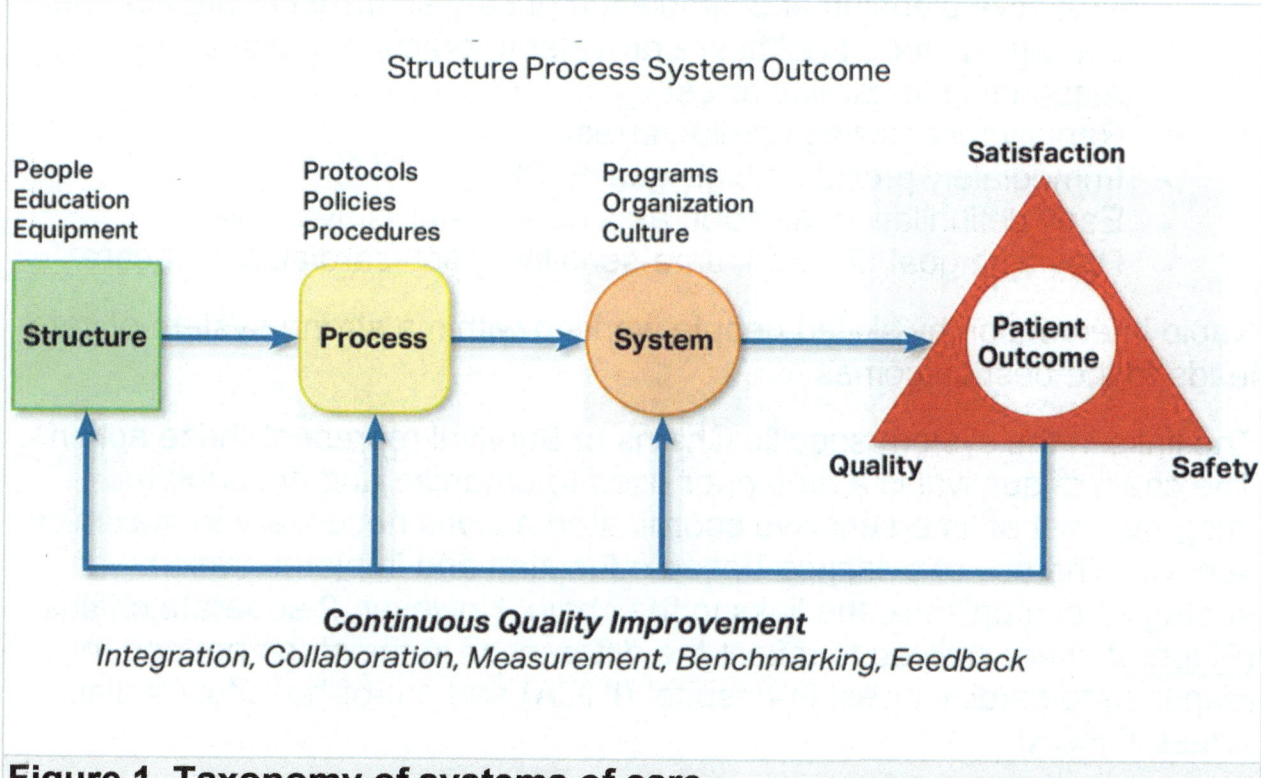

Figure 1. Taxonomy of systems of care.

These systems require individuals and groups to share information so that they can evaluate and improve their system. Leadership and accountability are important components of this team approach. Participants and leaders in systems of care must continually assess the performance of each system component; only after this assessment can they effectively intervene to improve outcomes.

The CQI process consists of an iterative cycle of
- Systematically evaluating resuscitation care and outcome
- Creating benchmarks with stakeholder feedback
- Strategically addressing identified deficiencies

Cardiac Arrest and Post–Cardiac Arrest Systems of Care

Successful resuscitation requires integrated, coordinated actions. Experts believe that high survival rates from both in- and out-of-hospital sudden cardiac death are possible with strong systems of care.

Several factors have been associated with improved survival in patients with cardiac arrest:
- Training healthcare providers to become more knowledgeable about what improves survival rates
- Proactive planning and simulation of cardiac arrest to provide the opportunity for a healthcare provider to practice and improve responding to cardiac arrest
- Rapidly recognizing cardiac arrest
- Immediately providing high-quality CPR
- Early defibrillation, as soon as a defibrillator is available
- Providing goal-directed, time-sensitive post–cardiac arrest care

Rapid intervention by skilled people working within a strong system of care leads to the best outcomes.

The links in the system-specific Chains of Survival represent these actions. The chain of survival is a metaphor used to organize and describe the integrated set of time-sensitive coordinated actions necessary to maximize survival. The use of evidence-based education and implementation strategies can optimize the links in the chain. However, 2 separate chains (Figure 2) were created to reflect the differences in the steps needed for response to cardiac arrest in-hospital (IHCA) and out-of-hospital cardiac arrest (OHCA).

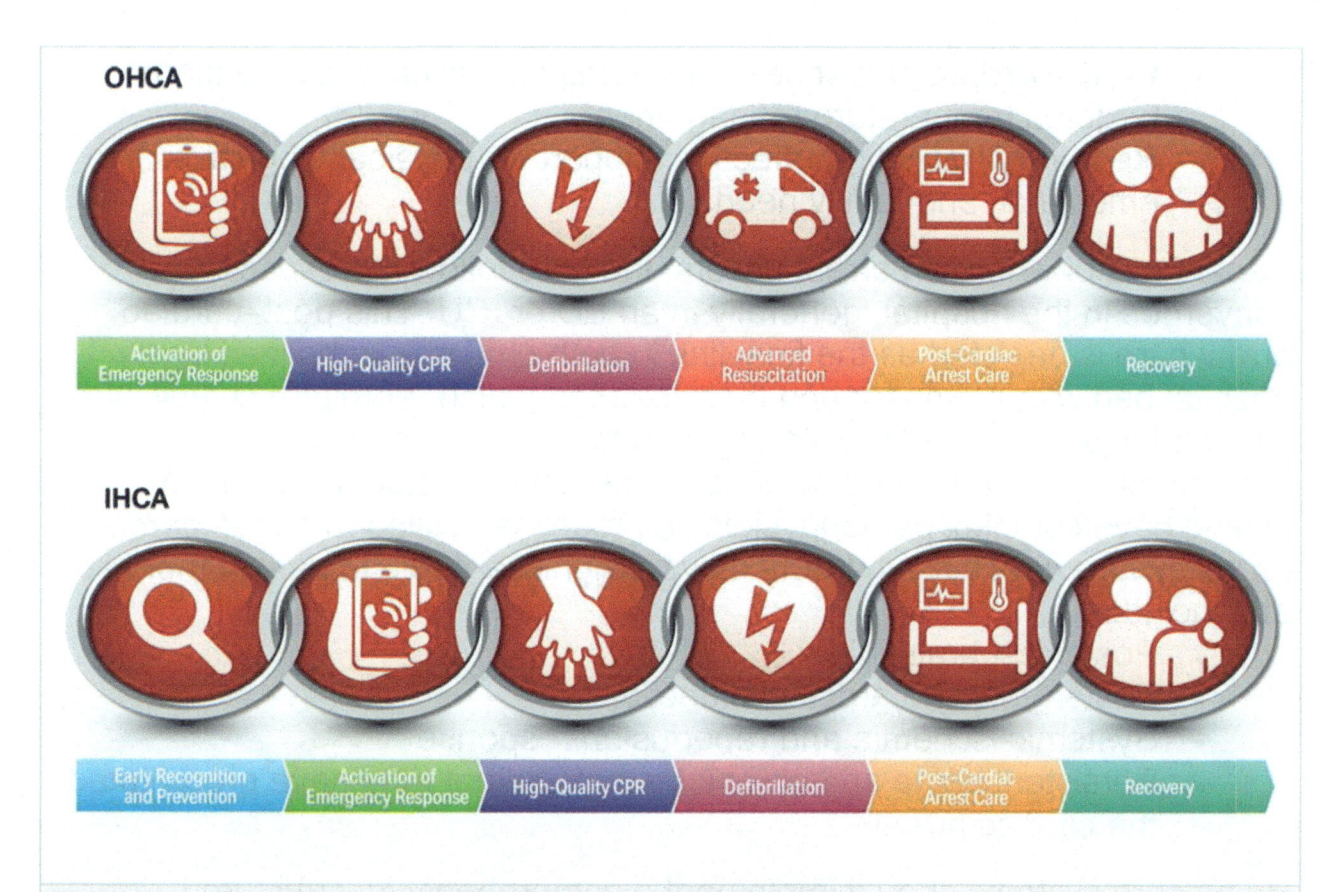

Figure 2. System-specific Chains of Survival.

Cardiac arrest can happen anywhere—on the street, at home, or in a hospital emergency department (ED), in-patient bed, or intensive care unit (ICU). Elements in the system of care and order of actions in the Chain of Survival differ based on the situation. Care will depend on whether the victim has the arrest outside the hospital or inside the hospital. Care also depends on whether the victim is an adult, child, or infant.

Chain of Survival Elements

Although there are slight differences in the Chains of Survival based on the age of the victim and location of the cardiac arrest, each includes the following elements:
- **Prevention and preparedness**, including responder training, early recognition of cardiac arrest, and rapid response
- **Activation of the emergency response system**, either outside of or within the hospital
- **High-quality CPR**, including **early defibrillation** of VF and pVT
- **Advanced resuscitation interventions**, including medications, advanced airway interventions, and extracorporeal CPR

- **Post–cardiac arrest care**, including critical care interventions and targeted temperature management
- **Recovery**, including effective support for physical, cognitive, emotional, and family needs

Regardless of where an arrest occurs, the care following resuscitation converges in the hospital, generally in an ED or ICU. This post–cardiac arrest care is depicted as the final link in both chains, symbolized by a hospital bed with a monitor and thermometer, which represent critical care interventions, advanced monitoring, and targeted temperature management. Patients who achieve ROSC after cardiac arrest in any setting have complex pathophysiologic processes called the *post–cardiac arrest syndrome*. This syndrome plays a significant role in patient mortality and includes

- Postarrest brain injury
- Postarrest myocardial dysfunction
- Systemic ischemia and reperfusion response
- Persistent acute and chronic pathology that may have precipitated the cardiac arrest[5]

Healthcare systems should implement a comprehensive, structured, consistent, multidisciplinary system of care for treating post–cardiac arrest patients. Programs should address ventilation and hemodynamic optimization, targeted temperature management (TTM), immediate coronary reperfusion with percutaneous coronary intervention (PCI) for eligible patients, neurologic care and prognostication, and other structured interventions. Individual hospitals that frequently treat cardiac arrest patients show an increased likelihood of patient survival when these interventions are provided.

As noted above, the structure and process elements before the convergence of the 2 chains vary significantly. Patients with OHCA depend on elements within the community for support. Lay rescuers must recognize the patient's arrest, call for help, and initiate CPR and early defibrillation (public-access defibrillation [PAD]) until a team of professionally trained emergency medical services (EMS) providers assumes responsibility and transports the patient to an ED and/or cardiac catheterization lab, followed by admission to an ICU for post–cardiac arrest care. Ideally, all victims of OHCA receive bystander CPR and defibrillation; if not, CPR and defibrillation won't occur until EMS personnel arrive, making the victim's chance of survival much lower. It is vital to measure and improve dispatch-aided CPR rates.

In contrast, patients with IHCA depend on a system of appropriate early recognition and prevention of cardiac arrest, which is represented by a magnifying glass in the first link. When cardiac arrest occurs, prompt activation of the emergency response system with a response to the cardiac arrest that provides high-quality CPR, early defibrillation, and advanced cardiovascular life support should result in the smooth interaction of a multidisciplinary team of professional providers, including physicians, nurses, respiratory therapists, and others. The last link is recovery and includes considerations for the postarrest needs of the patient and family. The chain metaphor endures: in any resuscitation, the chain is no stronger than its weakest link.

The classic resuscitation Chain of Survival concept linked the community to EMS and EMS to hospitals, with hospital care as the destination.[6] But patients with a cardiac emergency may enter the system of care at any point (Figure 3), including on the street; at home; or in the hospital's ED, inpatient bed, ICU, operating suite, catheterization suite, or imaging department. The system of care must be able to manage cardiac emergencies wherever they occur.

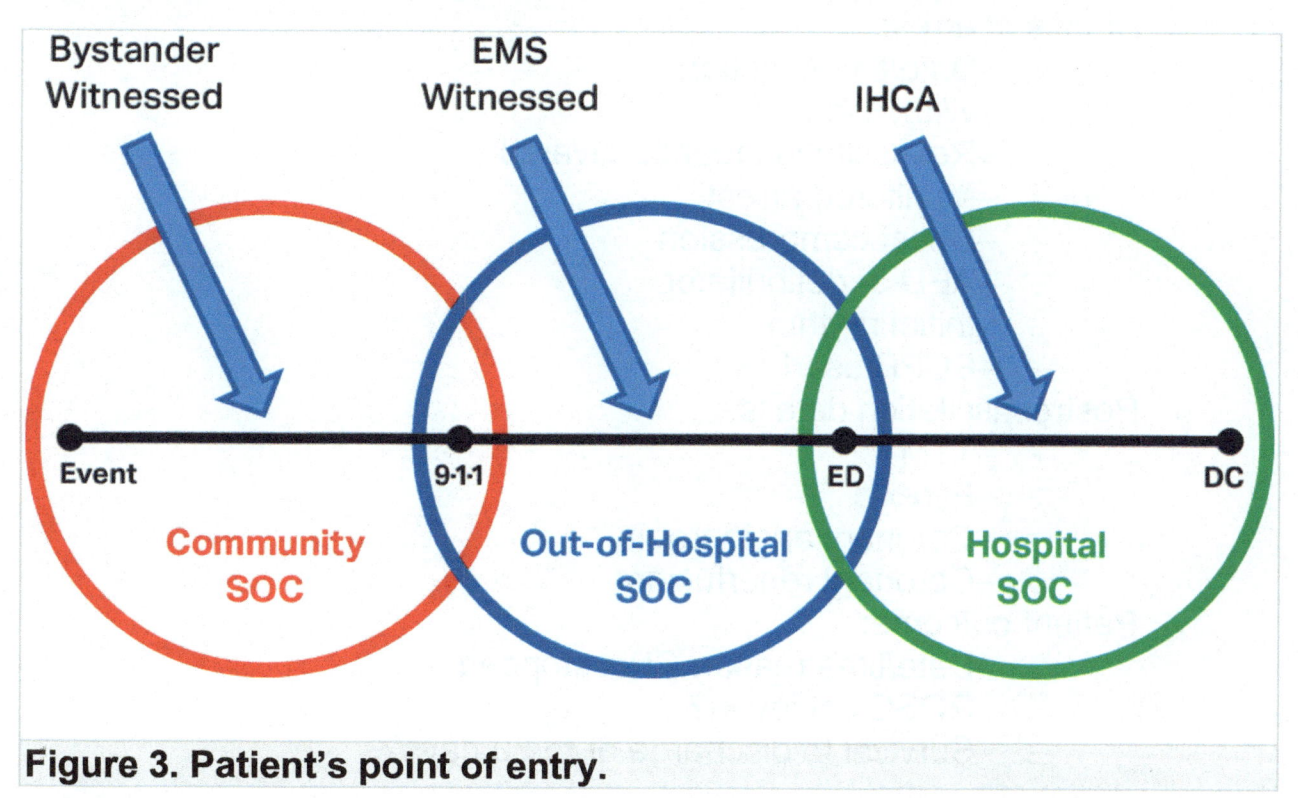

Figure 3. Patient's point of entry.

Abbreviations: DC, discharge; SOC, system of care.

Measurement

Systems that continually work to improve resuscitation outcomes capture and review data related to resuscitation education, processes, and outcomes to identify measures that can lead to better patient care. Quality improvement efforts rely on valid assessments of resuscitation performance and patient outcomes.

Utstein-style guidelines and templates allow for reporting resuscitation outcomes after trauma and drowning.[7] These OHCA guidelines[8] provide guidance for core performance measures, including

- Occurrence of bystander CPR
- Time interval from collapse to defibrillator placement
- Time interval to advanced airway management
- Time interval to first administration of resuscitation medication
- Survival to hospital discharge

These IHCA guidelines[9] provide guidance for core performance measures, including the following:

- Patient demographics
- Patient category (inpatient or outpatient) and illness category
- Details of arrest:
    - –Date/time/location
    - –Witnessed
    - –Resuscitation team activated
    - –Monitored arrest
    - –Chest compression
    - –AED or defibrillator
    - –Initial rhythm
    - –ECPR used
- Postresuscitation details:
    - –TTM
    - –Pyrexia
    - –Coronary angiography
    - –Coronary reperfusion
- Patient outcome:
    - –Date/time/reason CPR stopped
    - –ROSC achieved?
    - –Survival to discharge or to 30 days?

- —Neurologic outcome
- —Date/time of death
- —Organ donation

Physiologic end points are generally considered the best indicators of resuscitation effectiveness, and outside of a hospital setting, $ETCO_2$ is typically available. During CPR, $ETCO_2$ is a relative indicator of cardiac output and can also signal return of spontaneous circulation (ROSC), so this should be used if possible. CPR performance monitors are now widely available,[10] and they provide invaluable real-time feedback on the quality of CPR that rescuers deliver during resuscitation attempts. Other monitors of CPR performance are increasingly available and can provide real-time feedback to healthcare providers. After a resuscitation attempt, these monitors also provide data for debriefing and information for system-wide CPR CQI programs. Without a way to measure CPR and understand their performance, providers cannot improve.

Some CPR performance characteristics are available as immediate feedback while other characteristics are available only after CPR or not at all, given current technology. The ability to receive immediate feedback on the following items will depend on the level of technology available:

- Immediately available feedback
    - —Chest compression rate
    - —Depth
    - —Recoil
- Feedback for review
    - —Chest compression fraction
    - —Preshock, perishock, and postshock pauses
    - —Feedback that cannot be assessed adequately
    - —Ventilation rate
    - —Airway pressure
    - —Tidal volume
    - —Inflation duration
    - —Other physiological end points, if available (ie, $ETCO_2$, intra-arterial blood pressure, cardiac ultrasound)

Current CPR monitoring devices do not always provide optimal feedback. For example, accelerometers do not sense mattress compression, and their rigid algorithms do not realistically prioritize the order of feedback—they cannot measure depth if the provider leans too much, so the devices prioritize feedback to correct leaning before depth. Although some solutions currently exist, including software (automated algorithms) and hardware (smart backboard, dual accelerometers, reference markers, and others), continued improvements to performance require continued improvements to CPR monitoring.

Benchmarking and Feedback

Systems should review feedback data and compare the information to prior internal performance and similar external systems. Existing registries can help benchmark the data. Examples of these registries include
- Cardiac Arrest Registry to Enhance Survival (CARES) for OHCA
- Get With The Guidelines-Resuscitation program for IHCA

Change

Simply by measuring and benchmarking care, systems can positively influence outcome. However, they must also review and interpret the data to identify areas for improvement, such as
- Increased bystander CPR response rates
- Improved CPR performance
- Shortened time to defibrillation
- Citizen awareness
- Citizen and healthcare professional education and training

Over the past 50 years, rescuers have used the modern-era BLS fundamentals of early recognition and activation, early CPR, and early defibrillation to save hundreds of thousands of lives around the world. However, survival disparities identified years ago persist, so we must continue improving care to fulfill the potential of the Chain of Survival. Fortunately, we have the knowledge and tools—represented by the Chain of Survival—to address many of these care gaps, and future discoveries will offer opportunities to improve rates of survival.

STEMI Systems of Care

The goal of STEMI care is to minimize heart damage and maximize the patient's recovery. The STEMI links (Figure 4) indicate the actions that patients, family members, and healthcare providers can rapidly take to maximize STEMI recovery:
- Recognition and reaction to STEMI warning signs
- EMS dispatch and rapid EMS system transport and prearrival notification to the receiving hospital
- Assessment and diagnosis in the ED (or cath lab)

- Treatment

Figure 4. The STEMI Chain of Survival.

Starting With Dispatch

All dispatchers and EMS providers must train to recognize ACS symptoms along with the potential complications. When authorized by medical control or protocol, dispatchers should tell patients with no history of aspirin allergy or signs of active or recent gastrointestinal (GI) bleeding to chew aspirin (162 to 325 mg) while they wait for EMS providers to arrive.

Activating EMS

Prompt diagnosis and treatment offer the best chance for saving the heart, so healthcare providers must recognize patients with potential ACS and begin evaluation, triage, and management as quickly as possible.

EMS Components
- Obtain prehospital ECGs
- Notify the receiving facility of a patient with possible ST-segment elevation myocardial infarction (STEMI) ("STEMI alert")
- Activate the cardiac catheterization team to shorten reperfusion time
- Continuously review and improve quality

Hospital-Based Components
- ED protocols
  - –Provide a streamlined cardiac catheterization team process
  - –Admit to the coronary ICU

- - Provide quality assurance, real-time feedback, and healthcare provider education
- Emergency physician's role
  - - Select the most appropriate reperfusion strategy
  - - Activate the cardiac catheterization team when needed
- Hospital leadership role
  - - Must be involved in the process and committed to supporting rapid access to STEMI reperfusion therapy

Stroke Systems of Care

The goal of stroke care is to minimize brain injury and maximize the patient's recovery. The Stroke Chain of Survival (Figure 5) links the actions that patients, family members, and healthcare providers should take to maximize stroke recovery. These links are

- Rapid recognition of and reaction to stroke warning signs and symptoms
- Rapid use of 9-1-1 and EMS dispatch
- Rapid EMS recognition of stroke, triage, transport, and prehospital notification to the receiving hospital
- Rapid diagnosis and treatment in the hospital

Figure 5. The Stroke Chain of Survival.

Recent clinical trials suggest that all patients eligible for endovascular therapy (EVT) should be considered for that treatment in addition to IV alteplase. Regional stroke systems of care for acute ischemic stroke need to be in place so that eligible patients can be quickly transported from the field per local designation protocols or transferred from non-EVT centers to comprehensive or thrombectomy-capable stroke centers that offer these treatments.

Systematic Approach

For optimal care, healthcare providers use a systematic approach to assess and treat arrest and acutely ill or injured patients. For a patient in respiratory or cardiac arrest, high-performance teams aim to support and

restore effective oxygenation, ventilation, and circulation with return of intact neurologic function. An intermediate goal of resuscitation is ROSC. These teams guide their actions by using the following systematic approaches:
- **Initial assessment** (visualization and scene safety)
- **BLS Assessment**
- **Primary Assessment** (A, B, C, D, and E)
- **Secondary Assessment** (SAMPLE, H's and T's)

Before you approach any patient, rapidly verify scene safety (no threat to the provider). Once you've determined that the scene is safe, use the systematic approach (Figures 6 and 7) to determine the patient's level of consciousness.
- If the patient appears unconscious, use the BLS Assessment for the initial evaluation, and use the Primary and Secondary Assessments for more advanced evaluation and treatment.
- If the patient appears conscious, use the Primary Assessment for your initial evaluation.

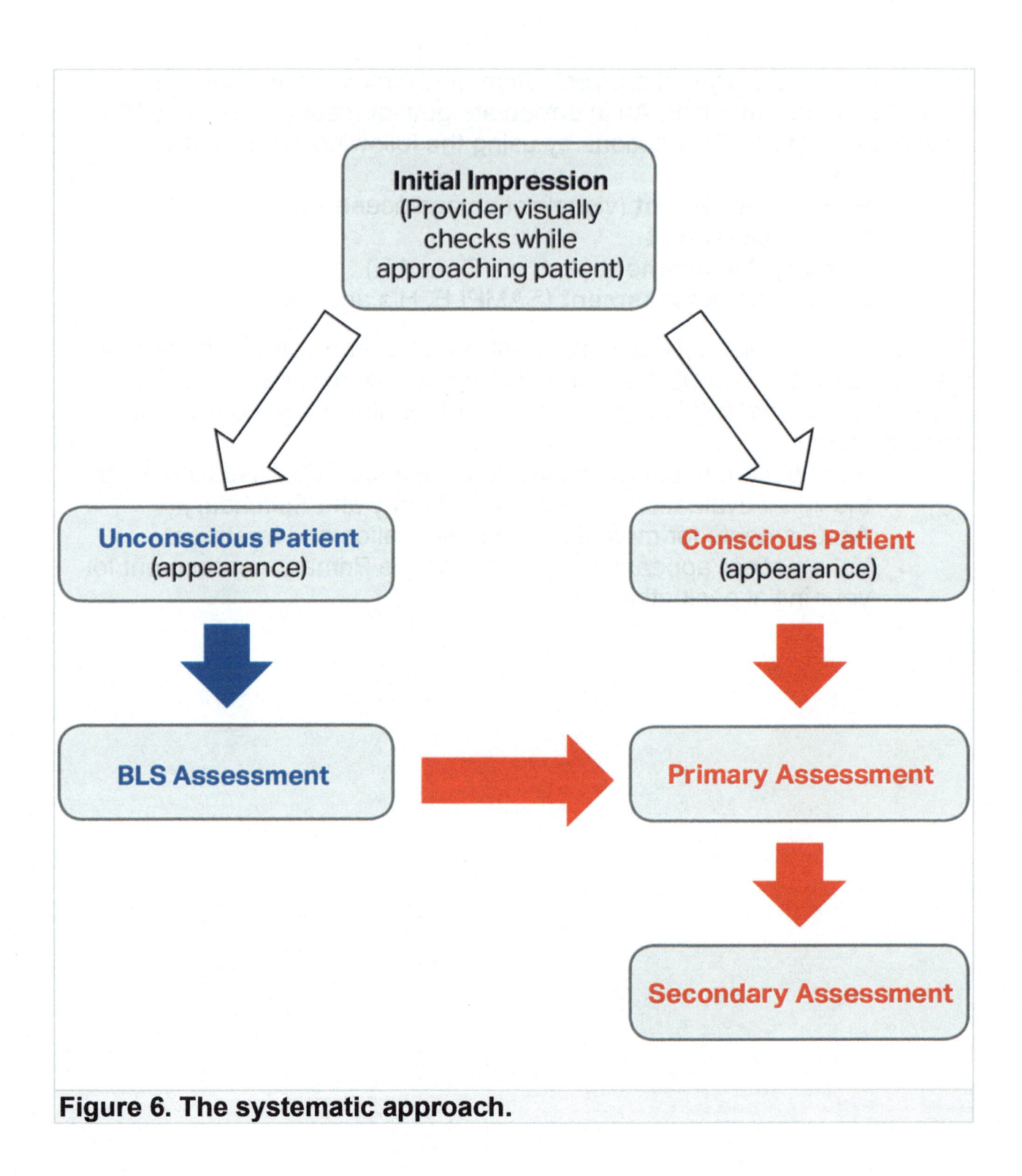

Figure 6. The systematic approach.

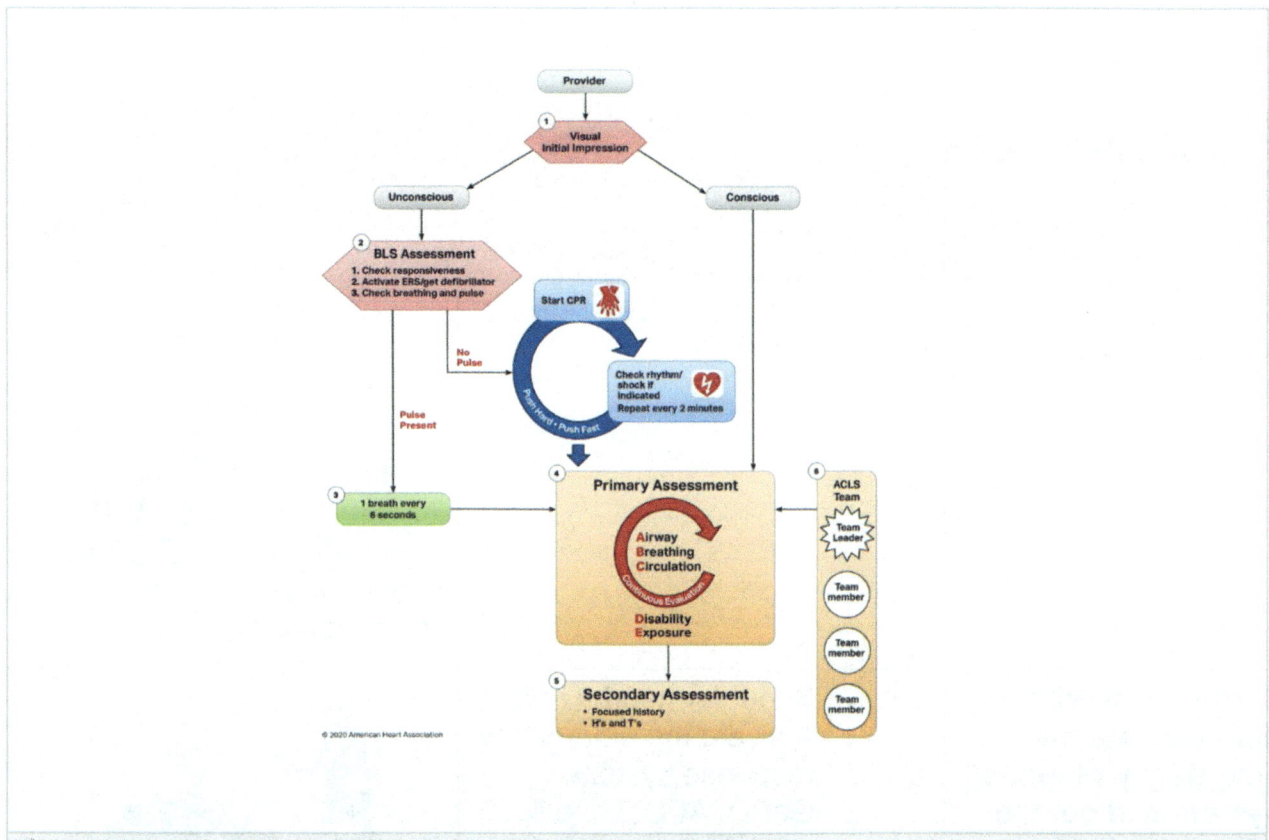

Figure 7. The expanded systematic approach.

BLS Assessment

The BLS Assessment is a systematic approach to BLS for trained healthcare providers. This approach stresses **early CPR with basic airway management and defibrillation** but not advanced airway techniques or drug administration. By using the BLS Assessment, any healthcare provider can support or restore effective oxygenation, ventilation, and circulation until the patient achieves ROSC or advanced providers intervene. Performing the BLS Assessment substantially improves a patient's chance of survival and a good neurologic outcome.

Remember to assess first, and then perform the appropriate action.

Although the BLS Assessment requires no advanced equipment, you can use readily available supplies, such as a bag-mask ventilation device if it is available. Whenever possible, place the patient faceup on a firm, flat surface to maximize the effectiveness of chest compressions. Table 2 is an overview of the BLS Assessment, and Figures 8 through 12 illustrate the steps needed during the BLS Assessment.

Table 2. BLS Assessment

Assessment	Assessment technique and action	Supporting image
Check responsiveness.	• Tap and shout, "Are you OK?"	Figure 8. Check for responsiveness.
Shout for nearby help/activate the emergency response system and get the AED/defibrillator.	• Shout for nearby help. • Activate the emergency response system. • Get an AED if one is available, or send someone to activate the emergency response system and get an AED or defibrillator.	Figure 9. Shout for nearby help/activate the emergency response system/get an AED.
Check for breathing and pulse.	• **To check for absent or abnormal breathing** (no breathing or only gasping) **scan the chest for rise and fall** for at least 5 but no more than 10 seconds. • Feel for a pulse for at least 5 but no more than 10 seconds. • Perform the pulse check simultaneously with the breathing	Figure 10. Check breathing and pulse simultaneously.

	check **within 10 seconds** to minimize delaying CPR. • If you find no breathing and no pulse within 10 seconds, start CPR, beginning with chest compressions. • If you find a pulse, start rescue breathing at 1 breath every 6 seconds. Check pulse about every 2 minutes.	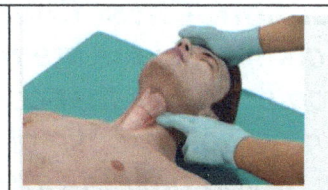 Figure 11. Check for a carotid pulse.
Defibrillate.	• If pulse is not felt, check for a shockable rhythm with an AED/defibrillator as soon as it arrives. • Provide shocks as indicated. • Follow each shock immediately with CPR, beginning with compressions.	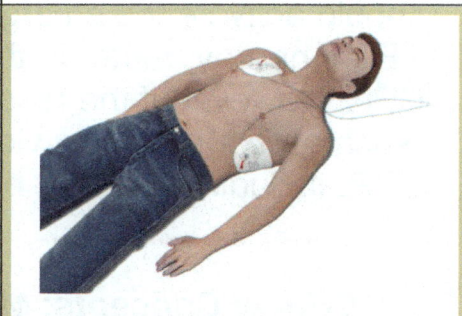 Figure 12. Defibrillation.

Critical Concepts: High-Quality CPR
To perform high-quality CPR, rescuers should
- *Compress the chest hard and fast at least 2 inches (5 cm) at a rate of 100 to 120/min (30:2 or another advanced protocol that maximizes CCF).*
- *Allow the chest to completely recoil after each compression.*
- *Switch compressors about every 2 minutes or earlier if fatigued— the switch should only take about 5 seconds.*
- *Minimize interruptions in compressions to 10 seconds or less (high CCF).*
- *Avoid excessive ventilation.*

Caution: Chest Compression Depth

Chest compressions are more often too shallow than too deep. However, research suggests that compressing deeper than 2.4 inches (6 cm) in adults may not be optimal for survival from cardiac arrest and may cause injuries. If you have a CPR quality feedback device, target your compression depth from 2 to 2.4 inches (5 to 6 cm).

Tailoring the Response

Single rescuers may tailor the sequence of rescue actions to the most likely cause of arrest. For example, a healthcare provider who sees an adolescent suddenly collapse (eg, after a blow to the chest) can assume that the patient has had a sudden cardiac arrest. In this case, the rescuer should activate the emergency response system via mobile device, get an AED if nearby, return to the patient to attach the AED, and then provide CPR. However, if the rescuer believes hypoxia caused the cardiac arrest (such as in a drowning victim), he or she may perform about 2 minutes of CPR, including breaths, before activating the emergency response system.

Critical Concepts: Minimizing Interruptions in Chest Compressions

When you stop chest compressions, blood flow to the brain and heart stops, so you must minimize the number of interruptions. Additionally, try to limit the duration of interruptions for defibrillation or rhythm analysis to no longer than 10 seconds unless you are moving the patient from a dangerous environment. Refer to Figure 13.

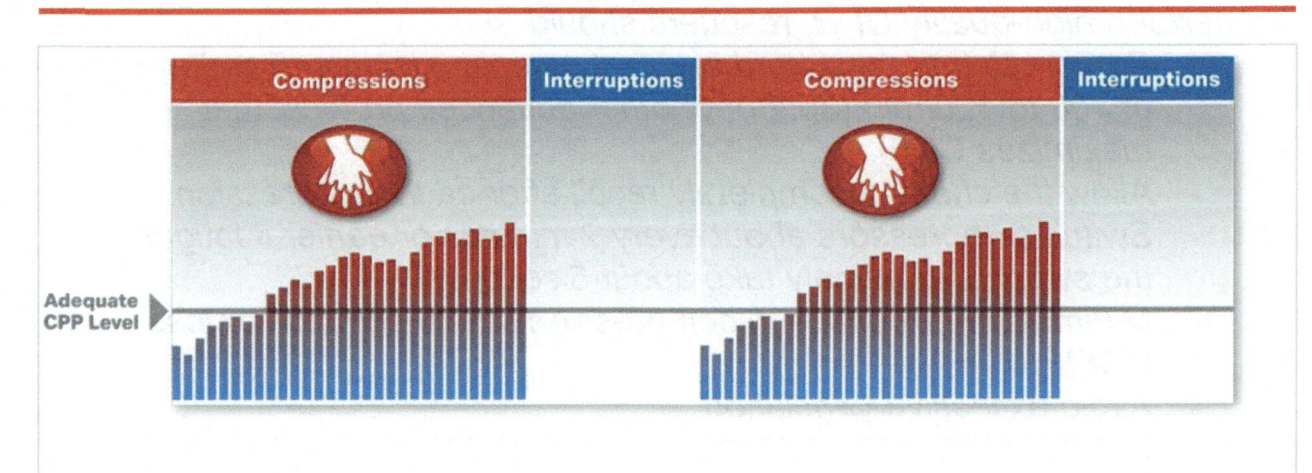

Figure 13. Relationship of quality CPR to coronary perfusion pressure demonstrating the need to minimize interruptions in compressions.

Avoid
- Prolonged rhythm analysis
- Frequent or inappropriate pulse checks
- Prolonged ventilation
- Unnecessary movement of the patient

Coronary perfusion pressure (CPP) is aortic relaxation (diastolic) pressure minus right atrial relaxation (diastolic) pressure. During CPR, CPP correlates with both myocardial blood flow and ROSC. In 1 human study, ROSC did not occur unless a CPP of 15 mm Hg or greater was achieved during CPR. Because $ETCO_2$ is related to cardiac output with chest compressions during cardiac arrest, ROSC is similarly unlikely with a persistent $ETCO_2$ of less than 10 mm Hg.

Starting CPR When You Are Not Sure About a Pulse

If you aren't sure whether you feel a pulse, start CPR. Unnecessary compressions are better than no compressions at all in a patient with no pulse, and delayed CPR reduces the chance of survival.

Agonal Gasps

You may see agonal gasps in the first minutes after sudden cardiac arrest, but agonal gasps are not normal breathing. They are a sign of cardiac arrest. A patient who gasps may appear to be drawing air in very quickly. The mouth may be open, and the jaw, head, or neck may move with gasps. These gasps may appear forceful or weak, and some time may pass between them because they usually happen at a slow, irregular rate. An agonal gasp may sound like a snort, snore, or groan. If you identify agonal gasps, begin chest compressions without delay.

Caution: Agonal Gasps
- *Agonal gasps may be present in the first minutes after sudden cardiac arrest.*
- *Agonal gasps are not normal breathing.*

Table 3. Primary Assessment

Assessment	Action

Airway
• Is the patient's airway patent?
• Is an advanced airway indicated?
• Have you confirmed proper placement of the airway device?
• Is the tube secured, and are you reconfirming placement frequently and with every transition?
	• Maintain an open airway in unconscious patients by using a head tilt–chin lift, an oropharyngeal airway, or a nasopharyngeal airway.
	• Use advanced airway management if needed (eg, laryngeal mask airway, laryngeal tube, endotracheal tube).
	   ◦ –Weigh the benefits of placing an advanced airway against the adverse effects of interrupting chest compressions. If bag-mask ventilation is adequate, you may defer inserting an advanced airway until the patient does not respond to initial CPR and defibrillation or until ROSC. Advanced airway devices such as a laryngeal mask airway, a laryngeal tube, or an esophageal-tracheal tube can be placed while chest compressions continue.
	   ◦ –If using advanced airway devices:
	      ▪ Confirm the proper integration of CPR and ventilation
	      ▪ Confirm the proper placement of advanced airway devices by physical examination and quantitative waveform capnography
	      ▪ Secure the device to prevent dislodgment
	      ▪ Monitor airway placement, effectiveness of CPR, and ROSC with continuous quantitative waveform capnography

Breathing
• Are ventilation and oxygenation adequate?
• Are quantitative waveform capnography
	• Give supplemental oxygen when indicated.
	   ◦ –For cardiac arrest patients, administer 100% oxygen.
	   ◦ –For others, adjust the oxygen administration to achieve oxygen saturation of 95% to 98% by pulse oximetry (90% for ACS and 92% to 98% for post–cardiac arrest care).

and oxyhemoglobin saturation monitored?	- Monitor the adequacy of ventilation and oxygenation by
	  - –Clinical criteria (chest rise and cyanosis)
	  - –Quantitative waveform capnography
	  - –Oxygen saturation
	  - –Avoid excessive ventilation

Circulation
- Are chest compressions effective?
- What is the cardiac rhythm?
- Is defibrillation or cardioversion indicated?
- Has intravenous (IV)/intraosseous (IO) access been established?
- Is ROSC present?
- Is the patient with a pulse unstable?
- Are medications needed for rhythm or blood pressure?
- Does the patient need volume (fluid) for resuscitation?
	- Monitor CPR quality.
	  - –Quantitative waveform capnography (if the partial pressure of CO_2 in exhaled air at the end of the exhalation phase, or $PETCO_2$, is less than 10 mm Hg, attempt to improve CPR quality). Waveform capnography should be as high as possible with improved CPR quality. Continuous quantitative waveform capnography provides an indirect measure of cardiac output during chest compressions because the amount of carbon dioxide exhaled is associated with the amount of blood that passes through the lungs. An $ETCO_2$ less than 10 mm Hg during chest compressions rarely results in ROSC.
	  - –A sudden increase in $ETCO_2$ to more than 25 mm Hg may indicate ROSC.
	  - –Intra-arterial pressure (if relaxation phase [diastolic] pressure is less than 20 mm Hg, attempt to improve CPR quality). Inter-arterial pressure should be as high as possible with improved CPR quality. If intra-arterial pressure monitoring is available, strive to optimize blood pressure. Relaxation phase (diastolic) pressures less than 20 during chest compressions rarely results in ROSC.
	- Attach monitor/defibrillator for arrhythmias or cardiac arrest rhythms (eg, VF, pVT, asystole, PEA).
	- Provide defibrillation/cardioversion.
	- Obtain IV/IO access.
	- Give appropriate drugs to manage rhythm and blood pressure.
	- Give IV/IO fluids if needed.

	• Check glucose and temperature. • Check perfusion issues.
Disability	• Check for neurologic function. • Quickly assess for responsiveness, levels of consciousness, and pupil dilation. • AVPU: Alert, Voice, Painful, Unresponsive
Exposure	• Remove clothing to perform a physical examination. • Look for obvious signs of trauma, bleeding, burns, unusual markings, or medical alert bracelets.

The gasp may sound like a snort, snore, or groan. Gasping is a sign of cardiac arrest.

Primary Assessment

In the Primary Assessment, you continue to assess the patient and perform appropriate actions until the patient is transferred to the next level of care. Members of a high-performance team often perform assessments and actions in ACLS simultaneously.

For unconscious patients in arrest (cardiac or respiratory), complete the BLS Assessment before the Primary Assessment. For conscious patients who may need more advanced assessment and management, conduct the Primary Assessment first. Table 3 provides an overview of the Primary Assessment.

Remember to assess first, and then perform the appropriate action.

Secondary Assessment

The Secondary Assessment involves the differential diagnosis, including a focused medical history and searching for and treating underlying causes (H's and T's). Gather a focused history of the patient, if possible. Ask specific questions related to the patient's presentation.

SAMPLE

Consider using the memory aid SAMPLE:
- **S**igns and symptoms
    - –Breathing difficulty
    - –Tachypnea, tachycardia
    - –Fever, headache

- o   –Abdominal pain
- o   –Bleeding
- **A**llergies
    - o   –Medications, foods, latex, etc
    - o   –Associated reactions
- **M**edications (including the last dose taken)
    - o   –Patient medications, including over-the-counter, vitamins, inhalers, and herbal supplements
    - o   –Last dose and time of recent medications
    - o   –Medications that can be found in the patient's home
- **P**ast medical history (especially relating to the current illness)
    - o   –Health history (eg, previous illnesses, hospitalizations)
    - o   –Family health history (in cases of ACS or stroke)
    - o   –Significant underlying medical problems
    - o   –Past surgeries
    - o   –Immunization status
- **L**ast meal consumed
    - o   –Time and nature of last intake of liquid or food
- **E**vents
    - o   –Events leading to current illness or injury (eg, onset sudden or gradual, type of injury)
    - o   –Hazards at scene
    - o   –Treatment during interval from onset of disease or injury until evaluation
    - o   –Estimated time of onset (if out-of-hospital onset)

The answers to these questions can help you quickly identify likely or suspected diagnoses. Look for and treat the underlying cause by considering the H's and T's to ensure that you are not overlooking common possibilities. The H's and T's create a guide for possible diagnoses and interventions for your patient.

H's and T's

The H's and T's are a memory aid for potential reversible causes of cardiac arrest and emergency cardiopulmonary conditions. The ACLS cases provide details on these components:

H's

- Hypovolemia
- Hypoxia

- Hydrogen ion (acidosis)
- Hypo-/hyperkalemia
- Hypothermia

T's

- Tension pneumothorax
- Tamponade (cardiac)
- Toxins
- Thrombosis (pulmonary)
- Thrombosis (coronary)

Critical Concepts: Common Underlying Causes of PEA
- *Hypovolemia and hypoxia are the 2 most common underlying and potentially reversible causes of PEA.*
- *Look for evidence of these problems as you assess the patient and treat immediately.*

Diagnosing and Treating Underlying Causes

Patients in cardiac arrest (VF/pVT/asystole/PEA) need rapid assessment and management to determine if an underlying, potentially reversible problem caused the arrest. If you can quickly identify a specific condition, you may achieve ROSC. Identifying the underlying cause is crucial in cases of cardiac arrest. Addressing the underlying cause will provide the best chance for a successful resuscitation. Ultrasound may help with identifying the underlying cause quickly and can also provide information to help determine the next step for treatment. Paying attention to the patient's response to interventions may also help you narrow the differential diagnosis.

To search for the underlying cause, do the following:
- Consider the underlying causes by recalling the H's and T's
- Analyze the ECG for clues to the underlying cause
- Recognize hypovolemia
- Recognize drug overdose/poisonings

Hypovolemia

Hypovolemia, a common cause of PEA, initially produces the classic physiologic response of a rapid, narrow-complex tachycardia (sinus tachycardia) and typically increases diastolic and decreases systolic pressures. As loss of blood volume continues, blood pressure drops, eventually becoming undetectable, but the narrow QRS complexes and rapid rate continue (ie, PEA).

Consider hypovolemia as a cause of hypotension, which can deteriorate to PEA. Providing prompt treatment can reverse the pulseless state by rapidly correcting the hypovolemia. Common nontraumatic causes of hypovolemia include occult internal hemorrhage and severe dehydration. Consider volume infusion for PEA associated with a narrow-complex tachycardia.

Cardiac and Pulmonary Conditions

ACS that involve a large amount of heart muscle can present as PEA, VF, pVT, or asystole. That is, occlusion of the left main or proximal left anterior descending coronary artery can present with cardiogenic shock rapidly progressing to cardiac arrest and PEA. However, in patients with cardiac arrest and without known pulmonary embolism (PE) or suspected PE or STEMI, giving routine fibrinolytic treatment during CPR shows no benefit and is not recommended.

Massive or saddle PE obstructs flow to the pulmonary vasculature and causes acute right heart failure. In patients with cardiac arrest due to presumed or known PE, it is reasonable to administer fibrinolytics.

Pericardial tamponade may be reversible with pericardiocentesis, and during periarrest, volume infusion may help while definitive therapy is initiated. Once you recognize tension pneumothorax, you should effectively treat it with needle decompression and chest tube insertion.

You cannot treat cardiac tamponade, tension pneumothorax, and massive PE unless you recognize them. A skilled provider can perform bedside ultrasound to help rapidly identify tamponade, pneumothorax, and echocardiographic evidence of PE.

Drug Overdoses or Toxic Exposures

Certain drug overdoses and toxic exposures may lead to peripheral vascular dilatation and/or myocardial dysfunction with resultant hypotension and cardiovascular collapse. Treat poisoned patients aggressively because the toxic effects may progress rapidly, but during this time, the myocardial dysfunction and arrhythmias may be reversible.

Treatments that can provide support include

- Prolonged basic CPR in special resuscitation situations (such as accidental hypothermia)
- Extracorporeal CPR
- Intra-aortic balloon pump therapy
- Renal dialysis
- Intravenous lipid emulsion for lipid-soluble toxins
- Specific drug antidotes (digoxin immune Fab, glucagon, bicarbonate)
- Transcutaneous pacing
- Correction of severe electrolyte disturbances (potassium, magnesium, calcium, acidosis)
- Specific adjunctive agents

Remember, if the patient shows signs of ROSC, begin post–cardiac arrest care.

References
1. 1.Abella BS, Alvarado JP, Myklebust H, et al. Quality of cardiopulmonary resuscitation during in-hospital cardiac arrest. *JAMA.* 2005;293(3):305-310. doi: 10.1001/jama.293.3.305
2. 2.Benjamin EJ, Muntner P, Alonso A, et al; for the American Heart Association Council on Epidemiology and Prevention Statistics Committee and Stroke Statistics Subcommittee. Heart disease and stroke statistics—2019 update: a report from the American Heart Association. *Circulation.* 2019;139(10):e56-e528. doi: 10.1161/CIR.0000000000000659
3. 3.Edelson DP, Abella BS, Kramer-Johansen J, et al. Effects of compression depth and pre-shock pauses predict defibrillation failure during cardiac arrest. *Resuscitation.* 2006;71(2):137-145. doi: 10.1016/j.resuscitation.2006.04.008
4. 4.Edelson DP, Litzinger B, Arora V, et al. Improving in-hospital cardiac arrest process and outcomes with performance debriefing. *Arch Intern Med.* 2008;168(10):1063-1069. doi: 10.1001/archinte.168.10.1063
5. 5.Neumar RW, Nolan JP, Adrie C, et al. Post-cardiac arrest syndrome: epidemiology, pathophysiology, treatment, and prognostication: a consensus statement from the International Liaison Committee on Resuscitation (American Heart Association, Australian and New Zealand Council on Resuscitation, European Resuscitation Council, Heart and Stroke Foundation of Canada, InterAmerican Heart Foundation, Resuscitation Council of Asia,

and the Resuscitation Council of Southern Africa); the American Heart Association Emergency Cardiovascular Care Committee; the Council on Cardiovascular Surgery and Anesthesia; the Council on Cardiopulmonary, Perioperative, and Critical Care; the Council on Clinical Cardiology; and the Stroke Council. *Circulation.* 2008;118(23):2452-2483. doi: 10.1161/CIRCULATIONAHA.108.190652

6. 6.Cummins RO, Ornato JP, Thies WH, Pepe PE. Improving survival from sudden cardiac arrest: the "chain of survival" concept: a statement for health professionals from the Advanced Cardiac Life Support Subcommittee and the Emergency Cardiac Care Committee, American Heart Association. *Circulation.* 1991;83(5):1832-1847. doi: 10.1161/01.cir.83.5.1832

7. 7.Jacobs I, Nadkarni V; and the ILCOR Task Force on Cardiac Arrest and Cardiopulmonary Resuscitation Outcomes. Cardiac arrest and cardiopulmonary resuscitation outcome reports: update and simplification of the Utstein templates for resuscitation registries: a statement for healthcare professionals from a task force of the International Liaison Committee on Resuscitation (American Heart Association, European Resuscitation Council, Australian Resuscitation Council, New Zealand Resuscitation Council, Heart and Stroke Foundation of Canada, InterAmerican Heart Foundation, Resuscitation Councils of Southern Africa). *Circulation.* 2004;110(21):3385-3397. doi: 10.1161/01.CIR.0000147236.85306.15

8. 8.Cummins RO, Chamberlain D, Hazinski MF, et al. Recommended guidelines for reviewing, reporting, and conducting research on in-hospital resuscitation: the in-hospital 'Utstein style'. *Circulation.* 1997;95(8):2213-2239. doi: 10.1161/01.cir.95.8.2213

9. 9.Nolan JP, Berg RA, Andersen LW, et al. Cardiac Arrest and Cardiopulmonary Resuscitation Outcome Reports: Update of the Utstein Resuscitation Registry Template for In-Hospital Cardiac Arrest: A Consensus Report From a Task Force of the International Liaison Committee on Resuscitation (American Heart Association, European Resuscitation Council, Australian and New Zealand Council on Resuscitation, Heart and Stroke Foundation of Canada, InterAmerican Heart Foundation, Resuscitation Council of Southern Africa, Resuscitation Council of

Asia). *Circulation*. 2019;140(18):e746-e757. doi: 10.1161/CIR.0000000000000710

10. 10.Meaney PA, Bobrow BJ, Mancini ME, et al; for the CPR Quality Summit Investigators, the American Heart Association Emergency Cardiovascular Care Committee, and the Council on Cardiopulmonary, Critical Care, Perioperative and Resuscitation. Cardiopulmonary resuscitation quality: improving cardiac resuscitation outcomes both inside and outside the hospital: a consensus statement from the American Heart Association. *Circulation*. 2013;128(4):417-435. doi: 10.1161/CIR.0b013e31829d8654

Part 2: Preventing Arrest

Recognition: Signs of Clinical Deterioration

Rapid Response

Often, nurses, physicians, or family members who are concerned that the patient is deteriorating will activate the rapid response system in the hospital. Some rapid response systems weigh, combine, and score specific physiologic criteria to determine when to act. The following list gives examples of such criteria for adult patients:
- Airway compromise
- Respiratory rate less than 6/min or more than 30/min
- Heart rate less than 40/min or greater than 140/min
- Systolic blood pressure (SBP) less than 90 mm Hg
- Symptomatic hypertension
- Unexpected decrease in level of consciousness
- Unexplained agitation
- Seizure
- Significant decrease in urine output
- Subjective concern about the patient

The wide variability in incidence and location of IHCA suggests potential areas for standardizing quality and preventing some cardiac arrests. More than half of IHCAs result from respiratory failure or hypovolemic shock, and changes in physiology such as tachypnea, tachycardia, and hypotension foreshadow most of these events. Therefore, IHCA often represents the progression of physiologic instability and a failure to quickly identify and stabilize the patient. This scenario is more common on the general wards—outside of critical care and procedural areas—where patient-to-nurse ratios are higher and monitoring of patients is less intense. In this setting, intermittent manual vital sign monitoring with less frequent direct observation by clinicians may increase the likelihood of delayed recognition.

Over the past decade, hospitals in several countries have designed rapid response systems to identify and treat early clinical deterioration in patients, improving patient outcomes through critical care expertise. The rapid response system has several components:
- Event detection and response-triggering arm
- A planned response arm, such as an RRT or MET

- Quality monitoring
- Administrative support

RRTs and METs

Hospitals established RRTs or METs to provide early intervention in patients whose conditions are deteriorating, with the goal of preventing IHCA.[1,2] These teams can include physicians, nurses, and respiratory therapists who have the critical care experience and skills to intervene in life-threatening situations. They are typically asked to see any patient who is identified as deteriorating, no matter who reports that deterioration: staff members, the family, or the patient. These teams bring monitoring and resuscitation equipment to perform a rapid patient assessment, and they initiate appropriate treatment and drug therapies to reverse physiologic deterioration and prevent poor outcomes, much like EMS services intervening when called in the prehospital setting.

Published Studies

Although the ideal composition of METs or RRTs is not known, many published before-and-after studies of METs or RRTs have reported a drop in the rate of cardiac arrests after these teams intervene.[3,4] Although some studies have not reported a decrease in overall mortality with the introduction of these teams,[5] there may be other benefits, such as improved end-of-life care, because these teams may initiate discussions with patients and families before cardiac arrest, preventing unwanted interventions in critically ill patients.

Additional documented benefits of these systems include the following:
- Decreased unplanned emergency transfers to the ICU
- Decreased ICU and total hospital length of stay
- Reduced postoperative morbidity and mortality rates
- Improved rates of survival from cardiac arrest

Implementing a Rapid Response System

Implementing any type of rapid response system requires a significant cultural change in most hospitals. Those who design and manage the system must pay particular attention to issues that may prevent the hospital from using the system effectively. Examples of such issues are insufficient resources, poor education, fear of calling the team, fear of losing control over patient care, and resistance from team members.

Implementing a rapid response system requires ongoing education, impeccable data collection and review, and feedback. Developing and maintaining these programs requires a long-term cultural and financial commitment from the hospital administration. Hospital administrators and healthcare professionals need to reorient their approach to emergency medical events and develop a culture of patient safety with a primary goal of decreasing morbidity and mortality.

Acute Coronary Syndromes

The Acute Coronary Syndromes Algorithm (Figure 16) will help guide your clinical strategy when patients have signs and symptoms of ACS, including possible acute myocardial infarction (AMI). To apply this algorithm effectively, you must have the basic knowledge to assess and stabilize patients with ACS.

The initial 12-lead ECG is used to classify patients into 1 of 2 ECG categories of myocardial infarction, with different strategies of care and management needs. These 2 ECG categories are outlined in the Acute Coronary Syndromes Algorithm:
- ST-segment elevation (STEMI)
- Non-ST–segment elevation ACS (NSTE-ACS)
    - –ST-segment depression, T-wave inversion, transient ST-segment elevation
    - –Nondiagnostic or normal ECG

The following focuses on the first category: STEMI, with time-sensitive reperfusion strategies.

You will
- Identify, assess, and triage acute ischemic chest discomfort
- Provide initial treatment of possible ACS
- Emphasize early reperfusion of the patient with ACS/STEMI

Goals for ACS Patients

The primary goals are as follows:
- Prevention of major adverse cardiovascular events such as death, nonfatal MI, and the need for urgent postinfarction revascularization
- Identification of patients with STEMI and triage for early reperfusion therapy

- Relief of ischemic chest discomfort
- Treatment of acute, life-threatening complications of ACS, such as VF/pVT, unstable bradycardia, ventricular wall rupture, papillary muscle rupture, decompensated shock, and other unstable tachycardias

Reperfusion therapy opens an obstructed coronary artery with either mechanical means or drugs. PCI, performed in the cardiac catheterization laboratory after coronary angiography, allows for balloon dilation or stent placement—or both—for an obstructed coronary artery.

Rhythms for ACS

Sudden cardiac death, ventricular tachycardias, and hypotensive bradycardia may occur with acute ischemia. Anticipate these rhythms, and be prepared for immediate interventions, including defibrillation or cardioversion as well as administration of drugs or pacing for stable bradycardias.

Drugs for ACS

Drug therapy and treatment strategies continue to evolve rapidly in the field of ACS, so be sure to keep up with important changes.

To treat ACS, you'll initially use these drugs to relieve ischemic discomfort, dissolve clots, and inhibit thrombin and platelets:
- Oxygen
- Aspirin
- Nitroglycerin
- Opiates (eg, morphine)
- Fibrinolytic therapy (overview)
- Heparin (unfractionated, low-molecular-weight)

Additional adjunctive agents that will not be discussed in this course include the following:
- β-Blockers
- Bivalirudin
- $P2Y_{12}$ inhibitors (clopidogrel, prasugrel, ticagrelor)
- Angiotensin-converting enzyme inhibitors
- HMG-CoA reductase inhibitors (statin therapy)
- Glycoprotein IIb/IIIa inhibitors

STEMI Chain of Survival

The STEMI Chain of Survival (Figure 14) is similar to the Chain of Survival for sudden cardiac arrest. Its links indicate the actions that patients, family members, and healthcare providers can rapidly take to maximize STEMI recovery:
- Recognition and reaction to STEMI warning signs
- EMS dispatch and rapid EMS system transport and prearrival notification to the receiving hospital
- Assessment and diagnosis in the ED (or cath lab)
- Treatment

Figure 14. The STEMI Chain of Survival.

OHCA Response

Half of ACS deaths occur before the patient reaches the hospital, with VF or pVT as the precipitating rhythm in the majority of cases. VF is most likely to develop during the first 4 hours after onset of symptoms, so communities should develop EMS and prehospital programs to respond quickly to ACS. Such programs should focus on
- Recognizing symptoms of ACS
- Activating the EMS system, with EMS providing prehospital notification
- Providing early CPR if cardiac arrest occurs
- Providing early defibrillation with AEDs available through public-access defibrillation programs and first responders
- Providing a coordinated system of care among the EMS system, the ED, cath lab, and cardiac specialists

Pathophysiology of ACS

Patients with coronary atherosclerosis may develop a spectrum of clinical syndromes that represent varying degrees of coronary artery occlusion. These syndromes include NSTE-ACS and STEMI. Sudden cardiac death may occur with any of these syndromes. Figure 15 illustrates the pathophysiology of ACS.

Figure 15. Pathophysiology of ACS.

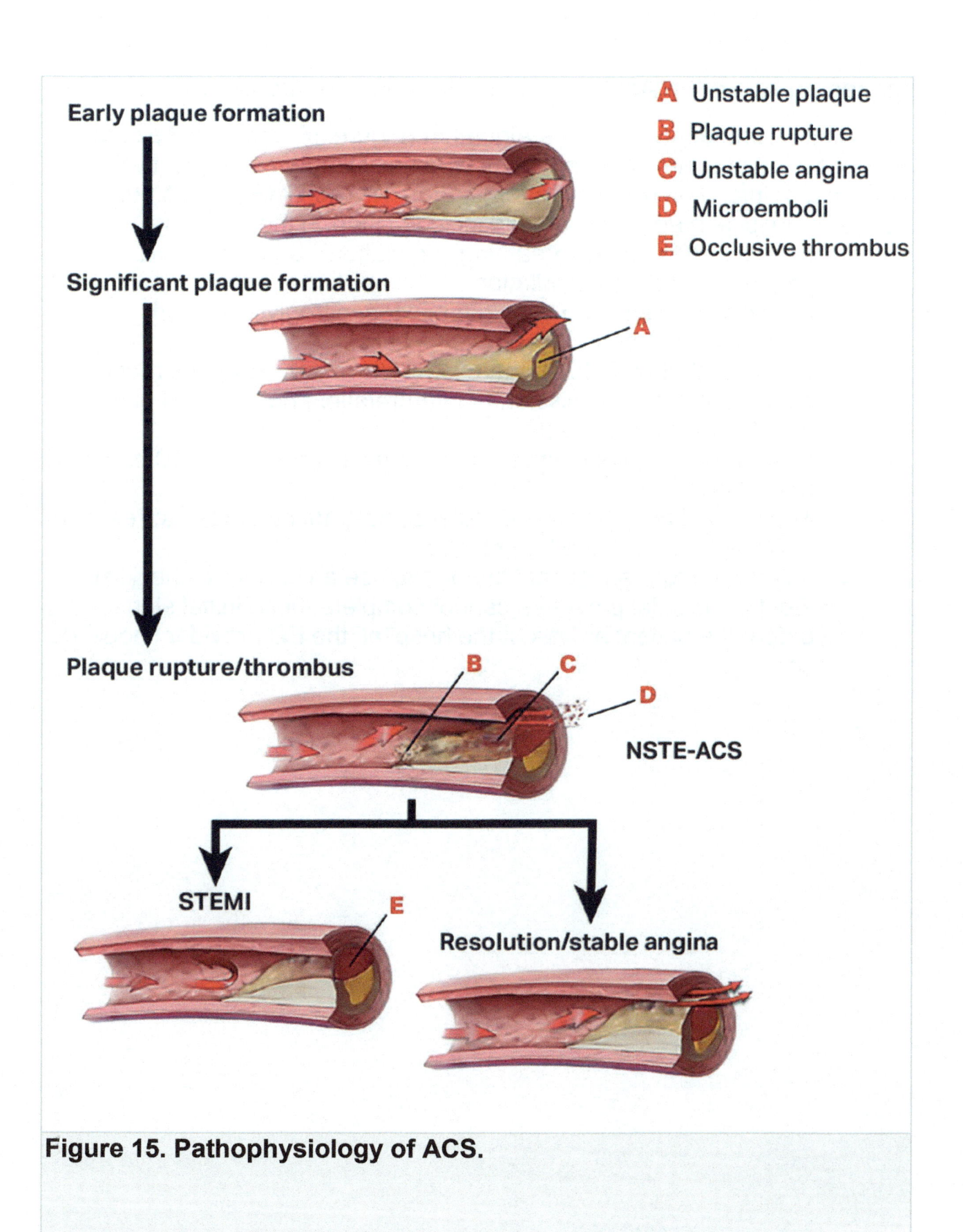

Managing ACS: The Acute Coronary Syndromes Algorithm

The Acute Coronary Syndromes Algorithm (Figure 16) outlines the steps for assessing and managing a patient who has symptoms suggestive of ischemia or infarction (ACS symptoms, Step 1). The EMS assessment and care and hospital preparation should include (Step 2) the following:
- Assess ABC (airway, breathing, circulation). Be prepared to provide CPR and defibrillation.
- Administer aspirin and consider oxygen, nitroglycerin, and morphine if needed.
- Obtain a 12-lead ECG. If there is ST elevation, notify the receiving hospital with a transmission or interpretation; note time of onset and first medical contact.
- Provide prehospital notification; on arrival, transport to ED/cath lab per protocol.
- The notified hospital should mobilize hospital resources to respond to STEMI and activate STEMI alert.
- If considering prehospital fibrinolysis, use a fibrinolytic checklist.
- If out-of-hospital providers cannot complete these initial steps before the patient arrives at the hospital, the ED provider should do so.

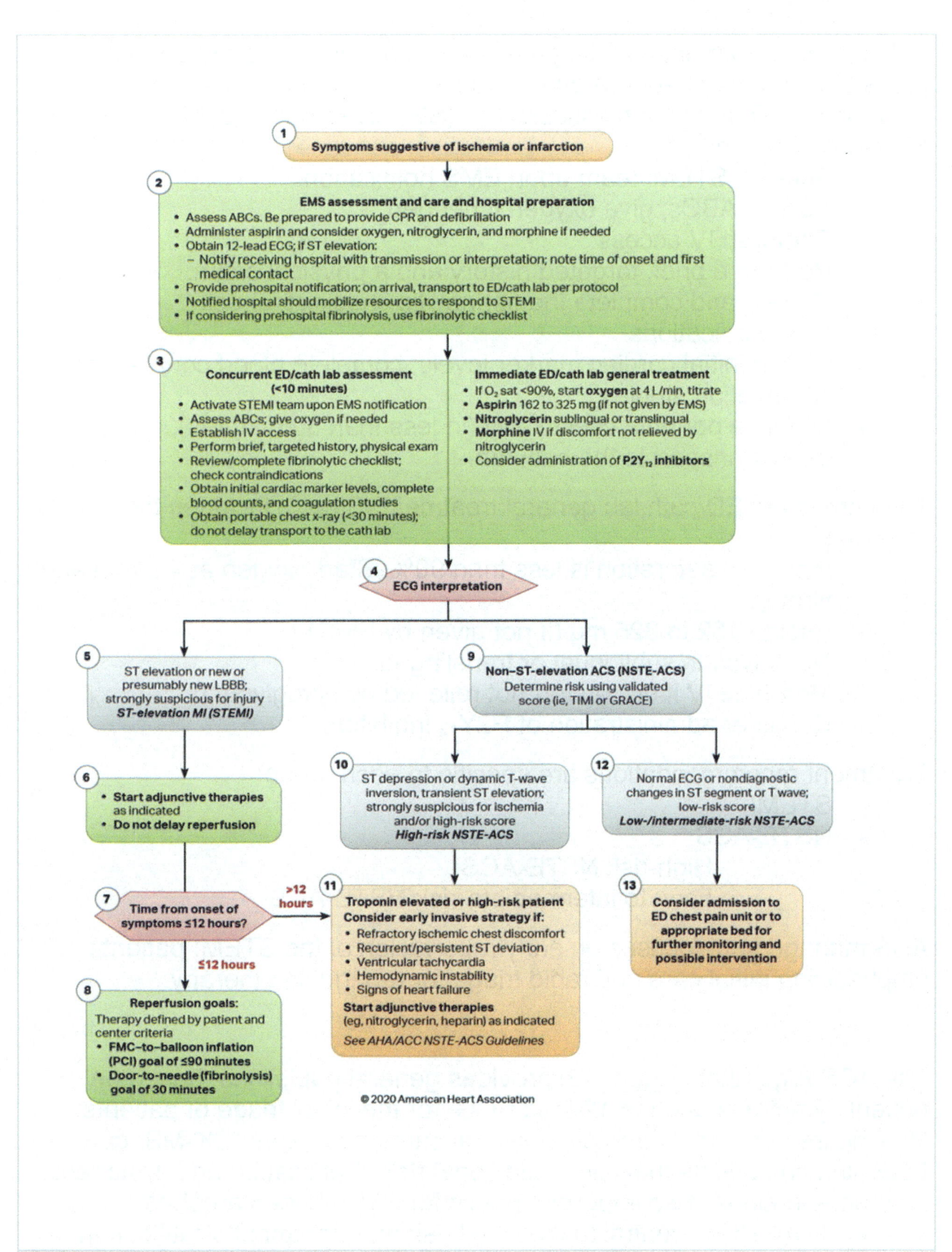

Figure 16. Acute Coronary Syndromes Algorithm.

Subsequent treatment may begin with EMS providers, based on local protocols, or it may begin when the patient arrives at the hospital. Concurrent ED or cath lab assessment (Step 3) should occur in less than 10 minutes and include

- Activate STEMI team upon EMS notification.
- Assess ABCs; give oxygen if needed.
- Establish IV access.
- Perform a brief, targeted history and a physical exam.
- Review and complete the fibrinolytic checklist; check contraindications.
- Obtain initial cardiac marker levels, complete blood counts, and coagulation studies.
- Obtain a portable chest x-ray (in less than 30 minutes); do not delay transport to the cath lab.

The immediate ED/cath lab general treatment (Step 3) includes the following:

- If oxygen saturation is less than 90%: Start oxygen at 4 L/min and titrate
- Aspirin 162 to 325 mg (if not given by EMS)
- Nitroglycerin sublingual or translingual
- Morphine IV if discomfort not relieved by nitroglycerin
- Consider administration of $P2Y_{12}$ inhibitors

Treatment recommendations are specific to each group:

- STEMI
- NSTE-ACS
    - –High-risk NSTE-ACS
    - –Low- to intermediate-risk NSTE-ACS

ACS management focuses on early reperfusion of the STEMI patient, emphasizing initial care and rapid triage for reperfusion therapy.

Important Considerations

The ACS Algorithm (Figure 16) provides general guidelines, based on patient symptoms and the 12-lead ECG, for the initial triage of patients. Healthcare personnel often obtain serial cardiac markers (CK-MB, cardiac troponins) in patients that allow additional risk stratification and treatment recommendations. Two important points for STEMI need emphasis:

- The ECG is central to the initial risk and treatment stratification process.

- For STEMI patients, you do not need evidence of elevated cardiac markers to decide to administer fibrinolytic therapy or perform diagnostic coronary angiography with coronary intervention (angioplasty/stenting).

Application of the ACS Algorithm

The steps in the algorithm guide assessment and treatment as follows:
- Step 1 is to identify symptoms suggestive of ischemia or infarction, such as chest or shoulder pain, dyspnea, or nausea.
- In Step 2, EMS assesses the patient and provides care, transport, and hospital prearrival notification. Prehospital ECG capture and evaluation is important.
- In Step 3, the ED/cath lab immediately assesses and treats the patient in less than 10 minutes. Next, the ED/cath lab provides immediate general treatment including oxygen and administration of drugs.
- After interpreting the ECG in Step 4, use Steps 5 and 9 to classify patients according to ST-segment analysis.
- If your analysis points to STEMI, use Steps 5 through 8 to treat the patient.

Symptoms Suggestive of Ischemia or Infarction

You should know how to identify symptoms that suggest cardiac ischemia (Step 1). Promptly conduct a targeted evaluation of every patient whose initial symptoms suggest possible ACS.

The most common symptom of myocardial ischemia and infarction is retrosternal chest discomfort. The patient may perceive this discomfort more as pressure or tightness than as actual pain.

Chest discomfort is the major symptom in most patients (both men and women) with ACS, but patients frequently deny or misinterpret this and other symptoms. The elderly, women, diabetic patients, and hypertensive patients are most likely to delay, in part because they are more likely to have atypical symptoms or presentations. The decision to call for an ambulance may also reduce delays in care. Other factors that can affect the interval between symptom onset and presentation to hospital include time of day, location (eg, work or home), and presence of a family member.

Symptoms that suggest ACS may also include

- Uncomfortable pressure, fullness, squeezing, or pain in the center of the chest lasting several minutes (usually more than a few minutes)
- Chest discomfort spreading to the shoulders, neck, one or both arms, or jaw
- Chest discomfort spreading into the back or between the shoulder blades
- Light-headedness, dizziness, fainting, syncope, sweating, nausea, or vomiting
- Unexplained, sudden shortness of breath, which may occur with or without chest discomfort
- Less commonly, the discomfort occurs in the epigastrium and is described as indigestion.

These symptoms may also suggest other life-threatening conditions, including aortic dissection, acute PE, acute pericardial effusion with tamponade, and tension pneumothorax.

Starting With Dispatch

All dispatchers and EMS providers must train to recognize ACS symptoms along with the potential complications. When authorized by medical control or protocol, dispatchers should tell patients with no history of aspirin allergy or signs of active or recent gastrointestinal (GI) bleeding to chew aspirin (162 to 325 mg) while they wait for EMS providers to arrive.

EMS Assessment, Care, and Hospital Preparation

Step 2 in the algorithm outlines EMS assessment, care, and hospital preparation. EMS responders may perform the following assessments and actions as they stabilize, triage, and transport the patient to an appropriate facility:

- Assess ABCs. Be prepared to provide CPR and defibrillation.
- Administer aspirin and consider oxygen, nitroglycerin, and morphine if needed.
- Obtain a 12-lead ECG. If there is ST elevation, notify the receiving hospital with a transmission or an interpretation; note time of onset and first medical contact.
- Provide prehospital notification; on arrival, transport to ED/cath lab per protocol.
- The notified hospital should mobilize hospital resources to respond to STEMI and activate STEMI alert.

- If considering prehospital fibrinolysis, use fibrinolytic checklist.

Assessing ABCs

Assessing ABCs includes
- Monitoring vital signs and cardiac rhythm
- Being prepared to provide CPR
- Using a defibrillator if needed

Administering Oxygen and Drugs

You should be familiar with the actions, indications, cautions, and treatment of side effects.

Oxygen

EMS providers should administer **oxygen** if the patient is dyspneic or hypoxemic, has obvious signs of heart failure, or has an arterial oxygen saturation that is less than 90% or unknown. Providers should adjust oxygen therapy to a noninvasively monitored oxyhemoglobin saturation 90% or greater. The usefulness of supplemental oxygen therapy has not been established in normoxic patients with suspected or confirmed ACS, so providers may consider withholding it in these patients.

Aspirin (Acetylsalicylic Acid)

A dose of 162 to 325 mg of non–enteric-coated or chewed aspirin causes immediate and near-total inhibition of thromboxane A_2 production by inhibiting platelet cyclooxygenase (COX-1). Platelets are one of the principal and earliest participants in thrombus formation. This rapid inhibition also reduces coronary reocclusion and other recurrent events independently and after fibrinolytic therapy.

If the patient has not taken **aspirin** and has no history of true aspirin allergy and no evidence of recent GI bleeding, administer aspirin (162 to 325 mg) to chew. In the initial hours of an ACS, aspirin is absorbed better when chewed than when swallowed, particularly if the patient has received morphine. Use rectal aspirin suppositories (300 mg) for patients with nausea, vomiting, active peptic ulcer disease, or other disorders of the upper GI tract. Aspirin is associated with a reduction in mortality for patients with ACS.

Nitroglycerin (Glyceryl Trinitrate)

Nitroglycerin effectively reduces ischemic chest discomfort, and it has beneficial hemodynamic effects. The physiologic effects of nitrates reduce left ventricular (LV) and right ventricular (RV) preload through peripheral arterial and venous dilation.

Give the patient 1 sublingual nitroglycerin tablet (or translingual dose) every 3 to 5 minutes for ongoing symptoms if permitted by medical control and no contraindications exist. You may repeat the dose twice (total of 3 doses). Administer nitroglycerin only if the patient remains hemodynamically stable: SBP is greater than 90 mm Hg or no lower than 30 mm Hg below baseline (if known) and the heart rate is 50 to 100/min.

Nitroglycerin is a venodilator; use it cautiously or not at all in patients with inadequate ventricular preload. These situations include

- **Inferior wall MI and RV infarction.** RV infarction may complicate an inferior wall MI. Patients with acute RV infarction depend on RV filling pressures to maintain cardiac output and blood pressure. If you cannot rule out RV infarction, use caution in administering nitrates to patients with inferior STEMI. If you confirm RV infarction by right-sided precordial leads, or if an experienced provider confirms it through clinical findings, then nitroglycerin and other vasodilators (morphine) or volume-depleting drugs (diuretics) are contraindicated as well.
- **Hypotension, bradycardia, or tachycardia.** Avoid using nitroglycerin in patients with hypotension (SBP less than 90 mm Hg), marked bradycardia (heart rate less than 50/min), or marked tachycardia.
- **Recent phosphodiesterase inhibitor use.** Avoid using nitroglycerin if you suspect or know that the patient has taken sildenafil or vardenafil within the previous 24 hours or tadalafil within 48 hours. These agents are generally used for erectile dysfunction or in cases of pulmonary hypertension, and in combination with nitrates, they may cause severe hypotension refractory to vasopressor agents.

There appears to be no association between nitroglycerin therapy and survival in patients with ACS.

Opiates (eg, Morphine)

Consider administering morphine for severe chest discomfort that does not respond to sublingual or translingual nitroglycerin if authorized by protocol or medical control. Morphine is indicated in STEMI when chest discomfort does not respond to nitrates. Use morphine with caution in NSTE-ACS because of an association with increased mortality. In addition, morphine may mask symptoms of myocardial ischemia and decrease absorption of important orally administered drugs, such as antiplatelets (P2Y$_{12}$ inhibitors). Currently there are no data to suggest an association between morphine and survival advantages in patients with ACS.

Morphine may be used to manage ACS because it
- Produces central nervous system analgesia, which reduces the adverse effects of neurohumoral activation, catecholamine release, and heightened myocardial oxygen demand
- Alleviates dyspnea
- Produces venodilation, which reduces LV preload and oxygen requirement
- Decreases systemic vascular resistance, which reduces LV afterload
- Helps redistribute blood volume in patients with acute pulmonary edema

Remember, morphine is a venodilator. As with nitroglycerin, use smaller doses and carefully monitor physiologic response before administering additional doses in patients who may be preload dependent. If hypotension develops, administer fluids as a first line of therapy.

Critical Concepts: Pain Relief With Nitroglycerin
Pain relief with nitroglycerin is not useful for diagnosing the cause of symptoms in ED patients with chest pain or discomfort. GI and other causes of chest discomfort can improve with nitroglycerin administration, so a patient's response to nitrate therapy is not diagnostic of ACS.

Caution: Nonsteroidal Anti-inflammatory Drugs
Do not use nonsteroidal anti-inflammatory drugs (except for aspirin), including nonselective and COX-2 selective drugs, during hospitalization for STEMI because of the increased risk of mortality, reinfarction, hypertension, heart failure, and myocardial rupture associated with their use.

Obtaining a 12-Lead ECG

The AHA recommends out-of-hospital 12-lead ECG diagnostic programs in all EMS systems, and all EMS systems should take the actions outlined in Table 4.

Table 4. EMS Actions per AHA Recommendations	
EMS action	**Recommendation**
Obtain a 12-Lead ECG if available.	The AHA recommends routine use of 12-lead out-of-hospital ECGs for patients with signs and symptoms of possible ACS.
Provide prearrival notification to the hospital.	Prearrival notification of the ED shortens the time to treatment (10 to 60 minutes has been achieved in clinical studies) and speeds reperfusion therapy with fibrinolytics or PCI or both, which may reduce mortality and minimize myocardial injury.
Complete a fibrinolytic checklist if appropriate.	If STEMI is identified on the 12-lead ECG, complete a fibrinolytic checklist if appropriate. Consider prehospital fibrinolysis per local protocol.

Immediate ED Assessment and Treatment

The ED and cath lab assessment should occur concurrently within the first 10 minutes. The high-performance team should quickly evaluate the patient with potential ACS on the patient's arrival and obtain a 12-lead ECG (if not already performed before arrival) and assess the patient.

The 12-lead ECG (example in Figure 17) is at the center of the decision pathway in managing ischemic chest discomfort and is the only way to identify STEMI.

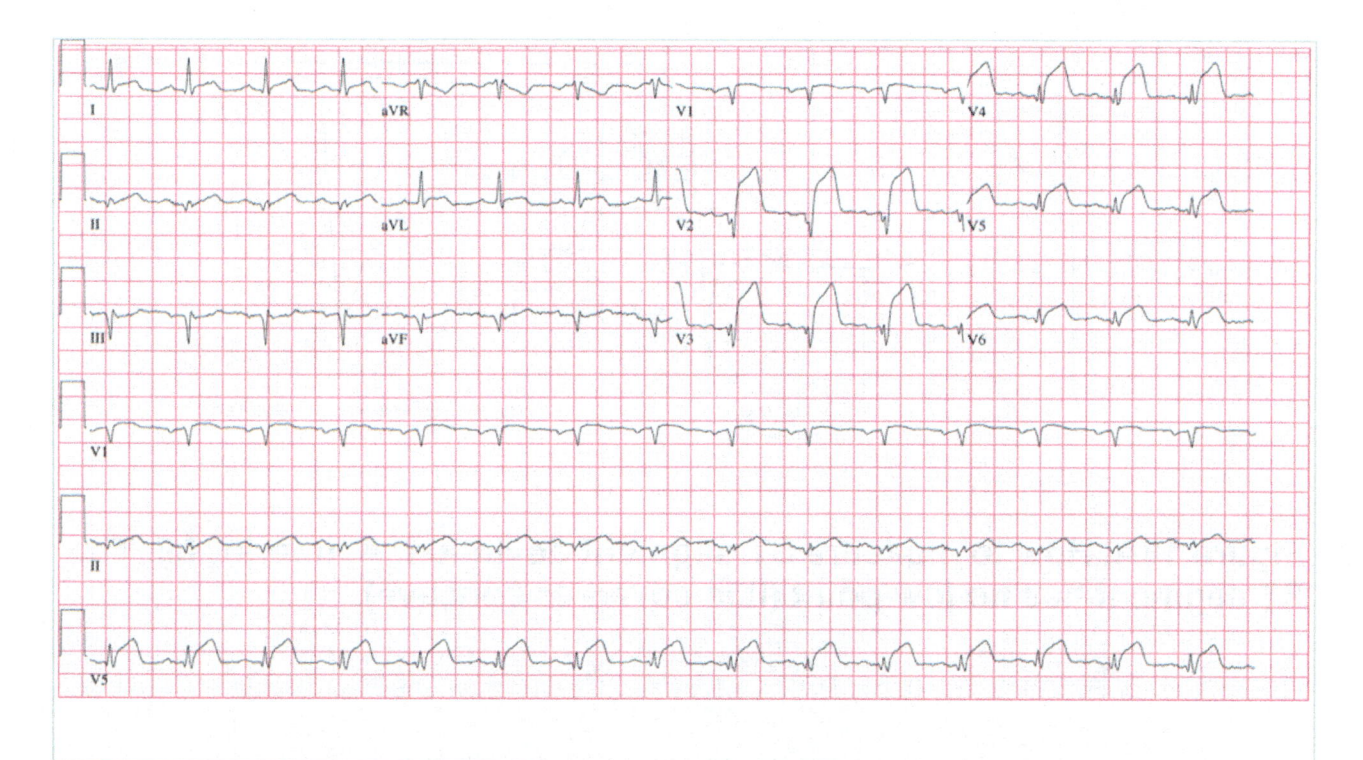

Figure 17. Anterior STEMI on a 12-lead ECG.

Assess ABCs, give oxygen (if needed), and establish IV access. Perform a brief targeted history and physical exam, focusing on chest discomfort, signs and symptoms of heart failure, cardiac history, risk factors for ACS, and historical features that may preclude the use of fibrinolytics. Review and complete fibrinolytic checklist and check contraindications. Obtain initial cardiac marker levels and complete blood counts and coagulation studies, and obtain a portable chest x-ray in less than 30 minutes (do not delay transport to the cath lab). For a patient with STEMI, the goals of reperfusion are

- PCI should begin within 90 minutes from first medical contact to balloon inflation
- Fibrinolytic administration should begin within 30 minutes of the patient's arrival in the ED

Figure 18 shows how to measure ST-segment deviation.

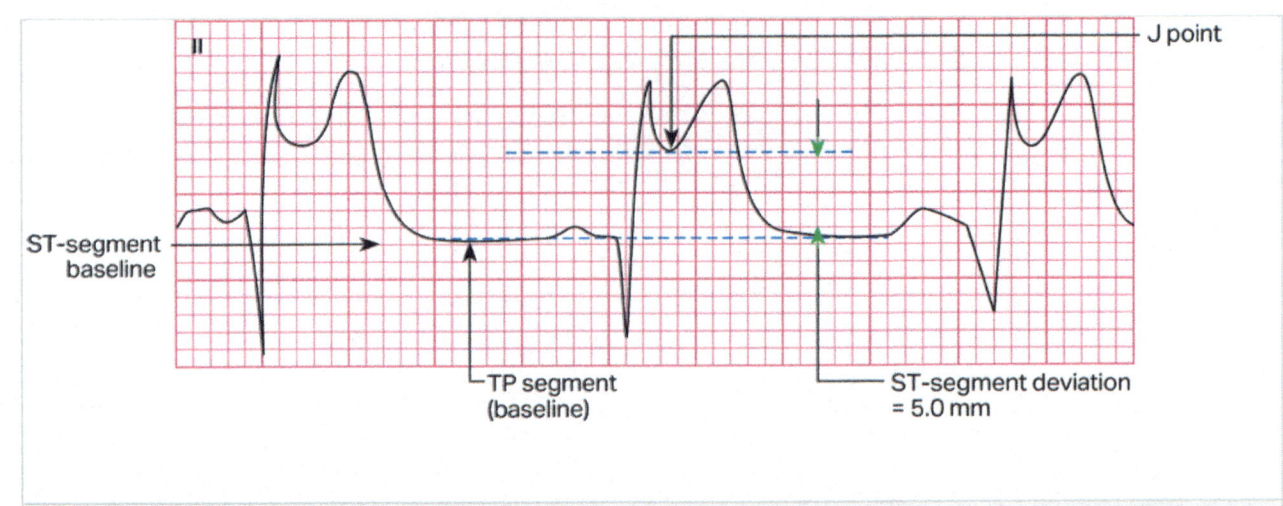

Figure 18A. How to measure ST-segment deviation. A, Inferior MI. The ST segment has no low point (it is coved or concave).

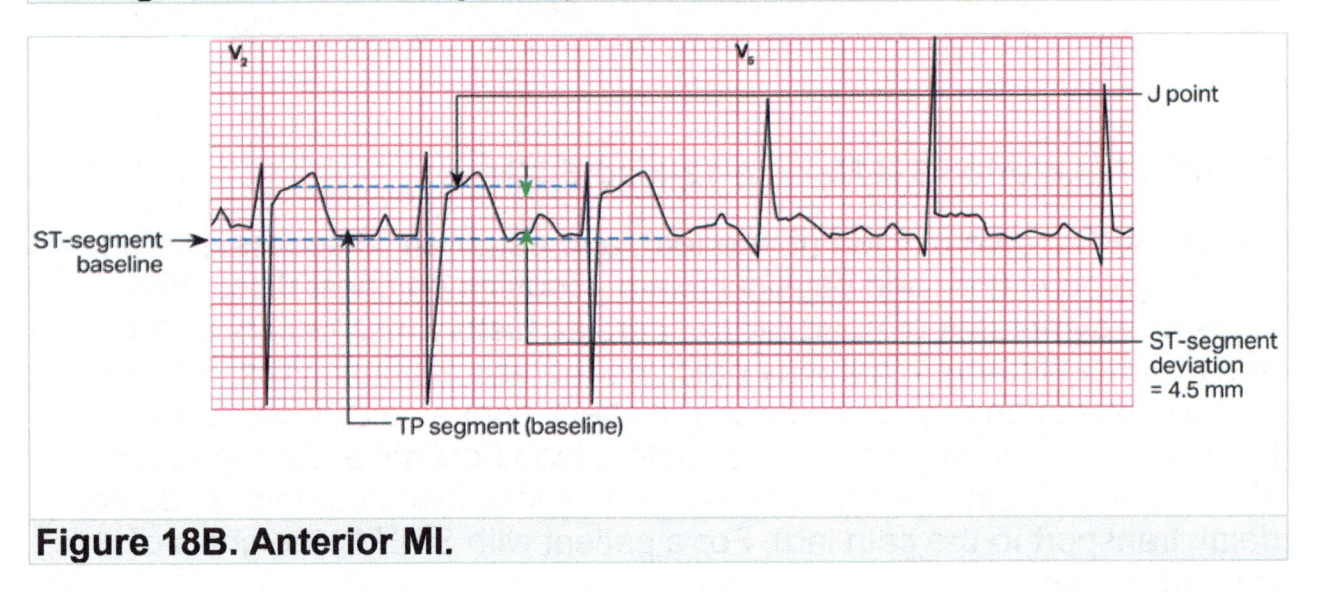

Figure 18B. Anterior MI.

The First 10 Minutes

Concurrent ED/cath lab assessment in the first 10 minutes:
- Activate STEMI team upon EMS notification.
- Assess ABCs; give oxygen if needed.
- Establish IV access.
- Perform brief, targeted history, physical exam.
- Review and complete fibrinolytic checklist; check contraindications.
- Obtain initial cardiac marker levels and complete blood counts and coagulation studies.
- Obtain a portable chest x-ray (in less than 30 minutes); do not delay transport to the cath lab. The results of cardiac markers, chest x-ray, and laboratory studies should not delay reperfusion

therapy unless clinically necessary, eg, suspected aortic dissection or coagulopathy.

Immediate ED and Cath Lab General Treatment

Unless allergies or contraindications exist, consider these 4 agents in patients with ischemic-type chest discomfort:
- If oxygen saturation is less than 90%: Start oxygen at 4 L/min and titrate.
- Aspirin 162 to 325 mg (if not given by EMS)
- Nitroglycerin sublingual or translingual
- Morphine IV if discomfort not relieved by nitroglycerin

Consider administration of P2Y$_{12}$ inhibitors. Because out-of-hospital providers may have given these agents already, administer initial or supplemental doses as indicated. (See the discussion of these drugs in EMS Assessment, Care, and Hospital Preparation.)

Critical Concepts: Oxygen, Aspirin, Nitrates, and Opiates
- *Unless contraindicated, initial therapy with aspirin, nitrates, and, if indicated, oxygen is recommended for all patients suspected of having severe ischemic chest discomfort. If pain is not controlled, consider morphine to minimize pain and the associated catecholamine release. However, morphine can decrease absorption of oral antiplatelet medications.*
- *The major contraindication to nitroglycerin and morphine is hypotension, including from an RV infarction. The major contraindications to aspirin are true aspirin allergy and active or recent GI bleeding.*

Classifying Patients by ST-Segment Deviation

Review the initial 12-lead ECG (Step 4) and classify patients into 1 of 2 following major clinical groups (Steps 5 and 9):
- *STEMI* is characterized by ST-segment elevation in 2 or more contiguous leads or new left bundle branch block (LBBB). Threshold values for ST-segment elevation consistent with STEMI are J-point elevation greater than 2 mm (0.2 mV) in leads V$_2$ and V$_3$ (2.5 mm in men younger than 40 years; 1.5 mm in all women)

and 1 mm or more in all other leads or by new or presumed new LBBB.
- NSTE-ACS (Step 9):
  - *–High-risk NSTE-ACS (Step 10)* is characterized by ischemic ST-segment depression 0.5 mm (0.05 mV) or greater or dynamic T-wave inversion with pain or discomfort. Nonpersistent or transient ST-segment elevation 0.5 mm or greater for less than 20 minutes is also included in this category. If troponin is elevated or if this is a high-risk patient, consider early invasive strategy if (Step 11)
    - Refractory ischemic chest discomfort
    - Recurrent/persistent ST-segment deviation
    - Ventricular tachycardia
    - Hemodynamic instability
    - Signs of heart failure

  - Start adjunctive therapies (eg, nitroglycerin, heparin) as indicated. Please refer to the "2014 AHA/ACC Guideline for the Management of Patients With Non–ST-Elevation Acute Coronary Syndromes: A Report of the American College of Cardiology/American Heart Association Task Force on Practice Guidelines" for more information.[6]

  - *–Low- to intermediate-risk NSTE-ACS (Step 12)* is characterized by normal or nondiagnostic changes in the ST segment or T wave that are inconclusive and require further risk stratification. This classification includes patients with normal ECGs and those with ST-segment deviation in either direction of less than 0.5 mm (0.05 mV) or T-wave inversion of 2 mm (0.2 mV) or less. Serial cardiac studies and functional testing are appropriate. Note that additional information (troponin) may place the patient into a higher risk classification after initial classification. Consider admission to the ED chest pain unit or to an appropriate bed for further monitoring and possible intervention (Step 13).

The ECG classification of ischemic syndromes is not exclusive—for example, a small percentage of patients with normal ECGs may have MI. If the initial ECG is nondiagnostic and clinical circumstances indicate (eg, ongoing chest discomfort), repeat the ECG. The use of a single ECG to classify patients with suspected ACS is not sufficient. Assessment of cardiac enzymes and serial ECGs in patients with ongoing symptoms is necessary to complete the acute assessment of patients suspected of having this condition.

STEMI

Patients with STEMI usually have complete occlusion of an epicardial coronary artery.

Treat STEMI by providing early reperfusion therapy achieved with primary PCI or fibrinolytics.

Reperfusion therapy for STEMI is perhaps the most important advancement for treating cardiovascular disease in recent years. Early fibrinolytic therapy or direct catheter-based reperfusion is an established standard of care for patients with STEMI who present within 12 hours after symptom onset with no contraindications. Reperfusion therapy reduces mortality and saves heart muscle; the shorter the time to reperfusion, the greater the benefit. In fact, providing fibrinolytic therapy in the first hour after symptom onset reduces mortality by 47%.

__Critical Concepts: Delay of Therapy__
- *Do not delay diagnosis and treatment to consult with a cardiologist or another physician except in equivocal or uncertain cases because delays are associated with increased hospital mortality rates.*
- *Potential delay during in-hospital evaluation may occur from door to data (ECG), from data to decision, and from decision to drug (or PCI). These 4 major points of in-hospital therapy are commonly referred to as the 4 D's.*
- *All providers must focus on minimizing delays at each of these points.*

Early Reperfusion Therapy

Rapidly identify patients with STEMI and use a fibrinolytic checklist to screen for indications and contraindications to fibrinolytic therapy, if appropriate.

The first qualified physician who encounters a patient with STEMI should interpret or confirm the 12-lead ECG, determine the risk/benefit of reperfusion therapy, and direct administration of fibrinolytic therapy or activation of the PCI team. Early activation of PCI may occur with established protocols. Use these recommended time frames:
- For PCI, the goal is first medical contact–to–balloon inflation time of 90 minutes or less. For patients at a non–PCI-capable hospital, time from first medical contact to device should be less than 120 minutes when considering primary PCI, but systems should strive to achieve the shortest time possible.
- If fibrinolysis is the intended reperfusion, the longest acceptable ED door-to-needle time (needle time is the beginning of infusion of a fibrinolytic agent) is 30 minutes, but systems should strive to achieve the shortest time possible.
- Consider patients who are ineligible for fibrinolytic therapy for transfer to a PCI facility, regardless of delay, but prepare for a door-to-departure time of 30 minutes.

Adjunctive treatments may also be indicated.

Choosing Primary PCI

The most common form of PCI is coronary angioplasty with stent placement, and primary PCI is preferred over fibrinolytic administration. Many studies have shown PCI to be superior to fibrinolysis in the combined end points of death, stroke, and reinfarction for patients presenting between 3 and 12 hours after onset.

Interventional strategies for the management of STEMI are as follows:
1. Primary PCI: The patient is taken to the catheterization laboratory for PCI immediately after hospital presentation.
2. Rescue PCI: The patient is initially treated with fibrinolytic therapy. The patient does not show signs of reperfusion (lack of ST resolution more than 50% after 1 hour of fibrinolytic therapy administration) and therefore is referred for rescue PCI.

3. Pharmacoinvasive strategy: The patient is initially treated with fibrinolytic therapy with the intention to perform coronary angiography and PCI, if appropriate.

Considerations for the use of primary PCI include the following:
- PCI is the treatment of choice for the management of STEMI when it can be performed effectively with first medical contact–to–balloon inflation time of 90 minutes or less by a skilled provider at a skilled PCI facility.
- Primary PCI may also be offered to patients presenting to non–PCI-capable centers if PCI can be initiated promptly within 120 minutes after first medical contact.
- For patients admitted to a non-PCI center, transferring for PCI vs administering on-site fibrinolytics may have some benefit in terms of reinfarction, stroke, and a trend to lower mortality when PCI is performed within 120 minutes after first medical contact.
- PCI is also preferred in patients with contraindications to fibrinolytics and is indicated in patients with high-risk features, heart failure complicating MI, or cardiogenic shock.

Using Fibrinolytic Therapy

Administer a fibrinolytic agent or "clot-buster" to patients with ST-segment elevation greater than 2 mm (0.2 mV) in leads V_2 and V_3 and 1 mm or more in all other leads or by new or presumed new LBBB (eg, leads III, aVF; leads V_3, V_4; leads I and aVL) without contraindications. Fibrin-specific agents achieve normal flow in about 50% of patients given these drugs. Examples of fibrin-specific drugs are alteplase, reteplase, and tenecteplase. Streptokinase was the first fibrinolytic used widely, but it is not fibrin specific.

Considerations for the use of fibrinolytic therapy are as follows:
- In the absence of contraindications and in the presence of a favorable risk-benefit ratio, fibrinolytic therapy is one option for reperfusion in patients with STEMI and *onset of symptoms within 12 hours after presentation* with qualifying ECG findings and if PCI is not available within 90 minutes after first medical contact.
- In the absence of contraindications, it is also reasonable to give fibrinolytics to patients with *onset of symptoms within the prior 12 hours* and ECG findings consistent with true posterior MI. Experienced providers will recognize this as a condition where ST-

segment depression in the early precordial leads is equivalent to ST-segment elevation in others. When these changes are associated with other ECG findings, it suggests a "STEMI" on the posterior wall of the heart.
- Fibrinolytics are generally not recommended for patients presenting *more than 12 hours after onset of symptoms*. But they may be considered if ischemic chest discomfort continues with persistent ST-segment elevation.
- Do not give fibrinolytics to the following patients:
  - —Those who present *more than 24 hours after the onset of symptoms*
  - —Those with ST-segment depression, unless a true posterior MI is suspected

Adjunctive Treatments

Other drugs are useful when indicated in addition to oxygen, sublingual or translingual nitroglycerin, aspirin, morphine, and fibrinolytic therapy. These include
- Unfractionated or low-molecular-weight heparin
- Bivalirudin
- $P2Y_{12}$ inhibitors (clopidogrel, prasugrel, and ticagrelor)
  - —Clopidogrel and prasugrel are thienopyridines that require liver biotransformation into active metabolites. Ticagrelor does not require liver biotransformation and is a reversible $P2Y_{12}$ inhibitor. The timing of administration of $P2Y_{12}$ should be at the discretion of local site practices.
- IV nitroglycerin
- β-Blockers
- Glycoprotein IIb/IIIa inhibitors

IV nitroglycerin and heparin are common for early management of patients with STEMI. We briefly discuss heparin and IV nitroglycerin, but we do not review bivalirudin, $P2Y_{12}$ inhibitors, β-blockers, and glycoprotein IIb/IIIa inhibitors. These agents require additional risk stratification skills and a detailed knowledge of the spectrum of ACS and, in some instances, continuing knowledge of the results of clinical trials.

Heparin (Unfractionated or Low-Molecular-Weight)

Heparin is a routine adjunct for PCI and fibrinolytic therapy with fibrin-specific agents (alteplase, reteplase, tenecteplase). If you use these drugs, you must be familiar with dosing schedules for specific clinical strategies.

Inappropriate dosing and monitoring of heparin therapy have caused excess intracerebral bleeding and major hemorrhage in STEMI patients. Providers using heparin must know the indications, dosing, and use in the specific ACS categories.

The dosing, use, and duration are derived from use in clinical trials. Specific patients may require dose modification. See the ECC Handbook for weight-based dosing guidelines, intervals of administration, and adjustment of low-molecular-weight heparin in renal function. See the American College of Cardiology/AHA guidelines for detailed discussion in specific categories.

IV Nitroglycerin

Routine use of IV nitroglycerin is not indicated and has not been shown to significantly reduce mortality in STEMI. However, IV nitroglycerin is indicated and used widely in ischemic syndromes and is preferred over topical or long-acting forms because it can be adjusted in a patient with potentially unstable hemodynamics and clinical condition. Indications for initiating IV nitroglycerin in STEMI are

- Recurrent or continuing chest discomfort unresponsive to sublingual or translingual nitroglycerin
- Pulmonary edema complicating STEMI
- Hypertension complicating STEMI

Treatment goals using IV nitroglycerin are as follows:

For relief of ischemic chest discomfort,
- Titrate to effect
- Keep SBP greater than 90 mm Hg
- Limit drop in SBP to 30 mm Hg below baseline in hypertensive patients

For improvement in pulmonary edema and hypertension,
- Titrate to effect
- Limit drop in SBP to 10% of baseline in normotensive patients

- Limit drop in SBP to 30 mm Hg below baseline in hypertensive patients

Acute Stroke

Overview

The identification and initial management of patients with acute stroke is within the scope of an ACLS provider.

Out-of-hospital acute stroke care focuses on critical EMS assessments and actions (Step 2):
- Assess ABCs; give oxygen if needed.
- Initiate stroke protocol.
- Perform physical exam.
- Perform validated prehospital stroke screen and stroke severity tool.
- Establish time of symptom onset (last known normal).
- Triage to most appropriate stroke center.
- Check glucose; treat if indicated.
- Provide prehospital notification; on arrival, transport to brain imaging suite.

Note: Refer to the Emergency Medical Services Acute Stroke Routing later in this section.

In-hospital acute stroke care occurs in the ED or brain imaging suite. It is best practice to bypass the ED and go straight to the brain imaging suite. The immediate general and neurologic assessment by the hospital or stroke team (Step 3) includes the following:
- Activate stroke team upon EMS notification.
- Prepare for emergent CT scan or MRI of brain upon arrival.
- Stroke team meets EMS on arrival.
- Assess ABCs; give oxygen if needed.
- Obtain IV access and perform laboratory assessments.
- Check glucose and treat if indicated.
- Review patient history, medications, and procedures.
- Establish time of symptom onset or last known normal.

Perform a physical exam and neurologic examination, including the NIH Stroke Scale or Canadian Neurological Scale. In 2010, the AHA/ASA launched Target: Stroke, a national quality improvement initiative with the

goal of reducing door-to-needle times for eligible patients with acute ischemic stroke. The most recent implementation of current best practices, Target Stroke: III, has established new, more aggressive target goals to give patients the best chance for a good recovery. Target Stroke: III time target goals for reperfusion strategies include the following:
- Achieve door-to-needle times within 60 minutes in 85% or more of acute ischemic stroke patients treated with IV thrombolytics.
- Achieve door-to-device times (arrival to first pass with thrombectomy device) within 90 minutes for direct-arriving patients and within 60 minutes for transfer patients in 50% or more of acute ischemic stroke patients treated with endovascular therapy (EVT).

Drugs for Stroke

Drugs for stroke include
- Approved fibrinolytic agent (alteplase)
- Glucose (D_{10}/D_{50})
- Labetalol
- Nicardipine
- Clevidipine
- Aspirin

Major Types of Stroke

Stroke is a general term. It refers to an acute neurologic impairment that follows interruption in blood supply to a specific area of the brain. Although expeditious stroke care is important for all patients, this section emphasizes reperfusion therapies for acute ischemic stroke.

The major types of stroke are
- Ischemic stroke: accounts for 87% of all strokes and is usually caused by an occlusion of an artery to a region of the brain (Figure 19)
- Hemorrhagic stroke: accounts for 13% of all strokes and occurs when a blood vessel in the brain suddenly ruptures into the surrounding tissue. Fibrinolytic therapy is contraindicated in this type of stroke. Avoid anticoagulants.

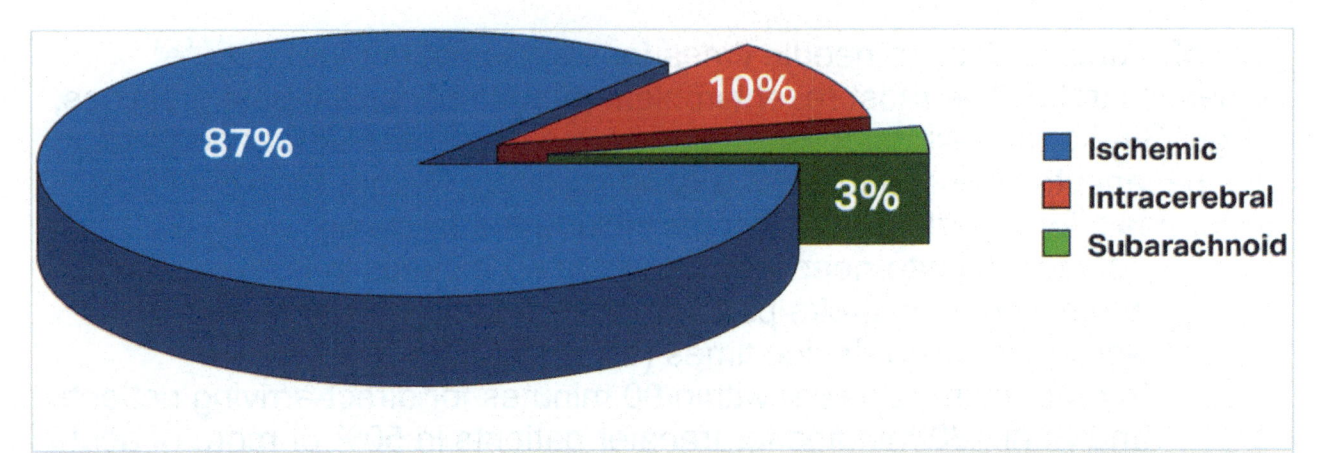

Figure 19. Types of stroke. Eighty-seven percent of strokes are ischemic and potentially eligible for reperfusion therapy if patients otherwise qualify. Thirteen percent of strokes are hemorrhagic, and the majority of these are intracerebral.

The male-to-female incidence ratio is 1.25 in persons 55 to 64 years of age, 1.50 in those 65 to 74, 1.07 in those 75 to 84, and 0.76 in those 85 and older. Blacks have almost twice the risk of first-ever stroke compared with Whites.

Approach to Stroke Care

Each year in the United States, about 795 000 people suffer a new or recurrent stroke. Stroke remains a leading cause of death as well as disability in the United States. Stroke risk increases with age, but approximately one third of people hospitalized for stroke are under age 65.[7]

Early recognition of acute ischemic stroke is critically important because time from symptom onset to reperfusion is key. IV fibrinolytic treatment should be provided as early as possible, generally within 3 hours after onset of symptoms, or within 4.5 hours after onset of symptoms for selected patients. EVT may be given within 24 hours after onset of symptoms in appropriately selected patients, but better outcomes are associated with shorter times to treatment. Although most strokes occur at home, only half of acute stroke patients use EMS for transport to the hospital, which delays time to evaluation and therapeutic interventions. Stroke patients often deny or try to rationalize their symptoms. Even high-risk patients, such as those with atrial fibrillation or hypertension, fail to recognize the signs of stroke. This delays activation of EMS and treatment, resulting in increased morbidity and mortality.

Community and professional education is essential, and it has been successful in increasing the proportion of eligible stroke patients treated with fibrinolytic therapy. Healthcare providers, hospitals, and communities must continue to develop regional stroke systems of care to improve the efficiency and effectiveness of stroke care.

Stroke Chain of Survival

The goal of stroke care is to minimize brain injury and maximize the patient's recovery. The Stroke Chain of Survival (Figure 20) described by the AHA and the American Stroke Association (ASA) is similar to the Chain of Survival for sudden cardiac arrest. It links the actions that patients, family members, and healthcare providers should take to maximize stroke recovery. These links are

- Rapid recognition of and reaction to stroke warning signs and symptoms
- Rapid use of 9-1-1 and EMS dispatch
- Rapid EMS recognition of stroke, triage, transport, and prehospital notification to the receiving hospital
- Rapid diagnosis and treatment in the hospital

Figure 20. The Stroke Chain of Survival.

The 8 D's of Stroke Care

The 8 D's of Stroke Care highlight the major steps in diagnosis and treatment of stroke and key points at which delays can occur:
- **D**etection: rapid recognition of stroke signs and symptoms
- **D**ispatch: early activation and dispatch of EMS by phoning 9-1-1
- **D**elivery: rapid EMS stroke identification, management, triage, transport, and prehospital notification
- **D**oor: emergent ED/imaging suite triage and immediate assessment by the stroke team
- **D**ata: rapid clinical evaluation, laboratory testing, and brain imaging
- **D**ecision: establishing stroke diagnosis and determining optimal therapy selection
- **D**rug/**D**evice: administration of fibrinolytic and/or EVT if eligible

- **D**isposition: rapid admission to the stroke unit or critical care unit, or emergent interfacility transfer for EVT

For more information on these critical elements, see the Adult Suspected Stroke Algorithm (Figure 21).

1. Identify signs and symptoms of possible stroke
Activate emergency response

2. Critical EMS assessments and actions
- Assess ABCs; give oxygen if needed
- Initiate stroke protocol
- Perform physical exam
- Perform validated prehospital stroke screen and stroke severity tool
- Establish time of symptom onset (last known normal)
- Triage to most appropriate stroke center
- Check glucose; treat if indicated
- Provide prehospital notification; on arrival, transport to brain imaging suite

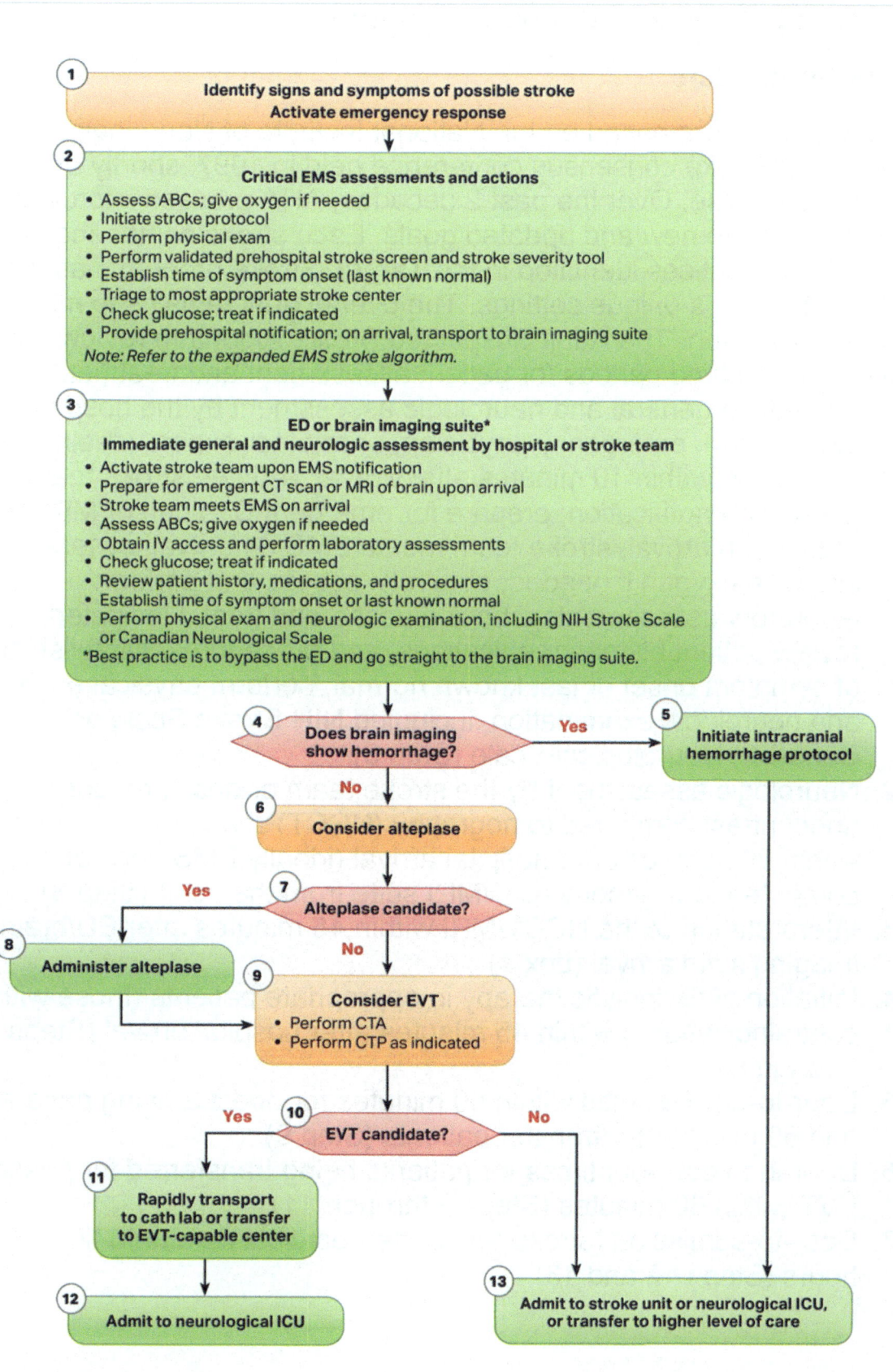

Note: Refer to the expanded EMS stroke algorithm.

3. ED or brain imaging suite*
Immediate general and neurologic assessment by hospital or stroke team
- Activate stroke team upon EMS notification
- Prepare for emergent CT scan or MRI of brain upon arrival
- Stroke team meets EMS on arrival
- Assess ABCs; give oxygen if needed
- Obtain IV access and perform laboratory assessments
- Check glucose; treat if indicated
- Review patient history, medications, and procedures
- Establish time of symptom onset or last known normal
- Perform physical exam and neurologic examination, including NIH Stroke Scale or Canadian Neurological Scale

*Best practice is to bypass the ED and go straight to the brain imaging suite.

4. Does brain imaging show hemorrhage?

5. Yes → Initiate intracranial hemorrhage protocol

No ↓

6. Consider alteplase

7. Alteplase candidate?

Yes → **8. Administer alteplase**

No ↓

9. Consider EVT
- Perform CTA
- Perform CTP as indicated

10. EVT candidate?

Yes → **11. Rapidly transport to cath lab or transfer to EVT-capable center** → **12. Admit to neurological ICU**

No → **13. Admit to stroke unit or neurological ICU, or transfer to higher level of care**

© 2020 American Heart Association

Figure 21. Adult Suspected Stroke Algorithm.

Goals of Stroke Care

Initial time goals were based on the National Institute of Neurological Disorders and Stroke consensus conference held in 1997, shortly after the approval of alteplase. Over the past 2 decades, AHA process improvement projects have led to new and updated goals. Each stroke center should adopt the best practices identified in the Target: Stroke programs as they apply to that center's unique settings. The overall goal remains to minimize delays to reperfusion. The Adult Suspected Stroke Algorithm reviews the critical in-hospital time periods for patient assessment and treatment:

1. Immediate general and neurologic assessment by the hospital or stroke team, emergency physician, or another expert, ideally upon arrival and within 10 minutes after arrival; activate stroke team upon EMS notification; prepare for emergent CT scan or MRI of brain upon arrival; stroke team meets EMS on arrival; assess ABCs and give oxygen if needed; obtain IV access and perform laboratory assessments; check glucose and treat if indicated; review patient history, medications, and procedures; establish time of symptom onset or last known normal; perform physical exam and neurologic examination, including NIH Stroke Scale or Canadian Neurological Scale (Step 3).
2. Neurologic assessment by the stroke team or designee and noncontrast computed tomography (NCCT) scan or MRI performed within 20 minutes after hospital arrival (ideally EMS goes directly to computed tomography (CT)/MRI suite from the field) (Step 3)
3. Interpretation of the NCCT/MRI within 45 minutes after ED/brain imaging suite arrival (box 4)
4. Initiation of fibrinolytic therapy in appropriate patients (those without contraindications) within 45 minutes after hospital arrival (Steps 6 through 8)
5. Door-to-device times within 90 minutes for direct arriving patients and 60 minutes for transfer patients (Step 9)
6. Door-in to door-out times for patients being transferred for possible EVT within 60 minutes (Steps 9 through 11)
7. Door-to-admission (stroke unit or neurocritical care unit) time of 3 hours (Steps 12 and 13)

Critical Time Periods

Patients with acute ischemic stroke have a time-dependent benefit for reperfusion therapy similar to that of patients with STEMI, but this time-dependent benefit is much shorter. The critical time period for administration of reperfusion therapies begin with the onset of symptoms. Critical time periods from hospital arrival are summarized here and represent maximum times:
- Immediate general assessment: **within 10 minutes**
- Immediate neurologic assessment: **within 20 minutes**
- Acquisition of CT/MRI of the head: **within 20 minutes**
- Interpretation of the CT/MRI scan: **within 45 minutes**
- Administration of fibrinolytic therapy, timed from ED/brain imaging suite arrival: **within 60 minutes**
- Administration of fibrinolytic therapy, timed from onset of symptoms: **within 3 hours, or 4.5 hours in selected patients**
- Administration of EVT, timed from onset of symptoms: **up to 24 hours for patients with large vessel occlusion (LVO): 0 to 6 hours requires eligible NCCT scan; 6 to 24 hours requires eligible penumbral imaging**
- Admission to a monitored bed: **3 hours**
- Interfacility transfers for EVT (door-in-door-out): **1 hour**

The Adult Suspected Stroke Algorithm (Figure 21) emphasizes important elements of out-of-hospital and in-hospital care for patients with possible stroke. In addition, the Emergency Medical Services Acute Stroke Routing (Figure 22) emphasizes an important evaluation to determine the best hospital to take the patient with a suspected stroke to. These actions include using a stroke screen and severity tool, and rapid transport to the hospital. As with ACS, notifying the receiving hospital in advance speeds the care of the stroke patient upon arrival.

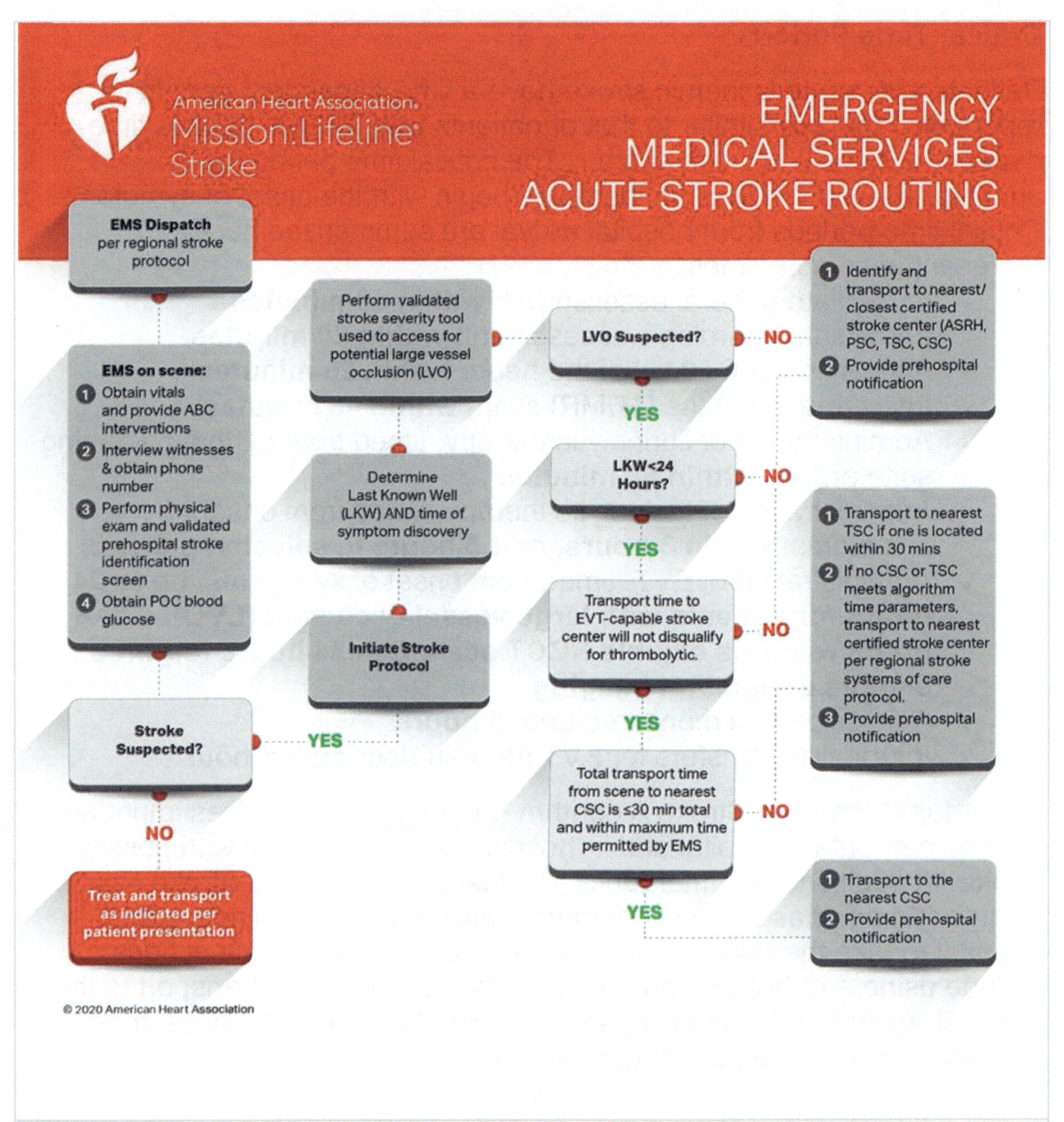

Figure 22. Emergency Medical Services Acute Stroke Routing Algorithm.

Application of the Adult Suspected Stroke Algorithm

We will now discuss the steps in the algorithm (as well as other related topics):
- Identification of signs and symptoms of possible stroke and activation of emergency response (Step 1)

- Critical EMS assessments and actions (Step 2)
- Immediate general and neurologic assessment by hospital or stroke team (ED or brain imaging suite) (Step 3)
- Brain imaging (CT/MRI scan) (Step 4): Does brain imaging show hemorrhage?
- Alteplase candidate? (Fibrinolytic therapy risk stratification of candidate) (Step 7)
- Considering EVT and patient's qualification as a candidate (Steps 9 and 10)
- Rapid transport to cath lab or transfer to EVT-capable center (Step 11)
- Admittance to neurologic ICU or stroke unit, or transfer to higher level of care (Steps 12 and 13)
- Additional imaging for presence of LVO and penumbra when indicated (Steps 9 and 10)
- General stroke care (Steps 12 and 13)

Identify Signs of Possible Stroke and Activate Emergency Response

Warning Signs and Symptoms

The signs and symptoms of a stroke may be subtle. They include
- Sudden weakness or numbness of the face, arm, or leg, especially on one side of the body
- Trouble speaking or understanding
- Sudden trouble seeing in one or both eyes
- Sudden trouble walking
- Dizziness or loss of balance or coordination
- Sudden severe headache with no known cause
- Sudden confusion

Activate EMS System Immediately

Currently half of all stroke patients are driven to the ED by family or friends. Thus, stroke patients and their families must be educated on potential signs or symptoms of stroke and the need to phone 9-1-1 and activate EMS as soon as they detect a possible stroke.

EMS provides the safest and most efficient method of emergency transport to the most appropriate stroke hospital. The advantages of EMS transport include the following:

- Emergency medical dispatchers play a critical role in timely treatment of potential stroke by
    - –Identifying possible stroke patients
    - –Providing high-priority dispatch
    - –Instructing bystanders in lifesaving CPR skills or other supportive care if needed while EMS providers are on the way
- Responding providers can assess ABCs and give oxygen as needed.
- EMS personnel can initiate stroke protocol, perform a physical exam, establish time of symptom onset (last known normal), and check glucose and treat if indicated.
- EMS can triage to the most appropriate stroke center on the basis of a validated prehospital stroke screen and a stroke severity tool and on patient characteristics following regional destination protocols.
- EMS can provide prehospital notification, enabling the hospital to prepare to evaluate and manage the patient more efficiently, and on arrival transport to the brain imaging suite.

Provide Critical EMS Assessments and Actions

Prehospital EMS providers must minimize the interval between the onset of symptoms and patient arrival in the ED/brain imaging suite. Specific stroke therapy can be provided only in the appropriate receiving hospital ED, so time in the field only delays (and may prevent) definitive therapy. More extensive assessments and initiation of supportive therapies can continue en route to the hospital or in the ED/brain imaging suite.

Critical EMS Assessments and Actions

To provide the best outcome for the patient with potential stroke, EMS providers should identify the signs and symptoms of possible stroke (Step 1). These include the following:
- Assess ABCs and give oxygen if needed to hypoxemic stroke patients (ie, whose oxygen saturation is 94% or less) or to those patients with unknown oxygen saturation.
- Initiate stroke protocol.
- Perform physical exam.
- Perform validated prehospital stroke severity tool. Perform a rapid prehospital stroke screen (eg, CPSS) and stroke severity

assessment for possible large vessel occlusion (eg, Los Angeles Motor Scale [LAMS], Rapid Arterial Occlusion Evaluation [RACE], Cincinnati Stroke Triage Assessment Tool [CSTAT], Field Assessment Stroke Triage for Emergency Destination [FAST-ED]).
- Establish time of symptom onset (last known normal). Determine the time of symptom onset or when the patient was last known normal or at neurologic baseline. This represents time zero. If the patient wakes from sleep with symptoms of stroke, time zero is the last time the patient was seen to be normal.
- Triage to most appropriate stroke center. Transport the patient rapidly and triage to an appropriate stroke center based on last known well, stroke severity tool, and regional stroke destination protocol. Support cardiopulmonary function during transport. If possible, bring a witness, family member, or caregiver with the patient to confirm time of onset of stroke symptoms.
- Check glucose if indicated. During transport, check blood glucose if protocols or medical control allows.
- Provide prehospital notification to the receiving hospital, and on arrival, transport to the brain imaging suite.

Table 5. The Cincinnati Prehospital Stroke Scale

Test	Findings
Facial droop: have the patient show teeth or smile (Figure 23).	**Normal**—both sides of the face move equally
	Abnormal—one side of the face does not move as well as the other side
Arm drift: patient closes eyes and extends both arms straight out, with palms up, for 10 seconds (Figure 24).	**Normal**—both arms move the same *or* both arms do not move at all (other findings, such as pronator drift, may be helpful)
	Abnormal—one arm does not move *or* one arm drifts down compared with the other
Abnormal speech: have the patient say, "you can't teach an old dog new tricks."	**Normal**—patient uses correct words with no slurring
	Abnormal—patient slurs words, uses the wrong words, or is unable to speak
Interpretation: if any 1 of these 3 signs is abnormal, the probability of a stroke is 72%.	

- The patient with acute stroke is at risk for respiratory compromise from aspiration, upper airway obstruction, hypoventilation, and (rarely) neurogenic pulmonary edema. The combination of poor perfusion and hypoxemia will exacerbate and extend ischemic brain injury, and it has been associated with worse outcome from stroke.

Both out-of-hospital and in-hospital medical personnel should provide supplemental oxygen to hypoxemic stroke patients (ie, those whose oxygen saturation is 94% or less) or patients for whom oxygen saturation is unknown.

Stroke Assessment Tools

The AHA recommends that all EMS personnel be trained to recognize stroke by using a validated, abbreviated out-of-hospital neurologic evaluation tool such as the Cincinnati Prehospital Stroke Scale (CPSS) (Table 5) or the Los Angeles Prehospital Stroke Screen.
Modified from Kothari RU, Pancioli A, Liu T, Brott T, Broderick J. Cincinnati Prehospital Stroke Scale: reproducibility and validity. *Ann Emerg Med.* 1999;33(4):373-378. With permission from Elsevier.

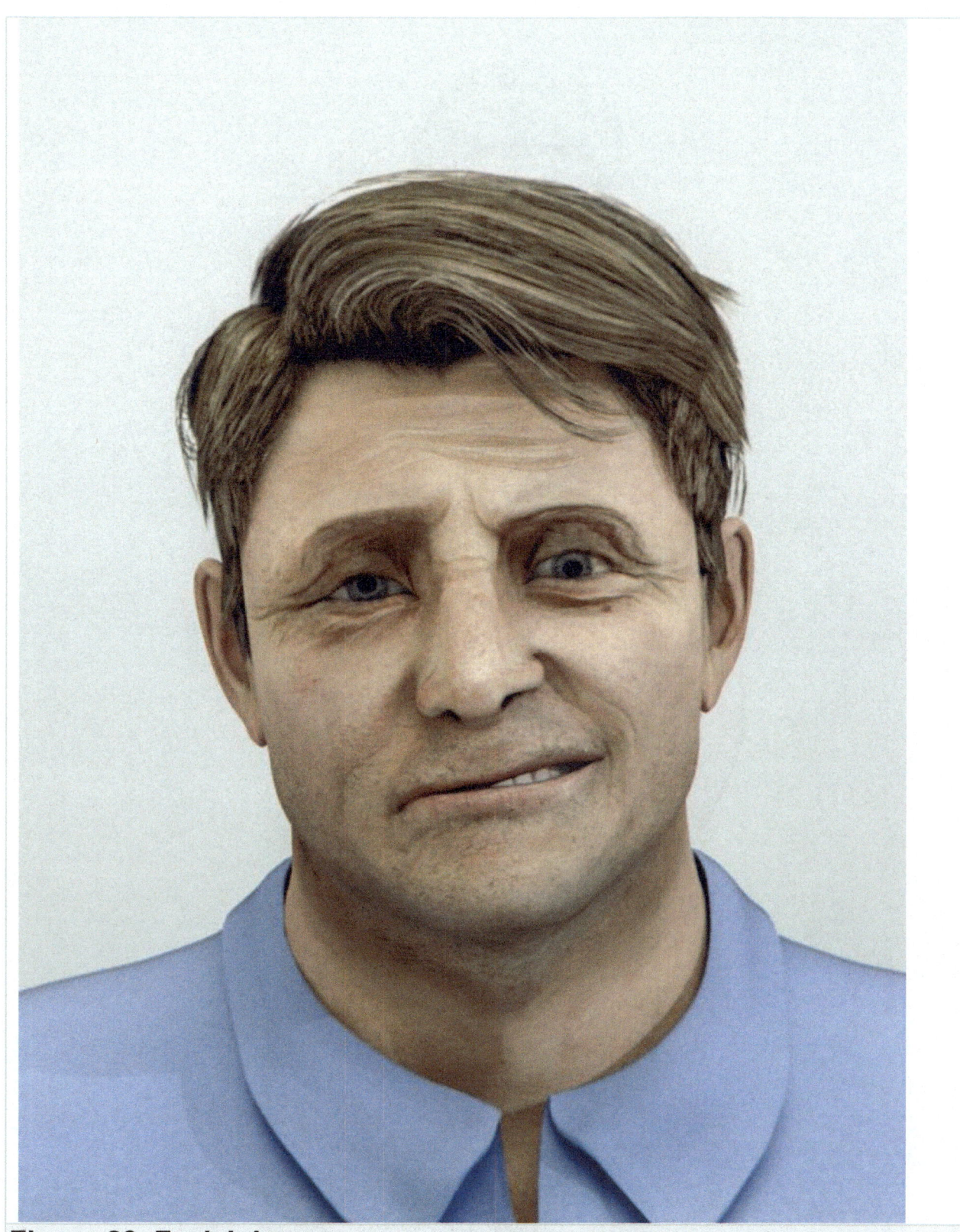

Figure 23. Facial droop.

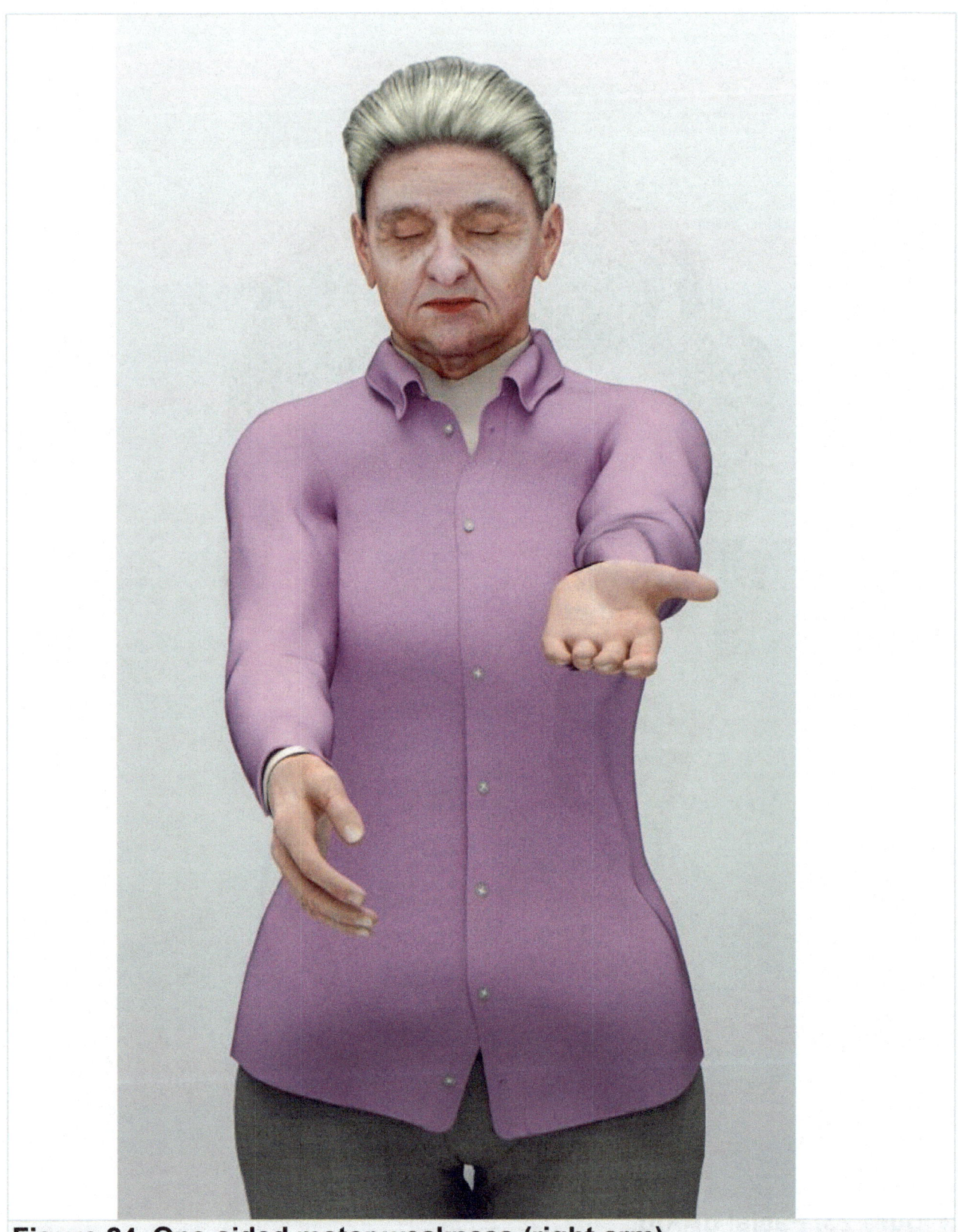

Figure 24. One-sided motor weakness (right arm).

Cincinnati Prehospital Stroke Scale

The CPSS identifies stroke on the basis of 3 physical findings:
- Facial droop (have the patient smile or try to show teeth)
- Arm drift (have the patient close eyes and hold both arms out, with palms up)
- Abnormal speech (have the patient say, "You can't teach an old dog new tricks")

By using the CPSS, medical personnel can evaluate the patient in less than 1 minute. The presence of 1 finding on the CPSS has an estimated probability of stroke of 72% when scored by prehospital providers.

The following list includes examples of prehospital stroke screens and stroke severity scores.

Prehospital stroke screens:
- Cincinnati Prehospital Stroke Scale (CPSS/FAST)
- Los Angeles Prehospital Stroke Screen (LAPSS)
- Melbourne Ambulance Stroke Screen (MASS)
- Miami Emergency Neurologic Deficit Score (MENDS)
- Recognition of Stroke in the Emergency Room Score (ROSIER)

Stroke severity score:
- National Institutes of Health (NIH) Stroke Scale
- Shortened National Institutes of Health Stroke Scale 5 and 8 (sNIHSS-5 and sNIHSS-8)
- Cincinnati Prehospital Stroke Severity Screen (CPSSS)
- Field Assessment Stroke Triage for Emergency Destination (FAST-ED)
- Los Angeles Motor Scale (LAMS)
- Rapid Arterial Occlusion Evaluation Score (RACE)
- Three Item Stroke Scale (3ISS)

Stroke Centers and Stroke Units

Evidence indicates a benefit from triage of stroke patients directly to designated certified stroke centers. Local stakeholders should create a stroke destination protocol based on regional stroke resources.

As stated in the "Guidelines for the Early Management of Patients With Acute Ischemic Stroke: 2019 Update to the 2018 Guidelines for the Early Management of Acute Ischemic Stroke," "Certification of stroke centers by an independent external body, such as Center for Improvement in Healthcare Quality, Det Norske Veritas, Healthcare Facilities Accreditation Program, and The Joint Commission, or a state health department, is recommended." This recommendation is supported by data that demonstrate that the development of stroke centers improves patient care and clinical outcomes. Table 6 shows the different levels and capabilities of hospital stroke designation. Currently, 4 levels of stroke certification exist, and certification is given on the basis of a hospital's specific capabilities.

Table 6. Levels and Capabilities of Hospital Stroke Designation

Hospital attributes	ASRH	PSC	TSC	CSC
Location	Likely rural	Likely urban/suburban	Likely urban	Likely urban
Stroke team accessible/available 24 hours/day, 7 days/week	Yes	Yes	Yes	Yes
Noncontrast CT available 24 hours/day, 7 days/week	Yes	Yes	Yes	Yes
Advanced imaging (CTA/CTP/MRI/MRA/MRP) available 24 hours/day, 7 days/week	No	Yes	Yes	Yes
Intravenous alteplase capable	Yes	Yes	Yes	Yes
Thrombectomy capable	No	Possibly	Yes	Yes
Diagnoses stroke pathogenesis/manages poststroke complications	Unlikely	Yes	Yes	Yes
Admits hemorrhagic stroke	No	Possibly	Possibly	Yes
Clips/coils ruptured aneurysms	No	Possibly	Possibly	Yes
Dedicated stroke unit	No	Yes	Yes	Yes
Dedicated neurocritical care unit/ICU	No	Possibly	Possibly	Yes

Abbreviations: ASRH, Acute Stroke Ready Hospital; CSC, Comprehensive Stroke Center; CTA, computed tomography angiography; CTP, computed tomography perfusion; MRA, magnetic resonance angiography; MRI, magnetic resonance imaging; MRP, magnetic resonance perfusion; PSC, Primary Stroke Center; TSC, Thrombectomy-Capable Stroke Center.

Acute Stroke Ready Hospital

Acute Stroke Ready Hospitals typically serve rural and under-resourced areas. Emergent identification and treatment of patients with alteplase, when indicated, is typically facilitated by telemedicine to provide access to acute neurologic expertise. Typically, patients are later transferred for admission to a stroke unit or for a higher level of care, as indicated.

Primary Stroke Center

The Primary Stroke Center is the cornerstone of stroke systems of care. These centers comprise a wide range of hospitals able to quickly identify stroke patients, provide alteplase therapy if indicated, and admit patients to a dedicated stroke unit. Roughly half of all stroke patients in the United States receive care in a Primary Stroke Center.

Thrombectomy-Capable Stroke Center

The Thrombectomy-Capable Stroke Center certification was jointly created by the AHA and the Joint Commission to recognize stroke centers that meet the same high-quality standards as a primary stroke center but are also capable of providing EVT for patients with LVO. The Thrombectomy-Capable Stroke Center designation was created to recognize these EVT-capable facilities in areas where a Comprehensive Stroke Center was not available.

Comprehensive Stroke Center

Hospitals achieving Comprehensive Stroke Center certification are capable of managing all forms and severities of stroke, both ischemic and hemorrhagic, and can provide 24/7 access to specialty care, such as neurosurgery, EVT, and neurocritical care. A Comprehensive Stroke Center typically serves as the hub of a regional stroke system of care, providing receiving capabilities for transferred patients and providing feedback and education for transferring sites.

Hospitals in a region should achieve stroke center certification to the highest level possible, and then use these levels of capabilities to design a regional stroke system of care. The hospitals' capabilities should be communicated to the regional EMS system and the community.

Once a patient arrives in the ED, a number of assessments and management activities must occur quickly. Protocols should be used to minimize delay in definitive diagnosis and therapy. Incorporating best practices from the Target Stroke programs has been shown to reduce overall door-to-needle times and improve clinical outcomes while maintaining overall safety. These practices have also been shown to decrease the various interval times first established by the 1997 National Institute of Neurological Disorders and Stroke consensus conference.

The goal of the stroke team, emergency physician, or other experts should be to assess the patient with suspected stroke within* 10 minutes *after arrival in the ED/brain imaging suite (Step 3): "time is brain."

Target: Stroke II Best-Practice Strategies

1. **EMS Prenotification:** EMS providers should provide early prenotification to the receiving hospital when stroke is recognized in the field.
2. **Use stroke tools:** A stroke toolkit containing rapid triage protocol, clinical decision support, stroke-specific order sets, guidelines, hospital-specific algorithms, critical pathways, NIH Stroke Scale, and other stroke tools should be available and used for each patient.
3. **Employ rapid triage protocol and stroke team notification:** Acute triage protocols facilitate the timely recognition of stroke and reduce time to treatment. Acute stroke teams enhance stroke care and should be activated as soon as there is hospital prenotification from EMS personnel of a stroke patient or the stroke patient is identified in the ED.
4. **Use a single-call activation system:** A single call should activate the entire stroke team.
5. **Attach a timer or clock to chart, clipboard, or patient bed:** Acute ischemic stroke care requires an accurate, timely, coordinated, and systematic evaluation of the patient. A universal clock visible to the healthcare providers is an enabling tool for improving the quality of care.
6. **Ensure EMS transfer directly to CT or MRI scanner:** Guided by prespecified protocols, providers can transport eligible stroke patients, if appropriate, from the ED triage area directly to the CT/MRI scanner for initial neurologic examination and brain imaging to determine tissue plasminogen activator eligibility, bypassing the ED bed.

7. **Rapidly acquire and interpret brain imaging:** It is essential to initiate a brain CT scan (or MRI) as soon as possible after patient arrival. Consider initial CT interpretation by a stroke neurologist, reserving advanced imaging for unclear cases only. Additional brain imaging may be acquired after alteplase consideration to determine the presence of an LVO and salvageable penumbra.
8. **Conduct rapid laboratory testing (including point-of-care testing if indicated):** When indicated, order laboratory tests such as glucose and testing for patients in whom coagulation parameters should be assessed because of suspicion of coagulopathy or warfarin treatment. International normalized ratio (prothrombin time)/partial thromboplastin time results should be available as quickly as possible and no later than 30 minutes after ED arrival.
9. **Prepare alteplase in advance:** Mix the drug and set up the bolus dose and 1-hour infusion pump as soon as a patient is recognized as a possible alteplase candidate, even before brain imaging.
10. **Provide rapid access and administration of intravenous alteplase:** Once eligibility has been determined and intracranial hemorrhage has been excluded, intravenous alteplase should be promptly administered without delay.
11. **Use a team-based approach:** The team approach based on standardized stroke pathways and protocols has proven to be effective in enhancing the number of eligible patients treated and reducing time to treatment in stroke.
12. **Provide prompt data feedback:** Accurately measuring and tracking prehospital times, door-to-needle times, IV alteplase and EVT treatment rates in eligible patients, other time intervals, and performance on other stroke performance/quality measures equip the stroke team to identify areas for improvement. A data monitoring and feedback system includes the use of the Get With The Guidelines-Stroke Patient Management Tool.

Immediate General and Neurologic Assessment

Table 7 show the steps by the hospital or stroke team in the ED or brain imaging suite (best practice is to bypass the ED and go straight to the brain imaging suite).

Table 7. Critical Actions in the Evaluation of Potential Acute Stroke

Step	Action
Activate stroke team	Activate stroke team upon EMS notification.
Obtain a CT brain scan or MRI scan	Prepare for emergent CT scan or MRI of brain upon arrival. Upon prehospital notification, order an emergent CT scan or MRI scan of the brain and have the patient taken directly to the CT/MRI suite. Have the CT/MRI read promptly by a qualified physician.
Meet stroke team	Stroke team meets EMS on arrival. Upon prehospital notification or arrival, activate the stroke team or arrange consultation with a stroke expert based on predetermined protocols.
Assess ABCs	Assess the ABCs and evaluate baseline vital signs; give oxygen if needed.
Obtain IV access	Obtain IV access and perform laboratory assessments. Do not let this delay obtaining a CT scan of the brain or administering alteplase.
Check glucose	Check glucose and promptly treat hypoglycemia (<60 mg/dL).
Obtain patient's history	Review patient history, medications, and procedures
Establish symptom onset	Establish time of symptom onset or last known normal
Perform physical and neurologic examinations	Perform physical exam and neurologic examination, including NIH Stroke Scale or Canadian Neurological Scale
Obtain a 12-lead ECG	Obtain a 12-lead ECG, which may identify a recent or ongoing AMI or arrhythmias (eg, atrial fibrillation) as a cause of embolic stroke. A small percentage of patients with acute stroke or transient ischemic attack have coexisting myocardial ischemia or other abnormalities. There is general agreement to recommend cardiac monitoring during the first 24 hours of evaluation in patients with acute ischemic stroke to detect atrial fibrillation and potentially life-threatening arrhythmias.

> Life-threatening arrhythmias can follow or accompany stroke, particularly intracerebral hemorrhage. If the patient is hemodynamically stable, treatment of non–life-threatening arrhythmias (bradycardia, VT, and atrioventricular [AV] conduction blocks) may not be necessary.
>
> ***Do not delay the CT/MRI scan to obtain the ECG.***

Immediate Neurologic Assessment by Hospital or Stroke Team

The stroke team, neurovascular consultant, or emergency physician does the following:
- Reviews the patient's history, medications, and procedures and establishes time of symptom onset or last known normal
- Performs a physical and neurologic examination, including the NIH Stroke Scale or Canadian Neurological Scale

The goal for neurologic assessment is within 20 minutes after the patient's arrival in the ED/brain imaging suite: "time is brain."

Establish Symptom Onset

Establishing the time of symptom onset or last known well may require interviewing out-of-hospital providers, witnesses, and family members.

Conduct Neurologic Examination

Assess the patient's neurologic deficits by using an established stroke scale, preferably the NIH Stroke Scale or Canadian Neurological Scale. The NIH Stroke Scale uses 15 items to assess and quantify neurologic deficits of a stroke patient. This is a validated measure of stroke severity based on a detailed neurologic examination.

Perform Brain Imaging (CT/MRI): Does Brain Imaging Show Hemorrhage?

A critical decision point in the assessment of the patient with acute stroke is the performance and interpretation of an NCCT/MRI to differentiate ischemic from hemorrhagic stroke. Assessment also includes identifying other structural abnormalities that may be responsible for the patient's symptoms or that represent contraindication to fibrinolytic therapy. The initial NCCT/MRI scan is the most important test for a patient with acute stroke.

- If an NCCT/MRI scan is not readily available, stabilize and promptly transfer the patient to a facility with this capability.
- The presence of intracranial hemorrhage is an absolute contraindication to alteplase and EVT.

Systems should be established so that brain-imaging studies can be performed within 20 minutes *after the patient arrives in the ED or brain imaging suite.*

Decision Point: Hemorrhage or No Hemorrhage

Additional imaging techniques such as CT perfusion, CT angiography, or MRI scans of patients with suspected stroke should be promptly interpreted by a physician skilled in neuroimaging interpretation. Obtaining these additional studies should not delay initiation of IV alteplase in eligible patients. The presence of hemorrhage vs no hemorrhage determines the next steps in treatment.

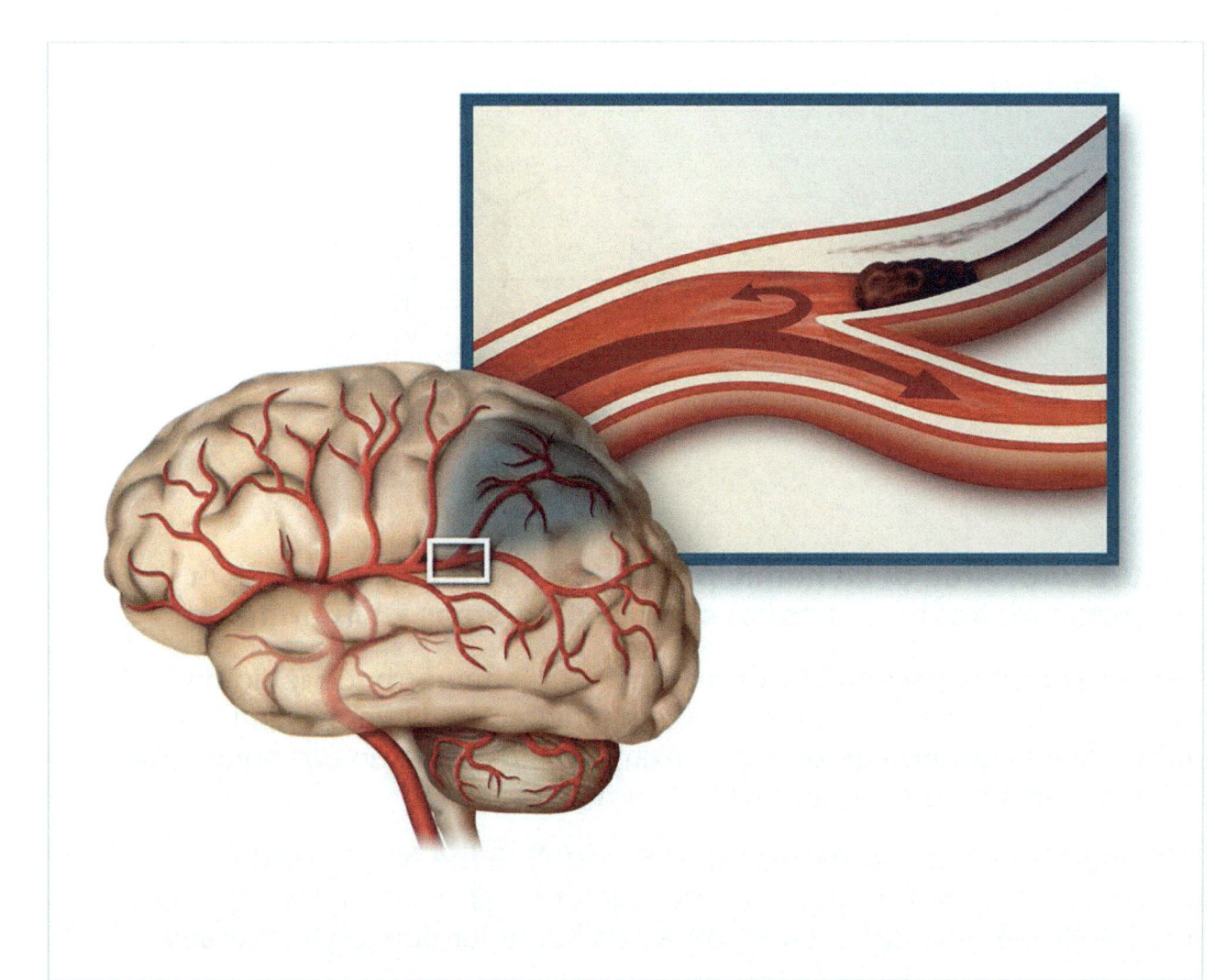

Figure 25A. Occlusion in a cerebral artery by a thrombus. A, Area of infarction surrounding immediate site and distal portion of brain tissue after occlusion.

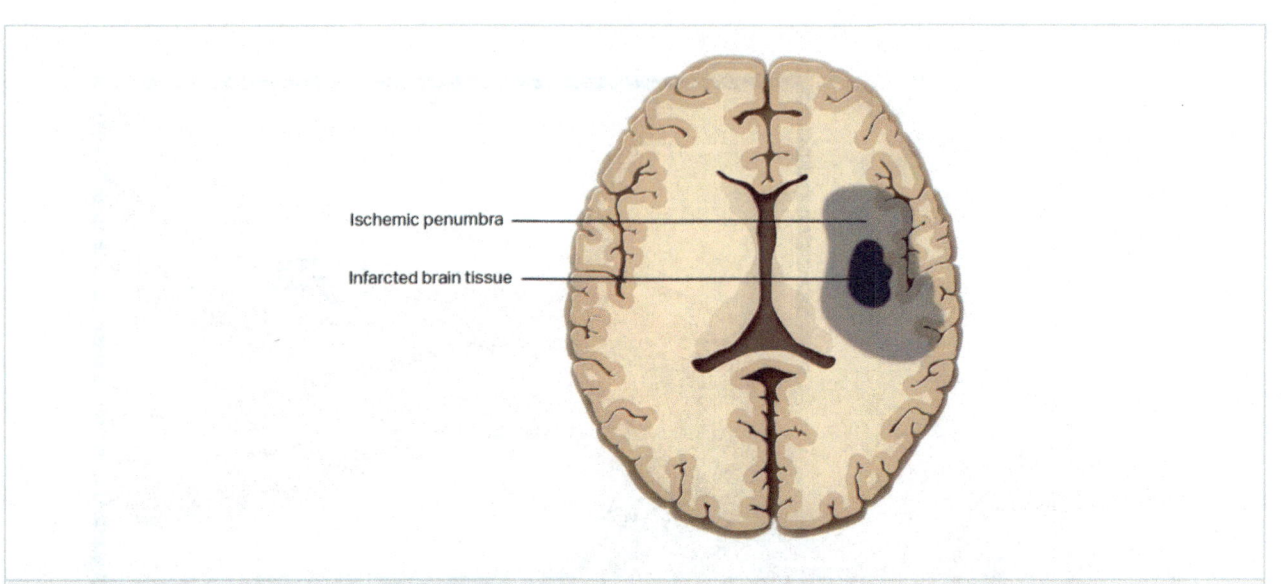

Figure 25B. Area of ischemic penumbra (ischemic, but not yet infarcted [dead] brain tissue) surrounding areas of infarction.

Hemorrhage is present (Steps 5 and 13). If hemorrhage is noted on the NCCT/MRI scan, the patient is not a candidate for fibrinolytics. Initiate intracranial hemorrhage protocol. Admit to the stroke unit or neurologic ICU, or transfer to a higher level of care.

Hemorrhage is not present (Step 6 and 8). If the NCCT/MRI scan shows no evidence of hemorrhage and no sign of other abnormality (eg, tumor, recent stroke), the patient may be a candidate for fibrinolytic therapy.

For patients with a suspected LVO, additional imaging is required. CT angiography will determine if an LVO is present. Less than 6 hours from symptom onset, penumbral imaging is not required. More than 6 hours from symptom onset, penumbral imaging (CT perfusion or multimodal MRI) is required to identify patients with salvageable penumbra. Advanced imaging, including perfusion imaging, should not delay administration of IV alteplase.

Figures 25A and B show an ischemic penumbra that is alive but dysfunctional because of altered membrane potentials. The dysfunction is potentially reversible. The goal of current stroke reperfusion treatments is to minimize the area of permanent brain infarction by preventing the areas of reversible brain ischemia in the penumbra from transforming into larger areas of irreversible brain infarction.

Fibrinolytic Therapy

Studies have demonstrated that there is a higher likelihood of good to excellent functional outcome when alteplase is given to adults with acute ischemic stroke within 3 hours after onset of symptoms, or within 4.5 hours after onset of symptoms for selected patients. Evidence from prospective randomized studies in adults also documents a greater likelihood of benefit the earlier treatment begins.

Table 8. Inclusion and Exclusion Characteristics of Patients With Ischemic Stroke Who Could Be Treated With Alteplase Within 3 Hours After Symptom Onset and Extended Window for Select Patient From 3 to 4.5 Hours*	
Indications (COR 1)	
Within 3 hours[‡]	IV alteplase (0.9 mg/kg, maximum dose 90 mg over 60 minutes with initial 10% of dose given as bolus over 1 minute) is recommended for selected patients who may be treated within 3 hours of ischemic stroke symptom onset or patient last known well or at baseline state. Physicians should review the criteria outlined in this table to determine patient eligibility.[‡] (COR 1; LOE A)
Within 3 hours—Age	For otherwise medically eligible patients ≥18 years of age, IV alteplase administration within 3 hours is equally recommended for patients ≤80 and >80 years of age.[‡] (COR 1; LOE A)
Within 3 hours—Severe stroke	For severe stroke, IV alteplase is indicated within 3 hours from symptom onset of ischemic stroke. Despite increased risk of hemorrhagic transformation, there is still proven clinical benefit for patients with severe stroke symptoms.[‡] (COR 1; LOE A)
Within 3 hours—Mild disabling stroke	For otherwise eligible patients with mild but disabling stroke symptoms, IV alteplase is recommended for patients who can be treated within 3 hours of ischemic stroke symptom onset or patient last known well or at baseline state. (COR 1; LOE B-R)[§]
BP	IV alteplase is recommended in patients with BP <185/110 mm Hg and in those patients whose BP can be lowered safely to this level with

	antihypertensive agents, with the physician assessing the stability of the BP before starting IV alteplase.‡ (COR 1; LOE B-NR)‖
CT	IV alteplase administration is recommended in the setting of early ischemic changes on NCCT of mild to moderate extent (other than frank hypodensity).‡ (COR 1; LOE A)

The AHA/ASA 2019 Guidelines for the Early Management of Patients With Acute Ischemic Stroke recommends giving IV alteplase to patients with acute ischemic stroke who meet the current eligibility criteria, if it is given by

- Physicians using a clearly defined institutional protocol
- A knowledgeable interdisciplinary team familiar with stroke care
- An institution with a commitment to quality stroke care

Evaluate for Fibrinolytic Therapy

If the CT/MRI scan is negative for hemorrhage, the patient may be a candidate for fibrinolytic therapy. Immediately perform further eligibility and risk stratification:

Additional recommendations for treatment with IV alteplase for patients with AIS (COR 2a)	And (COR 2b)
Wake-up and unknown time of onset	IV alteplase (0.9 mg/kg, maximum dose 90 mg over 60 minutes with initial 10% of dose given as bolus over 1 minute) administered within 4.5 hours of stroke symptom recognition can be beneficial in patients with AIS who awake with stroke symptoms or have unclear time of onset >4.5 hours from last known well or at baseline state and who have a DW-MRI lesion smaller than one third of the MCA territory and no visible signal change on FLAIR. (COR 2a; LOE B-R)§
Early improvement	IV alteplase treatment is reasonable for patients who present with moderate to severe ischemic stroke and demonstrate early improvement but remain moderately impaired and potentially disabled in the judgment of the examiner.‡ (COR 2a; LOE A)

| Stroke mimics | The risk of symptomatic intracranial hemorrhage in the stroke mimic population is quite low; thus, starting IV alteplase is probably recommended in preference over delaying treatment to pursue additional diagnostic studies.‡ (COR 2a; LOE B-NR)‖ |

Contraindications (COR 3: No Benefit)*	And (COR 3: Harm)
0 to 4.5-hour window—Mild nondisabling stroke	For otherwise eligible patients with mild nondisabling stroke (NIHSS score 0–5), IV alteplase is not recommended for patients who could be treated within 3 and 4.5 hours of ischemic stroke symptom onset or patient last known well or at baseline state. (COR 3: No Benefit, LOE B-R)§
CT	There remains insufficient evidence to identify a threshold of hypoattenuation severity or extent that affects treatment response to alteplase. However, administering IV alteplase to patients whose CT brain imaging exhibits extensive regions of clear hypoattenuation is not recommended. These patients have a poor prognosis despite IV alteplase, and severe hypoattenuation defined as obvious hypodensity represents irreversible injury.‡ (COR 3: No Benefit; LOE A)
ICH	IV alteplase should not be administered to a patient whose CT reveals an acute intracranial hemorrhage.‡ (COR 3: Harm; LOE C-EO)‖
Ischemic stroke within 3 months	Use of IV alteplase in patients presenting with AIS who have had a prior ischemic stroke within 3 months may be harmful.‡ (COR 3: Harm; LOE B-NR)‖
Severe head trauma within 3 months	In AIS patients with recent severe head trauma (within 3 months), IV alteplase is contraindicated.‡ (COR 3: Harm; LOE C-EO)‖
Acute head trauma	Given the possibility of bleeding complications from the underlying severe head trauma, IV alteplase should not be administered in posttraumatic infarction that occurs during the acute in-hospital phase.‡ (COR 3: Harm; LOE C-EO)‖ (Recommendation wording modified to match COR 3 stratifications.)
Intracranial/intraspinal surgery within 3 months	For patients with AIS and a history of intracranial/spinal surgery within the prior 3 months, IV alteplase is potentially harmful.‡ (COR 3: Harm; LOE C-EO)‖
History of intracranial hemorrhage	IV alteplase administration in patients who have a history of intracranial hemorrhage is potentially harmful.‡ (COR 3: Harm; LOE C-EO)‖

Subarachnoid hemorrhage	IV alteplase is contraindicated in patients presenting with symptoms and signs most consistent with an SAH.‡ (COR 3: Harm; LOE C-EO)‖
GI malignancy or GI bleed within 21 days	Patients with a structural GI malignancy or recent bleeding event within 21 days of their stroke event should be considered high risk, and IV alteplase administration is potentially harmful.‡ (COR 3: Harm; LOE C-EO)‖
Coagulopathy	The safety and efficacy of IV alteplase for acute stroke patients with platelets <100 000/mm^3, INR >1.7, aPTT >40 seconds, or PT >15 seconds are unknown, and IV alteplase should not be administered.‡ (COR 3: Harm; LOE C-EO)‖

(In patients without history of thrombocytopenia, treatment with IV alteplase can be initiated before availability of platelet count but should be discontinued if platelet count is <100 000/mm^3. In patients without recent use of OACs or heparin, treatment with IV alteplase can be initiated before availability of coagulation test results but should be discontinued if INR is >1.7 or PT is abnormally elevated by local laboratory standards.) (Recommendation wording modified to match COR 3 stratifications.) |
| **LMWH** | IV alteplase should not be administered to patients who have received a full treatment dose of LMWH within the previous 24 hours.‡ (COR 3: Harm; LOE B-NR)§‖

(Recommendation wording modified to match COR 3 stratifications.) |
| **Thrombin inhibitors or factor Xa inhibitors** | The use of IV alteplase in patients taking direct thrombin inhibitors or direct factor Xa inhibitors has not been firmly established but may be harmful.‡ (COR 3: Harm; LOE C-EO)‖ IV alteplase should not be administered to patients taking direct thrombin inhibitors or direct factor Xa inhibitors unless laboratory tests such as aPTT, INR, platelet count, ecarin clotting time, thrombin time, or appropriate direct factor Xa activity assays are normal or the patient has not received a dose of these agents for >48 hours (assuming normal renal metabolizing function). |

	(Alteplase could be considered when appropriate laboratory tests such as aPTT, INR, ecarin clotting time, thrombin time, or direct factor Xa activity assays are normal or when the patient has not taken a dose of these ACs for >48 hours and renal function is normal.) (Recommendation wording modified to match COR 3 stratifications.)
Concomitant Abciximab	Abciximab should not be administered concurrently with IV alteplase. (COR 3: Harm; LOE B-R)§

- If the CT/MRI scan shows no hemorrhage, the probability of acute ischemic stroke remains. *Review inclusion and exclusion criteria for IV fibrinolytic therapy (Table 8) and repeat the neurologic exam (NIH Stroke Scale or Canadian Neurological Scale).*
- If the patient's neurologic function is rapidly improving to normal, fibrinolytics may be unnecessary.

Alteplase Considerations in the 3- to 4.5-Hour Time Window in Addition to Those in the 0- to 3-Hour Window*

Indications (COR 1)	
3-4.5 hours‡	IV alteplase (0.9 mg/kg, maximum dose 90 mg over 60 min with initial 10% of dose given as bolus over 1 min) is also recommended for selected patients who can be treated within 3 and 4.5 hours of ischemic stroke symptom onset or patient last known well. Physicians should review the criteria outlined in this table to determine patient eligibility.‡ (COR 1; LOE B-R)‖
3-4.5 hours–Age	IV alteplase treatment in the 3- to 4.5-hour time window is recommended for those patients ≤80 years of age, without a history of both diabetes mellitus and prior stroke, NIHSS score ≤25, not taking any OACs, and without imaging evidence of ischemic injury involving more than one third of the MCA territory.‡ (COR 1; LOE B-R)‖
Additional recommendations for treatment with IV alteplase for patients with AIS (COR 2a)	**And (COR 2b)**
3-4.5 hours–Age	For patients >80 years of age presenting in the 3- to 4.5-hour window, IV alteplase is safe and can be as effective as in younger patients.‡ (COR 2a; LOE B-NR)‖

3-4.5 hours—Diabetes mellitus and prior stroke	In AIS patients with prior stroke and diabetes mellitus presenting in the 3- to 4.5- hour window, IV alteplase may be as effective as treatment in the 0- to 3-hour window and may be a reasonable option.‡ (COR 2b; LOE B-NR)‖
3-4.5 hours—Severe stroke	The benefit of IV alteplase between 3 and 4.5 hours from symptom onset for patients with very severe stroke symptoms (NIHSS score >25) is uncertain.‡ (COR 2b; LOE C-LD)‖
3-4.5 hours—Mild disabling stroke	For otherwise eligible patients with mild disabling stroke, IV alteplase may be reasonable for patients who can be treated within 3 and 4.5 hours of ischemic stroke symptom onset or patient last known well or at baseline state. (COR 2b; LOE B-NR)§

Abbreviations: AC, anticoagulants; AIS, acute ischemic stroke; aPTT, activated partial thromboplastin time; BP, blood pressure; COR, Class of Recommendation; CT, computed tomography; DW-MRI, diffusion-weighted magnetic resonance imaging; FLAIR, fluid-attenuated inversion recovery; GI, gastrointestinal; ICH, intracerebral hemorrhage; INR, international normalized ratio; IV, intravenous; LMWH, low-molecular-weight heparin; LOE, Level of Evidence; MCA, middle cerebral artery; NCCT, noncontrast computed tomography; NIHSS, National Institutes of Health Stroke Scale; OAC, oral anticoagulant; PT, prothromboplastin time.

*The relative contraindications are abbreviated. Modified from Table 8 in the "Guidelines for the Early Management of Patients With Acute Ischemic Stroke: 2019 Update to the 2018 Guidelines for the Early Management of Acute Ischemic Stroke: a Guideline for Healthcare Professionals from the American Heart Association/American Stroke Association."[8] Please see Table 8 for a full listing of specific considerations.

‡When uncertain, the time of onset time should be considered the time when the patient was last known to be normal or at baseline neurological condition.

‡Recommendation unchanged or reworded for clarity from 2015 IV Alteplase. See Table XCV in online Data Supplement 1 for original wording.

§See also the text of these guidelines for additional information on these recommendations.

‖LOE amended to conform with American College of Cardiology/AHA 2015 Recommendation Classification System.

COR amended to conform with American College of Cardiology/AHA 2015 Recommendation Classification System.

Unless otherwise specified, these eligibility recommendations apply to patients who can be treated within 0 to 4.5 hours of ischemic stroke symptom onset or patient last known well or at baseline state.

Clinicians should also be informed of the indications and contraindications from local regulatory agencies (for current information from the US Food and Drug Administration refer to http://www.accessdata.fda.gov/drugsatfda_docs/label/2015/103172s5203lbl.pdf).

For a detailed discussion of this topic and evidence supporting these recommendations, refer to the AHA scientific statement on the rationale for inclusion and exclusion criteria for IV alteplase in AIS.

Potential Adverse Effects

As with all drugs, fibrinolytics have potential adverse effects. At this point, weigh the patient's risk for adverse events against the potential benefit and discuss with the patient and family.
- Confirm that no exclusion criteria are present (Table 8).
- Consider risks and benefits.
- Be prepared to monitor and treat any potential complications.
- The major complication of IV alteplase for stroke is intracranial hemorrhage. Other bleeding complications may occur and may range from minor to major. Angioedema and transient hypotension may occur.

Patient Is a Candidate for Fibrinolytic Therapy

If the patient remains a candidate for fibrinolytic therapy (Step 8), discuss the risks and potential benefits with the patient or family if available. After this discussion, if the patient or family members decide to proceed with fibrinolytic therapy, give the patient alteplase. Begin your institution's stroke alteplase protocol, often called a *postalteplase pathway of care*.

Alteplase is considered the standard of care for eligible patients with acute ischemic stroke. Because of this treatment's proven benefit and the need to expedite it, healthcare providers are justified to proceed with IV thrombolysis in an otherwise eligible adult patient with a disabling acute ischemic stroke in situations where that patient cannot provide consent (eg, due to aphasia or confusion) and a legally authorized representative is not immediately available to provide proxy consent.

Do not administer anticoagulants or antiplatelet treatment for 24 hours after administration of alteplase, typically until a follow-up CT scan at 24 hours shows no intracranial hemorrhage.

Extended IV Alteplase Window: 3 to 4.5 Hours

Treatment of carefully selected patients with acute ischemic stroke with IV alteplase between 3 and 4.5 hours after onset of symptoms has also been shown to improve clinical outcome, although the degree of clinical benefit is smaller than that achieved with treatment within 3 hours. Data supporting treatment in this time window come from a large, randomized trial (ECASS-3 [European Cooperative Acute Stroke Study]) that specifically enrolled patients between 3 and 4.5 hours after symptom onset, as well as from a meta-analysis of prior trials.

The use of IV alteplase within the 3- to 4.5-hour window has not been approved by the US Food and Drug Administration (FDA), although it is recommended by the 2019 AHA acute ischemic stroke guidelines for those who meet the ECASS-3 eligibility criteria (Table 8).

Endovascular Therapy

Substantial new high-quality research on the clinical efficacy of endovascular treatments of acute ischemic stroke was published in 2015. In light of that research, although IV alteplase remains as a first-line treatment, the AHA now recommends EVT for select patients with acute ischemic stroke due to an LVO.

As with fibrinolytic therapy, patients must meet inclusion criteria to be considered for this treatment. Similarly, better clinical outcomes are associated with reduced times from symptom onset to reperfusion, but these new treatment options offer the added benefit of expanding the treatment window up to 24 hours from the onset of symptoms. Once you determine the patient is an EVT candidate, rapidly transport to cath lab or transfer to an EVT-capable center, followed by admittance to a neurologic ICU.

Mechanical Thrombectomy With Stent Retrievers

Mechanical thrombectomy has been demonstrated to provide clinical benefit in selected patients with acute ischemic stroke.

Patients arriving within 6 hours after symptom onset should receive EVT with a stent retriever if they meet all of the following criteria:
- Prestroke modified Rankin Score of 0 to 1
- Causative LVO of the internal carotid artery or proximal middle cerebral artery demonstrated on cerebrovascular imaging
- Age 18 years or older
- NIH Stroke Scale score of 6 or greater
- Alberta Stroke Program Early CT Score (ASPECTS) of 6 or greater (ASPECTS is an early, reliable tool that uses a 10-point quantitative topographic CT scan score to determine early ischemic changes.)
- Treatment can be initiated (groin puncture) within 6 hours after symptom onset or last known normal

In selected patients with acute ischemic stroke within 6 to 16 hours after last known normal who have LVO in the anterior circulation and meet other DAWN (Clinical Mismatch in the Triage of Wake Up and Late Presenting Strokes Undergoing Neurointervention With Trevo) or DEFUSE 3 (Endovascular Therapy Following Imaging Evaluation for Ischemic Stroke) eligibility criteria, mechanical thrombectomy is recommended.

In selected patients with acute ischemic stroke within 16 to 24 hours after last known normal who have LVO in the anterior circulation and meet other DAWN eligibility criteria, mechanical thrombectomy is reasonable.

Intra-Arterial Alteplase

Initial treatment with intra-arterial thrombolysis is beneficial for carefully selected patients with major ischemic strokes of less than 6 hours' duration caused by occlusions of the middle cerebral artery. Regarding the previous recommendations for intra-arterial thrombolysis, those data were derived from clinical trials that no longer reflect current practice, including the use of fibrinolytic drugs that are not available. A clinically beneficial dose of intra-arterial alteplase is not established, and alteplase does not have FDA approval for intra-arterial use. As a consequence, mechanical thrombectomy with stent retrievers is recommended over intra-arterial thrombolysis as first-line therapy. Intra-arterial thrombolysis initiated within 6 hours after stroke onset in carefully selected patients who have contraindications to the use of IV alteplase might be considered, but the consequences are unknown.

Stroke Systems of Care

Recent clinical trials suggest that all patients eligible for EVT should be considered for that treatment in addition to IV alteplase. Regional stroke systems of care for acute ischemic stroke need to be in place so that eligible patients can be quickly transported from the field per local designation protocols or transferred from non-EVT centers to comprehensive or thrombectomy-capable stroke centers that offer these treatments.

Begin General Stroke Care

After being considered for reperfusion strategies, all patients should be placed on an acute stroke pathway. The general care of all patients with stroke includes the following actions:
- Begin acute stroke pathway.
- Assess ABCs, and give oxygen if needed.
- Monitor blood glucose.
- Monitor blood pressure.
- Monitor temperature.
- Perform dysphagia screening.
- Monitor for complications of stroke and fibrinolytic therapy.
- Transfer to a higher level of care (EVT, neurological ICU) if indicated.

Begin Stroke Pathway

Admit patients to a stroke unit (if available) for careful observation, including monitoring of blood pressure and neurologic status. If neurologic status worsens, order an emergent CT scan. Determine if cerebral edema or hemorrhage is the cause; consult neurosurgery as appropriate.

Additional stroke care includes support of the airway, oxygenation, ventilation, and nutrition. Provide normal saline to maintain intravascular volume (eg, approximately 75 to 100 mL/h) if needed.

Monitor Blood Glucose

Hyperglycemia is associated with worse clinical outcome in patients with acute ischemic stroke. Although there is no direct evidence that active glucose control improves clinical outcome, here is evidence that insulin treatment of hyperglycemia in other critically ill patients improves survival rates. For this reason, consider giving IV or subcutaneous insulin to lower blood glucose in patients with acute ischemic stroke when the serum glucose level is greater than 180 mg/dL.

Monitor for Complications of Stroke and Fibrinolytic Therapy

Prophylaxis for seizures is not recommended. But treatment of acute seizures followed by administration of anticonvulsants to prevent further seizures is recommended. Monitor the patient for signs of increased intracranial pressure such as increasing lethargy or decreasing level of consciousness or increased blood pressure with a concurrent decrease in heart rate. Continue to control blood pressure to reduce the potential risk of bleeding.

Table 9. Options to Treat Arterial Hypertension in Patients With Acute Ischemic Stroke Who Are Candidates for Emergency Reperfusion Therapy[8]

COR 2b	LOE C-EO
Patient otherwise eligible for emergency reperfusion therapy except that BP is >185/110 mm Hg: • Labetalol 10-20 mg IV over 1-2 minutes, may repeat 1 time; or • Nicardipine 5 mg/h IV, titrate up by 2.5 mg/h every 5-15 minutes, maximum 15 mg/h; when desired BP reached, adjust to maintain proper BP limits; or • Clevidipine 1-2 mg/h IV, titrate by doubling the dose every 2-5 minutes until desired BP reached; maximum 21 mg/h • Other agents (eg, hydralazine, enalaprilat) may also be considered If BP is not maintained ≤185/110 mm Hg, do not administer alteplase.	
Management of BP during and after alteplase or other emergency reperfusion therapy to maintain BP ≤180/105 mm Hg: • Monitor BP every 15 minutes for 2 hours from the start of alteplase therapy, then every 30 minutes for 6 hours, and then every hour for 16 hours.	
If systolic BP >180-230 mm Hg or diastolic BP >105-120 mm Hg: • Labetalol 10 mg IV followed by continuous IV infusion 2-8 mg/min; or	

- Nicardipine 5 mg/h IV, titrate up to desired effect by 2.5 mg/h every 5-15 minutes, maximum 15 mg/h; or
- Clevidipine 1-2 mg/h IV, titrate by doubling the dose every 2-5 minutes until desired BP reached; maximum 21 mg/h

If BP not controlled or diastolic BP >140 mm Hg, consider IV sodium nitroprusside.

Hypertension Management in Alteplase Candidates

Although management of hypertension in the stroke patient is controversial, patients who are candidates for fibrinolytic therapy should have their blood pressure controlled to lower the risk of intracerebral hemorrhage after administration of alteplase. General guidelines for the management of hypertension are outlined in Table 9.

Abbreviations: AIS, acute ischemic stroke; BP, blood pressure; COR, Class of Recommendation; IV, intravenous; LOE, Level of Evidence.

Different treatment options may be appropriate in patients who have comorbid conditions that may benefit from rapid reductions in BP, such as acute coronary heart failure, aortic dissection, or preeclampsia/eclampsia. Data derived from Jauch et al.[9]

If a patient is eligible for fibrinolytic therapy, blood pressure must be 185 mm Hg or less systolic and 110 mm Hg or less diastolic to limit the risk of bleeding complications. Because the maximum interval from the onset of stroke until effective treatment of stroke with alteplase is limited, most patients with sustained hypertension above these levels will not be eligible for IV alteplase.

Managing arterial hypertension in patients not undergoing reperfusion strategies remains challenging. Data to guide recommendations for treatment are inconclusive or conflicting. Many patients have spontaneous declines in blood pressure during the first 24 hours after onset of stroke. Until more definitive data are available, the benefit of treating arterial hypertension in the setting of acute ischemic stroke is not well established (Class 2b; Level of Evidence C).[9] Patients who have malignant hypertension or other medical indications for aggressive treatment of blood pressure should be treated accordingly (revised from the previous guideline).[10]

Bradycardia

Overview

Bradycardia is generally defined as any rhythm disorder with a heart rate less than 60/min but for assessment and management of a patient with symptomatic bradycardia, it is typically defined as having a heart rate less than 50/min.

Managing bradycardia requires
- Differentiating between signs and symptoms caused by the slow rate vs those that are unrelated
- Correctly diagnosing the presence and type of atrioventricular (AV) block
- Using atropine as the drug intervention of first choice
- Deciding when to initiate transcutaneous pacing (TCP)
- Deciding when to start epinephrine or dopamine to maintain heart rate and blood pressure
- Knowing when to seek expert consultation about complicated rhythm interpretation, drugs, or management decisions or when to consider transvenous pacing
- Knowing the techniques and cautions for using TCP

Rhythms for Bradycardia
- Sinus bradycardia
- First-degree AV block
- Second-degree AV block: block of some, but not all, atrial impulses before they reach the ventricles. This block can be further classified as Mobitz type I or Mobitz type II second-degree AV block.
    - –Mobitz type I AV block:
        - Also known as *Wenckebach phenomenon*, typically occurs at the AV node. It is characterized by successive prolongation of the PR interval until an atrial impulse is not conducted to the ventricles (Figure 26B). The P wave corresponding to that atrial impulse is not followed by a QRS complex. The cycle of progressive lengthening of the PR interval until failure of conduction of the atrial impulse to the ventricles often repeats.
    - –Mobitz type II second-degree AV block (Figure 26C):

- Occurs below the level of the AV node. It is characterized by intermittent nonconduction of P waves (atrial impulses to the ventricle) with a constant PR interval on conducted beats. There can be a consistent ratio of atrial to ventricular depolarizations, eg, 2 P waves to 1 QRS complex.
- Third-degree AV block

You should know the major AV blocks because important treatment decisions are based on the type of block (Figure 26). Complete (or third-degree) AV block is generally the most clinically significant block because it is most likely to cause cardiovascular collapse and require immediate pacing. Recognizing a stable bradycardia due to AV block is a primary goal, and recognizing the type of AV block is secondary.

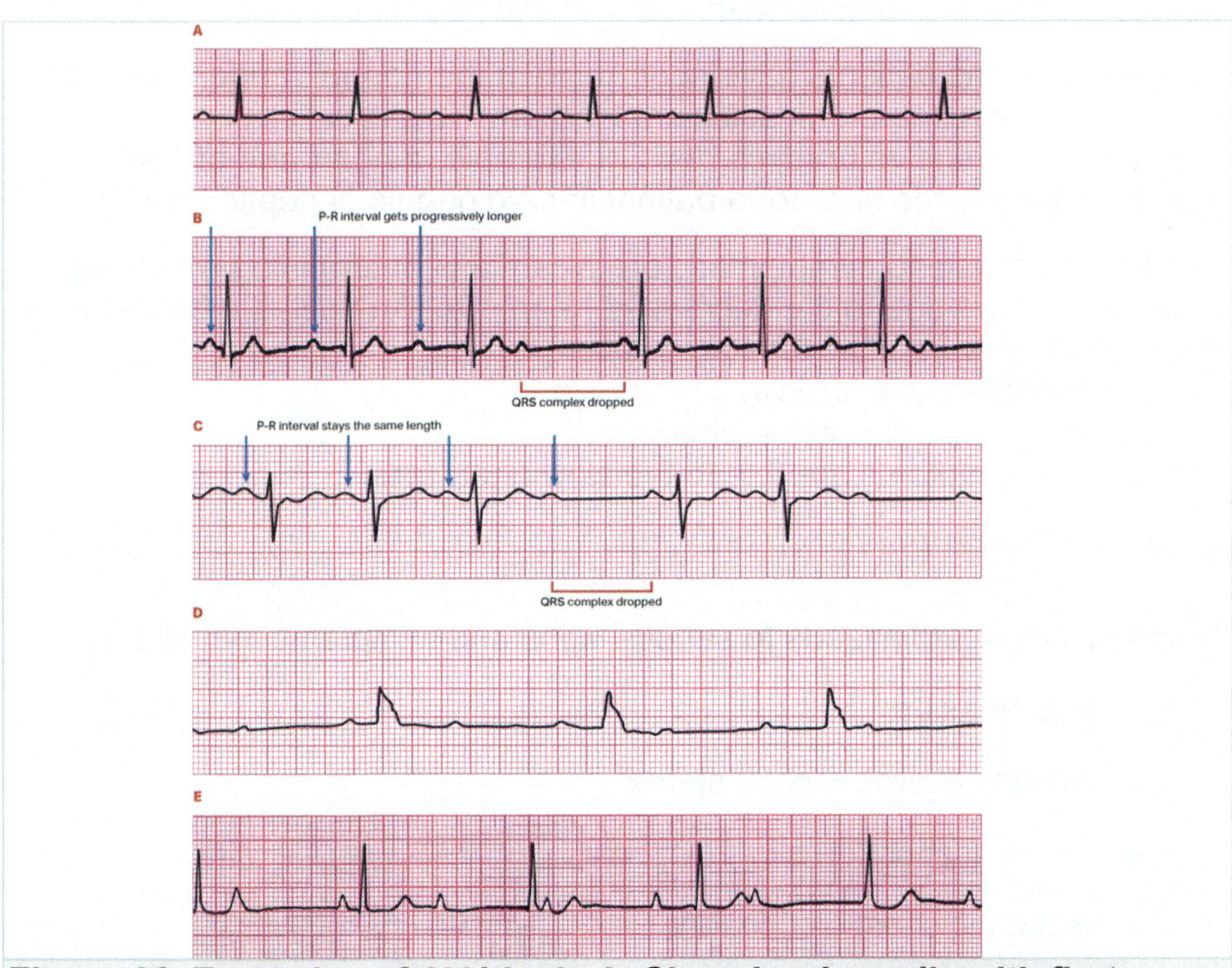

Figure 26. Examples of AV block. A, Sinus bradycardia with first-degree AV block. B, Second-degree AV block type I. C, Second-degree AV block type II. D, Complete AV block with a ventricular escape

pacemaker (wide QRS: 0.12 to 0.14 second). E, Third-degree AV block with a junctional escape pacemaker (narrow QRS: less than 0.12 second).

Drugs for Bradycardia

Drugs for bradycardia include
- Atropine
- Dopamine (infusion)
- Epinephrine (infusion)

Symptomatic Bradycardia

Bradycardia may have multiple causes, including some that are physiologic and require no assessment or therapy. For example, a healthy, well-trained athlete may have a resting heart rate less than 50/min.

In contrast, some patients have heart rates in the normal range, but these rates are inappropriate or insufficient for them. This is called a *functional* or *relative bradycardia*. For example, a heart rate of 70/min may be relatively too slow for a patient in cardiogenic or septic shock.

The key to managing symptomatic bradycardia is determining which signs or symptoms are due to the decreased heart rate. An unstable bradycardia exists clinically when 3 criteria are present:
1. The heart rate is slow.
2. The patient has symptoms.
3. The symptoms are due to the slow heart rate.

Signs and Symptoms

Unstable bradycardia leads to serious signs and symptoms that include

- Hypotension
- Acutely altered mental status
- Signs of shock
- Ischemic chest discomfort
- Acute heart failure
-

Managing Bradycardia: The Bradycardia Algorithm

The Adult Bradycardia Algorithm (Figure 27) outlines the steps for assessing and managing a patient who presents with unstable bradycardia with a pulse. Implementing this algorithm begins with identifying bradycardia (Step 1), which is typically when the heart rate is less than 50/min. First steps include the components of the BLS Assessment and the Primary Assessment.

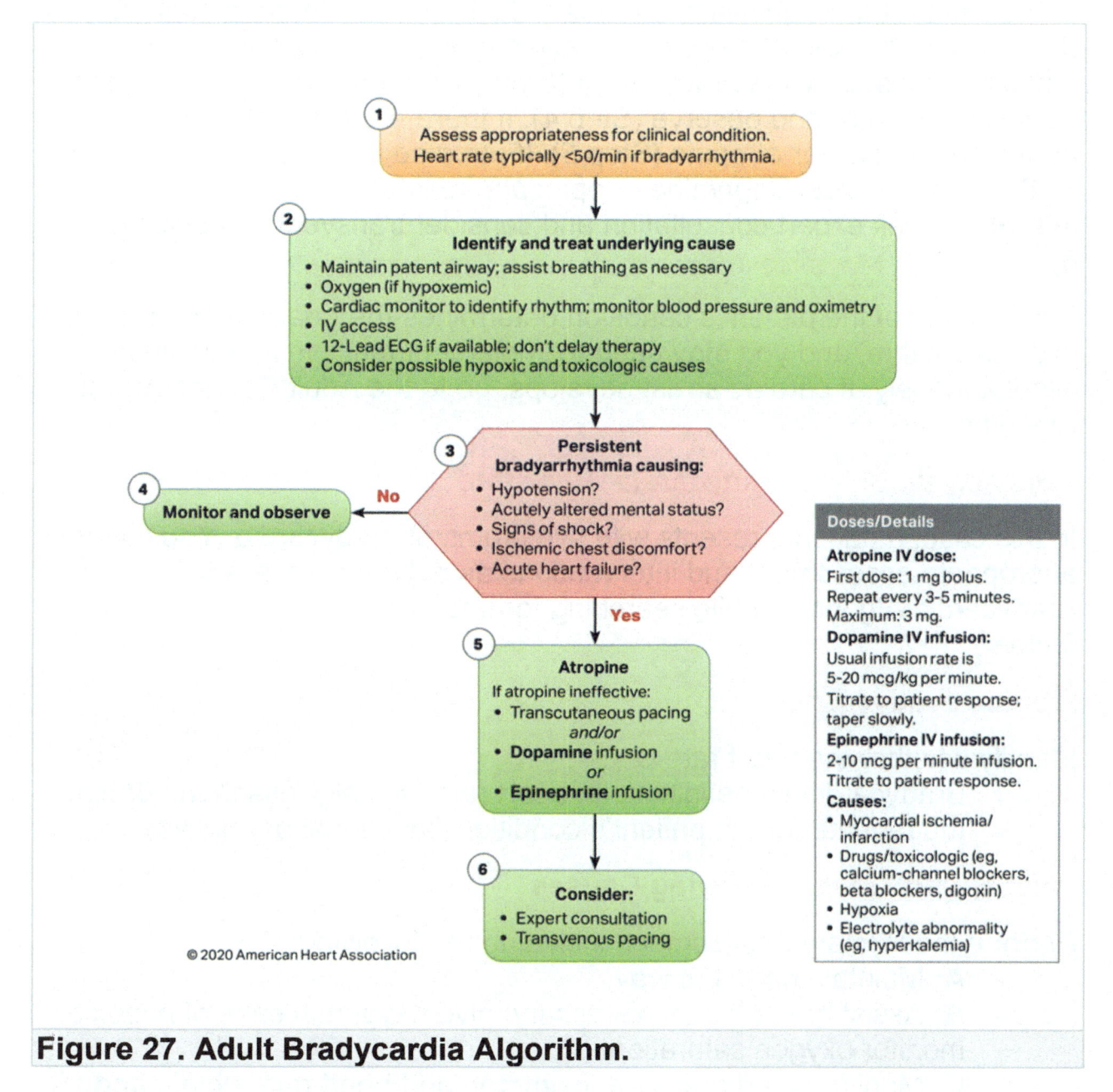

1. Assess appropriateness for clinical condition. Heart rate typically <50/min if bradyarrhythmia.

2. Identify and treat underlying cause
- Maintain patent airway; assist breathing as necessary
- Oxygen (if hypoxemic)
- Cardiac monitor to identify rhythm; monitor blood pressure and oximetry
- IV access
- 12-Lead ECG if available; don't delay therapy
- Consider possible hypoxic and toxicologic causes

3. Persistent bradyarrhythmia causing:
- Hypotension?
- Acutely altered mental status?
- Signs of shock?
- Ischemic chest discomfort?
- Acute heart failure?

4. No → **Monitor and observe**

5. Atropine
If atropine ineffective:
- Transcutaneous pacing and/or
- Dopamine infusion or
- Epinephrine infusion

6. Consider:
- Expert consultation
- Transvenous pacing

Doses/Details

Atropine IV dose:
First dose: 1 mg bolus.
Repeat every 3-5 minutes.
Maximum: 3 mg.

Dopamine IV infusion:
Usual infusion rate is 5-20 mcg/kg per minute.
Titrate to patient response; taper slowly.

Epinephrine IV infusion:
2-10 mcg per minute infusion.
Titrate to patient response.

Causes:
- Myocardial ischemia/infarction
- Drugs/toxicologic (eg, calcium-channel blockers, beta blockers, digoxin)
- Hypoxia
- Electrolyte abnormality (eg, hyperkalemia)

© 2020 American Heart Association

Figure 27. Adult Bradycardia Algorithm.

Identify and treat underlying causes (Step 2):

- Maintain patent airway; assist breathing as necessary.
- Give oxygen (if hypoxemic).
- Use a cardiac monitor to identify rhythm. Monitor blood pressure and oximetry.
- Establish IV access.
- Obtain a 12-lead ECG if available (Step 2).
- Consider possible hypoxic and toxicologic causes.

In the differential diagnosis, the primary decision point in the algorithm is to determine if the patient has signs or symptoms of poor perfusion and if these are caused by the bradycardia (Step 3). If there are no signs of poor perfusion, monitor and observe (Step 4). If there are signs of poor perfusion, administer atropine (Step 5). If atropine is ineffective, prepare for TCP and/or consider dopamine or epinephrine infusion (Step 5). If indicated, seek expert consultation and consider transvenous pacing (Step 6).

The severity of the patient's condition determines the treatment sequence in the algorithm, and you may need to implement multiple interventions simultaneously. If cardiac arrest develops, go to the Adult Cardiac Arrest Algorithm.

Applying the Adult Bradycardia Algorithm

In this case, a patient presents with symptoms of bradycardia. You conduct appropriate assessment and interventions as outlined in the Adult Bradycardia Algorithm while searching for and treating possible contributing factors.

Identify Bradycardia

Identify whether the heart rate is
- Bradycardia by definition, ie, heart rate typically less than 50/min
- Inadequate for the patient's condition (functional or relative)

Identify and Treat Underlying Causes

Perform the Primary Assessment, including the following:
- **A:** Maintain patent airway.
- **B:** Assist breathing as necessary; give oxygen in case of hypoxia; monitor oxygen saturation.
- **C:** Monitor blood pressure, oximetry, and heart rate; obtain and review a 12-lead ECG; establish IV access.

- **D and E:** Conduct a problem-focused history and physical examination; search for possible hypoxic and toxicologic causes, and treat possible contributing factors.

Critical Concepts: Bradycardia
- *Bradycardia can be a sign of life-threatening hypoxia.*
- *Bradycardia associated with hypertension can be a sign of a life-threatening increase in intracranial pressure, especially in the setting of stroke or brain injury.*

Are Signs or Symptoms Caused by Persistent Bradyarrhythmia

Look for these adverse signs and symptoms of the bradycardia:
- **Symptoms: acutely altered mental status, signs of shock, ischemic chest discomfort**
- **Signs: hypotension, acute heart failure**
- Are the signs and symptoms related to the slow heart rate?

Sometimes the symptom is not due to the bradycardia. For example, hypotension associated with bradycardia may be due to myocardial dysfunction rather than the bradycardia. Keep this in mind when you reassess the patient's response to treatment.

Critical Concepts: Bradycardia
The key clinical question is whether the bradycardia is causing the patient's symptoms or some other illness is causing the bradycardia.

Assess for Adequate Perfusion?

You must now decide if the patient has adequate or poor perfusion.
- If the patient has **adequate perfusion**, monitor and observe (Step 4).
- If the patient has persistent bradyarrhythmia causing **poor perfusion**, proceed to Step 5.

Treatment Sequence Summary

If the patient has poor perfusion secondary to bradycardia, treat as follows:
- Give atropine as first-line treatment: atropine 1 mg IV—may repeat to a total dose of 3 mg IV.

- *If atropine is ineffective,* provide transcutaneous pacing and/or dopamine 5 to 20 mcg/kg per minute infusion (chronotropic or heart rate dose) or epinephrine 2 to 10 mcg/min infusion.

The severity of the patient's clinical presentation determines the treatment sequence. For patients with unstable bradycardia, move quickly through this sequence. These patients may be in pre–cardiac arrest and may need multiple interventions simultaneously.

Avoid relying on atropine in type II second-degree or third-degree AV block or in patients with third-degree AV block with a new wide QRS complex where the location of the block is likely to be in infranodal tissue (such as in the bundle of His or more distal conduction system).

Treatment Sequence: Atropine

If you find no immediately reversible causes, atropine remains the first-line drug for acute stable bradycardia. Atropine sulfate acts by reversing cholinergic-mediated decreases in the heart rate and AV node conduction. Dopamine and epinephrine may be successful as an alternative to TCP.

For bradycardia, give atropine 1 mg IV every 3 to 5 minutes (maximum total dose of 3 mg IV). Note that atropine doses of less than 0.5 mg IV may further slow the heart rate.

Use atropine cautiously in the presence of acute coronary ischemia or myocardial infarction (MI). An atropine-mediated increase in heart rate may worsen ischemia or increase infarct size.

Do not rely on atropine in Mobitz type II second-degree or third-degree AV block or in patients with third-degree AV block with a new wide QRS complex. These bradycardias likely will not respond to reversal of cholinergic effects by atropine; preferably, treat them with TCP or β-adrenergic support as temporizing measures while the patient is prepared for transvenous pacing. Atropine administration should not delay external pacing or β-adrenergic infusion for patients with impending cardiac arrest.

A β-adrenergic infusion (ie, dopamine, epinephrine) is not a first-line agent for treating unstable bradycardia, but it can be used as an alternative when a bradycardia is unresponsive to treatment with atropine. You can also use a β-adrenergic infusion as a temporizing measure while the patient is prepared for transvenous pacing.

Vasopressors do not increase survival from bradycardia. Because these medications can improve aortic diastolic blood pressure, coronary artery perfusion pressure, and the rate of ROSC, the AHA continues to recommend their use.

Alternative drugs may also be appropriate in special circumstances such as the overdose of a β-blocker or calcium channel blocker. Do not wait for a maximum dose of atropine if the patient presents with second-degree or third-degree block; rather, move to a second-line treatment after 2 to 3 doses of atropine.

Treatment Sequence: TCP

TCP may be useful to treat unstable bradycardia. TCP is noninvasive and can be performed by ACLS providers. Consider immediate pacing in unstable patients with high-degree heart block when IV access is not available. It is reasonable to initiate TCP in unstable patients who do not respond to atropine.

After initiating TCP, confirm electrical and mechanical capture (Figure 28). Because heart rate is a major determinant of myocardial oxygen consumption, set the pacing to the lowest effective rate based on clinical assessment and symptom resolution. Reassess the patient for symptom improvement and hemodynamic stability. Give analgesics and sedatives for pain control. Note that many of these drugs may further decrease blood pressure and affect the patient's mental status. Try to identify and correct the cause of the bradycardia.

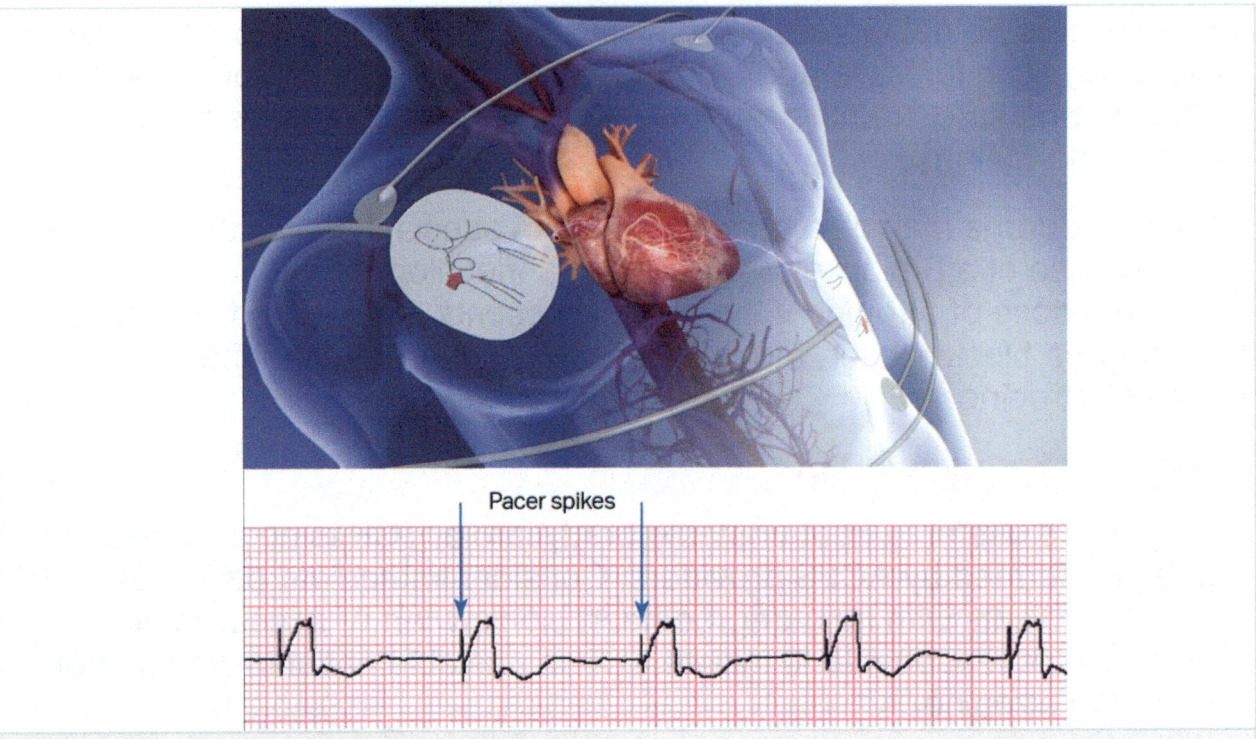

Figure 28. Transcutaneous pacing.

TCP has its limitations—it can be painful and may not produce effective electrical and mechanical capture. If bradycardia is not causing the symptoms, TCP may be ineffective despite capture. For these reasons, consider TCP as an emergent bridge to transvenous pacing in patients with significant sinus bradycardia or AV block.

If you chose TCP as the second-line treatment and it is also ineffective (eg, inconsistent capture), begin an infusion of dopamine or epinephrine and prepare for possible transvenous pacing by obtaining expert consultation.

Sedation and Pacing

Most conscious patients should be sedated before pacing. If the patient is in cardiovascular collapse or rapidly deteriorating, you may need to start pacing without prior sedation, particularly if sedation drugs are not immediately available. Evaluate the need for sedation in light of the patient's condition and need for immediate pacing. A review of sedation drugs is beyond the scope of this course, but the general approach could include the following:
- Give a parenteral narcotic for analgesia.
- Give parenteral benzodiazepine for anxiety and muscle contractions.

- Use a chronotropic infusion once available.
- Obtain expert consultation for transvenous pacing.

Treatment Sequence: Epinephrine, Dopamine

Although β-adrenergic agonists with rate-accelerating effects are not first-line agents for treating stable bradycardia, they are alternatives to TCP or in special circumstances, such as overdose with a β-blocker or calcium channel blocker.

Because epinephrine and dopamine are vasoconstrictors as well as chronotropes, healthcare providers must assess the patient's intravascular volume status and avoid hypovolemia when using these drugs. Dobutamine (a β-adrenergic agonist) is appropriate when vasoconstriction is not desired.

Either epinephrine infusions or dopamine infusions may be used for patients with stable bradycardia, particularly if associated with hypotension, for whom atropine may be inappropriate or after atropine fails.

Begin epinephrine infusion at a dose of 2 to 10 mcg/min and titrate to patient response; begin dopamine infusion at 5 to 20 mcg/kg per minute and titrate to patient response. At lower doses, dopamine has a more selective effect on inotropy and heart rate; at higher doses (greater than 10 mcg/kg per minute infusion), it also has vasoconstrictive effects.

Next Actions

After considering the treatment sequence in Step 5, you may need to
- Consider expert consultation—but do not delay treatment if the patient is unstable or potentially unstable.
- Prepare the patient for transvenous pacing.

Transcutaneous Pacing

Many devices can pace the heart by delivering an electrical stimulus, causing electrical depolarization and subsequent cardiac contraction, and TCP delivers pacing impulses to the heart through the skin via cutaneous electrodes. Most defibrillator manufacturers have added a pacing mode to manual defibrillators. Performing TCP is often as close as the nearest defibrillator, but you should know the indications, techniques, and hazards for using TCP.

Indications and Precautions

Indications for TCP are as follows:
- Hemodynamically unstable bradycardia (eg, hypotension, acutely altered mental status, signs of shock, ischemic chest discomfort, acute heart failure hypotension)
  - –Unstable clinical condition likely due to the bradycardia
- Bradycardia with stable ventricular escape rhythms

Precautions for TCP are as follows:
- TCP is contraindicated in severe hypothermia.
- Conscious patients require analgesia for discomfort unless delay for sedation will cause or contribute to deterioration.
- Do not assess the carotid pulse to confirm mechanical capture; electrical stimulation causes muscular jerking that may mimic the carotid pulse.

Technique

Perform TCP by following these steps:
1. Place pacing electrodes on the chest according to package instructions.
2. Turn the pacer on.
3. Set the demand rate to 60 to 80/min. You can adjust this rate up or down (based on patient clinical response) once pacing is established.
4. Set the current milliamperes output 2 mA above the dose at which consistent capture is observed (safety margin).

External pacemakers have either *fixed* rates (asynchronous mode) or *demand* rates.

Assess Response to Treatment

Signs of hemodynamic impairment include hypotension, acutely altered mental status, signs of shock, ischemic chest discomfort, acute heart failure, or other signs of shock related to the bradycardia. The goal of therapy is to improve these signs and symptoms rather than target a precise heart rate. Start pacing at a rate of 60 to 80/min. Once pacing is initiated, adjust the rate based on the patient's clinical response.

Consider giving atropine before pacing in mildly symptomatic patients. Do not delay pacing for unstable patients, particularly those with high-degree

AV block. Atropine may increase heart rate, improve hemodynamics, and eliminate the need for pacing. If atropine is ineffective or likely to be ineffective, or if IV access or atropine administration is delayed, begin pacing as soon as it is available.

Patients with ACS should be paced at the lowest heart rate that allows clinical stability. Higher heart rates can worsen ischemia because heart rate is a major determinant of myocardial oxygen demand. Ischemia, in turn, can precipitate arrhythmias.

If unstable bradycardia does not respond to atropine, consider a chronotropic drug infusion to stimulate heart rate as an alternative to pacing:
- Epinephrine: administer at 2 to 10 mcg/min infusion and titrate to patient response.
- Dopamine: administer at 5 to 20 mcg/kg per minute infusion and titrate to patient response.

Bradycardia With Escape Rhythms

A bradycardia may lead to secondary bradycardia-dependent ventricular rhythms. When a patient's heart rate falls, an electrically unstable ventricular area may "escape" suppression by higher and faster pacemakers (eg, sinus node), especially in the setting of acute ischemia. These ventricular rhythms often fail to respond to drugs. With severe bradycardia, some patients will develop wide-complex ventricular beats that can precipitate VT or VF. Pacing may increase the heart rate and eliminate bradycardia-dependent ventricular rhythms. However, an accelerated idioventricular rhythm (sometimes called AIVR) may occur in the setting of inferior wall MI. This rhythm is usually stable and does not require pacing.

Patients with ventricular escape rhythms may have normal myocardium with disturbed conduction. After correcting electrolyte abnormalities or acidosis, use pacing to stimulate effective myocardial contractions until the conduction system recovers.

Standby Pacing

Acute ischemia of conduction tissue and pacing centers can cause several bradycardic rhythms in ACS. Patients who are clinically stable may decompensate suddenly or become unstable over minutes to hours due to worsening conduction abnormalities, and these bradycardias may deteriorate to complete AV block and cardiovascular collapse. To prepare

for this clinical deterioration, place TCP electrodes on any patient with acute myocardial ischemia or infarction associated with the following rhythms:
- Symptomatic sinus node dysfunction with severe and symptomatic sinus bradycardia
- Asymptomatic Mobitz type II second-degree AV block
- Asymptomatic third-degree AV block
- Newly acquired left, right, or alternating bundle branch block or bifascicular block in the setting of AMI

Tachycardia: Stable and Unstable

Overview

The Team Leader in this case will assess and manage a patient with a rapid, unstable heart rate. You must be able to classify the tachycardia and intervene appropriately as outlined in the Adult Tachycardia With a Pulse Algorithm. You will be evaluated on your knowledge of the factors involved in safe and effective synchronized cardioversion as well as your performance of the procedure.

Rhythms for Unstable Tachycardia

This case involves these ECG rhythms (examples in Figure 29):
- Sinus tachycardia
- Atrial fibrillation
- Atrial flutter
- Supraventricular tachycardia (SVT)
- Monomorphic VT
- Polymorphic VT
- Wide-complex tachycardia of uncertain type

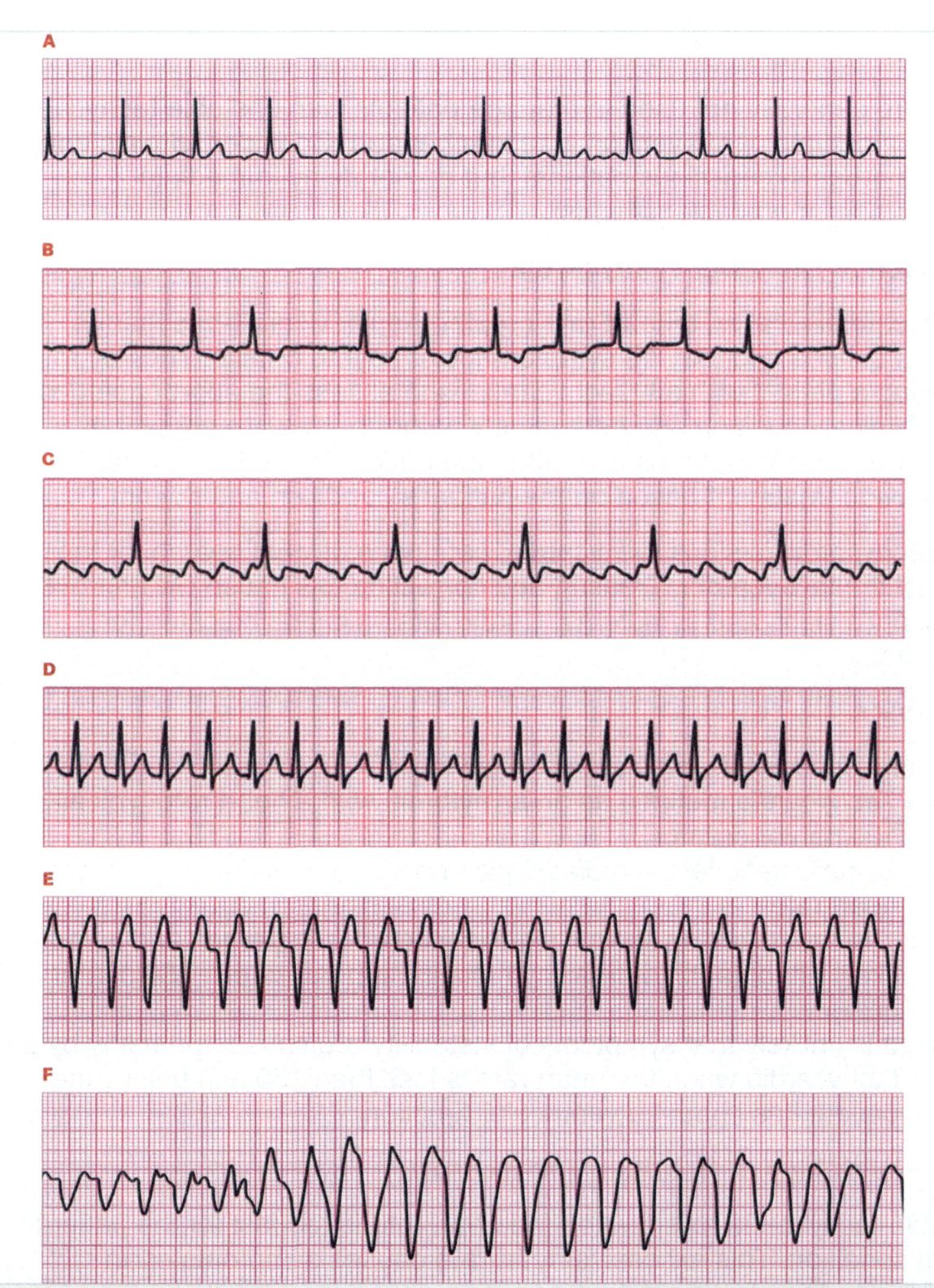

Figure 29. Examples of tachycardias. A, Sinus tachycardia. B, Atrial fibrillation. C, Atrial flutter. D, Supraventricular tachycardia. E, Monomorphic ventricular tachycardia. F, Polymorphic ventricular tachycardia.

Drugs for Unstable Tachycardia

Drugs are generally not used to manage patients with unstable tachycardia; rather, immediate cardioversion is recommended. Consider administering sedative drugs in conscious patients, but do not delay immediate cardioversion in unstable patients.

Approach to Unstable Tachycardia

A tachycardia—that is, a heart rate greater than 100/min—has many potential causes and may be symptomatic or asymptomatic. The key to managing a patient with any tachycardia is to assess the appropriateness for the clinical condition and determine whether pulses are present. If pulses are present, determine whether the patient is stable or unstable, and then provide treatment based on the patient's condition and rhythm.

If the tachycardia is sinus tachycardia, conduct a diligent search for the cause of the tachycardia. Treating and correcting this cause will improve the patient's signs and symptoms. Cardioversion is not indicated for tachycardia.

Definitions

Definitions used in this case are as follows:
- *Tachycardia:* defined as an arrhythmia with a heart rate typically 100/min or greater
- *Symptomatic tachycardia:* signs and symptoms due to the rapid heart rate
- The rate takes on clinical significance at its extremes and is more likely attributable to an arrhythmia if the heart rate is 150/min or greater.
- It is unlikely that symptoms of instability are caused primarily by the tachycardia when the heart rate is less than 150/min unless the patient has impaired ventricular function.

Pathophysiology of Unstable Tachycardia

Unstable tachycardia exists when the heart rate is too fast for the patient's clinical condition. This excessive heart rate causes symptoms or an unstable condition because the heart is
- *Beating so fast* that cardiac output is reduced; this can cause pulmonary edema, coronary ischemia, and hypotension with reduced blood flow to vital organs (eg, brain, kidneys)

- *Beating ineffectively* so that coordination between the atrium and ventricles or the ventricles themselves reduces cardiac output

Signs and Symptoms

Unstable tachycardia leads to serious signs and symptoms that include
- Hypotension
- Acutely altered mental status
- Signs of shock
- Ischemic chest discomfort
- Acute heart failure

Rapid Recognition

The 2 keys to managing unstable tachycardia are rapidly recognizing that
1. The patient is significantly symptomatic or even unstable
2. The signs and symptoms are caused by the tachycardia

Quickly determine whether the tachycardia is producing hemodynamic instability and the serious signs and symptoms *or* the serious signs and symptoms (eg, the pain and distress of an AMI) are the cause of the tachycardia.

Making this determination can be difficult. Many experts suggest that when a heart rate is less than 150/min, the symptoms of instability are not likely caused primarily by the tachycardia unless ventricular function is impaired. A heart rate typically less than 150/min is usually an appropriate response to physiologic stress (eg, fever, dehydration) or other underlying conditions.

Assess frequently for the presence or absence of signs and symptoms and for their severity.

Indications for Cardioversion

Rapidly identifying symptomatic tachycardia will help you determine whether to prepare for immediate cardioversion:
- At heart rates typically 150/min or greater, symptoms are often present and cardioversion is often required in unstable patients.
- If the patient is seriously ill or has underlying cardiovascular disease, symptoms may be present at lower rates.

You must know when cardioversion is indicated, how to prepare the patient for it (including appropriate medication), and how to switch the defibrillator/monitor to operate as a cardioverter.

Caution: Sinus Tachycardia
Never cardiovert a patient who has a sinus rhythm.

Managing Unstable Tachycardia: The Adult Tachycardia With a Pulse Algorithm

The Adult Tachycardia With a Pulse Algorithm simplifies initial management of tachycardia. The presence or absence of pulses is considered the key to managing patients with any tachycardia. If a pulseless tachycardia is present, then manage the patient according to the PEA pathway of the Adult Cardiac Arrest Algorithm (Figure 41). If pulses are present, assess appropriateness for the clinical condition and determine whether the patient is stable or unstable, and then provide treatment based on the patient's condition and rhythm Step 1). Identify and treat underlying causes by doing the following (Step 2):

- Maintain patent airway; assist breathing as necessary.
- Give oxygen (if hypoxemic).
- Use a cardiac monitor to identify rhythm; monitor blood pressure and oximetry.
- Obtain IV access.
- Obtain a 12-lead ECG (if available).

Determine if the persistent tachyarrhythmia is causing (Step 3)

- Hypotension
- Acutely altered mental status
- Signs of shock
- Ischemic chest discomfort
- Acute heart failure

To manage unstable tachycardia, ACLS providers should consider synchronized cardioversion and sedation, and, if regular narrow complex, adenosine 6 mg IV (follow with saline flush) (Step 4). If these interventions are not successful and if the tachycardia is refractory, providers should look for any underlying causes and consider the need to increase the energy level for the next cardioversion and add antiarrhythmic drugs. Providers should also obtain expert consultation (Step 5). Actions in the steps require advanced knowledge of ECG rhythm interpretation and antiarrhythmic therapy; these actions should take place in-hospital with expert consultation available.

The Adult Tachycardia With a Pulse Algorithm (Figure 30) outlines the steps for assessing and managing a patient presenting with symptomatic tachycardia with pulses. Implementation of this algorithm begins with the identification of tachycardia with pulses (Step 1). If a tachycardia and a pulse are present, identify and treat underlying causes and perform assessment and management steps guided by the BLS, Primary, and Secondary Assessments (Step 2). The key in this assessment is to decide whether the tachycardia is stable or unstable.

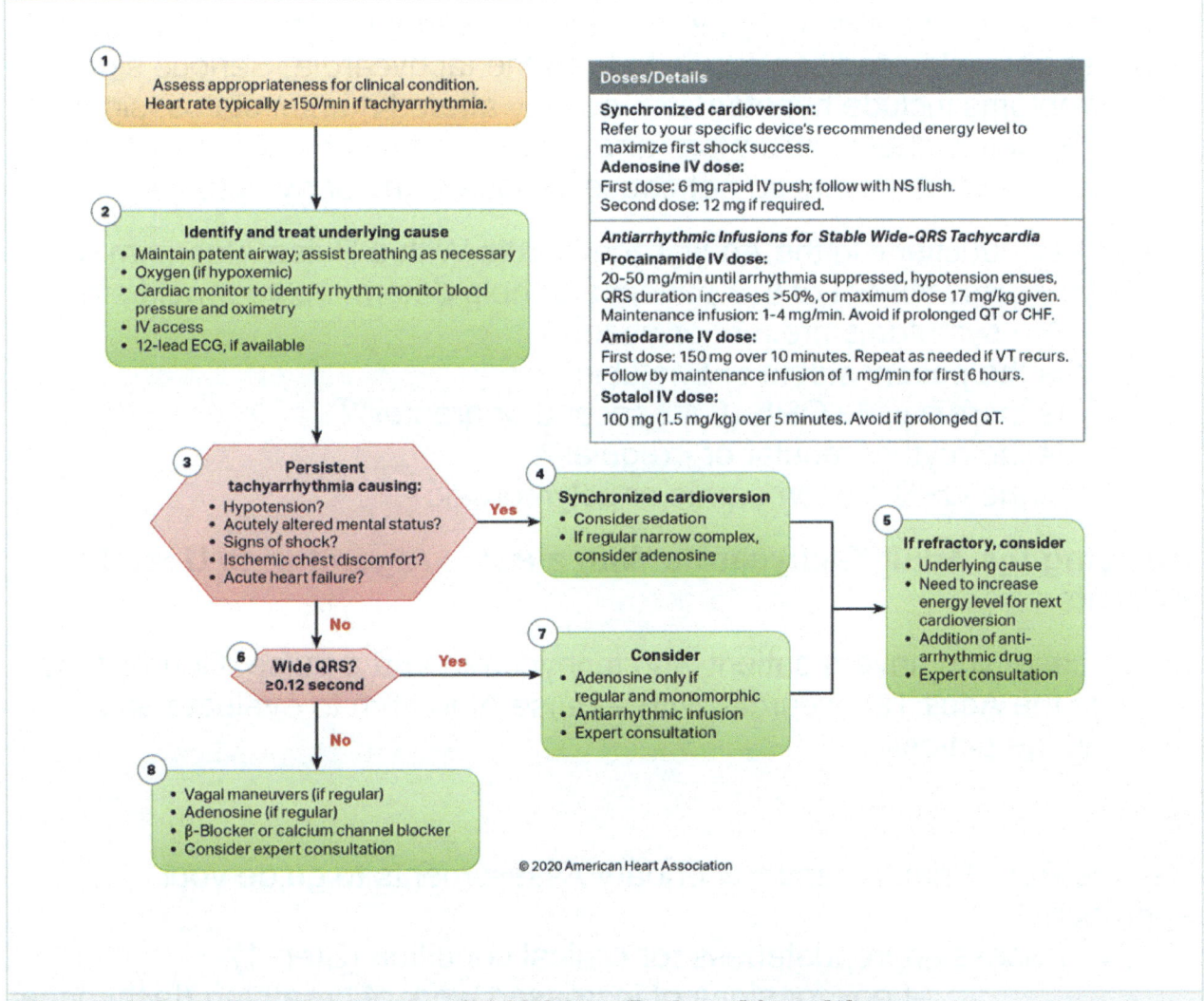

Figure 30. Adult Tachycardia With a Pulse Algorithm.

The tachycardia is unstable if signs and symptoms persist after maintaining the patent airway, assisting with breathing as necessary, the patient receives supplemental oxygen, *and* if significant signs or symptoms are due to the tachycardia (Step 3). In this case, immediate synchronized cardioversion is indicated (Step 4). If cardioversion is unsuccessful, consider next steps (Step 5).

If the patient is stable, evaluate the ECG and determine if the QRS complex is wide (0.12 second or greater) and whether it is regular or irregular (Step 6). (*Note:* the treatment of stable tachycardia is presented in the next case.)

Serious Signs and Symptoms, Unstable Condition

Intervention is determined by the presence of serious signs and symptoms or by an unstable condition resulting from the tachycardia. Serious signs and symptoms include hypotension, acutely altered mental status, signs of shock, ischemic chest discomfort, and acute heart failure. Ventricular rates less than 150/min usually do not cause serious signs or symptoms.

These key questions in the Adult Tachycardia With a Pulse Algorithm will guide your assessment of this patient and help determine your next steps:
- Are symptoms present or absent?
- Is the patient stable or unstable?
- Is there a wide QRS (0.12 second or greater)?
- Is the rhythm regular or irregular?
- Is the QRS monomorphic or polymorphic?

Applying the Adult Tachycardia With a Pulse Algorithm to Unstable Patients

In this case, you have a patient with tachycardia and a pulse. Conduct the steps in the Adult Tachycardia With a Pulse Algorithm to evaluate and manage the patient.

Assess Clinical Condition

Use the BLS, Primary, and Secondary Assessments to guide your approach.
- Assess appropriateness for clinical condition (Step 1):
  - —Look for signs of increased work of breathing (tachypnea, intercostal retractions, suprasternal retractions, paradoxical abdominal breathing), and hypoxemia as determined by pulse oximetry.

Identify and Treat the Underlying Cause

Identify and treat underlying cause (Step 2).

- Maintain patent airway; assist breathing as necessary.
- Give oxygen (if hypoxemic).
- Use a cardiac monitor to identify rhythm; monitor blood pressure and oximetry.
- Establish IV access.
- Obtain a 12-lead ECG if available.

If symptoms persist despite support of adequate oxygenation and ventilation, proceed to Step 3.

Critical Concepts: Unstable Patients
- *Obtain a 12-lead ECG (if available) early in the assessment to better define the rhythm.*
- *However, unstable patients require immediate cardioversion.*
- *Do not delay immediate cardioversion to acquire the 12-lead ECG if the patient is unstable.*

Decision Point: Is the Persistent Tachycardia Causing Serious Signs or Symptoms?

Assess the patient's degree of instability and determine if it is related to the tachycardia (Step 3).

Unstable

If the persistent tachyarrhythmia is causing the patient to demonstrate rate-related cardiovascular compromise with serious signs and symptoms, proceed to immediate synchronized cardioversion (Step 4).

Serious signs and symptoms are unlikely if the ventricular rate is less than 150/min in patients with a healthy heart. However, if the patient is seriously ill or has significant underlying heart disease or other conditions, symptoms may be present at a lower heart rate.

Stable

If the patient does not have rate-related cardiovascular compromise, proceed to Step 6. You'll have time to obtain a 12-lead ECG, evaluate the rhythm, determine the width of the QRS, and determine treatment options. For stable patients, seek expert consultation because treatment has the potential for harm.

Treatment Based on Type of Tachycardia

You may not always be able to distinguish between supraventricular and ventricular rhythms. Most wide-complex tachycardias are ventricular in origin, especially if the patient has underlying heart disease or is older. If the patient is pulseless, treat the rhythm as VF and follow the Adult Cardiac Arrest Algorithm.

If the patient has a wide-complex tachycardia and is unstable, assume it is VT until proven otherwise. The amount of energy required for cardioversion of VT is determined by the specific device's recommended energy level to maximize first shock success.

- If the patient is unstable but has a pulse with regular uniform wide-complex VT (monomorphic VT), treat with synchronized cardioversion. Follow your device's specific recommended energy level to maximize the success of the first shock. If the patient does not respond to the first shock, increasing the dose stepwise is reasonable. (This recommendation represents expert opinion.)
- Arrhythmias with a polymorphic QRS appearance (polymorphic VT), such as torsades de pointes, will usually not permit synchronization. If the patient has polymorphic VT, treat as VF with high-energy unsynchronized shocks (eg, defibrillation doses).
- If you have any doubt about whether an unstable patient has monomorphic or polymorphic VT, do not delay treatment for further rhythm analysis. Provide high-energy, unsynchronized shocks (defibrillation doses).

Perform Immediate Synchronized Cardioversion

- If possible, establish IV access before cardioversion and administer sedation if the patient is conscious.
- Do not delay cardioversion if the patient is extremely unstable.

If the patient with a regular narrow-complex SVT or a monomorphic wide-complex tachycardia is not hypotensive, healthcare providers may administer adenosine 6 mg IV (follow with saline flush) while preparing for synchronized cardioversion.

If cardiac arrest develops, see the Adult Cardiac Arrest Algorithm.

Cardioversion

You must know when cardioversion is indicated and what type of shock to administer (Figure 31). Before cardioversion, establish IV access and sedate the responsive patient if possible, but do not delay cardioversion in unstable or deteriorating patients.

1 Tachycardia
With serious signs and symptoms related to the tachycardia

2 If ventricular rate is >150/min, prepare for **immediate cardioversion**. May give brief trial of medications based on specific arrhythmias. Immediate cardioversion is generally not needed if heart rate is ≤150/min.

3 Have available at bedside
- Oxygen saturation monitor
- Suction device
- IV line
- Intubation equipment

4 **Premedicate whenever possible***

5 *Synchronized cardioversion*†‡
Refer to your specific device's recommended energy level to maximize first shock success.

Notes

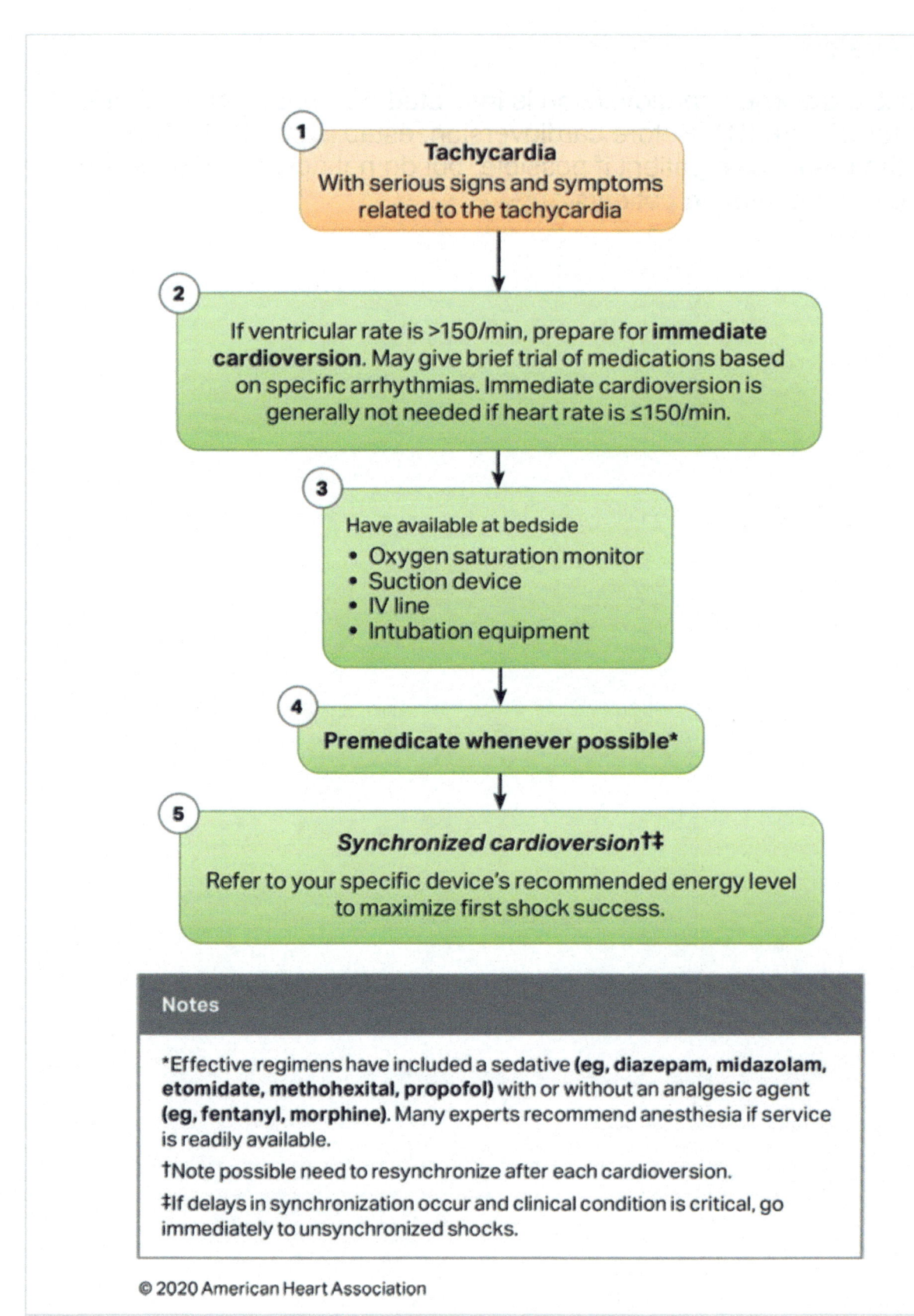

*Effective regimens have included a sedative **(eg, diazepam, midazolam, etomidate, methohexital, propofol)** with or without an analgesic agent **(eg, fentanyl, morphine)**. Many experts recommend anesthesia if service is readily available.

†Note possible need to resynchronize after each cardioversion.

‡If delays in synchronization occur and clinical condition is critical, go immediately to unsynchronized shocks.

© 2020 American Heart Association

Figure 31. Electrical Cardioversion Algorithm.

This section discusses the difference between unsynchronized and synchronized shocks, potential problems with synchronization, and energy doses for specific rhythms.

Unsynchronized vs Synchronized Shocks

Modern defibrillators and cardioverters can deliver unsynchronized or synchronized shocks. An *unsynchronized shock* means that the electrical shock is delivered as soon as you push the shock button on the device. These shocks may fall randomly anywhere within the cardiac cycle and use higher energy levels than synchronized shocks. *Synchronized cardioversion* uses a sensor to deliver a shock that is synchronized with a peak of the QRS complex. When you engage the sync option, pressing the shock button can result in a delay before shocking because the device synchronizes the shock to the peak of the R wave, and this may require analysis of several complexes. Synchronization avoids delivering a shock during cardiac repolarization (represented on the surface ECG as the T wave), a period of vulnerability in which a shock can precipitate VF. Synchronized shocks also use a lower energy level than attempted defibrillation. Always deliver synchronized shocks in patients with a pulse unless there is polymorphic VT, synchronization is impossible, or there is a delay to treatment in the unstable patient.

Potential Problems With Synchronization

In theory, synchronization is simple: just push the sync control on the face of the defibrillator/cardioverter. In practice, however, synchronization has potential problems:
- If the R-wave peaks of a tachycardia are undifferentiated or of low amplitude, the monitor sensors may be unable to identify an R-wave peak and therefore will not deliver the shock.
- Many cardioverters will not synchronize through the handheld quick-look paddles. An unwary practitioner may try to synchronize—unsuccessfully in that the machine will not discharge—and may not recognize the problem.
- Synchronization can take extra time (eg, if you need to attach electrodes or are unfamiliar with the equipment).

Recommendations

Synchronized shocks are recommended for patients with a pulse and tachycardias such as

- Unstable SVT
- Unstable atrial fibrillation
- Unstable atrial flutter
- Unstable regular monomorphic tachycardia with pulses

Unsynchronized high-energy shocks are recommended
- For a patient with no pulse (VF/pVT)
- For clinical deterioration (in prearrest), such as those with severe shock or polymorphic VT, when you think a delay in converting the rhythm will result in cardiac arrest
- For patients who are unstable or deteriorating and synchronization cannot be immediately accomplished
- When you are unsure whether monomorphic or polymorphic VT is present in the unstable patient

If the shock causes VF (occurring in only a very small minority of patients despite the theoretical risk), immediately attempt defibrillation.

Energy Doses for Specific Rhythms

For dosing, follow your specific device's recommended energy level to maximize the success of the first shock.

Synchronized Cardioversion

Synchronized cardioversion is the treatment of choice when a patient has a symptomatic (unstable) reentry SVT or VT with pulses and is recommended to treat unstable atrial fibrillation and flutter.

Cardioversion is unlikely to be effective for treating junctional tachycardia or ectopic or multifocal atrial tachycardia because these rhythms have an automatic focus arising from cells that are spontaneously depolarizing at a rapid rate. Delivering a shock generally cannot stop these rhythms and may actually increase the rate of the tachyarrhythmia.

In synchronized cardioversion, shocks are administered through adhesive electrodes or handheld paddles with the defibrillator/monitor in synchronized (sync) mode. The sync mode delivers energy just after the R wave of the QRS complex.

Follow these steps to perform synchronized cardioversion, modifying the steps for your specific device.

1. Sedate all conscious patients unless unstable or deteriorating rapidly.
2. Turn on the defibrillator (monophasic or biphasic).
3. Attach monitor leads to the patient and ensure proper display of the patient's rhythm. Position adhesive electrode (conductor) pads on the patient.
4. Press the sync control button to engage the synchronization mode.
5. Look for markers on the R wave indicating sync mode.
6. Adjust monitor gain if necessary until sync markers occur with each R wave.
7. Select the appropriate energy level. Deliver synchronized shocks according to your device's recommended energy level to maximize the success of the first shock.
8. Announce to team members: "Charging defibrillator—stand clear!"
9. Press the charge button.
10. Clear the patient when the defibrillator is charged.
11. Press the shock button(s).
12. Check the monitor. If tachycardia persists, increase the energy level (joules) according to the device manufacturer's recommendations.
13. Activate the sync mode after delivery of each synchronized shock. Most defibrillators default back to the unsynchronized mode after delivery of a synchronized shock. This default allows an immediate shock if cardioversion produces VF.

Figure 31 shows the steps to perform electrical cardioversion. First, determine if the patient has serious signs and symptoms related to tachycardia (Step 1). If the heart rate is greater than 150/min, prepare for immediate cardioversion and consider giving a brief trial of medications on the basis of the specific arrhythmias. Immediate cardioversion is generally not needed if heart rate is 150/min or less (Step 2).

At the bedside, the provider should have the following available (Step 3):
- Oxygen saturation monitor
- Suction device
- IV line
- Intubation equipment

Next, premedicate whenever possible (Step 4). Effective regimens have included a sedative (eg, diazepam, midazolam, etomidate, methohexital, propofol) with or without an analgesic agent (eg, fentanyl, morphine). Many experts recommend anesthesia if service is readily available.

Perform synchronized cardioversion (Step 5). Refer to your specific device's recommended energy level to maximize first shock success. Note possible need to resynchronize after each cardioversion. If delays in synchronization occur and the patient's clinical condition is critical, go immediately to unsynchronized shocks.

Stable Tachycardias

If the patient does not have rate-related cardiovascular compromise, proceed to Step 6. You'll have time to obtain a 12-lead ECG, evaluate the rhythm, determine if width of the QRS is 0.12 second or greater. In this case, consider adenosine only if the rhythm is regular and monomorphic, and consider antiarrhythmic infusion. Seek expert consultation because treatment has the potential for harm. If the rhythm is refractory, consider the underlying cause, the need to increase energy level for the next cardioversion, additional antiarrhythmic drugs, and additional expert consultation.

Determine the Width of the QRS Complex
- If the width of the QRS complex is 0.12 second or more, go to Step 7.
- If the width of the QRS complex is less than 0.12 second, go to Step 8.

In some cases, a "stable" tachycardia is actually an early sign that the patient is becoming unstable, and you should initiate a search for underlying causes early to avoid further deterioration.

You must be able to classify the type of tachycardia (wide or narrow; regular or irregular) and intervene appropriately as outlined in the Adult Tachycardia With a Pulse Algorithm. During this case, you will perform initial assessment and management of regular narrow-complex rhythms (except sinus tachycardia), and you'll treat them with vagal maneuvers, adenosine, β-blocker or calcium channel blocker.

If the rhythm does not convert, consider expert consultation. If the patient becomes clinically unstable, prepare for immediate unsynchronized shock or synchronized cardioversion.

Understanding Sinus Tachycardia

Sinus tachycardia is a heart rate that is greater than 100/min, has P waves, and is generated by sinus node discharge. The heart rate in tachycardia typically does not exceed 220/min and is age-related. Sinus tachycardia usually does not exceed 120 to 130/min, and it has a gradual onset and gradual termination. Reentry SVT has an abrupt onset and termination.

Note that sinus tachycardia is excluded from the Adult Tachycardia With a Pulse Algorithm. Sinus tachycardia is caused by external influences on the heart, such as fever, anemia, hypotension, blood loss, or exercise—systemic, not cardiac, conditions. Sinus tachycardia is a regular rhythm, although the rate may be slowed by vagal maneuvers. *In sinus tachycardia, the goal is to identify and correct the underlying systemic cause, and cardioversion is contraindicated.*

β-Blockers may cause clinical deterioration if the cardiac output falls when a compensatory tachycardia is blocked. This is because cardiac output is determined by the volume of blood ejected by the ventricles with each contraction (stroke volume) and the heart rate.

Cardiac output (CO) = Stroke volume (SV) × Heart rate

If a condition such as a large AMI limits ventricular function (severe heart failure or cardiogenic shock), the heart compensates by increasing the heart rate. If you attempt to reduce the heart rate in patients with a compensatory tachycardia, cardiac output will fall, and the patient's condition will likely deteriorate.

Rhythms for Stable Tachycardia

Tachycardia classifications include the appearance of the QRS complex, heart rate, and whether they are regular or irregular:
- Narrow–QRS complex (SVT) tachycardias (QRS less than 0.12 second) in order of frequency
    - –Sinus tachycardia
    - –Atrial fibrillation
    - –Atrial flutter
    - –AV nodal reentry
- Wide–QRS complex tachycardias (QRS 0.12 second or more)
    - –Monomorphic VT
    - –Polymorphic VT
    - –SVT with aberrancy

- Regular or irregular tachycardias
    - –Irregular narrow-complex tachycardias are probably atrial fibrillation

Drugs for Stable Tachycardia

Drugs for tachycardia include
- Adenosine 6 mg IV (follow with saline flush); second dose (if required) 12 mg IV (follow with saline flush)
- Several analgesic and sedative agents are also used during electrical cardioversion, but those agents are not covered in this course.

Approach to Stable Tachycardia

A *stable tachycardia* refers to a condition in which the patient has
- A heart rate greater than 100/min
- No significant signs or symptoms caused by the increased rate
- A potential underlying cardiac electrical abnormality that generates the rhythm

Questions to Determine Classification

Classification of the tachycardia requires the careful clinical evaluation of these questions:
- Are symptoms present or absent?
- Are symptoms due to the tachycardia?
- Is the patient stable or unstable?
- Is the QRS complex narrow or wide?
- Is the rhythm regular or irregular?
- Is the QRS monomorphic or polymorphic?
- Is the rhythm sinus tachycardia?

The answers guide subsequent diagnosis and treatment.

Managing Stable Tachycardia: The Adult Tachycardia With a Pulse Algorithm

As noted in the Unstable Tachycardia Case, the keys to managing a patient with any tachycardia are assessing the appropriateness for the clinical condition, identifying and treating underlying causes (Step 1), and determining whether pulses are present and, if so, whether the patient is stable or unstable and then providing treatment based on the patient's condition and rhythm. If the patient is pulseless, manage the patient according to the Adult Cardiac Arrest Algorithm (Figure 41). If the patient has pulses, manage the patient according to the Adult Tachycardia With a Pulse Algorithm (Figure 30).

If a tachycardia and a pulse are present, perform the steps of the BLS, Primary, and Secondary Assessments. Determine if serious signs or symptoms are present and due to the tachycardia. This will direct you to either the stable or unstable section of the algorithm.
- If significant signs or symptoms are due to the tachycardia, immediate cardioversion is indicated (see the Unstable Tachycardia Case).
- If the patient develops pVT or VF, deliver unsynchronized high-energy shocks (defibrillation energy) and follow the Adult Cardiac Arrest Algorithm.
- If the patient has polymorphic VT, treat the rhythm as VF and deliver high-energy unsynchronized shocks (ie, defibrillation energy).

In this case, the patient is stable, so you will manage according to the stable section of the Adult Tachycardia With a Pulse Algorithm (Figure 30). A precise identification of the rhythm (eg, reentry SVT, atrial flutter) may not be possible at this time.

Applying the Adult Tachycardia With a Pulse Algorithm to Stable Patients

In this case, a patient has stable tachycardia with a pulse. Conduct the steps in the Adult Tachycardia With a Pulse Algorithm to evaluate and manage the patient.

Patient Assessment

Step 1 directs you to assess the appropriateness for the patient's clinical condition. Typically, a heart rate greater than 150/min at rest is due to tachyarrhythmias other than sinus tachycardia.

BLS and ACLS Assessments

Using the BLS, Primary, and Secondary Assessments to guide your approach, identify and treat underlying causes (Step 2):
- Maintain patent airway; assist breathing as necessary.
- Give oxygen (if hypoxemic).

- Use a cardiac monitor to identify rhythm; monitor blood pressure and oximetry.
- Obtain IV access.
- Obtain 12-lead ECG if available.

If symptoms persist, proceed to Step 3. If the patient is stable, go to Step 8.

IV Access and 12-Lead ECG

If the patient with tachycardia is stable (ie, no serious signs or symptoms related to the tachycardia), you have time to evaluate the rhythm and decide on treatment options. Establish IV access if not already obtained. Obtain a 12-lead ECG (if available) or rhythm strip to determine if the QRS is narrow (less than 0.12 second) or wide (0.12 second or more).

Decision Point: Wide or Narrow

The path of treatment is now determined by whether the QRS is wide or narrow and whether the rhythm is regular or irregular. If a monomorphic wide-complex rhythm is present and the patient is stable, consider adenosine (only if regular and monomorphic), consider antiarrhythmic infusion, and seek expert consultation. Treat polymorphic wide-complex tachycardia with immediate unsynchronized shock.

Wide-Complex Tachycardias

Wide-complex tachycardias are defined as a QRS of 0.12 second or more, but consider seeking expert consultation for help identifying the rhythm. The most common forms of life-threatening wide-complex tachycardias likely to deteriorate to VF are
- Monomorphic VT
- Polymorphic VT

Determine if the rhythm is regular or irregular.
- A regular wide-complex tachycardia is presumed to be VT or SVT with aberrancy.
- An irregular wide-complex tachycardia may be atrial fibrillation with aberrancy, pre-excited atrial fibrillation (atrial fibrillation using an accessory pathway for antegrade conduction), or polymorphic VT/torsades de pointes. These advanced rhythms require additional expertise or expert consultation. In addition, consider adenosine (only if regular and monomorphic) and antiarrhythmic infusion.

If the rhythm is likely VT or SVT in a stable patient, treat based on the algorithm for that rhythm.

Recent evidence suggests that if the rhythm etiology cannot be determined and is regular in its rate and monomorphic, IV adenosine is relatively safe for both treatment and diagnosis. IV antiarrhythmic drugs may be effective. We recommend:

- Procainamide 20 to 50 mg/min IV until arrhythmia suppressed, hypotension ensues, QRS duration increases more than 50%, or maximum dose 17 mg/kg IV is given. Maintenance infusion: 1 to 4 mg/min IV. Avoid if prolonged QT or congestive heart failure.
- Amiodarone (first dose) 150 mg IV over 10 minutes. Repeat as needed if VT recurs. Follow by maintenance infusion of 1 mg/min IV for first 6 hours.
- Sotalol 100 mg (1.5 mg/kg) IV over 5 minutes. Avoid if prolonged QT.

In the case of irregular wide-complex tachycardia, management focuses on control of the rapid ventricular rate (rate control), conversion of hemodynamically unstable atrial fibrillation to sinus rhythm (rhythm control), or both. Seek expert consultation.

Treating Tachycardia

You may not always be able to distinguish between supraventricular (aberrant) and ventricular wide-complex rhythms, so be aware that most wide-complex (broad-complex) tachycardias are ventricular in origin.

If a patient is pulseless, follow the Adult Cardiac Arrest Algorithm.

If a patient becomes unstable, do not delay treatment for further rhythm analysis. For stable patients with wide-complex tachycardias, consider expert consultation because treatment has the potential for harm.

Critical Concepts: Drugs to Avoid in Patients With Irregular Wide-Complex Tachycardia

Avoid AV nodal blocking agents such as adenosine, calcium channel blockers, digoxin, and possibly β-blockers in patients with pre-excitation atrial fibrillation, because these drugs may cause a paradoxical increase in the ventricular response.

Narrow QRS, Regular Rhythm

The therapy for narrow QRS with regular rhythm is to attempt vagal maneuvers, give adenosine, give a β-blocker or calcium channel blocker, and consider expert consultation. Vagal maneuvers, adenosine, and β-blocker or calcium channel blockers are the preferred initial interventions for terminating narrow-complex tachycardias that are symptomatic (but stable) and supraventricular in origin. Valsalva maneuvers or carotid sinus massage alone will terminate about 25% of SVT, and adenosine is required for the remainder.

- If SVT does not respond to vagal maneuvers, give **adenosine** 6 mg IV (follow with saline flush) in a large (eg, antecubital) vein over 1 second, and elevate the arm immediately.
- If SVT does not convert within 1 to 2 minutes, give a second dose of **adenosine** 12 mg IV (follow with saline flush) following the same procedure above.

Adenosine increases AV block and will terminate approximately 90% of reentry arrhythmias within 2 minutes. Adenosine will not terminate atrial flutter or atrial fibrillation but will slow AV conduction, allowing you to identify flutter or fibrillation waves.

Adenosine is safe and effective in pregnancy, but it has several important drug interactions. Patients with significant blood levels of theophylline, caffeine, or theobromine may require larger doses, and you should reduce the initial dose to 3 mg IV for patients taking dipyridamole or carbamazepine. Due to recent case reports of prolonged asystole after adenosine administration to patients with transplanted hearts or after central venous administration, you may consider lower doses such as 3 mg IV in these situations.

Adenosine may cause bronchospasm, so generally, you should not give adenosine to patients with asthma or chronic obstructive pulmonary disease, particularly if patients are actively bronchospastic.

If the rhythm converts with adenosine, it is probable reentry SVT. Observe patients for recurrence, and treat any recurrence with adenosine or longer-acting AV nodal blocking agents, such as the non-dihydropyridine calcium channel blockers (verapamil and diltiazem) or β-blockers. Typically, you should obtain expert consultation if the tachycardia recurs.

If the rhythm does not convert with adenosine, it is possible atrial flutter, ectopic atrial tachycardia, sinus tachycardia, or junctional tachycardia, and you should obtain expert consultation about diagnosis and treatment.

Critical Concepts: What to Avoid With AV Nodal Blocking Agents
Do not use AV nodal blocking drugs for pre-excited atrial fibrillation or flutter because these drugs are unlikely to slow the ventricular rate and may even accelerate the ventricular response. Also, be careful when combining AV nodal blocking agents of varying duration, such as calcium channel blockers or β-blockers, because their actions may overlap if given serially and provoke profound bradycardia.

Tachycardia Algorithm: Advanced Management Steps

As an ACLS provider, you should be able to recognize a stable narrow-complex or wide-complex tachycardia, classify the rhythm as regular or irregular, and provide initial management. You may treat regular narrow-complex tachycardias initially with vagal maneuvers, adenosine, and β-blocker or calcium channel blocker, but if these are unsuccessful, you'll need to consider expert consultation.

If you have experience with the differential diagnosis and therapy of stable tachycardias that do not respond to initial treatment, you can review the Adult Tachycardia With a Pulse Algorithm for additional steps and pharmacologic agents used in the treatment of these arrhythmias, both for rate control and for termination of the arrhythmia.

If at any point you become uncertain or uncomfortable while treating a stable patient, seek expert consultation because treatment has the potential for harm.

References
1. 1.Devita MA, Bellomo R, Hillman K, et al. Findings of the first consensus conference on medical emergency teams. *Crit Care Med.* 2006;34(9):2463-2478. doi: 10.1097/01.CCM.0000235743.38172.6E
2. 2.Peberdy MA, Cretikos M, Abella BS, et al. Recommended guidelines for monitoring, reporting, and conducting research on medical emergency team, outreach, and rapid response systems: an Utstein-style scientific statement: a scientific statement from

the International Liaison Committee on Resuscitation (American Heart Association, Australian Resuscitation Council, European Resuscitation Council, Heart and Stroke Foundation of Canada, InterAmerican Heart Foundation, Resuscitation Council of Southern Africa, and the New Zealand Resuscitation Council); the American Heart Association Emergency Cardiovascular Care Committee; the Council on Cardiopulmonary, Perioperative, and Critical Care; and the Interdisciplinary Working Group on Quality of Care and Outcomes Research. *Circulation.* 2007;116(21):2481-2500. doi: 10.1161/CIRCULATIONAHA.107.186227
3. 3.Solomon RS, Corwin GS, Barclay DC, Quddusi SF, Dannenberg MD. Effectiveness of rapid response teams on rates of in-hospital cardiopulmonary arrest and mortality: a systematic review and meta-analysis. *J Hosp Med.* 2016;11(6):438-445. doi: 10.1002/jhm.2554
4. 4.Dukes K, Bunch JL, Chan PS, et al. Assessment of rapid response teams at top-performing hospitals for in-hospital cardiac arrest. *JAMA Intern Med.* 2019;179(10):1398-1405. doi: 10.1001/jamainternmed.2019.2420
5. 5.Chan PS, Khalid A, Longmore LS, Berg RA, Kosiborod M, Spertus JA. Hospital-wide code rates and mortality before and after implementation of a rapid response team. *JAMA.* 2008;300(21):2506-2513. doi: 10.1001/jama.2008.715
6. 6.Amsterdam EA, Wenger NK, Brindis RG, et al. 2014 AHA/ACC guideline for the management of patients with non-ST-elevation acute coronary syndromes: a report of the American College of Cardiology/American Heart Association Task Force on Practice Guidelines. *Circulation.* 2014;130(25):e344-426. doi: 10.1161/CIR.0000000000000134
7. 7.Hall MJ, Levant S, DeFrances CJ. Hospitalization for stroke in U.S. hospitals, 1989-2009. *NCHS Data Brief.* 2012(95):1-8.
8. 8.Powers WJ, Rabinstein AA, Ackerson T, et al. Guidelines for the Early Management of Patients With Acute Ischemic Stroke: 2019 Update to the 2018 Guidelines for the Early Management of Acute Ischemic Stroke: A Guideline for Healthcare Professionals From the American Heart Association/American Stroke Association. *Stroke.* 2019;50(12):e344-e418. doi: 10.1161/STR.0000000000000211

9. Jauch EC, Saver JL, Adams HP Jr, et al; for the American Heart Association Stroke Council, Council on Cardiovascular Nursing, Council on Peripheral Vascular Disease, and Council on Clinical Cardiology. Guidelines for the early management of patients with acute ischemic stroke: a guideline for healthcare professionals from the American Heart Association/American Stroke Association. *Stroke.* 2013;44(3):870-947. doi: 10.1161/STR.0b013e318284056a
10. Adams HP Jr, del Zoppo G, Alberts MJ, et al. Guidelines for the early management of adults with ischemic stroke: a guideline from the American Heart Association/American Stroke Association Stroke Council, Clinical Cardiology Council, Cardiovascular Radiology and Intervention Council, and the Atherosclerotic Peripheral Vascular Disease and Quality of Care Outcomes in Research Interdisciplinary Working Groups. *Stroke.* 2007;38(5):1655-1711. doi: 10.1161/STROKEAHA.107.181486

Part 3: High-Performance Teams

High-performance teams are essential to successful resuscitation attempts. High-performance teams carry out their roles in highly effective manners, resulting in superior performance and timing, which can translate to improved survival for patients in cardiac arrest. What distinguishes high-performance teams from others is that each team member is committed to ensuring the highest-quality performance of the team rather than simply following orders. To function effectively, a high-performance team needs to focus on

- **Timing:** time to first compression, time to first shock, CCF ideally greater than 80%,* minimizing preshock pause, and early emergency medical services (EMS) response time
- **Quality:** rate, depth, complete recoil, minimizing interruptions, switching compressors every 2 minutes or sooner if fatigued, avoiding excessive ventilation, and using a feedback device
- **Coordination:** team dynamics: team members working together seamlessly toward a common goal, proficient in their roles
- **Administration:** leadership, measurement, continuous quality improvement, and number of participating code team members

* High-performing systems target at least 60%, with 80% or higher being a frequent goal.

High-performance teams (Figure 32) will need to incorporate timing, quality, coordination, and administration of the appropriate procedures during a cardiac arrest. The team will need to consider their overall purpose and goals, skills each team member possesses, appropriate motivation and efficacy, as well as appropriate conflict resolution and communication needs of the team. In addition, high-performance teams measure their performance, evaluate the data, and look for ways to improve performance and implement the revised strategy.

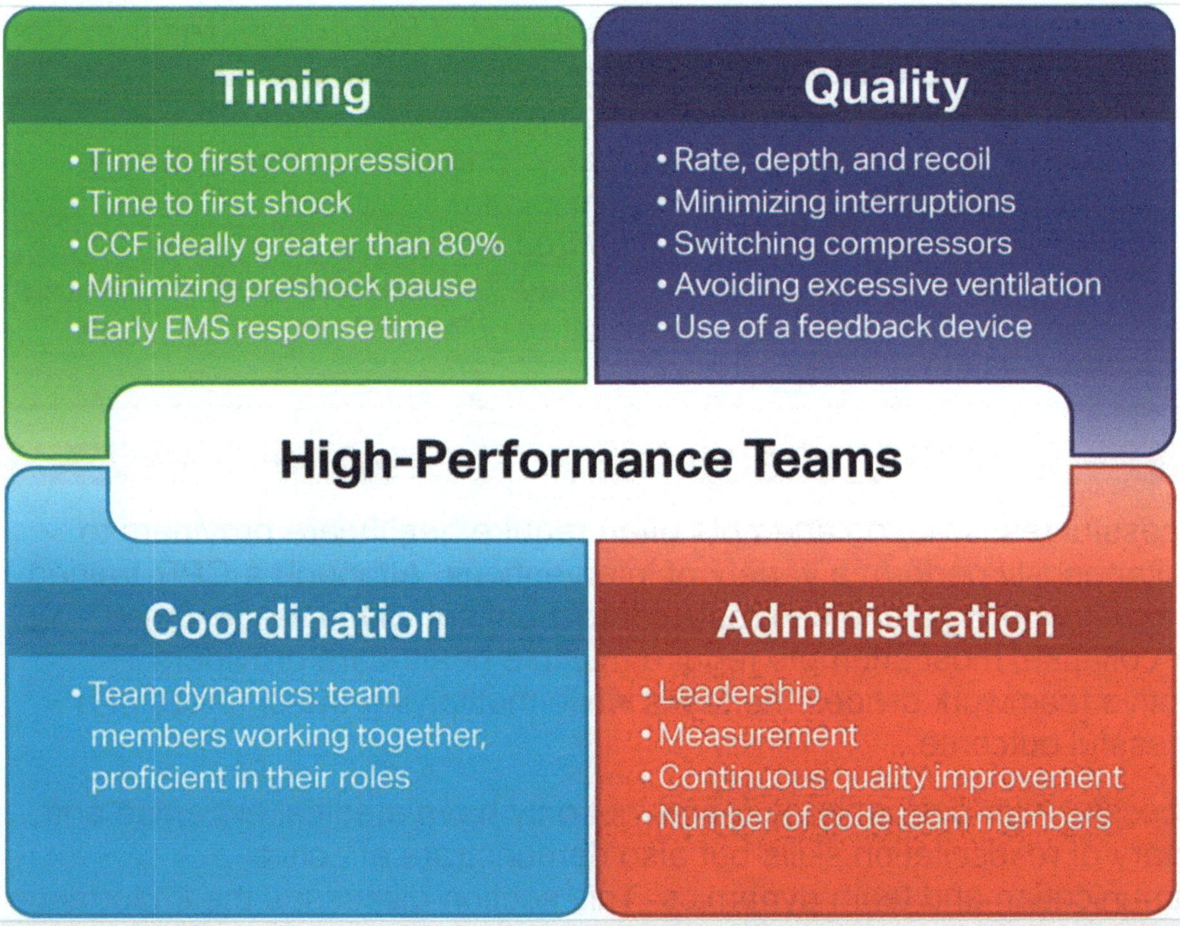

Timing
- Time to first compression
- Time to first shock
- CCF ideally greater than 80%
- Minimizing preshock pause
- Early EMS response time

Quality
- Rate, depth, and recoil
- Minimizing interruptions
- Switching compressors
- Avoiding excessive ventilation
- Use of a feedback device

High-Performance Teams

Coordination
- Team dynamics: team members working together, proficient in their roles

Administration
- Leadership
- Measurement
- Continuous quality improvement
- Number of code team members

Figure 32. Key areas of focus for high-performance teams to increase survival rates.

Critical Concepts: Ways to Increase Chest Compression Fraction
Whether you are a team member or the Team Leader during a resuscitation attempt, you should understand how a high-performance team can maximize CCF when performing CPR during a cardiac arrest. The team can achieve key metrics and increase CCF by doing the following:
- **Precharge the defibrillator** *15 seconds before a 2-minute rhythm analysis (deliver shock immediately if VF or pVT on the monitor). This makes it possible to conduct a rhythm analysis and give a shock (if needed) within 10 seconds or less.*
- *Perform a pulse check during the precharge phase in anticipation of an organized rhythm during analysis (a pulse check during compressions is not a reliable indicator of CPR quality).*

- *Compressor **hovers over the chest** (not touching it), ready to start chest compressions immediately after a shock, a rhythm analysis, or other necessary pauses in compressions.*
- **Have the next compressor ready to take over immediately.**
- *Intubate without pausing compressions.*
- *Deliver medications during compressions.*
- *Consider CPR protocols that deliver fewer pauses (eg, continuous compressions with asynchronous ventilation using a bag-mask device).*

High-Performance Team Roles and Dynamics

Successful resuscitation attempts often require healthcare providers to simultaneously perform a variety of interventions. Although a CPR-trained bystander working alone can resuscitate a patient within the first moments after collapse, most attempts require multiple healthcare providers. Effective teamwork divides the tasks while multiplying the chances of a successful outcome.

Successful high-performance teams not only have medical expertise and mastery of resuscitation skills but also demonstrate effective communication and team dynamics. This section discusses the importance of team roles, behaviors of effective Team Leaders and team members, and elements of effective high-performance team dynamics.

Critical Concepts: Understanding Team Roles
Whether you are a team member or a Team Leader during a resuscitation attempt, you should understand your role and the roles of other members. This awareness will help you anticipate
- *What actions will be performed next*
- *How to communicate and work as a member or as a leader of a high-performance team*

Roles in a High-Performance Team

Team Leader Role

Every high-performance team needs a leader to organize the efforts of the group. The Team Leader
- Organizes the group

- Monitors individual performance of team members
- Backs up team members
- Models excellent team behavior
- Trains and coaches
- Facilitates understanding
- Focuses on comprehensive patient care
- Temporarily designates another team member to take over as Team Leader if an advanced procedure is required (eg, advanced airway placement)

The Team Leader is responsible for making sure everything is done at the right time in the right way by monitoring and integrating individual performance of team members. The Team Leader should also help train future Team Leaders and improve team effectiveness. After resuscitation, the Team Leader can help analyze, critique, and practice for the next resuscitation attempt.

The Team Leader also helps team members understand why they must perform certain tasks in a specific way. The Team Leader should be able to explain why it is essential to
- Push hard and fast in the center of the chest
- Ensure complete chest recoil
- Minimize interruptions in chest compressions
- Avoid excessive ventilation

Whereas members of a high-performance team should focus on their individual tasks, the Team Leader must focus on comprehensive patient care.

Team Member Roles

For a successful resuscitation attempt, high-performance team members must be
- Proficient in performing the skills in their scope of practice
- Clear about role assignments
- Prepared to fulfill their role responsibilities
- Well-practiced in resuscitation skills
- Knowledgeable about the algorithms
- Committed to success

Team Member Role: CPR Coach

Many resuscitation teams now include the role of CPR Coach. The CPR Coach supports performance of high-quality BLS skills, allowing the Team Leader to focus on other aspects of clinical care. Studies have shown that resuscitation teams with a CPR Coach perform higher-quality CPR with higher CCF and shorter pause durations compared with teams that don't use a CPR Coach.

The CPR Coach does not need to be a separate role; they can be blended into the current responsibilities of the Monitor/Defibrillator. The CPR Coach's main responsibilities are to help team members provide high-quality CPR and minimize pauses in compressions. The CPR Coach needs a direct line of sight to the Compressor, so they should stand next to the Defibrillator. Below is a description of the CPR Coach's actions.

Coordinate the start of CPR: As soon as a patient is identified as having no pulse, the CPR Coach says, "I am the CPR Coach," and tells providers to begin chest compressions. The CPR Coach can adjust the environment to help ensure high-quality CPR. They can lower the bedrails or the bed, get a step stool, or roll the victim to place a backboard and defibrillator pads.

Coach to improve the quality of chest compressions: The CPR Coach gives feedback about performance of compression depth, rate, and chest recoil. They state the CPR feedback device's data to help the Compressor improve performance. This is useful because visual assessment of CPR quality is often inaccurate.

State the midrange targets: The CPR Coach states the specific midrange targets so that compressions and ventilation are within the recommended range. For example, they should tell the Compressor to compress at a rate of 110/min instead of a rate between 100 and 120/min.

Coach to the midrange targets: The CPR Coach gives team members feedback about their ventilation rate and volume. If needed, they also remind the team about compression-to-ventilation ratio.

Help minimize the length of pauses in compressions: The CPR Coach communicates with the team to help minimize the length of pauses in compressions. Pauses happen when the team defibrillates, switches Compressors, and places an advanced airway.

> ***Critical Concepts: CPR Coach Role***
>
> *The CPR Coach role is designed to help a high-performance team achieve the key metrics of high-quality CPR by providing feedback about*
> - *The Compressor's rate, depth, and recoil*
> - *Delivery of ventilations (rate and volume)*
> - *Compression pauses*
>
> *Working closely with the Team Leader, the CPR Coach should facilitate all compression pauses, including intubation. The CPR Coach should be integrated into the existing role of Monitor/Defibrillator on a high-performance team.*

Elements of Effective Team Dynamics as Part of a High-Performance Team

Roles

Clear Roles and Responsibilities

Every member of the team should know his or her role and responsibilities because each team member's role is important to the performance of the team. Figure 33 identifies 6 team roles for resuscitation. When fewer than 6 people are present, Team Leaders must prioritize these tasks and assign them to the healthcare providers present.

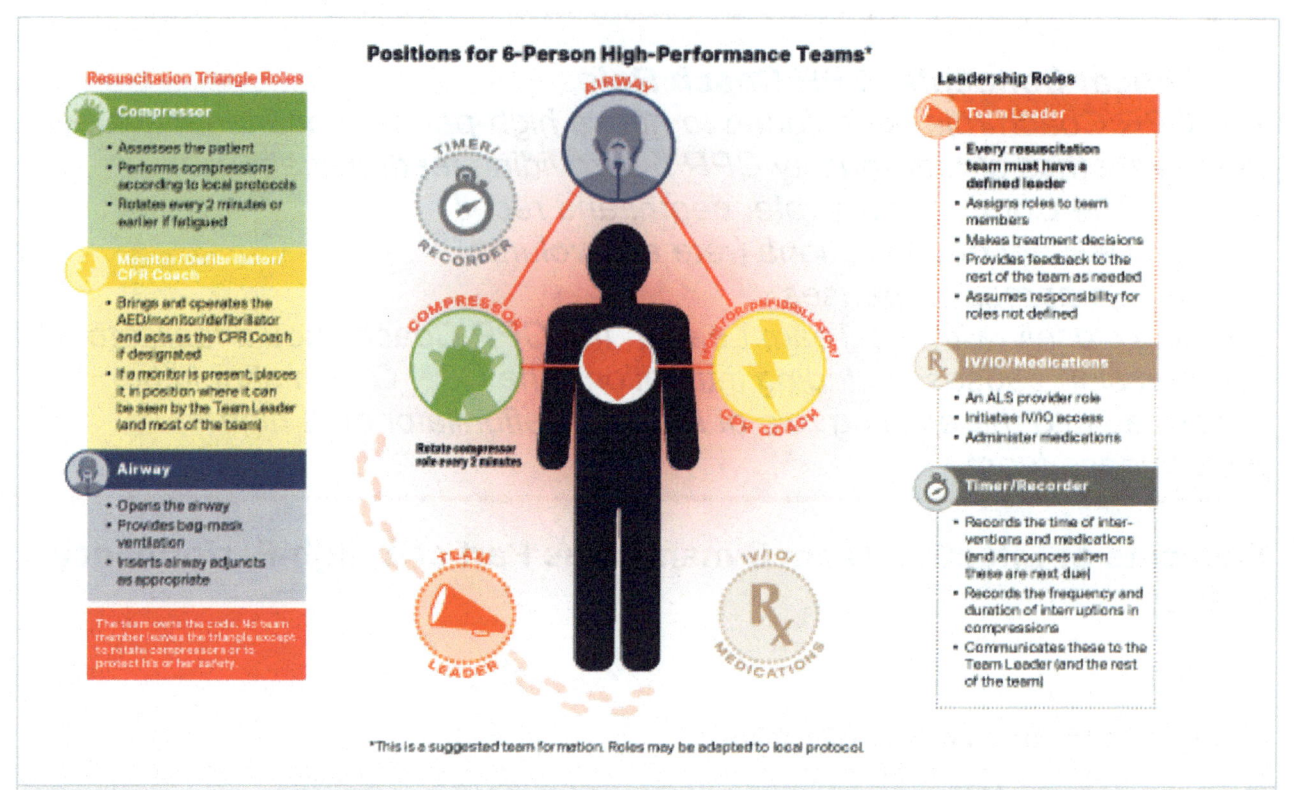

Figure 33. Suggested locations for the Team Leader and team members during case simulations and clinical events.

When roles are unclear, team performance suffers. Signs of unclear roles include
- Performing the same task more than once
- Missing essential tasks
- Assigning team members multiple roles when additional providers are available

For efficiency, the Team Leader must clearly delegate tasks. Team members should communicate when they can handle additional responsibilities. The Team Leader should encourage team members to participate actively and not simply follow directions. Table 10 lists some additional information about roles.

Table 10. Clear Roles and Responsibilities

Team member	Task
Team Leader	• Clearly define all team member roles in the clinical setting

140

	• Distribute tasks evenly to all available team members who are sure of their responsibilities
Team members	• Seek out and perform clearly defined tasks appropriate to their abilities • Ask for a new task or role if an assignment is beyond their level of expertise • Accept only assignments that are within their level of expertise

Knowing Your Limitations

Everyone on the team should know his or her own limitations and capabilities, including the Team Leader. This allows the Team Leader to evaluate resources and call for backup when necessary. High-performance team members should anticipate situations in which they need help and inform the Team Leader.

During the stress of an attempted resuscitation, do not practice or explore a new skill, especially without seeking advice from more experienced personnel. If you need extra help, request it early rather than waiting until the patient deteriorates further. Asking for help is not a sign of weakness or incompetence; it is better to have more help than needed rather than not enough help, which might negatively affect patient outcome. Table 11 lists some additional information about knowing your limitations.

Table 11. Knowing Your Limitations	
Team member	**Task**
Team Leader and team members	• Call for assistance early rather than waiting until the patient deteriorates • Seek advice from more experienced personnel when the patient's condition worsens despite primary treatment • Allow others to carry out assigned tasks, especially if the task is essential to treatment
Team members	• Seek advice from more experienced personnel before starting an unfamiliar treatment or therapy • Accept assistance from others when it is readily available

Constructive Interventions

During a resuscitation attempt, anyone on a high-performance team may need to intervene tactfully if a team member is about to take an inappropriate action. Team Leaders should avoid confrontation with team members and instead debrief afterward if needed. Table 12 lists some additional information about constructive interventions.

Table 12. Constructive Interventions

Team member	Task
Team Leader	• Ask that a different intervention be started if it has a higher priority • Reassign a team member who is trying to function beyond his or her level of skill
Team members	• Suggest an alternative drug or dose confidently • Question a colleague who is about to make a mistake • Intervene if a team member is about to administer a drug incorrectly

What to Communicate

Knowledge Sharing

Sharing information is critical to effective team performance. Team Leaders may become fixated on a specific treatment or diagnostic approach. Examples of these types of *fixation errors* are

- "Everything is OK."
- "This and only this is the correct path."
- "Do anything but this."

Table 13. Knowledge Sharing

Team member	Task
Team Leader	• Encourage information sharing

	• Ask for suggestions about interventions, differential diagnoses, and possible overlooked treatments (eg, intravenous access or drug treatments) • Look for clinical signs that are relevant to the treatment
Team members	• Share information with each other • Accept information that will improve their roles

When resuscitative efforts are ineffective, go back to the basics and talk as a team. Have conversations like, "Well, we've observed the following on the Primary Assessment…. Have we missed something?" High-performance team members should provide all available information about changes in the patient's condition to ensure that the Team Leader makes appropriate decisions. Table 13 lists some additional information about knowledge sharing.

Summarizing and Reevaluating

An essential role of the Team Leader is monitoring and reevaluating interventions, assessment findings, and the patient's status.

Team Leaders should periodically state this information to the team and announce the plan for the next few steps. Remember that the patient's condition can change. Be flexible to changing treatment plans, and ask for information and summaries from the Timer/Recorder as well. Table 14 lists some additional information about summarizing and reevaluating.

Table 14. Summarizing and Reevaluating

Team member	Task
Team Leader	• Continuously revisit decisions about differential diagnoses • Maintain an ongoing record of treatments and the patient's response • Change a treatment strategy when new information supports it • Inform arriving personnel of the current status and plans for further action
Team Leader and team members	• Note significant changes in the patient's clinical condition • Increase monitoring if patient's condition deteriorates (eg, frequency of respirations and blood pressure)

How to Communicate

Closed-Loop Communications

When communicating with high-performance team members, the Team Leader should use these closed-loop communication steps:

1. Give a message, order, or assignment to a team member.
2. Request a clear response and eye contact from the team member to ensure that he or she understood the message.
3. Confirm that the team member completed the task before you assign him or her another task.

Table 15 lists some additional information about closed-loop communications.

Table 15. Closed-Loop Communications

Team member	Task
Team members	• After receiving a task, close the loop by informing the Team Leader when the task begins or ends, such as, "The IV is in" • Only give drugs after verbally confirming the order with the Team Leader
Team Leader	• Always assign tasks by using closed-loop communication such as, "Give 1 milligram of epinephrine and let me know when it has been given" • Assign additional tasks to a team member *only* after receiving confirmation of a completed assignment

Clear Messages

Clear messages means concise communication spoken with distinctive speech in a controlled voice. All healthcare providers should deliver clear messages calmly and directly, without yelling or shouting. Distinct, concise messages are crucial for clear communication because unclear

Table 16. Clear Messages

Team member	Task
Team Leader	• Encourage all team members to speak clearly and use complete sentences
Team Leader and team members	• Repeat orders, and question them if the slightest doubt exists • Be careful not to mumble, yell, scream, or shout • Ensure that only 1 person talks at a time

communication can delay treatment or cause medication errors. Yelling or shouting can also impair effective high-performance team interaction. Table 16 lists some additional information about clear messages.

Mutual Respect

The best high-performance team members mutually respect each other and work together in a collegial, supportive manner. Everyone in a high-performance team must abandon ego and show respect during the resuscitation attempt, regardless of any additional training or experience that specific team members may have. Table 17 lists some additional information about mutual respect.

Table 17. Mutual Respect[1]

Team member	Task
Team Leader	• Acknowledge correctly completed assignments by saying, "Thanks—good job!"
Team Leader and team members	• Show interest and listen to what others say • Speak in a friendly, controlled tone of voice • Avoid displaying aggression if teammates do not initially understand each other

	• Understand that when one person raises his voice, others will respond similarly
	• Try not to confuse directive behavior with aggression

Respiratory Arrest

Overview

For respiratory arrest, this patient is unconscious and unresponsive and has a pulse, but respirations are completely absent or clearly inadequate to maintain effective oxygenation and ventilation. Do not confuse agonal gasps with adequate respirations. Use the BLS, Primary, and Secondary Assessments even though the patient is in respiratory but not cardiac arrest.

Drugs for Respiratory Arrest

Drugs for respiratory arrest include oxygen. Systems or facilities that use rapid sequence intubation may consider additional drugs.

Normal and Abnormal Breathing

The average respiratory rate for an adult at rest is about 12 to 20/min. Typically, a tidal volume of 6 to 8 mL/kg maintains normal oxygenation and elimination of CO_2.

Tachypnea is a respiratory rate above 20/min and *bradypnea* is a respiratory rate below 12/min. A respiratory rate below 6/min (*hypoventilation*), requires assisted ventilation with a bag-mask device or advanced airway with 100% oxygen.

Identifying Respiratory Problems by Severity

Identifying the severity of a respiratory problem will help you decide the most appropriate interventions. Be alert for signs of respiratory distress and respiratory failure.

Respiratory Distress

Respiratory distress is a clinical state characterized by abnormal respiratory rate or effort—either increased (eg, tachypnea, nasal flaring, retractions, and use of accessory muscles) or inadequate (eg, hypoventilation or bradypnea).

Respiratory distress can range from mild to severe. For example, a patient with mild tachypnea and a mild increase in respiratory effort with changes in airway sounds is in mild respiratory distress. A patient with marked tachypnea, significantly increased respiratory effort, deterioration in skin color, and changes in mental status is in severe respiratory distress. Severe respiratory distress can indicate respiratory failure.

Respiratory distress typically includes some or all of these signs in varying severity:
- Tachypnea
- Increased respiratory effort (eg, nasal flaring, retractions)
- Inadequate respiratory effort (eg, hypoventilation or bradypnea)
- Abnormal airway sounds (eg, stridor, wheezing, grunting)
- Tachycardia
- Pale, cool skin (however, some causes of respiratory distress, like sepsis, may cause warm, red, and diaphoretic skin)
- Changes in level of consciousness/agitation
- Use of abdominal muscles to help breathe

Respiratory distress is apparent when a patient tries to maintain adequate gas exchange despite airway obstruction, reduced lung compliance, lung tissue disease, or increase in metabolic demand (sepsis or ketoacidosis). As these patients tire or their respiratory function, effort, or both deteriorate, they cannot maintain adequate gas exchange and develop clinical signs of respiratory failure.

Respiratory Failure

Respiratory failure is a clinical state of inadequate oxygenation, ventilation, or both. Respiratory failure is often the end stage of respiratory distress. If the patient has abnormal central nervous system control of breathing or muscle weakness, she may show little or no respiratory effort despite being in respiratory failure. In these situations, you may need to identify respiratory failure based on clinical findings. Confirm the diagnosis with objective measurements, such as pulse oximetry or blood gas analysis.

Suspect *probable respiratory failure* if some of the following signs are present:
- Marked tachypnea
- Bradypnea, apnea
- No respiratory effort
- Poor to absent distal air movement

- Tachycardia (early); bradycardia (late)
- Cyanosis
- Stupor, coma (late)

Respiratory failure can result from upper or lower airway obstruction, lung tissue disease, and disordered control of breathing (eg, apnea or shallow, slow respirations). When respiratory effort is inadequate, respiratory failure can occur without typical signs of respiratory distress. Respiratory failure requires intervention to prevent deterioration to cardiac arrest. Respiratory failure can occur with a rise in arterial carbon dioxide levels (hypercapnia), a drop in blood oxygenation (hypoxemia), or both.

Respiratory distress can lead to respiratory failure, and respiratory failure can lead to respiratory arrest.

Respiratory Arrest

Respiratory arrest is the absence of breathing, usually caused by an event such as drowning or head injury. For an adult in respiratory arrest, provide a tidal volume of approximately 500 to 600 mL (6 to 7 mL/kg), or enough to produce visible chest rise.

Patients with airway obstruction or poor lung compliance may need higher pressures to produce visible chest rise. A pressure-relief valve on a resuscitation bag-mask device may prevent sufficient tidal volume in these patients, so ensure that you can bypass the device's pressure-relief valve and use high pressures, if necessary, to produce visible chest rise.

Caution: Tidal Volume

Most adult bag-mask devices provide a higher tidal volume than is recommended. Caution is advised. Consider using a pediatric bag-mask device.

Critical Concepts: Avoiding Excessive Ventilation

Avoid excessive ventilation (too many breaths or too large a volume) during respiratory arrest and cardiac arrest. Excessive ventilation can cause gastric inflation and complications such as regurgitation and aspiration. More important, excessive ventilation can be harmful because it
- *Increases intrathoracic pressure*
- *Decreases venous return to the heart*

- *Diminishes cardiac output and survival*
- *May cause cerebral vasoconstriction, reducing blood flow to the brain*

BLS Assessment

When evaluating a patient, proceed with the BLS Assessment after you verify scene safety.

Assess and Reassess the Patient

The systematic approach is assessment, and then action, for each step in the sequence. Check for responsiveness, shout for nearby help, and activate the emergency response system via a mobile device (if appropriate). Get an AED and emergency equipment (or send someone to do so). Look for no breathing or only gasping and check pulse (simultaneously) within 10 seconds.

Remember to assess first, and then perform the appropriate action.

Initial actions should include
- Checking for responsiveness
- Calling for additional help
- Assessing ABCs

Ventilation and Pulse Check

If a patient has respiratory arrest with a pulse, deliver 1 breath every 6 seconds, or 10 breaths/min using a bag-mask device or any advanced airway device. Each breath should be delivered for 1 second and achieve a visible chest rise. Be careful to avoid excessive ventilation. Check the pulse about every 2 minutes, taking between 5 and 10 seconds to check. If no pulse, start CPR.

If possible opioid overdose, administer naloxone, if available, per protocol.

Primary Assessment

Airway Management in Respiratory Arrest

If bag-mask ventilation is adequate, you may defer the decision to place an advanced airway until the Primary Assessment. Advanced airways include laryngeal mask airways, laryngeal tubes, and endotracheal (ET) tubes. If advanced airways are within your scope of practice, you may use them when appropriate and available.

Note: Ongoing quantitative waveform capnography will confirm and monitor placement of the advanced airway while the patient is intubated.

Managing Respiratory Arrest

Management of respiratory arrest includes both BLS and ACLS interventions. These interventions may include
- Giving supplemental oxygen
- Opening the airway
- Providing basic ventilation
- Using basic airway adjuncts (oropharyngeal airway [OPA] and nasopharyngeal airway [NPA])
- Suctioning the airway

Remember, for patients with a perfusing rhythm, deliver breaths once every 6 seconds.

Giving Supplemental Oxygen

Give oxygen to patients with acute cardiac symptoms or respiratory distress. Monitor their oxygen saturation, and adjust the supplemental oxygen to maintain at least 95% saturation (90% for ACS, and 92% to 98% for post–cardiac arrest care). Use 100% oxygen when treating patients in respiratory or cardiac arrest.

See the ACLS Student Resources for details on using oxygen for patients who are not in respiratory or cardiac arrest.

Opening the Airway

Common Cause of Airway Obstruction

The most common cause of upper airway obstruction in an unresponsive patient is loss of tone in the throat muscles (Figure 34 shows the airway anatomy). In this case, the patient's tongue falls back and obstructs the airway at the pharynx (Figure 35A).

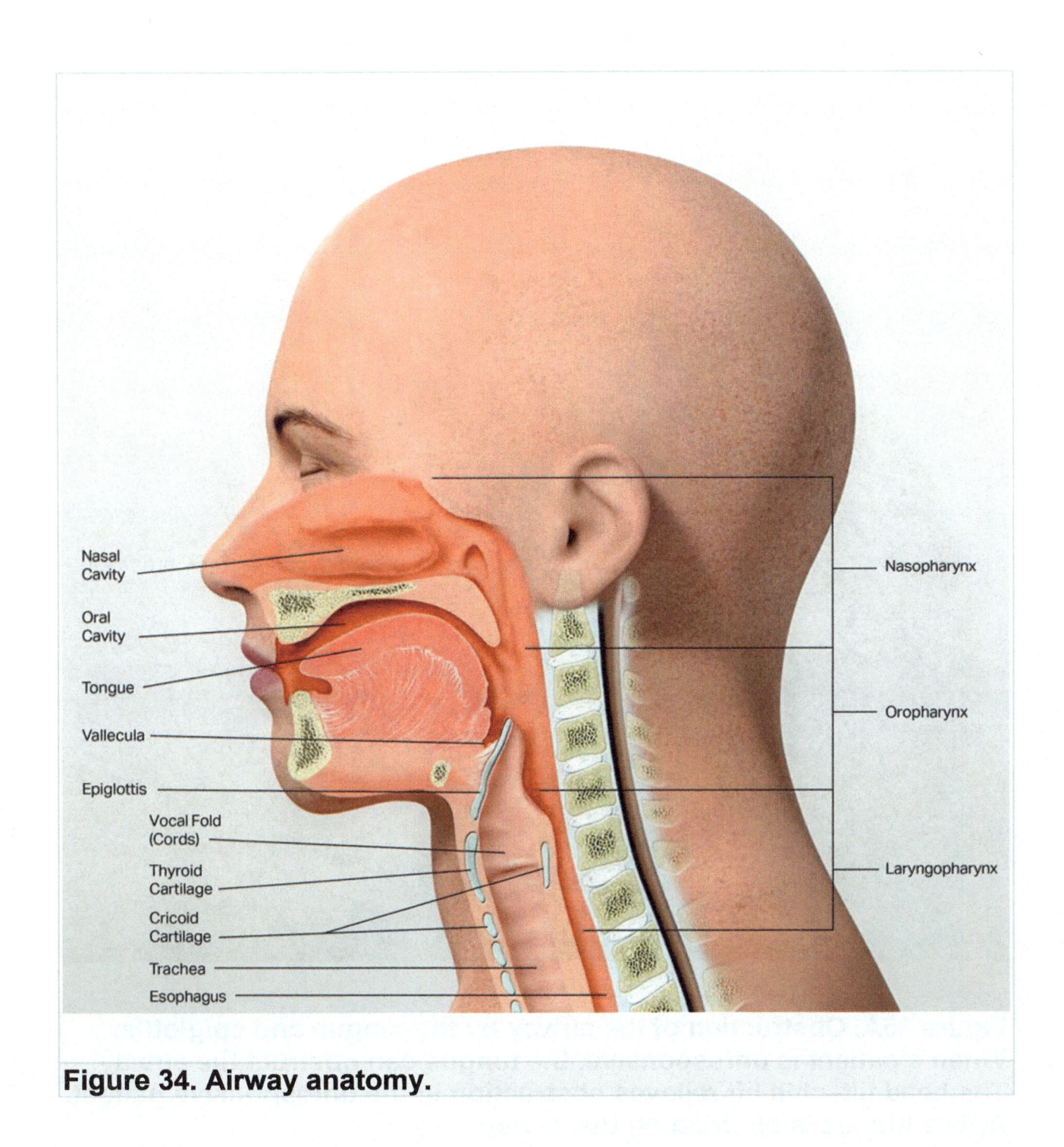

Figure 34. Airway anatomy.

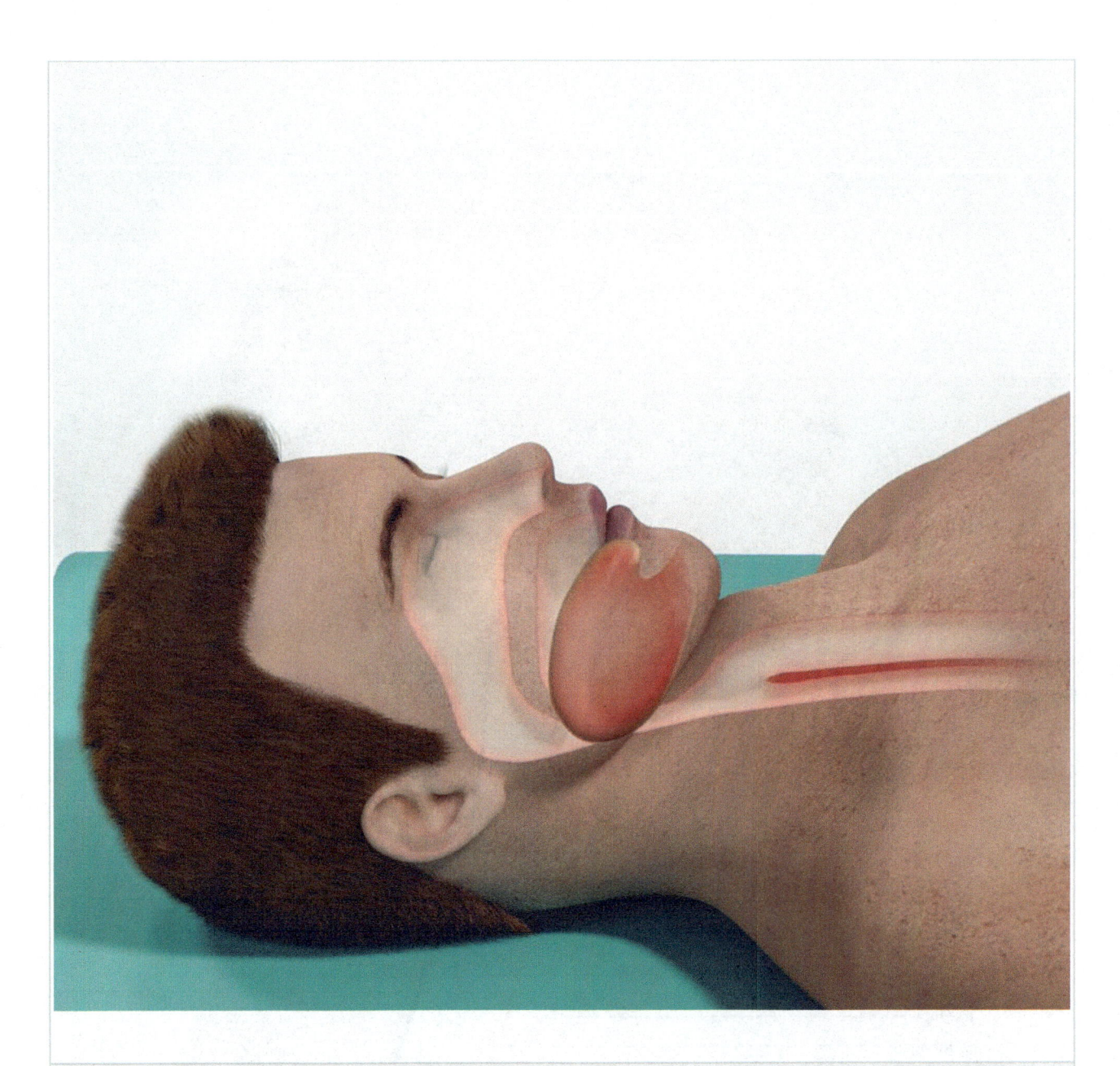

Figure 35A. Obstruction of the airway by the tongue and epiglottis. When a patient is unresponsive, the tongue can obstruct the airway. The head tilt–chin lift relieves obstruction in the unresponsive patient. A, The tongue is obstructing the airway.

Basic Airway Opening Techniques

Basic airway opening techniques relieve airway obstruction by the tongue or from relaxed upper airway muscles. One such technique requires tilting the head and lifting the chin: *the head tilt–chin lift* (Figure 35B).

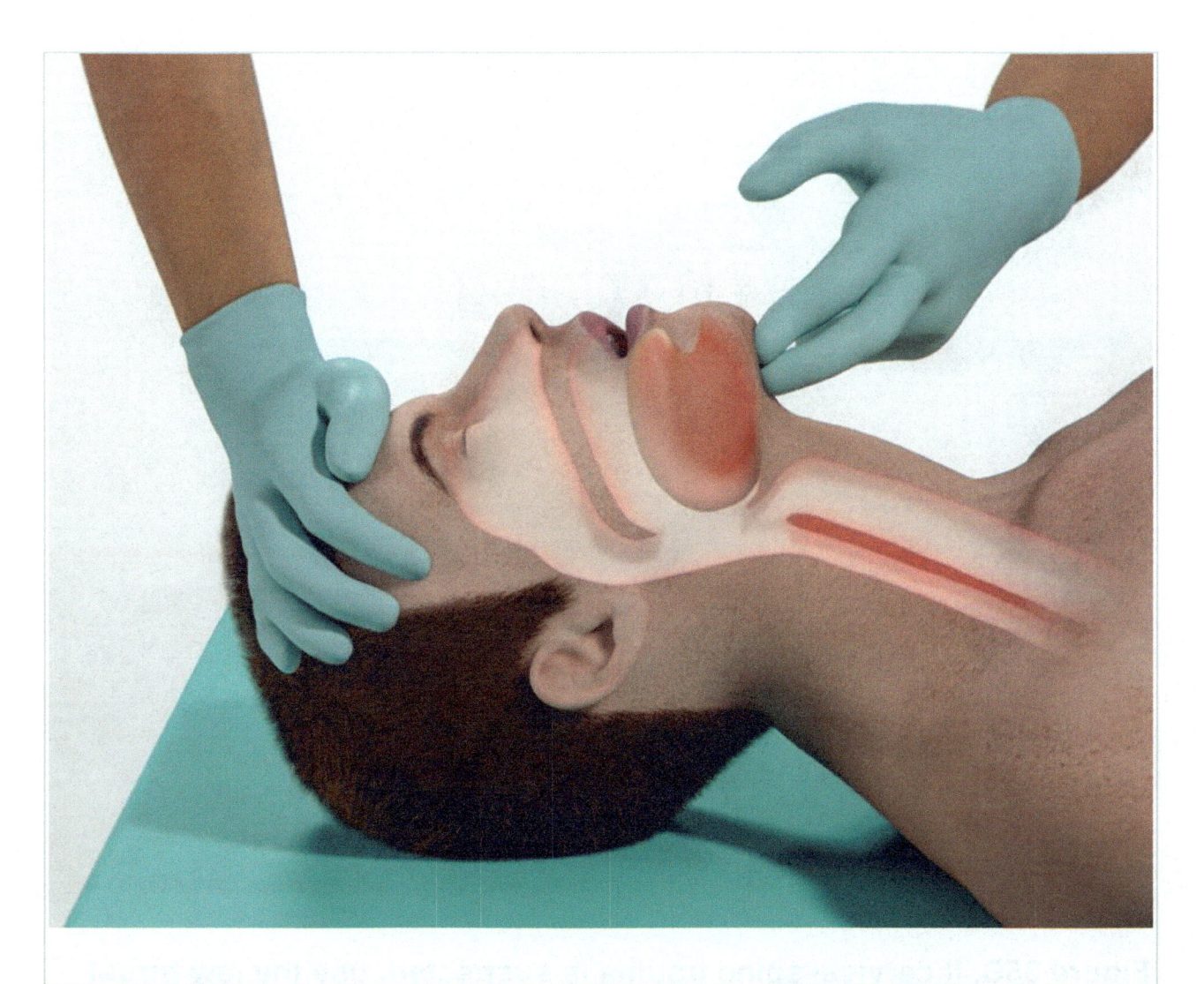

Figure 35B. The head tilt–chin lift lifts the tongue, relieving the obstruction.

In a trauma patient with suspected neck injury, try using a jaw-thrust technique that doesn't extend the head (Figure 35C). But because maintaining an open airway and providing ventilation is a priority, use the head tilt–chin lift if the jaw thrust does not open the airway.

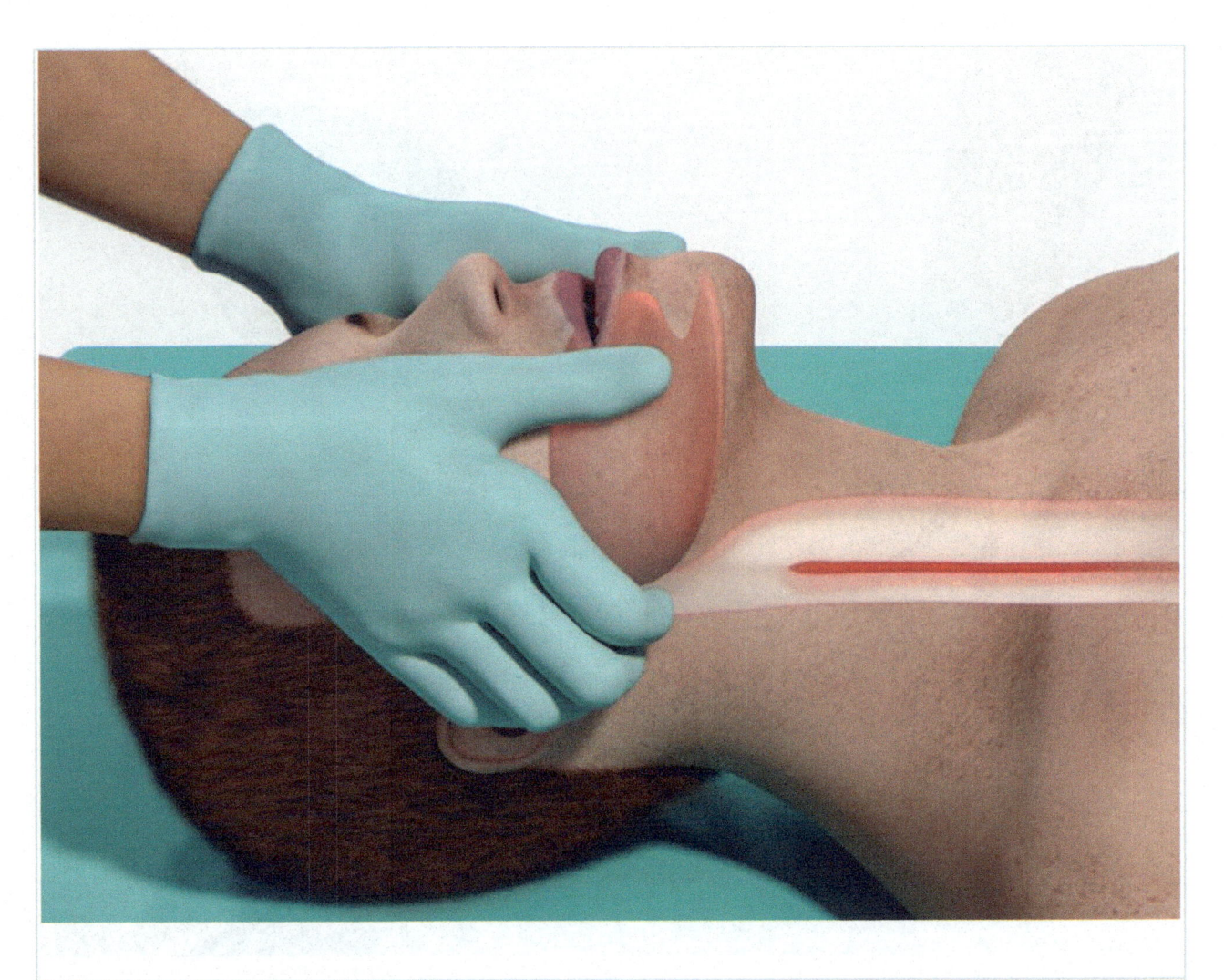

Figure 35C. If cervical spine trauma is suspected, use the jaw thrust without head extension.

Airway Management

Properly positioning the airway may be all you need to do for patients who can breathe spontaneously. In patients who are unconscious with no cough or gag reflex, insert an OPA or NPA to maintain an open airway.

If you find an unresponsive patient who was choking and is now in respiratory arrest, open the mouth wide and look for a foreign object. If you see one, remove it with your fingers. If you do not see a foreign object, start CPR. Each time you open the airway to give breaths, open the mouth wide, and look for and remove any foreign object. If you see no foreign object, resume CPR.

Providing Basic Ventilation

Basic airway skills used to ventilate a patient are
- Head tilt–chin lift
- Jaw thrust without head extension (suspected cervical spine trauma)
- Mouth-to-mouth ventilation
- Mouth-to-nose ventilation
- Mouth-to–barrier device ventilation (using a pocket mask)
- Bag-mask ventilation

Bag-Mask Ventilation

Bag-mask devices—which consist of a ventilation bag attached to a face mask—have been part of emergency ventilation for decades. These devices are the most common way to provide positive-pressure ventilation. When you use a bag-mask device, deliver approximately 500 to 600 mL tidal volume sufficient to produce chest rise over 1 second. Bag-mask ventilation is not the recommended method of ventilation for single rescuers during CPR. (A single rescuer should use a pocket mask for ventilation, if available.)

Providers can use the following techniques to hold the bag-mask device, depending on the number of rescuers:
- Use of the bag-mask device by 1 rescuer (Figure 36): The rescuer gets into position at the patient's head and circles the thumb and first finger around the top of the mask (forming a "C") while using the third, fourth, and fifth fingers (forming an "E") to lift the jaw. This is called the *E-C clamp technique*.
- Use of the bag-mask device by 2 rescuers (Figure 37): Two trained and experienced rescuers can more easily provide bag-mask ventilation. The rescuer at the patient's head tilts the patient's head and seals the mask against the patient's face, with the thumb and first finger of each hand creating a "C," to provide a complete seal around the edges of the mask. The rescuer uses the remaining 3 fingers (the "E") to lift the jaw (this holds the airway open). The second rescuer slowly squeezes the bag (over 1 second) until the chest rises. Both providers should observe chest rise.

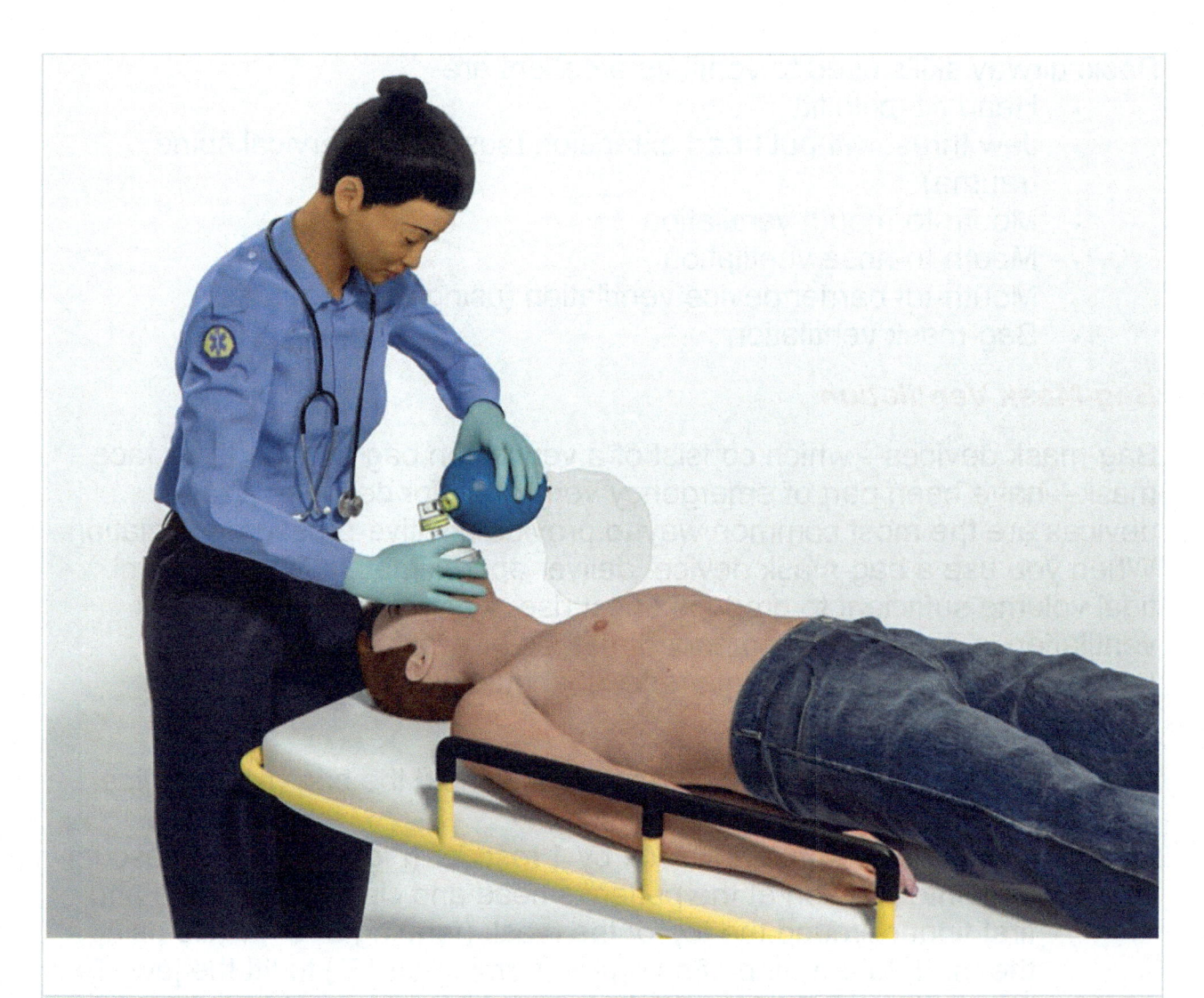

Figure 36. E-C clamp technique for holding the mask while lifting the jaw.

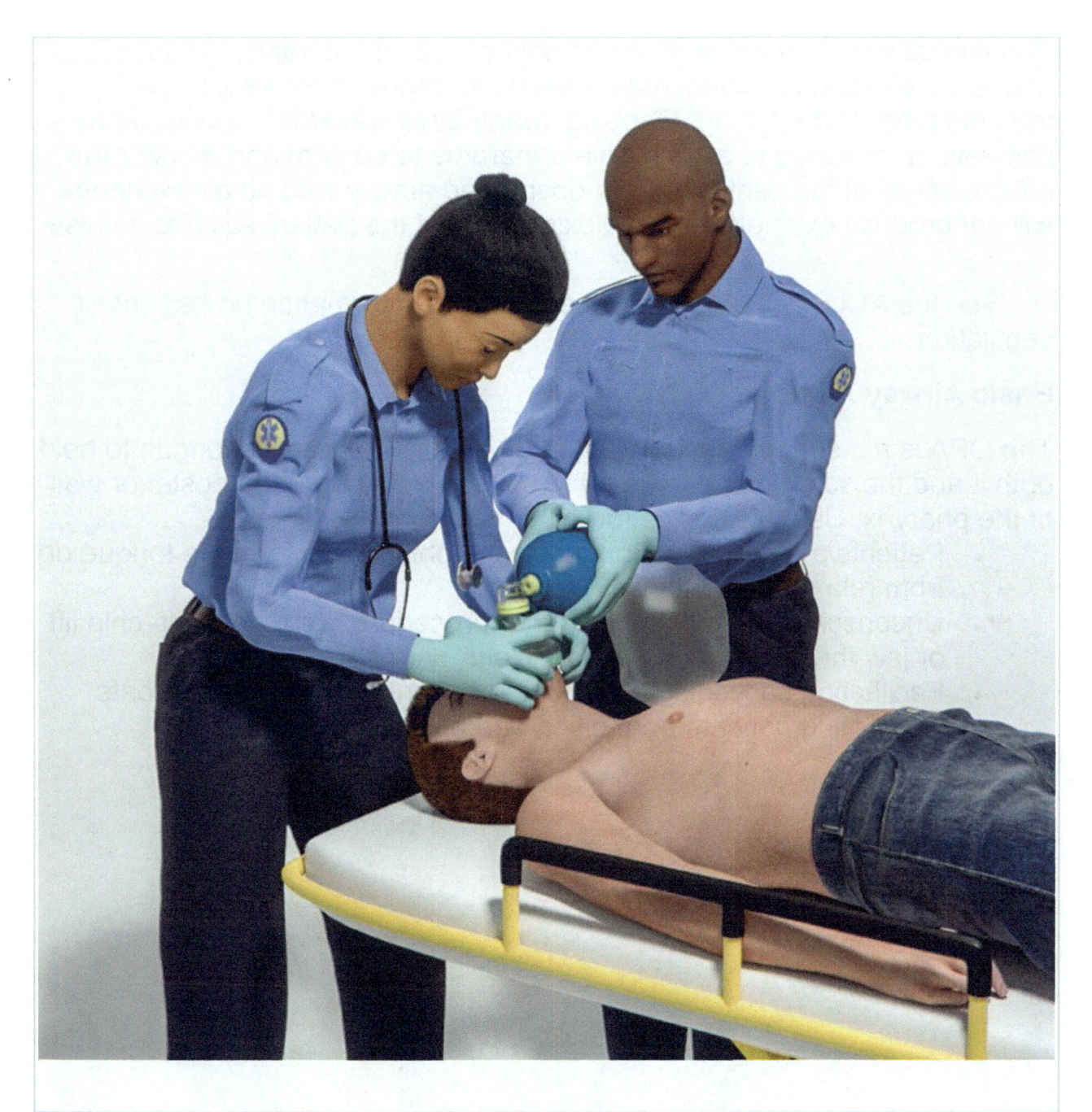

Figure 37. Two-rescuer use of the bag-mask device.

The universal connections on all airway devices allow you to connect any ventilation bag to numerous adjuncts. Valves and ports may include
- One-way valves to prevent the patient from rebreathing exhaled air
- Oxygen ports to administer supplemental oxygen
- Medication ports to administer liquid and other medications
- Suction ports to clear the airway
- Ports to provide quantitative sampling of $ETCO_2$

You can attach other adjuncts to the patient end of the valve, including a pocket face mask, laryngeal mask airway, laryngeal tube, esophageal-tracheal tube, and ET tube. Ongoing quantitative waveform capnography can also be attached to a bag-valve apparatus to confirm and monitor the effectiveness of the ventilation. An obstructed airway with no air exchange will not produce exhaled carbon dioxide, even if the patient still has a pulse.

See the ACLS Student Resources for more information on bag-mask ventilation.

Basic Airway Adjuncts: OPA

The OPA is a J-shaped device (Figure 38A) that fits over the tongue to hold both it and the soft hypopharyngeal structures away from the posterior wall of the pharynx. Use this device for
- Patients at risk of developing airway obstruction from the tongue or from relaxed upper airway muscles
- Unconscious patients when other procedures (eg, head tilt–chin lift or jaw thrust) fail to maintain a clear, unobstructed airway
- Facilitating suctioning of intubated patients' mouths and throats
- Preventing patients from biting and obstructing the ET tube

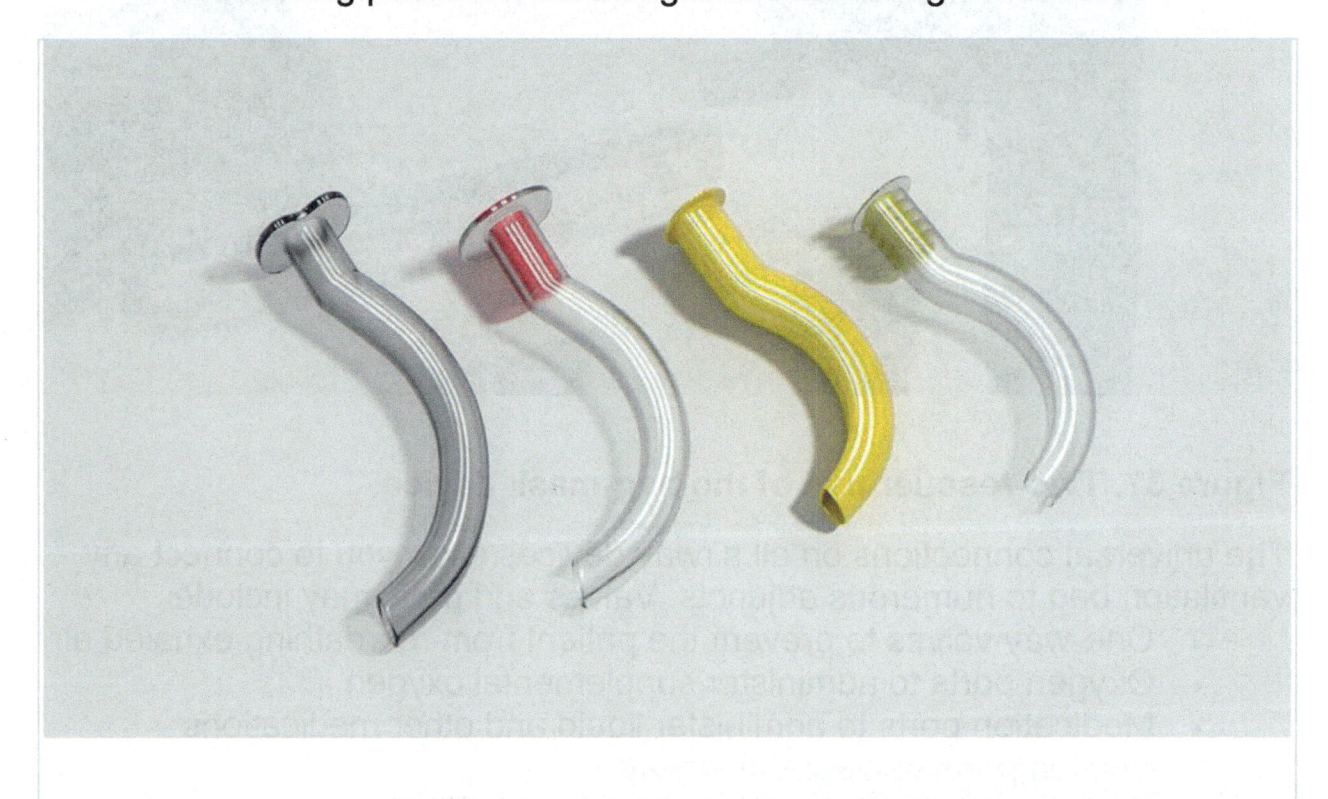

Figure 38A. Oropharyngeal airways. A, Oropharyngeal airway devices.

You may also use an OPA during bag-mask ventilation when a rescuer might unknowingly push down on the chin, blocking the airway.

However, do not use an OPA with a conscious or semiconscious patient because it may stimulate gagging and vomiting. Before using an OPA, check whether the patient has an intact cough and gag reflex. If so, do not use an OPA.

Technique of OPA Insertion

- Clear the mouth and pharynx of secretions, blood, or vomit by using a rigid pharyngeal suction tip if possible.
- Select the proper size OPA, and place it against the side of the face (Figure 38B). When the flange of the OPA is at the corner of the mouth, the tip is at the angle of the mandible. Insert the OPA so that it curves upward toward the hard palate as it enters the mouth.
- As the OPA passes through the oral cavity and approaches the posterior wall of the pharynx, rotate the device 180° into the proper position (Figure 38C). You can also insert the OPA at a 90° angle to the mouth and then turn it down toward the posterior pharynx as you advance the device.

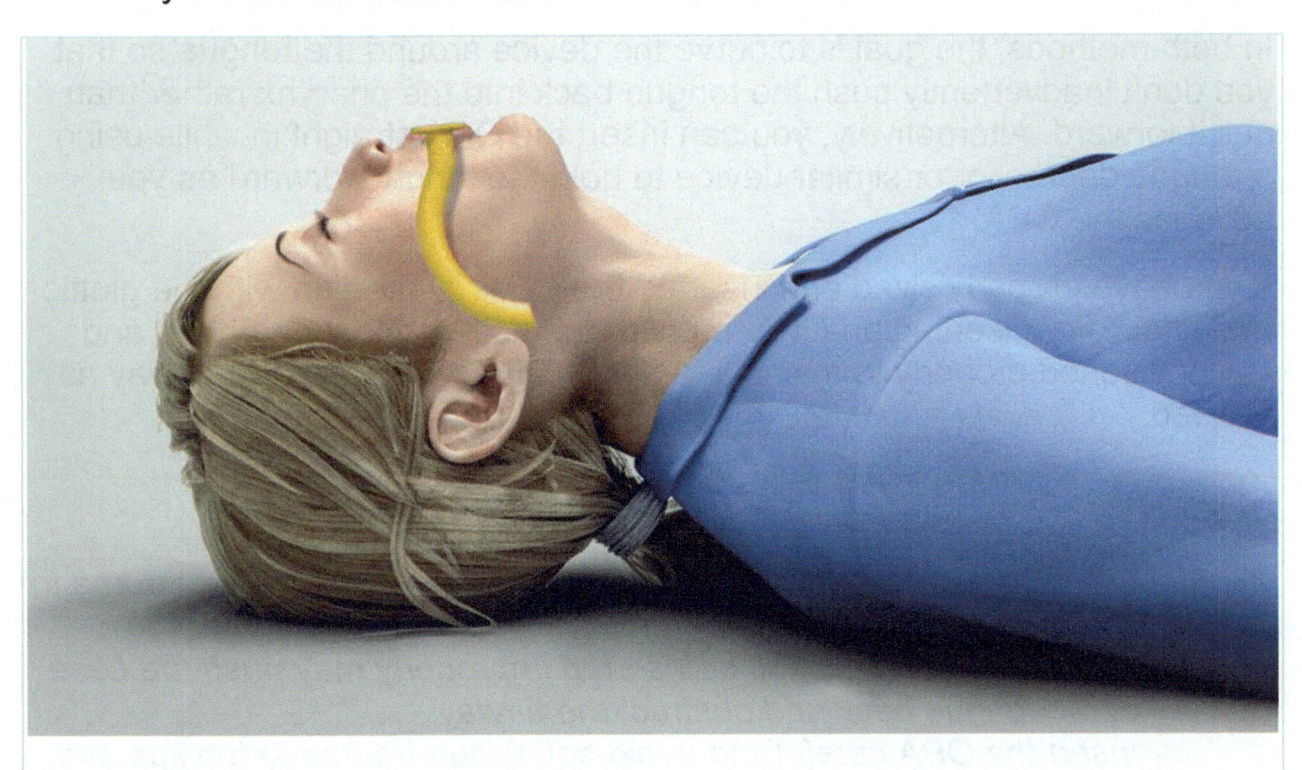

Figure 38B. Oropharyngeal airway device measurement.

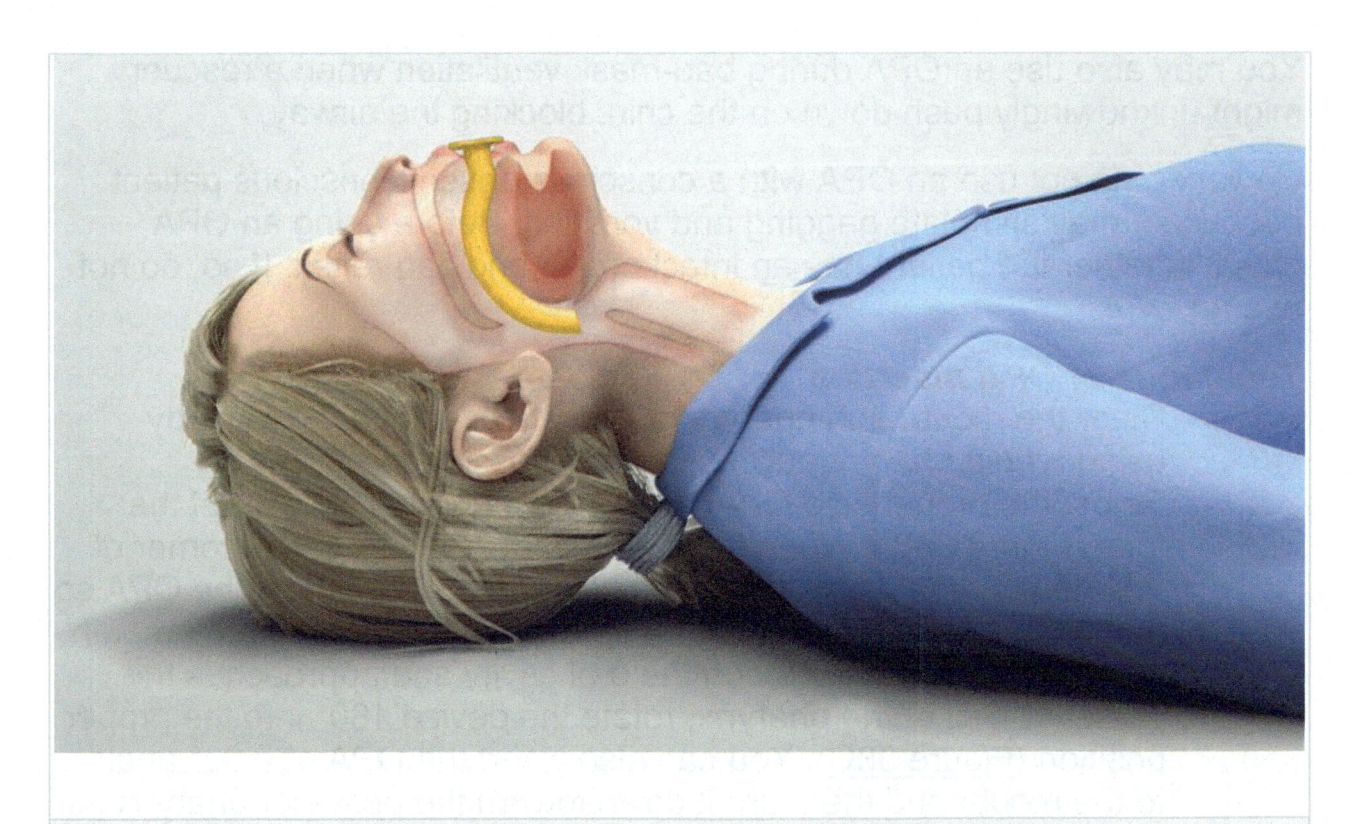

Figure 38C. Oropharyngeal airway device inserted.

In both methods, the goal is to curve the device around the tongue so that you don't inadvertently push the tongue back into the pharynx rather than pull it forward. Alternatively, you can insert the OPA straight in while using a tongue depressor or similar device to hold the tongue forward as you advance the OPA.

If you have properly sized and inserted the OPA, it will align with the glottic opening. After inserting an OPA, monitor the patient. Keep the head and jaw positioned properly to maintain a patent airway. Suction the airway as needed.

Caution: Using an OPA
- *OPAs that are too large may obstruct the larynx or cause trauma to the laryngeal structures.*
- *OPAs that are too small or inserted improperly may push the base of the tongue back and obstruct the airway.*
- *Insert the OPA carefully to avoid soft tissue trauma to the lips and tongue.*

- *Remember to use the OPA only in the unresponsive patient with no cough or gag reflex. If the patient has a cough or gag reflex, the OPA may stimulate vomiting and laryngospasm.*

Basic Airway Adjuncts: NPA

The NPA is used as an alternative to an OPA in patients who need a basic airway adjunct. The NPA is a soft rubber or plastic uncuffed tube (Figure 39A) that provides a conduit for airflow between the nostrils and the pharynx.

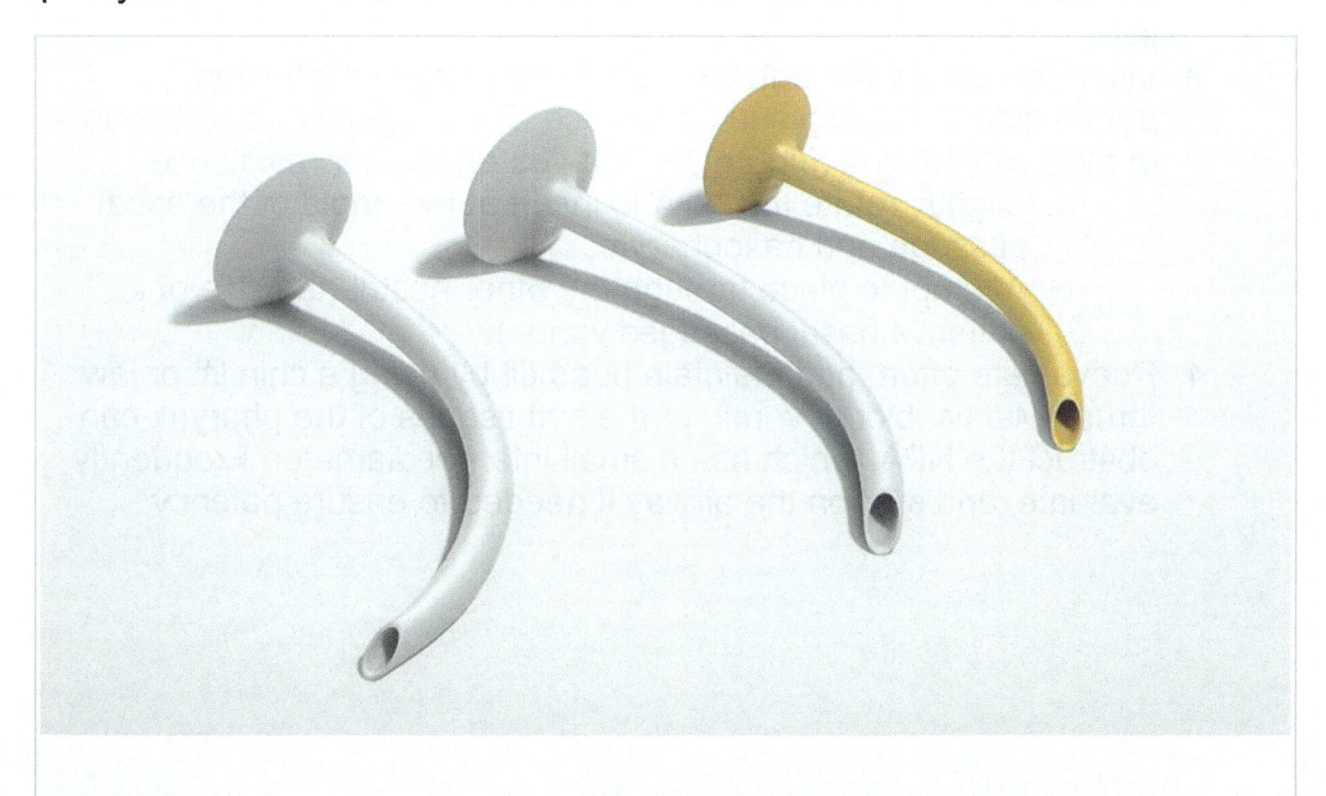

Figure 39A. Nasopharyngeal airways. A, Nasopharyngeal airway devices.

Unlike oral airways, NPAs may be used in conscious, semiconscious, or unconscious patients (patients with an intact cough and gag reflex). Use an NPA when inserting an OPA is technically difficult or dangerous, such as for patients with a gag reflex, trismus, massive trauma around the mouth, or wired jaws. You may also use NPAs in patients who are neurologically impaired with poor pharyngeal tone or coordination leading to upper airway obstruction.

Technique of NPA Insertion
1. Select the proper size NPA.
   a. Compare the outer circumference of the NPA with the inner opening of the nostrils. The NPA should not be so large that it causes sustained blanching of the nostrils. You can use the diameter of the patient's smallest finger as a guide for the proper size.
   b. The NPA should be as long as the distance from the tip of the patient's nose to the earlobe (Figure 39B).
2. Lubricate the airway with a water-soluble lubricant or anesthetic jelly.
3. Insert the airway through the nostril in a posterior direction perpendicular to the plane of the face. Pass it gently along the floor of the nasopharynx (Figure 39C). If you encounter resistance
   a. Slightly rotate the NPA to insert at the angle of the nasal passage and nasopharynx
   b. Attempt to place through the other nostril (the size of a patient's nasal passages varies)
4. Reevaluate often, and maintain head tilt by using a chin lift or jaw thrust. Mucus, blood, vomit, or the soft tissues of the pharynx can obstruct the NPA, which has a small internal diameter. Frequently evaluate, and suction the airway if needed to ensure patency.

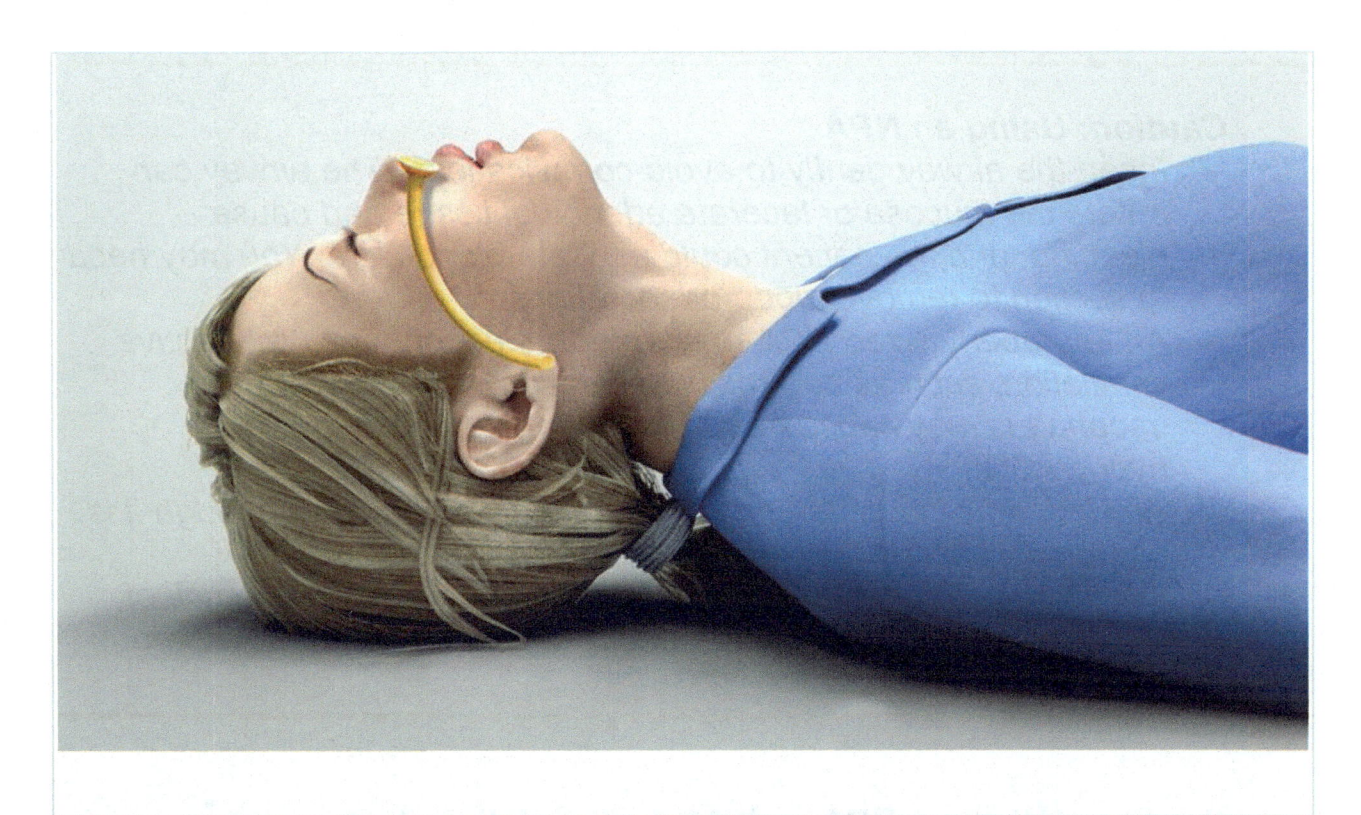

Figure 39B. Nasopharyngeal airway device measurement.

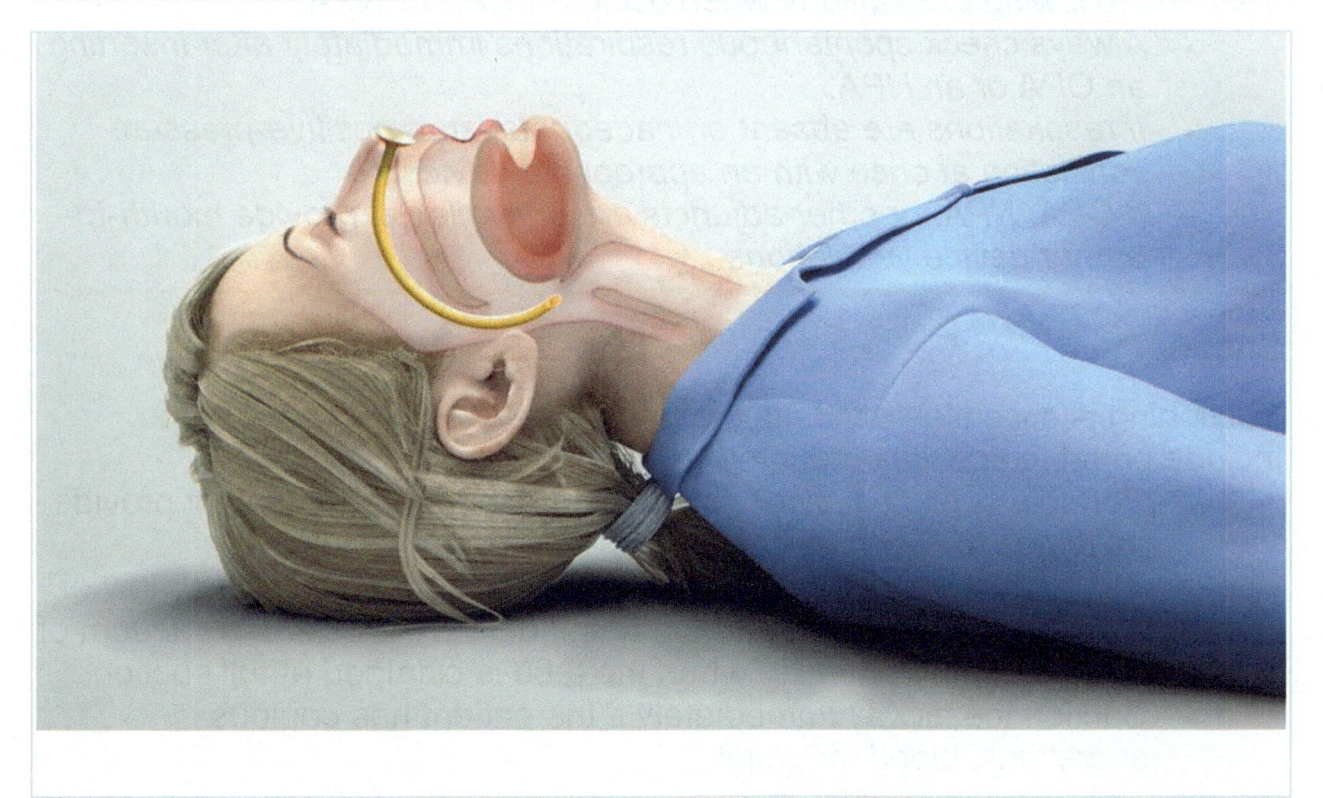

Figure 39C. Nasopharyngeal airway device inserted.

Caution: Using an NPA
- *Insert the airway gently to avoid complications. The airway can irritate the mucosa or lacerate adenoidal tissue and cause bleeding, and the patient could aspirate blood clots. You may need to suction to remove blood or secretions.*
- *An improperly sized NPA may enter the esophagus. With active ventilation, such as bag-mask ventilation, an NPA in the esophagus may cause gastric inflation and possible hypoventilation.*
- *An NPA may cause laryngospasm and vomiting, even though it is commonly tolerated by semiconscious patients.*
- *Use caution in patients with facial trauma because of the risk of misplacement into the cranial cavity through a fractured cribriform plate.*

Caution: Using an OPA or NPA Airway Adjunct
Take the following precautions when using an OPA or NPA:
- *Always check spontaneous respirations immediately after inserting an OPA or an NPA.*
- *If respirations are absent or inadequate, start positive-pressure ventilation at once with an appropriate device.*
- *If OPA, NPA, or other adjuncts are unavailable, provide mouth-to–barrier device ventilations.*

Suctioning

Suctioning is essential to maintain a patient's airway. Suction devices include portable and wall-mounted units.
- Portable suction devices are easy to transport but may not provide adequate suction power.
- Wall-mounted suction units should be able to provide an airflow of more than 40 L/min at the end of the delivery tube and a vacuum of more than −300 mm Hg when the tube is clamped at full suction.
- Suction the airway immediately if the patient has copious secretions, blood, or vomit.

Soft vs Rigid Catheters

For suctioning, you'll use both *soft flexible* and *rigid* catheters.

Use soft flexible catheters (available in sterile wrappers)
- In the mouth or nose
- For ET tube deep suctioning
- For aspiration of thin secretions from the oropharynx and nasopharynx
- To perform intratracheal suctioning
- To suction through an in-place airway (ie, NPA) to access the back of the pharynx in a patient with clenched teeth

Use rigid catheters (eg, Yankauer)
- To suction the oropharynx
- For suctioning thick secretions and particulate matter
- For more effective suctioning of the oropharynx

Oropharyngeal Suctioning Procedure

Follow these steps to perform oropharyngeal suctioning:
- Measure the catheter before suctioning.
- Gently insert the suction catheter or device into the oropharynx beyond the tongue. Do not insert it any further than the distance from the tip of the nose to the earlobe.
- Apply suction by occluding the side opening of the catheter while withdrawing with a rotating or twisting motion.
- If using a rigid suction device, place the tip gently into the oral cavity. Advance by pushing the tongue down to reach the oropharynx if necessary.
- Limit each suction attempt to 10 seconds or less.

ET Tube Suctioning Procedure

Patients with pulmonary secretions may require suctioning even after ET intubation. Follow these steps to perform ET tube suctioning:
- Use a sterile technique to reduce the likelihood of airway contamination.
- Gently insert the catheter into the ET tube but no further because it may injure the ET mucosa or stimulate coughing or bronchospasm. Be sure the side opening is not occluded during insertion.
- Apply suction by occluding the side opening only while withdrawing the catheter with a rotating or twisting motion.

- Do not exceed 10 seconds for a suction attempt. To avoid hypoxemia, precede and follow suctioning attempts with a short period of administration of 100% oxygen.

Monitor the patient's heart rate, pulse, oxygen saturation, and clinical appearance during suctioning. If bradycardia develops, oxygen saturation drops, or clinical appearance deteriorates, interrupt suctioning at once. Administer high-flow oxygen until the heart rate returns to normal and the clinical condition improves. Assist ventilation as needed.

Using Quantitative Waveform Capnography With a Bag-Mask Device

The AHA recommends using quantitative waveform capnography with a bag-mask device to confirm and monitor CPR quality. In addition to using feedback devices for CPR quality, using quantitative waveform capnography can help with real-time adjustment of CPR quality.

Pulse Oximetry

Oxygen saturation can be monitored noninvasively through pulse oximetry. This is a rapid tool to measure and monitor the amount of peripheral oxygen saturation (SpO_2), or oxygen in the blood. Normal pulse oximetry readings should be between 95% and 98%. Give supplemental oxygen when indicated. For cardiac arrest patients, give 100% oxygen. For other clinical conditions, adjust the oxygen administration to achieve an oxygen saturation as follows:
- ACS: 90%
- Stroke: 95% to 98%
- Post–cardiac arrest care: 92% to 98%

Providing Ventilation With an Advanced Airway

Selecting an advanced airway device depends on the high-performance team's training, scope of practice, and equipment. Advanced airways include
- ET tube
- Laryngeal tube
- Laryngeal mask airway

This course will familiarize you with these types of advanced airways but will not discuss how to place them. You will practice ventilating with an advanced airway already in place, and you'll integrate ventilation with chest compressions. To be proficient in using advanced airway devices, you must have adequate initial training and ongoing experience. Providers who insert advanced airways must participate in a process of CQI to document and minimize complications.

Caution: Advanced Airways
- *Some patients cannot be ventilated with a laryngeal mask airway, so be sure to have an alternative airway management strategy, such as a bag-mask device.*
- *For any advanced airway device, the ventilation rate is once every 6 seconds for respiratory or cardiac arrest.*
- *We **do not recommend** the routine use of cricoid pressure in cardiac arrest. Although cricoid pressure in nonarrest patients may protect the airway from aspiration and gastric insufflation during bag-mask ventilation, it also may impede ventilation and interfere with placing a tube or supraglottic airway.*

Only experienced providers should insert these advanced airways.

See ACLS Student Resources for more information about all the advanced airways listed here.

Endotracheal Tube

If you are assisting with *ET intubation*, refer to these basic steps for performing the procedure:
- Prepare for intubation by assembling the necessary equipment.
- Perform ET intubation (see ACLS Student Resources).
- Inflate the cuff or cuffs on the tube.
- Attach the ventilation bag.
- Confirm correct placement by physically examining the patient and using a confirmation device.
    - —Continuous waveform capnography is recommended (in addition to clinical assessment) as the most reliable method of confirming and monitoring correct placement of an ET tube. However, you may use colorimetric and nonwaveform carbon dioxide detectors when waveform capnography is not available.
- Secure the tube in place and monitor for displacement. Use the DOPE mnemonic (displacement, obstruction, pneumothorax, equipment failure) to help you troubleshoot.

Laryngeal Tube

The advantages of the *laryngeal tube* are similar to those of the esophageal-tracheal tube; however, the laryngeal tube is more compact and less complicated to insert. If you are trained to use a laryngeal tube, you may consider it as an alternative to bag-mask ventilation or ET intubation for airway management in cardiac arrest.

Laryngeal Mask Airway

The *laryngeal mask* airway is an advanced airway alternative to ET intubation and provides comparable ventilation for airway management in cardiac arrest.

Precautions for Trauma Patients

When you help ventilate patients with known or suspected cervical spine trauma, avoid moving their head, neck, or spine. This movement can irreversibly injure the spinal cord or worsen a minor spinal cord injury. Approximately 2% of patients with blunt trauma serious enough to require spinal imaging in the ED have a spinal injury, and the risk triples if the patient has a head or facial injury. Assume that any patient with multiple trauma, head injury, or facial trauma has a spine injury, and be particularly cautious if you suspect a cervical spine injury (eg, patients who were in a high-speed crash, fell from a height, or were injured while diving).

Follow these precautions if you suspect cervical spine trauma:
- Open the patient's airway by using a jaw thrust without head extension. But remember that maintaining a patent airway and providing adequate ventilation are your priorities, so use a head tilt–chin lift maneuver if the jaw thrust is not effective.
- Have another team member stabilize the patient's head in a neutral position as you manipulate the airway. *Restrict spinal motion manually rather than with immobilization devices.* Manual spinal immobilization is safer, and cervical collars may complicate airway management or even interfere with airway patency.

Spinal immobilization devices are helpful during transport.

Cardiac Arrest: VF/pVT

Overview

To be successful, any resuscitation attempt needs a strong base of high-quality CPR and defibrillation when the patient's ECG rhythm requires it. Leaders must also assess the performance of each system component, ensuring that system participants can effectively intervene to improve care. This process of quality improvement consists of an iterative and continuous cycle of

- Systematic evaluation of resuscitation care and outcome
- Benchmarking with stakeholder feedback
- Strategic efforts to address identified deficiencies

Another characteristic of high-quality CPR is minimal interruptions in chest compressions. Studies demonstrate that healthcare providers interrupt compressions far too often and for too long, in some cases spending 25% to 50% of a resuscitation attempt *without* delivering chest compressions.

Chest compression fraction (CCF) is the proportion of time during cardiac arrest resuscitation when the rescuer is performing chest compressions. CCF should be as high as possible: ideally greater than 80%. Data suggest lower CCF is associated with decreased ROSC and survival to hospital discharge.

Measurement

Quality improvement relies on valid assessment of resuscitation performance and outcome (refer to the Utstein guidelines in Part 1: Systems of Care).
- Share information among all links in the system of care, including
    - –Dispatch records
    - –EMS patient care report
    - –Hospital records

Benchmarking and Feedback

Systematically review and compare data internally to previous performance and externally to similar systems. Existing registries can help this benchmarking effort. Examples include the
- CARES for OHCA
- Get With The Guidelines®-Resuscitation program for IHCA

Change

By simply measuring and benchmarking care, systems can positively influence outcome, but they'll also need ongoing review and interpretation to identify areas for improvement, such as
- Citizen awareness
- Citizen and healthcare professional education and training
- Increased bystander CPR response rates
- Improved CPR performance
- Shortened time to defibrillation

Rhythms for VF/pVT
- VF (example in Figure 40)
- VT
- ECG artifact that looks like VF
- New LBBB

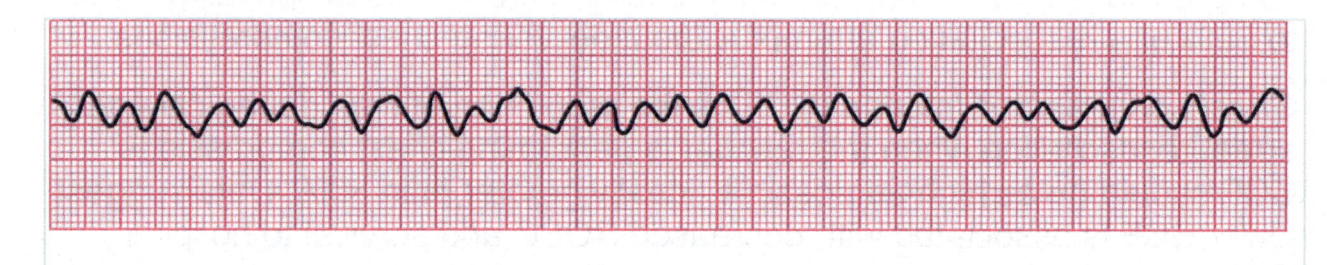

Figure 40. Example of VF.

Drugs for VF/pVT
- Drugs for VF/pVT include
- Epinephrine
- Amiodarone
- Lidocaine
- Magnesium sulfate
- Dopamine
- Oxygen
- Other medications, depending on the cause of the VT/pVT arrest

Managing VF/pVT: The Adult Cardiac Arrest Algorithm

You must know the most important algorithm for adult resuscitation: the Adult Cardiac Arrest Algorithm (Figure 41). This algorithm outlines all the steps to assess and manage a pulseless patient who does not initially

respond to BLS interventions, including a first shock from an AED. The algorithm consists of the 2 pathways for cardiac arrest:
- A shockable rhythm, displayed on the VF/pVT pathway of the algorithm
- A nonshockable rhythm, displayed on the asystole/PEA pathway of the algorithm

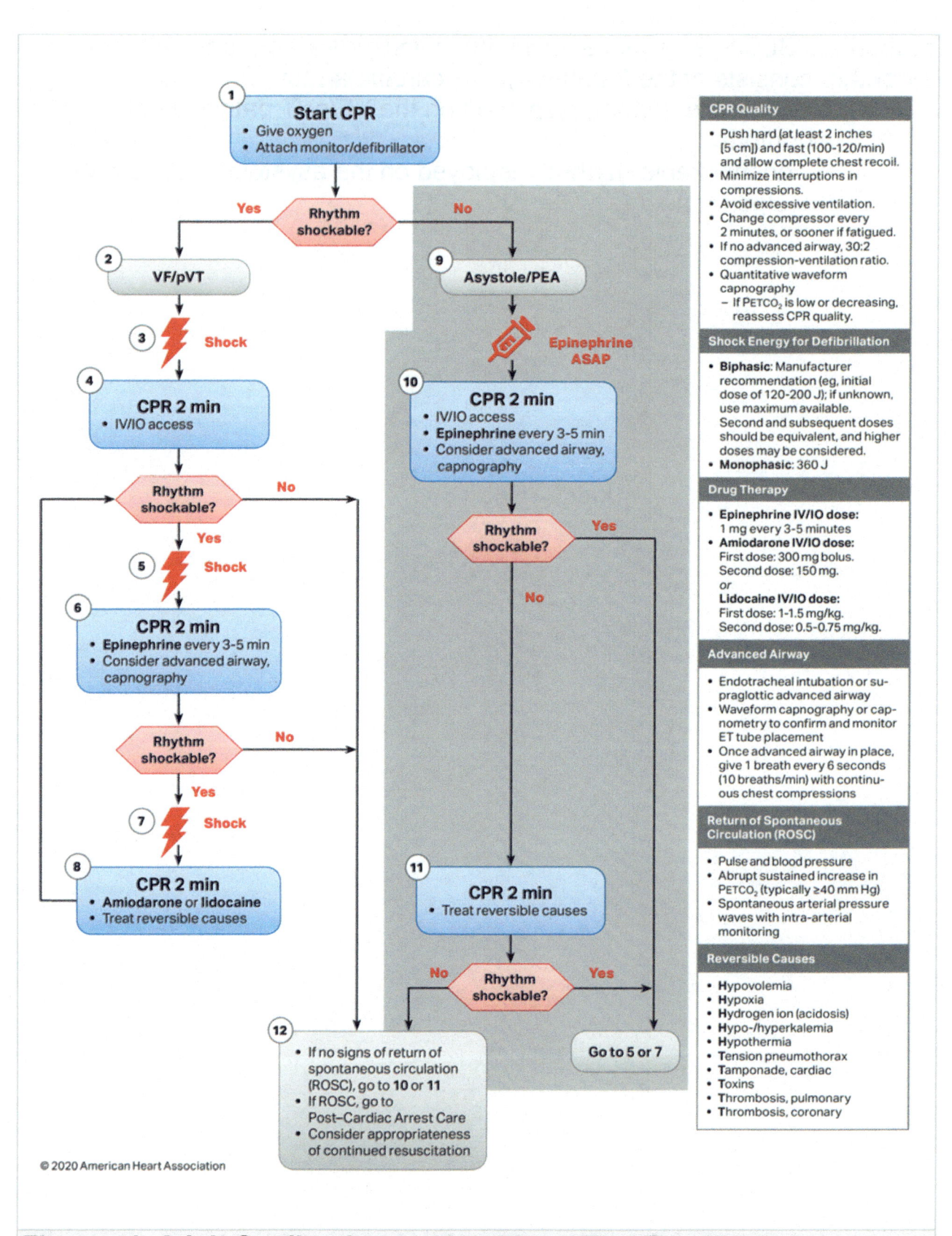

Figure 41. Adult Cardiac Arrest Algorithm, VF/pVT pathway.

Throughout the case discussion of the Adult Cardiac Arrest Algorithm, we will refer to Steps 1 through 12. These are the numbers assigned to the steps in the algorithm.

VF/pVT Path

Because many patients with sudden cardiac arrest demonstrate VF at some point in their arrest, most ACLS providers will often follow the VF/pVT pathway of the Adult Cardiac Arrest Algorithm (Figure 41). Rapidly treating VF according to this sequence is the best approach to restoring spontaneous circulation.

The algorithm includes pVT because it is treated as VF. VF and pVT require CPR until a defibrillator is available to deliver high-energy unsynchronized shocks.

Asystole/PEA Path

The asystole/PEA pathway of the algorithm outlines the sequence of actions to perform if the rhythm is nonshockable. You will practice this sequence in the Asystole and PEA Cases.

During the VF/pVT Case, you will practice performing rapid treatment on the VF/pVT pathway in the Adult Cardiac Arrest Algorithm.

Applying the Adult Cardiac Arrest Algorithm: VF/pVT Pathway

For this algorithm, healthcare providers should have already completed the BLS Assessment, including activating the emergency response system, performing high-quality CPR, attaching the manual defibrillator, and delivering the first shock (Steps 1 through 4). Now, the ACLS high-performance team intervenes and conducts the Primary Assessment. In this case, the team assesses the patient and takes actions as needed. The Team Leader coordinates the efforts of the high-performance team as they complete the steps listed in the VF/pVT pathway of the Adult Cardiac Arrest Algorithm.

> ***Caution: Agonal Gasps***
> - *Agonal gasps may be present in the first minutes after sudden cardiac arrest.*
> - *Agonal gasps are not normal breathing.*

A patient who gasps usually appears to be drawing air in very quickly. The mouth may be open and the jaw, head, or neck may move with gasps. Gasps may appear forceful or weak. Some time may pass between gasps because they usually happen at a slow, irregular rate. The gasp may sound like a snort, snore, or groan.
Gasping is a sign of cardiac arrest.

Start CPR
- Start CPR (Step 1)

The initial step in the Adult Cardiac Arrest Algorithm is to start CPR. As soon as the patient is found to be unresponsive with no breathing (or only gasping), shout for nearby help and activate the emergency response system, send for a defibrillator, check for a pulse, and start CPR, beginning with chest compressions. Attach the ECG monitor or AED pads as soon as they are available. Throughout the resuscitation attempt, provide high-quality CPR (give chest compressions of adequate rate and depth, allow complete chest recoil after each compression, minimize interruptions in compressions, and avoid excessive ventilation).
- Give oxygen.
- Attach the monitor/defibrillator.

Once the monitor/defibrillator is attached, check the rhythm to determine whether it is shockable (VF/pVT) or nonshockable (asystole/PEA) and follow the appropriate cardiac arrest pathway.

Minimize Interruption of Chest Compressions

A team member should continue to perform high-quality CPR until someone brings the defibrillator and attaches it to the patient. The Team Leader assigns roles and responsibilities and organizes interventions to minimize interruptions in chest compressions. This accomplishes the most critical interventions for VF or pVT: CPR with minimal interruptions in chest compressions and defibrillation during the first minutes of arrest. CPR quality should be measured in real time with an audiovisual feedback device, including CCF and quantitative waveform capnography, that captures the following information:
- Rate: 100 to 120/min
- Depth: at least 2 inches (5 cm)
- Chest recoil
- CCF: ideally greater than 80%

- Time to first defibrillation
- Time to first compression

Calculating CCF

Healthcare providers can calculate CCF using a feedback device, or they can calculate it manually by using 2 timers. Use one timer to measure the total code time, from code start until code stop, or until ROSC. Use a second timer to measure the total chest compression time. Each time chest compressions are stopped, pause the second timer until chest compressions are resumed. To calculate CCF, divide chest compression time by the total code time.

CCF = Actual chest compression time ÷ Total code time

The AHA does not recommend continued use of an AED (or the automatic mode) when a manual defibrillator is available and providers can adequately interpret rhythms. Rhythm analysis and shock administration with an AED may prolong the interruptions in chest compressions.

Additionally, while the manual defibrillator is charging, providers should resume CPR. Shortening the interval between the last compression and the shock by even a few seconds can improve shock success (defibrillation and ROSC), so practice efficient coordination between CPR and defibrillation.

For example, after you verify a shockable rhythm and initiate the charging sequence on the defibrillator, another provider should resume chest compressions and continue until the defibrillator is fully charged. You should deliver the shock as soon as the compressor removes his or her hands from the patient's chest and all providers are "clear" of contact with the patient. The same compressor should resume compressions immediately after the shock is delivered.

Note: although manual defibrillators can shorten the interruption needed for rhythm analysis, providers who are inexperienced with rhythm analysis should use an AED instead to avoid delays or inappropriate shocks.

Figure 42 illustrates the need to minimize interruptions in compressions. Coronary perfusion pressure (CPP) is aortic relaxation ("diastolic") pressure minus right atrial relaxation ("diastolic") pressure. During CPR, CPP correlates with both myocardial blood flow and ROSC. In 1 human study,

ROSC did not occur unless a CPP 15 mm Hg or greater was achieved during CPR.

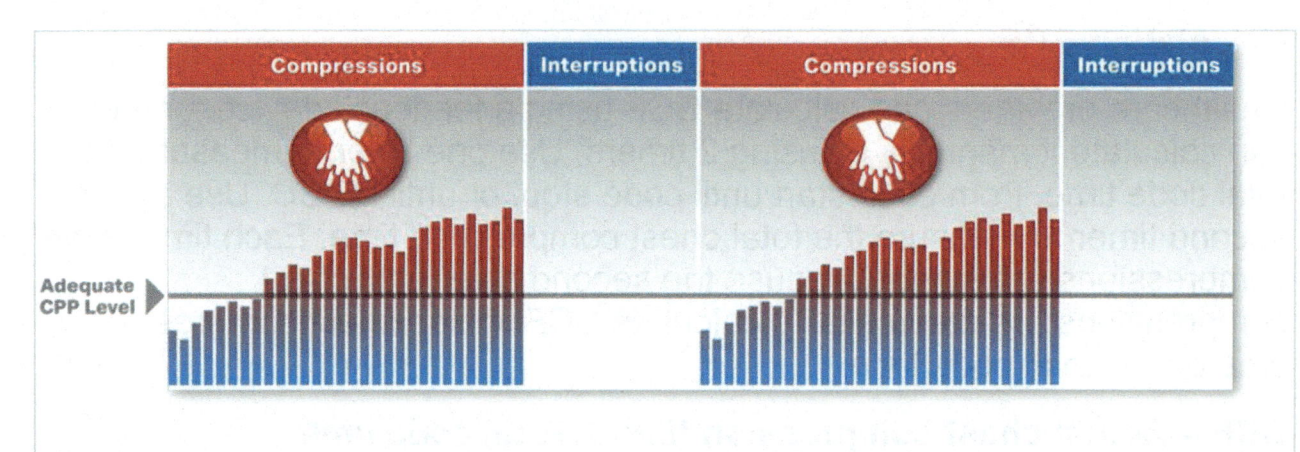

Figure 42. Relationship of quality CPR to CPP demonstrating the need to minimize interruptions in compressions.

Defibrillate (Shockable Rhythm: VF/pVT)

As soon as you determine that the rhythm is shockable (VF or pVT), deliver 1 shock. The appropriate energy dose is determined by the identity of the defibrillator—monophasic or biphasic.

If you are using a *monophasic* defibrillator, give a single 360-J shock. Use the same energy dose for subsequent shocks.

Biphasic defibrillators use various waveforms that effectively terminate VF over a specific dose range. When using biphasic defibrillators, providers should use the manufacturer's recommended energy dose (eg, initial dose of 120 to 200 J). Many biphasic defibrillator manufacturers display the effective energy dose range on the face of the device. If you do not know the effective dose range, deliver the maximal energy dose for the first and all subsequent shocks.

If the initial shock terminates VF but the arrhythmia recurs later in the resuscitation attempt, deliver subsequent shocks at the previously successful energy level.

For an AED, follow the device's prompts or know your device-specific manufacturer's recommendations. Healthcare providers should know how their defibrillator operates and limit pauses in chest compressions to rhythm analysis and shock delivery.

Immediately after the shock, resume CPR, beginning with chest compressions. Give 2 minutes of CPR. If there are available providers, IV or IO access should be established.

In adults experiencing sudden cardiac arrest due to VF or pVT, the heart is quivering but is not effectively pumping blood to vital organs. These patients have a much higher survival rate if they receive immediate chest compressions and early defibrillation. **Timing is critical.** Defibrillation stuns the heart—it doesn't restart the heart—to briefly terminate all electrical activity, including VF and pVT. If the heart is still viable, defibrillation may help the heart's normal pacemakers eventually resume electrical activity (return of spontaneous rhythm) that ultimately results in a perfusing rhythm (ROSC).

In the first 4 to 6 minutes after cardiac arrest, referred to as *clinical death*, no damage occurs to the brain. In the 6- to 10-minute period (biological death) after cardiac arrest, damage is likely to occur to the brain. Brain damage is usually irreversible after 10 minutes, except in special circumstances such as accidental hypothermia and cold-water drowning. Starting chest compressions immediately can delay these effects, and defibrillation can restore a perfusing rhythm. Again, time is critical. A defibrillator should be used as soon as it is available. If there are 2 or more providers present, CPR should be performed while the defibrillator pads are being attached to the patient's chest.

In the first minutes after successful defibrillation, any spontaneous rhythm is typically slow and may not create pulses or adequate perfusion. The patient needs CPR (beginning with chest compressions) for several minutes until adequate heart function resumes. Moreover, not all shocks will lead to successful defibrillation, so resume high-quality CPR beginning with chest compressions immediately after a shock.

The interval from collapse to defibrillation is one of the most important determinants of survival from cardiac arrest, and early defibrillation is critical:
- A common initial rhythm in out-of-hospital witnessed sudden cardiac arrest is VF.
- pVT rapidly deteriorates to VF, and then the heart quivers and does not pump blood.
- Electrical defibrillation is the most effective way to treat VF (delivery of a shock to stop the VF) and pVT.

- The probability of successful defibrillation decreases quickly over time.
- VF deteriorates to asystole if not treated.

The earlier defibrillation occurs, the higher the survival rate. When VF is present, CPR can provide a small amount of blood flow to the heart and brain but cannot directly restore an organized rhythm. Restoring a perfusing rhythm is more likely with immediate CPR and defibrillation within a few minutes after the initial arrest (Figure 43).

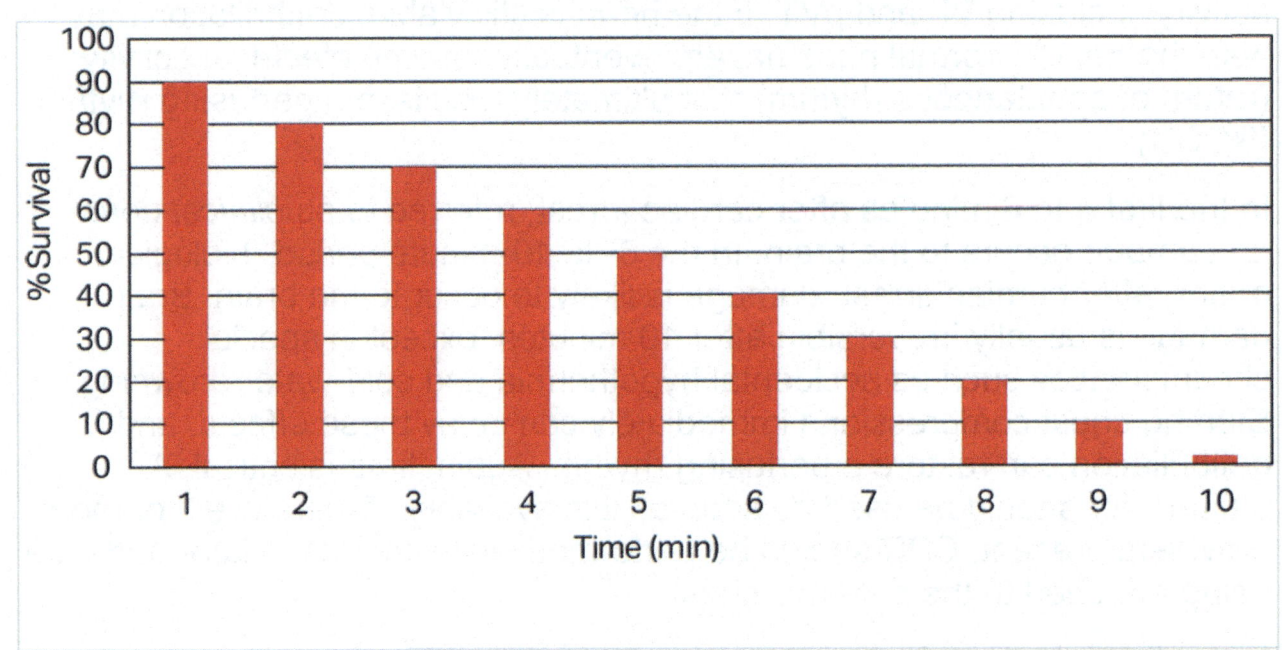

Figure 43. Relationship between survival from VF sudden cardiac arrest and time from collapse to defibrillation.

For every minute that passes between collapse and defibrillation, the chance of survival from a witnessed VF sudden cardiac arrest declines by 7% to 10% per minute without bystander CPR.[2] When bystanders perform CPR, the decline is more gradual and averages 3% to 4% per minute.[2-5] Early CPR can double[2,6] or triple[7] survival from witnessed sudden cardiac arrest at most defibrillation intervals.

Lay rescuer AED programs increase the likelihood of early CPR and attempted defibrillation and shorten the time between collapse and defibrillation for more patients with sudden cardiac arrest.

To ensure safety during defibrillation, always announce the shock warning. State the warning firmly and in a forceful voice before delivering each shock (this entire sequence should take less than 5 seconds):

- "Clear. Shocking." You do not need to use these exact words, but you must warn others that you are about to deliver shocks and that everyone must stand clear of the patient.
    - –Check to make sure you are clear of contact with the patient, the stretcher, or other equipment.
    - –Make a visual check to ensure that no one is touching the patient or stretcher.
    - –Be sure oxygen is not flowing across the patient's chest.
- When pressing the shock button, the defibrillator operator should face the patient, not the machine. This helps to ensure coordination with the chest compressor and to verify that no one resumed contact with the patient.

Resume CPR, Establish IV/IO Access, and Check Rhythm
- Perform CPR for 2 minutes.
    - –Immediately resume CPR, beginning with chest compressions. Do not perform a rhythm or pulse check at this point unless the patient is showing signs of life, such as ROSC.
- Establish IV/IO access.
    - –While CPR is being performed, if you do not already have vascular access (IV/IO), another member of the resuscitation team should establish vascular access to get ready for medications.

The Guidelines recommend that healthcare providers tailor the sequence of rescue actions based on the presumed etiology of the arrest. Moreover, ACLS providers can choose the best approach (functioning within a 2-minute cycle) for their high-performance team to minimize interruptions in chest compressions and improve CCF, including protocols such as
- Continuous chest compressions with asynchronous ventilation once every 6 seconds with the use of a bag-mask device
- Compression-only CPR in the first few minutes after arrest

Use a default compression-to-ventilation ratio of 30:2 for less-trained healthcare providers or if 30:2 is the established protocol. Figure 44 shows the progression from lay rescuers to highly trained and proficient healthcare providers.

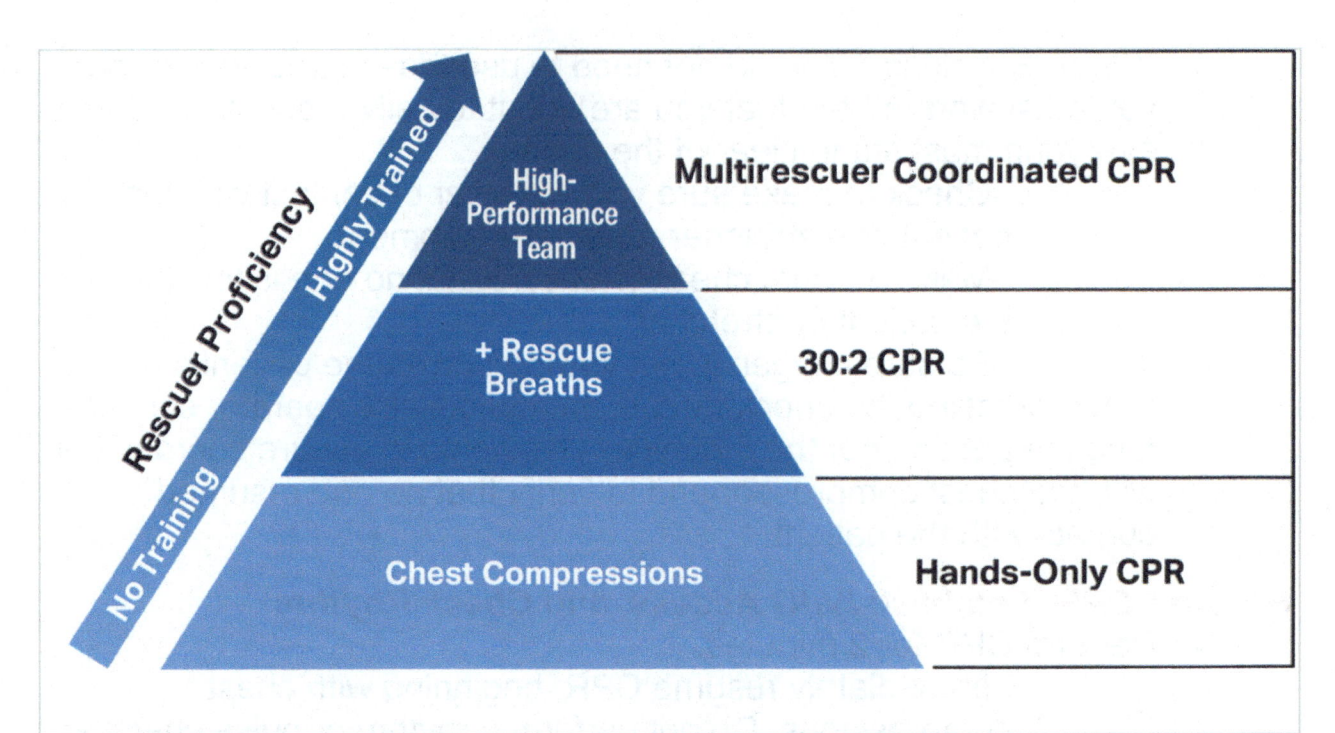

Figure 44. Progression from lay rescuers to highly trained healthcare providers for CPR delivery.

Perform a Rhythm Check

Check the rhythm after 2 minutes of CPR, but be careful to minimize interruptions in chest compressions.

Do not exceed 10 seconds for the pause in chest compressions to check the rhythm.
- If the rhythm is nonshockable and organized, try to find a pulse. If you have any doubt about the presence of a pulse, immediately resume CPR.

Remember to perform a pulse check—preferably during rhythm analysis—**only** if an organized rhythm is present.
- If the rhythm is organized and a pulse is felt, proceed to post–cardiac arrest care.
- If the rhythm is nonshockable and a pulse is not felt, proceed along the asystole/PEA pathway of the Adult Cardiac Arrest Algorithm (Steps 9 through 11).
- If the rhythm is shockable, give 1 shock and immediately resume CPR for 2 minutes after the shock.

Note: the AHA recommends routinely using self-adhesive pads during defibrillation because conductive materials (gel pads or self-adhesive pads) reduce transthoracic impedance—the resistance that the chest has on electrical current.

For persistent VF/pVT, give 1 shock and immediately resume CPR for 2 minutes, beginning with chest compressions.

Vasopressors

Vasopressors optimize cardiac output and blood pressure, and evidence shows that using vasopressors favors initial resuscitation with ROSC. However, research is still lacking on the effect that routinely using vasopressors during cardiac arrest has on the rates of survival to hospital discharge.

Epinephrine hydrochloride is used during resuscitation primarily for its α-adrenergic effects, ie, vasoconstriction. Vasoconstriction increases cerebral and coronary blood flow during CPR by increasing mean arterial pressure and aortic diastolic pressure. In previous studies, escalating and high-dose epinephrine administration did not improve survival to discharge or neurologic outcome after resuscitation from cardiac arrest.

When IV/IO access is available, give **epinephrine** 1 mg IV/IO during CPR after the second shock, and repeat every 3 to 5 minutes, or every 4 minutes as a midrange (ie, every other rhythm check). If additional team members are available, they should anticipate the need for drugs and prepare them in advance.

No known vasopressor (epinephrine) increases survival from VF/pVT. But because these medications can improve aortic diastolic blood pressure, coronary artery perfusion pressure, and the rate of ROSC, the AHA continues to recommend their use.

Perform a Rhythm Check

Check the rhythm after 2 minutes of CPR, but be careful to minimize interruptions in chest compressions. If the rhythm is shockable, give 1 shock and immediately resume CPR for 2 minutes after the shock.

Antiarrhythmics

Healthcare providers may consider giving antiarrhythmic drugs, either before or after the shock. The focus should be on administering medications quickly and so that defibrillation is not delayed. Evidence is still lacking on whether giving antiarrhythmic drugs during cardiac arrest is associated with improved survival to hospital discharge. Amiodarone or lidocaine may be considered for VF/pVT that is unresponsive to defibrillation. These drugs may be particularly useful for patients with witnessed arrest, for whom time to drug administration may be shorter.[8]

In ROC-ALPS (Resuscitation Outcomes Consortium–Amiodarone, Lidocaine or Placebo Study), a large out-of-hospital randomized controlled trial that compared captisol-based amiodarone with lidocaine or placebo for patients with VF/pVT refractory after at least 1 shock, there was no overall statistically significant difference in survival with good neurologic outcome or survival to hospital discharge.[9] In that study, ROSC was higher in patients receiving lidocaine compared with those receiving placebo but not for patients receiving amiodarone compared with patients receiving placebo. Among the subgroup of patients with bystander-witnessed cardiac arrest, survival to hospital discharge was higher for patients given amiodarone or lidocaine compared with those given placebo.[8]

Amiodarone or lidocaine may be considered for VF/pVT that is unresponsive to defibrillation. These drugs may be particularly useful for patients with witnessed arrest, for whom time to drug administration may be shorter.[8]

- **Amiodarone:** 300 mg IV/IO bolus, then consider 1 additional 150 mg IV/IO
    - –Amiodarone is considered a class III antiarrhythmic drug, but it possesses electrophysiologic characteristics of the other classes. Amiodarone blocks sodium channels at rapid pacing frequencies (class I effect) and exerts a noncompetitive antisympathetic action (class II effect). One of the main effects of prolonged amiodarone administration is lengthening of the cardiac action potential (class III effect).
- **Lidocaine:** 1 to 1.5 mg/kg IV/IO first dose, then 0.5 to 0.75 mg/kg IV/IO at 5- to 10-minute intervals, to a maximum dose of 3 mg/kg
    - –Lidocaine suppresses automaticity of conduction tissue in the heart by increasing the electrical stimulation threshold of the ventricle, His-Purkinje system, and spontaneous depolarization of the ventricles during diastole by a direct action on the tissues.
    - –Lidocaine blocks permeability of the neuronal membrane to sodium ions, which inhibits depolarization and the blockade of conduction.

Providers should consider magnesium sulfate for torsades de pointes associated with a long QT interval.

- **Magnesium sulfate** for torsades de pointes, loading dose 1 to 2 g IV/IO diluted in 10 mL (eg, D_5W, normal saline) given as IV/IO bolus, typically over 20 minutes
    - —Magnesium can be classified as a sodium/potassium pump agonist. Magnesium has several electrophysiological effects, including suppression of atrial L- and T-type calcium channels, and ventricular after-depolarizations. Routinely administering magnesium sulfate in cardiac arrest is not recommended unless torsades de pointes is present.

Search for and treat any treatable underlying cause of cardiac arrest, such as the H's and T's.

Cardiac Arrest Treatment Sequences

The Adult Cardiac Arrest Circular Algorithm (Figure 45) summarizes the recommended sequence of CPR, rhythm checks, shocks, and delivery of drugs based on expert consensus. We don't yet know the optimal number of CPR cycles and shocks to perform before starting pharmacologic therapy, but rhythm checks and shocks are organized around 5 cycles of CPR, or 2 minutes if a provider is timing the arrest. Do not delay shock. Continue CPR while preparing and administering drugs and charging the defibrillator. Interrupt chest compressions for only the minimum time required for ventilation (until an advanced airway is placed), rhythm check, and actual shock delivery.

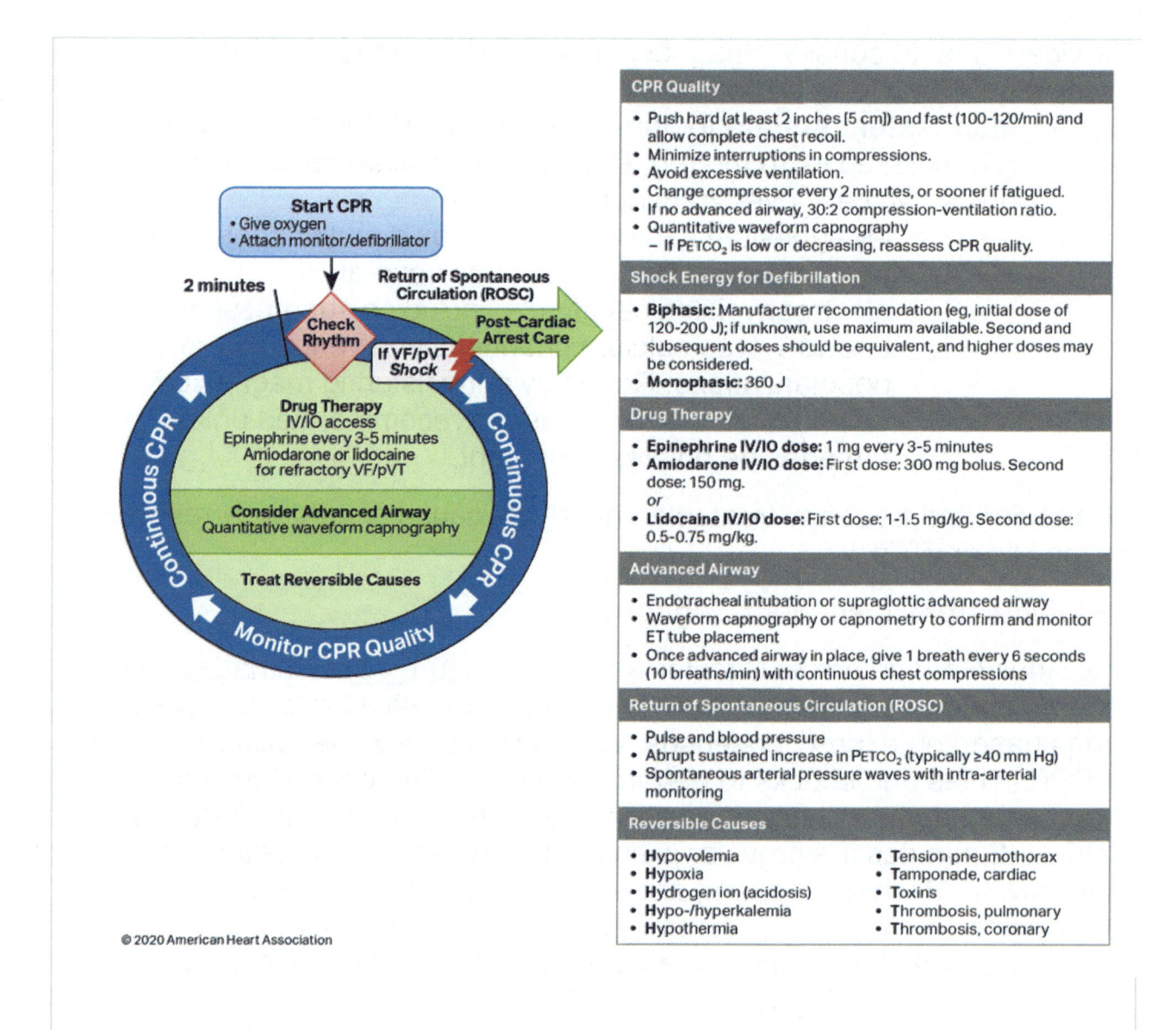

Figure 45. Adult Cardiac Arrest Circular Algorithm.

Physiologic Monitoring During CPR

For intubated patients, the AHA recommends using quantitative waveform capnography to monitor CPR quality (Figure 46), optimize chest compressions, and detect ROSC during chest compressions (Figure 47). The capnography tracing in Figure 47 displays PETCO$_2$ in millimeters of mercury on the vertical axis over time. This patient is intubated and receiving CPR. Note that the ventilation rate is approximately 10/min. Chest compressions are given continuously at a rate slightly faster than 100/min but are not visible with this tracing. The initial PETCO$_2$ is less than 12.5 mm Hg during the first minute, indicating very low blood flow.

PETCO₂ increases to between 12.5 and 25 mm Hg during the second and third minutes, consistent with the increase in blood flow with ongoing resuscitation. ROSC occurs during the fourth minute. ROSC is evident from the abrupt increase in PETCO₂ (visible just after the fourth vertical line) to greater than 50 mm Hg, which is consistent with a substantial improvement in blood flow.

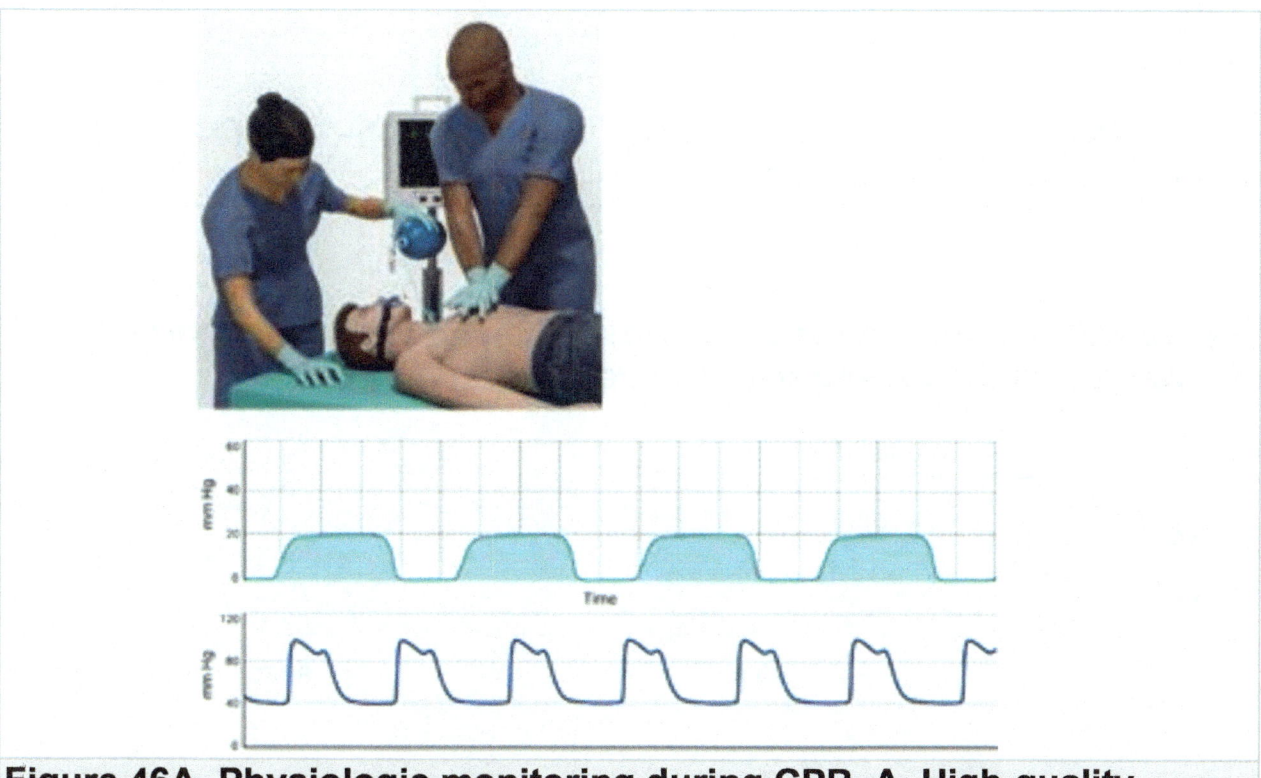

Figure 46A. Physiologic monitoring during CPR. A, High-quality compressions are shown through waveform capnography and intra-arterial relaxation pressure.

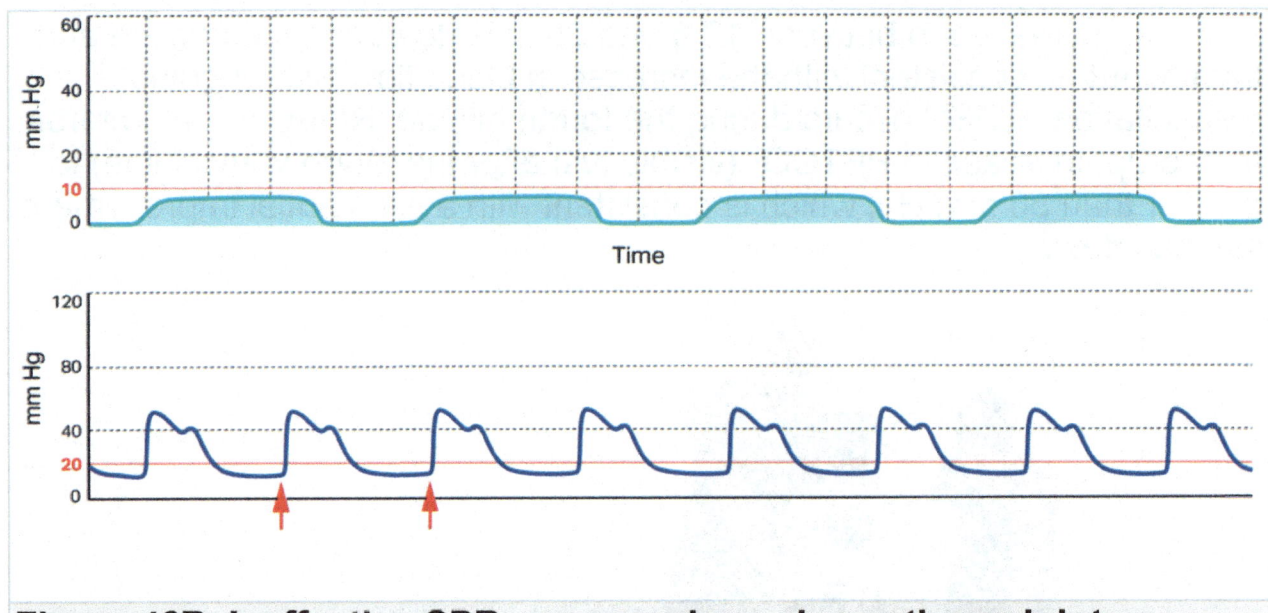

Figure 46B. Ineffective CPR compressions shown through intra-arterial relaxation pressure and waveform capnography.

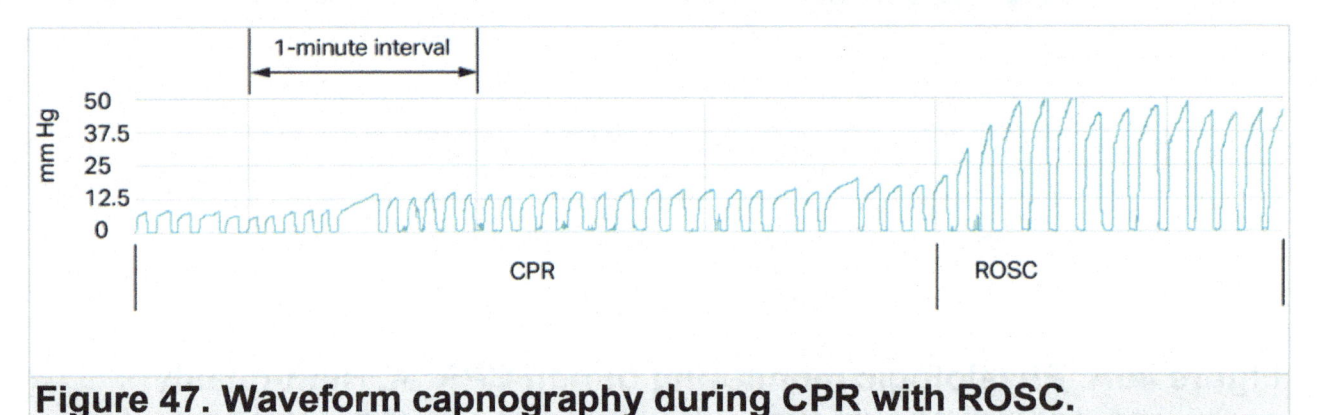

Figure 47. Waveform capnography during CPR with ROSC.

Although invasive monitors are usually not needed during CPR, physiologic parameters such as intra-arterial relaxation pressures (Figures 46A and B) and central venous oxygen saturation (SCVO$_2$) may help optimize CPR and detect ROSC.

Animal and human studies indicate that monitoring PETCO$_2$, CPP, and SCVO$_2$ provides valuable information on the patient's condition and response to therapy.[10-16] These physiologic parameters also correlate with cardiac output and myocardial blood flow during CPR, and when chest compressions fail to achieve identified threshold values, the patient rarely achieves ROSC. Furthermore, an abrupt increase in any of these parameters is a sensitive indicator of ROSC that you can monitor without interrupting chest compressions.

Although no clinical study has examined whether adjusting resuscitative efforts on the basis of physiologic parameters improves outcome, it is reasonable to use these parameters to optimize compressions and guide vasopressor therapy during cardiac arrest.

End-Tidal CO_2

The main determinant of $PETCO_2$ during CPR is blood delivery (cardiac output) to the lungs. Persistently low $PETCO_2$ values less than 10 mm Hg during CPR in intubated patients (Figure 46B) suggest that ROSC is unlikely, and it is reasonable to try to improve chest compressions and vasopressor therapy. If $PETCO_2$ abruptly increases to a normal value of 35 to 40 mm Hg or higher, it is reasonable to consider this an indicator of ROSC.

Coronary Perfusion Pressure or Arterial Relaxation Pressure

Increased coronary perfusion pressure (CPP) correlates with both myocardial blood flow and ROSC. A reasonable substitute for CPP during CPR is arterial relaxation ("diastolic") pressure, which you can measure with an intra-arterial catheter. If the arterial relaxation pressure is less than 20 mm Hg (Figure 46B), it is reasonable to try to improve chest compressions and vasopressor therapy.

Routes of Access for Drugs

The first priority during cardiac arrest is providing high-quality CPR and early defibrillation; inserting an advanced airway and administering drugs are secondary. There is no evidence that any drug used during cardiac arrest improves survival to hospital discharge with improved neurologic function.

Historically in ACLS, providers have administered drugs via IV or ET, but ET absorption of drugs is poor and optimal drug dosing is unknown. For these reasons, the IV route is preferred. When IV access is unsuccessful or not feasible, IO access may be considered.

Intravenous Route

Use a peripheral IV for drug and fluid administration unless central line access is already available. Central line access is not necessary during most resuscitation attempts, and it may cause interruptions in CPR and complications during insertion. These complications include vascular laceration, hematomas, bleeding, thrombosis, and infection. Inserting a central line in a noncompressible vessel is a relative (not absolute) contraindication to fibrinolytic therapy in patients with ACS.

You do not need to interrupt CPR to establish a peripheral IV line, but drugs typically take 1 to 2 minutes to reach the central circulation via the peripheral IV route. If you give a drug by the peripheral IV route, administer it as follows:
- Give the drug by bolus injection unless otherwise specified.
- Follow with a 20-mL bolus of IV fluid.
- Elevate the extremity for about 10 to 20 seconds to help deliver the drug to the central circulation.

Intraosseous Route

If IV access is not successful or feasible, you can safely and effectively deliver drugs and fluids during resuscitation via the IO route. Important points about IO access are that
- You can establish it in all age groups
- You can achieve it in 30 to 60 seconds
- It is preferable to ET and may be easier to establish in cardiac arrest
- Any ACLS drug or fluid that you administer via IV can be given IO

IO cannulation provides access to a noncollapsible marrow venous plexus, which serves as a rapid, safe, and reliable route during resuscitation for administering drugs, crystalloids, colloids, and blood. The technique requires a rigid needle, preferably a specially designed IO or bone marrow needle from an IO access kit. For more information on IO access, see the Access for Medications section in the ACLS Student Resources.

Endotracheal Route

IV and IO routes are preferred over ET, but if you consider administering drugs via the ET route during CPR, keep these concepts in mind:
- The optimal dose of most drugs given by the ET route is unknown.
- The typical dose of drugs administered via the ET route is 2 to 2½ times the IV route.
- You will need to stop CPR briefly so that the drug does not regurgitate up the ET tube.
- Drugs like epinephrine can negatively affect the colorimetric CO_2 detector's functionality.

Studies demonstrate that the circulatory system absorbs epinephrine, vasopressin, and lidocaine after administration via the ET route. When giving drugs via the ET route, dilute the dose in 5 to 10 mL of sterile water or normal saline, and inject it directly into the ET tube.

Fluid Administration

Adjust fluid administration and vasoactive or inotropic agents as needed to optimize blood pressure, cardiac output, and systemic perfusion. The optimal post–cardiac arrest blood pressure remains unknown; however, a mean arterial pressure 65 mm Hg or greater is a reasonable goal.

In hypovolemic patients, the ECF volume is typically restored with normal saline or lactated Ringer's solution, and avoid D_5W because it will reduce serum sodium too rapidly. Monitor serum electrolytes as appropriate.

Ultrasound for VF/pVT/Asystole/PEA

Ultrasound may be applied to patients receiving CPR to help assess myocardial contractility and identify potentially treatable causes of cardiac arrest, such as hypovolemia, pneumothorax, pulmonary thromboembolism, or pericardial tamponade. However, it is unclear whether routinely using ultrasound among patients experiencing cardiac arrest affects important clinical outcomes. If a qualified sonographer is present and use of ultrasound does not interfere with the standard cardiac arrest treatment protocol, then consider ultrasound as an adjunct to standard patient evaluation.

Return of Spontaneous Circulation

If resuscitative efforts successfully restore an organized rhythm (or you find other evidence of return of spontaneous circulation (ROSC), such as pulse and blood pressure, an abrupt and sustained increase in $PETCO_2$ (typically 40 mm Hg or higher) or spontaneous arterial pressure waves with intra-arterial monitoring, go to the Adult Healthcare Provider Post–Cardiac Arrest Care Algorithm.

If no signs of ROSC, resume CPR, administer epinephrine, and treat reversible causes. Consider appropriateness of continued resuscitation.

Cardiac Arrest: PEA and Asystole

Overview

During the BLS Assessment, high-performance team members will demonstrate high-quality CPR with effective chest compressions and ventilation with a bag-mask device. In the Primary Assessment, the Team Leader will recognize PEA or asystole and implement the appropriate interventions outlined in the Adult Cardiac Arrest Algorithm. Because correcting an underlying cause of PEA or asystole, if present and identified, is critical to patient outcome, the Team Leader will state the differential diagnosis while leading the high-performance team to find and treat reversible causes.

Rhythms for PEA

You will need to recognize the following rhythms:
- Rate—too fast or too slow
- Width of QRS complexes—wide vs narrow

Rhythms for Asystole (Lack of Rhythm)

You will need to recognize asystole (Figure 48) and slow PEA terminating in a bradyasystolic rhythm.

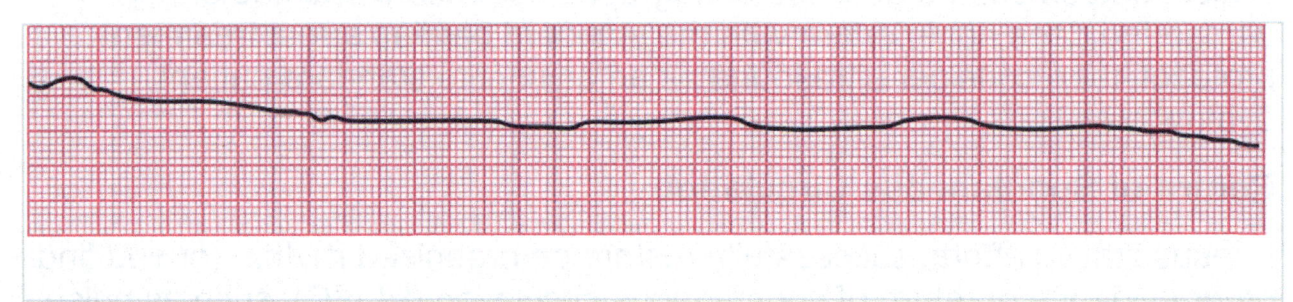

Figure 48. Example of asystole.

Drugs for PEA and Asystole

Drugs for PEA and asystole include
- Epinephrine
- Other medications, depending on the cause of the PEA and asystole arrest

Description of PEA

PEA refers to a situation where the heart generates electrical activity that should correspond to a pulse but no pulse can be palpated. PEA encompasses a heterogeneous group of rhythms that are organized or semiorganized. An organized rhythm consists of QRS complexes that are similar in appearance from beat to beat (ie, each has a uniform QRS configuration). Organized rhythms may have narrow or wide QRS complexes, they may occur at rapid or slow rates, and they may be regular or irregular.

Any organized rhythm without a pulse is defined as PEA, including sinus rhythm, atrial fibrillation or flutter, bundle branch blocks, and idioventricular or ventricular escape rhythms, etc. The heart is not pumping enough blood to sustain cardiac perfusion and the primary therapeutic approach relies on addressing the underlying cause of the arrest rather than converting to a different cardiac rhythm. Pulseless rhythms that are excluded include VF and pVT, which respond best to immediate electrical therapy, and asystole, which is treated similarly to PEA but is excluded by definition.

Differential Diagnosis in PEA

Previously, high-performance teams used the term *electromechanical dissociation* to describe patients who displayed electrical activity on the cardiac monitor but lacked apparent contractile function because of an undetectable pulse. That is, weak contractile function is present—detectable by invasive monitoring or echocardiography—but the cardiac function is too weak to produce a pulse or effective cardiac output. This is the most common initial condition present after successful defibrillation.

PEA also includes other conditions where the left ventricle of the heart is empty because of inadequate preload. In this case, the contractile function of the heart is adequate, but there is inadequate volume for the ventricle to eject. This may occur as a result of severe hypovolemia or as a result of decreased venous return from PE, cardiac tamponade, or tension pneumothorax.

If good CPR produces a strong pulse, relatively high $ETCO_2$ or blood pressure, it is more likely that the left ventricle is full and the cause of PEA is a poorly contractile left ventricle; conversely, if good CPR still does not produce evidence of good cardiac output, it is more likely that the left ventricle is relatively empty. This may help to focus the differential on the more likely causes when considering the H's & T's.

Approach to Asystole

Asystole is a cardiac arrest rhythm associated with no discernible electrical activity on the ECG (also called *flat line*). You should confirm that the flat line on the monitor is indeed true asystole by validating that the flat line is
- Not some other rhythm (eg, fine VF) masquerading as a flat line
- Not the result of an artifact associated with a disconnected lead or incorrect lead setting (eg, lead set to the pads when they are not on the patient)

Asystole and Technical Problems

Asystole is a specific diagnosis, but the term *flat line* is nonspecific and can result from several possible conditions, including absence of cardiac electrical activity, equipment failure, and operator error. Some defibrillators and monitors signal the operator when a lead or other equipment failure occurs, but some do not.

For a patient with cardiac arrest and asystole, quickly rule out any other causes of an isoelectric ECG, such as loose leads or leads that are not connected to the patient or defibrillator or monitor; no power; or amplitude or signal strength that is too low.

Asystole as an End Point

Often, asystole represents the final rhythm, including for a patient initially in VF or pVT. Cardiac function diminishes until electrical and functional cardiac activity finally stop and the patient dies.

Prolonged efforts are unnecessary and futile unless special resuscitation situations exist, such as hypothermia and drug overdose. Consider stopping if ETCO$_2$ is less than 10 mm Hg after 20 minutes of CPR and all reversible causes of cardiac arrest have been addressed.

Asystole: An Agonal Rhythm?

You will see asystole most often in 2 situations:
- As a terminal rhythm in a resuscitation attempt that started with another rhythm
- As the first rhythm identified in a patient with unwitnessed or prolonged arrest

Persistent asystole represents extensive myocardial ischemia and damage from prolonged periods of inadequate coronary perfusion. Prognosis is poor unless a special resuscitation circumstance or immediately reversible cause is present.

Managing Asystole/PEA: The Adult Cardiac Arrest Algorithm

The Adult Cardiac Arrest Algorithm consists of 2 cardiac arrest pathways (Figure 49): the treatment for a shockable rhythm (VF/pVT), and the treatment for a nonshockable rhythm (asystole/PEA). Because of the similarity in causes and management, the Adult Cardiac Arrest Algorithm combines the asystole and PEA pathways, but we will review these rhythms in separate cases. In both pathways, therapies are organized around 2-minute periods of uninterrupted, high-quality CPR.

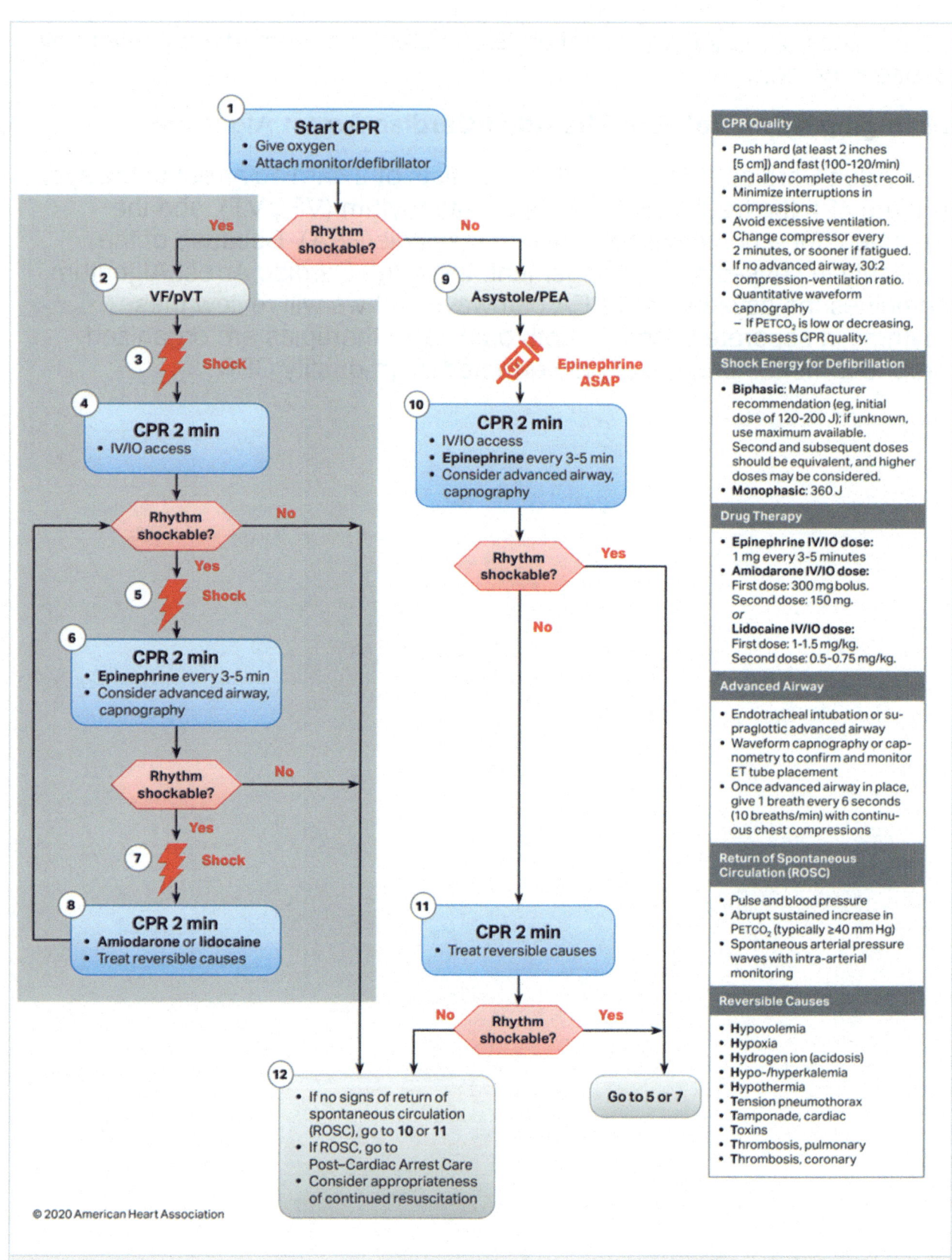

Figure 49. Adult Cardiac Arrest Algorithm, asystole/PEA pathway.

A good resuscitation outcome with return of a perfusing rhythm and spontaneous respirations requires the high-performance team to provide effective CPR and identify and correct the cause of PEA if present.

A high-performance team must seamlessly carry out the steps outlined in the algorithm while simultaneously working to identify and treat reversible causes of the arrest.

The Asystole/PEA Pathway of the Cardiac Arrest Algorithm

In this case, *the patient is in cardiac arrest*. High-performance team members initiate and perform high-quality CPR throughout the BLS, Primary, and Secondary Assessments. The team interrupts CPR for 10 seconds or less for rhythm and pulse checks.
- Start CPR (Step 1)

The initial step in the Adult Cardiac Arrest Algorithm is to start CPR. As soon as the patient is found to be unresponsive with no breathing (or only gasping), shout for nearby help and activate the emergency response system, send for a defibrillator, check for a pulse, and start CPR, beginning with chest compressions. Attach the ECG monitor or AED pads as soon as they are available. Throughout the resuscitation attempt, provide high-quality CPR (give chest compressions of adequate rate and depth, allow complete chest recoil after each compression, minimize interruptions in compressions, and avoid excessive ventilation).
- Give oxygen.
- Attach the monitor/defibrillator.

Once the monitor/defibrillator is attached, check the rhythm to determine whether it is shockable (VF/pVT) or nonshockable (asystole/PEA) and follow the appropriate cardiac arrest pathway.

Managing Asystole/PEA

This patient has an organized rhythm on the monitor but no pulse. The condition is PEA (Step 9). Resume chest compressions immediately. The Team Leader now directs the team in the steps outlined in the asystole/PEA pathway of the Adult Cardiac Arrest Algorithm (Figure 49).

Critical Concepts: Administer Epinephrine
Give epinephrine as soon as IV/IO access becomes available.

- *With respect to timing, for cardiac arrest with a nonshockable rhythm, it is reasonable to administer epinephrine as soon as feasible.*
- *Epinephrine 1 mg IV/IO—repeat every 3 to 5 minutes, or every 4 minutes as a midrange (ie, every other rhythm check)*

Administer drugs during CPR. Do not stop CPR to administer drugs. *With respect to timing, for cardiac arrest with a nonshockable rhythm, it is reasonable to administer epinephrine as soon as feasible. A recent systematic review found an association between earlier epinephrine and ROSC for patients with nonshockable rhythms, although improvements in survival were not universally seen.[17]*

Prioritize establishing IV/IO access over managing an advanced airway unless bag-mask ventilation is ineffective or hypoxia caused the arrest. All high-performance team members must search for an underlying and treatable cause of the PEA while they perform their assigned roles.

Perform a Rhythm Check

Check the rhythm and give 2 minutes of CPR after administering the drugs, but be careful to minimize interruptions in chest compressions.

Do not exceed 10 seconds for the pause in chest compressions to check the rhythm.

Consider advanced airway and capnography.

Nonshockable Rhythm

- If *no electrical activity is present* (asystole), repeat the sequence.
- If organized electrical activity is present, try to feel for a pulse. Take at least 5 seconds but no more than 10 seconds to check for a pulse.
- If *no pulse is present*, or if you have any doubt about the presence of a pulse, immediately resume CPR for 2 minutes, starting with chest compressions, and then repeat the sequence.
- If a pulse is present and the rhythm is organized, begin post–cardiac arrest care.
- Depending on the patient's status and the length of time you have been performing CPR, consider the appropriateness of continuing the resuscitation attempt.

Decision Point: Shockable Rhythm

- If the rhythm check reveals a shockable rhythm, resume CPR with chest compressions while the defibrillator is charging.
- Switch to the VF/pVT sequence in the algorithm, starting with Step 5 or 7.

Asystole/PEA Treatment Sequences

Figure 49 summarizes experts' recommended sequence of CPR, rhythm checks, and delivery of drugs for PEA and asystole.

Identifying and Correcting Underlying Causes

Treating asystole/PEA goes beyond the interventions in the algorithm. As you assess the patient, try to identify evidence of an underlying cause and correct it if present. Stop, think, and ask, "Why did this person have this cardiac arrest at this time?" You must search for and treat reversible causes of asystole/PEA for resuscitative efforts to be potentially successful. Use the H's and T's to recall conditions that could have contributed to asystole/PEA, and remember that hypovolemia and hypoxia are the 2 most common underlying, potentially reversible causes of asystole/PEA.

When in Doubt

If it is unclear whether the rhythm is fine VF or asystole/PEA, an initial attempt at defibrillation may be warranted. Fine VF may result from a prolonged arrest. At this time, the benefit of delaying defibrillation to perform CPR first is unclear. EMS system medical directors may consider implementing a protocol that allows EMS responders to provide CPR while preparing for defibrillation of patients who EMS personnel identify as being in VF.

Patients With DNAR Orders

During the BLS, Primary, and Secondary Assessments, you should be aware of reasons to stop or withhold resuscitative efforts. Some of these are
- Rigor mortis
- Indicators of do-not-attempt-resuscitation (DNAR) status (eg, bracelet, anklet, written documentation)
- Threat to the safety of providers

Out-of-hospital providers need to know EMS-specific policies and protocols applicable to these situations. In-hospital providers and high-performance teams should know of any advance directives or specific limits to resuscitation attempts that are in place. For example, a patient may consent to CPR and defibrillation but not to intubation or invasive procedures, and many hospitals will record this in the medical record. If the DNAR order is unclear or uncertain, resuscitation should be initiated and continued until it can be clarified.

Terminating Resuscitative Efforts

In-Hospital

If healthcare providers cannot rapidly identify an underlying cause and the patient does not respond to the BLS and ACLS interventions, consider terminating all resuscitative efforts.

The decision to terminate resuscitative efforts rests with the treating physician in the hospital and is based on many factors, including
- Time from collapse to CPR
- Time from collapse to first defibrillation attempt
- Comorbid disease
- Prearrest state
- Initial arrest rhythm
- Response to resuscitative measures
- $ETCO_2$ less than 10 after 20 minutes of high-quality CPR

None of these factors alone or in combination clearly predicts outcome, but the duration of resuscitative efforts is an important factor associated with poor outcome. The chance that the patient will survive to hospital discharge neurologically intact diminishes as resuscitation time increases. *Extracorporeal CPR* (ECPR) refers to the initiation of cardiopulmonary bypass during the resuscitation of a patient in cardiac arrest, with the goal of supporting end-organ perfusion while potentially reversible conditions are addressed. Consider the appropriateness of continued resuscitative efforts and stop the resuscitation attempt when you determine with a high degree of certainty that the patient will not respond to further ACLS and ECPR is not indicated or not available.

Out-of-Hospital

Continue out-of-hospital resuscitative efforts until 1 of the following occurs:
- Restoration of effective, spontaneous circulation and ventilation
- Transfer of care to a senior emergency medical professional
- Reliable criteria indicate irreversible death

- Exhaustion or dangerous environmental hazards prevent the healthcare provider from continuing
- Continued resuscitation places the lives of others in jeopardy
- A valid DNAR order is presented
- Online authorization comes from the medical control physician or there is prior medical protocol for termination of resuscitation

Duration of Resuscitative Efforts

The final decision to stop resuscitative efforts can never be as simple as an isolated time interval. If ROSC of any duration occurs, it may be appropriate to consider extending the resuscitative effort.

Experts have developed clinical rules to help decide whether to terminate resuscitative efforts for in-hospital and out-of-hospital arrests. Familiarize yourself with the established policy or protocols for your hospital or EMS system.

When deciding whether to extend resuscitative efforts, it may be appropriate to consider other issues, including drug overdose and severe prearrest hypothermia (eg, submersion in icy water). Special resuscitation interventions (such as ECPR) and prolonged resuscitative efforts may be indicated for patients with hypothermia, drug overdose, or other potentially reversible causes of arrest.

Ethical Considerations

High-performance teams must make a conscientious and competent effort to give patients a trial of CPR and ACLS, if the patient did not express a decision to forego resuscitative efforts and is not obviously dead (eg, rigor mortis, decomposition, hemisection, decapitation) (see the DNAR discussion in the ACLS Student Resources). The final decision to stop resuscitative efforts can never be as simple as an isolated time interval.

Human, Ethical, and Legal Dimensions of CPR in the ACLS Student Resources provides additional information on these considerations.

Transporting Patients in Cardiac Arrest

Emergency medical response systems should not require field personnel to transport every cardiac arrest patient to a hospital or an ED. However, transportation with continuing CPR is justified if personnel cannot perform interventions out-of-hospital that are available in the hospital and that are needed for special circumstances (ie, cardiopulmonary bypass or extracorporeal circulation for patients with severe hypothermia).

After OHCA with ROSC, transport the patient to an appropriate hospital with a comprehensive post–cardiac arrest treatment system of care that includes acute coronary interventions, neurologic care, critical care, and hypothermia. Transport in-hospital post–cardiac arrest patients to an appropriate critical care unit that can provide comprehensive post–cardiac arrest care.

Cardiac Arrest: Selected Special Situations

Treating VF/pVT in Accidental Hypothermia

Defibrillation is appropriate for cardiac arrest patients in VF/pVT with severe accidental hypothermia (a body temperature of less than 30°C [86°F]). If a patient does not respond to the initial shock, it is reasonable to perform additional defibrillation attempts by using BLS guidelines while actively rewarming. Hypothermic patients may have a reduced rate of drug metabolism, and drugs may accumulate to toxic levels with standard dosing regimens. It is reasonable to consider administering a vasopressor according to the standard ACLS algorithm while rewarming, although evidence does not support using antiarrhythmic drug therapy for hypothermic patients in cardiac arrest.

For patients in cardiac arrest with severe accidental hypothermia in-hospital, aim ACLS treatment at rapid core rewarming.

For patients in cardiac arrest with moderate hypothermia (30°C to 34°C [86°F to 93.2°F]), start CPR, attempt defibrillation, give medications according to local protocols, and, if in-hospital, provide active core rewarming.

Respiratory or Cardiac Arrest Associated With Opioid Overdose

- In the United States, between 2000 and 2014, there was a 200% increase in the rate of overdose deaths involving opioids.[18] In 2018, approximately 46 800 people died of opioid toxicity in the United States.[19] Most of these deaths were associated with prescription opioids. In Canada, more than 12 800 deaths were attributed to opioids between January 2016 and March 2019.[20]
- Isolated opioid toxicity is associated with central nervous system (CNS) and respiratory depression that can progress to respiratory

and cardiac arrest. Most opioid deaths involve ingesting multiple drugs or having medical and mental health comorbidities.[21-23] In addition, methadone and propoxyphene can cause torsades de pointes, and cardiotoxicity has been reported with other opioids.[24-30] Except in specific clinical settings (eg, unintended opioid overdose during a medical procedure), rescuers cannot be certain that the patient's clinical condition is due to opioid-induced CNS and respiratory depression toxicity alone.

- Naloxone is a potent opioid receptor antagonist in the brain, spinal cord, and GI system. Naloxone has an excellent safety profile and can rapidly reverse CNS and respiratory depression in a patient with an opioid-associated resuscitative emergency. Depending on their training and clinical circumstance, rescuers can administer naloxone intravenously,[31-34] intramuscularly,[31,32,35] intranasally,[33,35-39] or subcutaneously;[40] nebulize it for inhalation;[41,42] or instill it into the bronchial tree via ET tube.[43]

Management of Opioid-Associated Life-Threatening Emergency

Refer to the following steps in the Opioid-Associated Emergency for Healthcare Providers Algorithm (Figure 50) to manage an opioid-associated life-threatening emergency.

- Suspected opioid poisoning (Step 1):
    - –Check for responsiveness.
    - –Shout for nearby help.
    - –Activate the emergency response system.
    - –Get naloxone and an AED if available.
- Is the person breathing normally (Step 2)?
    - –Yes:
        - Prevent deterioration by checking for responsiveness (tap and shout), open airway and reposition, consider naloxone, transport to the hospital (Step 3).
        - Perform an ongoing assessment of responsiveness and breathing (Step 4).
    - –No. Does the person have a pulse (assess for 10 seconds or less) (Step 5)?

- If the person has a pulse, the provider should support ventilation by opening the airway and repositioning, providing rescue breathing or bag-mask ventilation, and giving naloxone (Step 6).
- If the person does not have a pulse, the provider should start CPR, use an AED, consider naloxone, and refer to BLS and ALS protocols (Step 7).

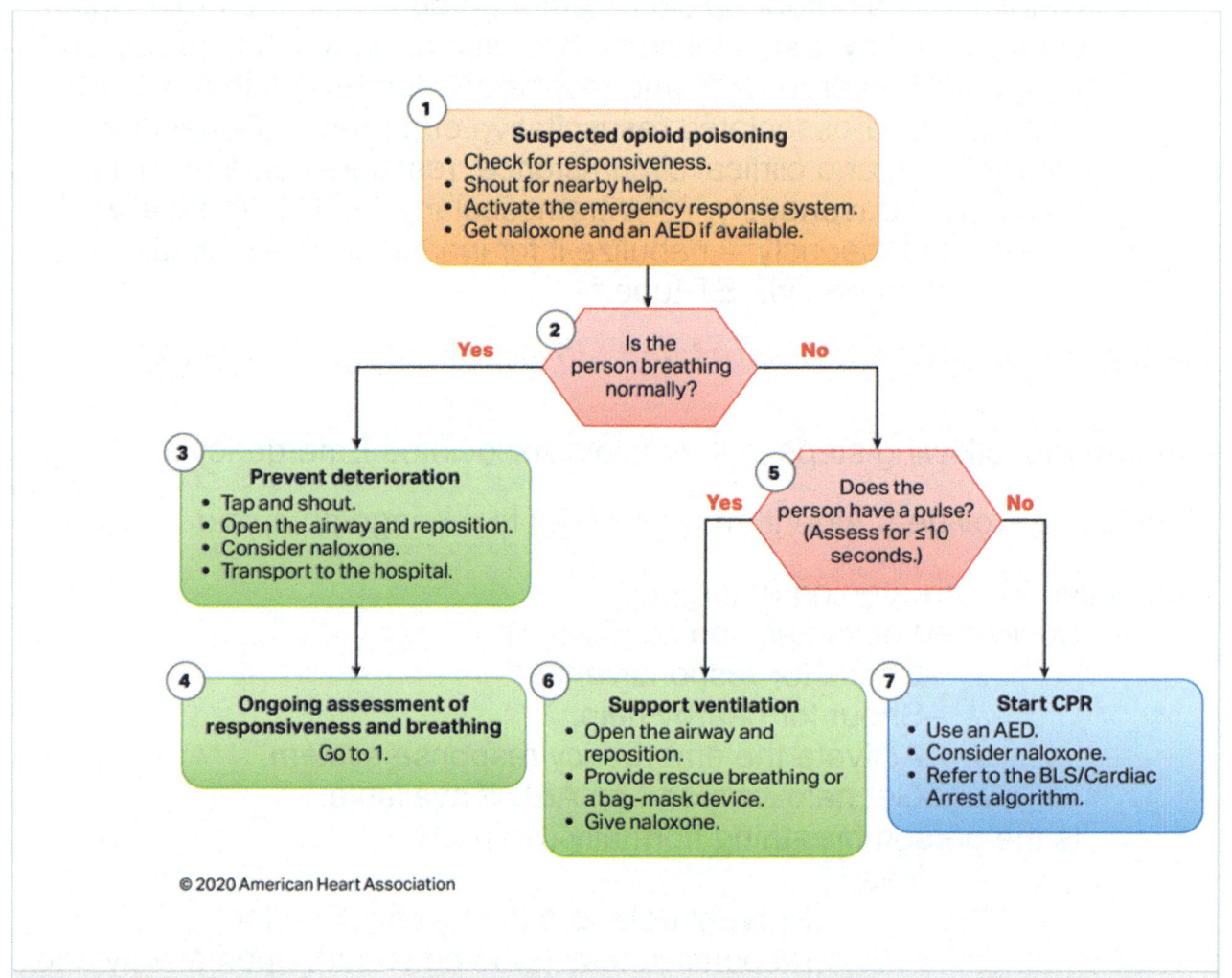

Figure 50. Opioid-Associated Emergency for Healthcare Providers Algorithm.

ECPR (for VF/pVT/Asystole/PEA)

ECPR refers to venoarterial extracorporeal membrane oxygenation during cardiac arrest. ECPR techniques require adequate vascular access and specialized equipment (Figure 51). By using ECPR, providers may support vital organs with perfusion and gas exchange while reversible causes of cardiac arrest (eg, acute coronary artery occlusion, PE, refractory VF, profound hypothermia, cardiac injury, myocarditis, cardiomyopathy, congestive heart failure, drug intoxication) are treated. ECPR can also serve as a bridge for LV assist device implantation or cardiac transplantation.

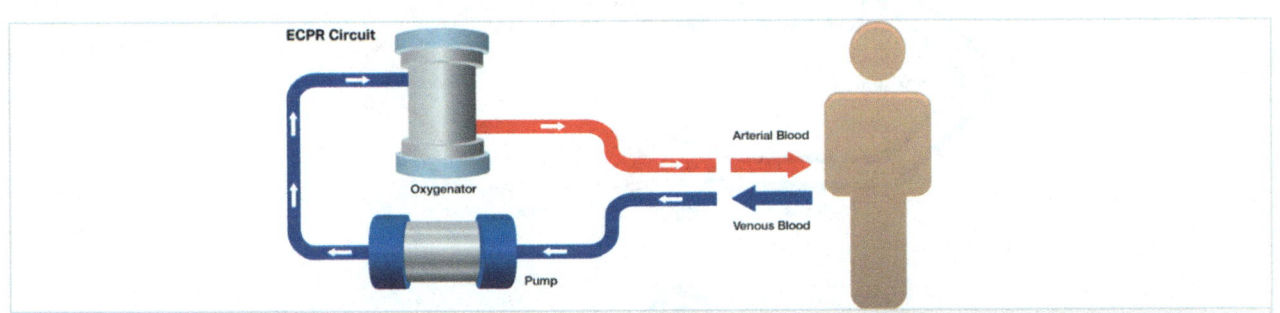

Figure 51. Schematic depiction of components of ECMO circuit as used for ECPR. Components include a venous cannula, a pump, an oxygenator, and an arterial cannula.

Abbreviations: ECMO, extracorporeal membrane oxygenation; ECPR, extracorporeal cardiopulmonary resuscitation.

Currently, ECPR requires vascular access with large bore cannulas inserted into the central vasculature, specialized equipment, and expertise in using ECMO, but evidence suggests a benefit to survival and favorable neurologic outcome with the use of ECPR when compared with conventional CPR in patients with refractory cardiac arrest.

Consider ECPR in settings where the necessary equipment and trained personnel can be deployed rapidly for select cardiac arrest patients with known or suspected reversible causes of cardiac arrest in whom conventional ACLS has failed.

Ventricular Assist Devices

Mechanical circulatory support devices, also called *ventricular assist devices* (VADs), can support the function of the ventricles with[44]
- A left ventricle with a left ventricular assist device (LVAD)
- A right ventricle with a right ventricular assist device (RVAD)
- Both ventricles with a biventricular assist device

Figure 52 shows the support intended with an LVAD, an RVAD, and a biventricular assist device. Most VADs are implanted inside the thoracic/abdominal cavity (intracorporeal, Figure 53). These devices pump blood from the weakened ventricle back into circulation. With an LVAD, blood enters the device from the left ventricle and is pumped to the central aortic circulation, assisting the heart.[44]

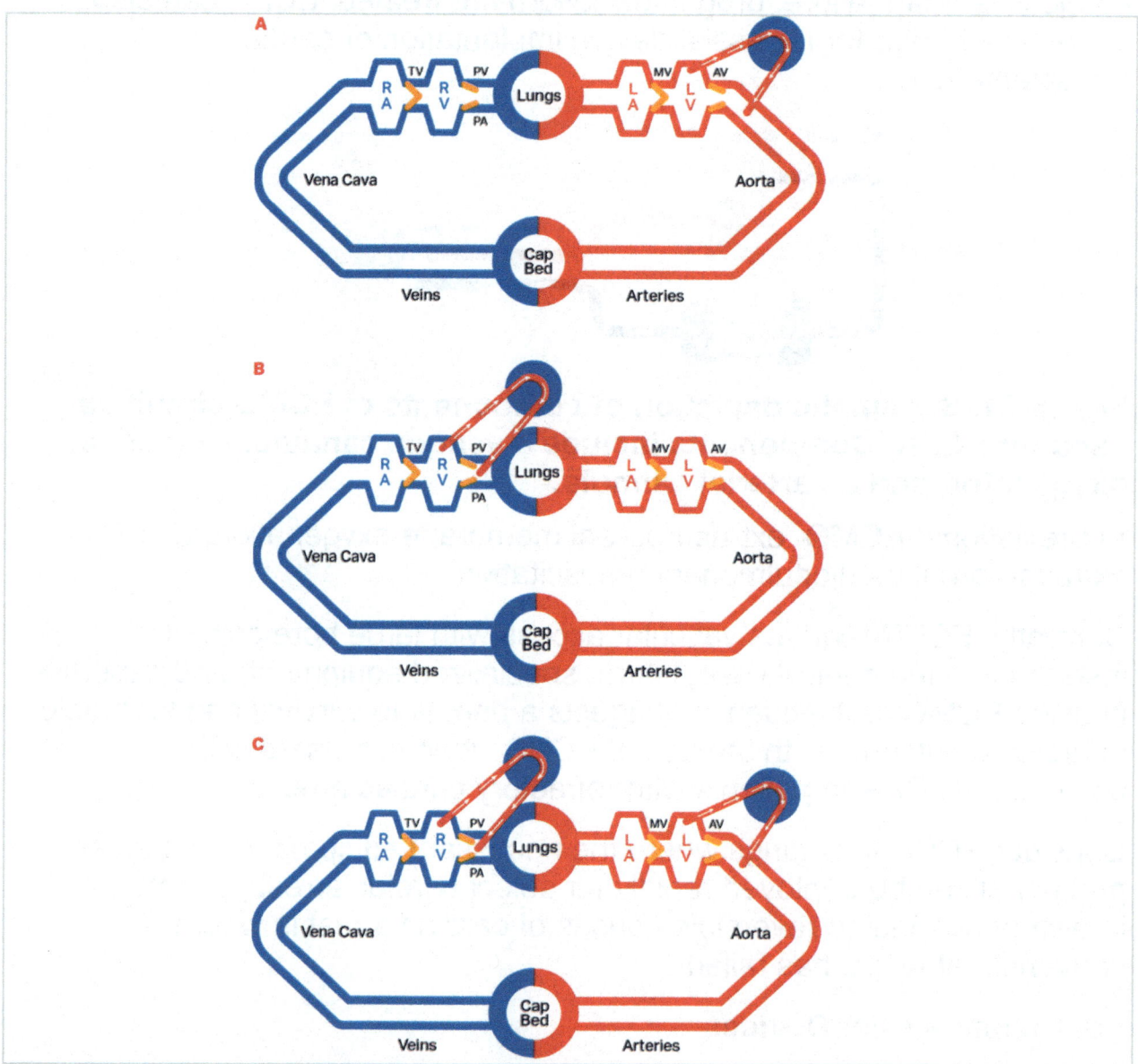

Figure 52. Ventricular assist device configurations of A, an LVAD; B, an RVAD; and C, a biventricular assist device.

Abbreviations: LA, left atrium; LV, left ventricle; RA, right atrium; RV, right ventricle.

Figure 53. Intracorporeal pumps.

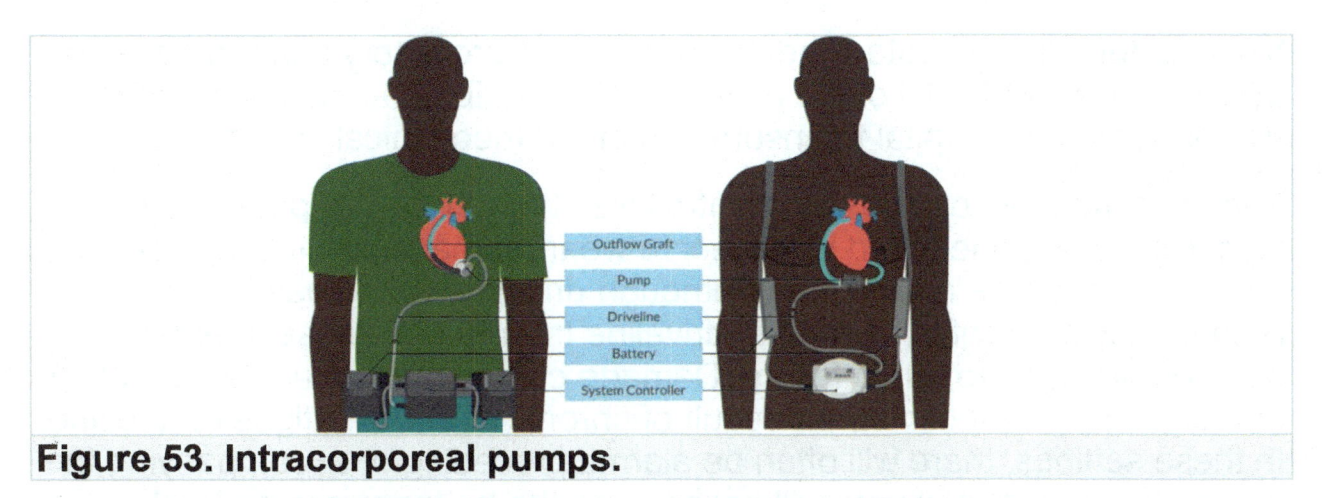

With an RVAD, the inflow is the right ventricle or atrium, and the outflow is the main pulmonary artery, just distal to the pulmonic valve. When an LVAD and an RVAD are used in the same patient simultaneously, the patient is referred to as having *biventricular support* or a *biventricular assist device*, indicating that both ventricles are supported mechanically.

A total artificial heart replaces the heart itself. Most patients who are discharged home with mechanical circulatory support currently have a durable LVAD.

LVADs can have 2 distinctly different mechanisms of blood flow and, therefore, are different physiologically:
- Pulsatile-flow LVADs (older technology, rarely used)
- Continuous-flow LVADs (the current generation of devices)

Because palpable pulses are often absent in patients with continuous-flow LVADs, it is important to understand the differences in the physical exam and in methods that can help rescuers determine if an unresponsive or mentally altered patient is, in fact, in cardiac arrest or circulatory collapse.

The 2 most common causes of pump failure are disconnection of the power or of the driveline. Therefore, the first step in assessing an unresponsive, mentally altered, or hypotensive VAD patient is to ensure that all connections are secure and an adequate power source is connected. Controller malfunction, damage, or disconnection can also lead to pump dysfunction or stoppage. All patients should have a backup controller with them, as well as backup batteries for emergency replacement, in case of damage or malfunction. EMS providers must keep patients and their backup equipment together at all times because replacement equipment may be limited or nonexistent at receiving hospitals, particularly at non-

VAD centers. To reiterate, when a mechanical circulatory support patient is transported by EMS, all of the patient's VAD equipment must accompany him or her to the hospital to ensure continued mechanical support.

The driveline that connects the controller to the device is a potentially vulnerable component and is subject to wear, damage, or kinking, which can result in device malfunction. Although driveline wiring has built-in redundancy as a safety measure, driveline trauma can cause internal damage and lead to pump failure. Damage can be acute, such as a cutting or crush injury, or it can be the result of chronic stress or fatigue on the line. In these settings, there will often be alarms preceding or accompanying the pump stoppage, but alarms will cease once the batteries are drained.

Management of the Patient With an LVAD (Figure 53)

Refer to the following steps in the Adult Ventricular Assist Device Algorithm (Figure 54) to manage a patient with an LVAD.
- Assist ventilation if necessary and assess perfusion (Step 1).
    - –Normal skin color and temperature?
    - –Normal capillary refill?
- Adequate perfusion (Step 2)?
    - –If yes, assess and treat non-LVAD causes for altered mental status, such as hypoxia, blood glucose, overdose, and stroke (Step 3).
        - Follow local EMS and ACLS protocols and notify VAD center and/or medical control and transport (Steps 4 and 5)
    - –If no, assess LVAD function by looking and listening for alarms and listening for the LVAD hum (step 6).
- Is the LVAD functioning (Step 7)?
    - –If yes, is the mean arterial pressure more than 50 mm Hg and or PETCO$_2$ more than 20 mm Hg (Step 8)?
        - If yes, do not perform chest compressions (Step 9); follow local EMS and ACLS protocols (Step 4) and notify VAD center and/or medical control and transport (Step 5).
        - If no, perform external chest compressions (Step 10) and follow local EMS and ACLS protocols (Step 4) and notify VAD center and/or medical control and transport (Step 5).

- –If no, attempt to restart LVAD and consider if the driveline and power source are connected. Do you need to replace the system controller (Step 11)?
    - If LVAD is not restarted, perform external chest compressions (Step 10) and follow local EMS and ACLS protocols (Step 4) and notify VAD center and/or medical control and transport (Step 5).
    - If LVAD has been restarted, follow local EMS and ACLS protocols (Step 4) and notify VAD center and/or medical control and transport (Step 5).

Adult Ventricular Assist Device Algorithm

Assist ventilation if necessary and assess perfusion
- Normal skin color and temperature?
- Normal capillary refill?

Adequate perfusion?

Yes → Assess and treat non-LVAD causes for altered mental status, such as
- Hypoxia
- Blood glucose
- Overdose
- Stroke

No → Assess LVAD function
- Look/listen for alarms
- Listen for LVAD hum

LVAD functioning?

Yes → MAP >50 mm Hg and/or PETCO₂ >20 mm Hg*?
- Yes → Do not perform external chest compressions
- No → Perform external chest compressions

No → Attempt to restart LVAD
- Driveline connected?
- Power source connected?
- Need to replace system controller?

LVAD restarted?
- No → Perform external chest compressions
- Yes → Follow local EMS and ACLS protocols

Notify VAD center and/or medical control and transport

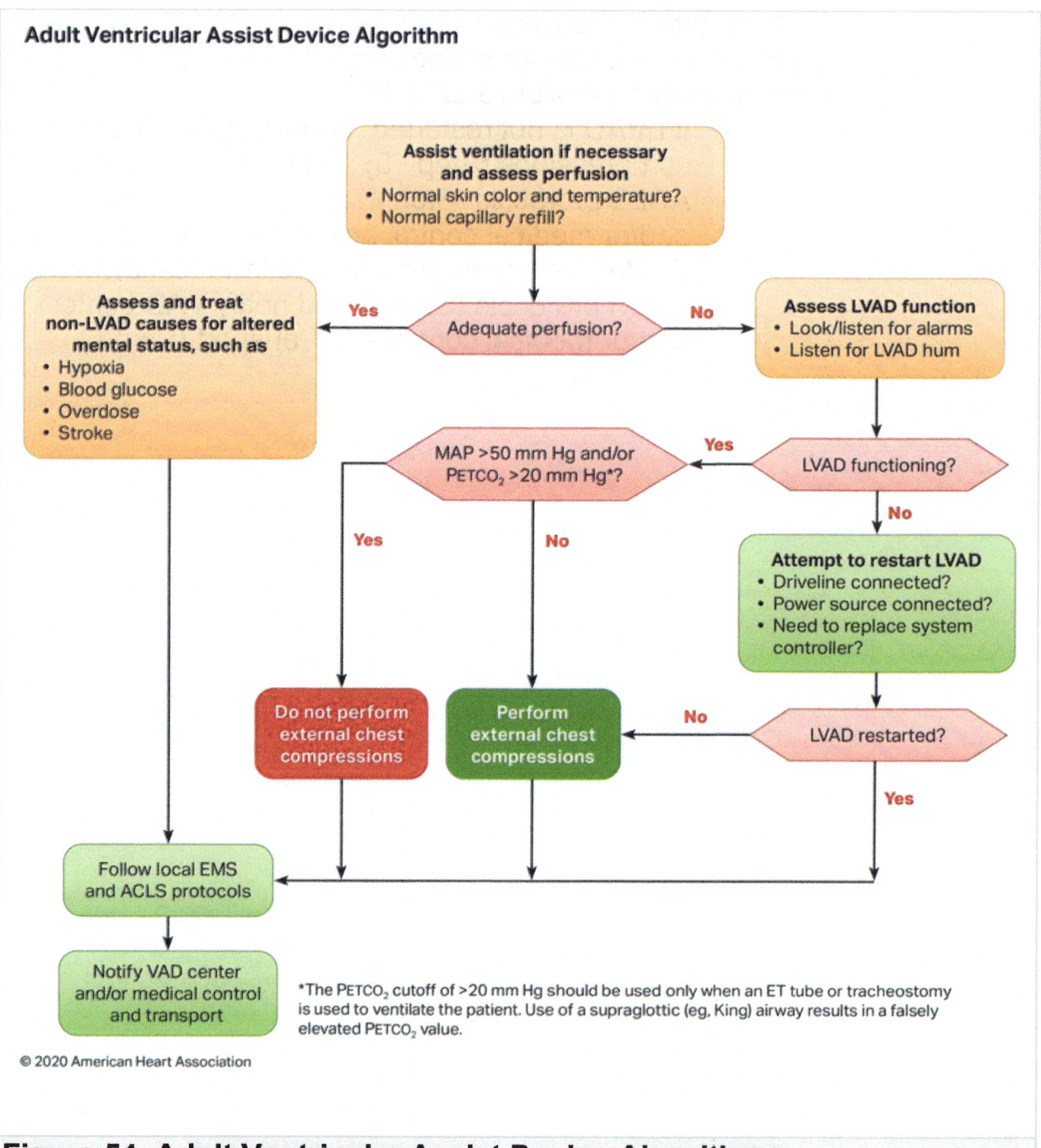

*The PETCO₂ cutoff of >20 mm Hg should be used only when an ET tube or tracheostomy is used to ventilate the patient. Use of a supraglottic (eg, King) airway results in a falsely elevated PETCO₂ value.

© 2020 American Heart Association

Figure 54. Adult Ventricular Assist Device Algorithm.

Abbreviation: MAP, mean arterial pressure.

Identifying the presence of mechanical circulatory support and code status is of initial importance. Some destination therapy patients with LVADs will have a legally executed, valid DNAR status and should be treated as any other patient with such a request. Obtain information from caregivers and medical alert identifications or wallet cards to ensure definitive patient identification. It seems reasonable for VAD centers to standardize their approach to patient identification. Medical alert bracelets and necklaces can help to identify VAD patients and their code or intubation status, and such medical jewelry should be kept with the patient during transport to the hospital.

If it is unclear whether the patient is an LVAD patient, establish care with standard BLS and ACLS protocols. Breathing should be supported as needed with supplemental oxygen, airway adjuncts, and intubation as indicated.

Once a patient is identified as an LVAD patient, EMS providers must recognize that their patient may be in a state of pseudo-PEA and not have a palpable pulse or measurable blood pressure yet have adequate perfusion. If there is adequate mental status, a provider should assess the VAD for function by auscultating for a VAD hum over the left chest/left upper abdominal quadrant, looking and listening for VAD alarms, ensuring secure connections to the VAD controller, and ensuring sufficient power for the VAD. Prompt notification of the VAD center and its personnel (eg, VAD coordinator) is strongly recommended.

Clinical emergencies in LVAD patients—as well as LVAD alarms, such as low flow, power spikes, suction events, and pulsatility alarms—most often occur as a result of processes that are extrinsic to the LVAD itself. Events within the LVAD also occur, but less frequently. By providing comprehensive assessment of cardiac anatomy and function, along with evaluation of LVAD function, echocardiography can provide critical information for physicians caring for acutely ill patients who have LVADs.

Cardiac Arrest Associated With Pregnancy

Background

During attempted resuscitation of a pregnant woman, providers have 2 potential patients: the mother and the fetus. The best hope for fetal survival is maternal survival. For the critically ill pregnant patient, rescuers must provide appropriate resuscitation with consideration of the physiologic changes due to pregnancy.

The Second Patient

A cardiovascular emergency in a pregnant woman creates a special situation for the ACLS provider. You must always consider the fetus when an adverse cardiovascular event occurs in a pregnant woman. At approximately 20 weeks or more of pregnancy (and possibly earlier), the size of the uterus begins to adversely affect the attempted resuscitation. At approximately 24 to 25 weeks of gestational age, the fetus may be able to survive outside the womb.

Decisions About Cesarean Delivery

The decision about whether to perform an emergency cesarean delivery must be made quickly when the mother is in cardiac arrest. Emergency cesarean delivery—also known as *hysterotomy*—may improve the outcome for both mother and child.

Key Interventions: Prevention of Cardiac Arrest in Pregnancy

To treat the critically ill pregnant patient:
- Place the patient in the left-lateral decubitus position to relieve possible compression of the inferior vena cava. Uterine obstruction of venous return can produce hypotension and could precipitate arrest in the critically ill patient.[45,46]
- Two methods of supporting the patient in the left-lateral decubitus position are (1) to use the angled backs of 2 or 3 chairs or (2) to use the angled thighs of several providers. Overturn a 4-legged chair so that the top of the chair back touches the floor. Align 1 or 2 more overturned chairs on either side of the first so that all are tilted in the same manner. Place the woman on her left side and align her torso parallel with the chair backs (Figure 55). Remember that this position will not be practical if chest compressions are needed.

Figure 55. Supporting the patient in the left-lateral decubitus position.

If cardiac arrest occurs, refer to the following steps in the Cardiac Arrest in Pregnancy In-Hospital ACLS Algorithm (Figure 57):
- Continue BLS and ACLS (Step 1):
    - –High-quality CPR
    - –Defibrillation when indicated
    - –ACLS interventions (eg, epinephrine)
- Assemble the maternal cardiac arrest team (Step 2).
- Consider the etiology of the arrest (Step 3).
    - –Perform maternal interventions (Step 4):
        - Perform airway management.
        - Administer 100% oxygen; avoid excessive ventilation.
        - Place IV access above the diaphragm.
        - If the patient is receiving IV magnesium, stop it and give calcium chloride or gluconate.
- Continue BLS/ACLS (Step 5).

- o –High-quality CPR
- o –Defibrillation when indicated
- o –Other ACLS interventions (epinephrine)
- Perform obstetric interventions (Step 6)
    - o –Provide continuous lateral uterine displacement.
    - o –Detach fetal monitors.
    - o –Prepare for perimortem cesarean delivery.
- Perform perimortem cesarean delivery (Step 7).
    - o –If no ROSC in 5 minutes, consider immediate perimortem cesarean delivery.
- Neonatal team to receive neonate (Step 8).

Team planning should be done in collaboration with the obstetric, neonatal, emergency, anesthesiology, intensive care, and cardiac arrest services. Priorities for pregnant women in cardiac arrest should include provision of high-quality CPR and relief of aortocaval compression with lateral uterine displacement.

The goal of perimortem cesarean delivery is to improve maternal and fetal outcomes. Ideally, perform perimortem cesarean delivery in 5 minutes, depending on provider resources and skill sets.

Assess for hypotension; maternal hypotension that warrants therapy is defined as an SBP less than 100 mm Hg or less than 80% of baseline.[47,48] Maternal hypotension can cause a reduction in placental perfusion.[49-51] In the patient who is not in arrest, both crystalloid and colloid solutions increase preload.[52]

Consider potential etiology and reversible causes of cardiac arrest, and identify any preexisting medical conditions that may be complicating the resuscitation.
- Anesthetic complications
- Bleeding
- Cardiovascular
- Drugs
- Embolic
- Fever
- General nonobstetric causes of cardiac arrest (H's and T's)
- Hypertension

Advanced Airway

In pregnancy, a difficult airway is common. Use the most experienced provider. Provide endotracheal intubation or supraglottic advanced airway. Perform quantitative waveform capnography or capnometry to confirm and monitor ET tube placement. Once an advanced airway is in place, give 1 breath every 6 seconds (10 breaths/min) with continuous chest compressions.

Techniques to Improve Maternal Hemodynamics

Shifting the Gravid Uterus

In cardiac arrest, the reduced venous return and cardiac output caused by the gravid uterus puts the mother at a hemodynamic disadvantage, thereby potentially reducing the effective coronary and cerebral perfusion produced by standard chest compressions. Therefore, when there is aortocaval compression, the effectiveness of the chest compressions may be limited.

Patient positioning has emerged as an important strategy to improve the quality of CPR and the resultant compression force and cardiac output.[53]

Patient Positioning During CPR

The gravid uterus can compress the inferior vena cava, impeding venous return, thereby reducing stroke volume and cardiac output. In general, aortocaval compression can occur for singleton pregnancies at approximately 20 weeks of gestational age,[54] at about the time when the fundus is at or above the umbilicus. Although chest compressions in the left lateral tilt position are feasible in a manikin study,[55] they result in decreased CPR quality (less forceful chest compressions) than is possible in the supine position.[56] Manual left lateral uterine displacement effectively relieves aortocaval pressure in patients with hypotension (Figure 56).[57]

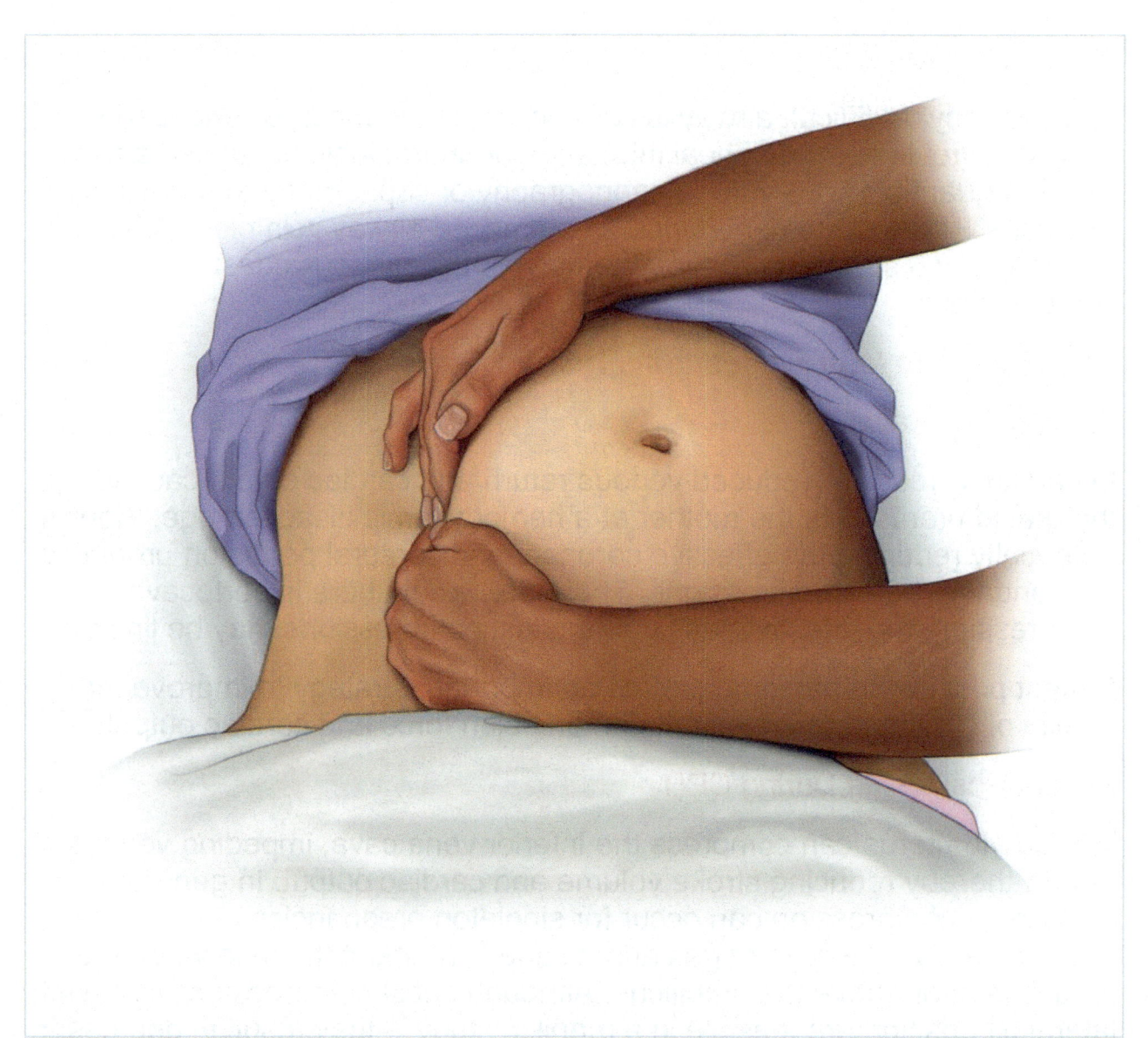

Figure 56A. Manual left uterine displacement, performed with the 2-handed technique.

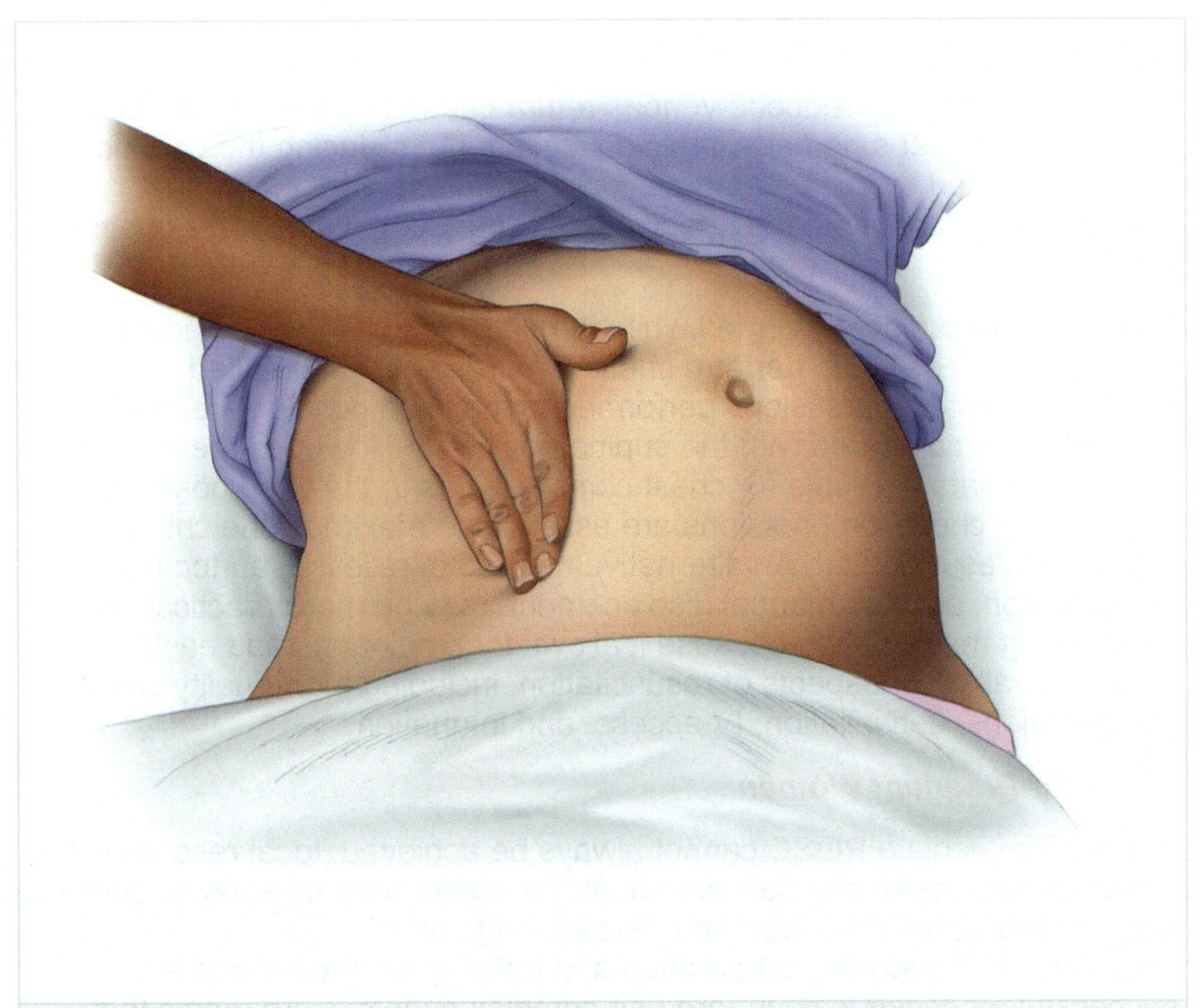

Figure 56B. One-handed technique during resuscitation.

Manual Left Uterine Displacement

Relieve compression of the inferior vena cava and the aorta by shifting the gravid uterus left and upward off the maternal vessels:
- Stand on the left side of the patient, level with the top of the uterus.
- Reach across the midline with both hands (Figure 56A) and pull the gravid uterus leftward and upward toward your abdomen.
- If it is not possible to stand to the left of the patient, use one hand to push the gravid uterus (Figure 56B) to the patient's left and upward.

Chest Compressions in the Left-Lateral Tilt

In cardiac arrest, the reduced venous return caused by the gravid uterus puts the mother at a hemodynamic disadvantage, reducing the cardiac output produced by chest compressions. Therefore, when there is aortocaval compression, the effectiveness of the chest compressions may be limited.

Chest compressions performed while the patient is tilted are not ideal. Although it is feasible to perform chest compressions in the tilted patient,[55] chest compressions performed in the tilted position are less forceful when compared with the supine position.[56] However, there are no physiologic data available for chest compressions in the tilted position. High-quality chest compressions are essential to maximize the chance of a successful resuscitation. An alternative method of relieving aortocaval compression, such as manual displacement, may be more practical and ideal during resuscitation because it allows for continuous and easier delivery of all other aspects of resuscitation, including high-quality chest compressions, defibrillation, IV access, and intubation.

ACLS for Pregnant Women

Because immediate ROSC cannot always be achieved, local resources for a perimortem caesarean delivery should be summoned as soon as cardiac arrest is recognized in a woman in the second half of pregnancy.[58] Systematic preparation and training are the keys to a successful response to such rare and complex events. Care teams that may be called upon to manage these situations should develop and practice standard institutional responses to allow for smooth delivery of resuscitative care.[53]

The treatments listed in the Cardiac Arrest in Pregnancy In-Hospital ACLS Algorithm include recommendations for defibrillation, medications, and intubation (Figure 57). The algorithm is divided into 2 focuses (maternal interventions and obstetric interventions) to reflect the simultaneous resuscitation interventions of both the maternal resuscitation team and the obstetrical/neonatal team to improve team performance, efficiency, and success.

Cardiac Arrest in Pregnancy In-Hospital ACLS Algorithm

1. Continue BLS/ACLS
- High-quality CPR
- Defibrillation when indicated
- Other ACLS interventions (eg, epinephrine)

2. Assemble maternal cardiac arrest team

3. Consider etiology of arrest

4. Perform maternal interventions
- Perform airway management
- Administer 100% O_2, avoid excess ventilation
- Place IV above diaphragm
- If receiving IV magnesium, stop and give calcium chloride or gluconate

5. Continue BLS/ACLS
- High-quality CPR
- Defibrillation when indicated
- Other ACLS interventions (eg, epinephrine)

6. Perform obstetric interventions
- Provide continuous lateral uterine displacement
- Detach fetal monitors
- Prepare for perimortem cesarean delivery

7. Perform perimortem cesarean delivery
- If no ROSC in 5 minutes, consider immediate perimortem cesarean delivery

8. Neonatal team to receive neonate

Maternal Cardiac Arrest
- Team planning should be done in collaboration with the obstetric, neonatal, emergency, anesthesiology, intensive care, and cardiac arrest services.
- Priorities for pregnant women in cardiac arrest should include provision of high-quality CPR and relief of aortocaval compression with lateral uterine displacement.
- The goal of perimortem cesarean delivery is to improve maternal and fetal outcomes.
- Ideally, perform perimortem cesarean delivery in 5 minutes, depending on provider resources and skill sets.

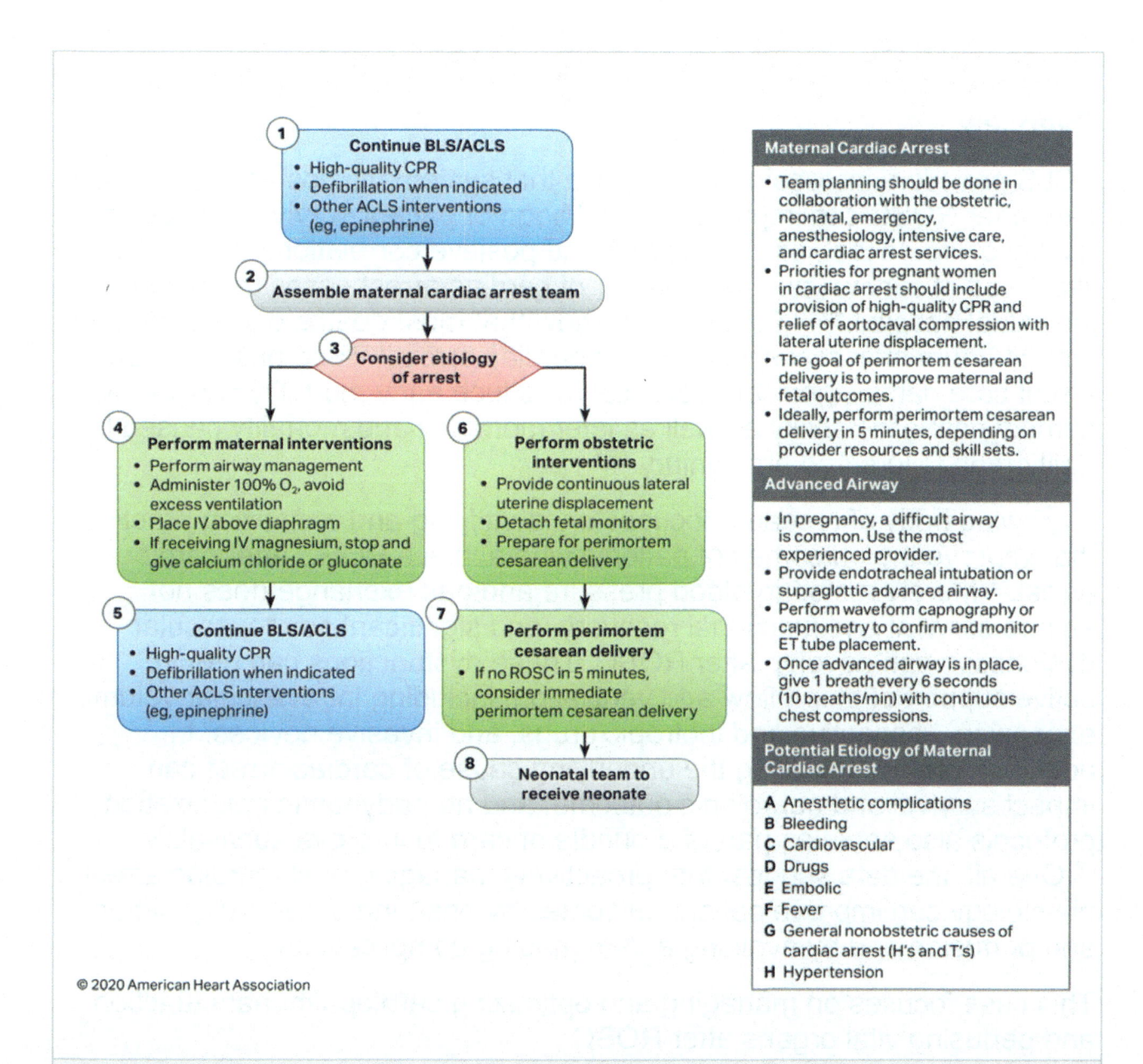

Advanced Airway
- In pregnancy, a difficult airway is common. Use the most experienced provider.
- Provide endotracheal intubation or supraglottic advanced airway.
- Perform waveform capnography or capnometry to confirm and monitor ET tube placement.
- Once advanced airway is in place, give 1 breath every 6 seconds (10 breaths/min) with continuous chest compressions.

Potential Etiology of Maternal Cardiac Arrest
A Anesthetic complications
B Bleeding
C Cardiovascular
D Drugs
E Embolic
F Fever
G General nonobstetric causes of cardiac arrest (H's and T's)
H Hypertension

© 2020 American Heart Association

Figure 57. Cardiac Arrest in Pregnancy In-Hospital ACLS Algorithm.

Post–Cardiac Arrest Care

Overview

ACLS providers increasingly recognize that systematic post–cardiac arrest care after ROSC can improve the likelihood of patient survival with good quality of life. In fact, studies have found positive correlations between the likelihood of survival and the number of cardiac arrest cases treated at any individual hospital.[59,60] Studies also show that most deaths occur during the first 24 hours after resuscitation from cardiac arrest,[61,62] so post–cardiac arrest care has a significant potential to reduce early mortality caused by hemodynamic instability as well as later morbidity and mortality caused by multiorgan failure and brain injury.[63,64]

A growing body of research focuses on identifying and optimizing practices that improve the outcomes of patients who achieve ROSC after cardiac arrest.[65] Merely restoring blood pressure and gas exchange does not ensure survival and functional recovery, and significant cardiovascular dysfunction can develop after ROSC. These dysfunctions can require active support of blood flow and ventilation, including intravascular volume expansion, vasoactive and inotropic drugs, and invasive devices. In addition, TTM and treating the underlying cause of cardiac arrest can impact survival and neurologic outcome, and hemodynamic optimization protocols also serve as part of a bundle of care to improve survival.[66-68] Overall, the data suggest that proactively managing post–cardiac arrest physiology can improve patient outcomes by ensuring organ oxygenation and perfusion and by avoiding and managing complications.

This case focuses on managing and optimizing cardiopulmonary function and perfusing vital organs after ROSC.

To ensure the success of post–cardiac arrest care, you must consider what interventions are needed for the initial stabilization phase as well as the continued management with additional emergent activities. Refer to the steps in the Adult Post–Cardiac Arrest Care Algorithm (Figure 58), as described below.

Initial stabilization phase: Resuscitation is ongoing during the post-ROSC phase (Step 1), and many of these activities can occur concurrently depending on the resources available.

However, if prioritization is necessary, follow this order (Step 2):

- Manage the airway: Place an ET tube early, and use quantitative waveform capnography or capnometry to confirm and monitor endotracheal tube placement.
- Manage respiratory parameters: Start 10 breaths/min (1 breath every 6 seconds); SpO_2 92% to 98%; $PaCO_2$ of 35 to 45 mm Hg.
- Manage hemodynamic parameters: Administer crystalloid and/or vasopressor or inotrope for goal systolic blood pressure of greater than 90 mm Hg or mean arterial pressure greater than 65 mm Hg.
- Obtain a 12-lead ECG (Step 3).

Continued management and additional emergent activities: These evaluations should be done concurrently so that decisions on targeted temperature management (TTM) receive high priority as cardiac interventions. Other critical care management activities include continuously monitoring core temperature (esophageal, rectal, bladder); maintaining normoxia, normocapnia, euglycemia; providing continuous or intermittent electroencephalogram (EEG) monitoring; and providing lung-protective ventilation.

- Consider emergent cardiac intervention if (Step 4)
    - –STEMI is present
    - –The patient has unstable cardiogenic shock
    - –Mechanical circulatory support is required
- Does the patient follow commands (Step 5)?
    - –Comatose (Step 6):
        - TTM: If the patient is not following commands, start TTM as soon as possible. Begin at 32°C to 36°C for 24 hours, using a cooling device with feedback loop.
        - Obtain brain CT.
        - Perform EEG monitoring.
        - Provide other critical care management, such as continuously monitoring core temperature; maintaining normoxia, normocapnia, and euglycemia; providing continuous or intermittent EEG monitoring, and lung-protective ventilation.
    - –Awake (step 7): Consider other critical care management.
- Evaluate and treat rapidly reversible etiologies and involve expert consultation for continued management (Step 8).

Consider the H's and T's:
- **H**ypovolemia
- **H**ypoxia
- **H**ydrogen ion (acidosis)
- **H**ypokalemia/hyperkalemia
- **H**ypothermia
- **T**ension pneumothorax
- **T**amponade, cardiac
- **T**oxins
- **T**hrombosis, pulmonary
- **T**hrombosis, coronary

Rhythms for Post–Cardiac Arrest Care

You will need to recognize the following rhythms:
- Rate—too fast or too slow
- Width of QRS complexes—wide vs narrow

Drugs for Post–Cardiac Arrest Care

Drugs for post–cardiac arrest care include
- Epinephrine
- Dopamine
- Norepinephrine infusions

Multiple System Approach to Post–Cardiac Arrest Care

To treat post–cardiac arrest patients, implement a consistent, comprehensive, structured, and multidisciplinary system of care. Programs should include management of airway and respiratory and hemodynamic parameters, TTM, immediate coronary reperfusion when indicated for restoration of coronary blood flow with PCI, neurologic diagnosis, critical care management, and prognostication.

Treat the precipitating cause of cardiac arrest after ROSC, and initiate or request studies that will further help identify and treat any cardiac, electrolyte, toxicologic, pulmonary, and neurologic precipitants of arrest.

Ensure an adequate airway and support breathing immediately after ROSC because unconscious patients usually require an advanced airway for mechanical support of breathing. Also, elevate the head of the bed 30° if tolerated to reduce the incidence of cerebral edema, aspiration, and ventilatory-associated pneumonia. Monitor the placement of an advanced airway, particularly during patient transport, by waveform capnography as described in the *2015 AHA Guidelines Update for CPR and ECC* and the *2020 AHA Guidelines for CPR and ECC*, and continuously monitor the patient's oxygenation with pulse oximetry.

Although 100% oxygen may have been used during initial resuscitation, adjust inspired oxygen to the lowest level required for an arterial oxygen saturation of 92% to 98% so that you avoid potential oxygen toxicity. Avoid hyperventilation, which is common during resuscitation attempts and can increase intrathoracic pressure, which decreases preload and lowers cardiac output. The decrease in $PaCO_2$ from hyperventilation can also decrease cerebral blood flow directly. Start ventilation at 10/min and adjust to achieve a $PaCO_2$ of 35 to 45 mm Hg.

Frequently reassess vital signs and monitor for recurrent cardiac arrhythmias by using continuous ECG monitoring. If the patient is hypotensive (SBP less than 90 mm Hg or mean arterial pressure of greater than 65 mm Hg), you can administer fluid boluses. If the patient's volume status is adequate, you may initiate infusions of vasoactive agents and adjust them to achieve a minimum SBP of 90 mm Hg or more or a mean arterial pressure of 65 mm Hg or more. Some experts advocate higher mean arterial pressures to promote cerebral blood flow.

Brain injury and cardiovascular instability are the major factors that determine survival after cardiac arrest.[69] Because TTM is currently the only intervention demonstrated to improve neurologic recovery, consider TTM for any patient who is comatose and unresponsive to verbal commands after ROSC. Obtain a CT brain scan, have EEG monitoring, and consider other critical care management. Transport the patient to a location that reliably provides this therapy in addition to coronary reperfusion (eg, PCI) and other goal-directed postarrest care therapies.

Treat the precipitating cause of cardiac arrest after ROSC and initiate or request studies that will further help evaluate the patient. You must identify and treat any cardiac, electrolyte, toxicologic, pulmonary, and neurologic precipitants of arrest. Overall, the most common cause of cardiac arrest is cardiovascular disease and associated coronary ischemia,[70,71] so obtain a 12-lead ECG as soon as possible to detect ST-segment elevation or LBBB. Perform coronary angiography right away (rather than later in the hospital stay or not at all) for OHCA patients with suspected cardiac etiology of arrest and ST-segment elevation on ECG. When you highly suspect AMI, activate local protocols for treatment and coronary reperfusion. Coronary angiography, if indicated, can be beneficial in post–cardiac arrest patients regardless of whether they are awake or comatose. It is unclear whether emergent coronary angiography is beneficial for post–cardiac arrest patients without STEMI. In the absence of evidence identifying the optimal timing for coronary angiography and PCI in post–cardiac arrest patients suspected of having ACS as the cause of their cardiac arrest but without ST-segment elevation, an interventional cardiologist should be consulted for each patient to determine timing of angiography and PCI based on local protocols. Concurrent PCI and TTM are safe, with good outcomes reported for some comatose patients who have undergone PCI.

Critical care facilities that treat patients after cardiac arrest should use a comprehensive care plan that includes acute cardiovascular interventions, use of TTM, standardized medical goal-directed therapies, and advanced neurologic monitoring and care. Determining neurologic prognosis is inaccurate during the first 72 hours after resuscitation in patients not treated with TTM. For those treated with TTM, you should wait 72 hours after the patient returns to normothermia. Prognostication using clinical examination may be confounded by sedation or paralysis, so these factors must be considered carefully before considering a withdrawal of life-sustaining therapy on the basis of neuroprognostication. Many initially comatose survivors of cardiac arrest have the potential for full recovery,[66,72,73] so it is important to place patients in a hospital critical care unit where experts can perform neurologic evaluation and appropriate testing to aid prognosis in a timely manner.

Managing Post–Cardiac Arrest Care: The Adult Post–Cardiac Arrest Care Algorithm

The Adult Post–Cardiac Arrest Care Algorithm (Figure 58) outlines the steps to immediately assess and manage post–cardiac arrest patients with ROSC. In this case, team members will continue to maintain good ventilation and oxygenation with a bag-mask device or advanced airway. You'll also use the H's and T's to recall conditions that could have contributed to the cardiac arrest. Throughout the case discussion of the Adult Post–Cardiac Arrest Care Algorithm, we will refer to Steps 1 through 8, the numbers assigned to the steps in the algorithm.

Initial Stabilization Phase

1. ROSC obtained
2. **Manage airway**
   Early placement of endotracheal tube

   Manage respiratory parameters
   Start 10 breaths/min
   SpO_2 92%-98%
   $PaCO_2$ 35-45 mm Hg

   Manage hemodynamic parameters
   Systolic blood pressure >90 mm Hg
   Mean arterial pressure >65 mm Hg
3. Obtain 12-lead ECG

Continued Management and Additional Emergent Activities

4. Consider for emergent cardiac intervention if
   - STEMI present
   - Unstable cardiogenic shock
   - Mechanical circulatory support required
5. Follows commands? — No / Yes
6. **Comatose**
   - TTM
   - Obtain brain CT
   - EEG monitoring
   - Other critical care management
7. **Awake**
   Other critical care management
8. Evaluate and treat rapidly reversible etiologies
   Involve expert consultation for continued management

Initial Stabilization Phase

Resuscitation is ongoing during the post-ROSC phase, and many of these activities can occur concurrently. However, if prioritization is necessary, follow these steps:
- Airway management: Waveform capnography or capnometry to confirm and monitor endotracheal tube placement
- Manage respiratory parameters: Titrate FIO_2 for SpO_2 92%-98%; start at 10 breaths/min; titrate to $PaCO_2$ of 35-45 mm Hg
- Manage hemodynamic parameters: Administer crystalloid and/or vasopressor or inotrope for goal systolic blood pressure >90 mm Hg or mean arterial pressure >65 mm Hg

Continued Management and Additional Emergent Activities

These evaluations should be done concurrently so that decisions on targeted temperature management (TTM) receive high priority as cardiac interventions.
- Emergent cardiac intervention: Early evaluation of 12-lead electrocardiogram (ECG); consider hemodynamics for decision on cardiac intervention
- TTM: If patient is not following commands, start TTM as soon as possible; begin at 32-36°C for 24 hours by using a cooling device with feedback loop
- Other critical care management
  – Continuously monitor core temperature (esophageal, rectal, bladder)
  – Maintain normoxia, normocapnia, euglycemia
  – Provide continuous or intermittent electroencephalogram (EEG) monitoring
  – Provide lung-protective ventilation

H's and T's

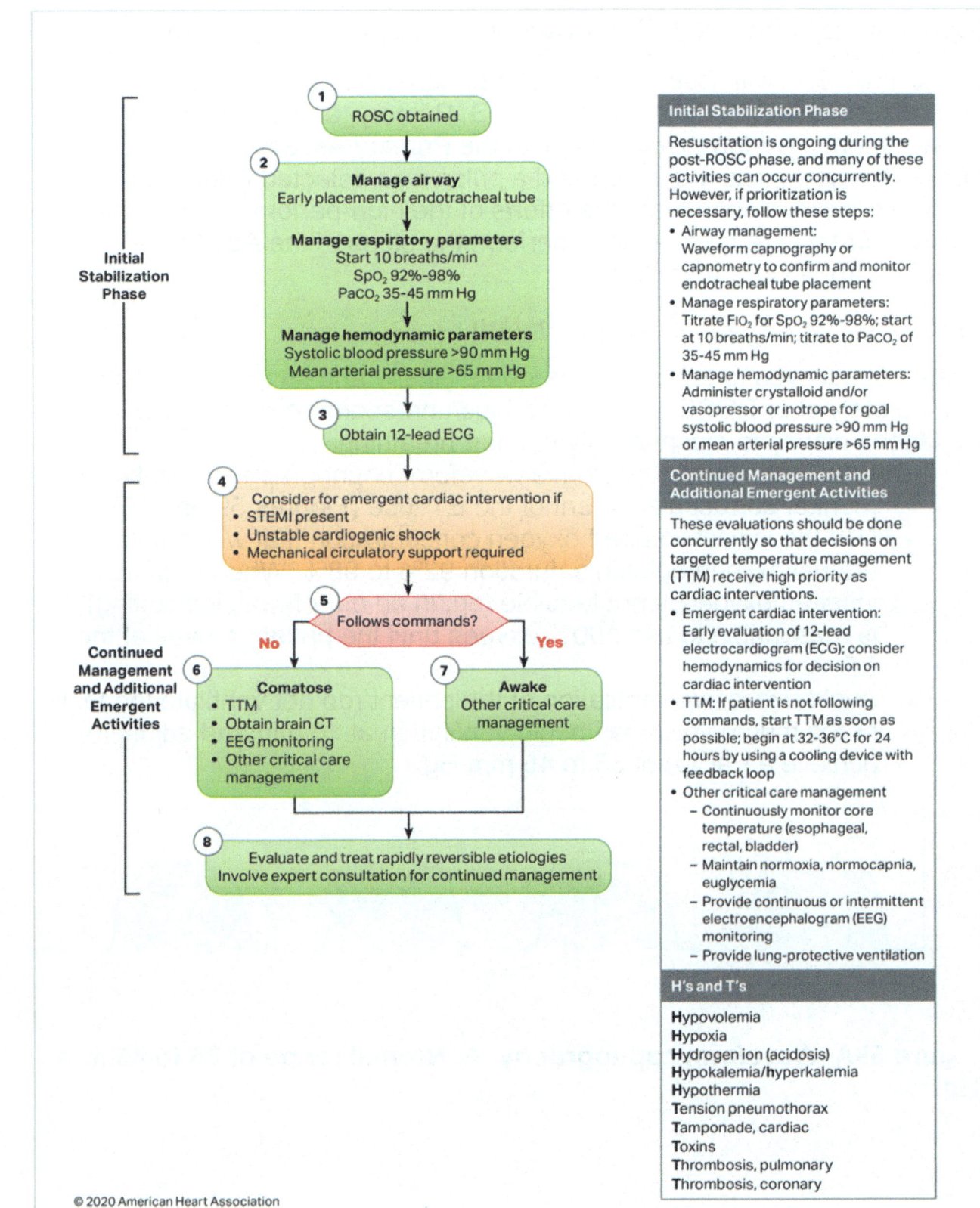

Hypovolemia
Hypoxia
Hydrogen ion (acidosis)
Hypokalemia/**h**yperkalemia
Hypothermia
Tension pneumothorax
Tamponade, cardiac
Toxins
Thrombosis, pulmonary
Thrombosis, coronary

© 2020 American Heart Association

Figure 58. Adult Post–Cardiac Arrest Care Algorithm.

Application of the Adult Post–Cardiac Arrest Care Algorithm

ACLS providers will assess and treat a patient who had cardiac arrest and was resuscitated with the use of the BLS, Primary, and Secondary Assessments. During rhythm check in the Primary Assessment, the patient's rhythm was organized and a pulse was detected (Figure 58). The Team Leader will coordinate the efforts of the high-performance post–cardiac arrest care team as they perform the steps of the Adult Post–Cardiac Arrest Care Algorithm.

Optimize Ventilation and Oxygenation

Step 2 directs you to ensure an adequate airway and support breathing immediately after ROSC. An unconscious/unresponsive patient requires an advanced airway to mechanically support breathing.

- Use continuous quantitative waveform capnography to confirm and monitor correct placement of the ET tube (Figures 59 and 60).
- Use the lowest inspired oxygen concentration that will maintain arterial oxyhemoglobin saturation 92% to 98%. When titrating inspired oxygen is not feasible (eg, in an out-of-hospital setting), it is reasonable to use 100% oxygen until the patient arrives at the ED.
- Avoid excessive ventilation of the patient (do not ventilate too fast or too much). You may begin ventilation at 10/min and adjust to achieve a PaCO$_2$ of 35 to 45 mm Hg.

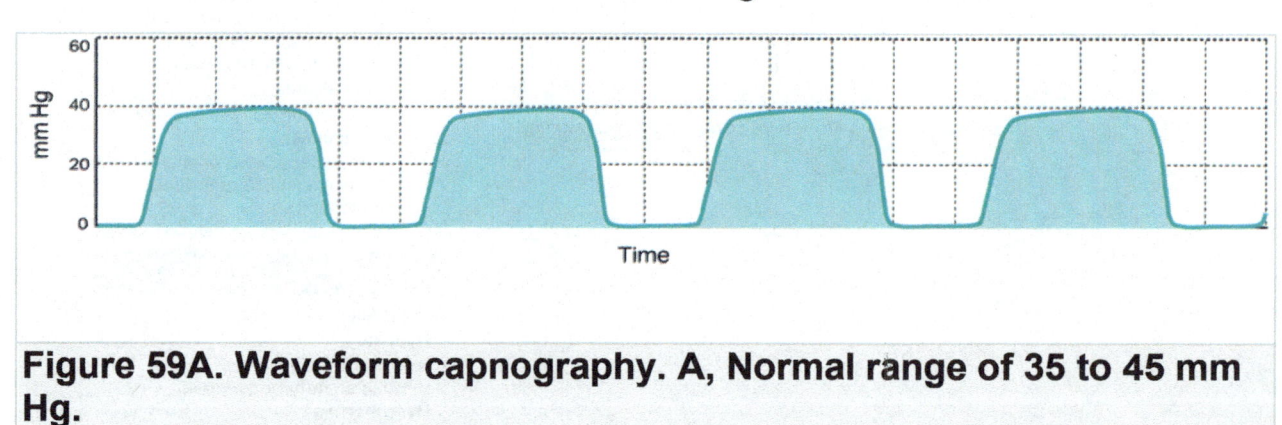

Figure 59A. Waveform capnography. A, Normal range of 35 to 45 mm Hg.

Figure 59B. 20 mm Hg.

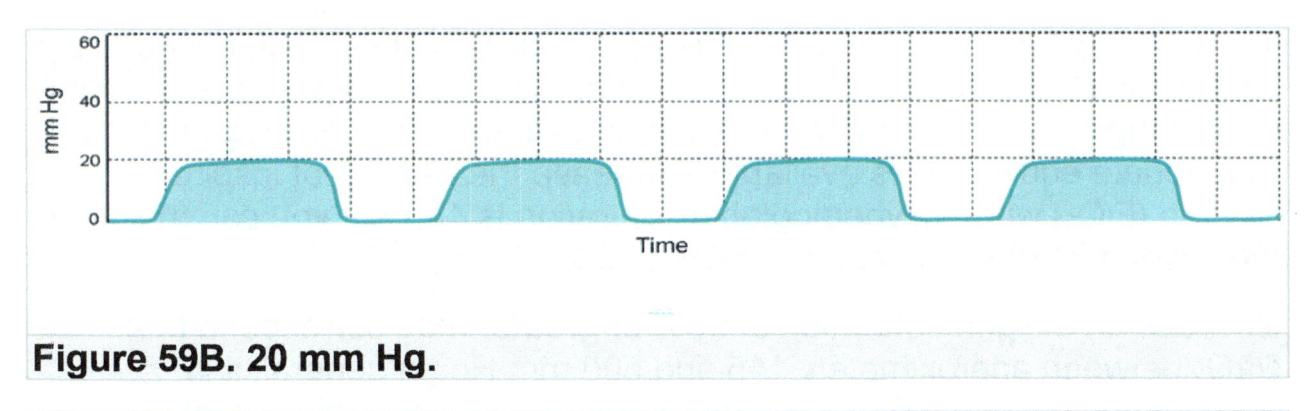

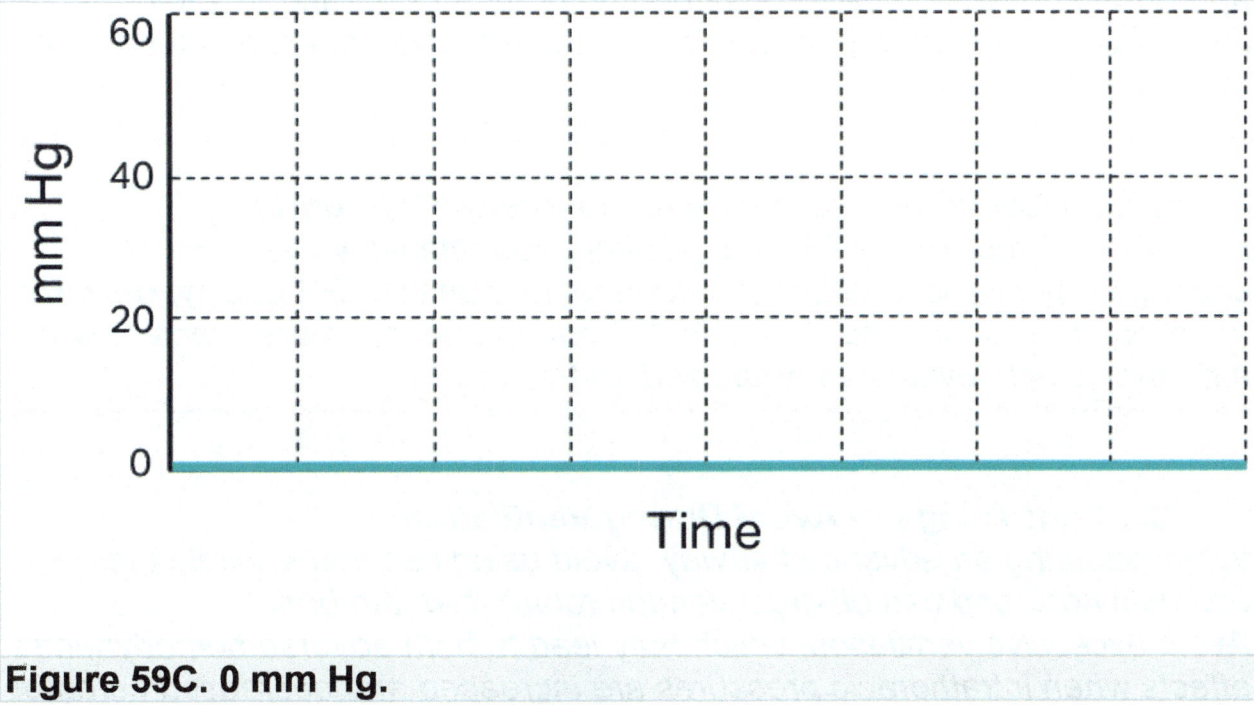

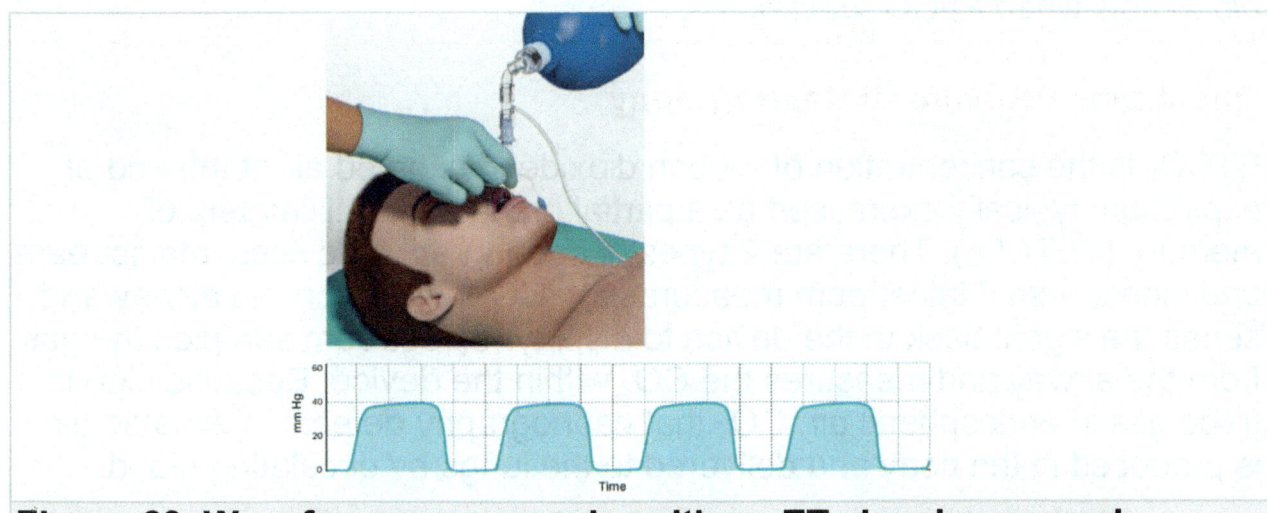

Figure 59C. 0 mm Hg.

Figure 60. Waveform capnography with an ET showing normal (adequate) ventilation pattern: PETCO$_2$ 30 to 40 mm Hg.

225

To avoid hypoxia in adults with ROSC after cardiac arrest, you may use the highest available oxygen concentration until you can measure the arterial oxyhemoglobin saturation or the partial pressure of arterial oxygen, if the appropriate equipment is available. Decrease the fraction of inspired oxygen (FiO$_2$) when oxyhemoglobin saturation is 100% if you can maintain the oxyhemoglobin saturation at 92% to 98%.

Because an oxygen saturation of 99% or greater may correspond to a PaO$_2$ between approximately 145 and 500 mm Hg, in general, it is appropriate to wean FiO$_2$ for a saturation of 98% or greater to avoid hyperoxia as long as the patient can maintain oxyhemoglobin saturation of 92% to 98%.

Critical Concepts: Quantitative Waveform Capnography
In addition to monitoring ET tube position, quantitative waveform capnography allows healthcare personnel to monitor CPR quality, optimize chest compressions, and detect ROSC during chest compressions or when a rhythm check reveals an organized rhythm.

Caution: Things to Avoid During Ventilation
When securing an advanced airway, avoid using ties that encircle the patient's neck and can obstruct venous return from the brain.
Avoid excessive ventilation, which may lead to both adverse hemodynamic effects when intrathoracic pressures are increased and decreased cerebral blood flow when PaCO$_2$ decreases.

Quantitative Waveform Capnography

ETCO$_2$ is the concentration of carbon dioxide in exhaled air at the end of expiration, typically expressed as a partial pressure in millimeters of mercury (PETCO$_2$). There are 2 types of capnography devices: mainstream and sidestream. Mainstream measures the CO$_2$ directly on the airway and sends the signal back to the device to display. Sidestream samples the gas from the airway and measures the CO$_2$ within the device. Because CO$_2$ is a trace gas in atmospheric air, CO$_2$ that capnography detects in exhaled air is produced in the body and delivered to the lungs by circulating blood.

Cardiac output is the major determinant of CO_2 delivery to the lungs. If ventilation is relatively constant, $PETCO_2$ correlates well with cardiac output during CPR.

Observe a persistent capnographic waveform with ventilation to confirm and monitor ET tube placement in the field, in the transport vehicle, on arrival at the hospital, and after any patient transfer to reduce the risk of unrecognized tube misplacement or displacement.

Although researchers have not studied capnography to confirm and monitor correct placement of supraglottic airways (eg, laryngeal mask airway, laryngeal tube, or esophageal-tracheal tube), effective ventilation through a supraglottic airway device should result in a capnography waveform during CPR and after ROSC.

Treat Hypotension (SBP Less Than 90 mm Hg)

Step 2 directs you to treat hypotension when SBP is less than 90 mm Hg. Obtain IV access if not already established, and verify that any IV lines are open. Continue ECG monitoring after ROSC, during transport, and throughout ICU care until deemed clinically not necessary. At this stage, consider treating any reversible causes that might have precipitated the cardiac arrest but persist after ROSC.

Treat hypotension as follows:
- **IV bolus:** 1 to 2 L normal saline or lactated Ringer's solution
- **Norepinephrine:** 0.1 to 0.5 mcg/kg per minute (in 70-kg adult: 7 to 35 mcg per minute) IV infusion adjusted to achieve a minimum SBP of greater than 90 mm Hg or a mean arterial pressure of greater than 65 mm Hg
    - —Norepinephrine (levarterenol), a naturally occurring potent vasoconstrictor and inotropic agent, may be effective for managing patients with severe hypotension (eg, SBP less than 70 mm Hg) and a low total peripheral resistance who do not respond to less potent adrenergic drugs such as dopamine, phenylephrine, or methoxamine.
- **Epinephrine:** 2 to 10 mcg per minute IV infusion adjusted to achieve a minimum SBP of greater than 90 mm Hg or a mean arterial pressure of greater than 65 mm Hg
    - —Epinephrine can be used in patients who are not in cardiac arrest but who require inotropic or vasopressor support.

- **Dopamine:** 5 to 20 mcg/kg per minute IV infusion adjusted to achieve a minimum SBP of greater than 90 mm Hg or a mean arterial pressure of greater than 65 mm Hg
  - —Dopamine hydrochloride is a catecholamine-like agent and a chemical precursor of norepinephrine that stimulates the heart through both α- and β-adrenergic receptors.

STEMI Is Present or High Suspicion of AMI

Both in-hospital and out-of-hospital medical personnel should obtain a 12-lead ECG as soon as possible after ROSC to identify those patients with STEMI or a high suspicion of AMI.

EMS personnel should transport these patients to a facility that reliably provides this therapy (Step 4).

Coronary Reperfusion

Begin aggressive treatment, including coronary reperfusion with PCI, if you detect STEMI after ROSC, regardless of coma or TTM. In cases of out-of-hospital STEMI, provide advance notification to receiving facilities.

Following Commands

Step 5 directs you to examine the patient's ability to follow verbal commands. If the patient does not follow commands, the high-performance team should consider implementing TTM, obtaining a brain CT, performing EEG monitoring, and providing other critical-care management (Step 6). If the patient can follow verbal commands, move to Step 7.

Targeted Temperature Management

TTM is the only intervention demonstrated to improve neurologic recovery after cardiac arrest. The optimal duration of TTM is at least 24 hours, and although comparative studies of the duration of TTM have not been performed in adults, hypothermia for up to 72 hours was used safely in newborns.

During TTM, monitor the patient's core temperature by using an esophageal thermometer, bladder catheter in nonanuric patients, or a pulmonary artery catheter if one is already in place for other indications. Axillary, oral, and rectal temperatures do not adequately measure core temperature changes.

TTM should not affect the decision to perform PCI, because concurrent PCI and hypothermia are reported to be feasible and safe.

To protect the brain and other organs, the high-performance team should start TTM in patients who remain comatose with ROSC after cardiac arrest.

For TTM, healthcare providers should select and maintain a constant target temperature between 32°C and 36°C for at least 24 hours. Although the optimal method of achieving the target temperature is unknown, any combination of rapid infusion of ice-cold, isotonic, non–glucose-containing fluid (30 mL/kg), endovascular catheters, surface cooling devices, or simple surface interventions (eg, ice bags) appears to be safe and effective.

Specific patient features may necessitate selecting one temperature over another for TTM. Higher temperatures might be preferable in patients for whom lower temperatures convey some risk (eg, bleeding), and lower temperatures might be preferable when patients have clinical features that worsen at higher temperatures (eg, seizures, cerebral edema). Of note, temperature control between 32°C and 36°C is not contraindicated in any patients, so all patients who require intensive care are eligible.

In the prehospital setting, do not routinely cool patients after ROSC with rapid infusion of cold IV fluids. Current evidence indicates no direct outcome benefit from these interventions, and IV fluid administration in the prehospital setting may increase pulmonary edema and rearrest. We don't yet know whether different methods or devices for temperature control outside of the hospital are beneficial.

Advanced Critical Care

After coronary reperfusion interventions, or if the post–cardiac arrest patient has no ECG evidence or suspicion of MI, the high-performance team should transfer the patient to an ICU.

Post–Cardiac Arrest Maintenance Therapy

No evidence supports continued prophylactic administration of antiarrhythmic medications once the patient achieves ROSC.

Other Postresuscitation Care
- Glucose management: The benefit of any specific target range of glucose management is uncertain in adults with ROSC after cardiac arrest. It is reasonable to manage blood glucose levels in

post-arrest patients using the same approach for the general critically ill population (eg, insulin therapy when needed to maintain a blood glucose of 150 to 180 mg/dL).
- Prophylactic antibiotics: The routine use of prophylactic antibiotics in postarrest patients is of uncertain benefit.
- Neuroprotective agents: The effectiveness of agents to mitigate neurologic injury in patients who remain comatose after ROSC is uncertain. There is no difference in any clinical outcomes with use of neuroprotective agents studied.
- Routine use of steroids: The routine use of steroids for patients with shock after ROSC is of uncertain value. There is no definitive evidence of benefit from steroids after ROSC.

Neuroprognostication

Hypoxic-ischemic brain injury is the leading cause of morbidity and mortality in survivors of OHCA, and it accounts for a smaller but significant portion of poor outcomes after resuscitation from IHCA.[69,74] Most deaths attributable to post-arrest brain injury are due to active withdrawal of life-sustaining treatment on the basis of a predicted poor neurologic outcome. Accurate neurologic prognostication is important to avoid inappropriate withdrawal of life-sustaining treatment in patients who may otherwise achieve meaningful neurologic recovery and also to avoid ineffective treatment when poor outcome is inevitable.[75]

Neuroprognostication relies on interpreting the results of diagnostic tests and correlating those results with outcome (Figure 61). Because a false positive test for poor neurologic outcome could lead to inappropriate withdrawal of life support from a patient who otherwise might have recovered, the most important test characteristic is specificity. Many of the tests considered are subject to error due to the effects of medications, organ dysfunction, and temperature. Furthermore, many research studies have methodological limitations, including small sample sizes, single-center design, lack of blinding, the potential for self-fulfilling prophecies, and the use of outcome at hospital discharge rather than a timepoint associated with maximal recovery (typically 3–6 months after an arrest).[75]

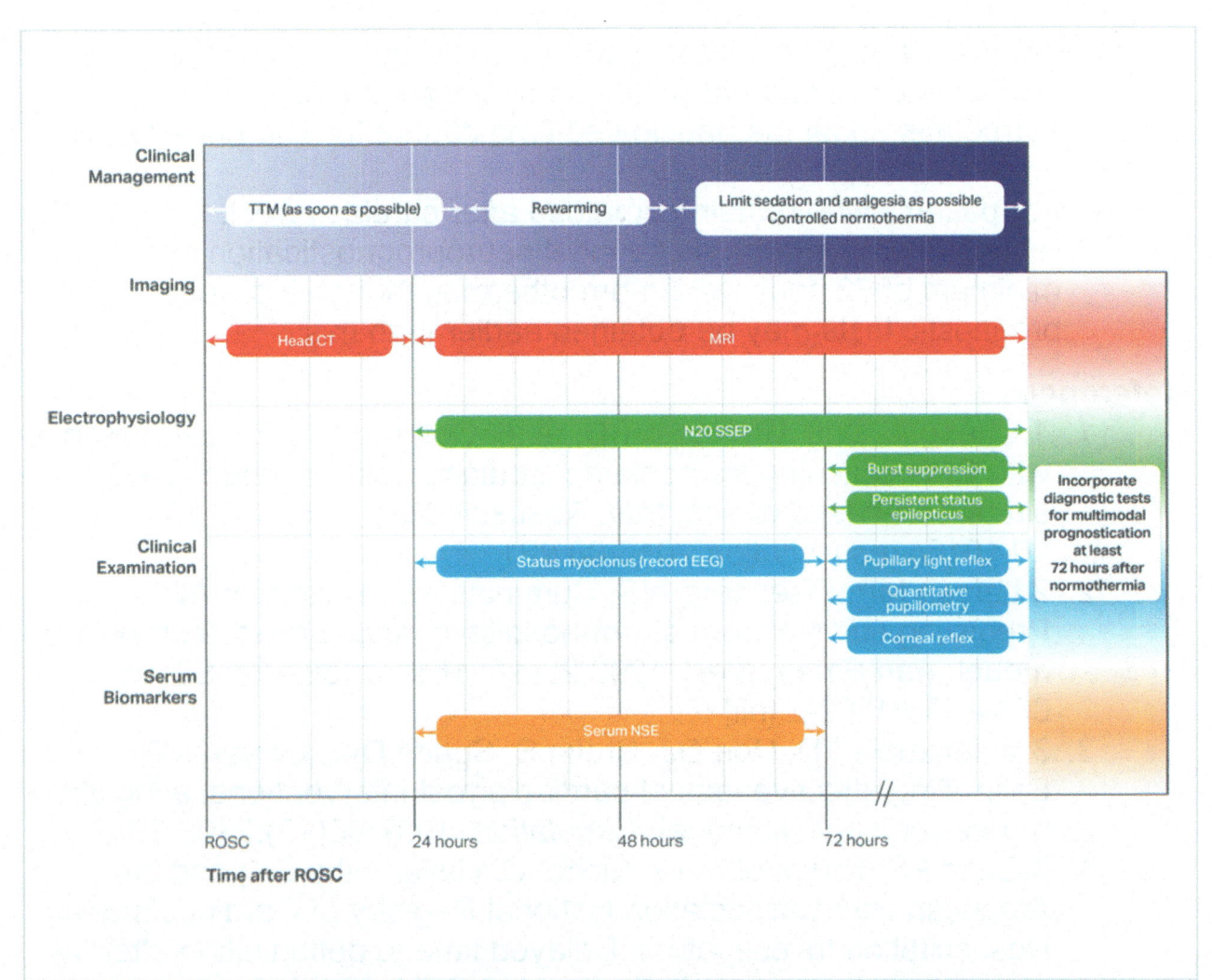

Figure 61. Schematic overview of a multimodal approach to neuroprognostication.

Because any single method of neuroprognostication has an intrinsic error rate and may be subject to confounding, multiple modalities should be used to improve decision-making accuracy.

General Considerations for Neuroprognostication
- In patients who remain comatose after cardiac arrest, neuroprognostication should involve a multimodal approach and not be based on any single finding.
- In patients who remain comatose after cardiac arrest, neuroprognostication should be delayed until adequate time has passed to ensure avoidance of confounding by medication effect or a transiently poor exam in the early postinjury period.

- Teams caring for comatose cardiac arrest survivors should have regular and transparent multidisciplinary discussions with surrogates about the anticipated time course for and uncertainties around neuroprognostication.
- For patients who remain comatose after cardiac arrest, it is reasonable to perform multimodal neuroprognostication at a minimum of 72 hours after normothermia, though individual prognostic tests may be obtained earlier than this.

References
1. 1.Cheng A, Duff JP, Kessler D, et al. Optimizing CPR performance with CPR coaching for pediatric cardiac arrest: A randomized simulation-based clinical trial. *Resuscitation.* 2018;132:33-40. doi: 10.1016/j.resuscitation.2018.08.021
2. 2.Larsen MP, Eisenberg MS, Cummins RO, Hallstrom AP. Predicting survival from out-of-hospital cardiac arrest: a graphic model. *Ann Emerg Med.* 1993;22(11):1652-1658. doi: S0196-0644(05)81302-2 [pii]
3. 3.Valenzuela TD, Roe DJ, Cretin S, Spaite DW, Larsen MP. Estimating effectiveness of cardiac arrest interventions: a logistic regression survival model. *Circulation.* 1997;96(10):3308-3313.
4. 4.Chan PS, Krumholz HM, Nichol G, Nallamothu BK; and the American Heart Association National Registry of Cardiopulmonary Resuscitation Investigators. Delayed time to defibrillation after in-hospital cardiac arrest. *N Engl J Med.* 2008;358(1):9-17. doi: 10.1056/NEJMoa0706467
5. 5.Stiell IG, Wells GA, Field B, et al; for the Ontario Prehospital Advanced Life Support Study Group. Advanced cardiac life support in out-of-hospital cardiac arrest. *N Engl J Med.* 2004;351(7):647-656. doi: 10.1056/NEJMoa040325
6. 6.Swor RA, Jackson RE, Cynar M, et al. Bystander CPR, ventricular fibrillation, and survival in witnessed, unmonitored out-of-hospital cardiac arrest. *Ann Emerg Med.* 1995;25(6):780-784.
7. 7.Holmberg M, Holmberg S, Herlitz J. Incidence, duration and survival of ventricular fibrillation in out-of-hospital cardiac arrest patients in Sweden. *Resuscitation.* 2000;44(1):7-17.
8. 8.Panchal AR, Berg KM, Kudenchuk PJ, et al. 2018 American Heart Association focused update on advanced cardiovascular life support use of antiarrhythmic drugs during and immediately after cardiac arrest: an update to the American Heart Association

guidelines for cardiopulmonary resuscitation and emergency cardiovascular care. *Circulation.* 2018;138(23):e740-e749. doi: 10.1161/CIR.0000000000000613

9. 9.Kudenchuk PJ, Cobb LA, Copass MK, et al. Amiodarone for resuscitation after out-of-hospital cardiac arrest due to ventricular fibrillation. *N Engl J Med.* 1999;341(12):871-878. doi: 10.1056/NEJM199909163411203

10. 10.Paradis NA, Martin GB, Rivers EP, et al. Coronary perfusion pressure and the return of spontaneous circulation in human cardiopulmonary resuscitation. *JAMA.* 1990;263(8):1106-1113.

11. 11.Levine RL, Wayne MA, Miller CC. End-tidal carbon dioxide and outcome of out-of-hospital cardiac arrest. *N Engl J Med.* 1997;337(5):301-306. doi: 10.1056/NEJM199707313370503

12. 12.Wayne MA, Levine RL, Miller CC. Use of end-tidal carbon dioxide to predict outcome in prehospital cardiac arrest. *Ann Emerg Med.* 1995;25(6):762-767. doi: 10.1016/s0196-0644(95)70204-0

13. 13.Halperin HR, Tsitlik JE, Gelfand M, et al. A preliminary study of cardiopulmonary resuscitation by circumferential compression of the chest with use of a pneumatic vest. *N Engl J Med.* 1993;329(11):762-768. doi: 10.1056/NEJM199309093291104

14. 14.Kern KB, Ewy GA, Voorhees WD, Babbs CF, Tacker WA. Myocardial perfusion pressure: a predictor of 24-hour survival during prolonged cardiac arrest in dogs. *Resuscitation.* 1988;16(4):241-250. doi: 10.1016/0300-9572(88)90111-6

15. 15.Lindner KH, Prengel AW, Pfenninger EG, et al. Vasopressin improves vital organ blood flow during closed-chest cardiopulmonary resuscitation in pigs. *Circulation.* 1995;91(1):215-221. doi: 10.1161/01.cir.91.1.215

16. 16.Little CM, Angelos MG, Paradis NA. Compared to angiotensin II, epinephrine is associated with high myocardial blood flow following return of spontaneous circulation after cardiac arrest. *Resuscitation.* 2003;59(3):353-359. doi: 10.1016/s0300-9572(03)00239-9

17. 17.Holmberg MJ, Issa MS, Moskowitz A, et al; for the International Liaison Committee on Resuscitation Advanced Life Support Task Force Collaborators. Vasopressors during adult cardiac arrest: a systematic review and meta-

analysis. *Resuscitation.* 2019;139:106-121. doi: 10.1016/j.resuscitation.2019.04.008
18. Rudd RA, Aleshire N, Zibbell JE, Gladden RM. Increases in drug and opioid overdose deaths—United States, 2000-2014. *MMWR Morb Mortal Wkly Rep.* 2016;64(50-51):1378-1382. doi: 10.15585/mmwr.mm6450a3
19. Centers for Disease Control and Prevention. America's drug overdose epidemic: data to action. https://www.cdc.gov/injury/features/prescription-drug-overdose/index.html. Accessed October 7, 2019.
20. Government of Canada. National report: apparent opioid-related deaths in Canada. September 2019; https://health-infobase.canada.ca/datalab/national-surveillance-opioid-mortality.html. Accessed October 7, 2019.
21. Paulozzi LJ, Logan JE, Hall AJ, McKinstry E, Kaplan JA, Crosby AE. A comparison of drug overdose deaths involving methadone and other opioid analgesics in West Virginia. *Addiction.* 2009;104(9):1541-1548. doi: 10.1111/j.1360-0443.2009.02650.x
22. Madadi P, Hildebrandt D, Lauwers AE, Koren G. Characteristics of opioid-users whose death was related to opioid-toxicity: a population-based study in Ontario, Canada. *PLoS One.* 2013;8(4):e60600. doi: 10.1371/journal.pone.0060600
23. Webster LR, Cochella S, Dasgupta N, et al. An analysis of the root causes for opioid-related overdose deaths in the United States. *Pain Med.* 2011;12(suppl 2):S26-S35. doi: 10.1111/j.1526-4637.2011.01134.x
24. Krantz MJ, Kutinsky IB, Robertson AD, Mehler PS. Dose-related effects of methadone on QT prolongation in a series of patients with torsade de pointes. *Pharmacotherapy.* 2003;23(6):802-805. doi: 10.1592/phco.23.6.802.32186
25. Eap CB, Crettol S, Rougier JS, et al. Stereoselective block of hERG channel by (S)-methadone and QT interval prolongation in CYP2B6 slow metabolizers. *Clin Pharmacol Ther.* 2007;81(5):719-728. doi: 10.1038/sj.clpt.6100120
26. Krantz MJ, Martin J, Stimmel B, Mehta D, Haigney MC. QTc interval screening in methadone treatment. *Ann Intern Med.* 2009;150(6):387-395. doi: 10.7326/0003-4819-150-6-200903170-00103

27. Stallvik M, Nordstrand B, Kristensen Ø, Bathen J, Skogvoll E, Spigset O. Corrected QT interval during treatment with methadone and buprenorphine—relation to doses and serum concentrations. *Drug Alcohol Depend.* 2013;129(1-2):88-93. doi: 10.1016/j.drugalcdep.2012.09.016
28. Chou R, Weimer MB, Dana T. Methadone overdose and cardiac arrhythmia potential: findings from a review of the evidence for an American Pain Society and College on Problems of Drug Dependence clinical practice guideline. *J Pain.* 2014;15(4):338-365. doi: 10.1016/j.jpain.2014.01.495
29. Lipski J, Stimmel B, Donoso E. The effect of heroin and multiple drug abuse on the electrocardiogram. *Am Heart J.* 1973;86(5):663-668. doi: 10.1016/0002-8703(73)90344-x
30. Labi M. Paroxysmal atrial fibrillation in heroin intoxication. *Ann Intern Med.* 1969;71(5):951-959. doi: 10.7326/0003-4819-71-5-951
31. Leach M. Naloxone: a new therapeutic and diagnostic agent for emergency use. *J Amer Coll Emerg Phys.* 1973;2:21-23.
32. Sporer KA, Firestone J, Isaacs SM. Out-of-hospital treatment of opioid overdoses in an urban setting. *Acad Emerg Med.* 1996;3(7):660-667. doi: 10.1111/j.1553-2712.1996.tb03487.x
33. Robertson TM, Hendey GW, Stroh G, Shalit M. Intranasal naloxone is a viable alternative to intravenous naloxone for prehospital narcotic overdose. *Prehosp Emerg Care.* 2009;13(4):512-515. doi: 10.1080/10903120903144866
34. Evans LE, Swainson CP, Roscoe P, Prescott LF. Treatment of drug overdosage with naloxone, a specific narcotic antagonist. *Lancet.* 1973;1(7801):452-455. doi: 10.1016/s0140-6736(73)91879-5
35. Kelly AM, Kerr D, Dietze P, Patrick I, Walker T, Koutsogiannis Z. Randomised trial of intranasal versus intramuscular naloxone in prehospital treatment for suspected opioid overdose. *Med J Aust.* 2005;182(1):24-27.
36. Barton ED, Colwell CB, Wolfe T, et al. Efficacy of intranasal naloxone as a needleless alternative for treatment of opioid overdose in the prehospital setting. *J Emerg Med.* 2005;29(3):265-271. doi: 10.1016/j.jemermed.2005.03.007

37. 37.Wolfe TR, Braude DA. Intranasal medication delivery for children: a brief review and update. *Pediatrics.* 2010;126(3):532-537. doi: 10.1542/peds.2010-0616
38. 38.Loimer N, Hofmann P, Chaudhry HR. Nasal administration of naloxone is as effective as the intravenous route in opiate addicts. *Int J Addict.* 1994;29(6):819-827. doi: 10.3109/10826089409047912
39. 39.Doe-Simkins M, Walley AY, Epstein A, Moyer P. Saved by the nose: bystander-administered intranasal naloxone hydrochloride for opioid overdose. *Am J Public Health.* 2009;99(5):788-791. doi: 10.2105/AJPH.2008.146647
40. 40.Wanger K, Brough L, Macmillan I, Goulding J, MacPhail I, Christenson JM. Intravenous vs subcutaneous naloxone for out-of-hospital management of presumed opioid overdose. *Acad Emerg Med.* 1998;5(4):293-299. doi: 10.1111/j.1553-2712.1998.tb02707.x
41. 41.Baumann BM, Patterson RA, Parone DA, et al. Use and efficacy of nebulized naloxone in patients with suspected opioid intoxication. *Am J Emerg Med.* 2013;31(3):585-588. doi: 10.1016/j.ajem.2012.10.004
42. 42.Weber JM, Tataris KL, Hoffman JD, Aks SE, Mycyk MB. Can nebulized naloxone be used safely and effectively by emergency medical services for suspected opioid overdose? *Prehosp Emerg Care.* 2012;16(2):289-292. doi: 10.3109/10903127.2011.640763
43. 43.Greenberg MI, Roberts JR, Baskin SI. Endotracheal naloxone reversal of morphine-induced respiratory depression in rabbits. *Ann Emerg Med.* 1980;9(6):289-292. doi: 10.1016/s0196-0644(80)80060-6
44. 44.Peberdy MA, Gluck JA, Ornato JP, et al; for the American Heart Association Emergency Cardiovascular Care Committee; Council on Cardiopulmonary, Critical Care, Perioperative, and Resuscitation; Council on Cardiovascular Diseases in the Young; Council on Cardiovascular Surgery and Anesthesia; Council on Cardiovascular and Stroke Nursing; and Council on Clinical Cardiology Cardiopulmonary resuscitation in adults and children with mechanical circulatory support: a scientific statement from the American Heart Association. *Circulation.* 2017;135(24):e1115-e1134. doi: 10.1161/CIR.0000000000000504
45. 45.Page-Rodriguez A, Gonzalez-Sanchez JA. Perimortem cesarean section of twin pregnancy: case report and review of the

literature. *Acad Emerg Med.* 1999;6(10):1072-1074. doi: 10.1111/j.1553-2712.1999.tb01199.x
46. 46.Cardosi RJ, Porter KB. Cesarean delivery of twins during maternal cardiopulmonary arrest. *Obstet Gynecol.* 1998;92(4, pt 2):695-697. doi: 10.1016/s0029-7844(98)00127-6
47. 47.Mendonca C, Griffiths J, Ateleanu B, Collis RE. Hypotension following combined spinal-epidural anaesthesia for Caesarean section: left lateral position vs. tilted supine position. *Anaesthesia.* 2003;58(5):428-431. doi: 10.1046/j.1365-2044.2003.03090.x
48. 48.Rees SG, Thurlow JA, Gardner IC, Scrutton MJ, Kinsella SM. Maternal cardiovascular consequences of positioning after spinal anaesthesia for Caesarean section: left 15 degree table tilt vs. left lateral. *Anaesthesia.* 2002;57(1):15-20. doi: 10.1046/j.1365-2044.2002.02325.x
49. 49.Alahuhta S, Jouppila P. How to maintain uteroplacental perfusion during obstetric anaesthesia. *Acta Anaesthesiol Scand Suppl.* 1997;110:106-108.
50. 50.Tamás P, Szilágyi A, Jeges S, et al. Effects of maternal central hemodynamics on fetal heart rate patterns. *Acta Obstet Gynecol Scand.* 2007;86(6):711-714. doi: 10.1080/00016340701252217
51. 51.Abitbol MM. Supine position in labor and associated fetal heart rate changes. *Obstet Gynecol.* 1985;65(4):481-486.
52. 52.Tamilselvan P, Fernando R, Bray J, Sodhi M, Columb M. The effects of crystalloid and colloid preload on cardiac output in the parturient undergoing planned cesarean delivery under spinal anesthesia: a randomized trial. *Anesth Analg.* 2009;109(6):1916-1921. doi: 10.1213/ANE.0b013e3181bbfdf6
53. 53.Lavonas EJ, Drennan IR, Gabrielli A, et al. Part 10: special circumstances of resuscitation: 2015 American Heart Association Guidelines Update for Cardiopulmonary Resuscitation and Emergency Cardiovascular Care. *Circulation.* 2015;132(18)(suppl 2):S501-518. doi: 10.1161/CIR.0000000000000264
54. 54.Ueland K, Novy MJ, Peterson EN, Metcalfe J. Maternal cardiovascular dynamics, IV: the influence of gestational age on the maternal cardiovascular response to posture and exercise. *Am J Obstet Gynecol.* 1969;104(6):856-864.
55. 55.Goodwin AP, Pearce AJ. The human wedge: a manoeuvre to relieve aortocaval compression during resuscitation in late

pregnancy. *Anaesthesia.* 1992;47(5):433-434. doi: 10.1111/j.1365-2044.1992.tb02228.x
56. 56.Rees GA, Willis BA. Resuscitation in late pregnancy. *Anaesthesia.* 1988;43(5):347-349. doi: 10.1111/j.1365-2044.1988.tb09009.x
57. 57.Cyna AM, Andrew M, Emmett RS, Middleton P, Simmons SW. Techniques for preventing hypotension during spinal anaesthesia for caesarean section. *Cochrane Database Syst Rev.* 2006(4):CD002251. doi: 10.1002/14651858.CD002251.pub2
58. 58.Benson MD, Padovano A, Bourjeily G, Zhou Y. Maternal collapse: challenging the four-minute rule. *EBioMedicine.* 2016;6:253-257. doi: 10.1016/j.ebiom.2016.02.042
59. 59.Callaway CW, Schmicker R, Kampmeyer M, et al; and the Resuscitation Outcomes Consortium (ROC) Investigators. Receiving hospital characteristics associated with survival after out-of-hospital cardiac arrest. *Resuscitation.* 2010;81(5):524-529. doi: 10.1016/j.resuscitation.2009.12.006
60. 60.Carr BG, Kahn JM, Merchant RM, Kramer AA, Neumar RW. Inter-hospital variability in post-cardiac arrest mortality. *Resuscitation.* 2009;80(1):30-34. doi: 10.1016/j.resuscitation.2008.09.001
61. 61.Laurent I, Monchi M, Chiche JD, et al. Reversible myocardial dysfunction in survivors of out-of-hospital cardiac arrest. *J Am Coll Cardiol.* 2002;40(12):2110-2116.
62. 62.Negovsky VA. The second step in resuscitation—the treatment of the 'post-resuscitation disease'. *Resuscitation.* 1972;1(1):1-7.
63. 63.Neumar RW, Nolan JP, Adrie C, et al. Post-cardiac arrest syndrome: epidemiology, pathophysiology, treatment, and prognostication: a consensus statement from the International Liaison Committee on Resuscitation (American Heart Association, Australian and New Zealand Council on Resuscitation, European Resuscitation Council, Heart and Stroke Foundation of Canada, InterAmerican Heart Foundation, Resuscitation Council of Asia, and the Resuscitation Council of Southern Africa); the American Heart Association Emergency Cardiovascular Care Committee; the Council on Cardiovascular Surgery and Anesthesia; the Council on Cardiopulmonary, Perioperative, and Critical Care; the Council on Clinical Cardiology; and the Stroke

Council. *Circulation.* 2008;118(23):2452-2483. doi: 10.1161/CIRCULATIONAHA.108.190652
64. 64.Safar P. Resuscitation from clinical death: pathophysiologic limits and therapeutic potentials. *Crit Care Med.* 1988;16(10):923-941.
65. 65.Skrifvars MB, Pettilä V, Rosenberg PH, Castrén M. A multiple logistic regression analysis of in-hospital factors related to survival at six months in patients resuscitated from out-of-hospital ventricular fibrillation. *Resuscitation.* 2003;59(3):319-328.
66. 66.Gaieski DF, Band RA, Abella BS, et al. Early goal-directed hemodynamic optimization combined with therapeutic hypothermia in comatose survivors of out-of-hospital cardiac arrest. *Resuscitation.* 2009;80(4):418-424. doi: 10.1016/j.resuscitation.2008.12.015
67. 67.Kirves H, Skrifvars MB, Vähäkuopus M, Ekström K, Martikainen M, Castren M. Adherence to resuscitation guidelines during prehospital care of cardiac arrest patients. *Eur J Emerg Med.* 2007;14(2):75-81. doi: 10.1097/MEJ.0b013e328013f88c
68. 68.Sunde K, Pytte M, Jacobsen D, et al. Implementation of a standardised treatment protocol for post resuscitation care after out-of-hospital cardiac arrest. *Resuscitation.* 2007;73(1):29-39. doi: 10.1016/j.resuscitation.2006.08.016
69. 69.Laver S, Farrow C, Turner D, Nolan J. Mode of death after admission to an intensive care unit following cardiac arrest. *Intensive Care Med.* 2004;30(11):2126-2128. doi: 10.1007/s00134-004-2425-z
70. 70.Anyfantakis ZA, Baron G, Aubry P, et al. Acute coronary angiographic findings in survivors of out-of-hospital cardiac arrest. *Am Heart J.* 2009;157(2):312-318. doi: 10.1016/j.ahj.2008.09.016
71. 71.Spaulding CM, Joly LM, Rosenberg A, et al. Immediate coronary angiography in survivors of out-of-hospital cardiac arrest. *N Engl J Med.* 1997;336(23):1629-1633. doi: 10.1056/NEJM199706053362302
72. 72.Hypothermia after Cardiac Arrest Study Group. Mild therapeutic hypothermia to improve the neurologic outcome after cardiac arrest. *N Engl J Med.* 2002;346(8):549-556. doi: 10.1056/NEJMoa012689
73. 73.Bunch TJ, White RD, Gersh BJ, et al. Long-term outcomes of out-of-hospital cardiac arrest after successful early

defibrillation. *N Engl J Med.* 2003;348(26):2626-2633. doi: 10.1056/NEJMoa023053

74. 74.Witten L, Gardner R, Holmberg MJ, et al. Reasons for death in patients successfully resuscitated from out-of-hospital and in-hospital cardiac arrest. *Resuscitation.* 2019;136:93-99. doi: 10.1016/j.resuscitation.2019.01.031

75. 75.Geocadin RG, Callaway CW, Fink EL, et al; for the American Heart Association Emergency Cardiovascular Care Committee. Standards for studies of neurological prognostication in comatose survivors of cardiac arrest: a scientific statement from the American Heart Association. *Circulation.* 2019;140(9):e517-e542. doi: 10.1161/CIR.0000000000000702

Appendix

Testing Checklists and Learning Station Checklists

Advanced Cardiovascular Life Support
Adult High-Quality BLS
Skills Testing Checklist

American Heart Association.

Student Name _____ Date of Test _____

Hospital Scenario: "You are working in a hospital or clinic, and you see a person who has suddenly collapsed in the hallway. You check that the scene is safe and then approach the patient. Demonstrate what you would do next."

Prehospital Scenario: "You arrive on the scene for a suspected cardiac arrest. No bystander CPR has been provided. You approach the scene and ensure that it is safe. Demonstrate what you would do next."

Assessment and Activation
- ☐ Checks responsiveness
- ☐ Shouts for help/Activates emergency response system/Sends for AED
- ☐ Checks breathing
- ☐ Checks pulse

Once student shouts for help, instructor says, "I am going to get the AED."

Compressions *Audio/visual feedback device required for accuracy*
- ☐ Hand placement on lower half of sternum
- ☐ Perform continuous compressions for 2 minutes (100-120/min)
- ☐ Compresses at least 2 inches (5 cm)
- ☐ Complete chest recoil. (Optional, check if using a feedback device that measures chest recoil)

Rescuer 2 says, "Here is the AED. I'll take over compressions, and you use the AED."

AED (follows prompts of AED)
- ☐ Powers on AED
- ☐ Correctly attaches pads
- ☐ Clears for analysis
- ☐ Clears to safely deliver a shock
- ☐ Safely delivers a shock
- ☐ Shocks within 45 seconds of AED arrival

Resumes Compressions
- ☐ Ensures compressions are resumed immediately after shock delivery
  - Student directs instructor to resume compressions *or*
  - Second student resumes compressions

STOP TEST

Instructor Notes
- Place a check in the box next to each step the student completes successfully.
- If the student does not complete all steps successfully (as indicated by at least 1 blank check box), the student must receive remediation. Make a note here of which skills require remediation (refer to instructor manual for information about remediation).

Test Results	Circle **PASS** or **NR** to indicate pass or needs remediation:	PASS	NR

Instructor Initials _____ Instructor Number _____ Date _____

© 2020 American Heart Association

Airway Management Skills Testing Checklist

American Heart Association

Student Name _____ Date of Test _____

Critical Performance Steps	Check if done correctly
BLS Assessment and Interventions	
Checks for responsiveness • Taps and shouts, "Are you OK?"	
Activates the emergency response system • Shouts for nearby help/Activates the emergency response system and gets the AED *or* • Directs second rescuer to activate the emergency response system and get the AED	
Checks breathing • Scans chest for movement (5-10 seconds)	
Checks pulse (5-10 seconds) **Breathing and pulse check can be done simultaneously** Notes that pulse is present and does not initiate chest compressions or attach AED	
Inserts oropharyngeal or nasopharyngeal airway	
Administers oxygen	
Performs effective bag-mask ventilation for 1 minute • Gives proper ventilation rate (once every 6 seconds) • Gives proper ventilation speed (over 1 second) • Gives proper ventilation volume (~half a bag)	

STOP TEST

Test Results	Circle **PASS** or **NR** to indicate pass or needs remediation:	**PASS**	**NR**

Instructor Initials _____ Instructor Number _____ Date _____

Instructor Notes
- Place a check in the box next to each step the student completes successfully.
- If the student does not complete all steps successfully (as indicated by at least 1 blank check box), the student must receive remediation. Make a note here of which skills require remediation (refer to Instructor Manual for information about remediation).

Test Results	Circle **PASS** or **NR** to indicate pass or needs remediation:	**PASS**	**NR**

Instructor Initials _____ Instructor Number _____ Date _____

© 2020 American Heart Association

Megacode Testing Checklist: Scenarios 1/3/8
Bradycardia → Pulseless VT → PEA → PCAC

Student Name _____ Date of Test _____

Critical Performance Steps						Check if done correctly
Team Leader						
Assigns team member roles						
Ensures high-quality CPR at all times	Compression rate 100-120/min ☐	Compression depth of ≥2 inches ☐	Chest compression fraction >80% ☐	Chest recoil (optional) ☐	Ventilation (optional) ☐	
Ensures that team members communicate well						
Bradycardia Management						
Starts oxygen if needed, places monitor, starts IV						
Places monitor leads in proper position						
Recognizes symptomatic bradycardia						
Administers correct dose of atropine						
Prepares for second-line treatment						
Pulseless VT Management						
Recognizes pVT						
Clears before analyze and shock						
Immediately resumes CPR after shocks						
Appropriate airway management						
Appropriate cycles of drug–rhythm check/shock–CPR						
Administers appropriate drug(s) and doses						
PEA Management						
Recognizes PEA						
Verbalizes potential reversible causes of PEA (H's and T's)						
Administers appropriate drug(s) and doses						
Immediately resumes CPR after rhythm checks						
Post–Cardiac Arrest Care						
Identifies ROSC						
Ensures BP and 12-lead ECG are performed and O_2 saturation is monitored, verbalizes need for endotracheal intubation and waveform capnography, and orders laboratory tests						
Considers targeted temperature management						

STOP TEST

Test Results Circle **PASS** or **NR** to indicate pass or needs remediation: **PASS** **NR**

Instructor Initials _____ Instructor Number _____ Date _____

Learning Station Competency
☐ Bradycardia ☐ Tachycardia ☐ Cardiac Arrest/Post–Cardiac Arrest Care ☐ Megacode Practice

© 2020 American Heart Association

Megacode Testing Checklist: Scenario 12
Bradycardia → VF → Asystole/PEA → PCAC

Student Name _____ Date of Test _____

Critical Performance Steps	Check if done correctly
Team Leader	
Assigns team member roles	
Ensures high-quality CPR at all times — ☐ Compression rate 100-120/min ☐ Compression depth of ≥2 inches ☐ Chest compression fraction >80% ☐ Chest recoil (optional) ☐ Ventilation (optional)	
Ensures that team members communicate well	
Bradycardia Management	
Starts oxygen if needed, places monitor, starts IV	
Places monitor leads in proper position	
Recognizes symptomatic bradycardia	
Administers correct dose of atropine	
Prepares for second-line treatment	
VF Management	
Recognizes VF	
Clears before analyze and shock	
Immediately resumes CPR after shocks	
Appropriate airway management	
Appropriate cycles of drug–rhythm check/shock–CPR	
Administers appropriate drug(s) and doses	
Asystole and PEA Management	
Recognizes asystole and PEA	
Verbalizes potential reversible causes of asystole and PEA (H's and T's)	
Administers appropriate drug(s) and doses	
Immediately resumes CPR after rhythm checks	
Post–Cardiac Arrest Care	
Identifies ROSC	
Ensures BP and 12-lead ECG are performed and O_2 saturation is monitored, verbalizes need for endotracheal intubation and waveform capnography, and orders laboratory tests	
Considers targeted temperature management	

STOP TEST

Test Results	Circle **PASS** or **NR** to indicate pass or needs remediation:	**PASS**	**NR**
Instructor Initials _____ Instructor Number _____ Date _____			

Learning Station Competency
☐ Bradycardia ☐ Tachycardia ☐ Cardiac Arrest/Post–Cardiac Arrest Care ☐ Megacode Practice

© 2020 American Heart Association

Megacode Testing Checklist: Scenario 9
Tachycardia → PEA → VF → PCAC

Student Name _____ Date of Test _____

Critical Performance Steps	Check if done correctly
Team Leader	
Assigns team member roles	
Ensures high-quality CPR at all times — Compression rate 100-120/min ☐ Compression depth of ≥2 inches ☐ Chest compression fraction >80% ☐ Chest recoil (optional) ☐ Ventilation (optional) ☐	
Ensures that team members communicate well	
Tachycardia Management	
Starts oxygen if needed, places monitor, starts IV	
Places monitor leads in proper position	
Recognizes tachycardia (specific diagnosis)	
Recognizes no symptoms due to tachycardia	
Considers appropriate initial drug therapy	
PEA Management	
Recognizes PEA	
Verbalizes potential reversible causes of PEA (H's and T's)	
Administers appropriate drug(s) and doses	
Immediately resumes CPR after rhythm check and pulse checks	
VF Management	
Recognizes VF	
Clears before analyze and shock	
Immediately resumes CPR after shocks	
Appropriate airway management	
Appropriate cycles of drug–rhythm check/shock–CPR	
Administers appropriate drug(s) and doses	
Post–Cardiac Arrest Care	
Identifies ROSC	
Ensures BP and 12-lead ECG are performed and O_2 saturation is monitored, verbalizes need for endotracheal intubation and waveform capnography, and orders laboratory tests	
Considers targeted temperature management	

STOP TEST

Test Results — Circle **PASS** or **NR** to indicate pass or needs remediation: **PASS**   **NR**

Instructor Initials _____ Instructor Number _____ Date _____

Learning Station Competency
☐ Bradycardia ☐ Tachycardia ☐ Cardiac Arrest/Post–Cardiac Arrest Care ☐ Megacode Practice

© 2020 American Heart Association

Megacode Testing Checklist: Scenarios 6/11
Bradycardia → VF → PEA → PCAC

Student Name _____ Date of Test _____

Critical Performance Steps						Check if done correctly
Team Leader						
Assigns team member roles						
Ensures high-quality CPR at all times	Compression rate 100-120/min ☐	Compression depth of ≥2 inches ☐	Chest compression fraction >80% ☐	Chest recoil (optional) ☐	Ventilation (optional) ☐	
Ensures that team members communicate well						
Bradycardia Management						
Starts oxygen if needed, places monitor, starts IV						
Places monitor leads in proper position						
Recognizes symptomatic bradycardia						
Administers correct dose of atropine						
Prepares for second-line treatment						
VF Management						
Recognizes VF						
Clears before analyze and shock						
Immediately resumes CPR after shocks						
Appropriate airway management						
Appropriate cycles of drug–rhythm check/shock–CPR						
Administers appropriate drug(s) and doses						
PEA Management						
Recognizes PEA						
Verbalizes potential reversible causes of PEA (H's and T's)						
Administers appropriate drug(s) and doses						
Immediately resumes CPR after rhythm checks						
Post–Cardiac Arrest Care						
Identifies ROSC						
Ensures BP and 12-lead ECG are performed and O_2 saturation is monitored, verbalizes need for endotracheal intubation and waveform capnography, and orders laboratory tests						
Considers targeted temperature management						

STOP TEST

Test Results	Circle **PASS** or **NR** to indicate pass or needs remediation:	**PASS**	**NR**
Instructor Initials _____	Instructor Number _____	Date _____	

Learning Station Competency
☐ Bradycardia   ☐ Tachycardia   ☐ Cardiac Arrest/Post–Cardiac Arrest Care   ☐ Megacode Practice

© 2020 American Heart Association

Megacode Testing Checklist: Scenarios 4/7/10
Tachycardia → VF → PEA → PCAC

Student Name _____ Date of Test _____

Critical Performance Steps						Check if done correctly
Team Leader						
Assigns team member roles						
Ensures high-quality CPR at all times	Compression rate 100-120/min ☐	Compression depth of ≥2 inches ☐	Chest compression fraction >80% ☐	Chest recoil (optional) ☐	Ventilation (optional) ☐	
Ensures that team members communicate well						
Tachycardia Management						
Starts oxygen if needed, places monitor, starts IV						
Places monitor leads in proper position						
Recognizes unstable tachycardia						
Recognizes symptoms due to tachycardia						
Performs immediate synchronized cardioversion						
VF Management						
Recognizes VF						
Clears before analyze and shock						
Immediately resumes CPR after shocks						
Appropriate airway management						
Appropriate cycles of drug–rhythm check/shock–CPR						
Administers appropriate drug(s) and doses						
PEA Management						
Recognizes PEA						
Verbalizes potential reversible causes of PEA (H's and T's)						
Administers appropriate drug(s) and doses						
Immediately resumes CPR after rhythm checks						
Post–Cardiac Arrest Care						
Identifies ROSC						
Ensures BP and 12-lead ECG are performed and O_2 saturation is monitored, verbalizes need for endotracheal intubation and waveform capnography, and orders laboratory tests						
Considers targeted temperature management						

STOP TEST

Test Results	Circle **PASS** or **NR** to indicate pass or needs remediation:	PASS	NR
Instructor Initials _____ Instructor Number _____ Date _____			

Learning Station Competency
☐ Bradycardia ☐ Tachycardia ☐ Cardiac Arrest/Post–Cardiac Arrest Care ☐ Megacode Practice

© 2020 American Heart Association

Megacode Testing Checklist: Scenarios 2/5
Bradycardia → VF → Asystole → PCAC

Student Name _____ Date of Test _____

Critical Performance Steps	Check if done correctly
Team Leader	
Assigns team member roles	
Ensures high-quality CPR at all times — ☐ Compression rate 100-120/min ☐ Compression depth of ≥2 inches ☐ Chest compression fraction >80% ☐ Chest recoil (optional) ☐ Ventilation (optional)	
Ensures that team members communicate well	
Bradycardia Management	
Starts oxygen if needed, places monitor, starts IV	
Places monitor leads in proper position	
Recognizes symptomatic bradycardia	
Administers correct dose of atropine	
Prepares for second-line treatment	
VF Management	
Recognizes VF	
Clears before analyze and shock	
Immediately resumes CPR after shocks	
Appropriate airway management	
Appropriate cycles of drug–rhythm check/shock–CPR	
Administers appropriate drug(s) and doses	
Asystole Management	
Recognizes asystole	
Verbalizes potential reversible causes of asystole (H's and T's)	
Administers appropriate drug(s) and doses	
Immediately resumes CPR after rhythm checks	
Post–Cardiac Arrest Care	
Identifies ROSC	
Ensures BP and 12-lead ECG are performed and O_2 saturation is monitored, verbalizes need for endotracheal intubation and waveform capnography, and orders laboratory tests	
Considers targeted temperature management	

STOP TEST

Test Results	Circle **PASS** or **NR** to indicate pass or needs remediation:	**PASS**	**NR**

Instructor Initials _____ Instructor Number _____ Date _____

Learning Station Competency
☐ Bradycardia ☐ Tachycardia ☐ Cardiac Arrest/Post–Cardiac Arrest Care ☐ Megacode Practice

© 2020 American Heart Association

ACLS Pharmacology Summary Table

This table provides information about common drugs used in ACLS.

Drug	Indications	Precautions and contraindications	Adult dosage
Adenosine	• First drug for most forms of stable narrow-complex SVT; effective in terminating those due to reentry involving AV node or sinus node • May consider for unstable narrow-complex reentry tachycardia while preparations are made for cardioversion • Regular and monomorphi	• Contraindicated in poison/drug-induced tachycardia or second- or third-degree heart block • Transient side effects include flushing, chest pain or tightness, brief periods of asystole or bradycardia, ventricular ectopy • Less effective (larger doses may be	**IV Rapid Push** • Place patient in mild reverse Trendelenburg position before administration of drug • Initial bolus of 6 mg given rapidly over 1 to 3 seconds followed by NS bolus of 20 mL; then elevate the extremity • A second dose (12 mg) can be given in 1 to 2 minutes if needed **Injection Technique** • Record rhythm strip during administration • Draw up adenosine dose in one syringe and flush in another; attach both syringes to the same or immediately adjacent IV injection ports nearest patient, with adenosine closest to patient; clamp IV tubing above injection port • Push IV adenosine as quickly as possible (1 to 3 seconds) • While maintaining pressure on adenosine plunger, push NS flush as rapidly as possible after adenosine • Unclamp IV tubing

| | | c wide-complex tachycardia, thought to be or previously defined to be reentry SVT
• Does not convert atrial fibrillation, atrial flutter, or VT
• Diagnostic maneuver: stable narrow-complex SVT | required) in patients taking theophylline or caffeine
• Reduce initial dose to 3 mg in patients receiving dipyridamole or carbamazepine, in heart transplant patients, or if given by central venous access
• If administered for irregular, polymorphic wide-complex tachycardia/VT, may cause deterioration (including hypotension)
• Transient periods of sinus | |

		<ul><li>bradycardia and ventricular ectopy are common after termination of SVT</li><li>Safe and effective in pregnancy</li></ul>	
Amiodarone	Because its use is associated with toxicity, amiodarone is indicated for use in patients with life-threatening arrhythmias when administered with appropriate monitoring:<ul><li>VF/pVT unresponsive to shock delivery, CPR, and a vasopressor</li><li>Recurrent, hemodynamically unstable VT</li></ul>With expert consultation, amiodarone may be used for treatment of some atrial and ventricular arrhythmias.	<ul><li>Rapid infusion may lead to hypotension</li><li>With multiple dosing, cumulative doses >2.2 g over 24 hours are associated with significant hypotension in clinical trials</li><li>Do not administer with other drugs that prolong QT interval (eg, procainamide)</li></ul>	**VF/pVT Cardiac Arrest Unresponsive to CPR, Shock, and Vasopressor**<ul><li>First dose: 300 mg IV/IO push</li><li>Second dose (if needed): 150 mg IV/IO push</li></ul>**Life-Threatening Arrhythmias** **Maximum cumulative dose:** 2.2 g IV over 24 hours. May be administered as follows:<ul><li>**Rapid infusion**: 150 mg IV over first 10 minutes (15 mg/min). May repeat rapid infusion (150 mg IV) every 10 minutes as needed</li><li>**Slow infusion**: 360 mg IV over 6 hours (1 mg/min)</li><li>**Maintenance infusion**: 540 mg IV over 18 hours (0.5 mg/min)</li></ul>

	Caution: **Multiple complex drug interactions**	• Terminal elimination is extremely long (half-life lasts up to 40 days)	
Atropine sulfate Can be given via endotracheal tube	• First drug for symptomatic sinus bradycardia • May be beneficial in presence of AV nodal block; **not likely to be effective for type II second-degree or third-degree AV block or a block in non-nodal tissue** • Routine use during PEA or asystole is unlikely to have a therapeutic benefit • Organophosphate (eg, nerve agent) poisoning:	• Use with caution in presence of myocardial ischemia and hypoxia. Increases myocardial oxygen demand • Unlikely to be effective for hypothermic bradycardia • May not be effective for infranodal (type II) AV block and new third-degree block with wide QRS complexes (in these patients	**Bradycardia (With or Without ACS)** • 1 mg IV every 3 to 5 minutes as needed, not to exceed total dose of 0.04 mg/kg (total 3 mg) **Organophosphate Poisoning** Extremely large doses (2 to 4 mg or higher) may be needed

	extremely large doses may be needed	may cause paradoxical slowing; be prepared to pace or give catecholamines)	
Dopamine IV infusion	• Second-line drug for symptomatic bradycardia (after atropine) • Use for hypotension (systolic blood pressure ≤70-100 mm Hg) with signs and symptoms of shock	• Correct hypovolemia with volume replacement before initiating dopamine • Use with caution in cardiogenic shock with accompanying CHF • May cause tachyarrhythmias, excessive vasoconstriction • Do not mix with sodium bicarbonate	**IV Administration** Usual infusion rate is 5-20 mcg/kg per minute. Titrate to patient response; taper slowly
Epinephrine Can be given via	• **Cardiac arrest:** VF, pulseless VT,	• Raising blood pressure and increasing	**Cardiac Arrest** • **IV/IO dose:** 1 mg (10 mL of 0.1 mg/mL solution) administered every 3-5 minutes during resuscitation; follow each dose

endotracheal tube Available in 1:10 000 and 1:1000 concentrations	asystole, PEA - **Symptomatic bradycardia:** Can be considered after atropine as an alternative infusion to dopamine - **Severe hypotension:** Can be used when pacing and atropine fail, when hypotension accompanies bradycardia, or with phosphodiesterase enzyme inhibitor - **Anaphylaxis, severe allergic reactions:** Combine with large fluid volume, corticosteroids,	heart rate may cause myocardial ischemia, angina, and increased myocardial oxygen demand - High doses do not improve survival or neurologic outcome and may contribute to postresuscitation myocardial dysfunction - Higher doses may be required to treat poison/drug-induced shock	with 20 mL flush, elevate arm for 10-20 seconds after dose - **Higher dose:** Higher doses (up to 0.2 mg/kg) may be used for specific indications (β-blocker or calcium channel blocker overdose) - **Continuous infusion:** Initial rate: 0.1-0.5 mcg/kg per minute (for 70-kg patient: 7-35 mcg/min); titrate to response - **Endotracheal route:** 2–2.5 mg diluted in 10 mL NS **Profound Bradycardia or Hypotension** 2-10 mcg/min infusion; titrate to patient response

	antihistamines		
Lidocaine Can be given via endotracheal tube	• Alternative to amiodarone in cardiac arrest from VF/pVT • Stable monomorphic VT with preserved ventricular function • Stable polymorphic VT with normal baseline QT interval and preserved LV function when ischemia is treated and electrolyte balance is corrected • Can be used for stable polymorphic VT with baseline QT-interval prolongation if torsades suspected	• Contraindication: Prophylactic use in AMI is contraindicated • Reduce maintenance dose (not loading dose) in presence of impaired liver function or LV dysfunction • Discontinue infusion immediately if signs of toxicity develop	**Cardiac Arrest From VF/pVT** • Initial dose: 1-1.5 mg/kg IV/IO • For refractory VF, may give additional 0.5-0.75 mg/kg IV push and repeat in 5-10 minutes; maximum 3 doses or total of 3 mg/kg **Perfusing Arrhythmia** For stable VT, wide-complex tachycardia of uncertain type, significant ectopy: • Doses ranging from 0.5-0.75 mg/kg and up to 1-1.5 mg/kg may be used • Repeat 0.5-0.75 mg/kg every 5-10 minutes; maximum total dose: 3 mg/kg **Maintenance Infusion** 1-4 mg/min (30-50 mcg/kg per minute)

| Magnesium sulfate | - Recommended for use in cardiac arrest only if torsades de pointes or suspected hypomagnesemia is present
- Life-threatening ventricular arrhythmias due to digitalis toxicity
- Routine administration in hospitalized patients with AMI is not recommended | - Occasional fall in blood pressure with rapid administration
- Use with caution if renal failure is present | **Cardiac Arrest (Due to Hypomagnesemia or Torsades de Pointes)**
1-2 g (2-4 mL of a 50% solution diluted in 10 mL [eg, D5W, normal saline] given IV/IO)
Torsades de Pointes With a Pulse or AMI With Hypomagnesemia
- Loading dose of 1-2 g mixed in 50-100 mL of diluent (eg, D5W, normal saline) over 5-60 minutes IV
- Follow with 0.5-1 g per hour IV (titrate to control torsades) |
|---|---|---|---|

Science Summary Table

This table compares topics from 2015 with 2020, providing a quick reference to what has changed and what is new in the science of advanced cardiovascular life support.

ACLS topic	2015	2020
Ventilation	<ul><li>1 breath every 5 to 6 seconds for respiratory arrest, with a bag-mask device</li><li>1 breath every 6 seconds for ventilation with an advanced airway in place</li></ul>	<ul><li>1 breath every 6 seconds for respiratory arrest with or without an advanced airway and also for cardiac arrest with an advanced airway (use this rate with a bag-mask device if your local protocol is continuous compressions and asynchronous ventilations for cardiac arrest)</li></ul>
Bradycardia	<ul><li>Atropine dose: 0.5 mg</li><li>Dopamine dosing: 2 to 20 mcg/kg per minute</li></ul>	<ul><li>Atropine dose: 1 mg</li><li>Dopamine dosing: 5 to 20 mcg/kg per minute</li></ul>
Tachycardia	<ul><li>Synchronized cardioversion initial recommended doses:<ul><li>–Narrow QRS complex, regular rhythm: 50 to 100 J</li><li>–Narrow QRS complex, irregular rhythm: 120 to 200 J</li><li>–Wide QRS</li></ul></li></ul>	<ul><li>Follow your specific device's recommended energy level to maximize the success of the first shock</li><li>Wide QRS complex, irregular rhythm: defibrillation dose (not synchronized)</li></ul>

	complex, regular rhythm: 100 J • Wide QRS complex, irregular rhythm: defibrillation dose (not synchronized)	
Post–Cardiac Arrest Care	• Titrate oxygen saturation to 94% or higher	• Titrate oxygen saturation to 92% to 98%
Adult Chain of Survival	• 5 links for both chains (IHCA and OHCA)	• 6 links for both chains (IHCA and OHCA): added a Recovery link to the end of both chains
IV/IO Access	• IV access and IO access are equivalent	• IV preferred over IO access, unless IV fails (then OK to proceed to IO)
ACLS topic	2020	
Cardiac Arrest	• Epinephrine 1 mg every 3 to 5 minutes or every 4 minutes as a midrange (ie, every other 2-minute rhythm check) • Amiodarone and lidocaine are equivalent for treatment (ie, either may be used) • Added maternal cardiac arrest information and algorithms (in-hospital) • Added ventricular assist device information (VAD: LVAD and RVAD) and algorithm • Added new prognostication diagram and information • Recommend using waveform capnography with a bag-mask device	
Stroke	• Revised stroke algorithm • New stroke triage algorithm for EMS destination • Focus on large vessel occlusion (LVO) for all healthcare providers • Endovascular therapy: treatment window up to 24 hours (previously up to 6 hours)	

	- Both alteplase and endovascular therapy can be given/performed if time criteria and inclusion criteria are met - Consider having EMS bypass the emergency department and go straight to the imaging suite (CT/MRI); initial assessment can be performed there to save time - Titrate oxygen saturation to >94%

Glossary

This table defines some common terms used in ACLS.

A	
Acute	Having a sudden onset and short course
Acute myocardial infarction (AMI)	The early critical stage of necrosis of heart muscle tissue caused by blockage of a coronary artery
Advanced cardiovascular life support (ACLS)	Emergency medical procedures in which basic life support efforts of CPR are supplemented with drug administration, IV fluids, etc
Asystole	Absence of electrical and mechanical activity in the heart
Atrial fibrillation	In atrial fibrillation the atria "quiver" chaotically and the ventricles beat irregularly
Atrial flutter	Rapid, irregular atrial contractions due to an abnormality of atrial excitation
Atrioventricular (AV) block	A delay in the normal flow of electrical impulses that cause the heart to beat
Automated external defibrillator (AED)	A portable device used to restart a heart that has stopped

B	
Basic life support (BLS)	Emergency treatment of a victim of cardiac or respiratory arrest through cardiopulmonary resuscitation and emergency cardiovascular care
Bradycardia	Slow heart rate, whether physiologically or pathologically

C	
Capnography	The measurement and graphic display of CO_2 levels in the airways, which can be performed by infrared spectroscopy
Cardiac arrest	Temporary or permanent cessation of the heartbeat
Cardiopulmonary resuscitation (CPR)	A basic emergency procedure for life support, consisting of mainly manual external cardiac massage and some artificial respiration
Coronary syndrome	A group of clinical symptoms compatible with acute myocardial ischemia. Also called coronary heart disease.
Coronary thrombosis	The blocking of the coronary artery of the heart by a thrombus

E	
Electrocardiogram (ECG)	A test that provides a typical record of normal heart action
Endotracheal (ET) intubation	The passage of a tube through the nose or mouth into the trachea for maintenance of the airway
Esophageal-tracheal tube	A double-lumen tube with inflatable balloon cuffs that seal off the hypopharynx from the oropharynx and esophagus; used for airway management

H	
Hydrogen ion (acidosis)	The accumulation of acid and hydrogen ions or depletion of the alkaline reserve (bicarbonate content) in the blood and body tissues, decreasing the pH
Hyperkalemia	An abnormally high concentration of potassium ions in the blood. Also called hyperpotassemia.
Hypoglycemia	An abnormally low concentration of glucose in the blood
Hypokalemia	An abnormally low concentration of potassium ions in the blood. Also called hypopotassemia.
Hypothermia	When the patient's core body temperature is below 96.8°F (36°C)
Hypovolemia	A decrease in the volume of circulating blood
Hypoxia	A deficiency of oxygen reaching the tissues of the body

I	
Intraosseous (IO)	Within a bone
Intravenous (IV)	Within a vein

M	
Mild hypothermia	When the patient's core body temperature is between 93.2°F and 96.8°F
Moderate hypothermia	When the patient's core body temperature is from 86°F and 93.2°F

N	
Nasopharyngeal (NPA)	Pertaining to the nose and pharynx

O	
Oropharyngeal airway (OPA)	A tube used to provide free passage of air between the mouth and pharynx

P	
Perfusion	The passage of fluid (such as blood) through a specific organ or area of the body (such as the heart)
Prophylaxis	Prevention of or protection against disease
Pulmonary edema	A condition in which fluid accumulates in the lungs
Pulseless electrical activity (PEA)	Continued electrical rhythmicity of the heart in the absence of effective mechanical function

R	
Recombinant tissue plasminogen activator (rtPA)	A clot-dissolving substance produced naturally by cells in the walls of blood vessels

S	
Severe hypothermia	When the patient's core body temperature is below 86°F
Sinus rhythm	The rhythm of the heart produced by impulses from the sinoatrial node
Supraglottic	Situated or occurring above the glottis
Synchronized cardioversion	Uses a sensor to deliver a shock that is synchronized with a peak in the QRS complex
Syncope	A loss of consciousness over a short period of time, caused by a temporary lack of oxygen in the brain

T	
Tachycardia	Increased heart rate, usually ≥100/min
Tamponade (cardiac)	A condition caused by accumulation of fluid between the heart and the pericardium, resulting in excess pressure on the heart. This impairs the heart's ability to pump sufficient blood.
Tension pneumothorax	Pneumothorax resulting from a wound in the chest wall which acts as a valve that permits air to enter the pleural cavity but prevents its escape

Thrombus	A blood clot formed within a blood vessel
U	
Unsynchronized shock	An electrical shock that will be delivered as soon as the operator pushes the shock button to discharge the defibrillator. Thus, the shock can fall anywhere within the cardiac cycle.
V	
Ventricular fibrillation (VF)	Very rapid uncoordinated fluttering contractions of the ventricles
Ventricular tachycardia (VT)	A rapid heart rate that originates in one of the lower chambers (ventricles) of the heart

Made in the USA
Coppell, TX
06 November 2022